Employment Law for Business and Human Resources Professionals

Alberta and British Columbia

FOURTH EDITION

Kelly Williams-Whitt

Adam Letourneau

TJ Schmaltz

Ryan Anderson

Kathryn J. Filsinger

emond ▪ Toronto, Canada ▪ 2021

Emond Montgomery Publications Limited
1 Eglinton Ave E, Suite 600
Toronto ON M4P 3A1
http://www.emond.ca/highered

Printed in Canada.

We acknowledge the financial support of the Government of Canada and the assistance of the Government of Ontario. Canada Ontario

Vice president, publishing: Anthony Rezek
Publisher: Lindsay Sutherland
Acquisitions editor: Laura Bast
Director, development and production: Kelly Dickson
Developmental editor: Lenore Gray Spence
Production supervisor: Anna Killen
Production editor: Natalie Berchem
Copy editor: Leanne Rancourt
Typesetter: Transforma
Permissions editor: Monika Schurman
Proofreader: Ward Jardine
Indexer: Andrew Little
Cover designer: Jordan Bloom
Cover image: ssguy/Shutterstock
Printer: Marquis

Library and Archives Canada Cataloguing in Publication

Title: Employment law for business and human resources professionals : Alberta and British Columbia / Kelly Williams-Whitt, Adam Letourneau, TJ Schmaltz, Ryan Anderson, Kathryn J. Filsinger.
Names: Williams-Whitt, Kelly, author. | Letourneau, Adam, 1974- author. | Schmaltz, T. J., 1978- author. | Anderson, Ryan, 1973- author. | Filsinger, Kathryn J., author.
Description: Fourth edition. | Includes bibliographical references and index.
Identifiers: Canadiana 20200271512 | ISBN 9781772556155 (softcover)
Subjects: LCSH: Labor laws and legislation—Alberta—Textbooks. | LCSH: Labor laws and legislation—British Columbia—Textbooks. | LCGFT: Textbooks.
Classification: LCC KE3247 . W52 2021 | LCC KF3457 .W52 2021 kfmod | DDC 344.712301—dc23ISBN 978-1-77255-615-5

Brief Contents

Detailed Contents

Detailed Contents

PART II

LEGAL ISSUES IN HIRING AND DURING THE COURSE OF EMPLOYMENT

PART III

THE END OF THE EMPLOYMENT RELATIONSHIP AND BEYOND

PART III

THE END OF THE EMPLOYMENT RELATIONSHIP AND BEYOND

Preface

From the initial recruitment stage to the end of employment, the law potentially affects every aspect of the employment relationship. As a human resources professional, you will not be expected to become an expert in all areas of employment law. However, you should have sufficient understanding of employment law so that, wherever possible, you can minimize legal risks and liabilities. You should be aware of the implications of actions proposed or taken and—most important—know when to seek expert legal advice.

The purpose of this book is to provide you with a fundamental and practical understanding of the key legal issues that arise between employers and employees. The book contains an extensive review of the underlying contractual relationship between the workplace parties, as well as the content and interpretation of employment-related statutes. Throughout the book, case summaries are used to help clarify and explain ideas and to provide you with a sense of how courts interpret the relevant laws.

Most of this text focuses on non-unionized employees—individuals whose terms and conditions of work are based on an individual contract of employment. It does, however, provide an in-depth description of the law governing unionized workplaces, both under provincial labour regimes (Chapter 3) and federal law (Chapter 4). There are specific provincial and federal statutes that govern unions, collective bargaining, and other union activity such as strikes. But there are also a number of statutes that apply to unionized and non-unionized employees alike. This book examines all the major statutory regimes, in addition to exploring the common law (judge-made law) rights and remedies, such as the right to sue for wrongful dismissal, that apply only to non-unionized employees.

The text is divided into three parts. Part I (Chapters 1 to 4) provides an overview of the legal and judicial framework within which employment laws are created and interpreted. Chapter 1 explains the sources of employment law, both statutory and judicial; the relevance of the *Canadian Charter of Rights and Freedoms*; and the issues related to constitutional jurisdiction in the employment area. Chapter 2 provides an explanation of the common law of employment (judge-made law) that affects non-unionized employees in the provincial jurisdiction. Common law issues are covered, including areas of potential liability for employers, the distinction between an employer–employee relationship and a principal–independent contractor relationship, and the legal implications of that distinction. Chapter 3 explores provincial labour relations legislation that affects employees who are unionized already or who would like to become unionized. The last chapter in Part I (Chapter 4) is an overview of the *Canada Labour Code*, legislation that only governs employees who work for the Government of Canada or in specific federally regulated industries (often called "industries of national importance").

Subsequent chapters are organized according to the chronology of the employment relationship. Part II (Chapters 5 to 11) addresses key legal issues that may arise in the hiring process and during the course of employment. Chapter 5 focuses on individual employment contracts and considers the benefits of written contracts of employment over oral ones. Common contractual terms are also reviewed. Chapter 6 provides an important overview of minimum employment standards that all employment contracts must meet. Chapter 7 discusses the significant impact that Alberta's and British Columbia's human rights legislation has throughout the employment relationship. Unlike the requirements of most employment laws, human rights requirements apply to pre-employment conduct as well as to all subsequent aspects of the employment relationship, and an understanding of those requirements is crucial for anyone involved in the hiring process.

Chapters 8 to 10 focus on laws that apply primarily during the course of an employment relationship. This includes an overview of the principal statutes that govern occupational health and safety, workers' compensation, and privacy rights and responsibilities within the employment relationship. Chapter 11 covers contractual issues that may arise during the course of employment, such as performance reviews and changes in the terms of employment agreements.

Part III (Chapters 12 to 15) reviews the key legal issues that arise at the end of an employment relationship. Chapter 12 deals with resignations and retirements. Chapters 13 and 14 review the common law concerning dismissal with and without cause, respectively, and related issues. Finally, Chapter 15 looks at post-employment obligations.

Acknowledgments

Without the achievement of Kathryn J. Filsinger, author of the Ontario editions, this text would not have been possible. Her work and that of the authors of the earlier Alberta and British Columbia editions remain both the inspiration and the template for this edition. We also express sincere thanks to Emond Publishing for their tireless and meticulous help.

Thank you also to the reviewers of the third edition of this text:

Marlize van Jaarsveld, British Columbia Institute of Technology
Brian Parker, Douglas College
Lora Freeman, Douglas College

Dr. Williams-Whitt would like to thank Dr. Daphne Taras and Dr. Allen Ponak for their invaluable expertise in labour and employment law and for their unwavering support throughout her career.

About the Authors

Dr. Kelly Williams-Whitt is the associate dean of the Dhillon School of Business at the University of Lethbridge and a professor of human resources and labour relations. She also has an active practice as a labour mediator and arbitrator. She is a former registered nurse, with an MBA and a PhD in human resource management and labour relations. Dr. Williams-Whitt teaches courses in occupational health and safety, labour relations, employment law, human resource management, and workplace diversity. She is also an active researcher working with colleagues from around the world conducting studies in management of workplace health, illness, and injury. Her work is published in peer-reviewed scientific journals and she has authored numerous books and book chapters on work disability and labour and employment law. Dr. Williams-Whitt holds an appointment with the Federal Mediation and Conciliation Service (Labour Program) as an adjudicator for cases falling under the *Canada Labour Code*. She sits on the editorial board of the *Journal of Occupational Rehabilitation* and is a member of the board of directors of Work Wellness Institute.

Adam Letourneau, QC, is an adjunct associate professor at the Dhillon School of Business at the University of Lethbridge, teaching various law and labour relations–related courses. He is also the managing partner of Letourneau LLP Lawyers | Arbitrators | Mediators.

Adam studied law at the University of Alberta and was called to the bar in 2006. In 2015, he completed an LLM degree in international dispute resolution at University College London and Queen Mary's University, University of London. Adam was appointed Queen's Counsel in 2015 and served as a bencher of the Law Society of Alberta in 2011 and from 2014 to 2018. He is a chartered arbitrator and chartered mediator.

Adam is the happy father of five lovely children and is a proud citizen of the Métis Nation of Alberta.

Terrence (TJ) Schmaltz has been a passionate part-time instructor with the British Columbia Institute of Technology's School of Business since 2005, teaching various law, business, and human resource management courses. He is also the chief people and legal officer for Prospera, Canada's sixth-largest credit union, with executive oversight for all human resource management, communications, and legal affairs.

TJ started his career as a labour and employment lawyer before transitioning into senior human resource management roles. He has extensive experience in mergers and acquisitions, leveraging his legal and business experience.

A chartered professional in human resources (CPHR) and a senior certified professional (SCP) with the US Society for Human Resource Management, TJ was granted the title of Fellow Chartered Professional in Human Resources (FCPHR) by CPHR Canada in 2018. He holds a bachelor of common law (LLB) and a bachelor of civil law (BCL) from McGill University.

He is the former chair of the board for CPHR BC & Yukon and became the chair of the board for CPHR Canada in 2020. He also serves on the board of directors for Ocean Wise.

TJ is a proud husband and father, living with his wife and son in Vancouver.

Ryan Anderson is a partner at the Vancouver office of Mathews, Dinsdale & Clark LLP. Ryan has worked in the human resources field for over two decades and advises employers in all areas of workplace law.

Ryan studied law at the University of British Columbia and was called to the bar in 2006. In 1999 he completed a master's degree in business administration and labour relations at Simon Fraser University, following his completion of a bachelor's degree in business administration and human resources management.

Ryan represents provincially and federally regulated employers concerning both labour relations and employment matters, primarily in British Columbia and Alberta. Ryan regularly assists employers and human resources professionals with the day-to-day challenges of managing employees. As an advocate, Ryan represents employers in a wide variety of forums, including administrative tribunals and labour arbitrations. In addition, Ryan provides practical training in all manner of human resource management topics.

Ryan has been a teacher in the human resources field for more than 20 years, most recently as an instructor at Simon Fraser University, teaching a labour and employment relations course to human resources professionals participating in the Certificate in Human Resources Management Program. Previously, Ryan was an instructor at Capilano University, where he taught a similar course to business students for over ten years.

PART I

The Legal Framework

The opening chapter of this textbook provides you with an overview of important concepts in employment law. You will learn about key statutes, how law is made and evolves, and the role that judges and administrative tribunals play in interpretation and enforcement. Workers in Alberta and British Columbia (BC) are protected by different laws depending on where they live; what kind of work they do; and whether they are classified as employees, contractors, unionized, or non-unionized. You will learn about the concept of jurisdiction and that employers in certain industries are covered by federal rather than provincial legislation.

Chapter 2 discusses judge-made employment law, which is called "common law." The chapter reviews the differences between employees and independent contractors and the legal implications of that distinction.

While the primary focus of this textbook is on non-unionized workplaces, employers in Alberta and BC should be aware of important differences that exist when employees are unionized or are attempting to become unionized. Chapter 3, therefore, explores the labour relations codes in both provinces. These codes regulate the process of unionization, collective bargaining, strikes, and other issues that may arise between employers and their unionized employees.

Chapter 4 is the final chapter in Part I and provides an overview of the *Canada Labour Code*, which protects employees who work for the government of Canada or who work in industries that are of national interest, such as transportation, telecommunications, and banking. You will learn that the Code is unique in that it includes sections addressing unionized workplaces, occupational health and safety, and minimum employment standards.

Overview of Employment Law

1

LEARNING OUTCOMES

After completing this chapter, you will be able to:

- Review the three main sources of employment law.
- Consider how and why employment law changes.
- Examine jurisdiction over employment law.
- Consider the relevance of the *Canadian Charter of Rights and Freedoms*.
- Review key employment-related statutes in British Columbia and Alberta, and in federal law.
- Look at the judicial and administrative systems that interpret employment laws.
- Learn how to locate relevant statutes and case law.

Introduction

Although most of this book looks at specific employment laws, Chapter 1 provides you with an overview of the legislative and judicial framework within which those employment laws are created. Knowing who makes, interprets, and enforces these laws is essential to understanding and applying them in the workplace. This chapter is intended to provide a context for everything else that you will learn in this book.

This text focuses primarily on non-unionized employees—individuals whose terms and conditions of work are based on individual contracts of employment between them and their employers. However, to help students understand the full legal context of employment in Alberta and BC, Chapter 3 highlights law that specifically applies to unionized employees, whose terms and conditions of employment are negotiated collectively.

This chapter provides an outline of the legal framework for employment law in BC and Alberta, but it is not a complete overview of the legal system and legal terminology. If you are unfamiliar with some of the terms, such as "Cabinet," you find in this chapter or the rest of the book, please consult <http://www.emond.ca/higher-education/glossary-of-legal-terms.html>.

Sources of Employment Law

statute law
a statute is a law passed (i.e., created) by the federal or provincial government

constitutional law
the *Canadian Charter of Rights and Freedoms*; the "supreme law of the land"

common law
law that has developed over the years through court decisions

There are three main sources of employment law in Canada: **statute law** (legislation passed by the government), **constitutional law** (in particular, the *Canadian Charter of Rights and Freedoms* [Charter][1]), and **common law** (judge-made law). The relative importance of each source depends on the particular area of law under consideration. Wrongful dismissal actions, for example, are based on the common law, while minimum employment standards and anti-discrimination laws are provided through statutes, though the common law gradually adopts many statute-based principles. A discussion of statute, constitutional, and common law is set out below.

Generally speaking, constitutional law and most employee rights contained in statutes apply to unionized and non-unionized employees alike. Common law rights and remedies, such as the right to sue for wrongful dismissal, normally apply only to non-unionized employees. Rights and remedies available only to unionized employees are contained within labour relations codes, collective agreements, and arbitral jurisprudence (decisions made by labour arbitrators)—see Chapter 3.

1 You can download a copy of the Charter from <https://www.canada.ca/en/canadian-heritage/services/download-order-charter-bill.htm>.

Statute Law

What Is a Statute?

A statute is a law created and passed by the federal or provincial government. Statutes are sometimes referred to as "legislation," "codes," or "acts." The *Alberta Human Rights Act*[2] and the BC *Human Rights Code*[3] are examples of statutes.

Why Are Statutes Passed? Why Are They Amended?

Employment statutes are usually passed because the government decides that employees require protections or rights beyond those that currently exist. Historically, employment legislation has provided minimum acceptable standards and working conditions, such as minimum wages and vacation entitlements. More recently, governments have implemented statutory requirements and protections, such as anti-discrimination legislation, that affect many facets of the employment relationship.

Factors that motivate change in employment law often relate to demographic shifts in society and changing social values. For example, the dramatic increase in the number of women in the paid workforce has led to significant new statutory requirements over the past 30 years, such as pay equity, increased pregnancy and parental leave, and prohibitions on discriminatory hiring and firing practices based on gender or family status. Changes in technology and the evolution of social media have led to enhanced privacy protection laws, while shifts within the economy and the nature of work have resulted in laws to better protect workers hired through temporary agencies.

FYI

Before There Were Employment Statutes ...

During the 19th and early 20th centuries, there were very few employment statutes; the relationship between an employer and employee was based almost entirely on the common law of contract. Under the common law, the parties were free to negotiate whatever terms of employment they could mutually agree on. But because an employee typically has much less bargaining power than an employer, in practice, this freedom of contract usually meant that the employer was free to set the terms it wanted. The employer was also free to select or discriminate against anyone it chose. Moreover, when legal disputes between an employer and employee arose, courts saw their role as strictly one of interpreting the existing employment agreement, not as one of trying to achieve a fairer balance between the parties' interests.

Over time, governments became convinced that leaving the employment relationship entirely to labour market forces (supply and demand) was unacceptable, and they intervened by passing laws in a broad range of areas. These included laws setting minimum employment standards, regulating workplace health and safety,

2 Access the full Act at <http://www.qp.alberta.ca/documents/Acts/A25P5.pdf>.

3 Access the full Act at <http://www.bclaws.ca/Recon/document/ID/freeside/00_96210_01>.

prohibiting discrimination based on key grounds, and creating a labour relations system that established the right of employees to join a union so that they could bargain with the employer collectively.

Today, although the non-union employment relationship is still premised on the basic principles of the common law of contract, the relationship between employers and employees is a highly regulated one, with numerous statutes affecting that relationship.

SOURCE: Based on lecture notes by Professor David Doorey as part of his Employment Law 3420 course, 2009, York University, Toronto.

Another factor prompting legislative change is a shift in the political party in power. For example, in the fall of 2002, the newly elected BC Liberal government made significant revisions to virtually every Act relating to employment law. In 2017, the New Democratic Party (NDP) was elected to government and has once again made significant changes to BC's employment legislation, including the BC *Employment Standards Act*, the BC *Human Rights Code*, and the BC *Labour Relations Code*. This includes establishing a schedule for annual increases to the minimum wage up to $15.21 per hour by June 2021, extending the timelines to file a human rights complaint, the re-establishment of the BC Human Rights Commission, and strengthening union successorship rights. These amendments will be discussed in later chapters.

In Alberta, the NDP, elected in 2015, made many changes to minimum employment standards, occupational health and safety regulations, as well as the *Labour Relations Code*. For example, they increased the minimum wage rate to $15 per hour. In 2019, the United Conservative Party was elected and immediately tabled a bill to roll back some of those changes, including a reduction in minimum wage for workers under the age of 18.

As various employment laws are discussed in this book, consider the policy issue that the law is meant to address, the goal of the legislation, and then the extent to which the law has been, or probably will be, effective in achieving that goal.

How Statutes Are Made: The Legislative Process

A statute first takes the form of a written bill. As in other provinces, a bill must pass three readings in the legislature to become a provincial statute in BC or Alberta. To become a federal statute, a bill must pass three readings in the House of Commons and must also be passed by the Senate in Ottawa. The following description of the legislative process concerns provincial legislation because the provinces pass most laws related to employment. (See Chapter 4 for a notable exception: employees governed by the federal *Canada Labour Code*.)

There are three types of bills. Although the majority of bills of general application are public bills, there are two other kinds of bills: private bills and private members' bills.[4]

4 The public can read or view webcasts of the debates and discussions about these bills in publicly available Legislative Assembly documents and records. Alberta Hansard (transcripts of debates) and Votes and Proceedings (under House Records) are available at <http://www.assembly.ab.ca/net/index.aspx?p=adr_home>, and select webcasts for past sittings are available at <http://assemblyonline.assembly.ab.ca/Harmony>. In BC, Debates (Hansard) are available at <https://www.leg.bc.ca>.

1. *Public bills.* Public bills are introduced in the legislature by the Cabinet minister who is responsible for the relevant subject matter. For example, bills concerning employment law are typically put forward by the Minister of Labour. A bill may contain either proposed amendments (changes) to a current statute or an entirely new piece of legislation. First reading introduces the bill. On second reading, the elected members of the legislative assembly (MLAs) debate the principles of the bill. If the bill passes second reading through a vote in the legislature, it goes to a committee of the legislature. Committees may hear witnesses and consider the bill clause by clause before reporting back to the legislature. Sometimes the bill is amended (revised) before its third and final reading to take into account input from the public or opposition parties. After third reading, there is a vote in the legislature, and if a majority of MLAs vote in favour of the bill, it is passed.
2. *Private bills.* Private bills cover non-public matters, such as changing corporate charters, and so are of limited scope and relevance.
3. *Private members' bills.* Private members' bills may deal with matters of public importance, but they are put forward by a private member of the legislature, not by a Cabinet minister. Therefore, they typically do not have much chance of becoming law and are often tabled to stimulate public debate on an issue or make a political point. Unless such bills win the support of the governing party, they usually "die on the order paper," which means that they never become law.

A bill becomes a statute once it receives royal assent. A statute may come into force in one of three ways:

1. *On royal assent.* The statute comes into force without the need for additional steps.
2. *On a particular date.* The statute itself names the date on which it comes into force.
3. *On proclamation.* The statute comes into force on a date chosen by Cabinet and announced later. Different sections of the statute may come into force at different times. For example, when additional time is required to prepare the regulations necessary to implement certain provisions of the law, those provisions may be proclaimed at a later date or the date may be set out in the statute.

When you are reading a statute, make sure that you have the current version. Statutes can be amended extensively, and sometimes entire sections are repealed (deleted) or added. The Canadian Legal Information Institute (CanLII, <http://www.canlii.org>) is a good place to find the most up-to-date version of employment-related statutes for each province. The site also contains past versions of the statutes and highlights changes enacted over time.

While statutes contain the main requirements of the law, detailed rules on how to implement or administer the statute are often found in **regulations**. Regulations

regulations
rules made under the authority of a statute

(also known as "delegated legislation") are rules made under the authority of a statute. For example, the BC *Employment Standards Act* and the Alberta *Employment Standards Code* state that there is a minimum wage for most occupations in BC and Alberta, respectively. However, the exact dollar amount of that minimum wage for various occupations is found in the regulations that accompany both statutes.

Although regulations are as legally binding as the statute that enables them, they are not made by a legislature. They are made by government officials and published in the *British Columbia Gazette* and the *Alberta Gazette*. Therefore, they are more easily made and amended than the actual statute itself.

Statutory Jurisdiction and Interpretation

members (of administrative tribunals) adjudicators appointed pursuant to a statute

Judges or **members of administrative tribunals** (adjudicators appointed pursuant to a statute, such as the BC Human Rights Tribunal) interpret legislation while adjudicating cases. There are two important points to note about the adjudication of legislation: whether the court or tribunal has jurisdiction and how it goes about the act of interpreting.

Jurisdiction

jurisdiction the authority granted to a legal body to administer justice within a defined area of responsibility; legislation applies only to a specific jurisdiction (area of responsibility), and courts and tribunals are limited to making decisions about issues that fall within a specific jurisdiction

Judges and tribunal members have a limited scope of authority or **jurisdiction**. Their jurisdiction is established by statute and restricts decision-making authority to specific issues and geographic areas. For example, the *Alberta Human Rights Act* applies only to the province of Alberta, and the Alberta Human Rights Commission may address only human rights issues. This means that the commission in Alberta cannot decide a case where the employer and employee are in BC at the time of the alleged violation. Conversely, the BC Human Rights Tribunal cannot hear cases involving violations that occur in Alberta. Their jurisdiction is also limited to the subject matters set out in the legislation. The Human Rights Commission and Tribunal are prohibited from deciding a case related to an occupational health and safety issue, since separate statutes govern these issues. However, several statutes may apply to a single situation. For example, an employee who is injured in the workplace and who wants to return to their pre-accident job may have remedies under both workers' compensation and human rights legislation against an employer who refuses to allow them to return. Whether or not a judge or administrative tribunal member has authority to decide a case may be a preliminary issue that is hotly debated by legal counsel prior to the main case being heard. Normally, the judge or tribunal member will decide whether they have the jurisdiction to hear the case.

Interpretation

Judges' interpretations of legislation, and to some extent those of tribunal members, may become precedents that influence later interpretations of the legislation. The first thing a judge will do when dealing with legislation is to look at past court decisions involving the same legislation and similar fact situations. Where a clear precedent does not exist, the judge must interpret and apply the legislation. When interpreting legislation, judges and tribunal members have developed several rules—such as the "mischief rule"—to help them. When using the mischief rule, they examine the problem, or mischief, that a statute was intended to correct and apply the corrective rationale to the issue. This approach seeks to ensure an appropriate context is applied when interpreting legislation. *1254582 Alberta Ltd v Miscellaneous Employees Teamsters Local Union 987 of Alberta* provides a good example of this approach to statutory interpretation.

CASE IN POINT

Court Uses Mischief Rule to Interpret Statute

1254582 Alberta Ltd v Miscellaneous Employees Teamsters Local Union 987 of Alberta, 2009 ABQB 127

Facts

In hopes of becoming the bargaining unit for airport taxi drivers in Edmonton, the Miscellaneous Employees, Teamsters Local Union 987 of Alberta made a certification application under the Alberta *Labour Relations Code*. The application failed because of lack of sufficient employee support, but the company that hired the drivers, Airport Taxi Service (ATS), objected to the classification of its drivers as employees in the first place. It claimed that the drivers were independent contractors. The Alberta Labour Relations Board and, upon judicial review, the Alberta Court of Queen's Bench considered the mischief rule to establish the appropriate classification of the taxi drivers as employees who were either in receipt of wages or entitled to wages, a requirement of the Code.

Relevant Issues

Whether the drivers working for ATS qualify as employees for the purposes of the Code, and whether passenger fares qualify as wages for the purposes of the Code.

Decision

The Alberta Court of Queen's Bench ruled that the Board's decision was reasonable when it determined that the ATS taxi drivers were employees, because ATS "controls the queue, the number of drivers, their vacation leaves, car use and generally dictates the terms of their relationship" (at para 20). Similarly, the Board was reasonable when it found that passenger fares qualified as wages to the taxi drivers when the mischief rule or purposive approach was applied to the Code's definition of wages: wages "includes any salary, pay, overtime pay and any other remuneration for work or services however computed or paid, but does not include tips and other gratuities" (s 1(a)).

The mischief rule was particularly useful in identifying the intent of the legislation. Both the Board and the Court quoted with approval a Nova Scotia case, which said:

> [The mischief rule] applies on the understanding that most legislative schemes that distinguish between employees and independent contractors are directed at providing needed benefits to employees. Therefore, it is understandable that the law should lean toward classification as an employee, at least in those cases where conventional analysis leads to an indeterminate conclusion. Everyone is aware that it is to the benefit of employers to outsource work traditionally undertaken by employees and this is the mischief that decision-makers must consider. (*Joey's Delivery Service v New Brunswick (Workplace Health Safety and Compensation Commission)* at para 98)

Courts and tribunals also use "internal aids" found in the statute itself to assist in its interpretation. Sections of a statute that define important terms, or an introduction or preamble that explains a statute's purpose, can help with interpretation. For example, the broad preamble to the *Alberta Human Rights Act*, which includes as its aim the "recognition of the inherent dignity and the equal and inalienable rights of all persons" (at 2) has led to an expansive interpretation of the rights contained in that statute.

External aids, such as legal dictionaries and scholarly articles, are also used to help interpret statutes.

What Level of Government Can Pass Employment-Related Statutes?

Canada is a federal state with three levels of government: federal, provincial, and municipal. Municipalities have no jurisdiction over employment, although they can pass by-laws on matters that affect the workplace, such as restrictions related to smoking.

The federal government has authority over only about 6 percent of employees in Canada. This is because in 1925 the Court ruled in *Toronto Electric Commissioners v Snider* that the federal government's legislative authority was limited to industries of national importance, such as banking, pipelines, telecommunications, railways, and transportation. Chapter 4 discusses the *Canada Labour Code*, which is the main employment legislation for employees in these federally regulated industries.[5]

The remainder of this text focuses primarily on provincial employment legislation in Alberta and BC. Although employment laws in all the provinces are similar in principle, they vary in detail, and the applicable statute should be referred to when issues related to employment arise.

Key BC and Alberta Employment Statutes

The following are the key employment statutes applied in BC and Alberta:

- The BC *Employment Standards Act* and the Alberta *Employment Standards Code* set out minimum rights and standards for employees, including minimum wages, overtime, hours of work, termination notice or termination pay, pregnancy and parental leave, vacation, and statutory holidays.
- The BC *Human Rights Code* and the *Alberta Human Rights Act* are aimed at promoting equity and preventing and remedying discrimination and harassment based on specified prohibited grounds.
- The BC *Labour Relations Code* and the Alberta *Labour Relations Code* deal with the right of employees to unionize and the collective bargaining process.
- The BC *Occupational Health and Safety Regulation* and the Alberta *Occupational Health and Safety Act* outline requirements and responsibilities for creating a safe workplace and preventing workplace injuries and accidents.
- The BC *Workers Compensation Act* and the Alberta *Workers' Compensation Act* provide no-fault insurance plans to compensate workers for work-related injuries and diseases. They also allow employers to limit their financial exposure to the costs of workplace accidents through a collective funding system.

5 A complete list of federally regulated business sectors is available on the Employment and Social Development Canada website at <https://www.canada.ca/en/employment-social-development/programs/employment-equity/regulated-industries.html>.

- The BC *Personal Information Protection Act* and the Alberta *Personal Information Protection Act* establish rules for private sector employers about the collection, use, and disclosure of employee information.

Federal Employment Statutes

As noted above, the federal government's legislative authority is limited to industries of national importance. Thus, federal employment law covers employees who work for a federally regulated company such as a bank or airline. The two main federal employment statutes are:

- the *Canada Labour Code*, which covers employment standards, collective bargaining, and health and safety (see Chapter 4); and
- the *Canadian Human Rights Act*, which covers human rights and pay equity.

FYI

Why Most Employees in British Columbia and Alberta Are Governed by Provincial, and Not Federal, Employment Law

When Canada became a nation on July 1, 1867, its founding document, the *Constitution Act, 1867*, set out the division of powers between the federal and provincial governments. However, it made no specific reference to employment matters. In the 1920s, a federal employment law was challenged in the courts in *Toronto Electric Commissioners v Snider* on the basis that the federal government did not have the constitutional authority to pass it. The Court held that employment law fell within the provinces' jurisdiction over "property and civil rights." As a result, federal jurisdiction over employment law became limited to industries of national importance, such as national transportation and communication. All other employers are provincially regulated.

Whether a company is federally or provincially incorporated does not determine whether it is provincially or federally regulated. Nor does a company's location affect the source of its regulation. Banks are federally regulated, and therefore the same federal employment statutes govern banks in Alberta and BC (it is noteworthy that most credit unions are provincially regulated because they do not meet the definition of a "bank"). In contrast, a provincially regulated employer that operates businesses throughout Canada will have its Alberta employees covered by Alberta's employment laws and its BC employees covered by BC's employment laws.

These statutes are similar in principle to their provincial counterparts, but there are some differences in the rights and protections granted.

The following federal laws apply to both federally and provincially regulated industries:

- *Canada Pension Plan*, which provides qualifying employees with pension benefits on retirement and permanent disability.
- *Employment Insurance Act*, which provides qualifying employees with income replacement during periods of temporary unemployment.

Constitutional Law

The Canadian Charter of Rights and Freedoms

Guaranteed Rights and Freedoms

One special statute that affects employment law in Canada is the *Canadian Charter of Rights and Freedoms*, which was adopted as part of the Constitution in 1982. Although the Charter does not address employment law specifically, it does set out guaranteed rights and freedoms that can affect the workplace whenever government action or legislation is involved. These include freedom of religion, association, and expression; democratic rights; mobility rights; legal rights; and equality rights.

As a constitutional document, the Charter is part of the "supreme law of the land." This means that other statutes must be in accord with its principles. If a court finds that any law violates one of the rights or freedoms listed in the Charter, it may strike down (rule invalid and unenforceable) part or all of the law and direct the government to change or repeal it. Before the Charter, the only basis on which the courts could overturn a law passed by a legislative body was a lack of legislative authority on the part of that body. The Charter has therefore greatly expanded the courts' role in reviewing legislation. From the perspective of employment law, the most important guarantee is the equality rights provision in section 15:

> 15(1) Every individual is equal before and under the law and has the right to the equal protection and equal benefit of the law without discrimination and, in particular, without discrimination based on race, national or ethnic origin, colour, religion, sex, age or mental or physical disability.
>
> (2) Subsection (1) does not preclude any law, program or activity that has as its object the amelioration of conditions of disadvantaged individuals or groups including those that are disadvantaged because of race, national or ethnic origin, colour, religion, sex, age or mental or physical disability.

Note that section 15(1) includes the words "in particular" before the list of protected grounds. Consequently, these grounds have been found not to be an exhaustive list of groups protected under the section; as seen in the *Vriend v Alberta* case, courts will add analogous (or comparable) grounds to protect members of groups who are seen as being historically disadvantaged.

The equality rights set out in section 15 also go beyond conferring the right to "formal" equality—that is, the right to be treated the same as others. The Supreme Court of Canada has repeatedly stated that the goal is "substantive equality." This means that in deciding if a law or government action is discriminatory, the courts should focus on the effect, not the intent. The test is whether the government has made a distinction that has the effect of perpetuating an arbitrary disadvantage on someone because of their membership in an enumerated or analogous group. In short, if the government action "widens the gap between the historically disadvantaged group and the rest of society rather than narrowing it, then it is discriminatory" (*Quebec (AG) v A* at para 332).

In one of the leading decisions on section 15, *Vriend v Alberta*, the Supreme Court of Canada had to decide whether the failure of Alberta's human rights legislation to include sexual orientation as a prohibited ground of discrimination was itself an infringement of the Charter's equality rights guarantee. This decision also illustrates the difference between "substantive" and "formal" equality rights.

CASE IN POINT

The Supreme Court of Canada Takes an Expansive Approach to Equality Rights

Vriend v Alberta, [1998] 1 SCR 493

Facts

Vriend was employed as a laboratory coordinator by a Christian college in Alberta where he consistently received positive evaluations and salary increases. However, shortly after he disclosed that he was gay, the college requested his resignation. When he refused, he was terminated. His subsequent attempt to file a complaint with the Alberta Human Rights Commission was unsuccessful because the province's human rights legislation at that time, the *Individual's Rights Protection Act* (IRPA), did not include sexual orientation as a protected ground. Vriend filed a motion for declaratory relief that the IRPA violated section 15 of the Charter because of its failure to include this ground. The trial judge agreed, but on appeal that decision was overturned. Vriend successfully applied to have his case heard by the Supreme Court of Canada.

Relevant Issue

Whether the omission of sexual orientation as a prohibited ground of discrimination under Alberta's human rights legislation violated section 15 of the Charter and was therefore unconstitutional.

Decision

The Supreme Court of Canada allowed Vriend's appeal, holding that sexual orientation should be "**read into**" Alberta's human rights law as a protected ground. In reaching this conclusion, the Court rejected the Alberta government's argument that the IRPA was not discriminatory because it treated homosexuals and heterosexuals equally since neither one was protected from discrimination on the basis of "sexual orientation" (i.e., formal equality). The Court noted that, looking at the social reality of discrimination against gay and lesbian Canadians, the omission of "sexual orientation" from the human rights statute clearly was far more likely to affect homosexual individuals negatively than heterosexual people. As a consequence, LGBT+ people were denied "the right to the equal protection and equal benefit of the law" as guaranteed by section 15(1), on the basis of a personal characteristic that was analogous to those grounds enumerated in the provision.

In *Vriend*, the Supreme Court actually read into a human rights law a category of people (based on sexual orientation) that a provincial legislature had previously excluded. In taking this activist approach, the Court commented that "[t]he denial by legislative omission of protection to individuals who may well be in need of it is just as serious and the consequences just as grave as that resulting from explicit exclusion" (para 98). As a decision of the Supreme Court, *Vriend* applied to other provinces, too. However, the BC government had, in 1992, already amended its human rights legislation to expressly prohibit discrimination on the basis of sexual orientation. After *Vriend*, the Alberta government also added sexual orientation to its statute.

read into
when it is determined there is extra meaning in the language of a piece of legislation, which may not have been originally intended

While the *Vriend* decision involved the courts reading in words to a statute, most successful challenges based on section 15 equality rights result in the courts striking down (nullifying) parts of the legislation. One example is the Supreme Court of Canada's 1999 decision in *M v H*. Although the facts of *M v H* had nothing to do with the workplace, the case has had a significant impact on employment law. As a result of this ruling, the provincial and federal governments were forced to change the definition of "spouse" to include same-sex partners in many pieces of legislation, including employment-related statutes.

CASE IN POINT

Definition of "Spouse" in the Family Law Act Violates Section 15 Charter Rights

M v H, [1999] 2 SCR 3

Facts

Two lesbian women, M and H, lived in a spousal relationship for several years. When they separated, M sought support payments on the basis of the role she had played in managing the home and assisting H with their advertising business during their years together. The Ontario *Family Law Act* provided that a spouse is entitled to support payments when a relationship ends. However, the definition of "spouse" was limited to married or cohabiting heterosexual couples.

Relevant Issue

Whether the *Family Law Act*'s definition of "spouse" contravened M's equality rights under section 15 of the Charter.

Decision

The Supreme Court of Canada held that the definition of "spouse" discriminated against same-sex partners and violated their equality rights. The purpose of the *Family Law Act* was to provide financial support for spouses whose relationship broke down, and excluding same-sex partners was contrary to the purpose of the law.

Accordingly, the word "spouse" is now defined in the BC *Family Law Act* to be gender-neutral: it includes married couples (which now include same-sex couples) and anyone in a "marriage-like relationship," regardless of gender. (Its predecessor, the *Family Relations Act*, had been more explicit, specifying that the "marriage-like relationship may be between persons of the same gender"). In Alberta, section 3(1) of the *Adult Interdependent Relationships Act* includes persons considered to be in a committed relationship other than marriage. The Alberta *Adult Interdependent Relationships Act* affirms that provincial legislation where partner status may be relevant applies to married and non-married interdependent couples regardless of sexual orientation. An example of this would be access to workers' compensation benefits for the partner of an employee who is injured or dies on the job.

Impact of the Charter on Private Sector Employers

The Charter directly applies only to government actions and conduct, such as passing legislation. It does not apply to the actions of individuals or private sector employers and employees. Therefore, an employee cannot use the Charter directly to challenge a private sector employer's employment decision or policy. However, an employee may be able to achieve the same result if the employer's decision or policy is based on, or allowed by, legislation that is found to contravene the Charter. For example, in the 1990 case *Douglas/Kwantlen Faculty Assn v Douglas College*, two faculty members wanted to prevent their employer from requiring them to retire at age 65 pursuant to its mandatory retirement policy as contained in the collective agreement. They challenged the constitutionality of BC's *Human Rights Code* because it failed to prohibit age-based discrimination in employment after age 64. This, they argued, contravened the Charter's equality rights provision. If they had succeeded in their argument, the Code's ceiling on age would have been declared unconstitutional, and the mandatory retirement policies of private and public sector employers would no longer be allowed. The Supreme Court of Canada agreed that the Code violated the equality rights in section 15 of the Charter. However, the faculty members were unsuccessful in their challenge at that time because of the "reasonable limits" provision found in section 1 of the Charter, which is discussed below.

Section 1: Charter Rights Subject to Reasonable Limits

The rights and freedoms guaranteed by the Charter are not unlimited. The courts may uphold violations of Charter rights if they fall within the provisions of section 1 of the Charter:

> The *Canadian Charter of Rights and Freedoms* guarantees the rights and freedoms set out in it subject only to such reasonable limits prescribed by law as can be demonstrably justified in a free and democratic society.

In the watershed case of *R v Oakes*, the Supreme Court of Canada set out a new test for determining when a law that limits a Charter right is a reasonable limit and therefore saved by section 1. A limitation of Charter rights is justifiable if:

1. the law relates to a pressing and substantial government objective; and
2. the means chosen to achieve the objective are "proportional" in that
    a. they are rationally connected to the objective;
    b. they impair the Charter right or freedom as little as possible ("minimal impairment"); and
    c. the benefits of the limit outweigh its harmful effects (in other words, the more severe the harmful effects of a measure, the more important the objective must be to justify it).

burden of proof
the obligation to prove a fact, a proposition, guilt, or innocence

Unless a law passes all parts of the test, the portion of the law that violates the Charter will be found to be unconstitutional. The **burden of proof** (i.e., the obligation to prove) lies with the government to show that the infringement is justified.

The application of the *Oakes* test is contextual and may evolve over time to reflect an appropriate balance between the rights of the individual and social objectives. For example, in the 2008 case *Association of Justices of the Peace of Ontario v Ontario (AG)*, Strathy J of the Superior Court in Ontario reached a different conclusion than the Supreme Court reached in *Douglas/Kwantlen Faculty Assn v Douglas College* and similar mandatory retirement cases. Justice Strathy found that although mandatory retirement was related to a pressing and substantial social objective, it failed the proportionality test. Minimal impairment was not established, and the harm was disproportionate to the desired objective. Justice Strathy's analysis (paras 177, 178) considered that the circumstances and views of Canadians had changed over the past two decades:

> [S]ociety's understanding of age discrimination, prohibited by the Charter, has evolved to the extent that practices considered acceptable 20 years ago are now prohibited. Our appreciation of the insidious effects of age discrimination has expanded. … [P]eople are living longer and they are working longer. While it is true that "everyone ages" and that there is, in general, a correlation between advancing age and physical and mental decline, improvements in medicine, physical and mental fitness and changed social attitudes have allowed people to make useful contributions to society well beyond the age that was once considered to be the time of retirement.

Mandatory retirement is a form of discrimination in both Alberta and BC, although this type of discrimination may be possible if an employer can show that it is a bona fide occupational requirement of a particular occupation (as has been the case with some roles in fire departments). Other aspects of age-based discrimination are covered in Chapter 7.

Section 33: The Notwithstanding Clause

The Charter contains a second potential limit on rights and freedoms through an override provision. Section 33 allows the federal or provincial governments to enact legislation "notwithstanding" (in spite of) a violation of the Charter. To invoke section 33, the government must declare that the law in question will operate notwithstanding the Charter, and this declaration must be renewed every five years. This section has rarely been invoked because few governments want to admit to knowingly infringing Charter rights. One of its rare uses occurred in June 2019, when Quebec passed Bill 21, *An Act respecting the laicity of the State*. Bill 21 is intended to maintain separation of church and state and prohibits employees in public sector positions (teachers, police officers, etc.) from wearing religious symbols while at work. This highly contested legislation discriminates based on religion and had previously been halted by an injunction that stated the law would cause "irreparable harm." It was subsequently revised and the notwithstanding clause of the Charter invoked to make legal challenges more difficult. Nonetheless, a constitutional challenge was filed immediately after the bill was passed. The legal fate and workplace impact of Bill 21 are yet to be determined.

Common Law

What Is the Common Law?

The third source of employment law is the common law, which is that part of the law that has developed over the years through court decisions. The common law is applied where there is no statute covering a particular area or where a governing statute is silent on a relevant point. For example, because most employment-related statutes define the term "employee" in general terms, judges and tribunals often look to previous **case law** to determine when an employment relationship exists and whether an individual is entitled to the statutory protections afforded employees. As noted above, even where legislation does exist, the courts' interpretations of the legislation form a body of case law that courts use to decide future cases involving that legislation.

case law
law made by judges, rather than legislatures, that is usually based on previous decisions of other judges

You can think of the sources of employment law as forming a pyramid, with the Constitution (including the Charter) at the top, because all statutes must conform to it. Regular statutes are in the middle. Common law is at the bottom because statute law takes precedence over judge-made law. Figure 1.1 illustrates this hierarchy.

FIGURE 1.1 Pyramid of Laws

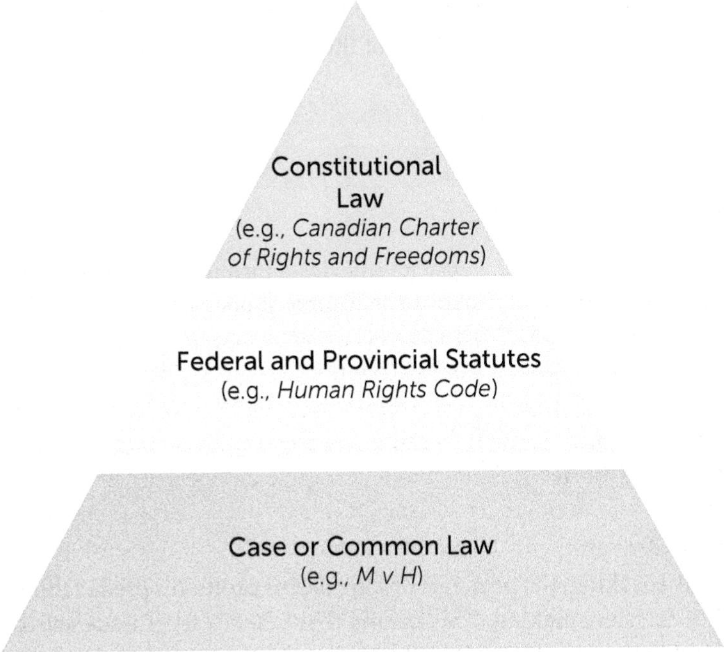

Constitutional Law (e.g., *Canadian Charter of Rights and Freedoms*)

Federal and Provincial Statutes (e.g., *Human Rights Code*)

Case or Common Law (e.g., *M v H*)

SOURCE: Adapted from Alexandrowicz et al, 2004, at 48.

precedent
what previous courts have decided in cases involving similar circumstances and principles

binding
requiring a lower court to follow a precedent from a higher court in the same jurisdiction (see also *stare decisis*)

stare decisis
a common law principle that requires lower courts to follow precedents emanating from higher courts in the same jurisdiction; Latin for "to stand by things decided"

persuasive
when a court is persuaded to follow a precedent from another jurisdiction or from a lower court, although it is not bound to do so

distinguishable
when the facts or other elements in the previous case are so different from those of the current case that the legal principle in the previous decision should not apply

Law formulated by the Supreme Court of Canada is the most significant. In BC, this is followed by law formulated by the British Columbia Court of Appeal, then the British Columbia Supreme Court, and finally the Provincial Court of British Columbia. In Alberta, a similarly tiered court structure exists, consisting of the Alberta Court of Appeal, the Alberta Court of Queen's Bench, and the Provincial Court of Alberta. More detail about Canadian courts is provided below under the heading "Judicial Framework."

Common Law Rules of Decision-Making

English-speaking Canada inherited the common law system from the British legal system, where it evolved over centuries.

To understand how the common law is applied, it is important to understand several principles of judicial decision-making. Under the common law, cases are decided by judges on the basis of **precedent**—that is, what previous courts have decided in cases involving similar circumstances and principles. Decisions made by higher courts are **binding** on lower courts in the same jurisdiction if the circumstances of the cases are similar. This principle is called ***stare decisis***, which means "to stand by things decided." A decision is considered **persuasive**, rather than binding, when a court is persuaded to follow a precedent from another jurisdiction or from a lower court, although it is not bound to do so.

In considering the weight to be given to previous cases, recent decisions tend to have more authority than older ones, and higher courts have more authority than lower ones. Where a lower court decides not to follow a previous decision from a higher court in the same jurisdiction, it may do so on the basis that the earlier case is **distinguishable**. In other words, it finds that the facts or other elements in the previous case are so different from those of the current case that the legal principle in the previous decision should not apply.

FYI

The Origin of Common Law

In the 12th century, King Henry II of England tried to bring greater consistency and fairness to the justice system. He trained a group of circuit judges who went from place to place and held assizes, or travelling courts, to hear local cases. Over time, these judges noted similarities in certain types of cases that allowed for similar judgments to be made and penalties to be assigned. At some point they began to write down their decisions and the reasons for them so that other judges could consult them. This became what we know today as case law or common law, because it allowed the law to be applied in a common fashion throughout the country (Alexandrowicz et al, 2004, at 42).

Generally speaking, the principle of *stare decisis* promotes predictability and consistency in decision-making. This means that when a legal issue arises, a lawyer knowledgeable in the field can usually predict the outcome (or range of outcomes) of the case based on the existing body of case law. However, consistency is not always achieved. For example, seemingly minor factual differences may lead to different legal results. Where, in a court's view, the application of case law would lead to an inappropriate result, the court may try to circumvent legal precedent, thus leading to apparent inconsistencies. When decisions are appealed to higher courts, the law may be clarified; otherwise, it remains unsettled until a similar case reaches an appellate court.

Occasionally there are watershed cases in which a high court decides to expand the boundaries of previous rulings or to depart entirely from a line of cases because, for example, it believes the cases no longer reflect social norms or economic realities. For example, in *British Columbia (Public Service Employee Relations Commission) v BCGSEU* (known as the *Meiorin* case), the Supreme Court of Canada reached a watershed decision in 1999 when it created a new, higher standard for employers defending a discriminatory job rule. In *Meiorin*, the Court criticized the way it and lower courts had previously analyzed discrimination cases under human rights legislation, and it redirected its interpretation. Among other things, the Court decided that an employer must accommodate employees affected by a discriminatory work rule or requirement, unless it is impossible to do so without undue hardship to the employer. Details of the case and the new approach taken by the Supreme Court are provided in Chapter 7 under the heading "Essential Requirements of the Job."

While the *Meiorin* decision is a particularly dramatic example of a case that changes the direction of the law, watershed decisions occur with some frequency in the employment arena. Changes in the composition of higher courts through the appointment of new judges may also lead to changes in the direction of case law.

Branches of the Common Law That Affect Employment

Two branches of the common law that affect employment are contract law and tort law.

Contract Law

The common law of contracts is fundamental to employment law because the legal relationship between employers and employees is contractual. An employer and a prospective non-unionized employee negotiate the terms and conditions of employment, and subject to legislative requirements their agreement forms the basis of their employment relationship. General principles of **contract law** determine whether an employer–employee relationship exists and what remedies apply to a breach of the employment agreement. While the relationship between the employer and unionized employees is also contractual, the interpretation and application of their employment contract (known as a collective agreement) is unique and covered in detail in Chapter 3. The discussion below illustrates that there are important differences between individual employment contracts and collective agreements.

contract law
an area of civil law that governs agreements between people or companies to purchase or provide goods or services

implied terms
default or mandatory rules that the courts assume are part of an employment agreement, even if they have not been expressly included in the employment contract

Most non-union employment contracts, whether written or oral (unless the parties expressly agree otherwise), contain a number of **implied terms**. Implied terms are default or mandatory rules that the courts assume are part of an employment agreement, even if they haven't been expressly included in the employment contract.

Examples include an employee's duty to be honest with the employer, and an employer's duty to provide a safe workplace. Implied terms are discussed more thoroughly in Chapter 5.

One of the implied terms that has a significant impact on individual employment law in Canada relates to dismissal. Employees in non-union, provincially regulated workplaces are entitled to reasonable notice of dismissal, or pay in lieu of notice, unless the dismissal is for **just cause** (serious misconduct). In other words, the employer must provide advance notice of dismissal or pay in lieu. Economic necessity does not relieve the employer of this obligation; employees who are laid off because of a shortage of work are entitled to reasonable notice or pay in lieu as well. This implied contractual term affects the Canadian approach to the entire employment relationship, including hiring, using written employment contracts, and managing job performance (Gilbert et al, 2011). It can be contrasted to the American approach, where in many states, employees are employed "at will," meaning that employment can be terminated without notice or cause.

just cause
serious employee misconduct that warrants dismissal without notice

In a successful lawsuit based on an individual employment contract, damages in the form of monetary compensation are awarded so that the plaintiff (the party suing) is placed in the same position that they would have been in if the defendant (the party being sued—i.e., the employer) had not breached the contract. In a wrongful dismissal action, for example, damages are awarded to reflect the wages and benefits that the plaintiff would have received had the employer provided reasonable notice of the termination.

The legal situation is different for unionized employees and those in federally regulated industries. Collective agreements require that the employer have just cause before disciplining or terminating an employee. The *Canada Labour Code* also has a just cause requirement for dismissals, which has been affirmed by the Supreme Court of Canada (see Chapter 4, Case in Point: *Wilson v Atomic Energy of Canada Limited*, 2016 SCC 29). In a non-unionized or provincially regulated workplace, the employer may end the employment relationship for any reason as long as the reason is not discriminatory and as long as the employer gives sufficient notice or pay in lieu of notice. In a unionized or federally regulated workplace, the employee must have engaged in misconduct before the employer can end the employment relationship.

The remedies available to an employee who is discharged without just cause are also different in the unionized or federal sectors. In a non-union environment, the remedies are normally monetary. In a unionized workplace they can be monetary, but the preferred remedy is to reinstate the employee to their original position. Reinstatement is rarely a remedy available to non-unionized employees in provincially regulated industries.

tort law
a branch of civil law (non-criminal law) that covers wrongs and damages that one person or company causes to another, independent of any contractual relationship between them

civil law
law that relates to private, non-criminal matters, such as property law, family law, and tort law; alternatively, law of jurisdictions, such as Quebec, that is not based on English common law

Tort Law

A tort is a wrong for which there is a legal remedy. **Tort law** is a branch of **civil law** (non-criminal law) and covers wrongs and damages that one person or company causes to another, independent of any contractual relationship between them. A tort can be either a deliberate action or a negligent action. To establish the tort of negligence, the plaintiff must show that:

1. the defendant owed the plaintiff a duty of care,
2. the defendant breached that duty and did not meet the expected standard of care, and
3. the plaintiff suffered foreseeable harm as a result.

Although tort law is typically applied when there is no contractual relationship, it may still have an impact at the workplace. An intentional tort is committed, for example, when an employer deliberately provides an unfair and inaccurate employment reference for a former employee. In this case, the former employee can sue the employer for committing the tort of defamation. A tort of negligence occurs, for example, when an employer carelessly misleads a prospective employee about the job during the hiring process and the employee suffers losses as a result of relying on the misrepresentation.

In a successful tort action, damages are awarded to the plaintiff for losses suffered as a result of the defendant's conduct. In the negligent misrepresentation situation, damages can be awarded to compensate the plaintiff for the costs of relocation (including losses on real estate) if the new job involves moving to a different city, the costs of a job search, and the emotional costs of distress.

Judicial Framework

The Court System

The court structure in Canada is hierarchical, as indicated in Figure 1.2. There are various levels of courts, the lowest being provincial courts and the highest being the Supreme Court of Canada. Parties who dislike the decision they receive in a lower court may appeal that decision under certain circumstances. The appeal system assists in the creation of consistent laws because a higher court may overturn the decision of a lower court that has failed to follow precedent.

The Supreme Court of Canada

Located in Ottawa, the Supreme Court of Canada is the final court of appeal. It hears cases from provincial courts of appeal and from the Federal Court of Appeal. However, it hears appeals only if it has granted leave to appeal. Because of its heavy workload, it grants leave to appeal only when a case is of general public importance or where the law requires clarification. Decisions of the Supreme Court of Canada bind all lower courts across Canada.

Other Courts

Each province has a court of appeal that hears appeals from decisions of the provincial superior courts. In BC, the court of appeal is called the British Columbia Court of Appeal, and in Alberta, it is called the Alberta Court of Appeal. The provinces' superior courts are the BC Supreme Court and the Alberta Court of Queen's Bench. Both have civil as well as criminal jurisdiction and are the primary trial courts.

They generally hear cases involving serious criminal offences, commercial or family matters, and appeals from lower courts for claims that exceed $35,000 in BC and $50,000 in Alberta.

FIGURE 1.2 The Structure of Federal and Provincial Court of Law

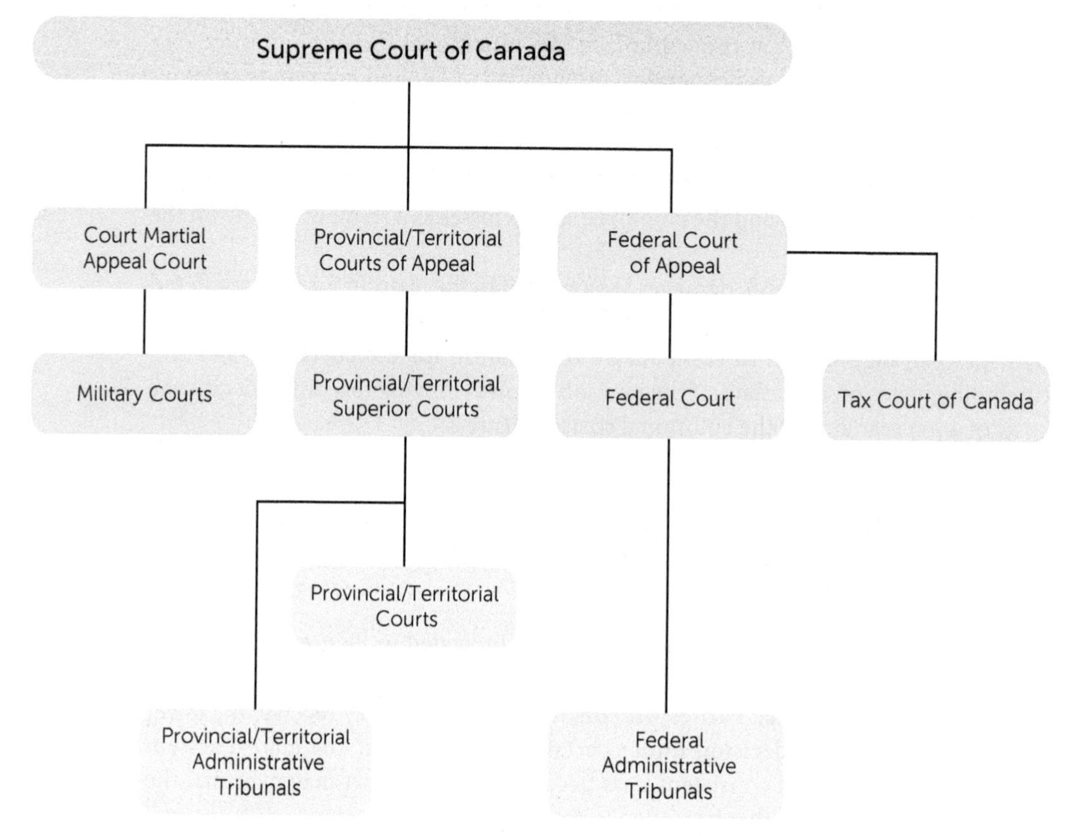

SOURCE: Based on Canada, Department of Justice, 2019.

Each province also maintains courts of special jurisdiction. These preside over matters such as small claims, family law (excluding divorce), juvenile offences, traffic violations, and trials of less serious criminal offences (Gilbert et al, 2011).

In Canada, judges are not elected. The federal or provincial government, depending on the level of court, appoints judges.

The Administrative System

Administrative Tribunals

administrative tribunals a quasi-judicial authority whose rules are typically governed by a subject-specific statute

Administrative tribunals have been established to make decisions in specialized areas, such as employment standards (e.g., the BC Employment Standards Tribunal) or discrimination (e.g., the Alberta Human Rights Commission). In employment law, administrative tribunals have primary jurisdiction over most matters. The main exception is the common law of wrongful dismissal, where disputes are heard in the traditional court system.

Tribunals act in a quasi-judicial manner, meaning that they observe the rules of procedural fairness and provide a full hearing, but they are less formal than courts, and their members are experts in employment matters. Although administrative tribunals are technically subordinate to the courts, appeals to the courts from their decisions are usually limited by statute in a provision called a **privative clause**. However, privative clauses do not displace the jurisdiction of the courts entirely, and courts may also overturn a tribunal's decision if it exceeded its jurisdiction, showed bias, or denied a party natural justice (Gilbert et al, 2011).

privative clause
a provision limiting appeals to the courts from decisions of administrative tribunals

A request to a court to review the decision of an administrative tribunal is called an application for **judicial review**. The Alberta Court of Queen's Bench and BC Supreme Court conduct judicial reviews. In Alberta, the Labour Relations Board became the appeal body for some parts of the *Occupational Health and Safety Act* and for the *Employment Standards Code* in 2019. In any appeal a decision may be overturned based on questions of fact or applying the facts to the law only if the decision was "unreasonable" (the stricter standard of "correctness" is only used in certain circumstances—see below). As the Supreme Court of Canada stated in *Dunsmuir v New Brunswick*, a decision will be found to be unreasonable only if it falls outside "a range of possible, acceptable outcomes which are defensible in respect of the facts and law" (at para 5). In other words, the reviewing court does not have to agree with the tribunal's decision as long as it is justifiable and supported with reasoning. This is a very deferential **standard of review** that recognizes the experience and expertise of specialized administrative bodies and the authority conferred on them by the legislature. However, for those relatively few cases that turn on a question of law that is outside the tribunal's area of expertise, such as constitutional law, reviewing courts will apply the "correctness" standard. This means that the court will substitute its own view if it does not agree with the tribunal's result.

judicial review
a request to a court to review the decision of an administrative tribunal

standard of review
the level of scrutiny that an appeal court will apply to the decision of a lower court or tribunal

More information concerning specific administrative processes and tribunals can be found in the chapters dealing with the related employment statutes.

Administrative Agencies

Below tribunals in the administrative hierarchy there are usually **administrative agencies** empowered to investigate complaints, make rulings, and sometimes issue orders. These agencies, or commissions, usually issue policy guidelines and perform an educational role in furthering the goals of a statute. For example, the Employment Standards Branch in BC and the Employment Standards Agency in Alberta play a key role in educating employers and employees about workplace issues and in administering the system in each province. There are also agencies and tribunals responsible for the physical well-being of employees, empowered under workers' compensation and occupational health and safety legislation (see Chapters 8 and 9).

administrative agencies
lower tribunals in the administrative hierarchy empowered to investigate complaints, make rulings, and sometimes issue orders

Individual employees may gain access to an administrative agency at no monetary cost to themselves; once a claim or complaint is initiated, the agency pursues the claim on behalf of the employee. An agency may have an internal appeal procedure, usually with the possibility of a further appeal to a board or tribunal (Gilbert et al, 2011). For example, in BC, there is an internal appeal procedure from a decision of the director of employment standards to the Employment Standards Tribunal, as set out in part 13 of the *Employment Standards Act*.

TABLE 1.1 Summary of Key Sources of Employment Law

Legal Source	Cause of Action	Initial Decision-Making
Individual employment contracts	Violating terms and conditions of individual employment contract—e.g., wrongful dismissal	BC & Alberta Small Claims Courts BC Supreme Court Court of Queen's Bench
Collective agreements	Violating terms and conditions of a collective agreement—e.g., unjust dismissal grievance	Arbitration board
Provincial employment standards legislation	Violating minimum employment standards—e.g., hours of work, vacation, minimum wage	Employment standards officer
Provincial human rights legislation	Discrimination in employment based on specified grounds—e.g., race or disability	Human Rights Tribunal
Provincial labour codes	Violation of the labour code by unions or employers—e.g., failing to bargain in good faith	Labour Relations Board
Canada Labour Code (federal)	Violation of the Labour Code affecting occupational health and safety, labour relations, and minimum employment standards	Canada Industrial Relations Board, adjudicator, or inspector
Provincial occupational health and safety legislation	Violating occupational health and safety legislation	Health and safety inspector
Provincial workers' compensation legislation	Provision of income replacement benefits to an employee with an illness or injury occurring at work	Workers' compensation board claims adjudicator
Provincial privacy legislation	Inappropriately accessing or releasing private employee information	Privacy Commissioner

Where to Find Employment Laws

Common Law

Court decisions are found in a number of case reporters—national, regional, provincial, and topical (see Table 1.1, above). These are periodical publications containing judges' written decisions. Because it is expensive to purchase case reporters, the Internet is now used more frequently to conduct legal research (Alexandrowicz et al, 2004, at 62-63). Discussions of case law can be found in encyclopedic digests, textbooks, loose-leaf reporting series, blogs, and newsletters. Links to a number of legal blogs specializing in Canadian labour and employment can be found at <http://www.lawblogs.ca/category/labour-employment>.

Reading and interpreting case citations is an important skill for researching legal cases. A **case citation** tells you how to locate a specific case. It sets out the case name, year in which the decision was made or in which it was published in the case reporter, volume number of the case reporter, series number, page number, and court. Consider the following case citation:

case citation
a reference for locating a case that sets out the case name, year in which the decision was made or in which it was published in a case reporter, volume number of the case reporter, series number, page number, and court

***Douglas/Kwantlen Faculty Assn v Douglas College*, [1990] 3 SCR 570**

- *Douglas/Kwantlen Faculty Assn v Douglas College.* Douglas/Kwantlen Faculty Assn is the plaintiff, and Douglas College is the defendant. In reports of older appeal cases, the first party named is the **appellant** (the party requesting the appeal), and the party named after the "v" ("versus") is the **respondent** (the party opposing the appeal), but courts have begun to simplify citations by always keeping the plaintiff's name first and the defendant's name after the "v" even on appeal cases—regardless of who is appealing.
- [1990]. Square brackets indicate the year that the case reporter volume was published. Sometimes parentheses are used in case citations to indicate the year in which a case was decided, if that year is different from the reporter year.
- 3 SCR. This refers to the case reporter volume and name. It indicates that the case can be found in the third volume of the 1990 Supreme Court Reports.
- 570. This is the page number.

appellant
the party requesting the appeal

respondent
the party opposing the appeal

A case may be published in several different case reporters, so you may see several alternate citations, called **parallel citations**. However, these are less important today given the use of Internet databases such as CanLII for finding cases and the adoption of neutral citations (see below).

parallel citations
references to a case published in two or more different case reporters

Many Internet citations, especially for provincial and territorial courts, use the following form or a variation of it:

***R v Tschetter* (7 May 2009), 080092455P10101-012 (Alta Prov Ct)**

This citation refers to a criminal case heard in the Alberta Provincial Court where judgment was issued on May 7, 2009. The number 080092455P10101-012 is a docket reference to the list of cases tried in Alberta. "R" is an abbreviation of "Regina," meaning the Queen or Crown.

neutral citation
a form of citation that includes the traditional case name; the core of the citation, containing the year of the decision, a court or tribunal identifier, and a number assigned to the decision; and possible optional elements, such as paragraph numbers or notes

Most Canadian courts have adopted a new method of citing judicial decisions. Since 2001, cases are assigned a **neutral citation**, which gives a unique identifier but does not refer to any case reporter. This neutral citation standard has three main parts: the traditional case name; the core of the citation, containing the year of the decision, a court or tribunal identifier, and a number assigned to the decision; and possible optional elements, such as paragraph numbers or notes. Consider the following example:

***Starson v Swayze*, 2003 SCC 32**

In this example, *Starson v Swayze* is the case name, 2003 is the year the decision was rendered, SCC (Supreme Court of Canada) is the court identifier, and 32 is the number of the decision—that is, the 32nd decision of the Supreme Court in 2003. The numbering sequence usually restarts each January 1.

Statute Law

The federal and provincial governments each publish their statutes and regulations. These can be purchased from the Queen's Printer and found in most public libraries and on the Internet.

Four useful Internet search sites are as follows:

- <http://www.canlii.org/en>
  The Canadian Legal Information Institute (CanLII) is a good source for federal and provincial statutes and regulations, as well as cases. The site is run by the Federation of Law Societies of Canada, which is the umbrella organization of Canada's 14 law societies.
- <http://laws.justice.gc.ca/eng>
  The federal Department of Justice offers a consolidation of federal statutes and regulations in a side-by-side bilingual PDF version. It also provides links to "Amendments Not in Force" and "Related Provisions."
- <http://www.bclaws.ca>
  The BC government's website provides statutes and regulations for the province, kept current to within two or three weeks (as noted at the top of each statute on the site).
- <http://www.qp.alberta.ca/laws_online.cfm>
  The Alberta government's website provides statutes and regulations for the province.

Staying Current

It is important to keep abreast of changes in the law. Newsworthy cases are often reported in newspaper articles, but you need legally focused sources as well, such as law firm newsletters, industry association publications, and employment reporting services.

KEY TERMS

administrative agencies, **23**
administrative tribunals, **22**
appellant, **25**
binding, **18**
burden of proof, **16**
case citation, **25**
case law, **17**
civil law, **20**
common law, **4**
constitutional law, **4**
contract law, **19**
distinguishable, **18**
implied terms, **19**
judicial review, **23**
jurisdiction, **8**
just cause, **20**
members (of administrative tribunals), **8**
neutral citation, **26**
parallel citations, **25**
persuasive, **18**
precedent, **18**
privative clause, **23**
read into, **13**
regulations, **7**
respondent, **25**
standard of review, **23**
stare decisis, **18**
statute law, **4**
tort law, **20**

REVIEW AND DISCUSSION QUESTIONS

1. Name a significant current demographic trend, and discuss the effect that it might have on employment law in the future.
2. In your opinion, what are some of the strengths and weaknesses of the common law system?
3. The *Canadian Charter of Rights and Freedoms* applies only where the government is involved. However, the Charter can indirectly affect private sector employers. How?
4. Describe two possible tools or rules that a judge or tribunal adjudicator can use in determining how to interpret a statute.
5. For each of the following situations, discuss what law (statute, common law, or constitutional law) applies. Do you believe the individual has a legitimate legal complaint? Why or why not? What do you think is the likely outcome and remedy if the employee files a complaint and is successful?
   a. Sheila worked at a BC location of a national restaurant chain for two years (making just above minimum wage). She has no written employment contract and is suddenly let go with no notice and no pay in lieu of notice. The employer simply says they are downsizing.
   b. Viktor is an engineer working for Big Oil Drilling Company in Alberta. He is discharged shortly after telling his employer he suffers from alcoholism. The reason Viktor admitted he had an alcohol addiction was because he had missed quite a lot of work recently and had been placed on an absence management program.
   c. Janice is a unionized registered nurse. She applied for another position in her hospital in BC but lost out to a male colleague. Janice had more experience and stronger qualifications.
   d. Bob is a senior sales manager who is let go after 12 years with his Alberta-based IT company. He has a contract that specifies notice well in excess of statutory minimums in addition to a severance package. Bob is not awarded the notice period, pay in lieu of notice, or the severance specified in his contract. The employer alleges just cause for poor performance, but all Bob's reviews were satisfactory.
   e. Sahana, a non-unionized window washer in Alberta, is suspended for one month without pay because she refused to work at a building until the harness on the washer's scaffolding was replaced. She felt the system was unsafe.
   f. Felix has been discharged from his job as a truck driver for a company that transports goods across the country. Although he has tried to be discreet, Felix gets fired within two weeks of attempting to organize his co-workers to become unionized. The employer does not provide a reason for the termination but provides pay in lieu of notice to Felix.

RELATED WEBSITES

The Canadian Legal Information Institute <http://www.canlii.org/en>

Federal legislation on the Justice Laws website <http://laws.justice.gc.ca/eng>

BC legislation <http://www.bclaws.ca>

The Alberta government's Queen's Printer website <http://www.qp.alberta.ca/laws_online.cfm>

REFERENCES

1254582 Alberta Ltd v Miscellaneous Employees Teamsters Local Union 987 of Alberta, 2009 ABQB 127.

Adult Interdependent Relationships Act, SA 2002, c A-4.5.

Alberta Human Rights Act, RSA 2000, c A-25.5.

Alexandrowicz, George, et al, *Dimensions of Law: Canadian and International Law in the 21st Century* (Toronto: Emond Montgomery, 2004).

Association of Justices of the Peace of Ontario v Ontario (AG), 2008 CanLII 26258 (Ont Sup Ct J).

British Columbia (Public Service Employee Relations Commission) v BCGSEU, [1999] 3 SCR 3.

Canada Labour Code, RSC 1985, c L-2.

Canada Pension Plan, RSC 1985, c C-8.

Canadian Charter of Rights and Freedoms, Part I of the *Constitution Act, 1982*, being Schedule B to the *Canada Act 1982* (UK), 1982, c 11.

Canadian Human Rights Act, RSC 1985, c H-6.

Department of Justice, "How the Courts Are Organized" (11 September 2019), online: *Government of Canada* <http://www.justice.gc.ca/eng/csj-sjc/ccs-ajc/02.html>.

Douglas/Kwantlen Faculty Assn v Douglas College, [1990] 3 SCR 570.

Dunsmuir v New Brunswick, 2008 SCC 9.

Employment Insurance Act, SC 1996, c 23.

Employment Standards Act, RSBC 1996, c 113.

Employment Standards Code, RSA 2000, c E-9.

Family Law Act, RSO 1990, c F.3.

Family Law Act, SBC 2011, c 25.

Family Relations Act, RSBC 1996, c 128 [repealed].

Gilbert, Douglas, et al, *Canadian Labour and Employment Law for the US Practitioner*, 3rd ed (Washington, DC: Bureau of National Affairs, 2011).

Human Rights Code, RSBC 1996, c 210.

Joey's Delivery Service v New Brunswick (Workplace Health, Safety and Compensation Commission), 2001 NBCA 17.

Labour Relations Code, RSA 2000, c L-1.

Labour Relations Code, RSBC 1996, c 244.

M v H, [1999] 2 SCR 3.

Oakes, R v, [1986] 1 SCR 103.

Occupational Health and Safety Act, RSA 2000, c O-2.

Occupational Health and Safety Regulation, BC Reg 296/97.

Personal Information Protection Act, SA 2003, c P-6.5.

Personal Information Protection Act, SBC 2003, c 63.

Quebec (AG) v A, 2013 SCC 5.

Toronto Electric Commissioners v Snider, 1925 CanLII 331 (UK JCPC).

Tschetter, R v (7 May 2009), 080092455P10101-0112 (Alta Prov Ct).

Vriend v Alberta, [1998] 1 SCR 493.

Workers Compensation Act, RSBC 1996, c 492.

Workers' Compensation Act, RSA 2000, c W-15.

Provincially Regulated Employers

Understanding Common Law

LEARNING OUTCOMES

After completing this chapter, you will be able to:

- Understand key common law issues related to hiring, including negligent misrepresentation.
- Understand the effect of using executive search firms in the recruitment process.
- Explain the legal implications of using background checks, including conducting Internet and social media searches.
- Understand differences in categories of employees, including full-time, part-time, and temporary employees.

Introduction

Although issues arising under human rights legislation present the most significant challenges facing employers during the hiring process, common law issues arise as well. For issues involving human rights, such as discrimination in the hiring process, see Chapter 7. This chapter's focus is on the rules for hiring found in the common law and in some legislation governing information sharing. The chapter begins by looking at the main areas of potential common law liability for employers and employees during the recruitment, selection, and hiring phases. These include misrepresentations by job candidates, the employer, and executive search firms; inappropriate inducements by employers to lure a job candidate; negligent hiring where an employer fails to conduct proper background checks; and anticipatory breach of contract.

The chapter then reviews the common law distinction between employees and independent contractors. Parties who intend to create a principal–independent contractor relationship must ensure they do not inadvertently create an employer–employee relationship. Such a mistake can have serious cost implications for both parties.

The chapter concludes by briefly discussing different categories of employees. Although in most situations the law does not distinguish one group of employees from another, categories such as full- and part-time employees are commonly referred to and are noted here for clarification.

Areas of Common Law Liability

Misrepresentation by Job Candidates

There is no legislation that requires job candidates to be honest during the application process. However, courts have held that misrepresentations made by employees before they are hired may justify dismissal if the misrepresentations go to the root of their qualifications for the job. In other words, if a false statement related to qualifications or work experience has a significant impact on the hiring decision, an employer can terminate an employee as a result of that misstatement, even if the employee is performing the job satisfactorily.

The question has also arisen as to whether legislation allows an applicant to omit information requested by the employer during the recruitment process. The courts' response has been that if the requested information is not provided within the time period specified, the omission may be equated to a misrepresentation and the employee may be terminated. In the 2006 arbitration decision *Union of Calgary Co-operative Employees v Calgary Co-operative Association Limited*, the nature of the employer's business required that employees be bondable. The employer's insurance policy stipulated that an employee must not have committed "any Fraudulent or Dishonest Act," either "before or after the date of employment." JJ, the grievor, had consented to a security check, and the offer of employment made to him was conditional on his supplying the security information to his potential employer. The Calgary Police Service waiver and release contained the proviso that

> in cases where an adult's record contains young offender information or a young offender requests a copy of his/her criminal record, the criminal

> record information WILL ONLY be given to the applicant. Individuals can disclose their own information to a third party, but even with consent, the Calgary Police Service is not legally permitted to disclose young offender information, other than to the applicant.

When JJ failed to deliver the security check results to his employer, the consequence was an administrative termination of his employment. Counsel for the grievor argued that the privacy rights of young offenders should be honoured and that the young person should be protected from "the stigma of societal response to convictions." But the Alberta Arbitration Board looked to the 1992 Supreme Court of Canada decision in *R v T (V)* and found instead that employers must be given "adequate information on a need-to-know basis" in order to meet due diligence requirements. A young person applying for employment, Arbitrator Beattie said, can choose whether the right to privacy is more important than the disclosure of a record. Once the young person decides to disclose the record, it becomes "authorized" and neither the express provisions nor the spirit of the legislation is breached. Instead, a required disclosure going to the root of the applicant's qualifications represents a balancing of the sound and legitimate concerns of the employer with the rights to privacy enshrined in the former *Young Offenders Act* and its successor, the *Youth Criminal Justice Act*.

This principle of misrepresentation by job candidates also applies to false statements that are not necessarily material to the hiring decision but that suggest an inherent lack of honesty, especially where the job requires a high degree of trust. If, for example, a candidate indicated that they had obtained a particular academic degree when in fact they had completed most of the course work but never graduated, dismissal may be justified. In *Cornell v Rogers Cablesystems Inc*, the Court found that dismissal was justified where the applicant misled the prospective employer into believing that he was still employed by his former employer.

On the other hand, minor misstatements that do not significantly misrepresent the applicant's qualifications or character do not usually justify dismissal without notice. In general, misstatements, even deliberate ones, that do not induce the employer to hire the applicant will not justify dismissal, even if they influence some of the terms of hiring. For example, if an applicant unintentionally misstated the length of time they had worked in a previous job and that misinformation was not significant to the employer, the employer probably could not dismiss the employee without reasonable notice. Likewise, misstatements about an applicant's previous salary may not justify dismissal, even if the misstatement was intentional. In the case of *Islip v Coldmatic Refrigeration of Canada Ltd*, the defendant company began talking with Islip about hiring him away from one of its competitors. Islip wrote out a proposed contract of employment, which Coldmatic accepted. In the proposal, Islip deliberately overstated his current salary by more than 20 percent, to gain a better salary with the new employer. Coldmatic later tried to claim it had the right to withdraw from the contract or to dismiss Islip with cause because of the misstatement. The British Columbia Court of Appeal found that the misstatement did not induce Coldmatic to hire Islip: it would have hired him at the higher salary even if it had known the truth. The Court also found that the misstatement was not a serious enough misrepresentation to justify dismissal for dishonesty. Statements about past salaries are less critical than statements about an applicant's qualifications to do the job. Cases in other provinces have similarly held that an applicant's misstatement of a current or past salary is not sufficiently misleading to support dismissal without notice (e.g., *Earle v Grant Transport*). (For the general rules regarding dismissal with or without notice, see Chapters 13 and 14.) Candidate misrepresentations during the hiring process of a more minor nature may not justify termination, but they still speak to a question of the individual's integrity and could justify disciplinary action by the employer, if the circumstances warrant.

attestation clause
a clause on a job application form that states that the information provided is true and complete to the applicant's knowledge and that a false statement may disqualify the applicant from employment or be grounds for dismissal

Employers who wish to emphasize the importance of honesty in filling out application forms and to buttress their legal position should include an **attestation clause** at the end of all job application forms. This clause should state that the information provided is true and complete to the applicant's knowledge and that the applicant realizes that a false statement may disqualify them from employment, may lead to disciplinary action, or may be cause for dismissal. The clause could also state that incomplete information may be cause for administrative dismissal, as was the consequence in the *Union of Calgary Co-operative Employees* case. Thus, if the employer subsequently discovers a serious misrepresentation, it can establish that the employee was forewarned about the possible consequences, including dismissal without notice. Similarly, if an employer believes that a certain educational or professional qualification is necessary for a particular job, it should state this in its job posting or hiring policy (Miedema & Hall, 2012, at 43).

Wrongful Hiring: Negligent Misrepresentation

Misrepresentation by an Employer

An employer also may be legally liable for inaccurate statements made during the hiring process. If the employer makes a misrepresentation that is relied on by a prospective employee and that employee suffers damages because of it, the employer may have to compensate the employee. It is irrelevant whether the employer sincerely believed that the misleading or inaccurate statements were true. The employer has an obligation to ensure that material statements made during the recruitment process are accurate.

The leading case in the area of negligent misrepresentation in hiring is *Queen v Cognos Inc*. It demonstrates the potential liability that exists when an employer fails to ensure the accuracy of statements made during the hiring process.

CASE IN POINT

Negligent Misrepresentation in Hiring

Queen v Cognos Inc, [1993] 1 SCR 87

Facts

Queen was living with his family in Calgary, where he had been practising as a chartered accountant for approximately eight and a half years, when he responded to the employer's advertisement for a position in Ottawa. During the interview, the employer's representative told him that the job involved a major project that was going to be developed over the next two years and that would be maintained by the individual hired. Although the representative was aware at the time of the interview that senior management had not yet approved funding for the project, he did not advise Queen that the job was dependent on the funding approval. Queen accepted the job, leaving a position that paid well and was secure. He signed a written contract of employment under which he could be terminated without cause on one month's notice or pay in lieu of notice. He moved his family from Calgary to Ottawa. However, funding for the project failed to materialize, and he was dismissed shortly thereafter. He brought an action for negligent misrepresentation in hiring.

Relevant Issue

Whether the employer was liable for negligent misrepresentation.

Decision

The Supreme Court of Canada held that the employer and its representative breached the duty of care owed to Queen during the hiring process. The Court found that to establish a negligent misrepresentation, the following test must be met:

- there must be a duty of care based on a special relationship between the party making the representation and the candidate;
- the representation must be untrue, inaccurate, and misleading;
- the party making the representation must have acted negligently in making the misrepresentation;
- the candidate must have reasonably relied on the negligent misrepresentation; and
- the reliance must have caused harm to the candidate.

The Supreme Court found that an employer owes a duty to a job candidate beyond merely being honest—it must also be careful that it does not mislead potential employees. It was apparent to the employer's representative that Queen was relying on the information provided during the interview in deciding to take the job. To meet the duty of care, the representative should have informed Queen of the precarious nature of senior management's financial commitment to the project.

Queen was entitled to damages of $50,000 for loss of income, the cost of obtaining other employment, the loss incurred on the sale of his Ottawa home, and general damages of $5,000 for emotional stress. This damage award is significant, particularly given Queen's short tenure and the value of money over time. The equivalent of this award in 2020 dollars would be approximately $88,000.

Actions for negligent misrepresentation in hiring are uncommon in Canada because employees recruited under false pretenses who are subsequently dismissed generally claim wrongful dismissal rather than negligent misrepresentation suits. However, in *Queen v Cognos Inc*, the candidate had signed a written contract of employment that limited his notice of termination to one month. The Court found that the fact that he had signed an employment contract did not remove the employer's liability for the misrepresentation made during pre-contract discussions. The written contract did not prevent the negligent misrepresentation action because the misrepresentation went to the "nature and extent" of the employment opportunity, and the contract did not cover this issue.

However, for a claim of negligent misrepresentation to succeed, the candidate's reliance on the negligent misrepresentation must be reasonable, as the case of *Beauchemin v Universal Handling Equipment Co* illustrates. When the plaintiff was 48 years old, he elected to leave his employer of 17 years at New Noble Cultivators in Nobleford, Alberta, for a job as an operations manager with the defendant, Universal, a light steel products company in Red Deer.

When after only five months of employment he was terminated, Beauchemin sued for wrongful dismissal and alleged that Universal had negligently misrepresented the nature of the job in pre-contract recruitment discussions. But after applying the test in *Queen v Cognos Inc*, the Alberta Court of Queen's Bench rejected Beauchemin's negligent misrepresentation claim. In addressing the first requirement of the test, the Court noted that the defendant had conceded that it owed Beauchemin a duty of care based on the "special relationship" between recruiters and job candidates. However, Universal denied that its statement that the operations manager position was "full-time permanent employment" should have been construed by Beauchemin as being in any way in the nature of a promise or guarantee to employ him until retirement, regardless of the suitability of his management style and quality of his job performance. The Court concluded that it had been unreasonable for the plaintiff to rely on that interpretation of the defendant's statement and determined that negligent misrepresentation had not been established.

There are a number of steps that an employer can take to fulfill its obligations and thereby mitigate liability. In fact, a judge, citing *Crisall v Western Pontiac Buick GMC (1999) Ltd*, said that "The burden on the employer to prove the employee's failure to mitigate is described as ' … a burden not lightly discharged'" (*D'Souza v Acero Engineering Inc* at para 85). As such, an employer should ensure that all information it provides in the pre-employment stage is accurate and complete. It should ensure that the job description is accurate and that all interviewers know what the prospective job and compensation package encompass. The employer's representatives must be candid about the job, providing a realistic preview. Attempts to make the job sound as attractive as possible should be avoided if they involve misleading a candidate in any way. If the interviewer does not know the answer to a question asked by a candidate, the interviewer should undertake to contact the candidate with the correct answer.

When a candidate is chosen, the employer should prepare a written employment contract that sets out the terms of employment. The contract should include a clause stating that all prior oral representations are void on the signing of the contract (this is known as an "entire-agreement" clause; see Chapter 5). Such a clause may override inaccurate statements and simple misunderstandings made in the hiring process.

There are limits to when an employer will be held liable for misstatements made during the hiring process. For example, employers will not be found liable where an employee's reliance on an employer's information is unreasonable. Where a reasonable person would have detected the inaccuracy or where the employee was in a position to verify the facts of a statement but failed to do so, the plaintiff will not be successful. Reliance on opinions or idle comments does not constitute grounds for a negligent misrepresentation claim, and misstatements that result in mere inconvenience do not establish a claim (Gilbert et al, 2011).

Recruitment and Executive Search Firm Misrepresentations

Employers often use recruitment agencies or executive search firms to recruit potential candidates. Most representations made by a recruitment firm are the legal responsibility of the employer. For example, if an overly zealous search firm recruiter promises a job candidate annual pay increases of 20 percent, that representation could bind the employer. If the pay increases do not materialize, it is possible that the employee could successfully sue the employer for breach of the employment contract.

Therefore, the employer's contract with the search firm should specify the position, compensation, and career potential for the job and restrict the firm to providing only that information to job candidates. Representations about the job should be limited to those authorized by the employer. The contract should also contain an **indemnity clause** establishing the search firm's liability in the event that it makes a misrepresentation to a candidate for which the employer is subsequently held liable.

indemnity clause
a provision in a contract under which one party commits to compensate the other for any harm, liability, or loss arising out of the contract

As shown in the case of *The Treaty Group Inc v Drake*, an executive search firm may also be legally responsible if it is negligent in the way it conducts its search and the employer suffers damages as a result.

CASE IN POINT

Executive Search Firm Liable in Both Contract and Tort

The Treaty Group Inc v Drake, 2007 ONCA 450, aff'g 2005 CanLII 45406 (Ont Sup Ct J)

Facts

Treaty retained Drake, a global personnel and training firm, to fill a position that involved bookkeeping and banking duties. Drake's marketing material promised that it would provide the "highest calibre of professional screening, evaluation and reference checking," and Treaty hired Drake's recommended candidate, Simpson. However, when Simpson resigned from her position two years later, Treaty discovered that she had defrauded the company of over $263,000. It turned out that Simpson had been twice criminally convicted of defrauding former employers, but Drake had not uncovered that information. In addition to taking action against Simpson, Treaty sued Drake, claiming damages on the basis of both breach of contract and tort for negligent misrepresentation concerning the quality of its service and negligence in failing to conduct proper reference checks.

Relevant Issue

Whether the executive search firm is liable for losses sustained by Treaty as a result of the employee's fraud.

Decision

The trial judge, upheld by the Court of Appeal, held that Drake was liable for Treaty's losses on the basis of both the tort of negligence and breach of contract because it was clear that had Drake properly checked Simpson's background, Treaty would not have hired her. However, damages were limited to 50 percent of the total amount of $263,324 on the principle of **contributory negligence**, because Treaty could have avoided the losses if it had supervised Simpson more carefully.

Inducement: Aggressive Recruiting

A tort known as "inducement," "allurement," or "enticement" occurs when an employee is lured from their current position through aggressive recruiting or inflated promises. Aggressive recruiting involves more than advertising a position. It requires a significant degree of pursuit, such as repeatedly contacting the candidate and encouraging them to leave their current job. The tort of enticement may also occur when the recruiter promises such things as promotions, salary increases, job security, or other benefits that never materialize.

contributory negligence
a common law defence in an action arising from negligence in which it is asserted that the plaintiff's own negligence directly caused or contributed to the injuries suffered

Where the tort of inducement is committed and the new employee is subsequently dismissed by the employer, the employee may be entitled to a larger award for wrongful dismissal damages than if there had been no inducement. Usually, in determining the length of notice of termination that a dismissed employee is entitled to, the court looks at length of service, age, position, and the availability of similar employment (see Chapter 14 for more details on calculating notice). However, where it finds that the employee was lured to a new job from a secure job, it considers additional factors in determining reasonable notice. It may extend the notice period on the basis of such factors as how secure the previous job was, whether the employee rejected other job offers that provided greater benefits, and whether the new job involved relocating. The rationale for this is that where a person is enticed to leave a secure position, it is unfair to wrongfully dismiss them after a short period of employment and then rely on a short notice entitlement.

For example, in *Crisall v Western Pontiac Buick GMC (1999) Ltd*, Crisall was given only one week's notice when she was dismissed by the defendant Edmonton car dealership that had recruited her for a position as a commissioned salesperson. Crisall sued for a greater notice period, and the Court looked at how she had been recruited. After having encountered Crisall while she was working at Denny Andrews Ford Sales, the Western Pontiac Buick business manager decided to phone her and encourage the 30 year old to attend a job interview with his dealership. She, however, was not seeking alternative employment, had a stable position, enjoyed her job, and enjoyed the people she was working with.

Although she voiced her reluctance to do so, she was nevertheless persuaded to attend an interview with Western Pontiac's business manager and general manager. Several weeks later she received messages from both men, who were seeking a second interview with her. She clearly stated that she intended to stay with Denny Andrews Ford, but was once again persuaded to attend an interview. Once more, she expressed reluctance to leave her employer. However, when Western Pontiac offered her a commission rate that was 5 percent higher than her current rate, a $350 per month car allowance, and a life and disability benefits package, she accepted.

But after only five months in her new position, she was suddenly terminated. A number of factors militated against the likelihood of Crisall's succeeding in a claim for an extension of damages based on the tort of inducement: (1) she had not had to relocate to accept the new job, because Western Pontiac Buick was right across the street from Denny Andrews Ford; (2) her length of service at Denny Andrews had been only ten months; (3) she had not rejected other job offers because she simply was not seeking employment; (4) despite the fact that she had three bachelor's degrees, it could not be argued that she held a management-level position at Western Pontiac; (5) she was only 30 years of age; and (6) similar employment was readily available, as evidenced by the fact that the day following her termination she made immediate efforts to become re-employed and had been offered a new job within a week (although the start date was not until two months later).

Despite these factors, the Alberta Court of Queen's Bench awarded an extension of notice to three months. The rationale for the extension was based on inducement, which the Court said went "beyond the ordinary degree of persuasion" (at para 62). The Court took a dim view of the recruitment style of the defendant, refused to minimize or trivialize Crisall's loss, and affirmed that employment is a defining characteristic in one's life, central to self-worth and identity.

An employer that overstates the features of a job may find that it has also committed the tort of negligent misrepresentation. Inducement and negligent misrepresentation are separate torts, but they can both arise from the same situation.

In summary, honesty and openness about the job being offered, especially in the area of job security and the possibilities for career advancement, are essential. It is never advisable for an employer to make specific promises with respect to long-term job security, such as "I guarantee you'll be in this job for at least five years."

The issue of the termination notice period should be addressed by the employer and employee in a written employment contract before the employee starts the job. For example, if the prospective employee is leaving a secure job of 18 years, the parties should state whether, or to what extent, this service will be recognized in determining reasonable notice of termination. It is better for both parties to negotiate this sensitive issue while they are on positive terms.

Restrictive Covenants

Many written employment contracts restrict the ability of employees to compete with their former employer, to solicit the former employer's employees or customers, or to use the former employer's confidential information. Before hiring an applicant, an employer should find out whether the applicant is subject to a **restrictive covenant**—that is, a promise not to engage in certain types of activities during or after employment—that might affect their ability to perform the new job.

restrictive covenant
a promise not to engage in certain types of activities during or after employment

Restrictive covenants are seen as a "restraint of trade" and are enforceable only if they are reasonable in the circumstances. The courts do not like contractual terms that inhibit or prevent someone from earning a living in their own field. Therefore, courts uphold a restrictive covenant only if an employer can show that it does not go beyond what is necessary to protect its legitimate interests. Courts consider a range of factors in determining what is legitimately necessary. These include the geographical area covered by the covenant, the length of time the restriction lasts, and the types of work prohibited. The greater these are in scope, the less likely they are to be reasonable. For example, it may be reasonable for an employer to restrict a former regional sales manager from competing in the same region as the employer for a short period of time after employment ends, but it would be unreasonable to restrict the manager from competing outside that region. A restrictive covenant may also be considered reasonable if the employer trained the employee in the trade (versus hiring a fully skilled employee) or provided the employee with trade secrets or other confidential information, such as customer lists. It is often reasonable to restrict the employee from using that training or those secrets to compete against the former employer.

The plaintiff in *Jones v Klassen*, for example, said it distinguished itself from competitors who ran large offices by providing investment services as a "storefront" company in small branch offices instead. In order to appropriately groom someone to run its one-person office, the plaintiff "invested" in the defendant: it trained him, paid for his Canadian securities course, and provided him with both the physical premises to run a business and a paid clerical assistant. Riley Klassen became "the face of Edward Jones" in St Albert, Alberta. But four years later, Klassen decided to join another storefront-style brokerage firm that was potentially a direct competitor with Edward Jones. On the weekend of his departure from Edward Jones, he wrote a letter to all of his clients, providing his cellphone number and suggesting that their interests might be better served by a "premium, independent, entirely Canadian-owned" investment firm. At the Edward Jones office, he also printed the client list, a "potential client" list, and thousands of pages of client data. During the six months following his resignation, client investment accounts totalling $3,393,101.10 in assets transferred to Klassen's new firm, which was approximately 37 percent of the former worth of the Edward Jones' accounts. Alleging breaches of its restrictive covenants with him, Edward Jones sued.

The Alberta Court of Queen's Bench found that Klassen had breached his contractual duty not to solicit clients, as well as a common law duty and a fiduciary duty to Edward Jones. (A fiduciary duty is a duty of good faith that some professionals and key employees hold toward clients or employers. For more, see Chapter 15.) In an initial employment agreement, Klassen had promised to "surrender to Edward Jones" all account records and client files if he ever left the company. He had promised that for six months following his termination or resignation, he would not "directly or indirectly solicit sales … or induce any customer" to leave Edward Jones. Finally, he had agreed that all such client information was confidential information that "constitute[d] a trade secret" and was therefore "the sole and exclusive property of Edward Jones." Klassen agreed, during pre-trial negotiations, to return the confidential information he had taken from the plaintiff. But when he did so, he retained photocopies of the originals. Finding this latter conduct "even more egregious" than his first breaches, the Court added $5,000 in punitive damages to its award of $13,464 in favour of the plaintiff, making it abundantly clear to Klassen that it was "the information [that] was the crucial proprietary property of Edward Jones, and not the paper on which it [was] printed" (at para 61).

The trend in the case law continues to be against the enforcement of restrictive covenants—even if the former employee is soliciting former clients and competing directly with the former employer—because of concerns about the former employee's ability to earn a living. However, as in the *Jones* case, the courts are much more sympathetic to employers when departing employees have confidential information from that employer and attempt to use it in their next job. In such cases, courts are willing to issue injunction or search-and-seizure orders against the ex-employee, prohibiting the individual from using that information or enabling the ex-employer to retrieve the information. Such orders protect the former employer without restraining the individual from earning a living. Recent examples of these orders are the BC case *Phoenix Restorations Ltd v Drisdelle* (injunction) and the Alberta case *Peters & Co Limited v Ward* (search and seizure).

An employer that is interested in recruiting a candidate who is subject to a restrictive covenant should obtain legal advice concerning the covenant's enforceability and the limits that it could place on the candidate's ability to perform the job. This is especially true if the new employer is a competitor of the former employer. The written employment contract should designate which party is legally responsible if the former employer successfully enforces this covenant.

Anticipatory Breach of Contract

An **anticipatory breach of contract** occurs when one party repudiates (rejects) the employment contract—through either its statements or its conduct—after the contract has been made but before employment begins. Although in principle this cause of action applies to both employer and employee, typically the employer is sued for wrongful dismissal damages when it changes its mind about an employment contract. For example, the employer may change its mind about the candidate's suitability or decide to eliminate a position after hiring someone to fill it because of changed circumstances. During the financial crisis in 2008, for instance, Ford Canada revoked hundreds of job offers made just before the crisis began, arguing that because of the rapidly deteriorating economy, it could no longer proceed with those hires. However, an employer's changed circumstances generally are not a defence against a claim for anticipatory breach of contract. At a minimum, an employee whose employment contract is revoked before starting the job will be entitled to "reasonable notice" damages, similar to the amount payable if an employee had already started work and been employed for a very short period. Moreover, where the individual has quit a secure job, relocated, or made some other change because of the job offer, the damage award will typically reflect these additional expenditures (Stefanik, 2010, at 4).

anticipatory breach of contract
when one party indicates it has no intention of living up to its obligations under the employment contract; this rejection—through either its statements or its conduct—is anticipatory because it occurs after the contract has been made but before employment begins

To be successful in an action for anticipatory breach of contract, the hired employee must show that:

- an offer of employment was made,
- the offer was accepted,
- the contract was then repudiated by the employer (by either word or conduct), and
- the employee suffered damages as a result.

If these criteria are met, the employee's entitlement to damages takes effect immediately upon the anticipatory breach: there is no need for the employee to wait until the date originally set for employment to begin before the employee seeks damages.

To protect itself against an action for anticipatory breach of contract, an employer should hire with care by determining the suitability of the candidate *before* an offer is made. Where the position depends on a particular set of circumstances unfolding in a certain way, the offer should be made conditional upon those circumstances occurring. Where an anticipatory breach *has* occurred as a result of changed circumstances, the employer may choose to help the employee find another, comparable job as quickly as possible to minimize the damages suffered and should certainly do nothing to hinder such a search. Finally, it is helpful to the employer to have a written employment contract that includes a reasonable termination notice clause that defines the amount of wrongful dismissal damages to which the employee is entitled. These clauses often provide for limited notice in the first few months of employment and likely could be relied on to reduce damages in an anticipatory breach situation (Stefanik, 2010, at 5).

That said, there may be situations in which an employer's repudiation of the employment contract is justified, and the employer will not be liable for damages for anticipatory breach of contract. For example, if driving is an essential part of the new position and the hired employee loses their licence after the job offer is made and accepted, the employer may, subject to any human rights obligations, be justified in refusing to honour the employment agreement.

Background Checking: Negligent Hiring

How important is it to investigate the information supplied by a job candidate? One large study found that 46 percent of the employment, education, and reference checks performed revealed inconsistencies between the information provided by the job applicant and the information uncovered through background checks (Miedema & Hall, 2012, at xi). Common misrepresentations found in resumés include listing family members as former supervisors, altering start or end dates to hide gaps in employment, providing incorrect job titles, and listing false academic credentials.

As noted above in the section "Misrepresentation by Job Candidates," an employer may (in rare cases) be able to dismiss an employee for cause for serious misrepresentations made during the hiring stage. However, the time and effort expended in doing so, as well as the costs of a "bad hire," underscore the desirability of verifying the information supplied and doing a background check *before* someone is hired.

Taking care in the hiring process is not just about avoiding the hiring (and later firing) of inadequate employees. The costs of a bad hire include potential liability for **negligent hiring** if that employee later causes foreseeable harm to a **third party** (someone other than the employer or employee).

negligent hiring
failing to take reasonable care in the hiring process that results in foreseeable injury to a third party

third party
someone other than the employer or employee

Reference Checks

Asking an applicant to supply references is a common and recommended practice. It is advisable to get references from a variety of sources, including supervisors, co-workers, and teachers, to get a well-rounded picture of the job candidate. An employer may also want to do further research about a job candidate, beyond the list of references the candidate provides. However, in doing so, employers run the risk of violating the BC or Alberta *Personal Information Protection Act* (PIPA), which arguably requires employers to notify applicants about any people the employer uses as references. (This legislation is discussed below, under the headings "Credit Checks" and "Internet and Social Media Searches.")

Although there have not been many Canadian cases on negligent hiring, there have been instances where an employer has been found liable to a third party when its failure to check references has resulted in harm to that third party. For example, in *Downey v 502377 Ontario Ltd*, two doormen employed at a bar beat a patron severely and caused serious brain injuries. One of the doormen had a history of violent actions. The employer was found liable for failing to properly check its employees' references. In another case, *Wilson v Clarica Life Insurance Co*, a life insurance company in BC was liable for negligent hiring when one of its authorized agents stole money from a client. This agent had a history of suspected theft—as one of Clarica's reference checks had revealed before it hired him.

The more a job exposes others to the risk of harm, the stronger the employer's duty to investigate becomes. The **standard of care** (the level of diligence the employee is expected to exercise) imposed on employers is the common law duty of **reasonable care**—the level of diligence that is reasonable under the circumstances. Hiring an employee who will be in a position of trust, such as those who work with vulnerable individuals (e.g., daycare providers or health care workers), or who may be required to use force, such as a security guard, requires a high standard of care. What that level of care is has not been firmly settled by the courts. However, in the *Drake* case discussed above, one expert suggested that standard practice in the executive search firm industry is to check the last five years of employment or the last three references (Miedema & Hall, 2012, at 21).

standard of care
the level of diligence the employee is expected to exercise

reasonable care
the level of diligence that is reasonable under the circumstances

Before checking references, an employer should obtain the written permission of the applicant. This authorization may be obtained through a statement on the application form where the applicant's signature indicates that permission has been given. The consent should be general enough that it allows the employer to contact any person who it believes is able to provide relevant information about the applicant. The employer should not be limited to making decisions based only on references named by the applicant. Note that if the applicant's current employer is to be contacted, specific consent should be obtained for that employer because the applicant may not have told the current employer that they are searching for another job. One way of handling this is to only obtain a reference from the current employer after a conditional offer of employment has been made (Miedema & Hall, 2012, at 21).

Employers should record the details of all steps taken when investigating candidates so that they will have a written record to use as evidence in the event of a lawsuit. A detailed paper trail should include references who did not respond and the information provided by those who responded. The same inquiries should be made of all applicants to ensure consistency and thoroughness and to avoid perceptions of discrimination. All information should be kept confidential. The reference checker should not share the comments of one reference with other references or tell references who the other references are (Miedema & Hall, 2012, at 22).

If a reference voluntarily offers information about the applicant that relates to a prohibited ground of discrimination, such as race or sexual orientation, the reference checker should indicate that they are not interested in that information. In addition, foreign references should not be treated as less valuable than Canadian references, because this could lead to a claim of discrimination (Miedema & Hall, 2012, at 26).

A common problem with reference checking is that former employers are hesitant to criticize a candidate, fearing that a negative reference could result in a lawsuit. In *Phutela v University of Alberta*, for example, the plaintiff claimed damages of $2 million against his former employer on the basis of what he alleged was slanderous information provided to a potential new employer, including a "libellous letter" to the effect that his employment had been terminated because of, among other things, dissatisfaction with his job performance. He claimed that malice was involved in the writing of the letter. The Alberta Court of Queen's Bench, however, refused to find malice and instead determined that both justification and **qualified privilege** applied to the comments made by the former employer. The Alberta Court of Appeal

qualified privilege
in the context of libel or slander, an exemption from liability for a statement made without malice, usually in the performance of a duty, and not communicated more widely than is appropriate

agreed. The reference letter, the appellate court said, had not been "voluntary," but rather was provided out of "a sense of obligation following a telephone interview." The defence of qualified privilege therefore applied to the letter. Furthermore, although "very serious allegations had been made against the plaintiff, allegations that would have considerable impact … on a prospective employer … there was no question about the truth" of those statements (at para 9), and thus the defence of justification also applied. As a result, the appeal was dismissed.

In reality, however, former employers are rarely sued for giving negative references. Still, many employers have adopted a "no references" policy, or they confirm only basic facts, such as the individual's job title and start and end dates of employment, as a means to avoid a tort claim of **defamation**. Despite this concern, an employer should conduct reference checks, especially where the position is one of trust and could reasonably result in harm to a third party. Moreover, even a reference that only confirms dates and job title can at the very least be helpful in revealing inconsistencies on a candidate's resumé (Miedema & Hall, 2012, at 23).

defamation
a tort claim based on a false statement or statements made to the detriment of an identified individual or organization and which are published or broadcast to an audience; defamation can be spoken (slander) or written (libel)

Education and Professional Credentials Checks

Another type of background check relates to education and professional or trade certification. Failure to perform these checks could result in negligence claims where a negligently hired employee causes harm or loss to a third party in the course of their employment because they lack the educational requirements necessary for the job. This is especially true where the applicant is required by law to hold a particular degree or certification, as in the case of engineers, accountants, and nurses (Miedema & Hall, 2012, at 31). Given the growth of "diploma mills" and fake degrees, the checker should call the institution cited on the resumé and speak directly with the records department or registrar's office to confirm a candidate's degree and date of graduation, or, where there is doubt about the institution itself, contact an independent source that evaluates educational institutions.

IN THE NEWS

Yahoo CEO Scott Thompson Resigns After Scrutiny of His Resumé

NEW YORK—Yahoo CEO Scott Thompson left the company four months into the job Sunday after more than a week of scrutiny into inaccuracies on his resumé and in company filings. …

Thompson's exit was encouraged by Third Point, the activist hedge fund that owns nearly 6 per cent of Yahoo shares. Third Point claimed that Thompson had padded his resumé with a degree in computer science from Stonehill College. Thompson did earn an accounting degree from Stonehill, a Catholic school near Boston, in 1979, a fact that Yahoo correctly lists. But he did not earn a computer science degree.

SOURCE: Rexrode, 2012. Used with permission.

Credit Checks

If an employer wants to check the candidate's credit situation, Alberta's *Credit and Personal Reports Regulation* requires that the employer obtain authorization from the applicant, in writing, of its intention before the check. The employer should include the request for authorization to conduct the credit check and provide notification on the application for employment (s 3.1(1)). When a reporting agency makes a disclosure or provides copies of particulars, it must inform the individual or the individual's representative of the individual's right to explain or protest any information contained in the reporting agency's file and the manner in which an explanation or protest may be made (s 3.1(4)).

In BC, the *Business Practices and Consumer Protection Act* allows reporting agencies to provide credit information about an individual to a party if the latter "intends to use the report for the purpose of evaluating the individual for employment, promotion, reassignment or retention as an employee" (s 108(1)(a)(iii)). However, the Act also stipulates that such information cannot be obtained from a reporting agency without the individual's consent (s 107(1)). Under section 107(2), consent can be given "by any method that permits the person to produce evidence that the individual consented, including by prominently displaying the information respecting the consent in a clear and comprehensible manner" in the employment application.

In Canada, most jobs do not require a credit check. Nonetheless, checking an applicant's credit history may be prudent where the position requires, for example, handling customers' money. However, because of the *Personal Information Protection Act* in BC and Alberta, it may be wise for an employer to conduct credit checks only where credit information is reasonably necessary for the position in question (Miedema & Hall, 2012, at 53). The *Mark's Work Wearhouse Ltd* report by the Alberta Office of the Information and Privacy Commissioner illustrates the risk.

CASE IN POINT

Pre-employment Credit Checks

Mark's Work Wearhouse Ltd, Investigation Report P2010-IR-001 (16 February 2010) (Alberta Office of the Information and Privacy Commissioner)

Facts

As part of a pre-employment screening process at Mark's Work Wearhouse (MWW), an applicant for a sales associate position was asked to sign a declaration of understanding and consent for a security clearance check and a credit check. He did so. Only a few hours after his in-person interview he received a phone call from the MWW human resources department asking him to explain how he intended to resolve his "credit issue." The applicant told the human resources representative that an error had occurred on the part of the federal government and his bank regarding his student loans but that, because of a lack of financial resources, he could not presently afford to address the matter. Despite seven years of experience working as a sales associate with another retail company, he was not offered the position at MWW. He later filed a complaint under Alberta's *Personal Information Protection Act*, alleging a breach of his privacy rights by MWW when it conducted what he believed was an unnecessary credit check.

Relevant Issues

1. Whether the information at issue was "personal information" or "personal employee information."
2. Whether MWW collected the complainant's personal information in compliance with section 11(1) of PIPA.

Decision

PIPA applies to provincially regulated private sector organizations in Alberta, and thus the privacy commissioner had jurisdiction to investigate the case against MWW.

1. Section 1(k) of PIPA defines personal information as "information about an identifiable individual." The information at issue in this case is the complainant's credit history. The report notes that the scope of information typically included by a credit reporting agency includes "an individual's occupation and current and past place of employment, past and present addresses, marital status, spouse or interdependent partner's name and age, number of dependents, education or professional qualifications, estimated income and assets, existing debts and paying habits, fines and restitution orders, cost of living responsibilities, and enquiries made by others" (at para 28).

   The privacy commissioner found that the information at issue was indeed "personal information" about an identifiable individual—the complainant. But the information was not "personal employee information," which, at the time, was defined in section 1(j) as

   > in respect of an individual who is an employee or a potential employee, personal information reasonably required by an organization that is collected, used or disclosed solely for the purposes of establishing, managing or terminating
   >
   > (i) an employment relationship ...
   >
   > between the organization and the individual but does not include personal information about the individual that is unrelated to that relationship.

   Although MWW argued that the credit check information provided "insight" into how an individual might handle the financial responsibilities of a sales associate based on how that person handled their own money, the privacy commissioner was "not persuaded that the Complainant's personal credit information [was] reasonably required for this purpose" (at para 37). She pointed out that there were "less privacy intrusive means by which to assess the Complainant's abilities" (at para 40), such as contacting the references he had provided about his performance over the past seven years in a similar work environment. Citing Arbitrator Steeves from *Vancouver (City) v Canadian Union of Public Employees Local 15* (12 November 2007), she was not persuaded by the mere *possibility* that someone's personal financial pressures might affect his performance at work:

   > A higher standard than "a possibility" is required to demonstrate that the information is not being collected simply because it might be useful in the future or convenient. ... A direct relationship between the work and this personal information is required. (at para 41)

2. Having established that the complainant's personal credit information was personal information according to PIPA, it remained for the commissioner to determine whether MWW's collection of that information was in compliance with section 11(1) of PIPA:

   > An organization may collect personal information only for purposes that are reasonable.

   Because MWW already had other controls in place for reducing in-store theft and fraud, such as closed circuit television cameras in 68 percent of its stores, a prohibition against employees processing their own sales or returns transactions, and a rule that only small amounts of cash were allowed to be kept in cash terminals, the commissioner concluded that MWW had failed to establish a reasonable connection between collecting the complainant's personal credit information and the company's stated purposes for collecting it.

Because the collection of personal credit information was not deemed reasonably necessary to assess an applicant's ability to perform sales associate duties at MWW, the privacy commissioner recommended that MWW cease collecting personal credit information as part of its hiring process for sales associate positions in all of its locations.

Police Records Checks

Where the position being applied for requires an employee to work with vulnerable people such as children, older adults, or people with disabilities, or involves substantial trust, employers should require candidates to provide a police records check. These can only be done with an applicant's consent. Such checks are actually required by law in certain industries or sectors or for certain jobs. For example, an employer who operates a group home for people with developmental disabilities must, before hiring an employee or volunteer who will work directly with residents, obtain a police records report. Similarly, a teacher applying for a teaching certificate must provide a "criminal record declaration" or verification (Miedema & Hall, 2012, at 103). The BC *Criminal Records Review Act* and regulations specify the organizations in BC that must conduct a criminal records check (or obtain a "criminal record check verification") for all employees and volunteers who will work with children or vulnerable adults. All police records checks require the prospective employee's informed consent.

There are several different types of police records searches, and an employer should be specific about the kind of search it requires for a particular position. For example, does the employer just want convictions, or does it want information related to charges and investigations as well? Certain types of criminal history will not be revealed unless a specific request is made. Where a police records check is advisable, an employer should ask its local police department about its practices and procedures (Miedema & Hall, 2012, at 105).

Over the past several years, the process of obtaining a police records check has become more restricted. There are now two ways to have a police records check completed: through a third-party background-screening firm (except for a vulnerable sector check, where the results will be released to the applicant only) or by sending the job applicant to a police station in the area where the applicant resides (Miedema & Hall, 2012, at 109). The police will not provide details about what offence a job applicant was convicted of to a background-checking firm, even with written consent from the applicant. However, where an applicant is asked to identify conviction details on the background-checking consent form, the police can confirm whether those conviction details are accurate (Miedema & Hall, 2012, at 102).

In many Canadian jurisdictions, including Alberta, an employer may refuse to hire someone who has a criminal record, even if the record does not relate to the job for which the individual is a candidate. However, in BC, Yukon, Quebec, and Prince Edward Island the record must relate to the job being applied for in order for an employer to refuse employment (Miedema & Hall, 2012, at 101; see also the discussion below and in Chapter 7). However, best practice in this area points to only conducting a criminal check where it is necessary for the position, documenting reasons for the hiring decision, and keeping the results confidential (Sherrard Kuzz LLP, 2012, at 2).

As will be noted in Chapter 7, BC employers are prohibited from discriminating against a person because that person has been convicted of a criminal or summary conviction offence that is unrelated to the employment of the individual, unless a clean record is a bona fide occupational requirement of the job. Similarly, an employer may not discriminate because of a criminal conviction for which a pardon has been granted. On the other hand, where the job applicant was charged with a criminal offence but not convicted, this does not fall within the specific definition of "record of offences" under human rights legislation or meet the definition of "a person [who] has been convicted." However, there is always a risk that an applicant will file a human rights complaint if they were not hired because of the charge, so an employer needs to approach this area with caution and keep thorough documentation of its decisions (Miedema & Hall, 2012, at 127).

Internet and Social Media Searches

A recent addition to the list of background checks that employers can perform relates to Internet and social media searches. The ease with which an employer can simply google candidates' names or check out their social media footprint makes this a tempting strategy. In fact, according to one study, 70 percent of employers use social networking sites to research job candidates and of those, 57 percent found content that caused them not to hire candidates (Hayes, 2018).

However, there are several potential pitfalls that an employer should be aware of if performing these types of searches. First, there is the possibility of mistaken identity, especially if the applicant has a relatively common name. Second, there is no "quality control" on the information located through a web-based search; anyone with a grudge or who is simply misinformed can post material on the Internet that is wrong, misleading, or one-sided. Clearly, it is unfair to reject someone on the basis of incorrect information, and an employer that relies on such information misses out on a potentially great candidate. Third, web-based searches often reveal information that touches on prohibited grounds of discrimination. For example, posted photographs can reveal religious affiliation or family status. As discussed in Chapter 7, having this type of information before the hiring decision is made opens an employer up to claims that the discriminatory information played a part in that decision (Miedema & Hall, 2012, at 172).

One way to address this concern is to have someone other than the decision-maker perform the search and ensure that person is aware of, and abides by, human rights requirements. In addition, an employer should carefully document its reasons for any hiring decision. Given the pitfalls discussed above, employers may conclude that the risk outweighs the benefits of this method of checking references.

Internet and social media searches also present potential privacy issues. However, to date, in the handful of cases where an employee's social media profile has been at issue, courts have found that individuals have no reasonable expectation of privacy where they have posted comments on sites to which hundreds of people have been given access (Miedema & Hall, 2012, at 172). Nonetheless, because of the breadth of the BC and Alberta *Personal Information Protection Acts*, employers in those provinces may want to review the guidelines for social media background checks that each province's information and privacy commissioner has published (see the References section at the end of this chapter, under Office of the Information and Privacy Commissioner).

FYI

Social Media Profile: UK Study Insights

A job candidate's social media profile can have a positive, as well as negative, effect on their employment prospects. For example, a search on LinkedIn, Twitter, and other sites can confirm an applicant's experience, qualifications, and connections within a particular industry, as well as convey the applicant's social media savvy. In a UK study, 68 percent of the employers surveyed indicated that they had hired a candidate because of what they saw on the individual's social networking site. At the same time, a similarly high percentage indicated that they had rejected candidates based on their social media profile. Reasons given include the posting of inappropriate photographs or comments (including disparaging comments about a former employer and discriminatory statements), posts that demonstrated poor communication skills, and posts that revealed criminal conduct.

When Background Checks Should Be Done

Like the pre-employment medical exam that will be discussed in Chapter 7, most types of background checks should only be done after a conditional offer of employment is made. The exception is job reference checks, and even then the *current* employer should be contacted only after a conditional offer, unless the candidate consents otherwise. Conducting background checks at the end of the process reduces risk of allegations of discrimination by unsuccessful job applicants. For example, credit checks require an applicant to provide their social insurance number, which can reveal information about place of origin, one of the prohibited grounds of discrimination under human rights legislation. It is easier to defend against an allegation of discrimination if the information was not obtained before a conditional offer of employment was made (Miedema & Hall, 2012, at xv).

In addition, many organizations now use third parties to carry out background checks after a conditional offer of employment has been made. With the applicant dealing directly with the third party, there is less risk that the employer will obtain information that touches on a prohibited ground of discrimination (Rudner, 2009, at 3).

Defining the Relationship

One basic issue that should be addressed early in the hiring process is the type of legal relationship that should exist between the individual who will perform the work and the hiring organization. Although an employer–employee relationship is the most common one, it is not the only possibility.

Independent Contractors Versus Employees

The parties should decide whether a principal–independent contractor relationship is better suited to their needs than a traditional employer–employee relationship. The hallmarks of a principal–independent contractor relationship are discussed below. Also examined are the numerous legal pitfalls that the parties may encounter if they do not identify or establish their relationship accurately. The legal rights and responsibilities of the parties depend on the nature of their relationship; a worker is not an independent contractor simply because the parties intend it to be so.

Indeed, there is always a risk that a relationship characterized by the parties as a principal–independent contractor relationship will be found to be an employer–employee relationship by a court or tribunal.

What Is a Principal–Independent Contractor Relationship?

independent contractor
a self-employed worker engaged by a principal to perform specific work; an independent contractor is not an employee

principal
the party who contracts for the services of an independent contractor; the party who can be bound by its agent

An **independent contractor** is a self-employed worker engaged by a **principal** to perform specific work. An independent contractor is not an employee. In some cases, the distinction between an independent contractor and an employee is obvious. For example, if a homeowner hires an individual to paint their house, the painter is not an employee but rather a self-employed contractor. However, there are other situations where it is much more difficult to make the distinction. For example, is a delivery driver who owns their own truck but delivers for only one business an employee of that business or an independent contractor? Despite the difficulty in some cases of distinguishing an employer–employee relationship from one of principal–independent contractor, the two relationships are treated very differently in law.

What Are the Advantages of a Principal–Independent Contractor Relationship?

There is an increasing trend for organizations to hire individuals as independent contractors rather than as employees. Many organizations like the fact that this relationship presents fewer ongoing legal obligations, less paperwork, and less expense than the employer–employee relationship. Reducing the "head count" is also a goal of many larger organizations.

Consider the following obligations that employers have to employees but not to independent contractors:

1. *Providing statutory benefits, such as vacation and overtime pay, and protections, such as pregnancy and parental leave, for employees.* Independent contractors generally are not entitled to employee statutory benefits. The terms of their contract determine their entitlement to benefits.
2. *Paying premiums for workplace health and safety insurance.* Independent contractors must arrange their own coverage.
3. *Providing reasonable notice of termination or pay in lieu (unless the employment contract states otherwise).* Independent contractors are entitled to notice of termination only if their contract so provides. There is no implied right to reasonable notice.
4. *Remitting appropriate health and income taxes and contributing to and remitting Canada Pension Plan (CPP) and employment insurance (EI) premiums.* Independent contractors remit their own statutory deductions and taxes. This reduces both costs and paperwork for the hiring organization. Also, the organization does not have to pay the "employer's" portion of CPP and EI premiums for independent contractors.
5. *Assuming liability for an employee's deliberate or negligent acts during the course of employment.* In contrast, independent contractors are generally liable to both the third-party victim and the hiring organization for misconduct or negligence while on the job (Levitt, 2002, at 1-23).

The individual being hired may also prefer independent contractor status to that of employee. There are tax benefits available to the self-employed: deducting expenses against income, no withholding of income tax at source, and fewer statutory deductions (such as EI premiums). Independent contractors also have greater flexibility in working for organizations other than the principal.

When May a Principal–Independent Contractor Designation Be Challenged?

If both parties agree that they want to create a principal–independent contractor relationship, how does the nature of their relationship become a legal issue? The parties' initial characterization may be challenged before a court or tribunal in several ways. A government agency (such as the Canada Revenue Agency) may question the parties' characterization because it thinks that statutory premiums for programs such as EI, workers' compensation, and CPP should have been remitted. An individual initially designated an independent contractor may subsequently wish to claim statutory benefits or protections that depend on employee status, such as EI benefits, workers' compensation coverage, or employment standards benefits (e.g., holiday pay and sick leave). This issue may also arise when an individual is terminated and seeks wrongful dismissal damages. Only in an employment relationship do courts find an implied duty to provide reasonable notice of termination or pay in lieu of notice.

What Happens if a Court or Tribunal Finds an Employer–Employee Relationship?

If a court or tribunal finds that the parties created an employment relationship, the "employer" may have to remit thousands of dollars to various government agencies for outstanding statutory premiums (potentially including those owed by the "employee"). Penalty and interest charges may also be incurred. Further, the employer may also have to pay the individual significant amounts of money for employment standards benefits, such as vacation and overtime premium pay or wrongful dismissal damages. At the same time, the individual will be liable for outstanding statutory premiums and income tax not deducted at source.

What Tests Establish an Employer–Employee Relationship?

Although several employment-related statutes contain a definition of "employee," the definitions are so brief that courts and tribunals fall back on the common law tests for distinguishing between an employer–employee and a principal–independent contractor relationship. The fundamental issue is whether the individual is an independent entrepreneur in business for themself or under the control and direction of the employer. The following tests have evolved under the common law to distinguish between an employee and an independent contractor. No single fact determines the matter; the facts of the case are assessed as a whole.

1. *Control test.* Does the organization control the individual's work, including where, when, and how it is performed? Is there permanence and exclusivity of the parties' relationship? Does the individual report to the organization during the workday? If the individual does not have autonomy, if day-to-day control over the work is maintained by the organization, and if the individual performs work over a long period of time and has no other clients, then courts are more likely to find an employment relationship.
2. *Risk test.* Does the individual bear any financial risk of profit or loss (other than fixed commissions)? For example, does the individual face the risk of not receiving payment for services performed? If not, that person is more likely to be considered an employee. And does the individual incur expenses that the alleged employer does not reimburse? If so, there is a greater chance the person is a contractor.
3. *Organization test.* Are the services rendered by the individual an integral part of the business? For example, an individual who writes a manufacturing company's newsletter is less likely to be an employee than a tool and die maker whose duties are central to the company's operations.
4. *Tools test.* Does the individual provide their own tools? If so, this favours independent contractor status, especially if a significant capital investment is involved, as in the case of a truck driver who supplies their own truck. The tools test is probably the least significant of the tests, but it is still relevant.

In applying the common law tests, *Wiebe Door Services Ltd v The Minister of National Revenue* (1986) and *671122 Ontario Ltd v Sagaz Industries Canada* (2001) are the leading cases. These and other cases demonstrate that courts look at the substance of the relationship (what happened in practice) rather than its form (what the written contract says). For example, the fact that an individual incorporates and declares themself self-employed for tax purposes is considered because it indicates the person's intent to be an independent contractor. However, this fact is not determinative if the other facts point to an employment relationship. *Pacific Rim Nutrition Ltd v Guardian Insurance Co of Canada* demonstrates how courts look at the specific facts of a case when deciding whether there is an employment relationship.

CASE IN POINT

Independent Contractor or Employee?

Pacific Rim Nutrition Ltd v Guardian Insurance Co of Canada (1995), 7 BCLR (3d) 251 (SC) aff'd 1998 CanLII 4986 (BCCA)

Facts

A bookkeeper working for the plaintiff company stole $180,000 from the company. This happened while the plaintiff was covered by liability policies with the defendant insurers. The bookkeeper's activities were finally discovered, she was dismissed, and the plaintiff sought indemnification under the insurance policies. Whether the insurers would pay out or not hinged on whether these acts were committed by an employee of the insured or an independent contractor. The insurers took the position that they were not obliged to pay out the losses because the bookkeeper was an employee; conversely, the insured argued that the bookkeeper was an independent contractor.

The insured argued the following as to why the bookkeeper was an independent contractor:

- The firm did not have control over the manner or method in which the bookkeeper carried out her bookkeeping duties because it did not have the necessary understanding and knowledge to do that.
- The firm did not make deductions for income tax, EI, or CPP from the bookkeeper's earnings.
- The bookkeeper did not receive any holiday pay, nor did she participate in any extended benefits plan.
- The bookkeeper chose her own method of bookkeeping ("synoptic journal") rather than the "one-write" system that had been in place prior to her working for the firm.
- The bookkeeper was paid an hourly rate for her services; this did not involve the firm's maintaining a record of the hours she worked, which was done for all the other workers. Furthermore, her remuneration was not recorded as "wages" but rather as "accounting expenses."
- The bookkeeper controlled the scheduling of hours that she worked, and she changed that schedule from time to time to suit herself.
- While providing her services, the bookkeeper never referred to herself as an "employee," as evidenced by her self-description in correspondence with the firm.
- The bookkeeper styled herself as being "self-employed" for income tax purposes, and in fact she provided similar services to other businesses.

Pacific Rim Nutrition (the plaintiff) argued the following as to why the bookkeeper was an employee:

- Her duties were normally associated with those of a bookkeeper employee, not a professional accountant, and they were essential to the day-to-day operations of the firm.
- She was subject to the direct control and supervision of the sole shareholder, director, and officer of the company, Mr Reid.
- She was not a member of any recognized professional association.
- She worked regular hours as directed by Mr Reid.
- Mr Reid regarded her at all times as his employee.
- The firm supplied all her necessary supplies and materials; she did not use any separately owned resources.
- She did not set the fees she should be paid but accepted the amount the firm paid her.
- At all times she worked on the firm's premises, never from her own office.
- The firm had the right to discharge her services and in fact gave her two weeks' notice of termination when it dismissed her.

Relevant Issue

Whether the dishonest bookkeeper was an employee or an independent contractor.

Decision

The Court found that

> the bookkeeper was an employee. Her day-to-day activities were controlled by the employer. She was an integral part of the business. The fact that she performed similar services for other businesses and that no "standard" deductions were made from her remuneration does not take away from the … substance of the relationship … between the plaintiff insured and the bookkeeper.

This case is an excellent example of how in many instances the issue of whether someone is an employee or an independent contractor is not that cut and dried. Many times, strong arguments can be advanced to support either finding.

How to Maintain a Principal–Independent Contractor Characterization

The list below outlines several ways to minimize the risks of having an independent contractor relationship subsequently characterized by a court or government agency as an employment relationship. Keep in mind that no single fact alone determines status. All the facts will be viewed together. In a large majority of cases, relationships that are purported to be principal–independent contractor relationships will, if challenged, be found to be employer–employee relationships.

1. A clearly written contract should include a statement that confirms the individual's independent contractor status. Although this statement is not conclusive, it indicates the original intent of the parties.
2. The contract should cover a fixed term and should include a fair mutual-termination clause, because independent contractors are typically hired for a specific project or period, while employees are usually hired on an indefinite basis.
3. The organization should not take any statutory deductions or remittances for income tax, CPP contributions, and EI contributions. The individual should acknowledge in the contract that the organization is not making these deductions and remittances.
4. The contract should include an indemnity provision stating that the independent contractor is responsible for any statutory remittances, such as for EI or workers' compensation premiums.
5. The contract should state that the independent contractor has no authority to create obligations on behalf of the organization, endorse cheques, or accept returns (Israel, 2003, at 2997).
6. The organization should not provide vacation, holiday, or overtime pay; health care benefits; or employee benefits, such as stock options or bonuses. Similarly, the organization should not provide a company uniform; business cards; company car; bookkeeping services; or office equipment, such as a computer, desk, or other facilities.
7. The contract should not restrict the individual from working for other clients, although it may require that the contractor dedicate a certain number of hours to the work being contracted for.
8. The organization should avoid reimbursing the independent contractor for expenses.
9. The organization should avoid setting hours of work.
10. The contractor should work offsite as much as possible. This is not, however, a guarantee of independent contractor status if the contractor works for only one employer and reports on a regular basis, electronically or otherwise.
11. The independent contractor should be entitled to accept or decline work when it is offered by the organization.
12. The independent contractor should purchase their own liability insurance.
13. The contract should not provide for performance reviews or disciplinary measures.
14. The contractor should consider becoming incorporated and obtaining a GST number, and they should make the appropriate tax returns. An individual who is incorporated, has a GST number, and makes the appropriate tax returns is more likely to be seen as an independent contractor.

15. The contract should reflect the reality of the relationship. If, for example, the organization exercises day-to-day control over the individual's work, that practical reality will undermine all the good work that went into preparing the contract.

Sometimes an individual may be considered an independent contractor for the purposes of taxes and government remittances and be designated an employee for the purpose of a wrongful dismissal action. This occurs when the facts of the case are not clearcut, and various agencies weigh those facts and the common law tests somewhat differently. Some government agencies may also tend to find that individuals are "employees" because it is easier to collect remittances from one employer than from hundreds of independent contractors.

Similarly, courts may be reluctant to characterize an individual, especially one with long years of service, as an independent contractor if it means that they may be terminated without any notice. In *Dynamex Canada Inc v Mamona*, an individual who successfully claimed to be an independent contractor for income tax purposes also successfully claimed to be an employee for the purposes of claiming holiday and vacation pay under employment standards legislation.

Agents

Another type of relationship is that of principal and agent. An **agent** can bind an organization to a contract with customers or other parties, even without the organization's knowledge. Common examples are real estate agents, travel agents, and insurance agents, as well as some individuals providing services as recruiters on a contract basis. An agent may be an independent contractor or an employee. For example, salespeople, buyers, and human resources managers who recruit employees are agents because they have the capacity to bind an organization in contracting with others. However, despite their agency status, they are usually categorized as employees and thus are eligible for reasonable notice of termination. Moreover, merely having a job title that includes the term "agent" does not make that individual an independent contractor. To determine whether an agent is an employee or an independent contractor, courts look at the established tests discussed above.

agent
a person who can bind an organization to a contract with customers or other parties, even without the organization's knowledge

Use of Temporary Employment Agencies

Sometimes an organization may choose to "hire" an individual through an employment agency. This individual is often referred to as an "agency employee" or a "temp." Unlike the situation where an executive search firm is used to recruit a new employee, agency employees are not actually hired by the organization where they work. They remain employees of the employment agency. They are paid by the agency, and the agency is liable for employment standards, such as vacation and public holiday pay.

Organizations usually use employment agencies when they need additional staff on a temporary basis—during peak seasons, when regular staff are on vacation or call in sick, or when particular projects need to be done. By using workers from an employment agency, organizations can avoid many of the costs associated with adding a person to the payroll.

Liability of Client Organizations for Agency Employees

There may be situations, especially where an agency employee has worked for an organization for a long time, where the organization itself becomes the employer for certain purposes. For example, if an individual hired through an agency is no longer needed by the organization after several years, a court may decide that the individual is an employee of the organization for wrongful dismissal purposes. The common law test to determine the true employer considers factors such as which party exercises control and direction over the worker, who pays the worker, and who has the authority to discipline or fire the worker (Moffatt, 2009, at 5).

Moreover, organizations have human rights and occupational health and safety responsibilities for their agency employees. Employers have a statutory obligation to create a safe work environment, and they are liable for any problems under occupational health and safety legislation. Similarly, under human rights legislation, employers have a responsibility to provide a work environment free from harassment and discrimination. Organizations should ensure that agency employees are treated no differently from actual employees when it comes to safety or human rights protections and internal complaints procedures.

Organizations can also be liable if an agency employee injures a third party in the course of the assignment. The courts will apply the common law test to determine who the employer is. Depending on the circumstances, either the employment agency or the organization will be found to be liable to the injured third party.

Different Types of Employees

An organization that decides to hire someone directly as an employee has the option of choosing which type of employee the person will be—for example, part-time, full-time, or temporary employee. For the most part, the law in Alberta and BC does not distinguish among different types of employees. Both full-time employees (those who work a full week) and part-time employees (those who work less than a full week) are entitled to statutory benefits and protections, although the monetary amount of benefits (such as vacation or termination pay) reflects the number of hours worked.

Temporary employees (direct hires, not hired through an agency) and casual employees (those who work intermittently as work is offered) are generally entitled to statutory benefits and protections as well. However, individuals who fall within the definition of temporary employee under the Alberta *Employment Standards Code* are not entitled to termination notice or pay in lieu of notice because these workers are aware of the temporary nature of their employment. Qualifications to the temporary employee exemption, such as that where the term is greater than 12 months, are discussed in Chapter 13. BC's *Employment Standards Act* does not define a "temporary employee" but does not compel an employer to provide any kind of notice or payment in lieu for termination of any worker who has been employed for less than three months.

To be eligible for benefits under the employment insurance system, an employee must have worked a minimum number of qualifying hours in insurable employment during the qualifying period. Thus, part-time or casual employees who have worked less than the minimum number of hours in the qualifying period are not eligible for benefits. However, where an employee has more than one job during the qualifying period, all insurable employment hours are added together to determine whether an employee qualifies for benefits.

Employees are commonly categorized by employers as follows:

1. *Permanent full-time employees.* These employees are hired for an indefinite period—that is, with no predetermined end to the employment relationship—and usually work 35 to 40 or 44 hours per week, depending on the province in which they reside. If a specific term of employment is not stipulated in an employment contract, the term of employment is assumed to be indefinite.
2. *Permanent part-time employees.* These employees are hired for an indefinite period to work less than full-time hours. There is no statutory definition of what constitutes a "part-time employee," although for the purposes of collective bargaining, part-time employees are usually those who work 24 hours per week or less.
3. *Temporary employees.* These employees work either full time or part time, but they are hired for a specific period or task rather than for an indefinite period like permanent employees. They may be called "fixed-term employees" because their employment contract is for a fixed period of time, such as six months. They may also be referred to as "contract workers." However, temporary employees are not independent contractors. Likewise, they are not "temps" or "agency employees," who remain employees of an employment agency.
4. *Casual employees.* These employees form a special category of temporary employees and work intermittently as work is offered. Both temporary and casual employees are sometimes referred to as "contract employees." Casual employees are often "elect-to-work employees," which means they can decline work when it is offered. Elect-to-work employees are not entitled to termination notice or termination pay under the BC and Alberta employment standards legislation.
5. *Agency employees or "temps."* These employees work for an employment agency at various places as arranged by the agency. The contract of employment is between the agency and the agency employee; an organization that uses the services of an agency employee pays the agency directly. The agency remains responsible for employment standards entitlements, such as vacation and public holiday pay. This topic is discussed above under the heading "Use of Temporary Employment Agencies."

KEY TERMS

REVIEW AND DISCUSSION QUESTIONS

1. Describe the circumstances when an employee may be terminated, without reasonable notice, for having provided inaccurate information on a job application form or during an interview. Is it fair that an employee may be terminated in these circumstances, even where they have been performing the job satisfactorily for some time? Why or why not?
2. Why might an employer prefer to hire an individual as an independent contractor rather than as an employee?
3. Why might an individual choose to work as an independent contractor rather than as an employee?
4. List ways that parties who want to create a principal–independent contractor relationship can minimize the risk that their relationship will be viewed as that of employer–employee.
5. Greg had worked for two years as a games supervisor at a casino, monitoring the dealers, when he was terminated for a serious incident of insubordination. Greg sued for wrongful dismissal damages. During his testimony at trial, Greg told the court that he had a degree from Arizona State University and that he had played football there. Counsel for the employer noticed that Greg seemed rather small for a football player and he asked Greg to name the coach of the football team or the team's nickname. At that point, Greg admitted that he had never in fact attended Arizona State even though he said he had on his resumé. In your view, would this misrepresentation on his resumé constitute just cause for his dismissal?
6. Brad began working at Lay-Z-Guy in 1981 as a customer service manager. In 1995 his employer started requiring him and other salespeople to sign a series of one-year agreements that stated they could be terminated on 60 days' notice. Three years later the employer required Brad to incorporate, and from that point forward, the agreements were between Lay-Z-Guy and Brad's corporation. The agreements defined Brad, and later his corporation, as an "independent marketing consultant" and expressly stated that the relationship was not one of employment, but rather of a principal–independent contractor. Brad paid for his own office space and remitted his own income taxes and workers' compensation premiums. At the same time, Lay-Z-Guy set prices, territory, and promotional methods, and Brad was limited to servicing Lay-Z-Guy exclusively. In 2003, Lay-Z-Guy terminated the agreement with 60 days' notice. Brad sued for wrongful dismissal damages, alleging that he was an employee.
   a. What arguments could Brad make to support his position that he was an employee?
   b. What arguments could Lay-Z-Guy make to support its position that Brad was an independent contractor?
   c. Which side do you think would be successful?
   d. Alternatively, do you think that Lay-Z-Guy could successfully argue that even if Brad was an employee, the contractual 60 days' notice provision governed and it was complied with?
7. Fiona has been offered a job as a marketing representative in a prestigious cosmetics firm called Beauty R Us. However, one week before she is to start her new job (and two weeks after she gave notice to her current employer) she receives a phone call from Beauty R Us stating that it has to withdraw its job offer. The firm tells Fiona that it just found out she is a high-profile activist for an animal rights group and some of its customers (such as those who sell fur coats) would be extremely uncomfortable dealing with her as a Beauty R Us marketing representative. Fiona is upset and wants to know what her legal rights are in this situation. Advise her. Explain your answer.

8. You asked a roofing company to make repairs to the roof of the building in which your firm operates its business. In the course of these repairs, one of the company's roofers carelessly dropped some shingles onto the head of a passerby of the building. The injured plaintiff is suing your firm, the roofing company, and the roofer for damages. In this situation there is both an employee and an independent contractor.

a. Identify who is the employee and who is the independent contractor in this situation and explain your answers.

b. Explain who is liable to the plaintiff for damages.

9. "It should be illegal for an employer to ask job applicants for their Facebook passwords." Do you agree with this statement? Why or why not?

REFERENCES

671122 Ontario Ltd v Sagaz Industries Canada Inc, 2001 SCC 59.

Beauchemin v Universal Handling Equipment Co, [1996] AJ No 128 (QL) (QB).

Business Practices and Consumer Protection Act, SBC 2004, c 2.

Cornell v Rogers Cablesystems Inc (1987), 17 CCEL 232 (Ont Dist Ct).

Credit and Personal Reports Regulation, Alta Reg 193/1999.

Criminal Records Review Act, RSBC 1996, c 86.

Crisall v Western Pontiac Buick GMC (1999) Ltd, 2003 ABQB 255.

Downey v 502377 Ontario Ltd, [1991] OJ No 468 (QL) (Gen Div).

D'Souza v Acero Engineering Inc, 2017 ABQB 775.

Dynamex Canada Inc v Mamona, 2003 FCA 248, leave to appeal to SCC refused, [2003] SCCA No 383 (QL).

Earle v Grant Transport, 1995 CanLII 7289 (Ont Sup Ct J).

Employment Standards Act, RSBC 1996, c 113.

Employment Standards Code, RSA 2000, c E-9.

Gilbert, Douglas, et al, *Canadian Labour and Employment Law for the US Practitioner* (Washington, DC: Bureau of National Affairs, 2011).

Hayes, Ladan Nikravan, "More than Half of Employers Have Found Content on Social Media that Caused Them Not to Hire a Candidate, According to Recent Career Builder Survey," *PR Newswire* (9 August 2018), online: <http://press.careerbuilder.com/2018-08-09-More-Than-Half-of-Employers-Have-Found-Content-on-Social-Media-That-Caused-Them-NOT-to-Hire-a-Candidate-According-to-Recent-CareerBuilder-Survey>.

Islip v Coldmatic Refrigeration of Canada Ltd, 2002 BCCA 255.

Israel, Peter, "Ensuring Independent Contractors Are Not Really Employees," *Canadian Employment Law Today* 384 (5 March 2003) at 2997.

Jones v Klassen, 2006 ABQB 41.

Levitt, Howard, *Quick Reference to Employment Law* (Toronto: International Reference Press, 2002).

Mark's Work Wearhouse Ltd, Investigation Report P2010-IR-001 (16 February 2010), online: *Alberta Office of the Information and Privacy Commissioner* <https://www.oipc.ab.ca/media/127959/P2010%E2%80%90001IR.pdf>.

Miedema, Adrian, & Christina Hall, *HR Manager's Guide to Background Checks and Pre-employment Testing*, 2nd ed (Toronto: Thomson Reuters, 2012).

Moffatt, Anthony, "The Fine Line Between Employee and Temp," *Canadian Employment Law Today* 533 (6 May 2009) at 4.

Office of the Information and Privacy Commissioner for British Columbia, *Conducting Social Media Background Checks* (May 2017), online: <http://www.oipc.bc.ca/guidance-documents/1454>.

Office of the Information and Privacy Commissioner of Alberta, *Guidelines for Social Media Background Checks* (December 2011), online: <https://www.oipc.ab.ca/media/383673/guide_social_media_background_checks_dec2011.pdf>.

Pacific Rim Nutrition Ltd v Guardian Insurance Co of Canada (1995), 7 BCLR (3d) 251 (SC) aff'd 1998 CanLII 4986 (BCCA).

Personal Information Protection Act, SA 2003, c P-6.5.

Personal Information Protection Act, SBC 2003, c 63.

Peters & Co Limited v Ward, 2015 ABCA 6.

Phoenix Restorations Ltd v Drisdelle, 2014 BCSC 1497.

Phutela v University of Alberta, 1996 ABCA 370.

Queen v Cognos Inc, [1993] 1 SCR 87.

Rexrode, Christina, "Yahoo CEO Scott Thompson Resigns After Scrutiny of His Resume," *Associated Press* (13 May 2012).

Rudner, Stuart, "Reference Letters Not So Risky," *Canadian Employment Law Today* 539 (29 July 2009) at 3.

Sherrard Kuzz LLP, "Criminal Record Checks: Managing Liability and Getting the Information You Need," *Management Counsel: Employment and Labour Law Update* XI:4 (August 2012) at 1, online: <http://www.sherrardkuzz.com/pdf/Vol_XI_4.pdf>.

Stefanik, Thomas, "Case in Point: Wrongful Dismissal, You're Hired! Wait, Check That … " *Canadian Employment Law Today* 555 (21 April 2010) at 4.

T (V), R v, [1992] 1 SCR 749.

The Treaty Group Inc v Drake, 2007 ONCA 450, aff'g 2005 CanLII 45406 (Ont Sup Ct J).

Union of Calgary Co-operative Employees v Calgary Co-operative Association Limited, [2006] CarswellAlta 910 (Arb Bd).

Wiebe Door Services Ltd v The Minister of National Revenue (1986), 87 DTC 5025 (FCA).

Wilson v Clarica Life Insurance Co, 2001 BCSC 1696, aff'd 2002 BCCA 502.

Youth Criminal Justice Act, SC 2002, c 1.

Unionized Workplaces

3

LEARNING OUTCOMES

After completing this chapter, you will be able to:

- Understand the main differences between a unionized and non-unionized workplace.
- Describe the evolution of labour law in Canada.
- Explain the process for certifying or decertifying a union.
- Understand the concept of exclusivity and explain its relevance to the system of labour relations in Canada.
- Describe activities that constitute unfair labour practices for unions and employers.
- Describe the contents of a typical collective agreement.
- Describe a typical grievance process, and understand the difference between grievance arbitration and interest arbitration.
- Understand the steps involved in calling a lawful strike or lockout, and the ways in which legislation and the common law regulate activity during strikes and lockouts.
- Understand the evolution in Charter case law involving union membership, collective bargaining, and strikes.

Introduction

individual employment contracts negotiated between an employer and each employee individually, without the involvement of an association or regulatory agency

This book outlines the law governing contracts of **individual employment**—that is, contracts negotiated between an employer and each employee individually, without the involvement of an association or regulatory agency. Of course, in the majority of non-unionized jobs, there isn't much negotiation between the employer and the employee. The employee applies for a job, and takes it as is—with the terms of work, including pay, set by the employer.

The reality is that there is an imbalance of power, as well as information, between employers and individual employees, which can lead to unreasonable terms of work in some cases. That is why Canadian law sets minimum standards for terms of work (Chapter 6), protects privacy (Chapter 10), and regulates workplace safety (Chapters 8 and 9). This imbalance has also prompted courts to find certain "implied terms" in all contracts of employment, such as the duty of fidelity, the duty of fair treatment, the requirement for reasonable notice in the event of a without-cause dismissal (Chapter 14), and other terms, such as a presumption against "restraint of trade" clauses (Chapter 15; and see generally Chapters 2 and 5).

Before most of these legislative and common law protections emerged, however, there was another movement that sought to rebalance the relationship between employers and employees. The labour movement that emerged before the Industrial Revolution (Webb & Webb, 1920) eventually established the right of workers to organize themselves into unions and to have the unions represent them at the negotiating table. The result was a more balanced negotiating position. Without a "collective agreement" in place for all its workers, an employer with a legally unionized workforce could not operate.

The ability of unions to negotiate employment terms that provide greater pay, job security, protections, and benefits to employees has raised employment standards generally through the regulations that governments began to adopt in the 20th century. But this ability was hard-won, facing initial resistance from courts and legislatures.

This chapter provides a fairly broad overview of labour law in British Columbia (BC) and Alberta, though it does illustrate the main principles with some of the specific rules in legislation and case law. The chapter has five sections. The first is on the history of collective bargaining law in Canada (which we will call "labour law"). The second looks at the establishment of a union in a particular workplace and the bargaining of a new union's first collective agreement. Next is an overview of collective agreements: their role in a unionized workplace, some mandatory and common terms in them, and the grievance arbitration procedure for interpreting and enforcing them. The fourth section reviews the use of strikes and lockouts, the ultimate form of economic pressure. The chapter concludes with a consideration of the role of the *Canadian Charter of Rights and Freedoms* (Charter), including several recent decisions that have considerably strengthened constitutional protection of unions.

Chapter 4 complements the following discussion of provincial labour law by outlining the labour law regime for federally regulated employers under the *Canada Labour Code*. Many of the principles in the federal statute are the same as those in BC and Alberta. Readers who would like a briefer overview of collective bargaining law in Canada can therefore read the "Canada Labour Code: Part I—Industrial Relations" section of Chapter 4.

History and Premises of Labour Law

The modern labour law regime in Canada did not emerge until the years immediately after the Second World War, and certain fundamental principles were still being established as recently as the 1970s. The history of labour law before the 1940s in England and Canada was one of initial hostility toward unions, followed by begrudging acceptance of the right to unionize, and finally, in the second half of the 20th century, protection and empowerment of unions.

One labour law scholar has identified three fundamental features of labour law in Canada:

1. The ability of individual employees to join together and form a union.
2. The ability of the union to force the employer to bargain with it, and not with individuals.
3. The ability of the union to resort to economic sanctions (chiefly, the withdrawal of labour through the exercise of the right to strike) to support bargaining demands (Rayner, 2007, at 2).

Until the post–Second World War era, Canadian law did not support the second of these features—which we will call "exclusive bargaining power." And since the union was not the exclusive bargaining agent for the employees it represented, the third feature, the "right to strike," was a much weaker bargaining tool. An employer could permanently hire other workers to replace those on strike.

Despite limitations on the bargaining power of unions before the Second World War, they were able to establish milestones in improvements to wages, hours of work, and workplace safety. These milestones began to set a template for early versions of employment standards legislation and thus influenced the development of individual employment law. Early employment legislation included statutes in the late 1800s in Ontario and Quebec that limited the hours of work for factory workers to a maximum of 60 per week. By the 1920s, collective bargaining gradually established the 8-hour workday and 48-hour workweek (a standard that the International Labour Organization endorsed in 1919)—though it was not until the 1940s that provinces began to adopt this standard in legislation for non-union workers. The late 1940s and early 1950s also began to see legislated standards for holidays and vacation pay, both of which had been a feature of collective agreements for decades.

Collective agreements also helped to spur minimum-wage laws. Unions were at first reluctant to see legislated minimum wages for a number of reasons, including the fear that these would reduce the importance of having a union. Nonetheless, such laws began to emerge before 1920. BC and Manitoba were the first, setting minimum wages for women (who were generally not working in unionized industries), followed by other provinces in 1919, 1920, and onward. The first minimum-wage law for men came in 1925 (Doorey, 2016, at 271-72).

The "Wagner Act Model" of Labour Law

In the 1930s, the US government passed a statute known as the *Wagner Act* that established a certification process enabling unions to exclusively represent employees in a defined unit and regulating the right to strike. Canada adopted this model in 1944, when Prime Minister William Lyon Mackenzie King used the *War Measures Act* to assert federal jurisdiction over labour, enacting order in council PC 1003. The principles established in PC 1003 became part of the *Industrial Relations and Disputes Investigation Act* in 1948, which eventually became the *Canada Labour Code* in 1967. Provinces soon followed with their own legislation.

Following is a list of the chief components of the *Wagner Act* model, as adopted by Canada in the 1940s and 1950s. Despite some variations from province to province, these principles continue to inform the statutes that each province has enacted:

1. The right of employees to join or form a union.
2. The process for certification of unions—and the duty of employers to bargain only with the union once it is certified ("exclusivity").
3. The establishment of the collective agreement as an enforceable contract that contains mechanisms to resolve disputes over the interpretation or application of the agreement without resorting to work stoppage.
4. The regulation of strike activity, including a prohibition against work stoppages during the term of a negotiated collective agreement.
5. The duty for both the union and employer to bargain in good faith.
6. The prohibition of "unfair labour practices."
7. The establishment of an administrative body (Labour Relations Board) to enforce labour relations codes.

The *Wagner Act* model considerably strengthened the position of unions and unionized workers in Canada, but it also involved trade-offs. The most significant gain for unions was the certification process, which grants unions the right to be the exclusive bargaining agent representing workers in a defined bargaining unit. In order to gain this right, union activists must persuade a majority of their co-workers to vote in favour of unionization. Once earned, this exclusivity strengthens the bargaining power of the union, particularly where the employer is not able to hire replacement workers (either because of a statutory prohibition or because worker skill is difficult to replace). Employers are also prohibited from negotiating special terms of employment with anyone in the bargaining unit. In other words, once the union has been certified, the group employment contract (collective agreement) that is negotiated applies to all members of the bargaining unit. The certification procedures under which employees democratically choose their union and that require the parties to bargain in good faith establish the "exclusivity" feature, which is arguably the strongest basis of union power in workplaces today.

The *Wagner Act* model also gave workers the right to strike without endangering their jobs. Employers are required to allow all striking employees to return to their jobs at the end of the strike. Whereas the previous regime merely legalized strikes (i.e., overrode the common law rules that made striking a tort and a crime), the new law created a special rule for unionized labour: they could go on strike without being treated as if they had quit. The *Wagner Act* model truly set labour law apart from the law of the individual contract of employment.

The trade-offs for the right to strike included mandatory conciliation before a strike or lockout could occur, the requirement of a strike vote by the workers, and a prohibition on strikes during the term of the collective agreement (known as the "peace obligation"). The second and third of these two restrictions make "wildcat strikes" illegal. Workers cannot simply walk off the job en masse in response to an act by the employer. Furthermore, there is a statutory "freeze" on the terms and conditions of employment during the period of conciliation. (Note: As discussed below, BC has dispensed with the conciliation process, replacing it with the option for the employer or union to request mediation.)

Establishing a Union

This section sets out the basic principles for establishing a union in a workplace that has not yet had one and for the negotiation of the first collective agreement. It also defines the most common types of unions and explains the concept of an "unfair labour practice," which is the basis for most labour relations board decisions. It is a high-level overview, so we will not explore the provincial legislation in depth. However, since this is a heavily regulated area of law, and since some readers may wish to look at the rules more closely, we have included references to many of the relevant sections of the *Labour Relations Code* in BC and Alberta (abbreviated as "LRC" or as the BC Code and Alberta Code).

Phases of Establishing a Union

The establishment of a union may be seen as having three phases:

1. *Organizing phase.* In this phase, employees begin talking among themselves about unionizing their workplace, or representatives from an existing union organization start to talk with workers about unionizing. There is no defined timeline for this phase, except that it ends when the employees or union apply for certification. Even during the organizing phase, before a union is in place, there are rules governing the behaviour of employers, employees, and unions. These appear primarily in sections 148–151 of the Alberta Code and sections 4–9 and 31 of the BC Code. See the section "Unfair Labour Practices," below, for further discussion.
2. *Certification phase.* This phase runs from the date of a union's application for certification (under division 5 of the Alberta Code and part 3, division 1, of the BC Code) to the date the Labour Relations Board decides whether or not to certify the union. This is normally the shortest phase, with fairly well-defined timelines (s 37 in the Alberta Code and ss 18 and 24–25 in the BC Code).

3. *Collective bargaining phase.* Collective bargaining occurs from the date a union or employer gives notice to commence bargaining until the date an agreement is achieved (or until decertification of the union, in the event the union fails to achieve an agreement and either the employees apply to decertify, the union simply ceases to exist, or another union tries to take it over). For unions and employers bargaining their first agreement, this phase starts after certification but does not start immediately upon certification. Whether it is a first agreement or collective bargaining that is occurring at the expiry of an existing agreement, one of the parties must give notice under sections 59–61 in Alberta and sections 45–47 in BC.

Types of Unions and Other Basic Terminology

Labour Relations Board (LRB)
the government agency responsible for interpreting, applying, and enforcing provincial labour relations codes; LRBs oversee certification and decertification processes and act as tribunals hearing disputes over unfair labour practices, strikes, lockouts, and any other matters related to the *Labour Relations Code*

bargaining unit
the group of employees for which the union negotiates a collective agreement

union member
a person admitted to membership in the union organization

- ***Labour Relations Board (LRB).*** The LRB is the government agency responsible for interpreting, applying, and enforcing provincial labour relations codes (LRCs). LRBs oversee certification and decertification processes and act as tribunals hearing disputes over unfair labour practices, strikes and lockouts, and any other matters related to the LRC. It is important to note that LRBs do not normally make decisions about the content of collective agreements. That is left to the parties to negotiate, and specially trained arbitrators typically adjudicate those disputes. Rather, the Board is responsible for ensuring fairness in certification, bargaining, strikes, and lockout processes.
- ***Bargaining unit.*** This is the group of employees for which the union negotiates a collective agreement. All employees who work in this "unit" are bound by the collective agreement, as is the employer. Being an *employee* within a bargaining unit does not make an employee a *union member*. Managerial employees are generally excluded from bargaining units to prevent the employer from interfering with a union's internal activities.
- *Membership.* As noted above, being an employee in the unit for which the union has exclusive bargaining rights does not automatically make a person a **union member**. Normally, employees will sign a card and pay a small membership fee to join. If an employee has a fundamental objection to being a member of the union, the employee may (in some cases) choose not to be a member. However, the union is still obligated to negotiate on behalf of that employee and is still required to represent that employee in disputes with the employer, and the employee is bound by the employment terms the union negotiates.

  Membership in the union enables a person to participate in the *governance* of the union itself. This includes the right to debate and vote on decisions the members make at general meetings of the union. Non-members do not generally have the right to participate in votes or decisions and may not attend general meetings.

  There are three votes that employees in the bargaining unit have the right to participate in even if they are not members:

- a *representation* vote, for the decision whether the union should be certified for that unit or decertified (s 58 of the Alberta Code; ss 24 and 33–34 of the BC Code)
- a *ratification* vote for approval of the first or renewed collective agreement (this is true only in BC, under ss 11(2) and 40; Alberta leaves it to the union to decide whether non-members can vote to ratify; note that neither province requires ratification—it is up to the union to decide whether to ask members to ratify)
- a *strike* vote (s 73 of the Alberta Code; s 40 of the BC Code). Section 39 of the BC Code also specifies that ratification votes (if held at all) and strike votes must be by secret ballot. In Alberta, all three types of vote are by secret ballot (s 15(2) of the Alberta Code).

- ***Union density/coverage***. This term simply refers to the percentage of workers who are unionized, as opposed to working under individual contracts of employment. We mention the term here mainly because it provides some context for the relevance of unions to workers across Canada. Union density in Canada has been relatively stable at around 30 percent since the late 1990s. Public sector work is the most highly unionized at around 70 percent, while the private sector is around 15 percent. Alberta has the lowest union coverage rate (24 percent) of any province; in BC, the union coverage rate is 29 percent (Statistics Canada, 2018).
- ***Union security***. This refers to any requirements in the collective agreement that employees in the bargaining unit either be members of the union or pay dues to the union. Almost all unions in Canada have some type of security clause.
- ***Union shop***. In a union shop, *all* employees in the bargaining unit *must* become members of the union within a specified period of time (usually after a probationary period). The employer does the hiring, but the employment is conditional on joining the union. If an employee refuses to join a union organization, the employee cannot work there.
- ***Closed shop***. In a closed shop, a person must be a member of the union before getting the job. The employer is only allowed to hire current members of the union to work in a particular bargaining unit. Today, closed shop unions have hiring-hall systems in place where employers contact the union to find workers for a specific job. Closed shops are less common than union shops and tend to be associated with the construction trades and film and music industries.
- ***Open shop/Rand formula shop***. In a true open shop union, membership is optional and payment of dues is also optional. The Rand formula shop is a variation of the open shop union. In a Rand formula shop, the employees do not have to be union members, but they are still required to have an amount equivalent to union dues deducted from their pay and remitted to a charitable organization agreed upon by the union and the employer (see s 29 of the Alberta Code and s 17 of the BC Code). The Rand formula was created to provide financial security to unions and prevent the problem of "free riders" who benefit from the union's work. As noted above, a union is required to

union density
the percentage of workers who are unionized, as opposed to working under individual contracts of employment; also called union coverage

union security
refers to any requirements in the collective agreement that employees in the bargaining unit either be members of the union or pay dues to the union

union shop
a type of union security whereby *all* employees in the bargaining unit *must* become members of the union within a specified period of time (usually after a probationary period); employment is conditional on joining the union

closed shop
a type of union security whereby a person must be a member of the union before getting the job; the employer is only allowed to hire current members of the union to work in a particular bargaining unit

open shop
a system whereby union membership is optional and payment of dues is also optional

Rand formula shop
a variation of the open shop union, and is what most labour legislation requires employers to accept if the union requests it; in a Rand formula shop, the employees do not have to be union members, but they are still required to have union dues deducted from their pay

represent all members of the bargaining unit, whether they are members or not. Representation can be a costly endeavour, and it was seen as unfair that a person who chose not to be a member would get all of the benefits without incurring any of the costs.

agency shop
a type of union security where non-members within the bargaining unit pay the union for the costs of collective bargaining, rather than pay regular dues that cover a broader range of union activities

- ***Agency shops***. This is where non-members within the bargaining unit pay the union for the costs of collective bargaining, rather than pay regular dues that cover a broader range of union activities. These are exceptionally rare in Canada—as are completely open shops (i.e., dues-optional shops).

Regardless of which type of shop applies, there are three principles to keep in mind:

1. *If you are in the bargaining unit, the union negotiates for you, whether you are a member or not and whether you pay dues or not.* Membership gives you more of a say in union governance, but non-membership does not exempt you from the union's authority to negotiate on your behalf and to pursue grievances on your behalf.
2. *The employer still does the hiring.* In a closed shop, however, the employee's admission to membership in the union is a prerequisite of employment. The union determines whether or not the individual has the necessary qualifications and skills for the job and the employer contacts the union to offer the job to the union member recommended by the union.
3. *For all unions, the employer normally deducts union dues from the employee's pay and remits them to the union.*

Certification Process

Basic Procedures

The process of certification is reasonably straightforward, aside from the political manoeuvring that can go on during the organizing period. There are a few steps and a few key requirements, some of which are strict (e.g., time limits and the percentage of employees who must support the application) and some of which are discretionary (e.g., the requirement that a bargaining unit be "appropriate for bargaining"). They are as follows:

1. A certain proportion of the employees in the proposed bargaining unit must indicate support for, or have already joined, the union. In BC, it must be 45 percent (see ss 18 and 24 of the BC Code). In Alberta, the proportion required is 40 percent (see s 33 of the Alberta Code). In BC, the workers must have joined the union; in Alberta, workers can either join or declare in writing their wish to have the union represent them.
2. Once a union signs up the required proportion of bargaining-unit workers, it applies to the Board for certification under section 18(1) of the BC Code and section 32 of the Alberta Code.

3. The Board then determines whether the proposed bargaining unit is "appropriate for bargaining." The BC and Alberta statutes give the LRBs complete discretion. LRBs will normally consider the following factors when evaluating bargaining-unit appropriateness:
   a. community of interest or similarity in skills, interests, duties, and working conditions;
   b. the nature of the employer's organization, including the physical and administrative structure of the employer;
   c. functional integration;
   d. geography (i.e., a preference for a unit in a small or connected area);
   e. the practice and history of the current collective bargaining relationship, if any relationship is in place;
   f. the practice and history of collective bargaining in the industry or sector;
   g. the viability of bargaining structures; most boards prefer larger units, rather than small and fragmented groups (British Columbia Labour Relations Board, "Guide to the Labour Relations Code");
   h. agreement of the parties; if the union and employer agree that a unit is appropriate, the Board may give that some weight in its decision (Alberta Labour Relations Board, "Information Bulletin").
4. Next, the Board confirms the number of employees in the unit (usually using the employer's payroll records) and confirms that the proofs of membership are valid and amount to at least 45 percent in BC or 40 percent in Alberta of the bargaining-unit employees.
5. The Board must then order a secret ballot representation vote. The BC Code states that the vote will take place within five business days of the application for certification. The Alberta Code requires that it occur within 20 working days (25 days for a mail-in vote).

   The outcome of a secret ballot vote will be determined on the basis of the ballots cast by the majority of employees who participated in the vote. If the majority vote in favour of the union, the Board will issue a certification order and all employees in the bargaining unit will become unionized. While this is the normal process for certification, it can occur where the employer voluntarily recognizes the union without requiring the voting procedures in the Code. The LRB can also order a remedial certification if the employer has engaged in an unfair labour practice that may have influenced the outcome of a certification drive.

   Recent changes to the BC Code have provided the Board with broader discretion to use certification as a remedy to an unfair labour practice. Previously, remedial certification was reserved for circumstances where the Board determined that "but for" the employer's unfair labour practice, the union's organizing efforts would likely have been successful. This required evidence of a downturn in union support or organizing momentum following the employer's unlawful activities. However, the new language in the BC Code (see s 14(1)) permits that the Board may remedially certify a union if the "board believes it is just and equitable in order to remedy the consequences of the prohibited act" (s 14(4.1)(c)). It is not yet clear how the Board will interpret and apply this newly widened discretion to order remedial certification.

The ability to use certification as a remedy to an unfair labour practice is also new to Alberta, and the *Widewaters* case establishes the framework the Board will use to determine when it is appropriate to apply this remedial action.

CASE IN POINT

Remedial Certifications in Alberta

United Food and Commercial Workers Canada Union (UFCW), Local 401 and Widewaters Calgary Hotel Management Company, ULC, 2018 CanLII 149047 (Alta LRB).

Facts

In this case the union filed an unfair labour practice complaint against the employer, Widewaters, for termination of Doncaster during an organizing campaign. The union argued that Doncaster was a key organizer. The employer alleged he was terminated for habitual lateness. During the hearing, Doncaster described himself as a "working-class anarchist" and a workers' advocate. He had tattoos of the words "union power" and "workers' rights" on his arms and had shown them to his employer. He began working as a dishwasher for Widewaters in November 2016. By August 2017, Doncaster had contacted UFCW to discuss the possibility of commencing a certification campaign. Two other employees joined Doncaster as internal organizers, and they began working toward unionization. In September 2017, Doncaster was verbally warned and received one letter regarding his tardiness. There was considerable dispute about the number of days he was late. Text messages were also sent in September indicating that the employer was aware of the organizing campaign. On September 21, Doncaster was terminated. The termination letter contained a number of errors regarding the alleged lateness. Evidence was submitted that other Widewaters employees knew about the union organizing drive but were "too scared to talk about it." One employee stated a person "got fired because of union activity" and another said that "someone from management told us we were not allowed to talk about that."

Relevant Issue

Was Doncaster discharged for his role in the organizing campaign?

Decision

The Board assessed four factors in its determination:

1. Whether the employer established a reasonable or credible explanation for the termination.
2. Whether the employer had knowledge of the organizing campaign and the employee's role in it.
3. Any pattern of anti-union activity by the employer.
4. The credibility of the witnesses.

While there was no pattern of anti-union activity, the Board found that Widewaters was aware of the organizing campaign and of Doncaster's involvement in the campaign. The timing of the decision to discharge Doncaster and the lack of a credible or reasonable explanation for his termination meant that the employer failed to establish that it did not discharge Doncaster because of his union organizing activities. The Board found Doncaster's evidence more credible than the evidence of his supervisors.

The Board stated that as a result of Doncaster's termination, the organizing campaign came to a halt and employees were not willing to risk their employment by speaking with the union or signing a petition in support of the union. The result was to undermine the union's legitimacy and chill its support in the bargaining unit. The Board ordered Doncaster be reinstated with compensation from the date of his termination to the date of the hearing.

In a subsequent decision, *UFCW, Local Union No 401 and Widewaters Calgary Hotel Management Company, ULC* (2018, CanLII 33689 Alta LRB), the Board ordered remedial certification and addressed the approach that should be taken. They rejected the idea that the actions of the employer needed to be "so outrageous and pervasive and with such dire consequences upon employees that any wish of those employees to organize would be totally frustrated" (at para 5). They also rejected the need to consider the viability of the potential collective bargaining relationship. Instead, they relied on the principles established by the Supreme Court of Canada in *Royal Oak Mines Inc* that when determining an appropriate remedy, the Board should take a contextual approach that focuses on the consequences of the unfair labour practice and how those consequences may be remedied or counteracted.

There are several notable factors about this case. First, the onus of proving anti-union animus was no longer a burden for the union and employee. New language in section 149 of the Alberta Code (passed in 2017) clearly placed the burden of proof on the employer, and this was the first case before the Board under the new legislative provisions. Second, the Board offers a lengthy discussion of remedial certification in the second part of the decision. Although this was the first remedial certification in Alberta, remedial certification has a much longer history in other provinces, including BC.

Effect of Certification

Certification has effects on the employer, on the union, and on other unions that may be interested in representing the same employees. The main effect, of course, is that the employer has to negotiate with that union and can no longer negotiate with individual employees in that bargaining unit. This is the exclusive right to bargain discussed above. It gives the unionized employees greater negotiating power, especially in BC, where it is illegal to hire replacement workers during a strike or lockout. This is not the case in all provinces. Alberta does not prohibit the employer from hiring replacement workers (often referred to by union activists as "scab labour"). However, if the workers are highly skilled or engage in dangerous work that requires extensive safety training, it may be difficult for employers to find replacements.

There are also effects on other unions, which face restrictions on their ability to "raid" the bargaining unit (i.e., try to take it over) once a union is certified. Although the law does allow other unions to attempt a takeover (and in so doing protects the right of employees who are unhappy with their union to switch to another one), it sets limits. For example, both provinces prohibit raiding for several months after a new certification or during a legal strike or lockout.

Decertification

There are four main reasons a union can lose its bargaining rights:

1. Employees no longer support the union and apply to decertify it.
2. The union or employer has ceased to operate.
3. Another union has raided it—that is, applied for certification to replace the existing union.
4. The LRB has ordered it under the BC Code. This may happen because of a violation of the BC Code by the union.

The process of decertifying or revoking the bargaining rights of a union is virtually identical to the process for certification. It requires support of the majority of employees in the bargaining unit, and the LRB will investigate to ensure that this is the case.

If another business buys a unionized employer, the new owner is bound by the collective agreement. It usually takes a complete shutdown of an operation to end the union's status as the certified bargaining agent for those employees. In the event of a merger of two corporations that each have unions in place, the Board has authority to determine a suitable new bargaining unit and to sort out certification status. (When a collective agreement is in place, the transfer of an operation to another city is not a closing down—it could be treated as an illegal lockout, unless the transfer and any layoffs follow the procedure in the collective agreement.)

Collective Bargaining

Part 4 (ss 45–55) of the BC Code and division 10 (ss 59–63) of the Alberta Code establish the processes for collective bargaining. The union or employer serves notice to the other party that it wants to start negotiating. Bargaining does not need to start right away upon certification. One party must give notice. In Alberta, if this is not a first contract and a collective agreement is already in place, notice to bargain must occur not less than 60 days and not more than 120 days prior to the expiry of the collective agreement (in the BC Code, s 46 just says that notice may be given any time within four months before an existing agreement expires). Once either party gives notice, bargaining must begin—the other party cannot refuse.

Bargaining Process

There is no specific time limit for negotiating the first or any subsequent collective agreement. The only requirement is that the parties meet and make every reasonable effort to enter into a collective agreement. The parties can bargain any issue that they deem relevant to the employment relationship, provided it does not violate other legislation. For example, a clause allowing discrimination on a ground prohibited by human rights legislation would not be enforceable.

There are two key requirements related to bargaining that are important to understand. First, when the parties are renegotiating an existing collective agreement that has expired, the terms and conditions of that collective agreement bridge until a new agreement is reached or until there is a strike or lockout. **Bridging** ensures that the employer continues to pay employees and abide by the terms and conditions of work that are already in place. The second important requirement is that the parties bargain in **good faith.** Bad-faith bargaining is a contravention of the Code that is evaluated on a case-by-case basis. The Alberta LRB Procedure Guide outlines common issues that arise in bad-faith bargaining, including the following:

- refusing to meet once notice to bargain has been served,
- refusing to attend meetings,
- attending meetings unprepared to bargain,
- undermining the union by negotiating directly with the employees,

bridging
refers to a collective agreement that applies to the parties at the time notice to bargain is served continuing to apply to the parties until (1) a new collective agreement is in place, (2) the right of the union to represent the employees is terminated, or (3) there is a strike or lockout

good-faith bargaining
the parties meet and make genuine efforts to reach agreement; this does not require that they agree to proposals from the other side, but they cannot deliberately sabotage bargaining efforts to avoid reaching agreement

- surface bargaining (e.g., reactivating signed-off proposals, adding new proposals late in the dispute, stalling), and
- illegal bargaining proposals (that conflict with other legislation or terms already agreed to by the parties).

There are generally three options available to the parties if bargaining is proceeding slowly or breaks down completely:

1. Either party can request that the Board appoint a mediator to assist them in settling the outstanding issues. A mediator will work with the parties to try to reach a mutually acceptable resolution. However, the recommendations of a mediator are not binding on the parties. If either party applies for mediation, it does not prevent a strike or lockout from occurring.
2. Either party can initiate job action to try to move bargaining forward. When it is initiated by the employer, it is a lockout. When it is initiated by the union it is a strike. Strikes and lockouts are discussed in more detail later in the chapter.
3. The parties can agree to voluntary interest arbitration. In this case the LRB will appoint an arbitrator who will request proposals from the parties and make a decision about the contents of the collective agreement. The decision of the arbitrator is binding on the parties. **Interest arbitration** is different than **grievance arbitration**, which occurs when a collective agreement is already in place and the parties have a disagreement about how it is interpreted.

It should be noted that special provisions of both the Alberta and BC codes apply when it is the first time the parties have negotiated an agreement after the union has been certified. Parties often have greater difficulty reaching their first agreement. Therefore, both the Alberta Code and the BC Code provide mechanisms for **first contract arbitration**. In Alberta, mandatory interest arbitration can only occur after a strike or lockout notice has been served and usually after attempts have been made to mediate a settlement between the parties. Recent changes to the BC Code have eliminated strike or lockout notice as a precondition for interest arbitration, which can (but not invariably) lead to a first collective agreement being imposed by an arbitrator.

Effect of Execution of the Collective Agreement

The main effect of a collective agreement is that the employer, employees, and union are bound by the terms and conditions they bargained. This may seem obvious, but the parties may still have disagreements about what they meant when they bargained the terms. This is why grievance mechanisms are included in all collective agreements. Collective agreements are generally much longer and more detailed than individual employment contracts. They may address wages and benefits, job requirements, scheduling, hours of work, vacation, procedures for hiring, promotion or

interest arbitration a form of dispute resolution that occurs when a collective agreement is being negotiated; the parties propose the terms and conditions of the collective agreement, and the arbitrator decides the content of any clauses that are in dispute

grievance arbitration also known as "rights arbitration," occurs when a collective agreement is in force; a form of dispute resolution where an arbitrator decides on the correct application or interpretation of an existing collective agreement clause

first contract arbitration a legislated requirement for interest arbitration in the place of a strike or lockout that applies only when a workplace is newly unionized and the parties are unable to reach their first agreement

transfer, and other important issues that may affect the employment relationship, such as harassment and discrimination. They tend to evolve and become more complex over time. Where an employment contract might be four or five pages long, a collective agreement may be 40 or 50 pages. It is also important to stress that all employees in the bargaining unit are bound by the agreement the union makes on their behalf, regardless of their membership status.

Another effect of concluding an agreement relates to raiding unions. Under section 19 of the BC Code, upon execution of the collective agreement a "collective agreement bar" kicks in. Alberta relies on the "certification bar" described above, but the effect is the same. In BC, once there is a collective agreement, another union may only apply for certification during the seventh or eighth month of the last year of the agreement if the agreement is in force for a term of three years or less, or during the seventh or eighth month of the third year of the agreement and thereafter in the seventh or eighth month in each subsequent year of the agreement if it is in force for a term of more than three years (s 19). This is known as the open period. Note that similar rules apply in the construction sector in BC, but the open periods are in July and August, rather than the seventh and eighth months of an agreement. After the agreement's expiry, another unit can apply at any time, even if the current union is negotiating a new agreement, but not during a strike or lockout and not for a period of 22 months after a raid application is dismissed by the Board. In Alberta, another union may attempt certification only if there is no collective agreement in place in the last two months of an existing collective agreement or in the 11th and 12th months each year of an existing agreement (s 37).

Finally, another important effect of the execution of a collective agreement is that the agreement bars strikes or lockouts for the term of the agreement. This is called the **peace obligation**. A union cannot call a strike, and an employer cannot lock employees out, during the term of a collective agreement.

peace obligation
a prohibition on strikes or lockouts during the term of the collective agreement

Unfair Labour Practices

Many of the disputes that labour relations boards hear in their roles as adjudicators are about unfair labour practices. These can include allegations that the employer or union has acted improperly during the organizing phase, during the certification phase, or later during the collective bargaining phase. There are many unfair labour practice cases involving allegations that the employer is trying to stop a union from becoming established or "bust" one that is already in place. Unions can also commit unfair labour practices, such as pressuring employees to join or censoring dissenters. Unfair labour practices also include bad-faith bargaining by either side.

General Rules for Unfair Labour Practices

From the organizing phase to the period after a collective agreement is signed, there are general obligations on both the employer and union that prohibit them from certain types of conduct (set out in ss 4–9 of the BC Code and ss 147–155 of the Alberta Code). Most unfair labour practice complaints heard by LRBs are against employers. Boards try to level the playing field as much as possible, especially when it comes to establishing a union and negotiating the first collective agreement, which is the time at which the union has the least amount of leverage. This is because the right to unionize is protected by the Charter and there is an inequality of power between employers and employees. The concern is that employers will use their power over not-yet-unionized employees to prevent the union from being established.

Most unfair labour practices committed by employers are in the realm of management decisions that affect employees. These range from acts that target individual employees to shutting down an entire operation. More specifically, employers are prohibited from any of the following actions:

- altering rates of pay or terms and conditions of employment during the certification process or after notice to bargain has been served;
- refusing to bargain in good faith with a certified union;
- participating or interfering in the formation or administration of a trade union, or contributing financial support to the union;
- refusing to employ or discriminating against someone because the person is a member of a trade union, indicates support for a trade union, participates in a strike, or files a complaint under the Code;
- intimidating, dismissing, or threatening to dismiss an employee for becoming a member of the union;
- suspending, disciplining, or discharging an employee for joining the union or for refusing to cross a picket line; or
- bargaining with any person or organization that is not the certified bargaining agent for the employees in the bargaining unit.

Students and employers are often surprised that it is an unfair practice for an employer to give the employees benefits during the union certification processes or during bargaining. The codes in both provinces are explicit about this: increases or decreases in wages are forbidden during these "freeze periods," as they are often referred to. Wage increases are as forbidden as decreases. The employer cannot make any changes during the freeze periods, unless those changes are things that are routinely done, such as regular merit-based pay increases (which labour boards may treat as a "business as usual" exception).

These rules don't prevent an employer from suspending, transferring, or laying off employees or from disciplining them where there is proper and sufficient cause. It is also important to note that employers are *not* prevented from expressing their views, so long as they do not use coercion, intimidation, threats, or undue influence. That said, recent changes to the BC Code now restrict an employer's freedom to communicate to employees such that the employer is only permitted to make statements of "fact or opinion reasonably held with respect to the employer's business" (s 8). Previously, employers in BC were expressly permitted to communicate its "views on any matter, including matters relating to an employer, a trade union or the representation of employees by a trade union, provided that the person does not use intimidation or coercion." It is yet to be seen how this subtle but significant new restriction will be interpreted and applied by the Board, but there is no doubt that employer communications with employees will be subject to greater scrutiny.

Unions have similar prohibitions that prevent them from intimidating employees or employers or restricting their right to communicate with each other. More specifically, unions are prohibited from engaging in any of the following:

- refusing to bargain in good faith;
- preventing a person from becoming a member for discriminatory reasons;
- attempting to compel an employer or employers' organization to bargain with a union that is not the certified bargaining agent for the employees in the bargaining unit;
- bargaining collectively or entering into a collective agreement when another union is the certified bargaining agent;
- attempting to organize workers on the employer's property without the permission of the employer (though s 7(1) of the BC Code does allow this activity during breaks);
- using coercion, intimidation, threats, or undue influence to encourage or discourage an employee from becoming a member of a union;
- requiring that an employer terminate an employee because the employee has been expelled or suspended from membership in the trade union (except where the employee failed to pay the fees uniformly required to be paid by all members as a condition of acquiring or retaining membership in the union); and
- disciplining or expelling a member for continuing to work during a strike or for refusing to engage in any activity that is a contravention of the legislation (e.g., refusing to participate in a wildcat strike).

It should also be noted that unions owe their members a "duty of fair representation." This generally means that they must carefully consider any grievance filed by a member and make a determination about carrying that grievance forward based on reasons that are not discriminatory or arbitrary.

Two important principles for unfair labour practices are *motive* and *onus*.

MOTIVE

Before or after the certification and collective bargaining freeze periods discussed above are in effect, an employer *is* allowed to increase or decrease wages, dismiss employees, or change working conditions as long as it does so for a valid business reason and is not violating the terms of a negotiated collective agreement. In other words, its motive cannot be to harm the union. This is often referred to as having an "anti-union animus." A non-unionized employer must, of course, comply with the common law and the *Employment Standards Act* or *Employment Standards Code*, and once a collective agreement is in place the employer must follow its rules. But even if the employer does comply with the law or the agreement, if its motive for a particular action is to try to break or undermine the union, that is an unfair labour practice.

ONUS

The question then becomes a matter of proving anti-union animus. Even in the case of an employer closing down an operation entirely, the employer may not have committed an unfair labour practice if the employer can show that it had valid business reasons for this decision.

Who has the onus? Generally, the onus (i.e., burden of proof) is on whoever files an unfair labour practice complaint. In practice, this can shift between the employer and the union. Labour boards have in some cases almost implicitly imposed a reverse onus on employers, provided the union can show some evidence of an anti-union animus. But in cases in which the union can only show that the employer has made a decision that is adverse to employees, it may not be enough.

However, there is a unique **reverse onus** clause in the BC Code (s 14(7)) that says for certain specified allegations of unfair labour practices, the employer has the primary onus of proving that it has *not* committed an unfair labour practice. The union need only prove that an employer's action has had some impact on an employee or set of employees, and the employer has to disprove unfairness.

reverse onus
a provision within a statute that shifts the burden of proof onto the individual specified to disprove an element of the information; typically, this provision concerns a shift in burden onto a defendant rather than the claimant

The Collective Agreement

This section provides an overview of collective agreements, focusing on three things:

1. the collective agreement's role surrounding all workplace relationships for the employees in the unit—and the residual role of other legal rules, including employment standards;
2. some of the standard terms in collective agreements, including terms that the BC and Alberta codes require to be included in agreements; and
3. grievance and arbitration procedures.

Collective Agreement as a "Collective Employment Contract"

We will first consider the definition of a collective agreement, and then look at the role of the agreement in relation to other legal principles, including the common law of contract, employment standards laws, workplace safety regulation, and human rights.

Definition of Collective Agreement

A collective agreement is a formal, often long and dense, document. The longer the union and employer have had a bargaining relationship, the longer the collective agreement is because the parties identify issues over time that they want to expressly address in their agreement. As the definitions below indicate, a collective agreement can also incorporate other documents, such as memoranda of understanding between the union and employer or terms in "common agreements" negotiated with outside organizations.

The Alberta Code defines a collective agreement (at s 1(1)(d)) as:

> an agreement in writing between an employer or an employers' organization and a bargaining agent [the union] containing terms or conditions of employment, and may include one or more documents containing one or more agreements.

The BC Code's definition (at s 1(1)) is:

> a written agreement between an employer, or an employers' organization authorized by the employer, and a trade union, providing for rates of pay, hours of work or other conditions of employment, which may include compensation to a dependent contractor for furnishing his or her own tools, vehicles, equipment, machinery, material or any other thing.

Beyond these definitions, there are some basic principles common to all collective agreements across Canada, which include:

- establishing the union as the certified bargaining agent and defining the size and scope of the bargaining unit;
- setting out terms of work, including pay, hours of work, safety matters, and other relevant conditions;
- providing the framework for dispute resolution, including the procedures for enforcing rules and how the parties work cooperatively to adapt the workplace to change;
- overriding any individual contracts as well as court claims to enforce individual rights (disputes must go through the collective agreement's grievance arbitration process); and
- imposing "peace" between the employer and union by requiring that there be no strikes or lockouts during the term of agreement (Rayner, 2007, at 363).

The Collective Agreement

Once a union is certified, it is not a mere agent (even though it is called a "bargaining agent"). It is the *principal*. That means it represents the employees and can make certain decisions regarding the administration of the collective agreement on its own, without the need to obtain approval from the employees, although this will depend to some degree on the constitution and by-laws of each individual union.

Once the employer and union have agreed on the terms of a tentative collective agreement, there is normally a process where employees in the bargaining unit have an opportunity to vote to accept or reject the contract. This is called **ratification.** If the tentative agreement is not ratified, the parties go back to the bargaining table. If it is ratified, it is signed by authorized representatives of the union and the employer and it becomes a binding contract. Individual employees are not required to sign a copy of the agreement. Furthermore, the labour relations codes in each province require that a copy of the collective agreement be submitted to the LRB.

ratification
a process where employees in the bargaining unit vote to accept or reject a contract negotiated by the union on their behalf

Collective Agreement as the Employment Contract

The most important point for readers to understand here is that the collective agreement is a legal contract and therefore a rule book that governs how employers manage their operations. It specifies not only the terms and conditions of work, but also the procedures for managing change in the workplace and the dispute resolution regime in the event of a disagreement over the interpretation or application of the agreement. With some limited exceptions, the parties do not look elsewhere for workplace rules. They do not rely on common law principles of contract or employment law, nor do they normally rely on general legislation unless it expressly applies to union workplaces or is compatible with collective bargaining. This does not mean that collective agreements can include terms that violate other work-related legislation. For example, a section of a collective agreement that violates occupational health and safety or human rights legislation would be considered null and void.

The leading case establishing the unique nature of the collective agreement is *McGavin Toastmaster Ltd v Ainscough*, a 1976 decision of the Supreme Court of Canada. This decision established that once a collective agreement is in place, there is no longer an individual employment contract. The collective agreement is not a collection of individual employment contracts; it is its own agreement, negotiated between the union and the employer, and enforced by the union and employer through the grievance and arbitration procedures contained within the agreement. In *McGavin Toastmaster*, the union went on a wildcat strike, which was a violation of the collective agreement. The employer treated this as a "fundamental breach" of the agreement, based on a principle from the common law of contract. It therefore fired all of the employees, ignoring the layoff procedures in the agreement. The Supreme Court ruled that the employer had no right to do so; even though the union had violated the agreement, the employer was required to use the remedies in the agreement in response to this violation.

Subsequent cases applied this rule and held that individual employees cannot take their employer to court over work-related matters. The collective agreement sets out all of the terms of the working relationship, and if a dispute involves the interpretation and application of the collective agreement, a dispute must go through the grievance and arbitration process that every agreement must include. Although *McGavin Toastmaster* said that "nothing remains" of an individual employment contract once a union reaches a collective agreement, a question that emerged in some cases was the extent to which arbitrators should apply general legal rules (from common law or legislation) to disputes in a unionized workplace, as opposed to using only the terms of the agreement. Some cases suggested that "general law" does apply, seeming to contradict the idea of the collective agreement as the complete code for that workplace.

In *Isidore Garon*, the Supreme Court reconciled *McGavin Toastmaster* with cases that seemed more flexible. The guiding takeaway from this decision is that a general legal rule that contradicts the general scheme or specific terms of the collective agreement cannot apply. An arbitrator can, however, apply a rule that is compatible with the collective agreement and that is a "supplementary or mandatory norm." Although this rule is abstract, the facts of the case provide some sense of what the Court means.

CASE IN POINT

General Legal Principles Only Apply if Compatible with Collective Bargaining

Isidore Garon ltée v Tremblay; Fillion et Frères (1976) inc v Syndicat national des employés de garage du Québec inc, 2006 SCC 2

Facts

Isidore Garon dealt with a pair of cases with similar facts. In them, the employers had shut down their businesses and dismissed the employees. The employers gave the employees the minimum amount of notice set out in Quebec's employment standards statute, *An Act Respecting Labour Standards*. (As you will see in Chapters 6 and 14, the amount of notice that such statutes require is very small, much lower than the common law standard that courts apply in wrongful dismissal cases.) The collective agreements set out no procedure for shutting down, though one of them did incorporate that Act's notice requirements by reference. The two unions each filed grievances. The question for the arbitrators was, how much notice must the employer give? The unions argued for one month per year of service, citing the *Civil Code of Québec* (CCQ, which is that province's equivalent of the common law requirement of reasonable notice). In this case it was the unions that wanted to apply a general legal rule that was not in the collective agreement. The arbitrators agreed with the unions and applied the CCQ. The employers applied for judicial review.

Relevant Issue

Can the notice requirements in the CCQ apply to dismissals of employees, despite the collective agreement's omission of a notice rule?

Decision

The majority ruled against the unions, stating that the CCQ scheme was, in fact, incompatible with the collective agreement scheme as a whole. The Court gave three reasons for this:

1. The collective agreement sets out in advance the rules of employment, so notice obligations beyond the legislated minimum employment standards are for the collective agreement, not for the CCQ (or the common law).
2. The collective agreement limits an employer's right to dismiss, so it must also limit an employee's right to reasonable notice.
3. The legislature had debated applying the CCQ to unionized workplaces and had chosen not to do so: there was no express legislative intent for this law to apply in this case.

The majority's reasoning implicitly placed the obligation on the union to negotiate proper notice procedures. If a union fails to do so, it must abide by the minimum standards set out in law and not on legal rules that are intended for non-unionized workplaces. Three judges dissented in the case. They argued that the CCQ can supplement the collective agreement—in other words, it should fill gaps. They took a less absolute view of whether the reasonable notice rules in the CCQ (which mirror those of the common law) were "compatible" with the collective agreement regime and concluded that there was no direct incompatibility. However, the majority of the Supreme Court judges upheld the idea of the collective agreement as a complete code, with very little room for general legal rules to apply.

Based on *Isidore Garon*, it is fair to say that most disputes in unionized workplaces are resolved according to the terms of the collective agreement, but that general legal principles may apply in some narrow situations. However, that ruling does not exclude legislative rules that expressly apply to unionized workplaces—for example, employment standards laws, workers' compensation and occupational health and safety regimes, and human rights statutes.

Common Terms in Collective Agreements

Here we will first review some basic terms that most labour relations codes, including those in BC and Alberta, require employers and unions to include in their collective agreements. Then we will consider some other terms that are not required but are found in most agreements.

The BC Code requires collective agreements to include the following terms, and often sets out default versions, which are "deemed" to be part of the agreement, if the actual agreement omits them:

- *Peace obligation* (ss 57–58)—stating that there will be no strike or lockout during the term of a collective agreement.
- *Just cause for discipline or dismissal* (s 84)—requiring that the employer have just and reasonable cause for any disciplinary action against an employee.
- *Arbitration* (s 84)—sending disagreements about the interpretation, operation, or violations of the collective agreement to arbitration or another dispute resolution method (discussed under the heading "Grievance Arbitration Process," below).
- *"Technological change" and joint consultation* (ss 53–54)—requiring a joint consultation committee (employer–union) and imposing on the employer the duty to give the union notice of changes in operations that will affect employees in the unit (known as "technological changes"—a term that means much more than changes in digital or mechanical technology and encompasses, for example, scheduling rearrangements). These clauses usually require the employer to meet with the union to develop an adjustment plan (usually through the joint committee).
- *Duration* (s 50)—specifying that all collective agreements must last for at least a year (they usually last for three to five but can vary).

The Alberta Code is less prescriptive, leaving the contents of a collective agreement up to the parties to negotiate. The Code itself prohibits strikes during the life of a collective agreement (ss 73–74), but there is no requirement that this be explicitly included in the agreement. Similarly, the Alberta Code does not mandate just cause provisions, though they are usually an implied term if not specified in a collective agreement. There is no requirement regarding technological change or joint consultation. The only collective agreement clause mandated by the Alberta Code is with respect to the inclusion of a dispute resolution mechanism. Section 135 indicates that collective agreements must contain a method of resolving differences in the interpretation, application, or operation of the collective agreement. However, there is no requirement that arbitration be the final step in that process. If a collective agreement does not include any type of dispute resolution mechanism, section 136 of the Code provides the clause that will be automatically included, which contains the process for binding arbitration. Finally, if the parties fail to negotiate the duration of a collective agreement, section 129 deems the term to be one year from the date the agreement commenced.

The following terms appear in many collective agreements, though they are not mandated by LRCs:

- *Recognition clause.* All agreements have a clause in which the employer formally recognizes the union as the representative of the employees in the union, even though it is not strictly necessary, since the Code already gives the union recognition. This clause typically includes a description of the bargaining unit.
- *Union security clause.* This clause specifies the type of union to be established (closed, union, open, etc.) and includes the obligation of the employer to collect dues from all employees in the unit.
- *Preamble.* Most collective agreements have a preamble that expresses the desire of the parties to work collaboratively to support the employment relationship and explains the purpose of the collective agreement.
- *Definitions.* The preamble may be followed by a series of definitions. For example, the collective agreement may specifically define what constitutes a "regular working day." It may include definitions for full-time, part-time, casual, or probationary employees. The more complex the workplace, the more common it is to see important terms defined so that they are easily interpreted by arbitrators.
- *Management rights.* Management rights clauses establish who makes decisions about issues that are not specifically addressed within the collective agreement. There are two perspectives regarding management rights. The "residual rights" view suggests that the employer has the unilateral right to make decisions about anything that is not included in the collective agreement. The "Laskin view" is based on a proposal by labour arbitrator Bora Laskin, who went on to become the chief justice of Canada in the 1970s. In a 1953 arbitration decision, Laskin argued that since the rest of the collective agreement was open to bargaining, these issues should also be resolved through bargaining (*International Chemical Workers Union, Local 279, in re Rexall Drug Co Ltd*). In practice, the residual rights view tends to prevail. However, these clauses generally:
  - ensure that the collective agreement takes precedence over general management rights,
  - require just cause before an employer can discipline or discharge an employee, and
  - require that the exercise of management rights be reasonable and consistent with the spirit of the collective agreement.
- *Just cause.* The agreement may set out specific procedures for establishing just cause, in addition to the basic obligation that the employer have just cause (noted above). The concept of just cause under collective agreements is distinct from the common law (discussed in Chapter 13), but in practice, arbitrators and LRBs apply similar principles. In disputes about just cause, the issue is often proportionality between the offence (the employee's

wrongdoing) and the penalty (dismissal or other discipline). One difference between union and non-union workplaces is that the right of a discharged employee to be *reinstated* is available as a remedy in unionized settings, and arbitrators use it regularly.

- *Grievance and arbitration.* As noted above, collective agreements are required to include some type of mechanism for resolving disputes about the contents of the collective agreement. These are referred to as *grievance mechanisms* and are discussed more thoroughly below.
- *Wages and working conditions.* A series of collective agreement clauses are generally needed to establish rules regarding hours of work and the details of compensation. These may include a range of wage structures (hourly, piecework, salary), increments for years of service (seniority), job performance requirements, bonuses, profit sharing, and benefits (long-term disability, health care, dental, pensions).
- *Internal labour market.* These clauses address how employees move from one role to another within the organization and what happens if they leave the organization for reasons unrelated to just cause (i.e., layoff or job loss due to contracting out). This may include rules about job postings (when and where), layoff procedures, bumping rights, severance pay, and contracting out. This is also where clauses regulating how the parties will manage the impact of technological change might appear.
- *Seniority.* Seniority protection is a cornerstone of most collective agreements. The agreements will often provide detailed formulas for calculating seniority. This is because seniority is normally a key factor in determining a range of rights within the collective agreement, such as wage increments, transfers, and promotions. More senior employees are given preference over junior employees, provided they have the requisite skills to do the job. Seniority also affects the order of layoff and recall and enables senior employees to "bump" more junior employees out of positions in the event of layoffs.
- *Work environment and behaviour.* These clauses address the physical work environment, safety, and other factors that are particular to the work done in the bargaining unit. This may include the establishment of joint committees for safety or whether employees have to wear uniforms. This is also where clauses that address human rights and prohibit harassment might be included.
- *Picket lines.* Many agreements permit employees to respect picket lines of other unions at the same workplace. This means the employee is entitled to refuse to cross the picket line and cannot be penalized for doing so—except that the employer is not required to pay employees who refuse to cross the line.

Given the number of different issues that can arise in the relationship between an employer and a group of employees, it is not difficult to see how these agreements can become quite lengthy and complex.

Grievance Arbitration Process

Basic Principles and Procedures

The grievance process is an essential part of a unionized workplace, and collective agreements usually set out quite a detailed regime for grievances, a regime that leads, if the disagreement is unresolved, to arbitration. Alberta and BC require at least a basic provision for arbitration in all agreements.

Most collective agreement grievance procedures contain a number of remedial steps or stages, where the parties try to resolve the issue prior to sending it to arbitration. This usually begins with informal meetings between the affected employee, the immediate supervisor, and a union representative. If this front-line group is unable to settle the grievance, there are several additional grievance stages with progressively more senior people involved (from both the employer and the union). Time limits are attached to each stage, and exceeding them may make a grievance inarbitrable.

It should be noted that arbitration is the last resort and is generally reserved for those situations where the parties need clarification of truly ambiguous terms in the collective agreement, or for when one side or the other wants to make an important point (even if they know they may lose). Arbitration is an expensive and lengthy process, though usually cheaper and faster than a court case at common law. In grievance arbitration, both sides share in the cost of a neutral third-party arbitrator (whom they must agree on). In addition, there is the time required to prepare for the arbitration hearing, the cost of legal counsel, and the costs associated with the attendance of witnesses. For this reason, the decision to proceed to arbitration (versus giving up and accepting the employer's position) belongs to the union, not the employee. In practice, the decision is normally made by union executives, though some unions may require a vote of members.

Arbitration is the main process for disputes about the collective agreement and the workplace generally. There are some areas of shared jurisdiction between the LRB and arbitrators in BC, but the default process is arbitration. The courts have little place here. Even where the decision of an arbitrator is reviewed by the courts (or the LRB in Alberta), there is considerable deference to the arbitrator's expertise. Review of a decision will only consider whether the arbitrator's decision was *reasonable* (except on questions of jurisdiction, general principles of law, or bad faith by the arbitrator—see *Dunsmuir v New Brunswick* [2008]).

Strikes and Lockouts

We come now to another important feature of labour law: the right of workers to go on strike and the concomitant right of the employer to lock out their workers. This feature is distinct from the rights of non-unionized workers, for whom "going on strike" means quitting. (At best, individuals who walk off the job because of a dispute can claim that the employer has constructively dismissed them—see Chapters 11 and 14). It should be noted that resorting to a strike or lockout is not taken lightly by either party. There are costs associated with this kind of job action that can include loss of pay for union members, loss of business for employers, negative impacts on the public, and damage to the culture of the organization.

If the employer and union cannot agree to terms for a collective agreement, the union can call a strike, or the employer can lock out their workers. The idea is to use economic pressure to get the other side to agree to less favourable terms and conditions than they would like. A strike or lockout will shut down most if not all of the operations in the bargaining unit. At the end of the strike or lockout, the workers return to their jobs. Although some provinces, including Alberta, allow employers to hire temporary replacement workers, the BC Code (s 68) has a strict prohibition on the practice. Section 68 even prohibits employers from forcing managers to fill in for striking workers. All jurisdictions prohibit the hiring of permanent replacements (in Alberta, the law entitles striking or locked-out workers to return to their jobs, bumping any replacement workers: s 90(1) of the Alberta Code).

This section sets out the basic rules around strikes and lockouts. It also outlines the BC and Alberta procedures for declaring certain workers to be performing **essential services**, and thus removing their right to walk off the job. This summary focuses on strikes, rather than lockouts. Many of the rules for when lockouts are allowed are similar, though there are some differences. For example, if there is a single employer, the employer does not need to hold a vote on whether to lock employees out. A lockout vote is only required where there is an association of employers.

essential services
public services that, if interrupted, would endanger the life, safety, or health of the public; this includes services necessary to maintain the rule of law and public security; essential services are defined in statute and may vary by province

The main rules for strikes and lockouts address two questions: (1) *When* is a strike or lockout allowed? and (2) *what activity* is allowed during a strike or lockout?

When Can a Strike or Lockout Occur?

As noted in the summary of the *Wagner Act* model earlier in this chapter, modern labour law allows strikes only at certain times. A strike that occurs at any other time is called a **wildcat strike**. Wildcat strikes are "untimely" and illegal. Below we will turn to two ways in which certain strike activity can become illegal: picketing at an *illegal location* and picketing in an *illegal manner*, which may involve torts such as intimidation or assault, or the crimes of assault or "watching and besetting."

wildcat strike
a work stoppage initiated by bargaining unit workers without proper authorization or approval; it may be started while the collective agreement is still valid or during bargaining but without notice being given or a strike vote taken

Certification Required

Employees cannot go on strike, and employers cannot lock out employees, until after a union has been certified. This means that unions cannot hold what is called a "representation strike" to try to pressure an employer and other workers to support the establishment of a union.

No Strike During the Term of the Collective Agreement

Both provinces stipulate that while a collective agreement is in force, there can be no strike or lockout.

Duty to Bargain in Good Faith, Appointment of Mediator, and Appointment of Disputes Inquiry Board

Once collective bargaining has begun, whether for the first agreement or a renewal, there is no specific time restriction or trigger for when a strike can be called. However, there are circumstances during bargaining when a strike or lockout might be considered unlawful:

- *Lack of good faith in bargaining.* When the union or employer goes through the motions but has no intention of actually reaching an agreement, this is called "surface bargaining" and is an unfair labour practice. In such a case, a strike or lockout is not automatically barred, but the other side can file a complaint with the LRB, which could prevent a strike or lockout.
- *Application for mediation.* If the talks are not going well, either side can apply for a mediator (or the Minister of Labour can also choose to appoint a mediator without a request from the parties). Once a mediator is appointed, there can be no strike or lockout. This rule is the same in both provinces (however, in BC the rule applies only to a mediator that the parties request under s 74, not to a special mediator that the Minister appoints). Alberta has an additional 14-day cooling-off period that commences on the day the mediator recommends terms for settlement or the day fixed by the mediator for accepting or rejecting the terms. The BC Code sets out slightly different procedures for negotiation of the first collective agreement (s 55) and renewal of the existing agreement (s 74). For the first agreement in Alberta, a request for a mediator can only be made if talks are at an impasse and the union has held a successful strike vote (i.e., its members have approved strike action). Recent amendments to the BC Code have eliminated the prerequisite of a strike vote—unions in BC can gain access to mediation for a first collective agreement without taking a strike vote or receiving majority support for it. In both provinces, the request for a mediator does not require a strike vote to have occurred when bargaining to renew or replace an existing agreement.

  It should also be noted that mediation cannot lead to an imposed agreement in either province. An imposed agreement is only possible in BC for the first agreement (s 55).
- *Disputes inquiry board.* In Alberta, the Minister of Labour may also decide to appoint a disputes inquiry board that will attempt to settle the dispute. This is not at the request of the parties. If there is a disputes inquiry board appointed, there can be no strike or lockout until ten days after the board makes its recommendations.

  Note that there is no required "conciliation" process in BC that resembles the disputes inquiry board in Alberta. The parties just rely on the mediation process described above.

Essential Services Agreement

In Alberta, a strike or lockout cannot occur until the parties have bargained an essential services agreement or have declared that there are no essential services in the bargaining unit. If an essential services agreement has been negotiated, it must be on file with the LRB. Similarly, in BC, the LRB may conduct an investigation, on its own motion or upon application by an employer or union, to determine if a strike or lockout would pose a threat to the health, safety, or welfare of the residents of the province. The results of that investigation are reported to the Minister of Labour, who may direct the Board to designate certain facilities, productions, and services as essential. That designation triggers obligations on the parties to negotiate an essential services agreement or otherwise abide by a board order to that effect before a strike or lockout can occur. Essential services are discussed in more detail below.

Strike Vote

Even when the parties have reached an impasse at the table and mediation has failed to solve it, the union cannot go on strike (and the employer cannot lock out) until the bargaining agent has followed the procedure for a strike or lockout vote. In the case of a lockout application from a single employer, the LRB will just poll the employer. If bargaining is occurring for a group of employers, the LRB will require a vote of the employers.

STRIKE VOTE PROCEDURE

The procedures for a strike vote are quite specific and strict. The vote is similar to a political election vote, with an election officer, voting stations, and secret ballots. Violations nullify the vote.

- *Secret ballot.* Votes must be by secret ballot and open to all those in the bargaining unit, regardless of union membership.
- *Results.* A majority of those who vote must vote in favour for there to be a strike.
- *72 hours' notice.* In BC no job action can start until 72 hours after the union has served written notice on both the employer and the LRB. In Alberta, the strike or lockout has to occur on the date and at the time and location specified in the strike or lockout notice, and notice must be served at least 72 hours prior to the start of the job action.
- *Mediation report.* In BC, if a mediator has been appointed, the union must ask the mediator to "report out" to the LRB, and the strike cannot start until at least 48 hours after the mediator has reported. In Alberta, the mediator must receive notice of the strike or lockout, but there is no specific time limit attached to the notice.
- *Limitation period.* A strike or lockout can only occur within three months of the date of the strike or lockout vote in BC or within 120 days in Alberta.
- *Time window.* In sum, strike activity can occur (or a lockout by a group of employers can start) in the window that *starts* 72 hours after notice to the employer or union and board (leaving aside any mediation report) and *ends* three months after the vote in BC or 120 days after the vote in Alberta.

- *After 72 hours' notice.* The strike need not start right away. In BC, the union's executive has wide discretion: it can choose when and what actions to take once it has given the 72 hours' notice. In Alberta, the date, time, and location of the strike must be specified in advance and must be included on the strike notice.

Last Offer Vote

In BC, there is one other way that a strike or lockout can be delayed—and possibly prevented entirely. Under section 78(1) of the BC Code, an employer can demand a "last offer vote," which requires the LRB to direct that the employer's latest offer be put directly to the employees for a vote. Under section 39, the vote is open to all in the bargaining unit and is by secret ballot. If a majority of those who vote are in favour, the agreement is constituted. Alberta has a similar procedure, under sections 69–70 of its Code, though in Alberta this procedure is available at any time after the parties have exchanged proposals, rather than on the eve of a strike (though it may be used only once during bargaining).

Summary

A strike or lockout may begin, and is therefore lawful, if the following conditions have been met:

- the parties have bargained in good faith but reached an impasse;
- the proper procedures for a strike or lockout vote have been taken;
- proper notice has been given;
- no mediator has been appointed (or the mediator has concluded their work);
- any essential services matters have been addressed; and
- in BC, there has been no demand for a last offer vote (or the members have voted to reject the employer's latest offer).

It should be apparent that the law does not treat the decision to strike or lockout lightly. Wildcat strikes are illegal, even if the employees walk off the job for a good cause. During the life of a collective agreement, any conflicts in the workplace, including disputes about alleged breaches of the agreement, no matter how serious, must be dealt with through the grievance and arbitration procedure in the agreement itself.

Bargaining Continues

The duty to bargain continues after a strike (or lockout) begins. The LRCs impose this duty, but it is also in the parties' interests. The purpose of the strike is to put pressure on the other party. The bargaining usually intensifies during job action—except in those cases in which talks have really broken down.

Note also that in BC, Alberta, and most other provinces, the LRBs can, at any point during negotiations, appoint fact-finders or mediators to assist the bargaining. Such appointments do not, however, stop the parties from striking or locking out.

What Activity Is Allowed During a Strike?

Actions Allowed by Strikers

During a strike, unions are allowed to do the following:

- withdraw services, on a scale from performing symbolic acts, or "working to rule" (i.e., performing only the absolute basic requirements of their jobs, no voluntary extras), to withdrawing certain services, to working reduced hours, to organizing a complete walkout from the job, accompanied by picketing;
- communicate their message to the public, which can include leafleting, even if there is not a walkout yet (i.e., employees continue to work), calling for a boycott on the employer's products or services, holding signs on picket lines, and posting information on websites, in advertisements, and so on as long as these actions do not shade into torts (see below);
- in BC, picket peacefully on public land or on private land "to which a member of the public ordinarily has access"—for example, at malls; and
- in Alberta, strike, but only at the striking or locked-out workers' place of employment and not elsewhere.

Picketing "secondary" sites is not allowed in Alberta and is subject to restrictions to protect third parties in BC, which raises some complex questions we will touch on under the heading "Unions and the Charter of Rights and Freedoms," below.

Actions Not Allowed by Strikers

Assuming the strike's timing makes it lawful, there are still restrictions on what the union can do. For example, picketers are not allowed to go on private land without permission of the landowner. Trespassing causes particular problems for unions when the employer's operation is in an office building or mall with other tenants. Similarly, it can be considered a "public or private nuisance" if picketing has an unreasonable adverse effect on the public or a property owner. Unions must take care not to inconvenience others too much. Courts today are, however, unlikely to consider peaceful picketing or actions such as leafleting a nuisance. Of course, being on strike does not entitle a person to hit a passerby with a sign (battery), make that passerby fear being struck (assault), or call customers who continue to do business with a struck employer defamatory names. There is a line that strikers cannot cross in their behaviour, from communicating their views to inducing a fear of violence. The larger the group of picketers, the greater the risk of this tort—though mere numbers are not enough if their behaviour is peaceful.

Actions Not Allowed by Employers

Employers are not allowed to defame union members or induce fear or violence either. Furthermore, there are restrictions in many provinces regarding hiring or having workers outside of the bargaining unit do the work of employees who are on strike. In Alberta, employers can hire temporary replacement workers. BC, however, prohibits employers from hiring them. Section 68 of the BC Code sets out this basic rule and goes on at some length to reinforce it by restricting the employer's use of existing employees who are not in the striking union's bargaining unit. BC rules are unusually strict, relative to the rules elsewhere in Canada.

Status of Workers on Strike

Striking workers are still employees and may not be fired during a strike or later for going on strike. Employers must continue to provide health and welfare benefits to employees who are on strike or locked out—as long as the union pays for the costs (e.g., a prorated portion of the premium, or other fees, depending on how the benefits are structured).

Essential Services

Most provinces have a procedure that enables the government to require certain workers to remain on the job during a strike or lockout. In Alberta and BC, this is accomplished through essential services requirements in their respective LRCs. Work that relates to public safety and security is often designated as essential services. This often includes police, fire, ambulance, correctional services, and hospitals. Prior to a 2015 Supreme Court decision in *Saskatchewan Federation of Labour v Saskatchewan*, which declared the right to strike a fundamental right protected by the Charter, Alberta prohibited employees like health care workers and police from strike or lockout (see below for further discussion of this case). Instead, they were required to settle a bargaining impasse through binding arbitration.

The *Saskatchewan Federation of Labour* decision prompted a review of legislation across Canada that prohibited strikes in particular occupations. Alberta made substantial revisions that included repealing several pieces of legislation, including parts of the LRC and the *Post-Secondary Learning Act*, which prohibited academic staff from going on strike.

Section 95 of the Alberta Code deals with essential services, which are defined as those services:

- the interruption of which would endanger the life, personal safety, or health of the public, or
- that are necessary to the maintenance and administration of the rule of law or public security.

Before any job action (strike/lockout) can take place, the parties must have applied for and received an exemption or negotiated an essential services agreement.

Exemptions may be granted by the Essential Services Commissioner where employees in the bargaining unit do not engage in essential services or where essential services can be maintained by other qualified persons who are not bargaining-unit members but already work for the employer. If neither of these conditions exist, the parties must negotiate an essential services agreement that:

- identifies the essential services that must be maintained during a strike or lockout,
- sets out the class and number of employees qualified to perform the essential services,
- explains how the qualified employees will be assigned during the strike or lockout,
- provides procedures to be followed for responding to emergencies,
- provides the terms and conditions of employment of qualified essential service employees, and
- identifies a list of umpires to resolve disputes should they arise during a strike or lockout.

Section 95 of the Alberta Code also provides the procedures for bargaining essential services agreements, as well as mediation if the parties are unable to reach agreement on the content of the essential services agreement. Once an agreement has been reached it is filed with the LRB and becomes binding on the parties.

Recent changes to the BC Code removed "educational programs" as a specifically designated essential service, consistent with the ruling in *Saskatchewan Federation of Labour*. The remainder of the essential services provisions in the BC Code provides a general procedure for all industries, one that contains a series of formal steps for a declaration of essential services to be made. First, an employer (or union, in the event of a lockout) must fill out an "essential services" application form, requesting that the LRB investigate whether some of the employer's "facilities, productions or services" (which we will here just call "services") are essential. (The LRB can also act on its own initiative and identify potential essential services.) The criterion for "essential" is that the labour dispute "poses a threat to … the health, safety or welfare of the residents of British Columbia" (s 72(1)(a) of the BC Code).

Second, the LRB investigates and decides whether the dispute does pose such a threat and reports to the Minister of Labour (s 72(1)(b)). The LRB does not at this point identify specific services that are essential—it just identifies whether the dispute poses a threat generally. Third, the Minister of Labour takes the LRB's report and considers whether there is a threat (s 72(2)). If the Minister sees a threat, the process goes to the fourth step: the Minister directs the LRB to determine what specific services must continue in the event of a work stoppage. It is then up to the employer and union to ensure that these services continue "in full" during any stoppage (s 72(8)). There are additional procedures for strikes or lockouts that have already begun when the question of essential services is raised.

It is worth noting that questions of essential services usually arise in disputes with public sector employees, such as emergency services. The general procedure, however, still applies to any sector, public or private. For example, a private business that maintains dangerous chemicals might be required to keep certain employees working to protect against potential hazards.

Unions and the Charter of Rights and Freedoms

The rules described so far in this chapter are all rules contained in labour legislation. The "rights" of unions and workers were, until some recent decisions under the Charter, merely entitlements provided by statute. Legislatures could modify or revoke almost all of those entitlements. However, since 2001 the Supreme Court of Canada has begun to use freedom of association, under section 2(d) of the Charter, to entrench certain aspects of collective bargaining law in the Constitution. This means that the Charter now provides some substantial protection for unions.

Until 2001, freedom of association only protected the right of workers to form a union. Neither the union itself, nor the collective of employees in the union, had any meaningful Charter rights except for some basic protection under freedom of expression. In other words, the Charter did not protect the union's right to do anything as a union except to express itself. If the government stripped or severely restricted the right to strike, the Charter had nothing to say about it. If the government modified the terms of existing collective agreements or abolished unions' rights to negotiate certain terms, such as seniority rules or restrictions on contracting out, a union could not challenge this change using the Charter.

A full study of how the Charter works is beyond the scope of this chapter, but the significance of recent Charter decisions on freedom of association makes it important to include in this discussion. Readers should be aware of four general points about Charter cases:

1. The Charter was created in 1982 as part of the *Constitution Act, 1982*. It is a constitutional document, so it overrides all other laws.
2. The Charter does not apply to private entities; it is a constitutional restriction on the federal and provincial governments. Thus, it can be used to challenge legislation (such as a labour relations code) or the actions of a government employer, but not to challenge the actions of a private employer.
3. All Charter cases involve two questions: (1) Has the government violated a Charter right? and (2) if so, is the violation "justifiable" under section 1 of the Charter? That section, seemingly innocuous on first reading, in fact allows governments to violate any Charter right. It means that these rights are not absolute. In applying section 1 to cases, the courts have created a "justification test" that balances the importance of the government's goal (e.g., the purpose of a piece of legislation, policy, or government action) and the effectiveness of the law in achieving that goal, on the one side, against the degree to which the law or government action restricts the Charter right, on the other side. It is a balancing test that courts perform whenever a government action is found to violate the Charter.

4. The Charter is focused mainly on individual rights and on "negative rights"—that is, the right of individuals to *not* have the government interfere with them. It does not entitle individuals to demand that the government provide them with, for example, a better standard of living. And until recently, courts were reluctant to consider the idea of "group rights" under the Charter. Recent union-related decisions, especially a pair of decisions from 2015 (discussed below), have begun to change this, at least when it comes to freedom of association.

The two Charter rights most relevant to unions are freedom of expression (s 2(b) of the Charter) and freedom of association (s 2(d)). The revolution in the courts' application of the Charter to unions has been in freedom of association, but a 2013 decision in Alberta has also expanded the scope of freedom of expression.

Freedom of Expression

The first major case involving unions was *RWDSU v Dolphin Delivery Ltd*, a 1986 decision of the Supreme Court of Canada. The case involved activity during a strike, and the decision upheld the right of workers to conduct primary picketing as a form of expression protected by section 2(b) of the Charter. It was an important decision for unions, since going on strike is a much less effective tool without the right to picket and carry out other expressive activity to bring pressure on the employer.

However, the decision was not a generous one for unions. The Supreme Court refused to overturn the common law rule against secondary picketing—that is, picketing at locations other than the worksite of the struck employer. The Court's formal reason was a reluctance to use the Charter against a rule that existed only in the common law (versus in legislation), but the language of the decision also suggested the Court's limited support for unions.

The Supreme Court also took time to exclude certain picketing activities from what section 2(b) protects:

- actual violence,
- threats of violence,
- other unlawful activity, and
- trespassing on private property.

Dolphin Delivery was just about expressive activity on picket lines. The case did not recognize a right to strike. The right to picket was limited to some extent by the fact that striking was, until the *Saskatchewan Federation* decision of 2015, a mere benefit that legislation conferred on unions and that provincial legislatures could decide to restrict or take away. Until the 2000s, *Dolphin Delivery* was the only real Charter protection that unions had: the right to picket and otherwise peacefully express themselves.

Starting at around the turn of the 21st century, Charter decisions began to shift in favour of unions. One small step in this shift came with the Supreme Court's 1999 decision in a BC freedom of expression case, *United Food and Commercial Workers,*

Local 1518 v KMart Canada Ltd. The Supreme Court ruled that the definition of "picketing" in section 1 of the BC LRC was unconstitutional because it included activities as benign as leafleting. The Court said that leafleting is obviously a form of expression deserving of protection, even under the narrow logic of *Dolphin Delivery*. But it was the factual context of the *KMart* case that mattered: the leafleting was happening at secondary sites (other KMart locations, where there was no strike under way). The Court said that to prohibit mere leafleting at secondary sites was an unjustifiable violation of section 2(b). However, this decision was not a dramatic break from previous decisions. It did not overturn the common law's general rule against picketing at secondary sites. Leafleting at a secondary site is not the same as picketing, and the Court spent much of its decision emphasizing how non-intimidating the activity was in this case.

A more dramatic shift came in 2002 with *RWDSU, Local 558 v Pepsi-Cola Canada Beverages (West) Ltd*, in which a union challenged the common law rule against secondary picketing. The Supreme Court overcame its reluctance to hold common law principles up to Charter scrutiny and nullified the rule. The judges' reasoning built on some of the language in *KMart* about the importance of work for individuals and the need to speak freely.

In the *Pepsi-Cola* decision, the Supreme Court threw out the old default rule of the common law, which made secondary picketing illegal unless the activity fit into one of the exceptions courts had defined. The Supreme Court flipped the rule upside down, saying that secondary picketing is, by default, lawful unless the specific picketing activity is tortious or criminal. This phrasing goes beyond extending section 2(b) to secondary picketing; it slightly broadens the scope of what kinds of activity freedom of expression protects, relative to *Dolphin Delivery*. The *Pepsi-Cola* decision means there is no common law barrier to peaceful picketing. BC and Alberta, however, still have in place legislative limits to secondary picketing (s 65 of the BC Code; s 84 of the Alberta Code).

The scope of expressive activity for unions seems to have broadened considerably with the Supreme Court's 2013 decision in *Alberta (Information and Privacy Commissioner) v United Food and Commercial Workers, Local 401* (*Alberta (IPC)*, also discussed in Chapter 10). Here a union was picketing the employer, a casino, during a ten-month-long strike. Some of the picketers were videotaping and photographing anyone who entered (customers, managers, other workers). The union posted screen shots of their faces on its website and made mocking posters using the image of a casino executive. One purpose of the videotaping was to deter people from dealing with the casino; another was to keep a record of activity, in case something went wrong, which is why the employer was also making videos.

Some individuals complained. The Information and Privacy Commissioner (IPC) accepted their complaints because the *Personal Information Protection Act* (PIPA) prohibits both the recording and publishing of images. The union challenged the IPC's decision in court, arguing that PIPA's prohibition violated its freedom of expression: both taking and publishing the videos and images were expressive acts. The Supreme Court agreed. It found these acts expressive and found the Act's prohibition of these expressive acts unjustifiable under section 1. PIPA was so broad in its scope, and so restrictive of legitimate uses of personal information such as those of the union, that the Court took the strong step of striking down the entire statute, forcing the government to rewrite it in a way that complies with the Charter. This is a rare remedy: usually the Court will find a specific provision unconstitutional or will "read in" a word or phrase to make the legislation comply with the Charter.

In applying the justification test to *Alberta (IPC)*, the Court underscored not only the role of strikes in creating negotiating leverage, but also the importance of unions in the lives of their members. The Supreme Court agreed that PIPA has an important goal, and the prohibitions in it serve that goal logically. However, the law failed the "proportionality" step of the justification test. As important as protection of privacy is, there are other interests that also matter. Those include enabling unions to use all reasonable methods to "alleviat[e] the presumptive imbalance between the employer's economic power and the relative vulnerability of the individual worker" (at para 32).

The Court in *Alberta (IPC)* did acknowledge that unions can cross the line into unacceptable activity that the law can legitimately prohibit (at para 38), but the Court gave the power to picket a robustness and primacy that was missing in the Charter case law of the 1980s and 1990s. *Alberta (IPC)* stresses the importance of unions to the protection of fundamental individual rights. Case law on freedom of association has shifted even more dramatically toward a recognition of this role for unions.

Freedom of Association

The First Era: The "Trilogy"

For unions, the early case law on freedom of association (s 2(d) of the Charter) was discouraging. It began in 1987 with a set of three Supreme Court decisions that are known as the "labour trilogy." These three decisions—*Reference re Public Service Employee Relations Act (Alta)* (*Alberta Reference*), *PSAC v Canada*, and *RWDSU v Saskatchewan*—were decidedly hostile to the idea that section 2(d) provides any meaningful protection to unions. (Students interested in this subject can read a summary of this trilogy of decisions in the *Mounted Police Association* and *Saskatchewan Federation* decisions described below.)

The most important of the three is the 1987 decision *Reference re Public Service Employee Relations Act (Alta)* (*Alberta Reference*). The majority of judges in that case focused on the *individual* nature of the right to associate and were only willing to concede two things to unions: the right of individual workers to join or form a union; and, perhaps, some sort of right of the union itself to do things that other Charter rights enable individuals to do. Harry Arthurs, a labour law specialist, dismissed this idea as the "right to golf"—by which he meant that it gave unions no more than the right to form a social club, one that lacks any constitutional rights to do anything on behalf of its members (Arthurs, 1988).

The trilogy, therefore, only protected the first modern feature of unions: the right of individuals to join or form a union, a protection that unions had gained in legislation (though not the Constitution) in the 1870s. As noted above, the right of individuals to join a union is insignificant if the union itself does not have rights—such as exclusive bargaining and the right to call strikes. Until recently, those two features were only available to unions via statutes. Under the trilogy's logic, legislatures could regulate those features as much as they wanted—and even abolish them.

Individual Challenges Against Unions—Lavigne (1991) and the Freedom Not to Associate

The trilogy also rejected, more fundamentally, the idea of group rights under the Charter. It emphasized the individual. In the late 1980s, unions began to worry that individuals would take up this signal from the Supreme Court and use the Charter to challenge unions' exclusivity of bargaining power. The *Lavigne* case was the first step in what could have been a series of such challenges.

CASE IN POINT

Requirement to Pay Union Dues Does Not Violate Individual's Freedom of Association

Lavigne v Ontario Public Service Employees Union, [1991] 2 SCR 211

Facts

Lavigne, an Ontario college professor, objected to his union's donation of money to the New Democratic Party in Ontario. His union was an "open shop," with a Rand formula union security clause, so he was not a member of the union, but he had to pay dues to it. He challenged the college's imposition on him of the duty to pay dues to the union. (The college was considered part of government, so he was able to challenge its rule that he had to pay dues.) His argument relied on the idea that freedom of association included not only the right *to* associate, but the right *not to* associate—the right to exclude himself from membership or financial contribution.

Relevant Issue

Did the college's requirement that Lavigne pay union dues violate a section 2(d) "freedom not to associate" with the union?

Decision

The Supreme Court's decision split three ways, but all agreed in the result, which was that the deduction of dues from Lavigne's paycheque did not unjustifiably violate the Charter.

- La Forest, Sopinka, and Gonthier JJ said freedom of association should be broadly construed to include the right not to be forced into an association, and therefore found that there had been a violation of the freedom of association. However, they turned to section 1 of the Charter and found that the Rand formula, requiring Lavigne to pay dues, was a justifiable violation of his freedom not to associate. The formula therefore did not violate the Charter.
- Wilson, Cory, and L'Heureux-Dubé JJ said there is no freedom from association and therefore no violation of the Charter at all, and even if there was, it would be saved by section 1. They similarly found that although the union's use of dues to support a political cause was expressive, this did not imply that Lavigne supported the party, nor did it prevent Lavigne from expressing his own political views. They did not view the Rand formula as a violation of any Charter right.
- McLachlin J took a middle approach, supporting the idea of a freedom not to associate but in a narrower conception. She found that there was no violation in this context. Just because some of his dues went to the NDP did not mean that Lavigne was personally forced to associate with the NDP cause.

All seven judges found that the Rand formula union security clause did not violate the Charter. However, four judges upheld the idea that freedom of association also includes the freedom not to associate. In doing so, they opened the door for future challenges against union shops, and possibly even for challenges to a union's exclusivity.

The challenges this case invited did not quite transpire during the 1990s, which lessened union fears after the trilogy that section 2(d) could be used for "union busting." However, it was not until the 2000s that section 2(d) began to be helpful to unions, rather than a potential threat.

The Turning Point: Dunmore (2001)

The turn away from the trilogy happened in 2001 with *Dunmore v Ontario (AG)*. The case follows a pattern that appears in several of the cases we will consider below. In 1994, the NDP government in Ontario extended the right to unionize to agricultural workers, who had been excluded in the past. In 1995, the Conservative Party took over the government in Ontario and repealed the NDP statute as part of the party's "common sense revolution." The repeal decertified the newly established agricultural worker unions, cancelled their collective agreements, and barred them from future certification. Several workers and the United Food and Commercial Workers Union applied to court, arguing that the law infringed their Charter rights. The lower courts applied the trilogy and rejected the claim. By a majority of 8–1, the Supreme Court allowed the union's appeal and ruled the new statute unconstitutional.

The Court's reasoning is a striking rebuttal of the thinking in the 1987 trilogy. Chief Justice Beverley McLachlin, writing for the majority, said that the trilogy's "traditional" approach to freedom of association did not capture the full range of activities that section 2(d) of the Charter protects. Freedom of association should sometimes protect activities that are inherently collective—that is, ones that individuals alone cannot perform. An individuals-only approach to section 2(d) will, she said, prevent unions from functioning effectively on behalf of individual employees.

Unions, she wrote, enable the "achievement of individual potential" through collective action. Denying "group" rights because of their collective nature would in fact hinder individual fulfillment, and thus hinder individual rights. This idea reverses the reasoning in the trilogy: it protects collective action, and not just the "right to join."

This decision did not overturn the trilogy, but the Supreme Court soon did so.

The Right to Bargain: Health Services (2007) and Fraser (2011)

In 2007, in the *Health Services* case from BC, the Supreme Court expressly overturned the trilogy, established Charter protection for meaningful collective bargaining, and created a test for striking down laws that "substantially interfere" with the right to bargain collectively.

CASE IN POINT

Freedom of Association Includes the Right to Bargain Collectively

Health Services and Support–Facilities Subsector Bargaining Assn v British Columbia, 2007 SCC 27

Facts

In 2002, soon after taking office after a decade of NDP government, the BC Liberal government passed a law designed to give health care employers more flexibility to organize their relations with employees as they saw fit. It did so by overriding the "constraints" of existing collective agreements.

This law did not go so far as to revoke the rights of health care workers (including nurses) to unionize. It did, however, take away many significant terms their unions had negotiated. The law changed collective agreement terms that gave employees rights regarding the following: transfers and multiple worksites; contracting out; job security programs; and layoffs and seniority-bumping rights. The statute replaced such terms in existing agreements and forbade the unions from renegotiating those terms in the next round of bargaining.

Relevant Issue

Did the revocation of rights to bargain on certain topics violate the unions' freedom of association?

Decision

Building on *Dunmore*, the Supreme Court ruled that the changes to contracting out and to layoffs and bumping rights violated section 2(d), but the other changes did not. McLachlin CJ and LeBel J, writing for a 7–1 majority, found that the violation of section 2(d) was unjustifiable under section 1, so those changes were unconstitutional. In doing so, the Court expressly overruled the 1987 trilogy, and specifically overturned *Alberta Reference*.

Although the Court did not overrule all the changes in the statute, it extended the content of section 2(d) to include a *right to bargain collectively*. It then suggested the following test for governmental interference with this right: legislation that "substantially interferes" with collective bargaining violates section 2(d) (at para 19). Such a violation might in some cases be saved by section 1, but not in this case.

As big a step as *Health Services* was, there was caution in the reasoning—such as the finding that some of the changes in the statute did not even amount to violations of the right to bargain collectively. In 2011, the Supreme Court's decision in *Ontario (AG) v Fraser* seemed to take an even more cautious approach and appeared to be a step back from *Dunmore* and *Health Services*.

In *Fraser*, the same union we saw in *Dunmore* appeared before the courts, challenging the new regime for agricultural workers in Ontario. After the *Dunmore* decision, the Ontario government did not restore agricultural workers to the *Labour Relations Act*'s regime (certified unions with exclusive bargaining power, etc.—the *Wagner Act* model). Instead, it created an *Agricultural Employees Protection Act*, which only allowed them to form an employees' association that would represent them in talks with employers. Employers did not need to negotiate with the associations; they just had to listen. The Act also prohibited employers from harassing, intimidating, or discriminating against workers and created a tribunal to enforce this limited form of protection. It did not allow certification; the associations had no right of exclusivity and no right to call strikes.

The Supreme Court upheld the law's validity, with one dissenting judge (Abella J), who would have struck it down. Chief Justice McLachlin, again writing for the majority of judges, affirmed *Dunmore* and *Health Services* but applied them narrowly. She wrote that section 2(d) protects association to achieve collective goals, but only said that this requires employers to *consider and discuss* employee proposals and complaints in good faith. The kind of bargaining activity that section 2(d) protects is a duty to meet in good faith and bargain on workplace issues, but section 2(d) does not require certification and exclusive bargaining power—it does not make the *Wagner Act* model a constitutional requirement. In this case, the Court felt that the law did oblige employers to fulfill this good-faith obligation and that the associations the law allowed were enough for employees' collective action.

The arguments before the Court in *Fraser* had amounted to an attack on the *Health Services* decision, so the Court's decision is significant in upholding that earlier ruling. However, in doing so, the Court also seemed to narrow the scope of the earlier decision, creating the possibility of a return to a more limited approach to freedom of association. The decision set the stage for the *Mounted Police Association* and *Saskatchewan Federation* decisions in 2015, which reinvigorated the Court's "purposive" approach to association, and suggest that future decisions will be even more strongly supportive of unions.

Mounted Police Association and Saskatchewan Federation (2015)

Mounted Police Association of Ontario v Canada (AG) was another challenge to the federal rules prohibiting RCMP members from unionizing. The government offered a consultation process instead, one with three components. The first was a Staff Relations Representative Program that RCMP management operated, through which members could raise work-related concerns. Second, the RCMP had established a Pay Council for concerns about pay and benefits. And third, RCMP members were allowed to create a Mounted Police Members' Legal Fund that provided individual members with legal assistance on employment-related issues. However, there was no organization with the authority to negotiate terms of work on behalf of all or a group of RCMP members.

By a 6–1 majority, the Supreme Court found that the prohibition on unions for RCMP members violated section 2(d) unjustifiably. The Supreme Court ruled that RCMP members ought to be able to form a union that could negotiate on their behalf with the employer, and struck down the federal laws that prevented RCMP members from doing so. McLachlin CJ and LeBel J wrote the majority's reasons for the decision and expressly affirmed that the trilogy is no longer good law. The Court adopted a purposive approach.

The purposive approach means that section 2(d) protects group rights, not just individual rights: "Recognizing group or collective rights complements rather than undercuts individual rights. … It is not a question of *either* individual rights *or* collective rights. Both are essential for full *Charter* protection" (at para 65). Thus, the Court reaffirmed its *Health Services* decision, and while it did not alter the decision in *Fraser*, it did clarify the meaning of that decision.

But what does the *Mounted Police Association* decision require the government to provide to RCMP members? The Court expressly states that the regime need not be the *Wagner Act* model (paras 93–97). In this respect, the decision affirms *Fraser*'s comments that the Charter does not require one specific labour relations model as long as there is opportunity for meaningful negotiation. And the Court went on (at paras 81–90) to give more detailed guidance about the model that the law requires, setting out two guiding criteria: *choice* and *independence*. Workers must have choice in which organization will represent them. And the body they choose must be independent from management. At paragraphs 91–99, the Court explained that there are a range of models that can satisfy the section 2(d) right, but any model must provide a "*meaningful process of collective bargaining*," which means "a process that gives employees meaningful input into the selection of their collective goals" (at para 99, emphasis added).

Saskatchewan Federation of Labour v Saskatchewan is a decision that the Supreme Court released two weeks after *Mounted Police Association*. This decision held that freedom of association also protects the right to strike. It overturned essential services rules in Saskatchewan that gave too much authority to the government to override strikes. The majority's decision, by Abella J, also provides a detailed historical summary of the evolution of law toward the *Wagner Act* model and the historical importance of strikes to unions and workers' rights and well-being.

This case began when the Conservative Party won a majority government in Saskatchewan and promptly passed two statutes that rolled back some of the pro-union legislation of its NDP predecessor. Some of these changes were adjustments to the procedure for certification of a union and did not amount to a violation of freedom of association. However, the Court struck down a new essential services statute that imposed too broad a designation of essential services on a wide range of public sector employees and set too absolute a no-strike rule for those services (at para 78). Not only did this law violate the newly established Charter right to strike, it completely failed the "justification" test under section 1 (see para 96).

What is clear is that the courts have adopted a radical shift in their approach to section 2(d) of the Charter. This shift protects the right to bargain collectively and the right to strike. It affects both unionized and not-yet-unionized workplaces, not only in the public sector but in the private one too. The Charter decisions since 2001 may prove to be as significant a milestone in the history of labour law as the adoption of the *Wagner Act* model in the late 1940s.

KEY TERMS

agency shop, 66
bargaining unit, 64
bridging, 70
closed shop, 65
essential services, 83
first contract arbitration, 71
good-faith bargaining, 70
grievance arbitration, 71
individual employment, 60
interest arbitration, 71
Labour Relations Board (LRB), 64
open shop, 65
peace obligation, 72
Rand formula shop, 65
ratification, 76
reverse onus, 75
union density, 65
union member, 64
union security, 65
union shop, 65
wildcat strike, 83

REVIEW AND DISCUSSION QUESTIONS

1. Name two ways the common law historically opposed unions. Are these still relevant today?
2. What is the difference between a closed shop and a union shop workplace? What do they have in common? Which is more common?
3. Can a union revoke an individual's membership, even if the revocation means job loss?
4. List two ways that labour laws motivate a newly certified union to negotiate an agreement.
5. Some employees are trying to organize a union. The employer becomes aware of this and announces, "To avoid the appearance of interference, we will not be issuing Christmas bonuses this year." Why would it do this? Is the move allowed if bonuses were an annual practice?
6. Explain three ways a union can become the certified bargaining agent for a group of employees.
7. Bernie works out a special arrangement with his employer to be paid triple-time if he is called in to work on holidays. Five years later, Bernie's workplace is unionized. The resulting collective agreement says the employer can call Bernie (and others) in on holidays and pay them double-time. The employer calls him in and pays him double. Can he sue for his usual triple-time pay?
8. Can an employee be exempted from paying dues to a union if the union donates money to a political party that the employee does not support?
9. As part of a new "austerity and efficiency" program, the BC government announces that it must change some of the terms of its collective agreement with the BC Government and Service Employees' Union. It passes legislation that overrides certain existing provisions in the agreement. The bill initially includes removal of the protections against contracting out and changes to the layoff rules, but the government removes those provisions in the face of political outcry. The bill takes away (1) job sharing (something a few dozen employees do); (2) flex time, which allows employees to work longer hours and take one day in ten off; (3) bumping rights that allowed employees in one region to take the job of employees in a different region; and (4) two of the six sick days that employees were allowed. The bill also says that similar provisions may not be included in renewal agreements.

   What might the union do? How would it argue its case? Assess its chances of success. What arguments might the government present in response?
10. Identify at least six types of clauses normally found in a collective agreement.
11. Herme works as a teacher with severely disabled students in Alberta. The Alberta Teachers' Association has been bargaining for the past six months, and it seems as though a strike is on the horizon. Herme thinks she should be classified as essential because her students have unique needs. A strike would be extremely disruptive for them, and there could be long-term impacts on their learning and development. Furthermore, this is a specialized field, and it is unlikely parents could find suitable alternative supervision in the event of a strike. Is Herme an essential services worker? What are the criteria for deciding whether Herme should be classified as essential?
12. What conditions need to exist in Alberta for a strike or lockout to be legal?
13. Consider what the freedom of association means in the *Charter of Rights and Freedoms*. How have court decisions impacted freedom of association for employees? What do you think of the Supreme Court's approach to collective bargaining and the right to strike as protected activities under the freedom of association? Do you think our current system of labour relations protects both the freedom to associate and the freedom *not* to associate? Why or why not?

REFERENCES

Agricultural Employees Protection Act, 2002, SO 2002, c 16.

Alberta (Information and Privacy Commissioner) v United Food and Commercial Workers, Local 401, 2013 SCC 62.

Alberta Labour Relations Board, "Information Bulletin: #9 Bargaining Unit Descriptions," online: <http://www.alrb.gov.ab.ca/bulletins/9bulletin.pdf>.

An Act Respecting Labour Standards, CQLR c N-1.1.

Arthurs, Harry, "The Right to Golf: Reflections on the Future of Workers, Unions and the Rest of Us Under the Charter" (1988) 13 Queen's LJ 17.

British Columbia Labour Relations Board, "Guide to the Labour Relations Code," online: <http://www.lrb.bc.ca/codeguide/chapter4.htm>.

Canada Labour Code, RSC 1985, c L-2.

Canadian Charter of Rights and Freedoms, Part I of the *Constitution Act, 1982*, being Schedule B to the *Canada Act 1982* (UK), 1982, c 11.

Civil Code of Québec, CQLR c C-1991.

Constitution Act, 1982, being Schedule B to the *Canada Act 1982* (UK), 1982, c 11.

Criminal Code, RSC 1985, c C-46.

Doorey, David J, *The Law of Work*, 2nd ed (Toronto: Emond, 2020).

Dunmore v Ontario (AG), 2001 SCC 94.

Dunsmuir v New Brunswick, 2008 SCC 9.

Employment Standards Act, RSBC 1996, c 113.

Employment Standards Code, RSA 2000, c E-9.

Health Services and Support–Facilities Subsector Bargaining Assn v British Columbia, 2007 SCC 27.

Industrial Relations and Disputes Investigation Act, SC 1948, c 54.

International Chemical Workers Union, Local 279, in re Rexall Drug Co Ltd (1953), 4 LAC 1468.

Isidore Garon ltée v Tremblay; Fillion et Frères (1976) inc v Syndicat national des employés de garage du Québec inc, 2006 SCC 2.

Labour Relations Code, RSA 2000, c L-1.

Labour Relations Code, RSBC 1996, c 244.

Lavigne v Ontario Public Service Employees Union, [1991] 2 SCR 211.

McGavin Toastmaster Ltd v Ainscough, [1976] 1 SCR 718.

Mounted Police Association of Ontario v Canada (AG), 2015 SCC 1.

Ontario (AG) v Fraser, 2011 SCC 20.

Personal Information Protection Act, SA 2003, c P-6.5.

Post-Secondary Learning Act, SA 2003, c P-19.5.

PSAC v Canada, [1987] 1 SCR 424.

Public Service Employee Relations Act, RSA 2000, c P-43.

Rayner, Wesley B, *Canadian Collective Bargaining Law*, 2nd ed (Toronto: LexisNexis Canada, 2007).

Reference re Public Service Employee Relations Act (Alta), [1987] 1 SCR 313.

RWDSU v Dolphin Delivery Ltd, [1986] 2 SCR 573.

RWDSU v Saskatchewan, [1987] 1 SCR 460.

RWDSU, Local 558 v Pepsi-Cola Canada Beverages (West) Ltd, 2002 SCC 8.

Royal Oak Mines Inc v Canada (Labour Relations Board), [1996] 1 SCR 369.

Saskatchewan Federation of Labour v Saskatchewan, 2015 SCC 4.

Statistics Canada, "Unionization Rates Falling," *The Daily* (17 May 2018), online: <https://www150.statcan.gc.ca/n1/pub/11-630-x/11-630-x2015005-eng.htm>.

United Food and Commercial Workers, Local 1518 v KMart Canada Ltd, [1999] 2 SCR 1083.

United Food and Commercial Workers Canada Union (UFCW), Local 401 and Widewaters Calgary Hotel Management Company, ULC, 2018 CanLII 149047 (Alta LRB).

United Food and Commercial Workers Canada Union (UFCW), Local 401 and Widewaters Calgary Hotel Management Company, ULC, 2018, CanLII 33689 Alta LRB.

Wagner Act [*National Labor Relations Act*], 29 USC.

Webb, Sydney, & Beatrice Webb, *The History of Trade Unionism, 1666–1920*. (Self-Published for the Trade Unionists of the United Kingdom, 1920).

Canada Labour Code

4

LEARNING OUTCOMES

After completing this chapter, you will be able to:

- Understand which employers and employees are governed by the *Canada Labour Code* (CLC).
- Identify and describe the subjects covered in each of the three parts of the CLC.
- Describe how employees in the federal sector can form a union.
- Discuss the right to strike and conditions that must exist before the employer can lock employees out or before employees can go on strike.
- Explain what is meant by the phrase "unfair labour practice" and give examples.
- Discuss key rights and responsibilities of employers and employees with respect to workplace health and safety.
- Discuss the unique unjust dismissal requirements of the CLC.
- Discuss the concept of danger as it is defined in part II the CLC and the legal test used to determine whether or not danger exists.
- Explain what is meant by the defence of "reasonable care and due diligence."
- Explain how minimum wage requirements work for employees covered by part III of the CLC.
- Identify the different types of leaves that are available to employees covered by the CLC.
- Discuss how part III of the CLC is enforced.

Introduction

The *Canada Labour Code* (CLC) is a unique piece of legislation that applies to employers and employees that operate under the jurisdiction of the federal government. This normally includes industries that are trans-provincial (operate across provincial boundaries) or are directly related to the work that is done by the government of Canada (e.g., Canada Post or the Canada Revenue Agency). In general, this means that if you are an employee of the federal government, or an employer or employee in the following industries, you are governed by this legislation (Government of Canada, 2020):

- banks;
- marine shipping, ferry and port services;
- air transportation, including airports, aerodromes, and airlines;
- railway and road transportation that involves crossing provincial or international borders;
- canals, pipelines, tunnels, and bridges (crossing provincial borders);
- telephone, telegraph, and cable systems;
- radio and television broadcasting;
- grain elevators, feed and seed mills;
- uranium mining and processing;
- businesses dealing with the protection of fisheries as a natural resource;
- many First Nation activities;
- most federal Crown corporations; and
- private businesses necessary to the operation of a federal act.

Although this seems like it would include a large number of employers and organizations, in actual fact this constitutes only about 6 percent of employees in Canada. It is a common misunderstanding that the CLC supersedes provincial labour codes. This is not true and can lead employers and employees astray when they are attempting to understand their rights and responsibilities with respect to the employment relationship.

The CLC is composed of three parts addressing subjects that are normally separate pieces of provincial legislation. Part I of the CLC addresses industrial relations issues, including unionization, the right to collective bargaining, and dispute resolution in unionized, federally regulated organizations. The provincial counterpart to part I of the CLC in Alberta is the Alberta *Labour Relations Code*, and in British Columbia (BC) it is the BC *Labour Relations Code*. Part II of the CLC addresses occupational health and safety in the federal sector and contains provisions that are similar though not identical to provincial legislation. Part III of the CLC addresses issues that are included in provincial employment standards legislation (in BC, the *Employment Standards Act*, and in Alberta, the *Employment Standards Code*), including hours of work, wages, vacations, and holidays. There are some unusual elements to part III that are not contained in most provincial legislation that will be discussed later in the chapter.

The reason we have included a new chapter addressing federal employees is that human resources managers in Alberta and BC need to be aware that their employers may in fact be operating in industries that are covered by the CLC, even if their head office or the majority of their business is conducted within one of the two provinces. Some larger corporations may have some parts of the business governed by provincial employment statutes while other parts are governed by federal employment law. It is therefore important that students know which legislation applies to which employees and which rules apply to them. The issue of jurisdiction is sometimes a contentious one, as illustrated by *Masterson v Manufacturers Life Insurance Co*.

CASE IN POINT

Life Insurance Company Not a Federal Undertaking

Masterson v Manufacturers Life Insurance Co, [2015] CLAD No 136 (QL)

Facts

Masterson was employed by Manufacturers Life Insurance (Manulife Financial) from March 2006 to June 2014. She worked in various positions and held the title of Major Accounts Client Manager at the Calgary branch office when she was dismissed. Her job involved developing and maintaining relationships with existing group benefit plan clients who had head offices in Alberta. Manulife is incorporated under the federal *Insurance Companies Act* (ICA) and has its head office in Toronto, where it is licensed under the applicable insurance legislation for the province. When Masterson was discharged, she filed a complaint under part III of the CLC alleging she was wrongfully dismissed and insufficiently compensated. An inspector with Employment and Social Development Canada made an initial finding that Manulife was subject to provincial rather than federal jurisdiction. Masterson disagreed, and the complaint was referred to an adjudicator.

Manulife argued that its insurance operation is not subject to the CLC because in order to apply, an entity must be a "federal work, undertaking or business" as defined in sections 2 and 167(1) of the CLC. Masterson argued that Manulife is governed by the ICA and is monitored by the Financial Consumer Agency of Canada, which shows that Manulife is not governed exclusively by the province and therefore the CLC should apply.

Relevant Issue

Does Manulife fall under federal or provincial jurisdiction for employment-related statutes?

Decision

The adjudicator noted that section 2 of the CLC defines a "federal work, undertaking or business" as

> [a]ny work, undertaking or business that is within the legislative authority of Parliament, including, without restricting the generality of the foregoing,
>
> (a) a work, undertaking or business operated or carried on for or in connection with navigation and shipping, whether inland or maritime, including the operation of ships and transportation by ship anywhere in Canada,
>
> (b) a railway, canal, telegraph or other work or undertaking connecting any province with any other province, or extending beyond the limits of a province,
>
> (c) a line of ships connecting a province with any other province, or extending beyond the limits of a province,
>
> (d) a ferry between any province and any other province or between any province and any country other than Canada,
>
> (e) aerodromes, aircraft or a line of air transportation,
>
> (f) a radio broadcasting station,
>
> (g) a bank or an authorized foreign bank within the meaning of section 2 of the *Bank Act*,
>
> (h) a work or undertaking that, although wholly situated within a province, is before or after its execution declared by Parliament to be for the general

advantage of Canada or for the advantage of two or more of the provinces,

(i) a work, undertaking or business outside the exclusive legislative authority of the legislatures of the provinces, and

(j) a work, undertaking or activity in respect of which federal laws within the meaning of section 2 of the *Oceans Act* apply pursuant to section 20 of that Act and any regulations made pursuant to paragraph 26(1)(k) of that Act.

In reaching a decision, the adjudicator relied on the language in the CLC and the well-established legal principle that presumes labour relations is a provincial matter, unless the nature, operations, and habitual activities of the organization are of an inherently federal nature. In applying this functional test to Manulife, the adjudicator found that it was clear the company provided life insurance, financial protection products, and wealth management services. While the province did not have exclusive authority over the insurance industry, per section 2(i), no other criteria from section 2 applied. Furthermore, the Supreme Court had already made it clear in 2007 (in *Canadian Western Bank v Alberta*) that the business of insurance falls within the jurisdiction of the provinces, even where an insurance company is operated interprovincially and federally incorporated. Since the main function of Manulife is the provision of insurance and insurance-related products, the adjudicator concluded that Manulife did not fall under the jurisdiction of the CLC. Masterson would have to pursue her complaint through the Alberta legal system.

In the remainder of this chapter we will explore each of the three parts of the legislation and provide examples of important cases that have helped define the parameters of the law and set precedents upon which future cases are likely to be decided. It should be noted that while decisions made by adjudicators applying the CLC may be cited in other jurisdictions, they will not be as relevant or persuasive as decisions made under the relevant provincial legislation. In other words, students should not construe the CLC as similar to the *Canadian Charter of Rights and Freedoms* (Charter), with which all other provincial legislation must comply.

Canada Labour Code: Part I—Industrial Relations

The preamble to part I of the CLC establishes the goals and objectives of the legislation and reflects an approach that balances the needs of the employer with the needs of employees to promote "the common well-being" and labour peace. The right of employees to join a union to bargain collectively with their employers, which is considered by the United Nations as a fundamental human right, is affirmed in the preamble:

> WHEREAS there is a long tradition in Canada of labour legislation and policy designed for the promotion of the common well-being through the encouragement of free collective bargaining and the constructive settlement of disputes;
>
> AND WHEREAS Canadian workers, trade unions and employers recognize and support freedom of association and free collective bargaining as the

> bases of effective industrial relations for the determination of good working conditions and sound labour-management relations;
>
> AND WHEREAS the Government of Canada has ratified Convention No. 87 of the International Labour Organization concerning Freedom of Association and Protection of the Right to Organize and has assumed international reporting responsibilities in this regard;
>
> AND WHEREAS the Parliament of Canada desires to continue and extend its support to labour and management in their cooperative efforts to develop good relations and constructive collective bargaining practices, and deems the development of good industrial relations to be in the best interests of Canada in ensuring a just share of the fruits of progress to all.

Part I of the CLC applies to all individuals employed in a federal undertaking (as defined above), their employers, and any union composed of those employees. Every employee is free to join the trade union of their choice and participate in the activities of the trade union. Employers are also free to join employers' organizations. The interpretation of part I of the CLC is guided by several regulations, including the *Canada Industrial Relations Board Regulations* and the *Canada Industrial Relations Regulations*.

Canada Industrial Relations Board: Powers and Duties

Division II of part I of the CLC is the portion of the legislation that establishes the Canada Industrial Relations Board (CIRB). The purpose of the CIRB is to settle any disputes relating to part I of the CLC. In other words, the main job of the CIRB is to deal with issues that arise in federally regulated workplaces where employees are already or wish to become unionized (or to decertify an existing trade union). This means the Board primarily deals with certification of trade unions, bargaining unit size and composition, disputes that arise as a result of collective bargaining, strikes, lockouts, and unfair labour practices.

In settling disputes regarding these issues, the CIRB has a number of powers, which are established in section 16 of part I and include the following:

1. conducting hearings;
2. compelling the attendance of witnesses to give testimony and to provide written evidence or other documents as requested by the Board;
3. examining any evidence put forward by the parties;
4. entering an employer's premises to observe work, materials, machinery, or other articles and to interrogate any person regarding a matter that is before the Board;
5. ordering or conducting representation votes for the purpose of certifying or decertifying a trade union;
6. determining whether the size and structure of a bargaining unit is appropriate for collective bargaining;

7. determining whether any unfair labour practice has been committed by the parties to a dispute; and
8. where an unfair labour practice has been committed, making legally binding decisions and ordering remedies as provided by the CLC.

Note that the CIRB does not enforce the orders it makes; enforcement occurs through the federal courts.

In the remainder of this section, we will review the basic requirements associated with the acquisition and termination of bargaining rights, collective bargaining, strikes and lockouts, and unfair labour practices.

Acquisition and Termination of Bargaining Rights

Any group of employees may form or join an existing trade union, and although it is not required, that union may apply for certification with the CIRB. Certification establishes that the union is the exclusive bargaining agent for the employees and will represent employees in negotiations with the employer regarding wages and working conditions. This means that employees cannot negotiate for themselves, and other uncertified unions cannot attempt to negotiate on behalf of the employees. Certification ensures that the status of the union is protected and any disputes that arise between the unionized employees and the employer are subject to the rules and regulations established in the CLC.

In order to become certified, the applicant union must demonstrate to the CIRB that a sufficient number of employees in a proposed bargaining unit support the union's application for representation rights. The union demonstrates support by collecting signed union membership cards from employees, which confirm each employee's desire to be represented by the union. If the CIRB is satisfied that a majority of the employees in the proposed bargaining unit have signed union membership cards, the CIRB will certify the union and all employees in the bargaining unit become unionized. If a union's application demonstrates that it has the support of not less than 35 percent and not more than 50 percent of the employees in the proposed bargaining unit, then the CIRB will order that a secret ballot vote be taken among the employees in the unit. The outcome of a secret ballot vote will be determined on the basis of the ballots cast by the majority of employees who participate in the vote.

You may wonder why employees would choose to unionize. The answer is not a simple one. However, it is most likely to occur when employees feel unfairly treated in terms of the economic benefits they receive or because they do not feel they have a voice that is being heard by the employer. By choosing to unionize and become certified, the employees have more power than when they bargain individually. Certification enables the employees to coordinate their activities, share knowledge, and use economic sanctions like job action or strikes (or the threat of economic sanctions) to buttress their negotiating position when bargaining is not progressing. Employers have similar rights under the CLC, including the right to join an employers' organization for the purpose of bargaining and the right to use economic sanctions (locking employees out) when bargaining is at an impasse. The CLC establishes rules regarding the exercise of these sanctions, with the overall goal of maintaining a level playing field between the parties to promote free and fair collective bargaining over the terms and conditions of employment.

Unions can be decertified in the same way they become certified. Employees wishing to decertify a union that represents them must establish that a majority of employees in the bargaining unit support decertification (referred to as "revocation" in the CLC). If the employees' application demonstrates majority support, the CIRB will usually order a secret ballot vote, the outcome of which will be determined on the basis of the ballots cast by the majority of employees who participated in the vote. In some instances, for example where the incumbent union does not challenge the application, the CIRB may revoke the certification without conducting a vote. Decertification may also occur if there is evidence that certification was obtained by fraud. Decertification cannot normally happen during a lawful strike or lockout.

If an employer sells all or part of a business, the union will continue to be the bargaining agent with the new employer. Therefore, an employer cannot decertify a unionized workforce by selling the business. Furthermore, the new employer is bound by any terms and conditions that are in a collective agreement (the group employment contract) at the time of the sale.

Collective Bargaining and Collective Agreements

Section 48 of the CLC requires that the parties bargain for the purpose of entering into a collective agreement. Collective bargaining normally begins after a union is newly certified, or within the last four months of an existing collective agreement where there is an ongoing union–management relationship. Either of the parties may give notice that they are prepared to commence bargaining. Where notice has been given, the parties have 20 days to meet and begin. Employers are not allowed to alter any terms and conditions of employment during the bargaining period, even if the collective agreement expires before a new agreement can be reached. Another way of saying this is that the parties follow the old collective agreement until they successfully agree on the terms and conditions for the new agreement.

The contents of a collective agreement, like the contents of any other contract of employment, are generally up to the two parties to negotiate. However, in the case of collective agreements subject to the CLC, there are some special requirements. First, if an employer plans to introduce a technological change that will substantially and adversely alter employment conditions or security for a number of employees, the legislation prescribes a procedure for providing notice and reopening the collective agreement to deal with the technology issue.

Second, section 57 of the CLC requires that every collective agreement include a provision for settling disputes about the interpretation, application, administration, or contravention of the collective agreement without resorting to work stoppage. This is generally referred to as a grievance process and means that the parties have to use the grievance mechanism to solve disputes when a collective agreement is in force, and it is illegal to strike during the life of a collective agreement. If a collective agreement does not include a grievance process, the CIRB will appoint an arbitrator (or arbitration board) to settle any issues that arise. An arbitrator has powers similar to those of the CIRB, and the decision made by the arbitrator is legally binding on the parties.

A final collective agreement clause that is mandated by the CLC is compulsory dues check-off. This clause requires that employers collect union dues from the wages of each employee in the bargaining unit. The amount collected is determined by the union and remitted to the union once collected. The only time this does not apply is when an employee has a religious conviction or belief and objects to joining a trade union. In this case, the dues that are collected are sent to a registered charity. This provision exists because the union is required to represent all employees in the bargaining unit, regardless of their preference for membership. This is called the *duty of fair representation*. Dues check-off exists to prevent "free-riders" from taking advantage of the duty of fair representation, which could eventually drain union coffers. This approach was established in a seminal labour arbitration decision by Rand J (a member of the Supreme Court of Canada) in 1946. The "Rand formula" is now the most common type of union membership clause that exists in Canada (Hebdon & Brown, 2012).

CASE IN POINT

Compulsory Union Dues Balance Freedom of Association with Union Responsibilities

Ford Motor Co of Canada v International Union United Automobile, Aircraft and Agricultural Implement Workers of America (UAW-CIO), [1946] OLAA No 1 (QL)

Facts

This is an arbitration settlement that arose in the context of a bitter strike by the union, which represented some 9,500 employees of the Ford Motor Company in Windsor, Ontario. At issue was a claim by the union for a particular type of union security called a union shop. In a union shop, new employees are required to become members of the union within a certain period of time. This can be contrasted to a closed shop, where the employer can only hire employees that are already part of a union, or an open shop, where employees are not required to become members of the union at all. The claim arose because Ford had accepted union shops with dues check-off in all of its American operations but was refusing to accept the same conditions on the Canadian side of the border.

Relevant Issue

Should employees in a legally certified bargaining unit be required to be members of the union?

Decision

Justice Rand determined he could not award a union shop because it could create strife within the union and between the employees and their employer. Furthermore, it would deny individuals the right to work independently of their association with any organized group. In other words, it would deny employees the right to the freedom of association, which would later be guaranteed in Canada's *Charter of Rights and Freedoms*.

However, Rand J also recognized (at para 26) that employees as a whole are beneficiaries of union action, and therefore it would not be inequitable to require that all employees contribute to the expense of maintaining the union and the costs incurred to ensure that their workplace rights are protected:

> I consider it entirely equitable then that all employees should be required to shoulder their portion of the burden of expense for administering the law of their

employment, the union contract; that they must take the burden along with the benefit.

Rand therefore awarded dues check-off, without the union shop status that would require employees to become members of the union. In the decision, Rand states that employers generally have greater power in the employment relationship than any individual employee or even union of employees. In order to maintain a balance of power between employers and employees, the union must be effective, and for that it must be financially viable. Rand dismissed Ford's arguments that it would be dangerous or unfair to entrust unions with the financial resources of membership dues, stating (at para 28), "those who control capital are scarcely in a position to complain of the power of money in the hands of labour." And thus, the Rand formula was born.

Conciliation and First Agreements

Division V of part I establishes the Federal Mediation and Conciliation Service, which exists to assist unions and employers who are unable to agree on the terms and conditions of a collective agreement. Either party can notify the Minister of Labour that they are unable to reach a resolution, at which point a conciliation officer will be appointed to work with the parties. The conciliation officer will provide a report with recommendations, though the parties are not bound by the recommendations unless they agree. If agreement is reached, the new collective agreement is drafted and put into effect. If agreement is not reached, the parties may pursue strike or lockout options, which are discussed in detail below.

It is not uncommon for employers and unions to have particular difficulty reaching an agreement when it is the first time they have negotiated. When the parties are inexperienced, the outcome may more often be a strike or lockout, which can have significant economic consequences for workers, the employer, and society as a whole. Therefore, the CLC has special provisions for settling first agreements. If the Minister considers it necessary or advisable, the CIRB can be directed to inquire into the dispute and determine the terms and conditions of employment for the parties. The employer and union are then bound by these for the life of the collective agreement, which the CLC mandates as two years in this circumstance. At the end of two years, the parties will try again to negotiate on their own. When the CIRB is appointed to settle a first contract dispute, section 80(3) of the CLC requires that

> (3) … the Board shall give the parties an opportunity to present evidence and make representations and the Board may take into account
>
> (a) the extent to which the parties have, or have not, bargained in good faith in an attempt to enter into the first collective agreement between them;
>
> (b) the terms and conditions of employment, if any, negotiated through collective bargaining for employees performing the same or similar functions in the same or similar circumstances as the employees in the bargaining unit; and
>
> (c) such other matters as the Board considers will assist it in arriving at terms and conditions that are fair and reasonable in the circumstances.

Strikes and Lockouts

If the union and employer cannot reach an agreement, and it is not the special circumstance of a first contract, there are several conditions that must exist for them to be in a position to strike or lockout. There are also rules that must be followed during the strike or lockout:

1. The collective agreement must be expired before a strike or lockout can occur.
2. Notice to bargain must have been given.
3. A conciliation officer must have been appointed and had 21 days to work with the parties.
4. The employer must give 72 hours' notice of a lockout, or the union must give 72 hours' notice of a strike.
5. For the union to go on strike, they must have had a secret ballot vote among employees in the bargaining unit sometime in the 60 days prior to the strike. The majority must approve of the strike.
6. During a strike or lockout, supply of services, operation of facilities, or production of goods must continue to the extent necessary to prevent immediate and serious danger to the health or safety of the public.
7. The employer cannot hire replacement workers to do the work of employees in the bargaining unit during a strike or lockout if the purpose is not for legitimate bargaining purposes but is to undermine the union's representational capacity.
8. Employers cannot discipline any employee who refuses to do the work of a striking or locked-out employee.
9. Employers cannot discontinue pension or other benefits during a strike or lockout as long as the bargaining agent is paying the necessary insurance premiums to maintain those benefits.
10. After the strike or lockout is over, the employer must reinstate employees in the bargaining unit who were on strike or lockout.

A strike that violates these conditions is unlawful, and the CIRB can order the employees back to work or the employer to end the lockout. The right to strike has been a contentious issue, particularly in the public sector or where a strike has the potential to disrupt services that are considered essential to public health and safety or to national economic interests. In the past, the government has intervened to order striking postal employees and airline pilots back to work. However, the Supreme Court of Canada decision in *Saskatchewan Federation of Labour v Saskatchewan* seems to have settled the right-to-strike question, firmly establishing that the right to strike is protected by the Charter.

IN THE NEWS

Right to Strike Is Protected by the Charter

The Supreme Court of Canada has revolutionized labour law in Canada by declaring that the right to strike is protected by the *Canadian Charter of Rights and Freedoms*. The ruling has broad implications across

Canada for provincial governments that limit the right of public sector workers to go on strike. Several provinces intervened, arguing that restricting public workers deemed "essential" (such as nurses or prison guards) from walking off the job is necessary to protect the public.

In earlier decisions, the Supreme Court took the view that freedom of association for workers did not equate to a right to collective bargaining or the right to strike. The Court now insists that governments can put only minimal limitations on those rights.

The majority 5–2 ruling written by Abella J stated that freedom of association must protect the right to the autonomy and dignity of vulnerable people and that the law must level the playing field between the parties in labour relations disputes: "attributing equivalence between the power of employees and employers … turns labour relations on its head, and ignores the fundamental power imbalance which the entire history of modern labour legislation has been scrupulously devoted to rectifying."

Dissenting Justices Rothstein and Wagner suggested that the majority's view of labour relations was stuck back in the early days of the Industrial Revolution, when workers were powerless: "Under the rubric of 'workplace justice,' our colleagues, relying on a 19th-century conception of the relationship between employers and workers, enshrine a political understanding of this concept that favours the interests of employees over those of employers and even over those of the public," they wrote.

The ruling came as the result of a public sector union challenge to a 2008 provincial law passed by the Saskatchewan Party that limited the right to strike for workers in essential services. The central concern with that particular piece of legislation was that the law gave the government the unilateral right to decide which workers were essential and also denied those workers access to an effective alternative to striking (such as arbitration).

Don Morgan, Saskatchewan's Labour Relations Minister said, "We do not feel that the safety and security of our citizens should be compromised by labour disruptions." But labour groups like the Canadian Union of Public Employees were elated with the decision because "without the right to strike, employers have an unfair advantage."

University of British Columbia law professor Joel Bakan suggested that the Court's views regarding the right to strike have changed over time. "The court recognizes that as workers' freedom of association is eroded by economic shifts and hostile governments, the judiciary becomes more essential for protecting this fundamental right. It's a classic case—like segregation in the US South, or abortion or sexual orientation equality in Canada—where governments cannot be relied upon to respect constitutional rights and freedoms, so the courts step in."

SOURCE: Fine, 2015.

Unfair Labour Practices

Section 94 of the CLC establishes a number of practices that are considered unfair labour practices in the relationship between the employer and the union. Many unfair labour practices apply to both parties, while some are specific to either the union or management. For example, it is considered an unfair labour practice for an employer to interfere in the formation or administration of a trade union. But it is also an unfair labour practice for a union to interfere in the formation or administration of an employers' organization. Neither party can attempt to intimidate, threaten, coerce, or impose a penalty on someone who files a complaint under the CLC. Employers are also prohibited from bargaining with a union that is not the certified bargaining agent. Similarly, a union that is not the certified bargaining agent is prohibited from attempting to bargain with the employer.

Raiding is another unfair labour practice. It occurs when one union attempts to displace another. There are lawful ways for employees to switch to a new union, but this requires that a proper certification process occur, and until that happens the new union is prohibited from bargaining with the employer. Section 96 makes it clear that no person or organization (union or employer) is allowed to intimidate or coerce a person to try to force them to become or not become a member of a union.

An example of an unfair labour practice that applies only to employers is discrimination against employees who wish to join a union or are part of a union. This means that an employer may not refuse to hire, fire, suspend, transfer, lay off, or otherwise discriminate against an individual because that person wishes to become or is already a member of a union. Employers are also prohibited from requiring that job candidates sign contracts promising to give up the right to unionize. Employers should be particularly careful about their human resources management practices during organizing campaigns. Threatening, intimidating, or disciplining an employee involved in an organizing drive is considered to be an unfair labour practice.

An important unfair labour practice that applies only to unions is attempting to unionize workers on employer property during working hours without first getting permission from the employer. Unions are also required to govern their affairs in a way that is non-discriminatory and non-coercive. They may not expel or suspend a union member for discriminatory reasons and, as noted above, are prohibited from using threats or intimidation to force workers to become unionized.

Where a party has been found to have engaged in an unfair labour practice, the CIRB may order a number of remedial actions, including the following:

- ordering that the offending party comply with the CLC;
- compensating, reinstating, or otherwise giving an employee anything that was denied as a result of the violation (e.g., awarding a transfer to another location, a salary increment, vacation, or any other benefit that the employee would have received if not for the unfair labour practice); and
- imposing fines.

Canada Labour Code: Part II—Occupational Health and Safety

In this section, a brief overview of part II is provided. The purpose of part II of the CLC is to prevent accidents and injuries that arise out of, are linked with, or occur in the course of employment. The CLC specifies that to prevent injury, employers should first try to eliminate the hazard. If that is not possible, the hazard should be reduced. Finally, if the hazard cannot be eliminated or reduced, the employer should provide personal protective equipment, clothing, devices, or materials. The CLC establishes the general rules and processes for the protection of workers, while specific requirements with respect to hazards that are common across many industries (e.g., noise, ladders, and excavations) are specified in the *Canada Occupational Health and Safety Regulations*. There are additional regulations specific to industries that have unique working conditions:

- *Aviation Occupational Health and Safety Regulations*, SOR/2011-87;
- *Coal Mining Occupational Health and Safety Regulations*, SOR/90-97;
- *Maritime Occupational Health and Safety Regulations*, SOR/2010-120;
- *Oil and Gas Occupational Safety and Health Regulations*, SOR/87-612; and
- *On Board Trains Occupational Health and Safety Regulations*, SOR/87-184.

As is the case with provincial health and safety legislation, the CLC allows an employee to withdraw from work and initiate a formal investigation if the employee reasonably believes the work is dangerous. Some risks are an inherent part of many jobs and can be particularly high in certain occupations, such as firefighting and policing. Where there are inherent dangers, employers are required to minimize the risk through all reasonable and practical measures. A work refusal would only be supported where the danger is not normally part of the job or where it is inherent but all reasonable and practical measures had not been taken to protect the worker. "Danger" is defined by the CLC as

> any hazard, condition or activity that could reasonably be expected to be an imminent or serious threat to the life or health of a person exposed to it before the hazard or condition can be corrected or the activity altered. (s 122(1))

This definition is quite broad in order to ensure a flexible interpretation that would capture danger that arises in a wide range of employment circumstances. It may also be complicated by the condition or health of the employee. In other words, a job task or activity may be hazardous for some employees but not for others. For example, the CLC contains special provisions for pregnant and nursing employees, who may refuse a task if they believe that it poses a risk to their health or to the health of their fetus or child. In this case, the employee is required to consult with a qualified medical practitioner to establish whether or not a risk exists. An interesting question about danger arises with this individualized approach, particularly where there is workplace conflict or bullying. Do these circumstances constitute danger under the meaning of the CLC? This very situation was addressed in the *Tryggvason* case, described below.

CASE IN POINT

No Danger Without Evidence That Workplace Conflict Causes Imminent Threat to Health

Nina Tryggvason v Transport Canada, 2012 OHSTC 10

Facts

Tryggvason was working as an employee of Transport Canada in Vancouver. According to Tryggvason, a number of changes had occurred in the workplace related to staffing and the distribution of work. In her opinion, the changes resulted in a form of workplace harassment and violence. She argued that her pre-existing medical conditions, combined with the conditions at work, placed her at risk and constituted danger within the meaning of the CLC. On June 9, 2010, Tryggvason invoked her right to refuse dangerous work, stating in an email:

> I am refusing to work under the Canada Labour Code Part 2—under the Health and Safety provisions and using the danger provisions to apply to emotional/physiological danger—including future danger to myself and others, and for the longer term negative impact on my health from the extreme workplace stressors. (at para 4)

Tryggvason claimed to have depression, chronic stress as a result of bullying and retribution by supervisors, suicidal thoughts, urges to harm colleagues, and diabetes (the management of which she alleged was affected by stress and depression). Management called the Vancouver Police to seek guidance. Tryggvason was taken to the hospital, where a psychological evaluation was undertaken and she was later released. The emergency room physician indicated that Tryggvason was not suicidal or homicidal and had good insight into her problems.

The health and safety officer (HSO) assigned to investigate the case concluded that Tryggvason's frustrations regarding her interpersonal relationships and work distribution did not amount to a condition of danger in the workplace. Tryggvason appealed the decision of the HSO.

At the appeal hearing, Tryggvason's counsellor (who had a PhD in social work, but was not a physician) indicated that Tryggvason met the tests for depression and post-traumatic stress disorder. Although the social worker was qualified to administer the tests, there was no supporting diagnosis from a physician.

Relevant Issue

Was the appellant exposed to danger, as defined by the CLC?

Decision

Appeals officer Michael Wiwchar determined that in this particular case Tryggvason was not exposed to danger as defined by the CLC. In reaching this conclusion, Wiwchar first considered whether the risk of psychological harm (as opposed to physical harm) could be considered a danger within the meaning of the legislation. Referencing a prior decision in *Tench v National Defence*, Wiwchar agreed (at para 66) that it could be

> that the alleged danger raised by the appellant in this case, that is, the alleged harassment, discrimination, bullying by co-workers, in her work place, are situations contemplated by the danger definition under subsection 122(1), when such acts have repercussions on the employee's psychological health.

The next step in the analysis was to determine whether the conditions detailed in the case could, per the definition of danger in the CLC, "reasonably be expected to be an imminent or serious threat to the life or health of a person exposed to it." In making this assessment, Wiwchar relied on a two-part test from *Tench*, which suggests that for a danger to exist, both of the following conditions must be met:

1. There must be persuasive evidence proving the employee's mental illness was present at the time.
2. There must be evidence proving that the illness was aggravated or could have been aggravated by a condition while at work.

After carefully examining the evidence brought forward at the appeal hearing, Wiwchar acknowledged the difficulty inherent in assessing the individual experience of danger, but found that Tryggvason had not met the requirements of the two-part test set out in the 2007 case *Alexander v Treasury Board*:

> 33. When others can observe the alleged danger in the workplace, there is no great difficulty in demonstrating that a danger may exist. However, if the danger is an individual experience, arbitrators have insisted that the employee must have solid evidence that can lead other reasonable individuals, examining the same circumstances, to conclude that the danger is indeed real. This is called an objective test. ...
>
> 35. Furthermore, where an employee refuses to perform work on medical grounds, which is the case here, it is incumbent upon that employee to satisfy his or her employer with documentary evidence from a physician that the work is a health hazard (see *United Automobile Workers, Local 636 v. F.M.C. of Canada Ltd, Link-Belt Speeder Division* (1971), 23 L.A.C. 234). In other words, the employee has the onus of producing the medical evidence that supports his or her claim that there is indeed a danger. (Emphasis removed.)

As the *Tryggvason* case shows, the CLC has taken a rather indirect approach to harassment and bullying in federally regulated workplaces. This changed rather dramatically in October 2018 when Bill C-65 received royal assent. Bill C-65 specifically addresses harassment and violence. Subsection 122(1) of the CLC adds a new definition for harassment and violence and establishes the importance of preventing harm that arises from harassment and violence:

> Harassment and violence means any action, conduct or comment, including of a sexual nature, that can reasonably be expected to cause offence, humiliation or other physical or psychological injury or illness to an employee, including any prescribed action, conduct or comment;
>
> The purpose of this Part is to prevent accidents, occurrences of harassment and violence and physical or psychological injuries and illnesses arising out of, linked with or occurring in the course of employment to which this Part applies.

In addition, Bill C-65 creates new duties for employers, which include the following:

- the duty to investigate, record, and report all occurrences of harassment and violence;
- the duty to take specific measures to prevent and protect against harassment and violence, and to respond to occurrences and offer support to affected employees; and
- the duty to ensure employees (including managers and supervisors) receive training in harassment and violence prevention, as well as their rights and obligations under this section of the CLC.

The CLC states that incidents of harassment and violence should not be investigated by a joint health and safety committee or safety representative. If someone is unhappy with the way that a complaint is being handled, that person may complain to the federal Minister of Labour. The Minister will investigate to see if the complaint has been dealt with appropriately or if the complaint is frivolous, trivial, or vexatious. If an employee is found guilty of harassment, the employer—not the employee—is held responsible for protecting workers.

The new *An Act to amend the Canada Labour Code (harassment and violence), the Parliamentary Employment and Staff Relations Act and the Budget Implementation Act, 2017, No 1* (SC 2018, c 22), establishes the detailed requirements for compliance with the new parts of the CLC. The regulation includes requirements for the qualifications that an investigator must have, time frames for resolving incidents, and requirements for dispute resolution processes and policies.[1]

It is interesting to consider whether the outcome in the *Trygvasson* case would have been different under the new harassment and violence provisions of the CLC. How adjudicators apply the new provisions, and the tests used to determine whether an employee has been harassed, remain to be seen.

1 More details on the regulation can be found here: <http://www.gazette.gc.ca/rp-pr/p1/2019/2019-04-27/html/reg1-eng.html>.

Health and Safety Responsibilities of Employers and Employees

Both employers and employees have general duties and responsibilities that are specified in sections 125 and 126 of the CLC. Employers are expected to protect the health and safety of every employee in every workplace controlled by the employer and for every work activity carried out by an employee in a workplace that is not controlled by the employer. This includes employees who work in third-party premises, employees who telework, and employees who have duties that are not conducted from a fixed location. For example, mail carriers and truck drivers perform the majority of their duties away from the employer's premises. However, even where employers do not have direct control over the worksite, they must still provide protective equipment and instruct employees in proper health and safety measures. This provision protects employees engaged in the multitude of activities on third-party premises and means that in an extreme situation, an employer may have to remove employees from unsafe locations.

There are 45 employer duties specified in the CLC, but they fall within the 12 main categories listed below:

1. Form policy health and safety committees with both employer and employee representatives (see below for details).
2. Develop and post health and safety policies, procedures, and regulations.
3. Notify employees of any known or foreseeable hazards.
4. Develop procedures for managing hazardous substances and post safety data sheets.
5. Train all employees in safe procedures and provide appropriate supervision.
6. Investigate and report all accidents, occupational diseases, or other hazards known to the employer.
7. Maintain health and safety records.
8. Ensure that workplace buildings and structures meet prescribed standards, including any guard rails, barricades, or fences.
9. Ensure that equipment, machinery, and vehicles are maintained, meet standards, and are operated in a safe manner.
10. Ensure that levels of ventilation, lighting, temperature, humidity, sound, and vibration meet prescribed standards.
11. Ensure that work stations and procedures meet ergonomic standards.
12. Provide first aid and health services, as well as sanitary and personal facilities with potable water.

The main duties of employees are outlined in section 126 and include the following:

1. Use safety equipment, materials, devices, and clothing as prescribed.
2. Follow safety procedures.
3. Report safety hazards to the employer.

These requirements are intended to increase the involvement of employees in occupational health and safety and to ensure the CLC is being followed. An employee who believes on reasonable grounds that there has been a contravention of the CLC, or that there is likely to be an accident or injury, is required to make a complaint to their supervisor. This process is mandatory. It is intended to ensure that employees' health and safety concerns are addressed by the employer without the employee needing to initiate the refusal-to-work process described above.

It should also be noted that employees cannot be found personally liable for anything done in good faith in providing first aid or in carrying out emergency measures. This is important for employees who volunteer to be fire or emergency wardens. Employers are required to ensure that these safety roles are filled (through volunteers or appointments) and that their specific duties are identified (see s 126(3)).

Safety Committees

The CLC requires that employers with more than 300 employees create a policy health and safety committee (PHSC). At least 50 percent of the PHSC must be made up of non-managerial employees. The PHSC is tasked with developing and monitoring health and safety policies and programs, including identification of hazards and employee education regarding health and safety matters. They are required to meet at least quarterly and have a key function in collecting and analyzing safety data for the organization.

Employers with 20 or more employees must have a workplace health and safety committee (WHSC). This is slightly different than the PHSC. The main duty of the WHSC is to conduct monthly inspections to identify hazards and to deal with complaints that arise. In other words, they enact the policies and programs developed by the PHSC. WHSCs are involved in investigations, inquiries, and inspections and are required to keep records of these events. If the workplace is small, and no PHSC exists, the WHSC may also be involved in policy development and employee training. WHSCs are required to meet at least nine times each year at regular intervals.

If an employer normally has fewer than 20 employees, the employer is required to appoint a health and safety representative. This person may not exercise managerial functions and generally participates in all of the activities of policy and workplace committees. This means they may be involved in program development, training, hazard identification, and investigations. The health and safety representative is required to inspect the workplace on a monthly basis, maintain records, and report hazards.

Complaint Resolution

As noted above, employees who believe there is likely to be an accident or injury to health resulting from the work they do may make a complaint to their supervisor and refuse to engage in the work until the complaint has been resolved. An employee cannot refuse to work if the hazard is a normal condition of employment. If the employee and supervisor do not agree, the matter is referred to the internal WHSC (see above), which will investigate. The committee will report to the employer and generally make a recommendation regarding the appropriate resolution of the issue. If the employee or employer disagrees with the committee, the matter can be referred to the Minister of Labour, who will appoint an investigator external to the organization. The employee can continue to refuse to work until the Minister's investigation is complete. If a complaint is made by an employee, an employer is prohibited from taking any action against that employee.

When conducting an investigation into a complaint or workplace accident, an investigator appointed by the Minister has, among other powers, the ability to enter the workplace, take samples and photographs, prevent anyone from disturbing the site of an accident, require that the employer produce documents, and take statements from employees. If a danger or hazard cannot be corrected or protected against, a stop-work order may be issued and will stay in effect until the problem can be addressed. Employers are prohibited from taking any action against employees who legally refuse dangerous work under this part of the CLC. They are also prohibited from penalizing employees who take part in the investigation of hazards or workplace accidents.

Offences and Punishment

The penalties for violating part II of the CLC can be severe if an individual is convicted of an offence. They include the potential of a fine up to $1 million or a prison term of up to two years (or both). This applies to officers, directors, agents, senior public officials, and any other person exercising managerial or supervisory functions in public administration.

As is the case in most provincial legislation, the defence of "reasonable care and due diligence" is available to individuals who are charged under the CLC. Provided a manager has done everything a reasonable person would do to prevent an accident, the manager is less likely to be charged, and if charged, they are more able to defend against the charge in court. The following are general recommendations for managers at differing levels to ensure they are exercising reasonable care and due diligence (Training for Work Place Committees and Health and Safety Representatives):

Senior management must:

- be aware of responsibilities and have written policies and directions in place
- ensure that system-wide programs are in place
- require regular reports and conduct periodic spot checks
- immediately act when made aware of potentially serious situations.

Senior managers are entitled to rely on their health and safety regime unless made aware that the system is defective.

Middle management should:

- be aware of responsibilities and issues
- ensure that the appropriate hazard prevention programs are in place

- where necessary, give specific direction
- report upward and manage downward
- exercise supervision and control over those they may normally be expected to influence or control.

Middle managers have a responsibility to not only give instructions but to also see that those instructions are carried out.

Line management should:

- ensure that hazard prevention program components are implemented;
- ensure that supervisors and employees are trained and that training is confirmed and recorded
- ensure that incidents are investigated and reported, corrective action is implemented, and follow-up is done.

Canada Labour Code: Part III—Standard Hours, Wages, Vacations, and Holidays

Part III of the CLC contains employment standards that are similar to the provisions in the BC *Employment Standards Act* and Alberta *Employment Standards Code* (see Chapter 6). In other words, it addresses minimum requirements in terms of hours of work, wages, vacations, leaves, termination of employment, and sexual harassment. Most of part III applies to any employer or employee within the federal jurisdiction as described at the start of this chapter. In the following paragraphs, the key requirements of the CLC will be explained, with special emphasis on some unique provisions that are not found in most provincial legislation.

Hours of Work

Standard hours of work for employees covered by the CLC are calculated as an average of 8 hours per day, not exceeding 40 hours per week. Employees can work more than 40 hours per week on average as long as the longer schedule is agreed to in writing by the union or at least 70 percent of the affected employees in non-unionized workplaces. A vote to change standard hours for non-unionized workplaces can be requested by any affected employee and is conducted by an inspector from Employment and Social Development Canada. The request must come within 90 days of the new hours taking effect, and the vote is conducted by secret ballot. In any case, the maximum number of hours that employees can be required to work is normally 48.

Sections 176 and 177 of the CLC allow employees to work in excess of the 48-hour maximum in exceptional circumstances. If the employer knows about the circumstances in advance, the employer is required to apply for a permit, ensure that the employees know about the application, and justify to the Minister of Labour the need for working in excess of the maximum. Employers do not need a permit if the situation is emergent and the employer could not have known about it in advance. Section 177(1) states:

> The maximum hours of work in a week specified in or prescribed under section 171, established pursuant to section 172 or prescribed by regulations made under section 175 may be exceeded, but only to the extent necessary to prevent serious interference with the ordinary working of the industrial establishment affected, in cases of
>
> (a) accident to machinery, equipment, plant or persons;
>
> (b) urgent and essential work to be done to machinery, equipment or plant; or
>
> (c) other unforeseen or unpreventable circumstances.

Furthermore, shifts must be scheduled so that employees have at least one full day of rest each week, and the CLC prescribes that, where possible, the day of rest should be a Sunday. Employees who work in excess of 40 hours per week are to be paid at least 1.5 times their regular rate of pay.

Bill C-86 added an entitlement for rest breaks. Employees are entitled to an unpaid break of at least 30 minutes for every five hours of work and a rest break of at least eight hours between shifts. Another change is that employers must provide 96 hours' written notice of the shift schedule, and employees can refuse shifts scheduled with less than 96 hours' notice (unless it's an emergency, a different shift schedule requirement is negotiated into a collective agreement, or the change was requested by the employee). Bill C-86 also provides employees with at least six months of service with the right to request a change to their work schedule, work location, number of hours, or other conditions and obligates the employer to respond in writing, specifying the reasons for declining the request (if applicable) in accordance with the permissible grounds listed in the legislation. Finally, Bill C-86 codifies an employee's right to refuse to work overtime requested by an employer in order to fulfill a family responsibility set out in the section that provides for family responsibility leave.

Minimum Wages

Division II of part III addresses minimum wage rates and takes a unique approach by establishing that the minimum rate should mirror that of the province in which the employee normally works.

Vacations

All employees are entitled to vacation, which they may start taking after being employed for ten months. Employees are entitled to at least two weeks of vacation (or 4 percent vacation pay) after one year of employment; three weeks (or 6 percent vacation pay) after five years; and four weeks (or 8 percent vacation pay) after ten years of employment. If a business is sold, merged, or leased, the employment of the affected employees is considered continuous and their vacation entitlements travel with them to the new employer.

General Holidays

There are nine general holidays established by the CLC:

1. New Year's Day,
2. Good Friday,
3. Victoria Day,
4. Canada Day,
5. Labour Day,
6. Thanksgiving Day,
7. Remembrance Day,
8. Christmas Day, and
9. Boxing Day.

Employees can work on a general holiday, but they must be paid at a rate of 1.5 times their regular rate of pay plus the holiday pay for that day. If the employee is a manager or other professional and is required to work on the general holiday, they will receive their normal rate of pay but must be given a day off with pay at another time. For employees who work part time, their holiday pay is calculated in proportion to the number of hours they normally work. Employees who do not work on the holiday are paid in accordance with the method they earn their wages (e.g., hourly, salary, or commission). The rate will normally equate to 1/20 of the wages they earned in the four weeks immediately prior to the holiday.

Reassignment, Maternity Leave, Parental Leave, Compassionate Care Leave, and Other Leaves of Absence

Employees in the federal sector are entitled to a number of different types of absence leaves. Where possible, the employee is required to give notice to the employer regarding the date of the leave as well as the expected return date. In cases where the leave is due to pregnancy or another circumstance that affects the health of the employee or a family member, the employee is required to provide a certificate from a qualified physician or specialist. While an employee is on leave, the employee continues to accrue pension and other benefits, though the employee is responsible for paying the premiums. The employee does not receive a wage but would normally receive some support through employment insurance. Employers are not allowed to discipline an employee because they have applied for or received a leave of absence, and the employee's position (or a comparable one) must be available to them when they return from the leave. The following leaves of absence are guaranteed under the CLC:

1. *Maternity and parental leave.* Families and pregnant women who work in the federal jurisdiction are entitled to a number of different supportive employment practices. First, a pregnant employee may be reassigned or have her job modified if there is medical evidence that any of her original job functions

could put the employee or her fetus at risk. If there is a medical reason the employee should not work at all during the pregnancy, the employee will be granted a leave of absence from the beginning of the pregnancy until 24 weeks after the birth. For a normal pregnancy, any employee who is pregnant is entitled to a leave of absence of up to 17 weeks, which can begin any time within the last 13 weeks of her estimated delivery date. If the newborn is hospitalized, the leave may be extended for the length of the child's hospitalization.

In addition to maternity leave, new parents of their own or an adopted child are entitled to a leave of absence of up to 63 weeks starting the day the child is born or comes into the care of the employee. Parental leave can be split between the parents if both work in the federal jurisdiction. However, the aggregate leave cannot exceed 71 weeks for the same birth or adoption. Should special medical circumstances exist where the child or parent is ill, the leave can be extended to 104 weeks.

The combined aggregate amount of maternity and parental leave that may be taken by more than one employee in respect of the same birth cannot exceed 86 weeks, but the combined aggregate amount of maternity and parental leave that may be taken by one employee in respect of the same birth cannot exceed 78 weeks.

2. *Compassionate care leave.* Employees who fall under the federal jurisdiction are entitled to take compassionate leave of

   > up to 28 weeks to provide care or support to a family member of the employee if a qualified medical practitioner issues a certificate stating that the family member has a serious medical condition with a significant risk of death within 26 weeks. (s 206.3(2))

   A family member can be:

   - a spouse or common law partner of the employee,
   - a child of the employee or a child of the employee's spouse or common law partner,
   - a parent of the employee or a spouse or common law partner of the parent, or
   - any other person who is classified as a "family member" in the *Employment Insurance Act.*

3. *Critical illness leave.* Employees in the federal sector are allowed 37 weeks of leave to care for a child that is critically ill. They are required to provide a medical certificate from a specialist indicating that the child requires the parent's care or support and the length of time the child will need that care and support.
4. *Death or disappearance leave.* This is a particularly unique section of the CLC that provides compassionate leave to parents of a child who has died or has disappeared and it is probable, considering the circumstances, that the death or disappearance is the result of a crime. The maximum leave for death is 104 weeks, and the maximum leave for disappearance is 52 weeks. In the case of a disappearance, the leave ends 2 weeks after the child is found alive. If the child is not found alive, the leave is extended for another 52 weeks. The leave also

ends when it becomes clear that the death or disappearance was not the result of a crime. An employee is not entitled to this leave if the employee is charged with the crime or it is likely that the child was a party to the crime.

5. *Bereavement leave.* Employees who fall under the federal jurisdiction are entitled to up to five days bereavement leave that may be taken during the period that begins on the day on which the death occurs and ends six weeks after the latest of the days on which any funeral, burial, or memorial service of the immediate family member occurs. This is the only leave where qualified employees are entitled to receive their regular rate of pay for a portion of the leave. Any employee who has worked for three or more months and loses a member of their immediate family is entitled to the first three days of bereavement leave with pay at their regular rate of wages for their normal hours of work. The definition of immediate family is not provided in the CLC. However, for the purposes of bereavement leave under the CLC, the *Canada Labour Standards Regulations defines* immediate family as follows:

   (a) the employee's spouse or common law partner
   (b) the employee's father and mother and the spouse or common law partner of the father or mother
   (c) the employee's children and the children of the employee's spouse or common law partner
   (d) the employee's grandchildren
   (e) the employee's brothers and sisters
   (f) the grandfather and grandmother of the employee
   (g) the father and mother of the spouse or common law partner of the employee and the spouse or common law partner of the father or mother
   (h) any relative of the employee who resides permanently with the employee or with whom the employee permanently resides.

   The *Canada Labour Standards Regulations* also clarify that "common law partner" means a person who has been cohabiting with an individual in a conjugal relationship for at least one year, or who had been cohabiting with the individual for at least one year immediately before the individual's death.

6. *Medical leave.* Employees who fall under the federal jurisdiction are entitled to a medical leave of absence of up to 17 weeks as a result of personal illness or injury, organ or tissue donation, or medical appointments during working hours. If a medical leave of absence is three days or longer, the employer may require that the employee provide a certificate issued by a health care practitioner certifying that the employee was incapable of working for the period of time they were absent from work.

   An employer is prohibited from dismissing, suspending, laying off, demoting, or disciplining an employee because the employee intends to take or has taken a medical leave of absence or taking such an intention or absence into account in any decision to promote or train the employee. As an exception to this general prohibition, an employer is allowed to accommodate an employee returning from illness or injury if the employee is unable to perform the same work that they performed prior to the absence. The employee may be assigned to a different position, with different terms and conditions of employment where necessary.

7. *Reserve force leave.* Federally regulated employees who are members of the reserve force and have completed at least three consecutive months of continuous employment with an employer are entitled to take a leave to participate in military operations or activities, including the following:
   - any operation in Canada or abroad—including preparation, training, rest, or travel from or to the employee's residence—that is designated by the Minister of National Defence;
   - Canadian Armed Forces military skills training;
   - any duties they are called upon to perform under the *National Defence Act*; and
   - treatment, recovery, or rehabilitation for a physical or mental health problem that has arisen as a result of their service.
8. *Family responsibility leave (personal leave).* Bill C-86 also introduced a new personal leave entitlement for federally regulated employees. This provision gives employees up to five days of annual leave, the first three of which are paid if the employee has three months or more of continuous service. Personal leave is allowed for illness or injury, responsibilities related to the health or care of a family member, responsibilities related to the education of a family member under the age of 18, any urgent matter concerning the employee or their family members, and attending a citizenship ceremony under the *Citizenship Act*.
9. *Family violence leave.* Federally regulated employees who are victims of family violence or who are the parents of a child who is the victim of family violence will be entitled to ten days' leave. Five days are paid leave for employees who have three consecutive months of continuous employment. Family violence leave days can be used to:
   - seek medical attention for physical or psychological injuries,
   - obtain services from organizations that provide services to victims of family violence,
   - obtain psychological or other professional counselling,
   - relocate (temporarily or permanently), and
   - seek legal advice or law enforcement assistance.

   Family violence leave does not apply to an employee who is charged with an offence related to the violence or if it is probable the employee committed the violence. Employers can request documentation to support the leave within 15 days of the employee's return to work, and the employee must provide it if it is reasonably practicable to do so.
10. *Leave for Traditional Aboriginal Practices.* A federally regulated employee who is an Indigenous person and who has been an employee for three

consecutive months may take a leave of up to five unpaid days per calendar year to engage in traditional Indigenous practices. This is another new leave created under Bill C-86 and may include Indigenous practices such as hunting, fishing, harvesting, or other practices prescribed by the regulation.

Group and Individual Terminations

Group Terminations

Another interesting and unique division of the CLC relates to the requirements surrounding mass terminations. Where an employer plans to terminate, either simultaneously or within any period not exceeding four weeks, 50 or more employees, the employer is required to notify the Minister of Labour at least 16 weeks in advance of the first termination. A copy of the notice is to be provided to the union (where a union is in place) and must be posted in a conspicuous spot at the workplace. Bill C-86 expressly provides the employer with the option of providing 48 hours' written notice and 16 weeks' pay in lieu of notice to effect the terminations on the same day. Individual notices of termination must be given as early as possible, but not less than two weeks before the termination date.

In addition to notifying the Minister, union, and employees, the employer is required to create a joint planning committee. There must be a minimum of four members of the committee, and at least half of the members must be elected representatives from the employees being terminated. The committee must be co-chaired by one representative of the employer and one representative of the redundant employees. The committee is required to meet not less than two weeks after notice of the group termination is provided to the Minister. According to section 221(1) of the CLC, the objective of the committee is to develop an adjustment program to either:

(a) eliminate the necessity for the termination of employment; or
(b) minimize the impact of the termination of employment on the redundant employees and to assist those employees in obtaining other employment.

The CLC requires that the union and employer cooperate with the committee and provide necessary information to them. An inspector can be assigned to attend committee meetings to monitor the process. If the committee is not able to develop a mutually agreeable plan, the members can request that an arbitrator be appointed by the Minister. The arbitrator may work with the committee to find a resolution or make a determination regarding the adjustment program. The arbitrator is not allowed to stop or delay the termination. Once the readjustment program is completed, the employer is required to implement it.

Individual Terminations

Employers who terminate an employee without just cause are required to provide the employee with a minimum of two weeks of notice that their employment will be terminated, or two weeks of pay in lieu of notice.

Severance

If an employee has worked for the employer for 12 months or more, and the employee is terminated without just cause, the employer is required to provide severance in addition to notice or pay in lieu of notice. The minimum severance required by the CLC is the greater of:

- two days' wages for each completed year of employment that is within the term of the employee's continuous employment by the employer, and
- five days' wages at the employee's regular rate of wages for their regular hours of work.

Work-Related Illness or Injury

Employers in the federal sector are not allowed to dismiss, suspend, lay off, demote, or discipline an employee because of absence from work due to work-related illness or injury. Furthermore, since there is no federal workers' compensation scheme (see Chapter 9 for a discussion of workers' compensation systems in Alberta and BC), the CLC requires that employers subscribe to an insurance plan that would provide wage replacement coverage if the employee is injured or becomes ill in the course of employment. This means that many employers subscribe to the workers' compensation scheme in their home province. The benefit of this is that the employee is barred from suing the employer for a workplace-based illness or injury. Employers are also required to return the employee to work, where possible, following the absence. If the employee is unable to perform the functions of their original position, the employer is allowed to place the employee in modified duties or an alternative position that matches the employee's medical restrictions.

Unjust Dismissal

Perhaps one of the most notable clauses in the CLC is the ability of employees to file a complaint with an inspector of Employment and Social Development Canada if they feel their dismissal has been unjust. This is a much simpler approach than that required if an employee pursues a case through the courts. It provides employees with a dispute resolution mechanism that is fast and relatively simple to navigate and does not require expensive legal representation. The employee is required to file the complaint within 90 days of the dismissal. The inspector will attempt to assist the parties to settle the dispute, but if this is not effective, the Minister of Labour will appoint an unjust dismissal adjudicator to hear the complaint and render a decision. The adjudicator will normally hold a hearing where the parties have an opportunity to present their cases and evidence. An unjust dismissal adjudicator has powers similar to those of the CIRB. If it is determined that the dismissal was unjust, a wide range of remedies are available whereby the employer may be ordered to:

- pay the person compensation not exceeding the amount of money that is equivalent to the remuneration that would, but for the dismissal, have been paid by the employer to the person;

- reinstate the person in their employ; and
- do any other like thing that it is equitable to require the employer to do to remedy or counteract any consequence of the dismissal.

The language used in the CLC regarding unjust dismissal has been the cause of some discord among adjudicators assigned to hear these cases. Over time, two streams of thought have developed. One stream of decisions has suggested that the language is intended to mean that an employee may not be dismissed without just cause. This is similar to the just cause requirements found in most collective agreements in unionized workplaces, wherein employers are required to prove that they had just cause before disciplining or discharging an employee. Just cause would normally include behaviours such as poor performance, theft, serious insubordination, or some other behaviour that is sufficiently serious that it damages the employment relationship beyond repair. The second stream of decisions follows the common law approach and takes the position that an employer does not require just cause per se; rather, the employer can sever the relationship at any time provided that appropriate notice, pay in lieu of notice, or severance is provided. In this case, a dismissal is only unjust if the employee, when terminated, was treated in a way that was unfair or discriminatory, or if the severance package was not reasonable. After decades of debate and judicial discord, the matter was conclusively addressed by a decision of the Supreme Court of Canada in *Wilson v Atomic Energy of Canada Limited.*

CASE IN POINT

Employers in Federal Sector Do Not Require Just Cause to Discharge Employees

Wilson v Atomic Energy of Canada Limited, 2016 SCC 29

Facts

Wilson had been employed by Atomic Energy of Canada Limited (AECL) as a procurement supervisor for about four and a half years. Although his title indicated he was a supervisor, he was not considered to hold a management position. Wilson was terminated without cause in November 2009. He was offered a severance package equating to approximately six months of salary. Wilson filed a complaint under part III of the CLC, and an adjudicator was appointed to hear the case. Wilson argued that employees in the federal jurisdiction cannot be dismissed without cause. AECL argued that dismissals without cause are not automatically unjust. The adjudicator decided in favour of Wilson, and AECL appealed to the Federal Court, which quashed the adjudicator's original decision. Wilson then appealed to the Federal Court of Appeal, which upheld the Federal Court's decision and confirmed that the unjust dismissal provisions of the CLC did not require just cause for dismissal. It is rare for courts to interfere in the decisions of administrative tribunals or individual adjudicators. However, in this case the Federal Court of Appeal noted that this was an issue of "persistent discord that has existed for many years" (at para 54 in *Wilson v Atomic Energy of Canada Limited,* 2015 FCA 17), and consequently Stratas J concluded that the Federal Court of Appeal was entitled to hear the case to determine which interpretation of the CLC was correct. The Federal Court of Appeal's decision was then appealed to the Supreme Court of Canada, which overturned the Court of Appeal's decision and restored the decision of the original adjudicator.

Relevant Issue

Was the employer entitled to lawfully terminate the employee on a "without cause" basis?

Decision

Justice Abella first addressed the standard of review for unjust dismissal adjudicators and clearly indicated that the standard is and should be "reasonableness." A decision is reasonable if it falls within a range of possible, acceptable outcomes that are defensible in respect of the facts and law. Justice Abella then went on to determine whether or not the adjudicator in the *Wilson* case was reasonable:

> Returning to this case, the issue is whether the Adjudicator's interpretation of ss. 240 to 246 of the *Code* was reasonable. The text, the context, the statements of the Minister of Labour when the legislation was introduced, and the views of the overwhelming majority of arbitrators and labour law scholars, confirm that the entire purpose of the statutory scheme was to ensure that non-unionized federal employees would be entitled to protection from being dismissed without cause under Part III of the *Code*. The alternative approach of severance pay in lieu falls outside the range of "possible, acceptable outcomes which are defensible in respect of the facts and law" because it completely undermines this purpose by permitting employers, at their option, to deprive employees of the full remedial package Parliament created for them. The rights of employees should be based on what Parliament intended, not on the idiosyncratic view of the individual employer or adjudicator. The Adjudicator's decision was, therefore, reasonable. (at para 10)

Justice Abella went on to affirm that the unjust dismissal sections of the statute should be interpreted to mean that just cause is required:

> The argument that employment can be terminated without cause so long as minimum notice or compensation is given, on the other hand, would have the effect of rendering many of the Unjust Dismissal remedies meaningless or redundant. Only by interpreting the Unjust Dismissal scheme as representing a displacement of the employer's ability at common law to fire an employee without reasons if reasonable notice is given, does the scheme and its remedial package make sense. That is how the 1978 provisions have been almost universally applied. It is an outcome that is anchored in parliamentary intention, statutory language, arbitral jurisprudence, and labour relations practice. To decide otherwise would fundamentally undermine Parliament's remedial purpose.

Sexual Harassment

Division XV.1 of the CLC establishes that every employee is entitled to employment free of sexual harassment, and that employers are required to take reasonable steps to ensure no employee is subject to sexual harassment, which is defined as

> any conduct, comment, gesture or contact of a sexual nature that ... is likely to cause offence or humiliation to any employee; or ... that might, on reasonable grounds, be perceived by that employee as placing a condition of a sexual nature on employment or on any opportunity for training or promotion. (s 247.1)

The employer's duties include issuing a policy statement that must contain:

- the definition of sexual harassment,
- a statement that every employee has the right to be free of sexual harassment and that the employer will take reasonable steps to ensure that employees are protected,

- a statement that disciplinary measures will be taken against any employee who subjects another person to sexual harassment,
- a process for bringing complaints to the attention of the employer,
- a statement indicating that the complainant's name will not be disclosed except where it is necessary for investigating the complaint or taking disciplinary measures, and
- a statement that directs employees to the *Canadian Human Rights Act* so that they understand their rights under the Act.

Enforcement

Enforcement of the provisions of the CLC is complaint-based. In other words, there is no regular inspection of employer practices that would identify problems. However, any employee covered by the legislation can make a complaint that their employer has contravened any provision of part III. The complaint must be made in writing and sent to an inspector. There are slightly different time frames and restrictions for different complaint types. For example, if the complaint is about non-payment of wages, the employee has six months from the date of the alleged non-payment to file a complaint. On the other hand, if the complaint is regarding an unjust dismissal, the employee must have been employed for at least 12 months, and the complaint must be filed within 90 days of the dismissal.

Inspectors are appointed by the minister of labour and have the authority to conduct investigations into complaints filed by employees within the requisite time frames. An inspector may require that the employer and complaining employee produce employment documents and records, typically including payroll and other records related to hours of work or conditions of employment. The CLC, in common with provincial employment standards legislation, requires that employers create and maintain certain employment records. These records must be kept for a minimum of 36 months after the work is performed. When wages are paid, the employer must include a statement that shows the pay period, hours worked, wage rate, deduction details, and total wage being paid. Employers are prohibited from making deductions other than those required by statute for taxes, the Canada Pension Plan, employment insurance, or union dues. Any other deductions must be authorized in writing by the employee.

If an inspector finds that an employer has failed to pay an employee wages or other amounts owed, the inspector can order payment. The inspector is also able to reject a complaint if the inspector feels that (1) they do not have jurisdiction, (2) the complaint is frivolous or vexatious, (3) the complaint has already been settled, (4) there is insufficient evidence to substantiate the complaint, or (5) the complaint is being dealt with in another forum (e.g., grievance arbitration in a unionized workplace). In any case, an appeal mechanism is in place should the losing party wish to dispute the decision of the inspector. If a payment order has been issued, the employer is not entitled to an appeal until the wages owed are paid to the minister, where they are held in trust until final adjudication of the complaint. Once this has occurred, a wage recovery referee will be appointed to adjudicate. The wages held in trust by the minister will be either returned to the employer or sent to the employee, in accordance with the decision of the wage recovery referee.

Any person who contravenes part III of the CLC; ignores or contravenes an order made by an inspector, referee, or adjudicator; or discharges or discriminates against someone who has filed a complaint is considered guilty of an offence. If convicted of the offence by a federal court, a corporation may be required to pay a fine of up to $50,000 for the first offence, $100,000 for a second offence, and $250,000 for each offence thereafter. An employee or unincorporated employer is liable for fines of up to $10,000, $20,000, and $50,000 for first, second, and third offences, respectively. Smaller fines ($1,000/day) apply for failing to keep or produce records for an inspector, while the $250,000 maximum is applied in cases where the employer has dismissed or disciplined an employee because of absence due to work-related illness or injury or where the employer has failed to purchase workers' compensation insurance.

REVIEW AND DISCUSSION QUESTIONS

1. Discuss employee rights with respect to unionization, the right to strike, and the right to bargain collectively.
   a. How is democracy a part of unionization?
   b. Is the right to unionize, bargain collectively, and go on strike necessary to balance power between employers and employees? Do other countries do it differently or better?
   c. What other ways can the power difference between employers and employees be balanced?
   d. What might occur if all employees were automatically unionized and could only decertify if they went through a decertification process?
2. Suzanne works for an oil and gas company as an engineer on pipeline projects, and her office is located in Calgary. While Suzanne is on a business trip in Vancouver, she slips and falls in the airport, breaking her leg. Is Suzanne's situation covered by federal or provincial legislation?
3. Compare the concept of "danger" in the occupational health and safety legislation in your province with that contained in the CLC. Are there any differences that could affect how the legislation is interpreted?
4. Barry was a 57-year-old truck driver who was dismissed after nearly ten years of service with XMD Trucking, a transportation company that carries goods across Canada and into the United States. Three years prior to his dismissal, he began experiencing difficulty with his back, which necessitated frequent rest breaks and a special seat that provided appropriate support. He was also unavailable to drive more often than when he was first hired. When Barry's back problem began to interfere with his schedule, XMD assigned him to an older truck and placed his seat in that truck. Barry was told he could "work on Barry time" and that this would be acceptable because the truck was paid off and every trip generated revenue. Seven months later, XMD terminated Barry's employment. Barry was given pay in lieu of notice and severance as required by the CLC, plus one extra week's salary. Barry filed a complaint alleging unjust dismissal. At the hearing, XMD argued that it was not required to have just cause, and as long as it paid him notice and severance that met the standards in the CLC, it was entitled to dismiss him. Was Barry unjustly dismissed?
5. AeroBC is a small passenger airline that primarily transports workers to and from the oil sands in Fort McMurray. The company had been booming for five years and expanded rapidly. When the price of oil took a dramatic downturn in 2018, the company's revenues went down along with it. It had 150 employees at the end of 2018, and in the early months of 2019, it determined it would have to lay off at least 40 percent of its workforce. None of AeroBC's employees is unionized.
   a. What procedure will the company have to follow in order to effect the termination without violating the CLC?
   b. What do you think might be included in an adjustment program?
6. Assume you are a finance manager for the Canadian Commercial Bank. You have noticed that the personality of one of your employees has changed drastically in the past few weeks. Melissa was always a happy employee, conscientious, and fun to be around. But she has been arriving to work late and is not herself. She rarely makes eye contact with anyone and has started sitting alone at lunch. She hasn't been to a company social function in almost six months. At first you thought it was because she was dating someone new and was spending all her time with him, but now you are not so sure. You call Melissa into your office to ask if there is something going on. At first she says she is fine, she promises she won't be late anymore, and then she starts to cry. You hand her a tissue and as she wipes away her tears, you see that she has a terrible bruise around her eye. When you ask her what happened she breaks down and tells you her new boyfriend hit her. They moved in together four months ago and he has become increasingly verbally abusive and now physically violent. What should you do? What is Melissa entitled to under the CLC?

REFERENCES

Alexander v Treasury Board (Department of Health), 2007 PSLRB 110.

Aviation Occupational Health and Safety Regulations, SOR/2011-87.

Canada Industrial Relations Board Regulations, 2012, SOR/2001-520.

Canada Industrial Relations Regulations, SOR/2002-54.

Canada Labour Code, RSC 1985, c L-2.

Canada Labour Standards Regulations, CRC c 986.

Canada Occupational Health and Safety Regulations, SOR/86-304.

Canadian Charter of Rights and Freedoms, Part I of the *Constitution Act, 1982*, being Schedule B to the *Canada Act 1982* (UK), 1982, c 11.

Canadian Human Rights Act, RSC 1985, c H-6.

Canadian Western Bank v Alberta, 2007 SCC 22.

Citizenship Act, RSC 1985, c C-29.

Coal Mining Occupational Health and Safety Regulations, SOR/90-97.

Employment Insurance Act, SC 1996, c 23.

Fine, Sean, "Canadian Workers Have Fundamental Right to Strike, Top Court Rules," *Globe and Mail* (30 January 2015), online: <https://www.theglobeandmail.com/news/national/top-court-upholds-canadian-workers-right-to-strike/article22717100/>.

Ford Motor Co of Canada v International Union United Automobile, Aircraft and Agricultural Implement Workers of America (UAW-CIO), [1946] OLAA No 1 (QL).

Government of Canada, "List of Federally Regulated Industries and Workplaces," online: <https://www.canada.ca/en/services/jobs/workplace/federally-regulated-industries.html>.

Hebdon, Robert, & Travor Brown, *Industrial Relations in Canada*, 2nd ed (Toronto: Nelson Education, 2012).

Insurance Companies Act, SC 1991, c 47.

Maritime Occupational Health and Safety Regulations, SOR/2010-120.

Masterson v Manufacturers Life Insurance Co, [2015] CLAD No 136 (QL).

National Defence Act, RSC 1985, c N-5.

Oil and Gas Occupational Safety and Health Regulations, SOR/87-612.

On Board Trains Occupational Health and Safety Regulations, SOR/87-184.

Saskatchewan Federation of Labour v Saskatchewan, 2015 SCC 4.

Tench v National Defence—Maritime Forces Atlantic, Nova Scotia, Decision No OHSTC-09-001.

Tryggvason v Transport Canada, 2012 OHSTC 10.

United Automobile Workers, Local 636 v FMC of Canada Ltd, Link-Belt Speeder Division (1971), 23 LAC 234.

Wilson v Atomic Energy of Canada Limited, 2016 SCC 29.

PART II

Legal Issues in Hiring and During the Course of Employment

Parties to an employment relationship must satisfy their legal obligations both during the hiring process and throughout the course of the relationship; these obligations, both common law and statutory, are examined in Part II.

The contractual agreement between an employer and an employee is the heart of the employment relationship in a non-union setting. It sets out the principal terms and conditions of employment. Chapter 5 examines the individual employment contract and associated common law issues and obligations.

Framing the employment relationship and providing additional legal boundaries are statutes that govern many of the rights and obligations of the workplace parties. These include employment standards statutes, human rights statutes, occupational health and safety statutes, and privacy statutes, among others. Unlike contractual obligations, these statutory requirements are non-negotiable; the parties cannot contract out of them. In British Columbia, the main statutes affecting individual employment relations are the *Employment Standards Act*, the *Human Rights Code*, the *Occupational Health and Safety Regulation*, the *Workers Compensation Act*, the *Labour Relations Code*, the *Freedom of Information and Protection of Privacy Act*, and the *Personal Information Protection Act*. Similarly, Alberta legislation includes the *Employment Standards Code*, the *Employment Standards Regulation*, the *Alberta Human Rights Act*, the *Occupational Health and Safety Act*, the *Occupational Health and Safety Code 2009*, the *Occupational Health and Safety Regulation*, the *Workers' Compensation Act*, the *Freedom of Information and Protection of Privacy Act*, and the *Personal Information Protection Act*. These statutes are examined in Chapters 6 through 10.

This part of the text frequently refers to unionized workplaces for several reasons. First, and most importantly, employment-related statutes, unlike the common law of individual employment contracts, apply to unionized and non-union employees alike. Therefore, how a particular legislative requirement affects the parties in the unionized context can illustrate how it applies in non-union workplaces as well. Second, where there are requirements that are unique to unionized workplaces, such as a union's duty to support accommodation measures under human rights legislation, briefly canvassing those requirements provides a broader understanding of the overall legislative framework. Finally, for some issues, such as workplace drug testing and privacy-related questions, the text touches on how these matters are typically dealt with by arbitrators under collective agreements to provide additional context.

Two federal statutes are also dealt with in this part. The *Employment Equity Act*, a federal statute, is considered in Chapter 7 because of its direct relevance to equity in the provincially regulated workplace. Chapter 10 focuses on the evolution of law related to privacy for employees, both on and off an employer's premises. The federal *Personal Information Protection and Electronic Documents Act* is relevant in this regard.

Finally, significant issues that are not covered by statute but that have legal implications under the common law, such as contractual amendments, performance management, discipline, and vicarious liability, are discussed in Chapter 11.

The Employment Contract

5

LEARNING OUTCOMES

After completing this chapter, you will be able to:

- Identify the legal requirements for a valid employment contract.
- Understand the advantages of a written employment contract over an oral contract.
- Identify common contractual terms and understand why they must be clearly drafted.
- Understand factors affecting the interpretation and enforceability of employment contracts, including lack of consideration, inequality of bargaining power, failure to meet statutory standards, and obsolescence.

Introduction

consideration
a mutual exchange of promises required, along with an offer and an acceptance, to create an enforceable contract; for example, in an employment contract, consideration is a promise of payment in exchange for a promise to perform the work

Every employment relationship is based on a contract, regardless of whether the contract is oral or written. Under the common law, three things are necessary to create a contract: an offer, acceptance of the offer, and **consideration** (something of value given or promised in exchange). A binding legal employment contract is created, therefore, wherever there is a job offer, an acceptance of that offer (noted by a clear "meeting of the minds" of the contracting parties), and the promise to exchange wages for work performed (the consideration). An oral contract that contains these elements is just as binding as a written one.

The employment relationship is, however, a special one within the law of contract, with its own history and particular legal issues. This chapter, therefore, both outlines the basic elements of all contracts and explores some of the legal issues that are particular to employment contracts.

Written Employment Contracts

Advantages of a Written Employment Contract

Despite the validity of an oral employment contract, a well-drafted written contract offers a number of significant benefits, which are set out below.

Reduces Risk of Misunderstandings

By specifying the rights and obligations of both the employer and the employee, a written contract reduces the risk of misunderstandings that could lead to disputes and lawsuits later on. It reflects a common understanding of the terms and conditions of employment that can always be referenced, even if the passage of time or staff changes make it difficult to recall the actual agreement made by the parties.

Addresses Potentially Contentious Issues Early

A written contract encourages the parties to deal with potentially contentious issues early in their relationship, when they are positively disposed to one another. Furthermore, because both the employer and the employee have a strong incentive to reach an agreement that is mutually satisfactory, contentious issues are likely to be dealt with in a constructive manner.

Reduces Uncertainty

If a dispute arises and the parties take the matter to court, a well-drafted employment contract provides the court with a clear record of the terms and conditions of employment. In contrast, the terms of an oral agreement are those that the court finds the parties agreed to and those that are implied by law. Where the matter in dispute relates to terms agreed to and an oral agreement was made, both parties will have the problem of convincing the court that, on a balance of probabilities, their version is the truest. For example, the employer and employee may, after the start of employment, disagree on how sales commissions are to be calculated. If the formula is not in writing, the parties may end up in court trying to prove that their own recollection of the agreement is more accurate than that of the other party.

Implied Terms

Where the issue in dispute was *not* addressed in an oral or written contract, a court will sometimes import **implied terms** into the agreement. This means that the court considers what terms the parties would likely have agreed on had they put their minds to the issue; it then deems those terms to be part of the contract. Because of the special nature of the employment relationship, by contrast to other contracts, the courts have also developed a set of standard implied terms that reflect what they believe the employer's and employee's rights and obligations ought to be, unless expressly stated otherwise in the agreement. These implied terms, long established at common law, are one of the reasons that employment contracts are often relatively short: the courts have already established some of the basic terms, so the employer and employee need not set those terms down in writing, unless they want to change them.

implied terms
default or mandatory rules that the courts assume are part of an employment agreement, even if they have not been expressly included in the employment contract

One of the most important implied obligations of an employer is reasonable notice of termination. This means that, in the absence of an express term relating to the contract's duration and termination notice (i.e., a termination clause), the courts will find that the contract implies an obligation of the employer to provide the employee with reasonable notice of termination in the absence of serious misconduct (referred to in this book as the "common law notice period"). Employers can instead give the employee pay in lieu of notice, an amount equal to the wages and benefits the employee would have received during the notice period (see Chapter 14). What constitutes "reasonable" notice depends on the particular facts of each case. Conversely, as the Supreme Court of Canada reconfirmed in the 2008 decision *RBC Dominion Securities Inc v Merrill Lynch Canada Inc*, employees have an implied duty to provide reasonable notice of resignation and can be liable for damages suffered if such notice is not given.

Employers also have an implied duty to provide the employee with the tools and training necessary to do the job properly and to provide a safe workplace (including a workplace free from harassment—see Chapter 7).

The most important implied term for an employee is the duty of good faith—that is, the duty to advance the interests of the employer while employed. An employee cannot, for example, compete with the employer during the term of the employment relationship or make improper use of the employer's confidential information. Employees also have a duty to do their work competently and honestly, which includes punctuality. Many of these implied duties are part of the law on just cause for dismissal. Chapters 13 and 14 explore these terms in the context of dismissal.

How Formal Should a Written Contract Be?

When a job is a senior position or when special issues are involved, the parties may want a written contract that is formal and comprehensive. For example, in the high-tech sector, it may be important to address confidentiality, non-solicitation, and non-competition obligations.

However, for most employment relationships, the written contract can be more basic. It often consists of a letter from the employer offering the employee a job and setting out the key terms and conditions, such as salary, benefits, start date, title, and job duties. Another essential element is the termination clause, since this can prevent costly **litigation** regarding reasonable notice. The offer letter may also specifically refer to the employer's policy manual, so that its policies covering such matters as discipline, probationary periods, absence, safety, and harassment are **incorporated by reference** into the employment contract, and thereby become part of the terms of employment. Incorporating the manual into the contract can be important in wrongful dismissal cases, since violations of the manual would support the employer's argument that it had just cause to fire the employee (but see the *ASM Corrosion Control* case below, under "Lack of Consideration," about the need to notify employees of changes to the manual).

litigation
legal action

incorporated by reference
when a second document is included as part of a first document because it is listed or named within the first document

Common Contractual Terms

In addition to being clearly drafted, written employment contracts should be customized to reflect the issues that are important to both the employer and the employee. Employers should be cautious of the temptation to use a single, standard contract for all employees. One size does not always fit all circumstances.

All employment contracts rest on the same general principles; however, the level of formality and detail varies. As noted above, for most employment relationships a letter of hire that sets out key terms and expressly incorporates the employer's policy manual may be sufficient. Key terms include the names of the parties, the date the job begins, a job title and description, the duration of the contract (if it is for a fixed term), the compensation offered, and the termination clause. For managerial positions, positions that involve a high degree of skill, and positions that require specific contractual terms (such as a non-competition clause), a formal contract is advisable. Executives and skilled employees may require the inclusion of details about bonuses, pension arrangements, stock options, and specifically negotiated **perks**.

perk
short for "perquisite," a bonus or benefit, particularly one owed to a job incumbent

The written contract provides both parties with the opportunity to set out their expectations, thereby reducing the risk of misunderstandings that can later lead to disputes and litigation. The employer may want to maintain sufficient flexibility so that, as circumstances change, it can make adjustments without risking a claim from the employee that it has fundamentally breached the contract. For example, where hours of work are included, the contract may stipulate that hours of work may vary from time to time.

A sample indefinite-term contract is set out in Appendix A to this text, and a sample fixed-term contract is set out in Appendix B.

An employment contract may include any terms that are not prohibited by law. The following are some of the more important topics that may be addressed in a written contract, along with suggestions for minimizing the risk of legal problems associated with them.

Job Description

Setting out the position and broad job duties clarifies the expectations of both parties and reduces the potential for misunderstandings. However, in the absence of contractual language that allows the employer to modify responsibilities, the employee is entitled to refuse to perform duties that fall outside the original agreement.

For example, in *Tanton v Crane Canada Inc*, the plaintiff had worked for the defendant in Edmonton as a warehouseman from January 1973 to July 1998. He was described by the Alberta Court of Queen's Bench as

> a person whose intellectual capacities would have been apparent to any other person of reasonable discernment. He had some difficulty understanding complex questions, and his memory capacity was limited. He … fit his position well, and … [was] a solid and steady employee, who could perform routine and even tedious and repetitive tasks.

The plaintiff also had physical incapacities involving one shoulder and one foot. When a new supervisor was hired to streamline operations and make the business more profitable, he altered the plaintiff's job assignment, purporting to "cross-train" him for other work, despite specific documentation on the plaintiff's past performance records indicating that "he is at his peak now" and "the ratings do not suggest ready capacity to take on new tasks." The plaintiff "quit under duress" and was unable to **mitigate** by finding other work, though he attempted unsuccessfully to get work at an institution for people with disabilities. The Alberta Court of Queen's Bench concluded that Lindsay Tanton had been constructively dismissed from the position he had steadfastly held for 25 years. He was awarded 24 months' notice. (For more information about constructive dismissal, see Chapters 11 and 14.)

mitigate
to make reasonable efforts to reduce damage or harm; the law imposes a duty to mitigate on anyone who suffers a loss, even if someone else is at fault; in employment law, mitigation means seeking a new job upon dismissal

Issues arising from an employer-modified job description can be lessened (but probably not eliminated entirely) with language in the contract that expressly allows the employer to change the duties of the job. For example, the contract could state that the employer may assign "any and all other duties as may be required from time to time."

Remuneration

The terms of an employment contract must at least match statutory minimum requirements. For example, a contract cannot contain a term that allows for overtime premium pay that is less than that required under provincial employment standards legislation. If it does, the term is null and void. (See Chapter 6 for a discussion of the requirements of employment standards legislation.)

There is no obligation to provide for future pay increases in the contract. The contract may be silent on this point or simply state that the employee's remuneration may increase or decrease in the future, based on performance evaluations. Contracts for executives may also contain details of bonus structures and stock options.

Term

An employment contract that covers a fixed period of time or a particular task must state the term or task. Otherwise, the contract is considered to cover an indefinite period. Hiring for a fixed term or task (as long as the task is well defined and of limited duration) relieves the employer of the obligation to provide reasonable notice of termination, because at the end of the term or task, employment simply ends. Creating a fixed-term or fixed-task contract limits the employer's liability and provides both parties with an opportunity to evaluate their working relationship.

However, there are various cautions to consider when creating and administering fixed-term contracts. Some are considered here. First, where the contract is, in substance, an indefinite one and the employer uses a series of rolling, fixed-term contracts simply to avoid statutory and common law termination requirements, courts are less likely to enforce the term. This was illustrated in the case of *Ceccol v Ontario Gymnastic Federation*, in which the employer provided a series of fixed-term one-year contracts. The Ontario Court of Appeal had little difficulty ruling the employment was indefinite and awarded common law notice for 17 years instead of the last one-year contract. It is prudent for the parties to negotiate a fair termination provision in an indefinite-term contract rather than attempt to frame the employment relationship with a series of fixed terms.

The second caution with fixed-term or fixed-task contracts is that monitoring and renewing them can pose an administrative challenge for employers, especially if the contracts expire at different times. If a renewal date is missed but the contract work nevertheless continues, a fixed-term contract becomes a contract for an indefinite term pursuant to employment standards legislation, which then requires an employer to provide the employee with common law notice, pay in lieu, or a combination of notice and pay in lieu. The contract may be written to address this matter by providing for automatic renewal. In this case, if the employer intends to terminate or alter the relationship at the end of the contract, it must do so in a timely manner, because the contract will otherwise be renewed automatically for the same fixed term.

Finally, employees hired on a fixed-term or fixed-task basis generally are required to be employed for the entire term or task. If an employer terminates an employee before the end of that period, damages are based on the remainder of the term, which might prove more costly to an employer than pay in lieu of common law notice for an indefinite-term employee. For example, if the employee's contract is for 12 months and the employer terminates the contract after only 2 months, the employer may be liable for the remainder of the contract (10 months) rather than for common law notice equivalent for a 2-month employee.

These issues can be addressed by including a termination clause in the fixed-term contract stating that either party is entitled to terminate the contract by giving the other party two (or three or four) weeks' written notice.

Termination

The amount of notice due to an employee on termination (without cause) is typically the most contentious issue in the employment contract (see Chapter 14). However, the benefits of dealing with the thorny issue up front, while the relationship between the parties is positive, are significant. Otherwise, the common law presumption of "reasonable notice" applies, and such notice is often more generous and less predictable than that provided for in most employment contracts.

To understand matters related to the enforceability of the termination clause, the parties should review their obligations regarding written contracts (discussed under the heading "Enforceability and Interpretation of Written Contracts," below), especially the requirement to meet or exceed the statutory minimum notice requirements. As illustrated by the decision in *Stevens v Sifton Properties Ltd*, termination clauses that fail to meet the statutory minimum standards *in every aspect and at any point in the employment relationship* are likely to be found to be invalid.

In addition, the termination clause should be clearly expressed because *clear language is required to rebut the common law presumption that an employee is entitled to reasonable notice*. Furthermore, the termination clause should be specifically brought to the employee's attention, and both parties should sign off on it before the employment relationship commences. This advice applies whether the termination clause is found in a formal written contract, a letter of hire, or the employer's policy manual that is incorporated into the employment agreement. *Christensen v Family Counselling Centre of Sault Ste Marie and District* shows the importance of clear language expressing the agreement of the parties when rebutting the common law presumption that an employee is entitled to reasonable notice.

contra proferentem
the doctrine of interpreting ambiguous contract language against the interests of the party that drafted the language

CASE IN POINT

Termination Provisions Insufficiently Clear to Rebut Common Law Presumption

Christensen v Family Counselling Centre of Sault Ste Marie and District, 2001 CanLII 4698 (Ont CA)

Facts

Christensen had worked as a therapist for the employer counselling centre for seven years when her employment was terminated as a result of funding cuts. On termination, she received ten weeks' pay. Her employment contract was the initial letter of offer, which did not address termination, except as it related to the probationary period. The contract referred to the policy manual, which was not sent with the letter of offer but which the employee received during her first week of work. The termination provisions in the manual were never explained to her. The trial judge found that the termination clauses were capable of at least four interpretations, and the Court applied the interpretation most favourable to the employee under the ***contra proferentem*** rule.

Relevant Issue

Whether the termination provisions limited Christensen's common law entitlement to reasonable notice or pay in lieu.

Decision

The Ontario Court of Appeal held that the key factor was whether the provision was sufficiently clear to rebut the common law presumption of reasonable notice. To rebut this presumption, the employer should have expressed its intention clearly and brought the clause to Christensen's attention when she was hired. An ambiguous notice provision cannot rebut the common law presumption in favour of reasonable notice. The Court awarded Christensen eight months' pay in lieu of reasonable notice of termination.

Termination Clauses and the Duty to Mitigate

The duty to mitigate refers to the obligation placed on a dismissed employee to look for a job that is comparable to the one from which the employee has been dismissed during the common law reasonable notice period. If the dismissed employee is successful, earnings from that new job will reduce any wrongful dismissal damages owed by the employer. (See Chapter 14 under the heading "The Duty to Mitigate.") This duty clearly applies where there is no enforceable termination provision in the employment contract and the period of reasonable notice is established as an implied term of the contract under the common law. However, until recently, case law has been mixed about whether the duty to mitigate applies where an employment contract specifically sets out the length of termination notice (or a specific amount of termination pay) and is silent on the duty to mitigate. However, in the 2012 case of *Bowes v Goss Power Products Ltd*, the Ontario Court of Appeal confirmed unequivocally that where an employment contract contains a stipulated entitlement on termination without cause and is silent on the duty to mitigate, the employee will not be required to mitigate. In the Court's view, in the context of the employment relationship, deciding otherwise would be unfair. As Winkler CJ notes:

> It is worthy of emphasis that, in most cases, employment agreements are drafted primarily, if not exclusively, by the employer. In my view, there is nothing unfair about requiring employers to be explicit if they intend to require an employee to mitigate what would otherwise be fixed or liquidated damages. In fact, what is unfair is for an employer to agree upon a fixed amount of damages, and then, at the point of dismissal, inform the employee that future earnings will be deducted from the fixed amount. (at para 55)

BC courts have affirmed that the rule in *Bowes* is equally well settled in the law of BC. In the 2014 decision *Maxwell v British Columbia*, the Court of Appeal again affirmed this, and went on to say:

> Where a contract provides for the effect of termination, generally the provisions of the contract prevail. Recourse to the common law is not required. In some circumstances, the contract may require mitigation, but where it does not the innocent party is entitled to what was agreed … .
>
> In the present case, the contract specifically provides that if the respondent was terminated without cause, "the College shall provide an all-inclusive payment in lieu of notice." It continues to specify the components of that payment. I see no basis on which it could be contended that the respondent was obliged to mitigate and that her failure to do so would relieve the appellants from their contractual obligations. (at paras 27 and 28)

To avoid the result in *Bowes*, *Maxwell*, and similar cases, an employer must make sure that its contractual termination provisions expressly establish a duty to mitigate. This applies whether the employment contract is for a fixed term or an indefinite period (Thompson & Lambert, 2013). However, it is important to note that an employee's minimum entitlement to pay in lieu of termination notice under employment standards legislation cannot be made subject to mitigation in a contract—those amounts are generally payable whether or not the dismissed employee mitigates.

Other Terms Related to the Termination Clause

In addition to specifying the termination notice owed to the employee on dismissal without cause—and the duty to mitigate—the parties may decide to include other terms related to termination. For example, the employer may want to include a definition of "just cause" to establish the conduct that would justify dismissal without notice or pay in lieu of notice.[1]

The termination clause may also set out the method by which termination pay is to be paid. For example, it could provide for payment by lump sum, salary continuance, or a combination of the two. The employer may also want to stipulate that salary continuance ends when the employee finds a comparable job, also known as "bridging."

Finally, the parties may want to address the issue of the employee's obligation to provide advance notice of resignation. This is especially important for an employer if the employee has specialized skills or holds a key position. Reasonable notice of resignation depends on the difficulty involved in finding a suitable replacement for the departing employee and does not directly equate with the length of notice that an employer may be required to provide to an employee. In *Torcana Valve Services Inc v Anderson*, the Alberta Court of Queen's Bench determined that while

> all employees are required to give reasonable notice, ... [i]n the absence of special circumstances, two weeks' notice in the case of an ordinary employee and four weeks' notice in the case of a more senior one

will generally be the appropriate common law standard (at para 79).

Probationary Period

Employers often want a period of time at the beginning of the employment relationship during which they may dismiss an employee without being obliged to provide reasonable notice under the common law. This gives the employer a window of time in which to evaluate the new employee's suitability for the position. Under the common law, however, a probationary period is not an implied term of an employment contract. Therefore, to incorporate a probationary period, the contract *must* expressly provide for it in writing.

It is somewhat unclear under the case law whether an employee may be summarily dismissed (i.e., dismissed without notice) during the probationary period at the employer's sole discretion, or whether the employer must provide objective reasons for its decision to avoid paying termination pay.

The tests to justify dismissing an employee during probation have been set forth by the Alberta Court of Appeal in *Rocky Credit Union Ltd v Higginson*. To justify the dismissal of an employee on probation, the employer need only establish that (1) the employee had been given a reasonable chance to show that they were suitable for

---

1 An example of a generic just cause clause would read something like "Notwithstanding any other paragraph of this Agreement, the Employer may end your employment at any time for just cause, without notice or pay in lieu of notice."

the position, based on standards the employer set out upon hiring; (2) the employer had found the employee to be unsuitable; and (3) the employer's decision was based on

> an honest, fair and reasonable assessment of the suitability of the employee, including not only job skills and performance but character, judgment, compatibility, reliability, and future with the company. (at para 6)

In cases of a probationary review, the Court added, it would not require the employer to establish actual cause. However, many contracts include a contractual provision concerning the probationary period that expressly allows the employer to terminate the employee at any time, and for any reason, within the first three months of employment without having to provide any notice or pay in lieu of notice (Israel, 2 April 2003).

In the absence of such a clause, however, employers likely have to be able to defend the dismissal by demonstrating that the employee was not suitable—and that the employee was given in advance some sense of what suitability entailed. This is apparent in the 2012 case *Geller v Sable Resources Ltd.* In this case, an employer dismissed a new employee without notice. The employee, an apprentice heavy-duty mechanic, balked when asked to work alone at a mine during his time off, without the supervision and on-the-job training he had been told to expect from a senior mechanic. The employer dismissed him without cause and justified the dismissal by saying that he was on probation. The BC Supreme Court applied the test in *Higginson* and determined that the dismissal was wrongful, since the dismissal was based on expectations that were contrary to what the employer had told the mechanic at the time of his hiring (the promised training and supervision by a senior mechanic) and contrary to the contract (asking him to work during his contractual time off). As this case demonstrates, dismissal during probation need not be for cause, but it must not run contrary to the expectations the employer gave the employee at the outset.

Probationary periods are typically three to six months, depending on the nature of the position. The assessment period is usually shorter for people employed to perform simple and repetitive tasks than it is for people who are employed in more demanding and varied positions (Echlin & Thomlinson, 2011, at 64).

Under Alberta's *Employment Standards Code* (s 55(2)(b)) and BC's *Employment Standards Act* (s 63(1)), employees who have been employed for three months or less are not entitled to statutory notice of termination or compensation. However, statutory notice or compensation is required after three months' service. Therefore, where the probationary period under a contract exceeds three months, the employer must give notice or compensation to an employee who is dismissed after three months unless the dismissal occurs for reasons exempted from the statutory requirements. For example, if the contract calls for a probationary period of six months and the employee is terminated after four months because the employer is dissatisfied with the employee's performance, the employer must provide one week's wages or notice of termination, in accordance with section 56(a) of the Alberta Act and section 63(1) of the BC Act. (In Alberta, it increases to two weeks after two or more years [s 58(1)(b)]. In BC, the required compensation for length of service [or notice instead of compensation] increases to two weeks after one year of consecutive employment, then three weeks after three years, then one additional week per year up to eight weeks [s 63(2)]. See Chapter 6 for more on these acts and Chapter 14 for a review of the statutory notice and compensation rules.)

This notice is necessary even though the termination occurs during the contractual probationary period and no reasonable notice is required under the common law. It is essential that the contractual provisions regarding notice of termination during any probationary period longer than three months take this statutory requirement into account; otherwise, the entire provision may be found unenforceable. A 2014 BC case illustrates this risk. In *Miller v Convergys*, an employee of three years was promoted. His new contract's termination clauses contained a typical probationary clause—apparently included by mistake, due to the careless use of a template for new employees—that said he could be dismissed during probation without notice or pay in lieu. It also specified the notice he was entitled to, if dismissed outside the probation period, setting that amount at the minimum standard in the *Employment Standards Act*. The employer dismissed him some time later and offered pay in lieu according to the contract's terms. The employee sued for common law notice, and argued that all of the termination provisions were invalid, since the probationary clause violated the Act: as an employee of three years at the time he started the new contract, the probationary "dismissal with no notice" rule violated section 63. His argument might have succeeded, but the contract also contained a severability clause, which stated that if any one clause was unenforceable, that clause would be severed, and the remainder of the contract would be valid (see the discussion under the heading "Severability Clause," below). The Court therefore upheld the employer's offered severance package, and the employee lost. The case is a good illustration of the importance of careful attention to employment contracts—as well as the value of a severability provision. (For more on the unenforceability of clauses that contradict basic employment standards legislation, see below).

Relocation

If a transfer to another city or region is a potential issue, the parties should address the matter in the contract. Otherwise, if the employer decides to transfer the employee, they could become embroiled in an unnecessary dispute about whether the right to relocate is an implied term of the contract. An employee could argue, for example, that the relocation constitutes a fundamental breach of contract and therefore amounts to constructive dismissal. (For more information about constructive dismissal, see Chapters 11 and 14.) However, if having the discretion to transfer the prospective employee is not significant to the employer but is a serious concern for the employee, the contract can expressly provide that there is no employer right to require relocation (Echlin & Thomlinson, 2011, at 65).

Benefits

Employment contracts can provide the details of benefit entitlements, including medical and dental benefits, vacation, and use of a company car, laptop computer, or other mobile device. Some benefit entitlements may not come into effect until several months after work begins. If this is the case, the delay should be set out in the contract so that the employee is not caught unaware.

The parties may also choose to establish how benefits will be dealt with in the event of dismissal or resignation.

Restrictive Covenants

Restrictive covenants are clauses that protect an employer's business interests by restricting what an employee can do during, and especially after, employment with regard to such matters as confidential information and customer lists. The three main types of restrictive covenants are set out below (see also Chapter 2):

1. *Non-disclosure clauses.* Also called confidentiality clauses, these clauses prevent a departing employee from using and disclosing confidential information related to the employer after employment ends.
2. *Non-solicitation clauses.* If enforceable, these clauses prevent a departing employee from soliciting the employer's customers, clients, or possibly employees. For example, an employee may agree that they will not initiate contact with their employer's customers for one year after employment ends.
3. *Non-competition clauses.* If enforceable, these clauses prevent a departing employee from competing with the employer. They are typically drafted to restrict competition for a specific time within a specific geographic area. For example, an employee could agree that they will not start up a business that competes with the employer's in the city where the employee has worked for the employer for 12 months after employment ends.

Non-disclosure clauses that simply limit the employee's use of the employer's confidential information are usually enforceable. The employer should clarify with employees what information it considers confidential and consistently enforce those guidelines. Confidential information includes such things as customer lists and information, intellectual property, and marketing plans.

FYI

New Frontiers—Who Owns the Customer Contacts on Social Media?

It is a long-standing principle in employment law that an employee cannot print a customer list, take it home (or email it to themself), and then use it to compete against their former employer (Pugen, 2013). But what if the competitive information is on social media sites such as LinkedIn? The law in this area is still developing. A 2013 decision in the United Kingdom found that the traditional obligation of an employee to not steal an employer's confidential or proprietary information applies to an employer's contacts on a LinkedIn page. However, this case did not deal with an employer's interest in an employee's personal LinkedIn account (Pugen, 2013). In *Eagle Professional Resources Inc v MacMullin*, the Ontario Court of Appeal decided that three employees who allegedly contacted their former employer's customers did not breach the non-solicitation provision in their employment contracts. The employees successfully argued that they relied only on publicly available information taken from social media sites such as LinkedIn, and the employer did not have a proprietary interest over the content (Stam, 2013).

Employees, especially those in sales, are often encouraged to use social media sites (Twitter, Facebook, LinkedIn, and so on) to connect with customers and prospective customers. Given the ease with which former employees can now reconnect with contacts made with or for an employer online, courts are having to make "awkward distinctions ... between information that could be memorized or in the public domain and information committed to writing or electronic storage" (Kempf, 2013).

To try to protect its interests in this unsettled area of the law, an employer should consider doing the following:

- Ensure that its databases and its presence on social media sites are maintained on its premises by employees who use only the employer's equipment and receive compensation for doing so (as per their job descriptions).
- Set clear privacy and confidentiality policy guidelines regarding its social media networking information *that is available to everyone who has access to this information.*
- Make all employees aware of its proprietary interest in all contact management software, including social media.
- Keep its social media groups and networking separate from employees' personal social media profiles or groups (Pugen, 2013).

Courts are more suspicious of non-solicitation and non-competition clauses because they affect a former employee's ability to earn a living in that person's area of expertise or in their usual geographic location. Courts will be seeking evidence to demonstrate that the restrictions only go as far as reasonably necessary to protect the legitimate business interests of the employer. In the case of a dispute over a non-solicitation clause, a court will examine the clause carefully to ensure that it is reasonable in the circumstances. The onus is on the employer to show that the clause is reasonable in the circumstances because, for example, the employee's job involved significant contact with and knowledge of customers and suppliers and that its business would be impacted by a breach of the non-solicitation clause.

Understanding that a company's stock-in-trade may not be a fleet of trucks, a herd of cattle, or a unique set of production machinery, but rather may be business information and knowledge, the protection of that information from competitors in the same field could rely heavily on the enforceability of restrictive covenants. Freight forwarding and logistical services in Calgary and Western Canada were at the heart of a non-solicitation and non-competition dispute in *Unified Freight Services v Therriault.* Unified Freight was a broker, locating transport companies to move commodities from one location to another. Michael Therriault was a company supervisor and a key employee known to be considering alternative employment options. He was observed on a number of occasions removing client information from the office in violation of express provisions in the company policy manual. The owner of Unified Freight sought advice from a lawyer and from the Calgary Police Service Economic Crimes Unit. He then terminated Therriault, advising him that he must return all documents removed from the office or deal with the police. The owner accompanied Therriault to his residence in Calgary, where confidential company records, including a 150-page master client list, were retrieved from four different locations: the garage, a storage room, a home office, and a company vehicle.

Despite having signed non-solicitation and non-competition clauses when he was terminated, Therriault wrote to a number of clients just ten days later, eventually advising them how to get in touch with him. The Alberta Court of Queen's Bench determined that as a key employee Therriault was a fiduciary, and that Unified

Freight was left in a particularly vulnerable position after Therriault's removal of its proprietary client information (see the discussion under the heading "Implied Duty to Maintain Confidentiality," below). The breadth and extent of the infraction was seen as confirmation that Therriault had breached his contractual obligations repeatedly and deliberately, with the motive of expediting a later return to the marketplace either on his own or with a competing employer. Accordingly, the Court found for the plaintiff and awarded Unified Freight $96,711.75 for its loss.

Courts take a stringent approach with non-competition clauses because they actually prevent former employees from working in a particular area for a fixed time. These clauses are viewed as a restraint of trade, and they are presumed invalid unless the employer shows that:

- the non-competition clause is necessary to protect the employer's legitimate business interests,
- the non-competition clause covers a reasonable length of time and geographic area, and
- a non-solicitation clause would not adequately protect the employer's legitimate interests in the circumstances (Israel, 2004).

When allegations of a breach of a confidentiality clause or non-solicitation agreement are made, it is not uncommon for employers to request an interim injunction. However, employers should not expect the injunction to provide sweeping restrictions on the activities of the former employees. Courts have ruled that injunctions should not be unnecessarily broad—otherwise, they may have the same effect as a non-competition clause. Two relatively recent, successful interim injunction cases in BC and Alberta, respectively, are *Phoenix Restorations Ltd v Drisdelle* and *Peters & Co Limited v Ward*. In each case, the former employees had emailed themselves and photocopied client lists and other information before leaving employment, in hopes of using that information in the new workplace. In a more recent BC case, *Quick Pass Master Tutorial School Ltd v Zhao,* the Court clarified (citing *Phoenix*):

> The Confidential Information Clause is not a restrictive covenant. Rather, it is "intended to protect the right of a business to keep confidential the information it hopes will help it to compete, so the usual relatively low threshold applies to it." This means that Quick Pass need only prove that its claim with respect to this clause is not frivolous or vexatious and the court need not engage in an extensive review of the merits of the claim. (at para 30)

The key to creating enforceable restrictive covenants is to be clear and to go no further than is necessary to protect the employer's legitimate business interests. For example, in industries where state-of-the-art information changes rapidly, a non-competition clause that extends beyond 12 months is probably unenforceable. There must also be a reasonable link between the employee's expertise or position and the scope of the clause. It is inadvisable to use a standard clause for all employees.

Another consideration is whether the duration and scope of the clause is the industry norm. Clauses that are more restrictive than those typical of the industry are less likely to be enforced by the courts. *Mason v Chem-Trend Limited Partnership* provides an example of a court weighing both the duration and scope of the non-competition clause in determining reasonableness.

CASE IN POINT

"Less Is More" in Non-Competition Clauses

Mason v Chem-Trend Limited Partnership, 2010 ONSC 4119

Facts

Mason was a salesperson at a chemical products manufacturer. After 17 years of service he was dismissed, allegedly for cause. His employment contract contained the following non-competition clause that prohibited him from competing with the employer for one year after termination—with no geographic restriction:

> I agree that if my employment is terminated for any reason by me or by the Company, I will not, for a period of one year following the termination, directly or indirectly, for my own account or as an employee or agent of any business entity, engage in any business or activity in competition with the Company by providing services or products to, or soliciting business from, any business entity which was a customer of the Company during the period in which I was an employee of the Company, or take any action that will cause the termination of the business relationship between the Company and any customer, or solicit for employment any person employed by the Company.

Mason applied to court for a declaration that the non-competition clause was unenforceable. The application judge upheld the restriction, finding that the unlimited geographic scope was reasonable: the employer's business was global, as a salesperson Mason had extensive access to confidential customer information, and one year was a relatively short period of time for non-competition clauses within the industry. The Court also noted that the clause was clearly worded and understood by the employee when he signed it. Mason appealed the Court's decision.

Issue

Whether the non-competition clause was enforceable.

Decision

The Court of Appeal found that although the non-competition clause was clearly written, and the one-year limit was well within the industry norm for salespeople, the clause was overly broad in other respects. Completely prohibiting Mason from competing for one year anywhere in the world constituted an unreasonable geographic scope. Furthermore, preventing him from doing business with "any business entity which was a customer of the Company" was an unworkable restriction. Mason had no way of knowing every customer the employer had had during his 17-year tenure. Finally, the employer's legitimate interest in its trade secrets and other confidential information was already protected by the non-disclosure clauses within the agreement.

As well, a court is more likely to find the restrictive covenant valid if the employee had a genuine opportunity to negotiate its terms, including the opportunity to seek independent legal advice.

Finally, the restrictive covenant's wording must be unambiguous. In *Shafron v KRG Insurance Brokers (Western) Inc*, the restrictive covenant prohibited the defendant insurance broker from competing with the employer within the "Metropolitan City of Vancouver" for a period of three years after leaving its employ. The trial judge refused to enforce the agreement, finding that the term "Metropolitan City of

Vancouver" was ambiguous because there was no such legal municipal entity. The BC Court of Appeal agreed that the term was ambiguous but decided that it could be made enforceable if the Court notionally severed part of that term from the agreement and read down the geographic scope so that it would be reasonable. On appeal, the Supreme Court of Canada overturned that decision. Noting the potential power imbalance between employees and employers, it reasoned that employers should not be allowed to negotiate overly broad non-competition clauses and then rely on the courts to read them down to the broadest scope that they consider reasonable. The Court concluded that restrictive covenants should be strictly construed; an ambiguous covenant is, by definition, unreasonable and unenforceable.

Given the long-standing reluctance of courts to enforce non-competition clauses in employment contracts, employers can mitigate their exposure by using non-solicitation clauses. Not only are non-solicitation clauses more likely to be enforced (although, as noted above, they too have to pass the "reasonableness" test), but they also enable former employees to look for work in the same industry as part of mitigating their losses (Levitt, 2013). Employers can also use customized contractual language that is detailed, specific, reasonable, and unambiguous.

Ownership of Intellectual Property

Intellectual property, such as inventions, patents, and copyright, is important for many companies, including those that develop electronics or computer software. An ownership clause deals with the ownership of intellectual property or inventions developed by the employee in the course of employment. It is useful to establish ownership of intellectual property early in the employment relationship to avoid potentially bitter disputes later if the employee develops a commercially viable product. The ownership clause typically provides that intellectual property that the employee invents or develops during the normal course of employment belongs to the employer (see *Seanix Technology Inc v Ircha*).

CASE IN POINT

Employer Rightful Owner of Invention Created on the Job

Seanix Technology Inc v Ircha, 1998 CanLII 6772 (BCSC)

Facts

Ircha, a mechanical engineer and designer, was employed to design computer cases and to comment on subcontractors' design work on such cases. While so employed, he invented a "computer case with swing-out motherboard/backplane support." The employee conceived and developed the basic idea for the invention at home, since he did not have design facilities at work. In early 1996, Ircha showed the design to his employer to demonstrate that he could do design work. In June 1996, he started an application for a patent for the swing-out apparatus, in his own name. Over the summer and fall, he negotiated with Seanix a better salary and even a joint venture with his employer in the production of new cases based on his design. However, Ircha was dissatisfied with the results of those negotiations, and he left Seanix's employment in November 1996. By August of the following year, the patent office was demanding further particulars, but the employer took the position that the patent belonged to it.

The parties went to court on an application for summary judgment in the BC Supreme Court to resolve the matter.

Relevant Issue

Whether patent rights to something invented by an employee while employed belong to the employee or the employer after the employment is terminated.

Decision

The Court ruled that the employer company was the rightful owner of the invention and was entitled to patent rights in it. The mere fact that an invention occurs while an employee is an employee is not what gives the employer a *prima facie* right to the intellectual property: it is that the invention is the product of the very work that the employee is paid to do. The judge repeated *obiter dicta* from an earlier BC Supreme Court decision (*Spiroll Corp Ltd v Putti*), subsequently adopted and applied by the Federal Court of Canada, which said

> a court must first find *what* the employee is engaged to do and, if he invents something while performing that function, it belongs to the employer. If he is employed to design then it would be a "normal incident" of his contract of employment that he should do so and that the result of his ingenuity should belong to his employer. (at 292-93)

In factual contrast to the *Ircha* case, a 2014 BC decision held that a college instructor did own intellectual property he created at his place of employment, since its creation was not specifically part of his duties. In *Mejia v LaSalle College International Vancouver Inc*, Mejia, the plaintiff, was a computer design and photography instructor who took a photograph in a classroom of a college student participating in a college event. The college used the image in its marketing materials, including its Facebook page. When the college fired the instructor for reasons unrelated to the photograph, he sued for wrongful dismissal and violation of copyright. It was unclear whether the photograph was taken during actual class time, but what decided the case for the Court was that the instructor's contract specified that he was paid to teach. His duties did not include taking photographs. Citing *Ircha*, the Court held that in this case the employee had not created intellectual property "in the course of employment." The instructor won damages, albeit a small amount in this case.

Choice of Law

A choice-of-law clause specifies the jurisdiction whose laws govern the contract. Often the jurisdiction is obvious. An employment contract between an Alberta-based employer that hires an Alberta-based employee is interpreted according to the laws of Alberta. However, where an Alberta employer hires an employee to work in another province or country or where someone from another jurisdiction is hired to work in Alberta, jurisdiction could be disputed. For this reason, an employment contract should stipulate which jurisdiction's laws govern its terms. The same applies for BC.

In BC, since 2003, an Act called the *Court Jurisdiction and Proceedings Transfer Act* has been in effect. This legislation is an important codification of basic principles relating to choice of law. Section 11(2) lists six major circumstances that a court will consider before deciding whether it or a court outside BC is the appropriate forum for that matter.

One consideration in determining which law should govern the contract is costs. A party who becomes involved in a legal dispute in another jurisdiction can incur significant additional litigation costs. On the other hand, where the employment contract has some connection with the United States—if, for example, an employee is hired to work in the US—an Alberta employer may prefer that the contract be governed by US law. This is because, unlike the situation in Canada, most US states do not require employers to provide reasonable notice of termination and instead allow termination at will.

However, for a choice-of-law clause to be upheld, there needs to be a reasonable connection between the employment contract and the chosen jurisdiction. Where there is no choice-of-law clause, a contract is interpreted according to the law of the jurisdiction that is most closely connected to the employment relationship.

Corporate Policies

In most circumstances, an employer wants a new employee to be contractually bound by its general policies, which are usually found in an employer's policy manual. The employer should arrange for a candidate to receive a copy of the manual some time before signing the contract so that they have time to review it. The employee should acknowledge, in writing, that the employee has read the policies and agrees to be governed by them. The best approach is for the written employment contract to include a provision that recites this agreement. If there are certain policies from which the employee wishes to be exempt, and the employer agrees, these should be specified in the written contract.

Entire-Agreement Clause

This clause states that the signed contract constitutes the entire agreement between the parties. Previous conversations, negotiations, and promises that may have been made during the hiring process are not binding on either party. This clause is intended to ensure that in case a dispute arises, a court is restricted to the words of the contract in settling the dispute. The decision in *McNeely v Herbal Magic Inc* demonstrates the impact this clause can have.

CASE IN POINT

Entire-Agreement Clause: Impact on Earlier Representations

McNeely v Herbal Magic Inc, 2011 ONSC 4237

Facts

McNeely had been a senior executive at Herbal Magic, a weight loss management company, for two years when it was purchased by TorQuest. During the sales negotiations, TorQuest's president told McNeely that he was a vital part of the deal and he would become the president and CEO of the new firm, Herbal Magic Inc. In light of these oral representations, McNeely invested $2.5 million in the new company's stock. However, only seven months after he became president and CEO, McNeely's employment was terminated.

Although the employer paid him severance pay according to his employment agreement, McNeely argued that the representations made to him before the purchase created a "collateral agreement" and he was entitled to damages for its breach. The employer countered that the entire-agreement clause in McNeely's employment contract precluded him from relying on any and all oral representations made that were not part of the signed contract.

Relevant Issue

Whether the contract's entire-agreement clause precluded the employee from claiming damages for oral statements made during pre-contract discussions.

Decision

The Court held for the employer. The inclusion of an entire-agreement clause showed that the parties intended the contract documents to be the whole of their agreement, notwithstanding any prior oral representations or discussions regarding the subject matter of the agreement. Negotiated by commercially sophisticated parties, the entire-agreement clause explicitly covered "all prior agreements, understandings, representations or warranties, negotiations and discussions, whether oral or written." As a result, the employee could not rely on any statements made during such discussions to claim damages for negligent misrepresentation.

Although the employer in *McNeely* was successful, it is important to note that an entire-agreement clause does not guarantee that a court will ignore evidence of all previous discussions, especially in the face of serious or fraudulent misrepresentations on the part of the employer. However, it does provide a legal basis for an argument to exclude prior discussions from a court's consideration.

Inducement

This clause addresses whether the employee's service with a previous employer is recognized by the contracting employer for severance purposes. If the employee was arguably induced to leave secure employment, the parties should negotiate and expressly state whether those previous years of service will be recognized for the purpose of benefits and calculating termination notice in the event that employment is terminated.

Independent Legal Advice

This clause states that the employee has had the opportunity to seek independent legal advice before signing the contract. The statement must, of course, be true and include sufficient time for an employee to pursue such advice if they wish. An employee who has had an opportunity to obtain independent legal advice will find it difficult to challenge the contract later on the basis that they were unaware of its terms or of their legal meaning, as it will likely be assumed that a lawyer fully explained the terms of the contract and explained the law surrounding the particular items in the contract. Such a provision may be less important for senior management employees, who are assumed to have the requisite knowledge and leverage to protect themselves during negotiations. Offering the opportunity for an employee to seek independent legal advice is particularly important when an employer includes contract provisions that restrict individual rights an employee would otherwise normally have (e.g., a termination clause or a restrictive covenant). Doing so will increase the likelihood such clauses will be enforced (assuming the clauses are reasonably drafted).

Severability Clause

This clause provides that if a court invalidates part of the employment contract, it will not affect the validity of the remainder of the agreement. An unenforceable clause will simply be severed from the rest of the agreement. A severability clause may be especially important where there is a non-competition provision in the contract, to ensure that if the non-competition clause is found invalid, the rest of the contract will remain in force.

Golden Parachute

A unique feature that has evolved in executive employment contracts is the "golden parachute." Golden parachutes provide for substantial economic compensation in the event that an executive's employment is terminated under certain specified circumstances. Typically the triggering event is a change in the ownership or control of the employer, as a result of which the executive loses their job or is justified in leaving the employer.

The rationale behind the golden parachute is to permit the executive to act in the interests of the employer during the transitional period without being distracted by its effect on them personally.

Implied Duty to Maintain Confidentiality

Even in the absence of restrictive covenants in employment contracts, employers and workers should be aware of numerous contractual relationships that are considered to be of a *fiduciary nature*. This is a legal relationship of trust between the parties that transcends the contractual relationship and imposes a duty of care upon the party in whom trust is reposed. In the context of an employment contract, this trust would be owed by a key employee, for example, or someone entrusted to handle large sums of money or property belonging to the employer, or someone in possession of confidential information. The law imposes a positive duty on employees to respect that confidentiality. Ideally, this relationship of confidentiality should be written into the employment contract, but its absence will not prevent employers from suing an employee for breach of trust or breach of confidentiality, where circumstances so warrant, because the fiduciary duty is deemed to be an implied term of the contract. The *Barton Insurance v Irwin* case illustrates some of the considerations courts use to assess whether a fiduciary duty exists. Fiduciary employees and the corresponding obligations of these individuals are explored extensively in Chapter 15.

CASE IN POINT

Confidentiality an Implied Term in Employment Contract

Barton Insurance Brokers Ltd v Irwin, 1999 BCCA 73

Facts

Irwin had been employed with an insurance agency in Prince George since 1980. She remained employed after that firm was absorbed by acquisition with the plaintiff employer in 1992, at which time she held the position of general office supervisor. She did not have the power to hire or fire; she had never been an officer, director, or shareholder of the existing or former firm; and she needed to get approval from an administrator for any expenditure or decisions related to the business. There was no written contract of employment between the parties. When she left the firm in 1994, she almost immediately began to work for Porter & McMillan, a competitor of her former employer. Her new employer asked her to recollect as many people as she could remember as customers and to contact them to solicit their business. Although she did not have any list from her former employer to do this, she was successful from memory in obtaining the business of over 200 former insurance clients. Subsequently, the plaintiff observed a significant falling off of its business and attributed this to Irwin's contacting former clients. It sued both Irwin and her new employer for damages for loss of commissions.

Relevant Issue

Whether a former employee giving names of clients and contacts from her previous employment to her new employer was in breach of confidentiality.

Decision

The Court stated that whether it is called a fiduciary duty, a duty of good faith, or a duty of confidence, a former employee may be in breach of that duty to a former employer. The Court noted that this duty is not limited to an employee's current employment: "After leaving employment, an employee may be obligated not to pursue certain activities to the detriment of the former employer" (at para 18). However, the courts have to balance that obligation with the freedom that former employees should have to pursue new opportunities in their employment. The courts must also take into account the position of the former employee, whether that person was a key or senior employee or a director of a firm. In this case, Irwin's status was not identified as equivalent to that of a key employee and so she was bound to a lower standard of care that applies to ordinary employees. Accordingly, the Court found that she was not in breach of confidentiality for giving the names of clients and contacts from her previous employment to her new employer.

Enforceability and Interpretation of Written Contracts

Even after agreement on the terms is reached and the contract is signed, there are a number of issues that can affect the enforceability and interpretation of written employment contracts. A party who is unhappy with the terms of an employment contract may challenge the contract's enforceability by raising one of the issues described below. For example, a written contract may restrict the amount of notice of termination to which an employee is entitled. If terminated, the employee may argue that the specified term is unenforceable because it does not meet minimum statutory standards, and therefore common law notice—which is usually much more generous than the notice specified in a written employment contract—should apply. Both parties to the employment contract need to be aware of the following issues so that they can avoid these pitfalls.

Lack of Consideration

It is a basic principle of contract law that for a contract to be enforceable there must be an offer, acceptance, and consideration. Consideration is something of value that each party exchanges. In the employment context, consideration is usually provided by the promised exchange of payment for work performed. A lack of consideration can become a problem for an employment contract in two ways. The first is when an employee begins work before the contract (and therefore all of the duties of the employee) is finalized. The second is when the employer changes some of the employee's duties later in the employment relationship.

Where an employee begins working before the contract is finalized, the employee may allege that the contract, signed after work began, is unenforceable because the employer provided no new consideration in exchange for those terms. Any significant terms that limit the employee's rights or impose duties on the employee that were not already agreed to before work began may prove to be unenforceable. In *Francis v Canadian Imperial Bank of Commerce*, a decision that has been followed in a number of BC and Alberta cases, the employee had already accepted employment with the bank before signing the bank's contract. The Court found that the employer could not rely on the three months' notice clause in the contract because there was no new consideration for the added term. The employee was therefore entitled to common law notice of 12 months.

The other, more common, challenge arises when an employer wants to add a new term to a contract during the course of the employment relationship. To do so, the employer must offer something additional (fresh consideration) to the employee. Amending contracts by adding or changing duties and rights without providing fresh consideration will usually make the new terms unenforceable—and may even amount to constructive dismissal. It is, however, possible to set up an employment contract in a way that enables changes without the need for fresh consideration. If the employer incorporates a document (such as a list of employee expectations or a code of conduct) by reference into the original employment offer, and makes that offer conditional upon the prospective employee's acceptance of the terms in the incorporated document, then changes to the contract during the course of employment may be permitted—as long as the employer notifies employees of the changes when they are made. It is also advisable to specify in the offer that the document may be amended during the period of employment.

In *ASM Corrosion Control Ltd v George*, the defendant was an instrument technician who was the "manager of Alberta operations" for the plaintiff. He resigned a month after travelling to Texas to take an employer-funded course, triggering the engagement of an employer-reimbursement clause in the policy manual incorporated by reference into his indefinite-term unwritten employment offer about eight years earlier. An amendment to that policy had occurred about three years after he began working. The amendment required employees who resigned within a year of benefiting from an employer-funded course to pay back not only the actual cost of the course, as was previously required, but also travel and other costs associated with attending it. Furthermore, employees were required to pay back the amount of their salary paid to them while the course was in progress. The defendant claimed to be unaware of these obligations.

In finding in favour of the employer, the Alberta Provincial Court observed that ASM Corrosion had taken the following steps to ensure that employees were made aware of any new policies: clear language was used to articulate each policy, new manuals were provided to each employee after each update, employees were required to sign acknowledgment-of-receipt forms after every revision, and a master copy of the policy was made readily accessible for reference at all times. Moreover and in particular, in discussions with the defendant prior to his leaving for Texas, the plaintiff had reminded him of the relevant policy regarding reimbursement obligations.

To prevent a contract term from being found unenforceable because of a lack of consideration, employers should ensure that the formal written employment contract is finalized before the hiring process is completed or before the employee is allowed to begin work. And if a policy manual is incorporated by reference into an initial employment offer made conditional upon an employee's acceptance of policy manual terms, care and forethought should go into deciding how to ensure that employees are made aware of any amendments. Once the employee begins work, it is too late to ask them to sign the contract, unless the employer is prepared to provide some new consideration, such as a signing bonus. *Watson v Moore Corp* illustrates some of the pitfalls employers can run into when changes are made to the employment contract without new consideration.

CASE IN POINT

Continuing Normal Employment Not Valid Consideration for Changes to Original Contract

Watson v Moore Corp, 1996 CanLII 1142 (BCCA)

Facts

Watson had worked for the defendant employer for 25 years. For the first 13 years, the parties did not have a written employment contract. Then over the course of the remaining 12 years of her employment, she was asked to sign several variations to the contract, including some changes that were less beneficial to her than before: the amount of notice she would be entitled to if she were dismissed was reduced and she was asked to accept an onerous non-competition covenant. Eventually, Watson was dismissed without cause and given 20 weeks' pay in lieu of notice; she sued for wrongful dismissal, claiming that she was entitled to greater notice of termination.

Her employer took the position that she was required to sign the various changes to her contract as a condition of her continued employment. Watson argued that she signed the last two contracts because she assumed that if she did not, she would lose her job. The trial Court ruled that the continuing of her employment was good consideration for the modification of the contract even where such changes were not necessarily beneficial to the employee. Watson appealed the decision to the BC Court of Appeal.

Relevant Issue

Whether continued employment constitutes adequate consideration in an employment contract.

Decision

The Court of Appeal said there was no consideration for the changes that were made to the original employment contract. It said that continuation of a worker's normal employment duties does not alone constitute consideration for a change in the worker's employment contract. Had there been some evidence of some forbearance on the employer's part from dismissing the worker, then there could be consideration. Because the changes that were not favourable to the employee were not supported by consideration, the employee was entitled to claim a longer period of notice for her dismissal.

The *Watson* decision has been applied in a number of recent cases across Canada in which employers have attempted to add new terms after employment began, including non-competition clauses imposed on employees once they have moved up to more senior positions (see e.g. *Skana Forest Products v Lazauskas* and *National Bank Financial Inc v Canaccord Genuity Corp*).

As mentioned above, there is another legal risk of changing a policy manual or other aspects of employees' working conditions. Even with sufficient notice, which can eliminate the "lack of consideration" risk, changes may amount to constructive dismissal if they are substantial enough. (For more on changes in employment terms and constructive dismissal, see Chapters 11 and 14.)

Inequality of Bargaining Power

unconscionable in the context of an employment contract, something that is unreasonably one-sided

Written employment contracts can be challenged on the basis of the parties' alleged inequality of bargaining power at the time the contract is negotiated. Courts have been sympathetic to these arguments where the terms of a contract are **unconscionable** (unreasonably one-sided) and the employee did not understand them. This could occur, for example, where the employee has little education or the employer applied undue pressure.

However, apparent inequality in bargaining power does not in itself render a contract unenforceable. To show inequality of bargaining position, the transaction, when viewed as a whole, must, as the BC Court of Appeal specified in *Harry v Kreutziger*, be "sufficiently divergent from community standards of commercial morality" (at para 26) that it should be set aside as unjust.

However, failure to draw an employee's attention to a key term of the contract will not necessarily render a contract unenforceable. For example, in *Wallace v Toronto Dominion Bank*, the Ontario Court of Appeal rejected the argument that a termination clause that provided for only four weeks' notice of termination or pay in lieu for a senior manager with eight years of service was invalid because of the parties' unequal bargaining power. Although the termination provision was not brought to the employee's attention at the time of hiring, the Court found that no special circumstances, such as lack of understanding of the terms of the contract or oppressive conduct by the employer, undermined the contract.

To minimize the risk of a challenge on the basis of inequality of bargaining power, there are several things the employer can do:

- Ensure that the terms of the contract represent a reasonable balance between the interests of both parties.
- Provide the candidate with a written copy of the proposed contract and give the candidate enough time to read it and obtain independent legal advice before signing. This allows the person to carefully review the terms of the contract and to understand them or have them explained fully so that the employee cannot later claim to have been unaware of a term or its meaning.
- Include a provision in the contract stating that the candidate had the opportunity to obtain independent legal advice before signing.
- Include a certificate of independent legal advice for the lawyer to review and sign confirming that they have fully explained the terms and laws referred to in the contract.
- Draw the candidate's attention to key terms such as non-competition, non-solicitation, and termination notice clauses and have the candidate initial them.

Obsolescence

A contract may be challenged on the ground of obsolescence where its terms no longer reflect the realities of an employee's position within the organization. In *Lyonde v Canadian Acceptance Corp*, the employee had been promoted over a 24-year period from a junior position to vice-president of administration. The Court refused to enforce a termination provision that provided no notice of termination. It found that his position within the organization had changed so dramatically that the essence of the employment contract was now fundamentally different. He was awarded 21 months' notice of termination.

In 2003, the Ontario Court of Appeal in *Irrcher v MI Developments Inc* examined a termination clause in a ten-year-old contract where an employee's responsibilities and remuneration had changed substantially since the time the contract was signed. Recently, in *McKercher v Stantec Architecture Ltd*, the Saskatchewan Court of Queen's Bench, citing *Irrcher v MI Developments Inc*, examined a termination clause in an 11-year-old contract where an employee's responsibilities and remuneration had changed substantially since the time the contract was signed.

CASE IN POINT

"Simply Not the Same Job": Employment Contract Found to Be Obsolete

McKercher v Stantec Architecture Ltd, 2019 SKQB 100

Facts

This was an application by McKercher against Stantec Architecture Ltd for damages for wrongful dismissal. The 51-year-old McKercher was dismissed without cause from his employment as an architect after 11 years. When he started the job, he was focused on project design and project administration, with no supervisory or budgetary responsibilities. Over time, he received promotions and, at the date of dismissal, his responsibilities included business strategy, financial growth, managing and expanding the client base, business development forecasting, attending networking events to promote the business, human resources and staff supervision, signing authority on proposals, and operational responsibilities. The employer argued to the Court that McKercher's entitlement to damages should be limited by the original employment agreement's termination provisions, which provided for a maximum of three months' notice or pay in lieu of notice.

Relevant Issue

Whether the termination provisions of the original contract of employment prevailed after McKercher's job function changed.

Decision

The Saskatchewan Court of Queen's Bench found that the termination provisions of the original employment contract did not apply. The changes and advancement in McKercher's responsibilities overtook the notice limit in the agreement. There was no evidence before the Court that Stantec made it clear to McKercher that the notice limit was intended to apply to the positions to which he was promoted. The Court found that a reasonable notice period was 12 months, given McKercher's age, years of service, level of responsibility, and his difficulty in finding similar employment after termination of his employment.

To ensure that old contracts do not become invalid, the parties should update the employment agreement whenever there is a promotion or other significant change in duties. Promotions or salary increases could be made conditional on the execution of an amended employment contract (Israel, 28 May 2003). Similarly, the employment contract could include a provision that allows it to be reviewed and updated periodically.

The termination clause usually states that the employee is entitled to a certain number of weeks' notice for each completed year of service, with a certain maximum and minimum total notice period. This type of clause protects against obsolescence in most cases. For greater certainty, employers may choose a clause that also states that it applies despite any changes in duties that arise over the life of the contract. Employees may balk at such a clause, but if they accept the clause, and were given time to read the contract, the clause may be enforceable.

Failure to Meet Minimum Statutory Standards

Employers must ensure that the terms of an employment contract at least meet minimum statutory standards. Otherwise, a contract term that fails to meet the statutory standard will be null and void. In the leading case of *Machtinger v HOJ Industries Ltd*, the Supreme Court of Canada examined a contract that specified a notice of termination period that failed to meet the statutory minimum notice requirements of the Ontario *Employment Standards Act*. The Court held that the provision was invalid and ordered that the employer provide not merely the statutory minimum, but full reasonable notice under the common law. (As you will see in Chapter 6, the minimum standards in legislation are just that: minimums. In cases of wrongful dismissal, the notice periods that courts award are usually much longer.)

CASE IN POINT

Employment Contract Fails to Meet Statutory Minimum Notice Requirements

Machtinger v HOJ Industries Ltd, [1992] 1 SCR 986, rev'g 1988 CanLII 4645 (Ont CA)

Facts

The severance provisions in the written employment contract provided for two weeks' termination notice or pay in lieu, whereas the Ontario *Employment Standards Act* required four weeks' notice or pay in lieu for someone with Machtinger's length of service. The employee argued that the provision was invalid for failing to meet the statutory minimum. He sued for common law damages for pay in lieu of reasonable notice. The trial judge agreed and awarded reasonable notice pay of seven months. The Court of Appeal allowed the employer's appeal, holding that the employee was entitled only to the statutory minimum. The employee appealed to the Supreme Court of Canada.

Relevant Issues

1. Whether the employer's attempt to contract out of the termination provision of the *Employment Standards Act* nullified the termination provisions of the employment contract.
2. Whether an employee is entitled to common law damages for pay in lieu of reasonable notice when an employment contract is silent on the issue of termination notice.

Decision

The Supreme Court held that the employer could not "contract out" of the minimum statutory notice requirement (i.e., override it). Furthermore, it refused simply to substitute the legislative requirement of four weeks' notice. The contractual termination provisions were void for all purposes, and the employer was liable for pay in lieu of reasonable notice under the common law. The employer was required to provide the employee with seven and one-half months' notice rather than the two weeks' notice set out in the contract.

The Court held that to rebut the common law presumption of pay in lieu of reasonable notice on termination, the contract of employment must clearly specify another period of notice. If a contract does not comply with the statutory requirements for termination notice, the common law presumption is not rebutted.

The parties to an employment contract can avoid the result in *Machtinger* by at least matching minimum statutory requirements in all employment contracts. As KPMG, the trustee in bankruptcy for the defendant in *Noble v Principal Consultants Ltd (Bankrupt)*, discovered, even a declaration of bankruptcy by an employer will not deprive an earlier-dismissed employee of his entitlement to damages or allow the employer to avoid the rule in *Machtinger*. Noble was senior vice-president of finance for the prairie region when he was terminated without cause after 18 years, just two months and six days before his employer filed for bankruptcy. The Alberta Court of Appeal found that the chambers judge had erred in characterizing the bankruptcy as an event that reduced Noble's notice-period entitlement. Citing Iacobucci J in *Re Rizzo & Rizzo Shoes Ltd*, the Alberta Court of Appeal underscored the importance of not creating distinctions among employees dismissed without cause:

> [T]he impetus behind the termination of employment has no bearing upon the ability of the dismissed employee to cope with the sudden economic dislocation caused by unemployment. As all dismissed employees are equally in

> need of the protections provided by the [*Employment Standards Act*], any distinction between employees whose termination resulted from the bankruptcy of their employer and those who have been terminated for some other reason would be arbitrary and inequitable. (at para 34)

Again, to avoid the result in *Machtinger*, some contracts include graduated notice requirements that provide for increasing periods of notice as an employee's period of service lengthens. To safeguard against changes to the termination requirements in employment standards legislation, the termination clause could state that the employee is entitled to the greater of the notice specified in the contract and the notice required by the legislation. Another approach is for the parties to revisit employment contracts at regular intervals to ensure they still meet or exceed statutory requirements.

Because employees have rights in the employment contract both under common law and under the provisions of employment standards legislation, the question arises whether they can pursue the enforcement of their statutory rights (such as overtime pay) in a civil action against an employer where they are also seeking to enforce their common law rights in the employment contract (such as claiming damages for wrongful dismissal). Initially, the BC Supreme Court in *Macaraeg v E Care Contact Centers Ltd* said employees could pursue both in a civil action, but that decision was reversed by the Court of Appeal.

CASE IN POINT

Employment Standards Legislation Can Be Enforced Only by the Director of Employment Standards, Not in Civil Actions

Macaraeg v E Care Contact Centers Ltd, 2008 BCCA 182

Facts

The plaintiff started working for the defendant corporation as a customer service representative in May 2004. The contract of employment stipulated that her rate of pay was $27,600 per annum. Nothing was stated in the contract about whether she was expected to work overtime or how much she would get if she did. Shortly after her employment began, the plaintiff found herself working on average 12 hours per day on weekdays and 8 hours on Saturdays. When she asked about her entitlement to overtime for these extra hours, her employer told her it did not pay overtime for extended workdays. The plaintiff was dismissed without cause in February 2006, at which time she was given two weeks' pay in lieu of notice. The plaintiff sued her employer for damages for wrongful dismissal in a civil action. She claimed to be entitled to not only more notice of termination but also payment for all the overtime hours she had worked. Her employer argued that the courts do not have jurisdiction to hear claims for overtime pay and that claims for overtime pay should be made to the director of employment standards instead. It argued that the Supreme Court of Canada's *Machtinger* decision did not apply here because the employee's right to overtime came from the BC *Employment Standards Act*, not from the common law or the terms of the contract. *Machtinger*, it said, applies to situations where there is a pre-existing common law right to fill the void if the terms of the contract do not protect the worker.

Relevant Issue

Whether the minimum employment rights protected by the *Employment Standards Act* comprise part of the implied terms in the contract of employment, and, if they do, whether those statutory rights are enforceable by way of a civil action like other terms in the employment contract.

Decision

The Court found that the minimum overtime payment requirements under the *Employment Standards Act* were not implied terms in the parties' employment contract and that the director of employment standards has exclusive jurisdiction to enforce the terms of the Act. Because payment for overtime was covered by the Act but not covered by the parties' employment contract, the employee had to seek recourse under the Act by applying to the director of employment standards, not by suing for such in a civil action.

The *Macaraeg* decision is significant in that it underscores that the rights granted by employment standards legislation are not automatically incorporated into the terms of an employment contract, regardless of what the intention of the parties to the employment contract happened to be. The minimum requirements of the legislation are not implied terms of the contract of employment. Employers and employees should therefore define as much as possible all the significant terms of the employment contract.

Use of Ambiguous Language: Contra Proferentem Rule

In preparing an employment contract, employers should use clear and unambiguous terms. If a court finds that the terms of a contract can bear two possible interpretations, it may apply a rule called *contra proferentem*. Under the *contra proferentem* rule, ambiguous language is interpreted against the party who drafted the agreement, because that is the party who could have avoided the problem by being clearer. In other words, if there is ambiguity or vagueness in the contract, the courts choose an interpretation that favours the party that did not write the contract. Because the drafter is usually the employer, as was the case in *Duxbury v Training Inc*, most contractual ambiguities are interpreted to benefit the employee.

CASE IN POINT

Contractual Ambiguities Interpreted Against Drafter

Duxbury v Training Inc, 2002 ABPC 24

Facts

When Debra Duxbury and Michelle Tucker were hired to step in as instructors for a certified esthetician program in Lethbridge, Alberta, Training Inc's classes had already begun, the program was in disarray, students were upset, and the former teacher was being terminated. Both Duxbury and Tucker were led to believe by the president of Training Inc that their teaching positions would be ongoing, but the defendant later sought to hire other instructors at a lower salary just before the commencement of the new semester, effectively terminating Duxbury's and Tucker's employment.

Relevant Issue

Whether the employment contracts were for definite or indefinite terms.

Decision

The Alberta Provincial Court found that there was ambiguity in the wording of the contracts. To determine the intention of the parties, the Court turned to an examination of the surrounding circumstances. It noted that between semesters the plaintiffs assisted the defendant with recruitment, attended "meet the students" socials, prepared the course syllabus, and redesigned exams—facts consistent with their belief that Training Inc had employed them indefinitely. The Court concluded that because the contracts were not explicit about duration, the lack of clarity should be interpreted strictly against the interests of the drafter in accordance with the *contra proferentem* rule. Accordingly, it treated the contracts as being for indefinite terms. This entitled the plaintiffs to common law damages in lieu of notice.

Employers should keep the following tips in mind when drafting employment contracts to reduce the risk that a contract, or a term of a contract, will be ruled unenforceable by a court:

1. *Use clear language.* The *contra proferentem* rule may result in ambiguous language being interpreted in favour of the other party.
2. *Be fair when negotiating terms.* Evidence of unfairness or undue influence in negotiating terms may render the contract void.
3. *Give the other party time to read, understand, and seek independent legal advice about the contract before signing it.*
4. *Meet or exceed the minimum statutory standards.*
5. *Bring critical terms to the other party's attention.* For example, an employer who drafts an agreement should bring clauses related to a probationary period to an employee's attention and have the employee initial those clauses.
6. *Provide additional consideration if the employer wants a new term included in the contract after it is signed or after employment begins.*
7. *Customize contracts rather than use a standard form.* It is important that the parties consider special issues that need to be addressed.

KEY TERMS

consideration, 136
contra proferentem, 141
implied terms, 137
incorporated by reference, 138
litigation, 138
mitigate, 139
perk, 138
unconscionable, 158

REVIEW AND DISCUSSION QUESTIONS

1. What are the advantages of a written employment contract over an oral one? Are there any disadvantages?
2. If a dispute arises out of an oral employment contract, how does a court establish the terms and conditions of the contract?
3. What are the main legal issues that can affect the enforceability of an employment contract?
4. What is the *contra proferentem* rule of interpretation? Does this rule seem fair to you? Why or why not?
5. Explain the difficulties that an employer may face with a fixed-term contract.
6. Why are courts generally wary of restrictive covenant clauses?
7. What contractual terms do you think an employee may have the most difficulty with?
8. An employee may challenge the enforceability of an employment contract on several grounds. Review the sample indefinite-term employment contract in Appendix A. Identify three ways in which the employer has drafted this contract to help it successfully defend a challenge to its enforceability based on the grounds discussed in the chapter. Explain your answer.
9. The morning Maria started her new job, the employer handed her a copy of the firm's policy manual and told her to look it over, informing her that its terms and conditions would apply to her employment contract. This was the first time the manual had been mentioned to her. Four months later Maria was terminated without notice on the basis that she was not suitable for the job. The employer stated that it did not owe her any notice of termination or pay in lieu because the policy manual established a probationary period of six months during which time she could be terminated for any reason without notice. Do you think Maria is bound by the terms set out in the policy manual? Provide reasons for your answer.
10. In a non-competition clause, a martial arts instructor was restricted from teaching at, owning, or operating a martial arts school within a ten-kilometre radius of his employer's business for one year after leaving employment. The instructor quit within two months and opened a martial arts school half a block from his former employer. Is the non-competition clause enforceable? Discuss.
11. The following clauses were found in Mark's employer's policy manual, which formed part of his employment contract:

    > Termination notice must be in writing from the Executive Director, and professional staff will receive one month's notice … and/or notice as established by legislation.
    >
    > This Personnel Code is to be considered a guideline for the minimum expectations of employment and benefits obtaining therefrom.

    When Mark was terminated without cause, the employer argued that according to the termination clause, it only had to meet the termination requirements of the provincial employment standards statute. Mark sued for wrongful dismissal damages under the common law. In your opinion, which party would likely be successful? Explain your answer.

REFERENCES

ASM Corrosion Control Ltd v George, 2002 ABPC 118.
Barton Insurance Brokers Ltd v Irwin, 1999 BCCA 73.
Bowes v Goss Power Products Ltd, 2012 ONCA 425.
Ceccol v Ontario Gymnastic Federation, 2001 CanLII 8589 (Ont CA).
Christensen v Family Counselling Centre of Sault Ste Marie and District, 2001 CanLII 4698 (Ont CA).
Court Jurisdiction and Proceedings Transfer Act, SBC 2003, c 28.
Duxbury v Training Inc, 2002 ABPC 24.

Eagle Professional Resources Inc v MacMullin, 2013 ONCA 639, aff'g [2013] OJ No 2656 (QL) (Sup Ct J).

Echlin, Randall, & Christine Thomlinson, *For Better or For Worse: A Practical Guide to Canadian Employment Law*, 3rd ed (Toronto: Canada Law Book, 2011).

Employment Standards Act, 2000, SO 2000, c 41.

Employment Standards Act, RSBC 1996, c 113.

Employment Standards Code, RSA 2000, c E-9.

Francis v Canadian Imperial Bank of Commerce, 1994 CanLII 1578 (Ont CA).

Geller v Sable Resources Ltd, 2012 BCSC 1861.

Harry v Kreutziger, 1979 CanLII 393 (BCCA).

Irrcher v MI Developments Inc, 2003 CanLII 27685 (Ont CA).

Israel, Peter, "Ask an Expert: Are Employment Agreements Valid if the Position and Salary Change?" *Canadian Employment Law Today* 390 (28 May 2003) at 3044.

Israel, Peter, "Ask an Expert: Does an Employer Have the Right to Terminate Probationary Employees Without Pay in Lieu of Notice?" *Canadian Employment Law Today* 386 (2 April 2003) at 3012.

Israel, Peter, "Ask an Expert: Preventing Former Employees from Competing," *Canadian Employment Law Today* 409 (17 March 2004) at 3196.

Kempf, Alfred, "Social Media and Trade Secrets" (22 November 2013), online: Pushor Mitchell LLP <http://www.pushormitchell.com/law-library/article/social-media-and-trade-secrets>.

Levitt, Howard, "Non-Competes Have Their Pros and Cons" *Financial Post* (10 December 2013).

Lyonde v Canadian Acceptance Corp (1983), 3 CCEL 220 (Ont H Ct J).

Macaraeg v E Care Contact Centers Ltd, 2008 BCCA 182.

Machtinger v HOJ Industries Ltd, [1992] 1 SCR 986, rev'g 1988 CanLII 4645 (Ont CA).

Mason v Chem-Trend Limited Partnership, 2010 ONSC 4119.

Maxwell v British Columbia, 2014 BCCA 339.

McKercher v Stantec Architecture Ltd, 2019 SKQB 100.

McNeely v Herbal Magic Inc, 2011 ONSC 4237.

Mejia v LaSalle College International Vancouver Inc, 2014 BCSC 1559.

Miller v Convergys CMG Canada Limited Partnership, 2014 BCCA 311.

National Bank Financial Inc v Canaccord Genuity Corp, 2018 BCSC 857.

Noble v Principal Consultants Ltd (Bankrupt), 2000 ABCA 133.

Peters & Co Limited v Ward, 2015 ABCA 6.

Phoenix Restorations Ltd v Drisdelle, 2014 BCSC 1497.

Pugen, Daniel, "Customer Contacts on LinkedIn = Property of the Employer," *Ontario Employer Advisor* (24 September 2013), online: <https://blog.firstreference.com/customer-contacts-on-linkedin-property-of-the-employer/#.XrQdHKhKhHZ>.

Quick Pass Master Tutorial School Ltd v Zhao, 2018 BCSC 683.

RBC Dominion Securities Inc v Merrill Lynch Canada Inc, 2008 SCC 54.

Rizzo & Rizzo Shoes Ltd (Re), [1998] 1 SCR 27.

Rocky Credit Union Ltd v Higginson, 1995 ABCA 132.

Seanix Technology Inc v Ircha, 1998 CanLII 6772 (BCSC).

Shafron v KRG Insurance Brokers (Western) Inc, 2009 SCC 6.

Skana Forest Products v Lazauskas, 2014 BCSC 759.

Spiroll Corp Ltd v Putti, 1975 CanLII 1077 (BCSC), aff'd 1976 CanLII 1146 (BCCA).

Stam, Lisa, "Who Owns 'Publicly Available' Social Media Content?" *Employment and Human Rights Law in Canada* (22 October 2013), online: <http://www.canadaemploymenthumanrightslaw.com/2013/10/articles/social-media/who-owns-publicly-available-social-media-content>.

Stevens v Sifton Properties Ltd, 2012 ONSC 5508.

Tanton v Crane Canada Inc, 2000 ABQB 837.

Thompson, Martin, & Kyle Lambert, "'You Can't Have Your Cake and Eat It (Part) 2': An Update on Mitigation and Employment Contracts," *Employment and Labour Bulletin* (December 2013), online: <http://www.mcmillan.ca/You-Cant-Have-Your-Cake-and-Eat-it-Part-2-An-Update-on-Mitigation-and-Employment-Contracts>.

Torcana Valve Services Inc v Anderson, 2007 ABQB 356.

Unified Freight Services v Therriault, 2006 ABQB 93.

Wallace v Toronto Dominion Bank, 1983 CanLII 1907 (Ont CA), leave to appeal to SCC refused (1983), 52 NR 157n.

Watson v Moore Corp, 1996 CanLII 1142 (BCCA).

Employment Standards Legislation 6

LEARNING OUTCOMES

After completing this chapter, you will be able to:

- Understand the purpose of Alberta's *Employment Standards Code* and British Columbia's *Employment Standards Act* in setting minimum rights for employees.
- Identify the minimum standards that apply to wages, hours of work, statutory or general holidays, overtime pay, vacation, and statutory leaves.
- Identify the protections available to employees who exercise their rights to statutory leaves, including maternity or pregnancy leave, parental leave, family leave, bereavement leave, compassionate care leave, and reservist/reservists' leave.
- Understand how the statutory rights and protections are enforced.

Introduction

Employment standards legislation sets out minimum terms and conditions of work, including hours of work, overtime premium pay, statutory holidays, vacation time and pay, and maternity or pregnancy leave and parental leave. It also establishes minimum requirements with respect to termination notice and termination pay, which are discussed in Chapters 13 and 14. An employer is free to exceed these statutory minimum standards, but it may not, even with the employee's agreement, fail to meet them.

For example, employment standards legislation requires that employees receive overtime pay after working a certain number of hours in a week. (In Alberta the number is 44 hours, and in British Columbia [BC] it is 40 hours.) If the employer and employee agree that overtime pay is required after only 35 hours, the parties are bound by this more generous term. However, if they agree that the employer is not required to provide overtime pay until the employee works 48 hours, the agreement contravenes the legislation and is not enforceable. If the employee subsequently files a complaint, or the province's employment standards agency learns of the statutory contravention in some other way, the employer must pay the employee the overtime premium pay owing, plus interest, and may have to pay a penalty to the government, through the Employment Standards Branch (BC) or Employment Standards (Alberta). The employee's initial agreement to the lower term will not be a defence.

To a certain extent, employment standards legislation displaces the common law principle that the parties are free to negotiate their own terms and conditions of employment. Its rationale is that many employees lack the bargaining power to negotiate acceptable working conditions with the employer. The government is thus setting and enforcing minimum rights that we, as a society, require in the interests of fairness in the workplace. Employment standards legislation can have a significant impact on both employers and employees, and because it affects minimum wages and working conditions it is frequently reviewed by governing parties in all provinces. Changes are made to address social and economic conditions or to reflect the ideology of the party in power at a given time. It is important that employers keep abreast of the changes to ensure they are in compliance with any revisions to employment standards minimums. Changes to employment standards in Alberta's Bill 2 and BC's Bill 8 (see the following In the News boxes) are examples of this evolution. Note that both Bill 2 and Bill 8 have since been passed.

IN THE NEWS

Ground Shifting Again for Alberta Employers—Premier Announces Employment and Labour Changes Under Bill 2—An Act to Make Alberta Open for Business

Bill 2: *An Act to Make Alberta Open for Business,* was put forward to Alberta's legislative assembly yesterday afternoon, May 27, 2019. At the press conference to announce the changes, Premier [Jason] Kenney said the changes aim to "bring fairness and balance back to the workplace" and to "get Albertans back to work."

Under Bill 2, the United Conservative Party government proposes to make various changes, many of which have the effect of undoing some of the legislative changes brought about by the NDP government in 2017, through their introduction of Bill 17: *The Fair and Family Friendly Workplaces Act*. These changes will almost certainly be welcome news to employers in Alberta. Changes to employment standards that will be of most interest to employers are summarized below:

Student Youth Minimum Wage—to take effect June 26, 2019

- The minimum wage will be reduced to $13 per hour for workers aged seventeen or younger (currently $15 per hour). The new lower wage will apply for the first 28 hours worked in a week by a student while school is in session. For every additional hour worked in a week after that, they must be paid the full $15 minimum hourly wage. However, during breaks from school and summer holidays, the new $13 an hour youth rate will apply to all hours worked by a student.

Employment Standards Code—to take effect September 1, 2019

- The method for calculating general holiday pay will again recognize the distinction between the general holiday occurring on a regular and irregular workday (this distinction was previously removed under the NDP government's Bill 17).
- In order to be eligible for general holiday pay an employee must work for at least 30 days in the 12 months preceding the general holiday (this eligibility requirement was previously removed under Bill 17).
- Overtime will be permitted to be banked at a 1:1 rate under an overtime agreement (currently, employers are required to give those hours at a ratio of 1.5 hours off for every overtime hour banked, as a result of Bill 17). This means no more Flexible Averaging Agreements.

SOURCE: Mathews Dinsdale, 28 May 2019.

IN THE NEWS

An Overhaul of BC's Employment Standards Legislation: Bill 8—What Employers Need to Know

Bill 8: *Employment Standards Amendment Act, 2019*, was introduced to the legislative assembly yesterday afternoon, April 29, 2019. The Bill contains extensive amendments to the *Employment Standards Act* (the "ESA"), the core piece of legislation governing British Columbia's non-unionized workplaces.

The Bill, which is not yet law, is expected to pass in the near future. This is a significant development with far reaching cost and operational implications for employers. The more notable changes include:

Application of the ESA to Unionized Workplaces: Currently, unionized workplaces are largely exempt from the application of the ESA. This will no longer be the case. Going forward, any collective agreement provision dealing with issues like overtime, hours of work, statutory holidays, the treatment of gratuities, vacation time/pay, seniority retention, entitlements upon termination of employment, and temporary/permanent layoff must meet or exceed the entitlements set out in the ESA. If they do not, or if a collective agreement is silent on these issues, the ESA entitlements will be deemed to be incorporated into the collective agreement.

Wage Deductions: While the ESA will continue to permit employers to deduct money from wages to pay off debts owed by an employee, going forward only certain categories of debt may be paid off in this manner.

Tips: New requirements will be introduced governing the treatment of tips and gratuities. Employers will be prohibited from withholding, deducting from, or requiring an employee to return any gratuities which are received. There is a limited exception for "tip pools," which are permitted, but which, in most cases, an employer (including any shareholder or director of an employer) will not be permitted to participate in such pools.

New Leave Periods: The Bill creates two new job-protected unpaid leave periods, as follows:

- *Critical illness or injury leave*—which provides for job-protected leave where an employee is required to provide care and support to a family member whose life is at risk. This new leave period provides for up to 36 weeks of leave, where the family member at risk of death is a minor, and 16 weeks in the case of an adult.
- *Leave respecting domestic violence*—which provides for up to 10 days of leave for victims of domestic violence to seek various assistance associated with the domestic violence. Victims of domestic violence will be additionally entitled to a further 15 weeks of unpaid leave.

Temporary Help Agencies: Temporary help agencies will be required to be licensed under the ESA. If an employer engages the services of an unlicensed agency, the employer will be deemed to be the employer of each employee who performs work on their behalf for all purposes under the ESA.

Filing Time Limits: The Director will be entitled to extend the current 6-month time limit for filing complaints in certain prescribed circumstances.

Ability to Conduct Broad Workplace Inspections: The Director will be permitted to conduct broad investigations, even in the absence of a complaint, to ensure workplaces are compliant with the ESA.

Wage Recovery: In the case of unpaid wages, employees will be entitled to recover all wages payable for a period of 12 months (currently 6 months) preceding their cessation of employment or the date the complaint is filed, whichever is earlier. This may be extended to a period of 24 months, in certain circumstances.

Information Concerning Employee Rights: Employers will be required to provide employees, in a form approved by the Director, information about the rights of employees under the ESA.

Record Keeping: Employers will be required to retain workplace payroll records for a period of 4 years following the date on which the records are created (currently the requirement is to maintain them for a period of 2 years following the termination of employment). Employers will also be required to retain averaging agreements and written assignments of wages for a 4 year period.

Employing Youth: Subject to limited exceptions, youth under the age of 14 will be prohibited from working generally, and children under the age of 16 will be prohibited from working in "hazardous industries," or from performing "hazardous work," which will be further defined by regulation.

All of the proposed changes referenced above will have significant impacts on British Columbia employers should they take effect. Once implemented, these items may result in significant cost implications to employers and increased regulatory and administrative requirements.

SOURCE: Mathews Dinsdale, 30 April 2019.

It is also important to remember that these are minimum standards. Individual employment agreements (and collective agreements) often set higher standards, and court decisions set higher standards for certain matters covered by the employment standards statutes. The most notable example of courts setting higher standards is in cases of wrongful dismissal. The minimum notice periods in the legislation are far lower than what courts award (see Chapter 13).

The 2008 BC Court of Appeal case *Macaraeg v E Care Contact Centers Ltd* has clarified the issue as to what extent the minimum requirements of the *Employment Standards Act* should be deemed to be implied terms of all or most employment contracts. (See the Case in Point in Chapter 5.) The Court ruled that the minimum requirements of the statute are *not* implied terms of the employment contract. If an employee is seeking some redress under the Act for a term that was not covered by the employment contract, the employee must apply to the Employment Standards Branch for a remedy, not sue the employer in court. Likewise, appeals of decisions by the branch are heard by the BC Employment Standards Tribunal, not the courts. The case is similar in Alberta regarding the referral of complaints to its Employment Standards branch rather than the courts.

This case does not, however, mean that employment contracts can avoid or lower the minimum standards set in legislation. Under section 4 of the Alberta *Employment Standards Code* (ESC) and section 4 of the BC *Employment Standards Act* (ESA), minimum standards cannot be avoided by the agreement of the parties; nor can they be avoided by the silence of the parties. Further, the language of section 3 of the ESC indicates that nothing in the Code affects any civil remedy of an employee or employer or "an agreement, a right at common law or a custom" that provides to an employee benefits that are "at least equal" to those under the ESC or "imposes on an employer an obligation or duty greater" than those provided under the legislation (s 3(1)(b)). There is no similar provision in the ESA, but the same principles apply in BC.

While minimum statutory standards apply to all employees, they are most relevant in entry-level positions and lower-paying jobs, where individual employees often lack bargaining power. However, the legislation has evolved over time, and it now contains a range of statutory standards and protections, such as maternity or pregnancy leave and parental leave provisions, that set the standard for most workplaces. Moreover, legislative changes are ongoing. For example, in BC, provisions concerning compassionate care leave were introduced in 2006. These provisions specify circumstances in which employees are entitled to unpaid leave of up to 8 weeks in a 26-week period to care for a gravely ill family member. Legislation of a similar nature was introduced in Alberta in 2014. However, in Alberta, to be eligible, an employee must have worked at least 52 consecutive weeks with the employer.

FYI

Key Features of Employment Standards Legislation

1. Alberta's *Employment Standards Code* and British Columbia's *Employment Standards Act* set minimum *standards*; an employee cannot waive their rights under these statutes and agree to standards of work that are less generous than those in the legislation. These standards include minimum wages (referenced in the regulations), hours of work and overtime, vacation entitlement, statutory holidays, statutory leaves of absence, and termination notice or termination pay.
2. If an employer promises an employee *a greater right or benefit* than that provided under the employment standards legislation, the greater right or benefit will be enforced if there is a complaint. Enforcement is carried out by employment standards officers in Alberta and BC. A greater right or benefit must be related to a specific entitlement. For example, an employer cannot forgo paying employees for statutory holidays by insisting that the overall compensation scheme is "a greater right or benefit" because the employees receive $10 per hour above minimum wage.
3. The legislation covers most *employees*. However, specific exemptions apply to certain occupations

and industries. For example, the hours of work standards do not apply to managerial and supervisory employees, and independent contractors are not covered.

4. Enforcement of rights is a complaint-based process. Employees who believe their rights have been infringed must file a complaint with the Employment Standards Branch (BC) or Employment Standards (Alberta).
5. Unionized employees are covered by employment standards legislation. However, the ESC in Alberta states that most of the significant minimum standards in the statutes do not apply to employees under a collective agreement (e.g., hours of work provisions). In BC, if a collective agreement contains any provision respecting the following matters, and the provisions meet or exceed the requirements of the ESA, the corresponding parts of the ESA do not apply:
   - hours of work and overtime;
   - statutory holidays;
   - annual vacations; and
   - seniority retention, recall, termination or layoff, and liability resulting from length of service.

   If a collective agreement *does not contain any provision* relating to one of these subject areas, or if it does not meet or exceed the requirements of the ESA, the corresponding part or section of the ESA is deemed to be incorporated into the collective agreement. The rest of the ESA applies to unionized employees in BC (with the exception of the enforcement provisions, as noted immediately below).

   In both provinces, unionized employees must usually follow the grievance procedure in their collective agreement to pursue their rights, rather than file a complaint with the Employment Standards Branch (BC) or Employment Standards (Alberta) (see Chapter 3).
6. With a few exceptions, such as group termination provisions in BC (s 64 of the ESA), employment standards legislation binds all employers, regardless of size.

General Requirements

Application

In Alberta, the *Employment Standards Code* applies to "all employers and employees, including the Crown in right of Alberta and its employees, except as otherwise provided in this Part" (s 2(1)). Close to 90 percent of employees employed in Alberta fall under the jurisdiction of the ESC.

The following is a list of groups of workers who are outside the jurisdiction of Alberta's Code:

- employees covered by another Act to the extent that the other Act states that the ESC or a provision of it does not apply to them (except for any provisions relating to maternity leave, parental leave, or reservist leave); these employees include academic staff employed by institutions covered by the *Post-secondary Learning Act* or employees who are members of a municipal police service appointed pursuant to the *Police Act*, among others;
- employees who fall under federal jurisdiction and who are already covered by the *Canada Labour Code*, including those employed in chartered banking, broadcasting and telecommunications, interprovincial and international pipelines, grain elevators, airports and air transportation, railways, First

Nations activities, and federal government departments and agencies, among others;
- international employees and interprovincial employees who are working out of the province (generally, the jurisdiction is based on the location where the work is performed);
- employees whose terms and conditions of employment are incorporated into the terms of a collective agreement covered by the Alberta *Labour Relations Code*, unless the collective agreement does not provide for the minimums set out in the ESC, in which case the terms of the ESC apply; and
- individuals who are determined to be independent contractors or self-employed workers (according to established tests, as discussed in Chapter 2).

In BC, the *Employment Standards Act* applies to "all employees other than those excluded by regulation," according to section 3. Sections 31–32 of the BC *Employment Standards Regulation* (ESR) list persons who are not covered by the ESA as follows:

- members of professional associations, such as doctors, lawyers, architects, and engineers (a total of 16 professions are identified);
- persons receiving employment insurance benefits while working under job creation projects;
- secondary school students working in a work experience program authorized by their school board or working for a school board;
- a "sitter" (employed solely to attend to a child or a disabled, infirm, or other person in a private residence, not a day care facility); and
- persons receiving income assistance or benefits under the *Employment and Assistance Act* while participating in an on-site training or work experience program.

Sections 33–45 of British Columbia's ESR go on to exempt a wide variety of employees who are *exempt only from some parts* of the Act or are subject to special rules. For example, managers and supervisory employees are not covered by the hours of work and overtime pay provisions. To fall within the scope of the exemption, the position must be truly managerial, carrying the power to hire and make independent decisions. Simply giving an employee the title of "manager" will not make them exempt from those requirements. Similarly, professional employees, such as teachers and college instructors, as well as firefighters and police officers, are exempt from provisions regarding minimum wage, maximum hours of work, overtime pay, paid statutory holidays, and vacation pay.

Record Keeping

In both Alberta and BC, all employers, regardless of size, are required to keep accurate records about employees. In Alberta, these records must be made available to employment standards officers, according to section 77 of the ESC. In BC, section 28 of the ESA specifies a range of employee records that employers must keep at their principal place of business and retain for four years after the date on which they were created. There can be significant penalties for failing to keep these records.

Accurate records can assist the parties in resolving disputes. For example, if an employee alleges that an employer owes them overtime pay and the employer has no reliable records, an adjudicator will usually accept the employee's claim.

Both provinces impose specific requirements concerning the information that an employer must record about each employee and the length of time that the records must be kept (ss 14 and 15 of the ESC; s 28 of the ESA). In Alberta, employee records must be kept for at least three years from the date that each record is made. For example, an employer must keep the name and address of each employee for three years after employment ends and must keep the information contained in each wage statement for three years after giving that information to the employee.

In BC, employee records need to be retained by the employer for four years after the date on which they were created. For example, employers must keep copies of employees' agreements to work excess hours and to average hours of work in calculating overtime pay for four years from the date the agreements were made. (See the section entitled "Variances from Standard Employment Arrangements," below.)

Wages

Payment of Wages

Both provinces require employers to establish regular pay periods. In BC, section 17 of the ESA requires payment of all wages at least semi-monthly and within eight days after the end of the pay period on or before the regular payday. In Alberta, the ESC provides employers with a little additional time. Payment of wages must be made no later than ten consecutive days after the end of each pay period (s 8(1)). By contrast to the ESA's semi-monthly rule, the ESC further states that a pay period must not be longer than one work month (s 7(2)).

Payment may be by cash, cheque, draft, money order, or (if certain conditions are met) by direct deposit into the employee's account at a bank or other financial institution. Partial payment is prohibited.

In BC, when employment ends there are two rules. If the employer terminates the employment, it must pay all wages owed within 48 hours of termination. If the employee terminates, the wages are due within six days (s 18).

In Alberta, when employment ends payment must be made no later than ten consecutive days after the last day of employment (ss 9(2) and 10(2)), unless the employer or the employee has given notice of termination in accordance with the termination notice provisions specified in the ESC (ss 56 and 58). If such notice of termination is given, the employer must pay the employee's earnings not later than three consecutive days after the last day of employment (ss 9(1) and 10(1)). In the case of an employee who terminates the relationship without providing the required notice to the employer, the employer must pay the earnings not later than ten consecutive days after the date on which the notice would have expired had it been given (s 10(3)).

Deductions from Wages and Vacation Pay

Section 12 of Alberta's ESC and sections 21–22 of BC's ESA prohibit an employer from withholding or deducting any wages payable to an employee unless the deduction is:

1. permitted or required by statute, as in the case of deductions for income taxes, employment insurance (EI) premiums, and Canada Pension Plan contributions;
2. permitted or required by a court order, as in the case of a garnishment order requiring the money to be paid to a third party to whom money is owing (e.g., a child support payment);
3. authorized by a collective agreement to which the employee is bound; or
4. personally authorized in writing by the employee (such authorizations must be clear and specific regarding the amount to be deducted; in BC, this exception is, by section 22(4), limited to assignments of wages to meet certain credit obligations).

Despite any written authorization by an employee, an employer in Alberta cannot make a deduction from wages to pay for faulty workmanship. Similarly, an employer cannot make a deduction for cash shortages or loss of property unless the employee is the only one with access to and total control over the cash or property. For example, if more than one person has a key to a locker where tools are kept, an employee cannot be held financially responsible for loss of the tools from the locker. Nor could an employer deduct from a waiter's paycheque the cost of dishes he broke in a restaurant.

Hutchins v Atlantic Provincial Security Guard Service Ltd shows that employers generally are restricted from making wage deductions unless they fall within one of the specific statutory exemptions. In *Hutchins*, the Court ruled against an employer that deducted money from an employee's wages because of unexplained damage to a rented vehicle in the employee's possession. The Court ruled against the employer because the damages did not fall within the statutory provisions.

CASE IN POINT

Employer's Ability to Deduct Wages Limited

Hutchins v Atlantic Provincial Security Guard Service Ltd, 1995 CanLII 8876 (NBLEB)

Facts

Hutchins, an employee of Atlantic Provincial Security Guard Services, was in possession of a rented van during the course of his employment when his shift ended on Friday. He obtained permission from his employer to keep the minivan for personal use on Saturday and Sunday. The employer failed to inform Hutchins that he would be responsible for the $40 cost of the weekend rental. After another rental in the course of his employment, he returned the vehicle with a damaged back door. The cost to repair the door was $424. Hutchins, who was the only driver of the vehicle, denied all knowledge of the damage. The employer demanded that he pay for the damage through a deduction from wages. When

Hutchins refused, the employer terminated his employment. The employer withheld both the $40 and the $424 from his final pay.

Relevant Issue

Whether the employer violated the ESA by deducting $40 and $424 from the employee's wages in these circumstances.

Decision

The Board found that the $40 deduction was appropriate since the employee requested the use of the van and derived a personal benefit from the employer's goodwill. However, the $424 deduction was inappropriate. There was no evidence to suggest that the employee damaged the van negligently or intentionally. Because the New Brunswick ESA (like the Alberta ESC) provides for employer deductions only in clear and carefully defined circumstances, the employer was not entitled to deduct the $424. The appropriate remedy for the employer was to pay the wages owing and to sue the employee for damages.

In BC, an employer cannot make a deduction from wages to pay any of the employer's business costs, even if the employee has agreed to it (s 21(2)). That section allows for exceptions to be made by regulation, but the current regulations do not make any exceptions.

Another difference between the two provinces is that in Alberta, employers are permitted to recover a genuine wage advance or an unintentional overpayment, whereas in BC, such a deduction is forbidden unless the employee authorizes it in writing (*Health Employers Assn of BC v BC Nurses' Union*). In the absence of such an agreement, the employer would have to file a grievance or bring a claim against the employee and prove the overpayment. Although Alberta does allow such deductions without authorization, employers must follow several rules: Alberta employers must document calculations of such a deduction and disclose them on the statement of wages, overpayments should be recovered from the employee as soon as possible, and any recoveries should be handled in a manner that is consistent for all affected employees and that minimizes the disruption to the affected employees.

Wage Statements

Both provincial statutes specify the information that an employer must provide on each wage statement and when it must be provided. An employer must furnish the employee with a written statement (or emailed statement if the employee is able to make a paper copy) on or before the employee's payday.

In Alberta, under section 14 of the ESC, the statement must include the following information (among other details):

- the period for which the wages are paid;
- the regular and overtime hours of work;
- the wage rate and the overtime rate;
- the earnings paid, showing separately each component of the earnings for each pay period;
- the amount and purpose of each deduction;
- time off instead of overtime pay provided and taken; and
- the net wage amount.

In BC, under section 27 of the ESA, the statement must include the following (among other details), unless the wage statement would be identical to the previous statement (in which case a new detailed statement is not required until there is a change):

- the hours worked by the employee in the pay period (regular and overtime);
- the wage rate (regular and overtime);
- the gross and net wage amount and how they were calculated; and
- the amount and purpose of each deduction.

Special requirements apply to vacation pay statements.

Variances from Standard Employment Arrangements

In Alberta, section 74 of the ESC provides the director of employment standards with discretion to grant a variance with respect to a scheme of employment in particular situations. The director may also revoke, amend, or vary an approval at any time.

In BC, sections 72 and 73 of the ESA allow for an employer and its employees to apply to the director of employment standards for a variance of at least ten requirements under the Act that can differ from the legislated minimum standard. Employers and employees can agree to vary these standards in such matters as:

1. the minimum daily hours of work and maximum hours before overtime is due,
2. overtime wages,
3. the hours that employees must be free from work,
4. split shifts, and
5. special clothing requirements.

The director of employment standards has wide discretion to grant the application for variance. The director must be satisfied that a majority of the employees who will be affected by the variance are aware of its effect and consent to it. The director has the power to attach certain conditions to the variance.

Minimum Employment Standards

Minimum Wage

Minimum wage is the lowest hourly wage that an employer can pay an employee. Most employees are subject to minimum wage requirements, regardless of whether they are full-time, part-time, or casual employees and regardless of whether they are paid on an hourly basis or on commission, piece rate, flat rate, or salary.

In Alberta, minimum wage requirements are referenced in section 138(1)(f) of the ESC and are addressed in the accompanying regulation; in BC, they are referred to in section 16 of the ESA and specified by regulation. The minimum wage rates are set out in the regulations to each statute and are typically raised every few years to keep up with inflation and the increased cost of living, though the rates tend to increase in fits and starts and are sometimes a source of intense political debate.

In BC, the minimum wage was the highest in the country in 2001, at $8 per hour, but the government froze the rate at that amount for a decade, citing concerns about the risk of job loss and businesses going bankrupt. By 2011 the BC minimum wage was the lowest in the country. That year, the government announced a stepped increase from $8 to $10.25 by 2012 (s 15 of the ESR). In 2015, the government announced another increase, to $10.45, an amount that disappointed those such as the BC Federation of Labour, which that year began to advocate for a $15 minimum wage with effective results.

As of June 1, 2019, the minimum wage in BC is $13.85. This is an increase from the rate of $12.65 that was in effect from June 1, 2018, until May 31, 2019. The minimum wage in BC increased again to $14.60 on June 1, 2020 and is scheduled to increase to $15.20 on June 1, 2021.[1]

In 2015, the government of Alberta announced its intention to raise the Alberta minimum wage (in a series of steps) to $15 by 2018. At the time of the announcement, Alberta's minimum wage was one of the lowest in the country. The first step in the series became effective on October 1, 2015, raising the general rate to $11.20 per hour ($10.70 for liquor servers). When this change was implemented, the Alberta minimum wage became the third highest in the country. On June 26, 2019, the government of Canada implemented a new job creation wage of $13 per hour for students aged 13 to 17.[2]

Minimum Reporting Pay

On occasion, employees who come in to work their scheduled shift are sent home before the end of the shift because, for example, business is slow or an expected shipment does not arrive. In this situation, a special rule applies.

In Alberta it is called the "three-hour rule," because an employer must pay an employee who is sent home after working less than three hours the greater of three hours at the applicable minimum wage or the employee's regular wage for the time worked. The following example illustrates how the calculation works:

> Yassi is scheduled to work an eight-hour shift at a retail store in Alberta. Business is slow, and the employer decides to send her home after only two hours. Yassi earns $13 per hour, so payment at her regular rate would be 2 × $13, or $26. If the applicable minimum wage is $11.20 per hour, the three-hour rule means that she is entitled to receive 3 × $11.20, or $33.60, because that amount is greater than $26.

---

1 To find the minimum wage rates in BC, visit <https://www2.gov.bc.ca/gov/content/employment-business/employment-standards-advice/employment-standards/wages/minimum-wage>.

2 To find the current minimum wage rates in Alberta, visit <https://www.alberta.ca/minimum-wage.aspx>. For a historical summary of minimum wage rates across Canada, organized by decade, see <http://srv116.services.gc.ca/rpt2.aspx?lang=eng>.

This rule does not apply to an employee who reports to work after being advised in advance not to report, an employee who is only available to work for less than three hours, or an employee who works from home. It is also inapplicable if the employer has no control over the reason that work is unavailable, as in the case of a fire or power failure. There are some (limited) categories of employees for whom the three-hour minimum is reduced to two hours—for example, school bus drivers, caregivers who provide home care, and adolescents who are 12 to 14 years of age when employed on a day that they are required to attend school, among others.

In BC, the special rule is called the "two-hour rule," but it is somewhat different. The rule is that there is a minimum of two hours for which an employer must pay an employee scheduled to work on a given day—regardless of how long the scheduled shift is. In the event that the employer cancels a scheduled shift or sends an employee home early, two rules apply, depending on the shift length: (1) if the employee was scheduled to work eight hours or less, the two-hour rule applies; (2) if the shift was for more than eight hours, a four-hour minimum payment rule applies. In all cases, these rules do not apply if the employee is unfit to work or violates health and safety rules—or fails to report to work. The four-hour rule is reduced to a two-hour rule if an employer must send an employee home or cancel a shift in advance due to reasons "completely beyond the employer's control" (e.g., unsuitable weather conditions or a power outage; s 34(2)(b)). Of course, if the employee actually works more than the minimum amount (two or four hours) before being sent home, the employer must pay for the entire period actually worked (s 34(4) of the ESA).

Hours of Work and Rest

Employment standards legislation in each province makes some provision for the maximum hours that an employer may assign to an employee or that an employee may agree to work in a given time period. In some provinces, including Alberta, the rules for "maximum hours of work" and "overtime" are separate issues. The maximum hours rule sets an absolute limit on the hours in a day or week that an employer can have the employee work; overtime refers to the threshold when overtime premium pay is required. BC takes a different approach, as you will see below.

General Rule

In BC, there is no fixed maximum number of hours in a day or week that an employee may work. The only absolute restriction on the number of hours an employee may work is set out in section 39 of the ESA: "an employer must not require or … allow an employee to work excessive hours or hours detrimental to the employee's health or safety."

There is no definition in the ESA or ESR of "excessive," and BC courts have not interpreted section 39. The BC Employment Standards Tribunal has considered section 39 in several cases, and in each case rejected the employee's claim that hours were excessive or detrimental to health. Two decisions of the Tribunal provide guidance on the meaning of section 39, albeit in general language (*Kenneth Johnston* BC EST # D071/10; and *Deepthi Perera* BC EST # D125/12, confirmed on reconsideration in BC EST # RD071/13). The Tribunal emphasized that any claim under section 39 of excessive or detrimental hours requires particular proof—that is, evidence specific to the employee who has filed the complaint. "Excessive hours" are those greater than "necessary" or "usual and proper" for the particular job. In considering whether hours are excessive, the Tribunal considered the nature of the work, specific job responsibilities, the period of time over which the hours were worked (e.g., how often the employee worked more than regular hours), and any other circumstances related to the job and the work hours. The Tribunal rejected the argument that "excessive" can be defined by the ESA's rules for the number of hours above which overtime is due, or by reference to any arbitrary limit (e.g., working more than 12 hours in one day). "Excessive" depends on the circumstances. To prove that hours have been "detrimental to the employee's health or safety," a complainant would have to provide evidence, such as a doctor's report, that links an employee's medical condition to the work hours. The director of employment standards and the Tribunal would not consider general studies about, for example, the effect of working night shifts: the evidence must be specific to the employee who has lodged the complaint.

In Alberta, employees may be required to work up to 12 hours per day and even longer when an accident occurs, urgent work is required, other unforeseeable or unpreventable circumstances occur, or the director of employment standards issues a permit authorizing extended work hours (s 16 of the ESC).

Agreement to Work Excess Hours

In Alberta, section 128(b) of the ESC prohibits an employer from requiring any worker to work hours in excess of the hours of work permitted under the Code. In BC, as noted above, section 39 of the ESA also prohibits "excessive hours" (without specifying a number) or hours detrimental to health or safety.

Hours Free from Work

Employees are entitled to have a certain number of hours free from work. In Alberta, this involves the following, at minimum:

- eight consecutive hours off work between shifts (s 17(2)); or
- one day of rest every workweek, or two consecutive days of rest in each period of two consecutive workweeks, or three consecutive days of rest in each period of three consecutive workweeks, or four consecutive days of rest in each period of four consecutive workweeks. This means that an employee can work up to 24 consecutive days, but then must take at least four consecutive days of rest (s 19).

In BC, the minimum hours free of work are as follows:

- eight consecutive hours off work between shifts (s 36(2)); or
- thirty-two consecutive hours off work every workweek, or else the employee is paid one and a half times the regular wage for time worked during the 32-hour period the employee should have been free from work (s 36(1)).

Emergencies

In BC, section 36(3) of the ESA makes an allowance for employers to call in workers to work before their eight consecutive hours free from work have gone by in the event of an emergency. This exception does not override the requirement of 32 hours off each week.

Eating Periods and Breaks

Generally, the employer must provide a 30-minute eating period after a maximum of five consecutive hours of work. In Alberta, the employer may require an employee to work longer without a break if an accident occurs, urgent work is needed, or other unpreventable or unforeseeable circumstances arise (s 18). Also in Alberta, breaks can be paid or unpaid at the employer's discretion. If breaks are unpaid, the employer cannot place restrictions on the employee during the break time, such as staying on the premises. Finally, in Alberta, a number of employees are exempt from the hours of work and rest period provisions, including managers, supervisors, farmworkers, specified professionals, and certain categories of salespeople, among others.

In BC, the rules and exemptions are essentially the same, but an employer can require an employee to work, or be available for work, during a meal break, as long as the meal break is counted as time worked by the employee.

An employer is not required to provide coffee breaks. However, if it does so and employees are required to remain at the workplace during the break, they are entitled to payment for this time.

Overtime

General Overtime Pay Rule

The purpose of overtime pay is to compensate employees for additional time spent working and to discourage employers from requiring employees to work excessive hours. The higher overtime rate applies to hours worked over a prescribed threshold amount.

In Alberta, section 21 of the ESC provides for a threshold of 8 hours on each workday in the workweek or 44 hours per week (called "the basic 8/44 rule"). Under section 22(1), employers must pay employees overtime pay at the rate of 1.5 times their regular rate of pay after they work in excess of 8 hours on each workday or 44 hours in the workweek, whichever is greater. For example, an employee who makes $14 per hour is entitled to overtime pay of $21 (1.5 × $14) for every hour worked after 44 hours in the workweek.

In BC, section 35 of the ESA provides for a threshold of 8 hours per day or 40 hours per week—unless the employer and employee have made an "averaging agreement" (discussed under the heading "Averaging Agreements (British Columbia)," below). The way the daily versus weekly overtime is calculated is similar to the system in Alberta, with two differences. First, the weekly threshold is lower in BC: 40 hours. Second, there are two daily thresholds in BC. Under section 40 of the ESA, employers must pay employees overtime pay at the rate of 1.5 times their regular rate of pay for all hours worked above 8 hours in a given day, and double the regular rate if the employee works more than 12 hours in one day. (Recall that, unlike Alberta, BC does not set an absolute maximum number of hours of work per day.)

As in Alberta, the calculation of overtime for hours worked during the week is separate. For calculating the number of hours worked per week, section 40 counts only the first 8 hours worked each day, since employees already receive overtime for daily hours above 8 (s 40(3)). This means that an employee would have to work more than five days in a week to cross the weekly overtime threshold, even if the employee works 10 hours per day during the five-day workweek. Of course, in that scenario, there would be no difference: in BC, this employee would earn overtime for 10 hours that week: 2 hours per day × 5 days.

Why, then, do Alberta and BC set two thresholds (weekly and daily) rather than just a weekly threshold? The distinction protects both employees who work fewer days per week but longer hours (who benefit from the daily threshold), and employees who work more days per week but fewer hours per day (who benefit from the weekly threshold).

In some cases, a collective agreement or company policy may provide for overtime pay at a lower threshold, such as for all hours worked in excess of 35 hours per week. As with any agreement that exceeds the ESA's or ESC's requirements, this lower threshold for overtime overrides the minimum requirements of the legislation.

An employer cannot lower an employee's regular wage to avoid paying overtime. For example, if an employee's regular pay is $15 per hour, the employer cannot lower the rate to $14 and then pay 1.5 × $14 for overtime hours worked. And as noted above, employees cannot "contract out" of the minimum standards under legislation, so they cannot give up their right to overtime pay.

Some job categories do not qualify for overtime pay under the legislation. The most significant of these exemptions relates to any person whose work is supervisory or managerial in character, but there are quite a number of jobs that are excluded from overtime pay and other rules governing hours of work, as the next section explains.

Occupations Not Affected by Overtime Rules

There are a number of occupations for which an employer is not obliged to pay workers overtime or for which the legislation specifies a different calculation of overtime.

Alberta's ESR lists persons, including managers, to whom the employer is not obliged to pay overtime or keep records of hours of work and overtime, such as architects, accountants, chiropractors, dentists, engineers, lawyers, optometrists, psychologists, veterinarians, and information systems professionals, among others.

BC's ESR also lists persons, including managers, to whom the employer is not obliged to pay overtime (and to whom none of the "hours of work" rules in part 4 of the ESA apply). These persons range from taxi drivers to teachers and professors to wilderness guides.

Since these rules change over time, employers should always check with their local Employment Standards office if they have any doubts about whether an employee is entitled to the regular overtime provisions. Employers should also take care not to make the common mistake of assuming that employees who are paid a salary rather than an hourly wage are excluded from overtime. As the next section of this chapter indicates, salaried employees are just as entitled to overtime pay as hourly wage earners. The exemption from overtime depends on the nature of the work, not on the means of payment.

Managers and supervisors are the largest category of employee that is not entitled to overtime pay. There is considerable case law on the exact definition of "manager." One of the trickiest issues in this case law is how to classify a person in a managerial or supervisory role who also performs non-supervisory or non-managerial tasks—and vice versa: workers whose responsibilities sometimes include supervision of other employees. This can be a difficult question, especially when an employee's job responsibilities change, as the Ontario case of *Tri Roc* illustrates.

CASE IN POINT

Overtime Pay for Managerial Employees

Tri Roc Electric Ltd v Butler, 2003 CanLII 11390 (Ont LRB)

Facts

Butler began to work for the employer in 1999. By the end of 2000, he became involved with several large electrical projects. In addition to his regular duties, he assumed some supervisory and administrative functions. He became responsible for keeping track of all hours worked by the employees at his site. He approved their time sheets, occasionally made recommendations for hiring and firing, and suggested wage rates for the new employees.

Although Butler consistently worked more than 44 hours a week, his employer refused to pay him overtime because it viewed him as being employed in a supervisory capacity.

Relevant Issue

Whether the employee was a supervisory or managerial employee and thus exempt from the overtime pay requirements of the Ontario ESA.

Decision

The Board held that under the old ESA, Butler was not entitled to overtime pay because the essential character of the job was managerial. Consequently, he was not entitled to any overtime pay for work performed before September 4, 2001 (the time at which Ontario's new ESA came into force).

However, from September 4, 2001, on Butler's duties could no longer be classified as supervisory or managerial because he "regularly" performed non-managerial duties, such as working with tools and completing electrical work, in the ordinary course of his employment. He was therefore entitled to receive overtime premium pay for work performed after the new statutory wording related to the supervisory/managerial exemption came into force.

Tri Roc established that under the ESA in Ontario, any employee who regularly performs non-managerial duties is eligible for overtime premium pay. The same principle applies in both Alberta and BC.

Salaried Employees

Salaried employees, whose wages are not based on the number of hours worked but rather on an annual salary, and who do not fall within the managerial or supervisory exemption, are entitled to overtime pay if they work more than the applicable threshold number of hours per week. In Alberta, this is 44 hours per week, and in BC, it is 8 hours per day or 40 hours per week, as described above. For example:

Thuy works in Alberta. Her salary is $600 per week. Because she worked 50 hours this workweek, she is entitled to 6 hours at the overtime rate. To calculate her overtime pay, divide $600 by 44 hours to determine her hourly rate ($600 ÷ 44 = $13.64 per hour). Thuy's overtime rate is therefore $20.46 per hour (1.5 × $13.64). Her total overtime pay is $122.76 ($20.46 × 6 hours). If Thuy worked in BC, a different threshold would apply for when overtime is triggered (40 hours for the week), but the same calculation would convert her salary to the appropriate hourly overtime rate.

Averaging Agreements (British Columbia)

British Columbia's ESA permits an employer and employee to agree in writing that the employee's hours of work may be averaged for the purpose of determining the employee's hours of work with respect to entitlement to wages or overtime pay. To be valid, such agreements must meet a number of requirements stipulated in section 37 of the ESA. Overtime pay is then payable after the employee has worked an average of 40 hours a week over the agreed period, which can be anywhere from one to four weeks.

Averaging agreements have obvious advantages for the employer because they potentially lower the amount of overtime pay. At the same time, employees may find an averaging agreement attractive if they prefer to work excess hours in some weeks and fewer in others. An averaging agreement makes this schedule more practical.

An averaging agreement must be in writing, set out the employee's work schedule, be signed by both the employer and employee, and include an expiry date. Section 37 of the ESA sets out a number of specifications as to how these agreements should work, so it is a good idea for any employer who intends to use an averaging agreement to check the applicable ESA section carefully to ensure that the agreement is in compliance with those specifications. Employers must retain records of any averaging agreement for four years after the employment terminates.

An expiry date does not prevent an employer and employee from agreeing to renew or replace the averaging agreement. However, the agreement cannot be revoked or cancelled before the expiry date unless both parties agree in writing.

Unlike what is required in some provinces, in BC the parties are not compelled to get approval from the director of employment standards for implementing an averaging agreement.

FYI

Class Actions and Overtime Claims

Overtime pay is a common source of employment standards claims. The provisions can be complicated to apply. For example, an employer may misclassify an employee as a manager when they are not or fail to keep track of overtime hours worked. Overtime claims have also become headline news. Two legal developments in Ontario and elsewhere in Canada have contributed to this:

1. Amendments to the law have made it easier to file class action claims. A class action is a form of lawsuit in which a group of plaintiffs who have a common complaint combine their claims and sue the defendant in a single lawsuit (Bongarde Media Co, 2009, at 3). As a result, the dollar amounts involved in class actions are often in the millions (or hundreds of millions).
2. Since the *Macaraeg v E Care Contact Centers Ltd* decision, in BC, employees are restricted to filing ESA claims, including claims for overtime, through the Employment Standards Branch. They may not pursue entitlements of the ESA through the civil courts, whether as class action suits or not. The employer's obligation to meet the ESA's requirements is not in fact an implied term of every employment contract but is instead a statutory right to be enforced through the proper administrative agency.

A review of recent class action claims based on overtime pay illustrates their potential magnitude. For example, a claim for $600 million was made against CIBC on the basis that the employer routinely refused to pay overtime to tellers and other front-line workers (*Fresco v Canadian Imperial Bank of Commerce*). In *McCracken v Canadian National Railway Company*, a claim was made for $300 million on the basis that employees were incorrectly classified as supervisors and managers.

Not all class action claims are allowed to proceed. For a class action to be brought, a plaintiff representing the class has to get a civil court judge to "certify" it. This requires the plaintiff to prove that, among other things, there are common issues of law or fact involved, a representative plaintiff will adequately represent the class, and a class action is the preferred proceeding.

In *Corless v KPMG LLP*, employees claimed $30 million on the basis that managers set performance targets that could not be met in a standard workweek, but the resulting overtime was never paid. The *Corless* litigation was certified as a class action proceeding in 2009 as part of a $10 million settlement to current and former KPMG employees. In *Fresco v Canadian Imperial Bank of Commerce*, the Ontario Court of Appeal certified the claim in 2012, overturning the Ontario Superior Court's refusal to do so. In that case, Fresco, the representative plaintiff, claimed that she was owed some $50,000 for the 2 to 15 hours a week of additional work she was required to perform as a teller and personal banker since 1998. Although the case involves literally thousands of current and former non-management employees, each with specific facts regarding unpaid overtime, the Court was satisfied that there was a common issue capable of being determined on a class-wide basis. *Fulawka v Bank of Nova Scotia* is another case in which an Ontario court certified a class action claim for overtime. Scotiabank and the employees reached a settlement in 2014, worth about $95 million.

By contrast to those three overtime cases, in *McCracken v Canadian National Railway Company* the Ontario Court of Appeal refused to certify the claim because the defendant argued that many of the claimants were managers, and thus not entitled to overtime. Even though all of the plaintiffs held the same job title ("first line supervisor"), there were in fact 70 different positions grouped under the title. The Court concluded that determining their managerial status required a position-by-position assessment, so proceeding as a class action would not avoid duplication of fact-finding and legal analysis.

Arguments about managerial status were not, however, a barrier to certification in *Rosen v BMO Nesbitt Burns Inc*, another case involving plaintiffs who might be classified as managers. In this decision from 2013, the employees had enough in common for the Court to hear arguments about whether they were managers or not as a class, rather than individually.

These cases suggest that lawsuits based on overtime claims will likely remain a significant issue in larger workplaces. That fact and the proliferation of smartphones, tablets, and other devices that enable employees to extend their workday underscore the need for employers to ensure that their overtime policies and practices comply with the requirements of employment standards legislation.

Employers should take the following steps to ensure compliance:

1. Make sure that employees are classified properly so that only those who are truly managers or supervisors are exempt from overtime pay. (Note that even employees who are exempt by statute may be entitled to overtime pay under their employment contract or an office policy.)

2. If possible, don't schedule non-managerial employees for more than 40 hours a week in BC or 44 hours a week in Alberta (or whatever the limit for non-overtime hours is under the terms of their employment agreement), and make sure that employees leave work at the end of those hours. Allowing an employee to stay late, even though it is not required or asked of the employee, potentially makes the employer liable for paying any resulting overtime.
3. Review job descriptions and performance targets to determine whether overtime hours are inherent in the workload.
4. Ensure that agreements to extend the hours of work or to average overtime pay fully comply with employment standards legislation—"almost" in compliance does not count.
5. Maintain accurate records of the hours worked and the amount paid. Without documentation, it will be difficult to prove that legislative requirements were met.
6. Have a clear policy regarding travel time and the amount of electronic work being done during off hours. Some employers ban the use of smartphones or similar devices for work purposes between certain hours or limit them to emergency use (Loewenberg & Lisi, 2008, at 5).
7. Clearly communicate and consistently enforce the overtime policy.

Banking of Overtime Pay

In Alberta, section 23 of the ESC allows an employer and employee to agree that the employee will receive paid time off work instead of overtime pay. An employee or the majority of a group of employees may enter into an overtime agreement with the employer. Under such an agreement, the employee takes time off with pay instead of receiving overtime pay. For this time off, the employee is paid at the same wage rate that they would have been paid had they worked and received "straight-time" wages from the employer.

In BC, section 42 of the ESA allows an employer and employee to agree that the employee will receive paid time off work or credit overtime work to a time bank instead of overtime pay. Such agreements can arise at the written request of the employee, and the employee must receive 1.5 hours of paid time off for each hour of overtime worked (and double hours if the employee works more than 12 hours in a single day). For example, if the employee works 48 hours in a week and therefore is entitled to 8 hours at the overtime rate, that employee may agree in writing to take 12 hours (1.5 × 8 hours) of paid time off in lieu of overtime pay. Without such a written agreement, the employer must provide overtime pay (at 1.5 times the employee's regular rate of pay) to compensate for overtime hours worked.

In both provinces, if an employee requests to close the time bank or leaves employment, the employer must pay any banked overtime owing. In Alberta, amendment or termination of the agreement is permitted with at least one month's written notice to the other party (s 23(2)(d) of the ESC).

Vacation

Vacation pay and vacation time are separate entitlements. An employee may be entitled to vacation pay but not vacation time, depending on whether the employee has worked a full year for the employer. The relevant provisions in Alberta's ESC are sections 34–44, and in BC's ESA the relevant provisions are sections 57–60.

Vacation Time

Employees in both provinces are entitled to at least two weeks' vacation time per year after they have worked for an employer for a full 12 months. In both Alberta and BC, the minimum increases to three weeks after five consecutive years of employment. An employee who resigns before completing a full year of employment is not entitled to vacation time, only vacation pay.

In Alberta, employees may take two weeks' vacation in an unbroken period (within the 12 months after it is earned), unless they request otherwise, in which case the vacation may be taken in periods of not less than one day. If the employer and the employee are unable to agree on a mutually satisfactory date to start the employee's annual vacation, the employer is entitled to decide when vacation time will be taken. In these cases, the employer must provide at least two weeks' written notice of the date on which the employee's annual vacation is to start. In some cases, an employer is entitled to decide when a vacation must be taken, regardless of the employees' preferences. For example, the employer can designate a plant shutdown for a week at Christmas, during which all employees take a vacation. However, the employer must give the vacation time within 12 months after it is earned.

In BC, an employer must allow its employees to take their vacation time in periods of one or more weeks, at the employee's discretion. Although the ESA does not specifically say so, the employer is entitled to decide when vacation time will be taken—as in the above example of a plant shutdown for a week at Christmas. Also, as in Alberta, the employer must give the vacation time within 12 months after the employee becomes entitled to it. For example, if Carlos starts work on January 1, 2020, he becomes entitled to two weeks' vacation after December 31, 2020, and his employer is required to provide him with two weeks' vacation to be taken by December 31, 2021.

PERIODS OF INACTIVE SERVICE

In Alberta, section 44 of the ESC states that an employee's annual vacation can be reduced in proportion to the number of days that the employee was absent from work. This includes maternity and parental leaves and other leaves.

In BC, inactive service (including that arising from layoff, sickness, injury, approved leaves, or statutory leaves such as jury, pregnancy, parental, family responsibility, compassionate care, or reservists' leave) is included in calculating the 12 months' employment (s 56 of the ESA). An employee who is on a statutory leave does not lose the right to take vacation time, although the employer may choose not to give vacation pay for that time. Vacation leave may be taken after the statutory leave expires or at a later date if the parties agree. The employee does not have to shorten the statutory leave or risk losing some or all of their vacation time.

Vacation Pay

Under the legislation in both provinces, employees are entitled to vacation pay that is at least equal to 4 percent of wages earned (excluding the vacation pay) during the 12-month period for which the vacation pay is given. However, after five consecutive years of employment, vacation pay is paid at 6 percent of total wages. For example, if Eli earns $25,000 a year within the first five years of his employment (starting with his date of commencement), he is entitled to receive 4 percent of that amount as vacation pay, which is $1,000. For full-time employees, 4 percent of earnings typically equals two weeks' pay. Where an employee works irregular hours, has worked many hours, or was laid off in the previous 12 months, 4 percent of earnings could be considerably more or less than two weeks' wages.

For the purposes of determining vacation pay in Alberta, "wages" do not include overtime earnings (unless there is an overtime agreement in place allowing for banked overtime hours to be paid at straight time when they are given; these straight-time earnings are included as wages when calculating vacation pay). Also excluded are general holiday pay, pay in lieu of termination notice, and unearned bonuses.

For the purposes of determining vacation pay in BC, "wages" do include overtime pay, statutory holiday pay, termination pay, and commissions.

The entitlement to vacation pay begins from the first hour of employment. An employee who leaves at any time must be given all vacation pay earned to that point. For example, an employee who works only seven days is entitled to 4 percent of the wages earned during those seven days. However, in BC (not Alberta) the employee must have been employed for at least five calendar days.

Many employers offer more vacation time and pay than the statutory minimum. In fact, employers usually provide at least three weeks' vacation time and 6 percent vacation pay even before five years of service. The workplace trend is toward recognizing the importance of leisure time. Even four weeks' vacation at an 8 percent rate is becoming more common for employees with as little as three to five years of service.

In Alberta, section 41 of the ESC permits an employer to pay vacation pay at any time, but no later than the next regularly scheduled payday after the vacation has commenced. If it is requested by the employee, vacation pay must be paid in full at least one day prior to the start of the vacation. In BC, section 58(2) stipulates that vacation pay must be paid at least seven days before the beginning of the employee's annual vacation, or on the employee's scheduled paydays, if such was agreed to in a written contract or collective agreement.

Vacation Entitlement and Statutory Leaves of Absence

In Alberta, section 44 of the ESC states that an employer can reduce an employee's vacation time and vacation pay in proportion to the number of days that they were, or would normally have been, scheduled to work but did not. As noted above, in BC an employee continues to earn credits toward vacation time during statutory leaves of absence, such as pregnancy, parental, and bereavement leaves.

In both cases, the impact of those leaves on vacation pay depends on the terms of the contract of employment. For example, where either a collective agreement or an individual contract provides that the employee earns two paid vacation days for every month of service, both vacation time and pay are earned through service and therefore continue to accumulate during statutory leaves.

However, where vacation pay is based on earnings, the amount of vacation pay is affected by statutory leaves because it is calculated as a percentage of wages earned, and an employee does not usually earn wages during a leave. For example, an employee on maternity or parental leave for the year preceding the vacation time would probably have no earnings from the employer. Therefore, vacation pay would not be owing.

General Holidays (Alberta)

General holidays (called "statutory holidays" in BC) are particular days, specified in the employment standards legislation, as paid days off for most workers in most circumstances. Sections 25–33 set out the provisions relating to general holidays in the ESC.

Nine General Holidays

As set out in the definitions in section 25 of Alberta's ESC, the nine paid general holidays that employees are entitled to each year in Alberta are New Year's Day, Alberta Family Day, Good Friday, Victoria Day, Canada Day, Labour Day, Thanksgiving Day, Remembrance Day, and Christmas Day. Section 25 also provides that other days may be designated as general holidays by the Lieutenant Governor in Council or by agreement between the employer and employees or by the employer.

Qualifying for Paid General Holidays

Most employees in Alberta are eligible for general holidays. However, employees who work in certain industries, such as hotels, restaurants, and hospitals, may be required to work on a general holiday.

If a holiday falls on a day that is normally a workday for the employee and the employee did not work on the holiday, they are entitled to their average daily wage.

If a holiday falls on a day that is not normally a workday for the employee and they work on the holiday, they are still entitled to 1.5 times their regular wage rate for hours worked.

If a holiday falls on a day that is normally a workday for the employee and they worked on the holiday, they are still entitled to the same amount of general holiday pay as before. There are two options for paying employees holiday pay:

1. The employee gets 1.5 times their regular wage for hours worked and average daily wage.
2. The employee gets their regular wage rate for hours worked and average daily wage with one day off work.

The following four examples show how the Alberta provisions work:

Izumi works eight hours a day, five days a week, earning $200 per day and $1,000 per week. She qualifies for the general holiday and has been given a day off on the general holiday, so her holiday pay is $200—in other words, she receives her typical day's pay.

Owen earns $20 per hour working part time on an as-required basis. Some days he works eight hours while others he works two or three hours. In the relevant nine-week period before the public holiday he worked a total of 15 days and earned $1,000, and 5 of those 15 days fell on the same day of the week on which the general holiday falls. His holiday pay is $66.67 ($1,000 ÷ 15). This reflects his average daily wage over the period before the holiday.

Joshua is in the middle of his parental leave. Although he receives parental benefits under the federal employment insurance program, he has no wages from his employer in the relevant period. He is not entitled to public holiday pay since he did not earn any wages or vacation pay during that period.

Fatima works eight hours a day, five days a week, earning $25 per hour or $1,000 per week. Her employer has asked her to work on a general holiday, and she works eight hours that day. Her employer is obliged to pay her $500 for that day (1.5 × $200 = $300 plus $200, an average day's pay). Alternatively, she may receive her daily pay rate of $200 and be provided an additional day off with pay at her regular daily rate.

Statutory Holidays (British Columbia)

Sections 44–48 of the ESA set out the rules for statutory holidays in BC.

Ten Statutory Holidays

As set out in the definitions in section 1 of the ESA, the ten paid statutory holidays that employees are entitled to each year are New Year's Day, Family Day (third Monday in February), Good Friday, Victoria Day, Canada Day, British Columbia Day (first Monday in August), Labour Day, Thanksgiving Day, Remembrance Day, Christmas Day, and Family Day.

Qualifying for Paid Statutory Holidays

Most employees in BC are eligible for statutory holidays. However, employees who work in certain industries, such as hotels, restaurants, and hospitals, often work on a statutory holiday. Section 44 of the ESA stipulates that every employee in BC who has been employed for at least 30 calendar days before a statutory holiday and who has worked or earned wages for 15 of the 30 calendar days preceding the statutory holiday (or worked under a corresponding averaging agreement) qualifies for statutory holiday pay.

If an employee is given a day off on the statutory holiday, or else is given a day off on another day of the year instead of the statutory holiday, that employee must be paid an amount equal to at least an average day's pay for that day off. The amount to be paid is determined by a formula (set out in s 45(1) of the ESA) based on the amount paid or payable to the employee for work done and wages earned over the 30-calendar-day period preceding the holiday divided by days worked over that period. This average day's pay applies whether or not the statutory holiday falls on the worker's regularly scheduled day off.

If the employer asks the employee to work on a statutory holiday, section 46 requires that the employer must pay (1) 1.5 times the regular wage for the time worked up to 12 hours, (2) double the regular wage for time worked beyond 12 hours, and (3) an average day's pay as per the formula in section 45(1). The following three examples show how the BC provisions work:

Mark earns $20 per hour working part time on an as-required basis. Some days he works eight hours; on others he works two or three hours. Suppose that Mark does not work on the statutory holiday, and that in the 30-calendar-day period before the statutory holiday he worked a total of 15 days and earned $1,000. His holiday pay would be $66.67 ($1,000 ÷ 15). This reflects his average daily wage over the period before the holiday. Note that if he had worked fewer than 15 days within the 30-calendar-day period before the statutory holiday, he would not be entitled to any holiday pay.

Ali works eight hours a day, five days a week, earning $25 per hour. His employer has asked him to work on a statutory holiday, and he works eight hours that day. In the previous 30 days he worked 20 days, earning $4,000, making his average day's pay $200. His employer must pay him $500 for the statutory holiday (1.5 × $200 = $300, plus $200, an average day's pay). If Ali had worked over 12 hours on that statutory holiday, say, 14 hours, he would be paid $750 (1.5 × $25 × 12 = $450, plus 2 × $25 × 2 = $100, plus $200).

Sucheta qualifies for statutory holiday pay, and she has agreed to take a day off on another day of the year instead of the statutory holiday. That other day is treated as if it is a statutory holiday. If in the 30-day period before the substituted day of holiday she works 20 days and earns $4,000, the employer must pay her $200 ($4,000 ÷ 20), an average day's pay. (A common example of such a switch is when a holiday such as Remembrance Day occurs mid-week, and the employee and employer wish to shift the holiday to make a long weekend.)

The ESA allows employers to substitute another day off for the statutory holiday if both the employer and employee agree to the substitution (s 48). However, that does not affect the employer's obligations or employee's rights with respect to the substituted day—that is, that day must still be treated as if it were a statutory holiday (s 45).

Statutory Leaves of Absence (Alberta)

A statutory leave allows an employee to take time off work for a specified purpose. An employer is not required to pay an employee while the employee is on statutory leave. However, employees who exercise their right to statutory leave are entitled to certain other statutory rights and protections, most importantly the right to return to work at the end of the leave period.

Alberta's ESC provides for a wide range of leaves, including maternity and parental (which covers adoption), reservist, compassionate care, death or disappearance of a child, critical illness of a child, long-term illness and injury, domestic violence, personal and family responsibility, and bereavement leaves. Collective agreements and employment agreements may provide for some additional leave days, such as short-term disability or personal days. Also, section 23 of the *Jury Act* states that an employee must be allowed sufficient leave to serve as a juror when summoned.

Maternity Leave

Sections 45–49, 52, and 53 of the ESC govern maternity leave. A pregnant employee has the right to take up to a combined total of 62 weeks of statutory leave, including 16 weeks' unpaid time off work for maternity leave and 37 weeks for parental leave. The employee may be eligible for employment insurance benefits during this time, but the employer is not required to pay the employee during the leave.

Section 45 of the ESC stipulates that a pregnant employee who has been employed by the employer for at least 90 days is entitled to maternity leave without pay. She must provide six weeks' written notice of the date she will start her maternity leave, according to section 47.

It is up to the employee, not the employer, to decide when to start her maternity leave. However, section 46 does set some parameters on when maternity leave may be taken. The earliest a maternity leave can begin is 13 weeks before the employee's due date, and the latest it can begin is on the actual birth date. If during the 13 weeks immediately preceding the estimated due date, the pregnancy of the employee interferes with the performance of her duties, the employer may give the employee written notice requiring her to start her leave (s 49). The leave must last until at least six weeks following the date of delivery unless the employee and the employer agree to shorten the period and the employee obtains a medical certificate indicating that resumption of work will not endanger her health (s 46(2)).

If an employee needs to leave her job early for health reasons, she does not have to start her maternity leave when she stops working; she may go on sick leave if she chooses. If any portion of an individual's absence before or after the birth of a child is related to a bona fide medical condition, the employee is entitled to short-term disability benefits if available under an existing employee benefit plan.

FYI

Maternity Leave

Pregnancy was once considered just cause for dismissal. In 1921, BC led the nation by several decades when it introduced maternity leave to protect women's right to employment during and after pregnancy. The next province to follow was New Brunswick in 1964. It wasn't until the late 1980s when women in all provinces were granted the same protection.

In 1971, the federal government instituted income replacement to women on leave, and in 1990 these benefits were also made available to fathers and adoptive parents who took time off from work to care for their children.

As noted earlier, a pregnant employee is supposed to give her employer at least six weeks' written notice before beginning her leave. However, there is no penalty for failing to provide this notice, and it may in fact be provided within two weeks after she ceases to work, by providing her employer with a medical certificate. If the employer requests it, the employee must provide a medical certificate stating the due date and the date of birth, stillbirth, or miscarriage.

For most employees, a maternity leave is 15 weeks, although an employee may take a shorter leave if she wishes. Once maternity leave begins, it must be taken all at once. An employee who returns to work early gives up the right to take the remainder of the leave.

FYI

Use It or Lose It Paternity Leave

WOULD MORE MEN TAKE A "USE IT OR LOSE IT" PATERNITY LEAVE?

Rather than focusing on ways to bring women back into the workforce after having children, it's worth exploring how to provide incentives for men to step out.

In Norway, fathers receive 12 weeks of paternity leave that is non-transferable to the mother: dads must "use it or lose it." In Sweden, fathers get about eight weeks of non-transferable paternity leave. In Quebec, they get five weeks. …

"Daddy quotas" carry a lingering, positive impact on fathers. A study by Ankita Patnaik, a doctoral student at Cornell University, found that men who took advantage of parental leave spent more time on child care and domestic obligations even years later. And their female partners spent more time working outside the home.

SOURCE: Eichler, 2013.

Parental Leave

Sections 50 and 51, the parental leave provisions of Alberta's ESC, were enacted in 2001. Unlike maternity leave, which is available only to birth mothers, parental leave is available to any new parent. It is intended to give new parents time to adjust to their new family roles. This leave can be up to 37 consecutive weeks within 53 weeks after the child's birth, or in the case of adoption, up to 37 consecutive weeks within 53 weeks after the child is placed with the adoptive parent. To qualify, the statute states that an employee must have been hired at least 90 days before the leave begins. An employee must provide at least six weeks' written notice of the date the employee will start the parental leave, unless there are extenuating circumstances that preclude notice being provided.

The term "parent" includes a birth mother, a birth father, or an adopting parent. A birth mother who takes maternity leave must start her parental leave as soon as her maternity leave ends if she had applied for maternity leave. That leave is 37 consecutive weeks beginning immediately after the end of her maternity leave. If the birth mother had not applied earlier for maternity leave, she is entitled to 37 consecutive weeks, beginning after the child's birth and within 53 weeks after the birth.

A birth father's parental leave must begin within 90 days after the child is born and can extend to 37 consecutive weeks of unpaid leave, which must be completed within 53 weeks of the birth or placement. A father's parental leave does not necessarily have to start immediately after a mother's maternity leave ends, for example.

Parental leave may be taken wholly by one parent or may be shared between two parents, but the total combined leave cannot exceed 62 weeks. If both employees are with the same employer, the employer is not required to grant parental leave to more than one employee at a time (s 50(3)). As with maternity leave, the employee must take the leave in an unbroken period. If both maternity and parental leave are being taken by the same employee, they must be taken consecutively. If the employee returns to work early, they forfeit the remainder of the leave.

Employees are required to give their employer at least six weeks' written notice before beginning a parental leave or before changing the proposed leave date. However, there is no penalty for failing to give this notice.

Both parents are entitled to take parental leave. Their leaves may overlap, or the mother's partner could begin parental leave as the mother is returning from her leave. Alternatively, both the mother and her partner could take their leaves at the same time.

For employment insurance benefit purposes, one or both parents may apply for the 35 weeks of EI parental benefits. However, if they both apply, their combined benefits claim cannot exceed 35 weeks. However, only one two-week waiting period need be served before benefits begin.

FYI

Fathers Taking EI Parental Leave on the Rise

In 2000, only 3 percent of fathers claimed or planned to claim paid parental benefits. A 2012 study found a higher proportion of Canadian fathers who had taken some sort of parental leave (76 percent for fathers in Quebec and 26 percent elsewhere in Canada). This is not only a statistically significant increase, but a socially significant one as well.

This claim rate for fathers moves Canada ahead of many other countries, but still leaves it considerably behind those that offer non-transferable leave to fathers. In Norway, for example, almost 80 percent of fathers take parental leave.

Previously, fathers were required to serve a two-week waiting period if they wished to share benefits with the mother, who also had to serve a two-week period at the beginning of her claim for maternity benefits. The father is no longer required to serve the second waiting period.

SOURCES: Statistics Canada, 2003; Findlay & Kohen, 2012.

Section 52 of the ESC prohibits an employer from terminating the employment of or laying off an employee who has started maternity leave or who is entitled to or has started parental leave, unless the employer has discontinued the business or activity, in whole or in part, in which the employee was employed.

When the employee is entitled to resume work, they must provide written notice to the employer at least four weeks in advance of the date they intend to resume work, unless failure to notify the employer was due to unforeseeable or unpreventable circumstances (ss 53(1) and (6)).

Section 53(7) provides that employees returning from maternity or parental leave are to be reinstated to the position they occupied when the leave started, or to a comparable position, at not less than the earnings and benefits they had when the leave started.

In the event that the discontinued operation, referenced above, resumes within 52 weeks of the end of the leave, the employer must reinstate the employee to the position they held at the start of the maternity or parental leave, at no less earnings or benefits, or provide alternative work in accordance with an established seniority system or practice in place at the time the leave commenced (s 53.1).

Reservist Leave

Effective June 30, 2009, the Alberta ESC was amended to provide employees who are reservists with unpaid, job-protected leaves of absence when they are deployed on operations outside Canada (including pre- and post-deployment responsibilities), or when they are deployed to assist with emergencies within Canada (ss 53.2–53.8). In addition, reservists are entitled to unpaid leave to participate in annual training for up to 20 days in a calendar year.

Reservists are members of the reserve force of the Canadian Forces as defined in the *National Defence Act*. Employees who are reservists and who have completed at least 26 consecutive weeks of employment with an employer are entitled to reservist leave.

Eligible employees who are planning to take reservist leave must give their employer at least four weeks' written notice identifying the start date and the date of return (estimated or actual). If urgent circumstances render such notice impractical, the employee must give notice as soon as is reasonable and practicable.

Employers are restricted from terminating an employee on reservist leave. Employees who have been granted such leave must be reinstated to the same position or a comparable position upon their return to work. If an employer suspends or discontinues its business in whole or in part during the leave, but the business operation subsequently resumes within 52 weeks following the end of the leave, the employer must reinstate the employee to the position occupied by the employee prior to the leave (with at least the same earnings and benefits), or provide alternative work in accordance with the prevailing practice or seniority system that was in place when the employee's leave started (with no loss of seniority or benefits).

Compassionate Care Leave

Sections 53.9–53.94, the compassionate care leave provisions of Alberta's ESC, were enacted in 2014. The Alberta legislation is similar to that in place in other provinces and in the *Canada Labour Code* for federally regulated employers. However, unlike the legislation in most other jurisdictions, the Alberta legislation requires that a lengthy prior employment relationship exist before employees are deemed eligible for compassionate care leave.

Section 53.9(2) provides that an employee who has worked for an employer for at least 90 days and who is the primary caregiver of a seriously ill family member can take unpaid, job-protected leave of up to 27 weeks.

The definition of "family member" in the ESC includes a spouse or common law partner, a child of the employee or a child of the employee's spouse or common law partner, a parent of the employee or the parent's spouse or common law partner, and any other classes of persons designated in the regulations. The regulations expand on the definition to include siblings, grandparents, grandchildren, aunts, uncles, nephews, nieces, and any other person considered to be like a close relative of the employee.

To be eligible for compassionate care leave, the employee must provide their employer with a physician's certificate stating that the family member has a serious medical condition with a significant risk that they will die within 26 weeks of the day the certificate is issued (s 53.9(4)).

The employee must provide at least two weeks' notice of their intention to take leave, unless circumstances necessitate a shorter notice period (s 53.9(5)). On return, an employee must provide two weeks' notice of their planned date of return to work, unless the employer agrees to a shorter notice period.

As with other statutory job-protected leaves, employers are restricted from terminating an employee who is on compassionate care leave. Employees who have been granted such leave must be reinstated to the same position or a comparable position upon their return to work (s 53.92(2)). If an employer suspends or discontinues its business in whole or in part during the leave, but the business operation subsequently resumes within 52 weeks following the end of the leave, the employer must reinstate the employee to the position occupied by the employee prior to the leave (with at least the same earnings and benefits), or provide alternative work in accordance with the prevailing practice or seniority system that was in place when the employee's leave started (with no loss of seniority or benefits) (s 53.93).

Employees may qualify for employment insurance while on compassionate care leave.

Death or Disappearance of Child Leave

Section 53.95 of Alberta's ESC provides an unpaid leave of up to 52 weeks to the parent of a child who has disappeared and it is probable, considering the circumstances, that the child disappeared as a result of a crime. The leave is up to 104 weeks if the child has died and it is likely that this is the result of a crime. In either case, the child must be under the age of 18. The employer may not terminate or lay off an employee who has taken a leave under this section of the Code. When the employee returns to work, the employer is required to reinstate the employee to the position the employee held prior to the leave or to provide alternative work of a comparable nature.

Critical Illness of a Child Leave

Under section 53.96 of the Code, an employee who is the parent of a critically ill child is entitled to unpaid leave of up to 36 weeks to provide care and support to the child. The employee is required to provide the employer with a medical certificate stating (1) that the child is critically ill and requires the care/support of one or more parents, (2) the start date of the period during which the care is required, (3) the end date of the period the care is required, and (4) the day the leave started (if it started before the certificate was issued). Similar to other types of leave, the employer must reinstate the employee to their original position or an alternative job of a comparable nature after the leave has ended.

Long-Term Illness and Injury Leave

This leave is for an employee who becomes ill or injured. Like other leaves, the employee must have worked for the employer for at least 90 days before they are entitled to long-term illness/injury leave. Medical documentation must be provided, and the employee may be provided up to 16 weeks in a calendar year. When the employee is ready to return, they must provide at least one week's written notice.

Domestic Violence Leave

Section 53.98 of the Alberta ESC allows an employee who is the victim of domestic violence up to ten calendar days of unpaid leave per year. According to the ESC, domestic violence occurs when an employee or the employee's dependant is subjected to any acts or omissions listed in the Code. These include (1) intentional acts or omissions that cause injury or property damage or that intimidate or harm, (2) acts or threats that intimidate a person by creating a reasonable fear of property damage or injury, (3) conduct that constitutes psychological or emotional abuse, (4) forced confinement, (5) sexual contact of any kind that is coerced by force or by threat of force, and (6) stalking.

The person engaging in the acts or omissions must be someone who is or was in an intimate relationship with the employee or has resided with the employee; someone who is dating the employee; a biological or adoptive parent of one or more children with the employee; is related by blood, marriage, or adoption to the employee; or who resides with the employee and has care or custody over the employee.

An employee can take the leave to seek medical attention for themselves or their children. They may also need it to access assistance from a victim services organization, to relocate, or to seek legal/law enforcement assistance. The requirements for notice and documentation from professionals are less specific than they are for other types of leave under the ESC. The only requirement specified is that the employee give the employer as much notice as is reasonable and practical. This allows both employers and employees some flexibility when managing these highly sensitive and risky situations.

Personal and Family Responsibility Leave

Employees in Alberta are entitled to five unpaid leave days per calendar year to manage their own health or to meet the health care responsibilities for a family member. This may include caregiving responsibilities for children or dependant adults. Before taking this leave, the employee must provide as much notice as is reasonably practical.

Bereavement Leave

Bereavement leave in Alberta is unpaid and up to three days per calendar year for the death of a family member.

Statutory Leaves of Absence (British Columbia)

A statutory leave in BC allows an employee to take time off work for a specified purpose. An employer is not required to pay an employee while the employee is on statutory leave. However, employees who exercise their right to statutory leave are entitled to certain other statutory rights and protections, most importantly the right to return to work at the end of the leave period.

British Columbia's ESA provides for 11 types of leave: maternity, parental, family responsibility, compassionate care, reservists', child disappearance, child death, domestic or sexual violence, critical illness or injury, bereavement, and jury duty.

Note that there is no statutory right to sick leave, paid or unpaid. An employer may agree to provide sick leave but is not required to do so.

Maternity Leave

Section 50 of the ESA governs maternity leave. A pregnant employee has the right to take up to 17 weeks' unpaid time off work. The employee may be eligible for employment insurance benefits during this time, but the employer is not required to pay the employee during the leave.

The ESA does not explicitly impose a minimum period of work for eligibility for maternity leave. Although section 50(4) states that an employee has an obligation to provide four weeks' notice in writing of her intention to go on leave, it has been clearly established that there are no consequences to an employee who fails to provide this notice.

It is up to the employee, not the employer, to decide when to start her maternity leave. However, the ESA does set some parameters on when maternity leave may be taken. The earliest the 17-week maternity leave may begin is 13 weeks before the employee's due date, and the latest it may begin is on the actual birth date. Employees can, however, request leave after the birth of the child or the termination of the pregnancy—in which case they are entitled to six weeks of leave (s 50(2)). If the employer requests it, the employee must provide a medical certificate stating the due date and the date of birth, stillbirth, or miscarriage.

If an employee needs to leave her job early for health reasons, she does not have to start her leave when she stops working; she may go on sick leave if she chooses. If any portion of an individual's absence before or after the birth of a child is related to a bona fide medical condition, the employee is entitled to short-term disability benefits if available under an existing employee benefit plan.

For most employees, a maternity leave is 17 weeks, although an employee may take a shorter leave if she wishes. Once maternity leave begins, it must be taken all at once. An employee who returns to work early gives up the right to take the remainder of the leave. In the case of miscarriages or stillbirths, the maternity leave may slightly exceed 17 weeks, because leave ends on the later of 17 weeks after it begins or 6 weeks after the stillbirth or miscarriage. An employee is also entitled to an additional 6 consecutive weeks of unpaid leave if for reasons related to the birth or termination of the pregnancy she is unable to return to work (s 50(3)).

Parental Leave

Section 51, the parental leave provision of British Columbia's ESA, was passed in 1995, almost 25 years after maternity leave was first enacted. Section 51 came in response to the creation of parental leave benefits under federal employment insurance. Unlike maternity leave, which is available only to birth mothers, parental leave is available to any new parent, including birth mothers, birth fathers, same-sex partners, and adopting parents. It is intended to give new parents time to adjust to their new family roles. The leave is 62 consecutive weeks for all parents except mothers who took maternity leave, who are entitled to 61 consecutive weeks immediately following the maternity leave.

As with maternity leave, the ESA does not impose a minimum period of work for eligibility for parental leave. Note that there are no consequences for an employee who fails to provide four weeks' notice of the intention to go on leave.

Section 51(1) sets out the entitlement to leave. First, it specifies that a birth mother who takes maternity leave must start her parental leave as soon as her maternity leave ends if she had applied for maternity leave, unless she and the employer agree otherwise (s 51(1)(a)). That leave is 61 consecutive weeks beginning immediately after the end of her maternity leave. If the birth mother had not applied earlier for maternity leave, she is entitled to the same form of parental leave as any non-adopting parent, as described below.

Under section 51(1)(b), a parent other than an adopting parent may take up to 62 consecutive weeks of parental leave. This leave must start within 78 weeks after the birth. The term "parent" is not defined in the ESA, but BC now has a broad definition under the new *Family Law Act*, which took effect in 2013. It includes not only birth mothers and fathers but same-sex partners and others who assume the role of parent, and includes the possibility of more than two parents.

An adopting parent is entitled to up to 62 consecutive weeks of unpaid leave beginning within 78 weeks after the child is placed with the parent (s 51(1)(d)).

The employee must take parental leave in an unbroken period, unless the employer agrees otherwise. If the employee returns to work early, they forfeit the remainder of the leave.

As mentioned above, there is no penalty for employees who fail to give their employer at least four weeks' written notice before beginning a parental leave or before changing the proposed leave date. In fact, section 123 of the ESA states that a technical irregularity will not invalidate any proceeding under the Act, and the BC Employment Standards Tribunal and the courts have said that failure to give written notice does not affect the employee's entitlement to the leave. Both parents are entitled to take the full period of parental leave. If the mother and the mother's partner, for example, both work for the same employer, the employer is required to provide 78 weeks of combined pregnancy/parental leave for the birth mother and 62 weeks of parental leave for the mother's partner. Their leaves may overlap, or the mother's partner could begin parental leave as the mother is returning from her leave. Alternatively, both the mother and her partner could take their leaves at the same time. And as noted above, the birth mother's parental leave does not have to start immediately after the birth, unless she takes maternity leave. If she does not take maternity leave, her parental leave can start at any time within 78 weeks after the birth.

Under federal law on employment insurance benefits, one or both parents may apply for the 35 weeks of EI parental benefits. However, if they both apply, their combined benefits claim cannot exceed 35 weeks. However, only one two-week waiting period need be served before benefits begin.

Family Responsibility Leave

Section 52 allows any employee up to five days of unpaid leave every year they are employed to meet responsibilities related to the care or health of a child in the employee's care or any other member of the employee's immediate family. It also allows such leave for responsibilities relating to the education of that employee's child. So the latter, for example, would allow a parent to attend a child's graduation ceremony.

Compassionate Care Leave

Section 52.1 of the ESA deals with compassionate care leave. This provision, first created in 2006, permits an employee to take up to 27 weeks of unpaid leave in a 52-week period to provide care or support to a family member who has been certified by a medical practitioner or nurse practitioner to have a serious medical condition and to be at significant risk of death within that 26-week period. Should the family member survive after that period but continue to be at significant risk within a further 26-week period, the employee can take an additional leave of up to 27 weeks.

"Family member" has been defined very broadly in the regulation pertaining to this leave, and it can encompass many relationships, including someone "like a close relative."

Reservists' Leave

Under section 52.2 of BC's ESA, which was added in 2008, employees who are reservists in the military and who are deployed, either internationally or domestically, are entitled to unpaid leave for the time required to engage in the operation. The employee must give the employer four weeks' notice if possible, or a reasonable amount of notice if the deployment occurs in less than four weeks. The notice must include the date the employee will begin and end the leave.

Leave Respecting the Disappearance of a Child

Section 52.3 of the ESA deals with leave respecting the disappearance of a child. If a child of an employee disappears and it is probable, in the circumstances, that the child's disappearance is a result of a crime, and the employee requests leave under this section, the employee is entitled to unpaid leave for a period of up to 52 weeks. This leave is not available to an employee who is charged with a crime that resulted in the disappearance of the employee's child.

The employee may take leave in more than one unit of time, with the employer's consent.

The leave must be taken during the period that starts on the date the child disappears and ends on the date that is 53 weeks after the date the child disappears. However, the leave may end on the earliest of the following dates, if any apply:

- the date on which circumstances indicate it is no longer probable that the child's disappearance is a result of a crime;
- the date the employee is charged with a crime that resulted in the disappearance of the child;
- the date that is 14 days after the date on which the child is found alive;

- the date on which the child is found dead (in which case the employee is entitled to leave respecting the death of a child under s 52.4); or
- the date that is the last day of the last unit of time in respect of which the employer consents.

If requested by the employer, the employee must, as soon as practicable, provide to the employer reasonably sufficient proof that the employee's child has disappeared in circumstances in which it is probable the disappearance is a result of a crime. A crime means an offence under the *Criminal Code*.

Leave Respecting the Death of a Child

Section 52.4 of the ESA deals with leave respecting the death of a child. If a child of an employee dies and the employee requests leave under this section, the employee is entitled to unpaid leave for a period of up to 104 weeks. This leave is not available to an employee who is charged with a crime that resulted in the death of the employee's child.

The employee may take leave in more than one unit of time, with the employer's consent.

The leave must be taken during the period that starts on the date the child dies or on the date the child is found dead, in the case of the child disappearing before the child dies, and the leave ends 105 weeks after the date the leave began. However, the leave may end on the earliest of the following dates, if any apply:

- the date the employee is charged with a crime that resulted in the death of the child, or
- the date that is the last day of the last unit of time in respect of which the employer consents.

If requested by the employer, the employee must, as soon as practicable, provide to the employer reasonably sufficient proof that the employee's child has died.

Leave Respecting Domestic or Sexual Violence

Section 52.5 of the ESA deals with leave respecting domestic or sexual violence. An employee or eligible person who experiences domestic or sexual violence may request leave for one or more of the following purposes:

> (a) to seek medical attention for the employee or eligible person in respect of a physical or psychological injury or disability caused by the domestic or sexual violence
>
> (b) to obtain for the employee or eligible person victim services or other social services relating to domestic or sexual violence
>
> (c) to obtain for the employee or eligible person psychological or other professional counselling services in respect of a psychological or emotional condition caused by the domestic or sexual violence

(d) to temporarily or permanently relocate the employee or eligible person or both the employee and eligible person

(e) to seek legal or law enforcement assistance for the employee or eligible person, including preparing for or participating in any civil or criminal legal proceeding related to the domestic or sexual violence

(f) any prescribed purpose (none have been prescribed as of yet).

If an employee requests leave under this section, the employee is entitled, during each calendar year, to up to ten days of unpaid leave in units of one or more days or in one continuous period and, in addition, up to 15 weeks of unpaid leave. The employee may take leave in more than one unit of time, with the employer's consent.

An employee is not eligible for this leave respecting an eligible person if the employee commits the domestic violence against the eligible person.

If requested by the employer, the employee must, as soon as practicable, provide to the employer reasonably sufficient proof in the circumstances that the employee is entitled to the leave.

Critical Illness or Injury Leave

Section 52.11 of the ESA deals with critical illness or injury leave, which provides for unpaid leave to care for a family member whose health has significantly changed due to critical illness or injury, such that the life of the family member is at risk. An employee may take up to 36 weeks of unpaid leave within a period of 52 weeks to care for a family member who is under the age of 19, and 16 weeks within a period of 52 weeks for a family member who is 19 years of age or older.

A request for critical illness or injury leave need not be in writing, but an employee must provide the employer with a certificate from a medical practitioner or nurse practitioner. The certificate must confirm that the baseline state of health of the family member has significantly changed and the life of the family member is at risk as a result of an illness or injury. The certificate must also establish that the care or support required by the family member can be met by one or more persons who are not medical professionals, and it must set out the time period for which the family member requires care or support.

The leave ends on the last day of the week that the family member dies, after the maximum amount of leave is taken, or 52 weeks after the leave begins.

If the life of the family member remains at risk 52 weeks after the first leave began, the employee may take a further leave after obtaining a new certificate.

Bereavement Leave

Section 53 allows any employee up to three days of unpaid leave on the death of a member of their immediate family. "Immediate family" is defined in section 1 of the ESA as being

(a) the spouse, child, parent, guardian, sibling, grandchild, or grandparent of an employee

(a.1) the child or parent of an employee's spouse;
(b) any person who lives with an employee as a member of the employee's family.

Jury Duty

Section 55 allows any employee required by law to attend court as a juror to be granted leave with the same obligations as apply to the other forms of leave we have discussed so far.

Employee Rights During Statutory Leaves

Employees who take statutory leave have considerable rights and protections. These are found in sections 52, 53, 53.4, 53.5, 53.91, 53.92, and 53.93 of Alberta's ESC, and in sections 54 and 56 of BC's ESA. They are designed to ensure that employees are put in the same position they would have been in if they had not taken leave. This reflects the public policy that no employee should suffer negative consequences because they exercise the right to take a statutorily guaranteed leave. The following rights are guaranteed under the two statutes, with slight variation between them.

Right to Reinstatement

When a statutory leave ends, an employer must reinstate the employee in the same or a comparable position. For a job to be "comparable," the salary must be at least equal to what the employee received before taking leave. There should be no significant change in duties, level of responsibility, location, hours, job security, and opportunity for promotion.

An employer is relieved of the obligation to reinstate a returning employee only if (1) their employment was terminated for reasons unrelated to the leave, such as the elimination of their job because of downsizing, and (2) there is no comparable position. The onus is then on the employer to prove that there was no connection between the leave and the termination of employment. The test is whether or not the employee would have lost their job even if they had not taken leave.

Because maternity and parental leaves can last for more than a year, employers may be required to hold a position open for several years in a row. An employee or the employee's spouse may become pregnant while on leave, and leaves may be taken back to back.

An employee who is not reinstated as required under the legislation, or who is terminated shortly after reinstatement, may file a claim with the Employment Standards Branch (BC) or Employment Standards (Alberta), and the employer may be ordered to immediately reinstate the individual to the pre-leave position.

The following case of *PSS Professional Salon Services* illustrates the high standard that an employer has to meet to justify a decision not to reinstate an employee after a statutory leave. Although the employee chose to pursue her claim under human rights legislation, rather than employment standards legislation, the employer's onus of proof and the issues involved are similar.

CASE IN POINT

"But For" the Leave, Would She Have Been Dismissed?

PSS Professional Salon Services Inc v Saskatchewan (Human Rights Commission), 2007 SKCA 149, leave to appeal to SCC refused, 2008 CanLII 32715 (SCC).

Facts

Hitchings worked for PSS, a small distributor of hair care products. She performed her job duties fairly well, but a few months after she started work other employees began to complain about working with her. A co-worker came to the owner, Campbell, in tears to say she found working with Hitchings stressful; Hitchings' own supervisor confided that Hitchings' attitude was giving her stomach aches. Campbell chose not to bring the matter up with her at that time because Hitchings was just about to go on pregnancy leave. He later admitted that had he spoken to her then, he would have disciplined rather than terminated her.

However, after Hitchings went on her leave, Campbell heard about more incidents of misconduct. He was told that she had often tried to undermine his authority, had used crude language when referring to him, and had insulted other employees. He was also told that she encouraged employees to leave work an hour early because that's when her supervisor left. Months later, when Hitchings contacted Campbell with her return date, her supervisor told him that she did not want Hitchings back and a co-worker said that if Hitchings returned, she would quit. Campbell decided not to let Hitchings return to work; instead, he terminated her employment with two weeks' pay in lieu of notice.

Hitchings filed a human rights complaint on the basis of gender discrimination. The employer responded that her termination was in no way related to her leave. Many employees in its female-dominated workplace had taken leaves and returned without incident, and her replacement had been hired on a temporary basis. Her dismissal, Campbell argued, was entirely due to the negative reports he had received while she was on leave.

The Saskatchewan Human Rights Tribunal found for Hitchings. It stated that the onus was on the employer to show that Hitchings' dismissal was totally unrelated to her leave and that it had not met this burden of proof. The Tribunal did not believe that the employer would have dismissed her without any investigation or warnings had she been at work rather than on pregnancy leave. Hitchings was awarded approximately $4,400 for loss of income and for injury to her feelings.

The employer's appeal to the Saskatchewan Court of Queen's Bench was denied; it then appealed to the Saskatchewan Court of Appeal.

Relevant Issue

Whether the employer's refusal to reinstate was justified.

Decision

In a majority decision, the employer's appeal was allowed. The Court noted that even Hitchings testified that it was likely that she was dismissed because she "rocked the boat," rather than because she went on pregnancy leave. The majority noted that the employer's decision to dismiss rather than discipline Hitchings was based on the information it received *after* Hitchings began her leave.

However, in a dissenting opinion, one appeal judge agreed with the Tribunal's finding that the employer's refusal to reinstate was unjustified. Although Hitchings' leave may not have been the primary reason for her termination, "but for" her leave, she would not have been dismissed, especially not before she had been given an opportunity to give her side of the story. The fact that Hitchings was no longer in the workplace made it easier for the employer to simply dismiss her rather than deal with her alleged misconduct, and therefore the leave was relevant to her dismissal.

Although in this case the employer was eventually successful, the rulings described show that a refusal to reinstate an employee after a statutory leave will attract a high degree of scrutiny. Certainly, in relying on pre-leave misconduct, an employer will have to explain why it failed to deal with the misconduct before the leave began. In *PSS Professional Salon Services*, the fact that the employer only found out about certain behaviour after the employee's leave began was crucial in the Appeal Court's decision.

Right to Salary Plus Increases

In BC, the returning employee must be paid at least as much as they were earning before the leave, *plus* any raises they would have received if they had worked throughout the leave (s 56(3) of the ESA). In Alberta, the remedy is limited to reinstatement to the former position (or a comparable position) at the *same* earnings and benefits that had accrued to the employee at the time the leave started. (Potential raises are not considered.)

Right to Retain Benefits

In BC only, the employer must continue to pay its share of the premiums during the leave for benefit plans such as pension, life insurance, accidental death benefits, extended health insurance, and dental plans offered before the leave (except when an employee elects, in writing, not to pay their share of the premiums required by these plans). The only type of leave to which this right does not apply is reservists' leave (s 56(5) of the ESA). A birth mother may be able to collect disability benefits during the part of the leave when she would otherwise have been absent from work for health reasons related to the pregnancy or birth. Alberta employers do not have these obligations under the ESC. (However, depending on the benefit plans in place, an employer may have some obligations under human rights legislation.)

Right to Vacation Entitlement

A BC employee on leave does not lose any vacation-time entitlement (s 56(1)); the employee may defer vacation until after the leave ends or later, if the employer agrees. In Alberta, there is no statutory provision requiring the continued accrual of vacation while an employee is on a statutory leave.

Right to Be Free from Reprisals

Employees cannot be penalized in any way for taking, planning to take, or being eligible to take a statutory leave.

Right to Accrue Seniority

In BC (but not Alberta), employees on statutory leave continue to accrue seniority and earn credit for service and length of employment as if they had not taken leave. For example, an employee who works for three years and then takes a year's leave is considered to have four years' service.

Termination Notice and Pay in Lieu of Notice

Minimum statutory requirements for termination notice or pay in lieu of notice are dealt with in Chapters 13 and 14.

Administration and Enforcement

Filing a Complaint in Alberta

An employee who believes their rights under Alberta's ESC have been infringed is first encouraged to attempt to resolve the matter with the employer before filing a complaint. However, if the matter is not resolved, the employee may file a claim with an officer of Employment Standards.

After the employee fills out a form concerning the details of the claim, an employment standards officer is assigned to investigate the complaint if it is covered by the ESC. When the complaint is accepted for investigation, the employer is notified, provided with a copy of the complaint, and asked to respond. Upon receiving the employer's response, the officer assesses the matter and may investigate further.

1. Under section 82(2), the time limit for filing a complaint relating to any of the employer's obligations under the ESC is any time during employment or, if the employment relationship has ended, within six months after the last day of employment. The director may extend the period for filing a complaint (either before or after the six-month time limit expires) if there are extenuating circumstances; however, complaints should be filed as soon as possible. Complaints must be in writing, and they must be delivered to an employment standards officer.
2. Under section 90, no order may be made with respect to earnings after one year from the date on which the earnings should have been paid if the employee is still employed by the employer; nor after one year from the date that employment terminated if the employee is no longer employed by the employer. In addition, the ESC sets out time limits on how far back an order can go in directing payment of earnings or compensation. The limit is six months for the payment of wages or overtime or both, and the limit is two years for the payment of vacation or general holiday pay or both.

Upon receiving a complaint, an employment standards officer must accept and review that complaint. However, under section 83, the officer may refuse to "accept or investigate" any complaint where:

1. the officer considers that
   a. the complaint is frivolous,
   b. there is insufficient evidence, or
   c. there are other means available to the employee to deal with the subject matter of the complaint; or
2. the employee is proceeding with another action with respect to the subject matter of the complaint or the employee has sought recourse before a court, tribunal, or arbitrator.

Similarly, an employee cannot file a claim for termination or termination pay and sue an employer for wrongful dismissal relating to the same termination. If an employee decides to start a court action after filing a claim with Employment Standards, the employee must withdraw the claim or the court action will be barred.

It is important to note that no employer may terminate or restrict the employment of an employee because the employee has made a complaint under the ESC or ESR (s 125).

Filing a Complaint in British Columbia

An employee who alleges a violation of rights under the ESA may file a claim with the director of employment standards with the province's Employment Standards Branch. Complaints must be in writing, and they must be delivered to an office of the Employment Standards Branch. After the employee submits a form describing the claim, an employment standards officer investigates the complaint, provided that it is covered by the ESA, meets the time limits, and does not fall within a list of exceptions (described below).

There are two situations in which the ESA imposes a time limit for establishing a claim:

1. Under section 74(3), six months after the last day of employment is the time limit for filing a complaint relating to any of the employer's obligations under the ESA, other than those identified under sections 8, 10, and 11.
2. Under section 74(4), the time limit is six months after the date of contravention where the employer has failed to comply with sections 8, 10, or 11. These relate to matters occurring during the hiring process, such as the employer making a false representation to the employee relating to the availability of the position, the type of work, wages, or conditions of employment.

Section 76 states that the director of employment standards must accept and review all complaints, unless the complaint falls within a list of exceptions. These include complaints that are outside the time limits above, outside the scope of the Act, lacking in evidence, made in bad faith, subject to a current or past court case, or otherwise already resolved. This section does not, however, bar an employee from filing a claim for termination or termination pay *and* suing an employer for wrongful dismissal relating to the same termination, as the 2007 case *Colak v UV Systems Technology Inc* affirms. In *Colak*, the BC Court of Appeal ruled that the "compensation for length of service" under section 63 of the ESA is a form of "deferred compensation" that is paid for work (at para 5). It is not the same as the money that courts award for an employer's failure to give sufficient notice, known as "payment in lieu of notice." A claim to the Employment Standards Branch for payments under section 63 is, therefore, separate from a wrongful dismissal claim in court.

The Investigative Process in Alberta

Alberta's Employment Standards branch encourages employees to resolve issues directly with their employers if possible. Various approaches are used, including initiating and encouraging the use of alternative dispute resolution mechanisms (s 73). Also, an officer may mediate between the employer and the employee (s 84).

If the officer determines that the complaint warrants further action but they are unable to mediate, settle, or have the parties reach a compromise on the difference, the officer must refer the complaint to the director (s 86) or issue an order to resolve the matter (s 87).

Once a complaint is lodged with the Employment Standards branch, the director may proceed with an investigation. The director is obliged to give any employer under investigation an opportunity to respond. The director's powers and authority to conduct the investigation are described throughout part 3 of the ESC, in sections 68–94. They include the power to:

- summon witnesses, to enforce those summons, and to punish with contempt those who fail to comply;
- engage the services of others to perform services for and otherwise assist the director;
- certify and appoint officers; or
- under section 71, delegate the performance or exercise of any function, power, or duty, except that the director may not delegate the director's power to issue a reinstatement or compensation order under section 89 (s 71(3)).

Officers may enter and inspect the workplace or the place where the employer carries on its business, stores its assets, or keeps its records, either with the employer's consent or under the authority of a warrant (s 77). The officer can examine and require production of relevant records, remove those records, and question individuals on relevant matters.

Even where no complaint has been filed, an employment standards officer may inspect an organization, with or without advance notice to the employer, to review payroll and other employment records and examine employment practices to ensure the ESC is being complied with (s 77(1)).

The Investigative Process in British Columbia

The Employment Standards Branch encourages employees to resolve issues directly with their employers if possible. Once a complaint is lodged with the Employment Standards Branch, the director may proceed with an investigation. The director is obliged to give any employer under investigation an opportunity to respond. The director's powers and authority to conduct the investigation are consistent with those of decision-makers under other statutes, which were harmonized in 2007, when the government passed the *Public Inquiry Act* (see ss 84–84.3 of the ESA). The general investigative powers include the authority to summon witnesses and to punish those who fail to comply. The director may also enter and inspect the workplace or the place where the employer carries on its business, stores its assets, or keeps its records, either with the employer's consent or under the authority of a warrant (s 85). The director can examine and require production of relevant records, remove those records, and question individuals on relevant matters.

Even where no complaint has been filed, a director may inspect an organization, with or without advance notice to the employer, to review payroll and other employment records and examine employment practices to ensure compliance with the ESA (s 76(2)).

Director's Decision in Alberta

If, after investigating a claim, the director of employment standards does not find a contravention of the ESC, the employee's complaint will be dismissed (s 88(5)).

If the director finds that there was a contravention, the ESC gives the director wide powers under sections 88, 89, and 90 to impose a remedy or penalty by issuing one or more of the following orders:

1. *Comply with the requirement.* Compliance orders require individuals to perform or cease performing actions that are contrary to the ESC. They are designed to enforce non-monetary violations, such as requiring employees to work excess hours, failing to keep accurate records, or failing to post material required by the ESC.
2. *Remedy or cease doing some improper act.*
3. *Pay wages to an employee.* Where wages are found owing to an employee, the officer may order the employer to pay wages to the employee in an amount not exceeding the sum that the employee would have earned if the employment had not been suspended or terminated, or if the employee had not been laid off (ss 89(2) and (3)).
4. *Reinstate an employee.* This could be joined with the employee's being paid any wages lost because of the contravention (ss 89(2) and (3)).
5. *Make any other decision or order that could have been made by an officer* (s 88(4)).

Where the employer contravenes any other provision of the ESC, the penalties can range up to $100,000 in the case of a corporation or up to $50,000 in the case of an individual (s 132).

Director's Determination in British Columbia

If, after investigating a claim, the director of employment standards does not find a contravention of the ESA, the director will dismiss the employee's complaint (s 79(8)).

If the director finds that there was a contravention, the ESA gives the director wide powers under section 79 to issue a decision, called a "determination," requiring an employer to do one or more of the following:

1. *Comply with the requirement.* The director may require individuals to perform or cease performing actions that are contrary to the ESA. These orders are designed to enforce non-monetary violations, such as requiring employees to work excess hours, failing to keep accurate records, or failing to post material required by the ESA.
2. *Remedy or cease doing an act.*
3. *Pay wages to an employee.* The officer may order the employer to pay outstanding wages plus a mandatory administrative penalty (s 29 of the ESR).

Interest on money owing by an employer is set as being equal to the prime lending rate on the 15th of the month immediately preceding a three-month period (s 25 of the ESR).

4. *Post a notice of contravention.* The director has the power to issue notices of contravention or post a notice regarding any other information about the ESA's requirements. This notice must be posted in a form and location specified by the director.
5. *Reinstate or compensate an employee.* For some violations of the ESA, an officer can order the employer to reinstate or compensate an employee. Reinstatement is rare, because the employment relationship is usually found to be irreparably harmed. However, compensation in these cases is a "make-whole" remedy, designed to put the employee in the position they would have been in if the contravention had not occurred. Awards can cover the full amount owing, including back pay for wages lost, amounts for future earnings until such time as the employee would reasonably have found another job, and out-of-pocket expenses that can be documented. Violations that attract a make-whole remedy can arise in the context of
   a. pregnancy, parental, family, bereavement, compassionate care, reservists', and jury duty leaves;
   b. false representations as to the availability of a position, the type of work, wages, or the conditions of employment (s 8); and
   c. reprisals when an employee exercises rights under the ESA.
6. *Issue other orders.* Section 79 of the ESA gives the director other powers as well, in addition to those stated above. For example, the director may order the employer to pay any costs of the director in connection with inspection or investigations under the ESA.

Where the employer contravenes any other provision of the ESA, the penalties range from $500 to up to as much as $10,000, depending on a number of variables, as set out in section 29 of the ESR.

Section 86 of the ESA authorizes the director to modify or cancel a determination about a complaint.

Appeals of Director's Decision in Alberta

A person who has a right to appeal to an umpire may appeal by serving the registrar a written notice specifying the reasons for the appeal. The notice of appeal must be served within 21 days after the date of service on the appellant (s 95). If an employer does not apply for a review within the time specified, the order or notice is final and binding on the employer.

Section 107 of the ESC gives to the umpire the right to decide whether a matter should be reconsidered, confirmed, varied, or revoked. There is no appeal from the umpire's decision if the matter falls within its exclusive jurisdiction and the decision is not open to question or review in any court (s 107(3)). However, a judicial review of the decision is possible if the requirements for such a review are met. The legal framework for judicial review is complex, and a legal opinion is warranted before pursuing this course.

Appeals of Director's Determination in British Columbia

Either party may appeal the director's determination to the Employment Standards Tribunal. An employee or employer may appeal the director's determination within 21 or 30 days, depending on whether the determination was served on the party personally or by registered mail, respectively (s 112 of the ESA). If an employer does not appeal within the time specified, the determination is final and binding on the employer. In the event of an appeal, the director's power under section 86 to modify or cancel a decision still applies for 30 days after receiving the request to appeal.

Section 116 of the ESA gives the Tribunal the right to decide whether a matter should be reconsidered, confirmed, varied, or cancelled. There is no appeal from the Tribunal's decision if the matter falls within its exclusive jurisdiction and the decision is not open to question or review in any court (s 110(2)). However, the parties may apply to the BC Supreme Court for judicial review of the decision. Because the Supreme Court will overturn the Tribunal's decision only if it was patently unreasonable, rather than merely wrong, applications for judicial review are rarely successful. In *British Columbia Securities Commission v Burke*, an employer unsuccessfully applied for a judicial review (that case was about the timing of parental leave; the BC government subsequently amended the ESA in 2013 to clarify the ambiguity about timing).

Offences and Penalties in Alberta

Any person who contravenes or fails to comply with the ESC or its regulations or fails to comply with an authorizing or enforcement instrument is guilty of an offence (s 130). When a corporation commits an offence under the ESC, every director or officer of the corporation who directed, authorized, assented to, permitted, participated in, or acquiesced in the commission of the offence is guilty of the offence, whether or not the corporation has been prosecuted for or convicted of the offence (s 131). Those corporations and individuals who commit an offence are liable to a fine of up to $100,000 for a corporation or up to $50,000 for an individual.

Offences and Penalties in British Columbia

In addition to specific offences under the ESA, section 125 states that it is an offence to violate any of the requirements in parts 2–8 of the ESA (ss 8–71). Those who do so are, under the *Offence Act*, liable to a fine of up to $2,000 or to imprisonment for up to six months or both. However, in practice, the Employment Standards Branch does not use the *Offence Act* penalties. The administrative penalties under the ESA and its regulations make them unnecessary.

It should also be noted that directors and officers of corporations found liable for unpaid wages can be held *personally* liable for up to two months' unpaid wages for each unpaid employee. The director of employment standards often uses this power.

Information Provided by the Employment Standards Branch in Alberta

Helpful information about employment standards is available on the Alberta Employment Standards website at <https://www.alberta.ca/employment-standards.aspx>. Besides the actual content of the ESC and its regulations, the website also has a variety of tools and contacts to assist people who want to know more specific information about the legislation.

Information Provided by the Employment Standards Branch in British Columbia

The BC government has a helpful website with useful information about the ESA at <https://www2.gov.bc.ca/gov/content/employment-business/employment-standards-advice/employment-standards>. Besides the actual content of the Act and its regulations, the website has an online manual and a keyword index to help people find specific information about the legislation (<https://www2.gov.bc.ca/gov/content/employment-business/employment-standards-advice/employment-standards/forms-resources/igm>). There is also a website for the BC Employment Standards Tribunal at <http://www.bcest.bc.ca>. The website contains all decisions rendered by the Tribunal since November 1995, as well as tribunal decisions that have been judicially reviewed.

REVIEW AND DISCUSSION QUESTIONS

1. You want to improve your company's hiring process. Is it legal to require a job applicant to go to the work-site and perform the job for two or three hours to get a first-hand look at what the job entails? Would you need to pay the applicant, or could you consider the exercise to be part of the hiring process? Discuss.
2. Your employer asks your opinion on the following situation. An employee has been on pregnancy/parental leave for the past year and is scheduled to return next month. However, this employee's performance has been unsatisfactory, and she has received numerous verbal and written warnings in the past. The employer wants to know whether it can offer this employee a voluntary termination package (i.e., a mutually agree-able term of settlement for terminating the employ-ment relationship). Discuss.
3. How do the BC and Alberta employment standards statutes define "parents"? Can two parents take the full period of parental leave? What if they work for the same employer?
4. **a.** Under what two circumstances can an employer in BC or Alberta make deductions from an employ-ee's wages?

   b. In Alberta, what are two additional exceptions where an employer is permitted to make deduc-tions from an employee's wages?
5. Are the protections provided under BC and Alberta employment standards statutes available to employees regardless of the size of the employer?
6. Who determines when vacation time is taken: the employer or the employee?
7. Discuss the key protections available to employees who take statutory leave.
8. Under what conditions and for what purposes are employees entitled to take reservist/reservists' leave?
9. Sponge Bob works part time as a dishwasher at the KrustyKrab restaurant, where he earns $12 per hour. He works the same hours every week: four hours on Thursdays, three hours on Fridays, and five hours on Saturdays. Sponge Bob took Remembrance Day off. Calculate how much public holiday pay Sponge Bob is entitled to receive for Remembrance Day, not includ-ing vacation pay.
10. You are approached by a friend, Chantel, who manages a local shoe store in Vancouver. She explains that she is working very long hours (50 to 60 hours a week) because she does everything in the store—hiring, fir-ing, preparing shift schedules, serving customers, and so on. She is paid an annual salary. At the time she was hired, Chantel understood that there would be no additional compensation for overtime, but now she does not think this is fair. Chantel wants to know if her employer has to give her overtime pay. Based on your knowledge of employment law, is Chantel entitled to receive overtime pay in these circum-stances? Explain your answer.
11. Jason, a university student, was hired as a part-time sales clerk in a retail store on October 26, 2019. His spouse is ill, and she needs Jason to drive her to the hospital for an important medical procedure. Jason wants to know the following information:

    a. Is he entitled to take a leave in these circumstances under your province's employment standards legislation? Explain your answer.

    b. Assuming for this part of the question that Jason *is* eligible for this leave, is he entitled under provincial legislation to be paid by the employer for this time off from work?

    c. Again, assuming that Jason is eligible for this leave, under your province's employment standards legislation how many more days (or partial days) from work can Jason take off for such responsibil-ities in that year?
12. Allison worked as a bartender and cashier in a bar. She occasionally had to leave the bar but would lock the till before doing so and leave the key between two registers. One evening, Allison's cash was short $300. She urged the employer to call the police, but the employer did not. The next week her till was short $1,000 and she was fired. The employer withheld her last paycheque as compensation for its losses. Allison filed a complaint with the director of employment standards for the deduction from her wages. The employer pointed to a form Allison had signed when she was hired that stated "If a shortage occurs, full pay-ment is due immediately. If for any reason this agree-ment cannot be met, I authorize the employer to deduct the shortage in full from my next pay." Did the employer violate the employment standards legislation by deducting the till shortages from Allison's final pay in these circumstances? Explain your answer.
13. Should there be a differential in minimum wages, either based on age or on the type of position? Explain your rationale.

RELATED WEBSITES

The website for the BC Employment Standards Branch <https://www2.gov.bc.ca/gov/content/employment-business/employment-standards-advice/employment-standards>

The website for the Employment Standards branch of the Alberta Ministry of Labour <http://work.alberta.ca/employment-standards.html>

REFERENCES

An Act to Make Alberta Open for Business, SA 2019 c8.

Bongarde Media Co, "Paying Wages: Are You at Risk of an Overtime Class Action?" *HR Compliance Insider* 5:3 (March 2009).

British Columbia Securities Commission v Burke, 2008 BCSC 1244.

Canada Labour Code, RSC 1985, c L-2.

Colak v UV Systems Technology Inc, 2007 BCCA 220, leave to appeal to SCC refused, 2007 CanLII 66743 (SCC).

Corless v KPMG LLP, 2008 CanLII 39784 (Ont Sup Ct J).

Criminal Code, RSC 1985, c C-46.

Deepthi Perera (22 November 2012), BC EST # D125/12, confirmed on reconsideration BC EST # RD071/13.

Eichler, Leah, "Would More Men Take a 'Use It or Lose It' Paternity Leave?" *Globe and Mail* (12 April 2013), online: <https://www.theglobeandmail.com/report-on-business/careers/career-advice/life-at-work/would-more-men-take-a-use-it-or-lose-it-paternity-leave/article11156542>.

Employment and Assistance Act, SBC 2002, c 40.

Employment Standards Act, RSBC 1996, c 113.

Employment Standards Amendment Act, 2019, Bill 8.

Employment Standards Code, RSA 2000, c E-9.

Employment Standards Regulation, Alta Reg 14/1997.

Employment Standards Regulation, BC Reg 396/95.

Family Law Act, SBC 2011, c 25.

Fresco v Canadian Imperial Bank of Commerce, 2012 ONCA 444, leave to appeal to SCC refused, 2013 CanLII 14331 (SCC).

Fulawka v Bank of Nova Scotia, 2012 ONCA 443 (certifying claim), 2014 ONSC 4743 (approving settlement).

Health Employers Assn of BC v BC Nurses' Union, 2005 BCCA 343.

Hutchins v Atlantic Provincial Security Guard Service Ltd, 1995 CanLII 8876 (NBLEB).

Jury Act, RSA 2000, c J-3.

Kenneth Johnston (2 July 2010), BC EST # D071/10.

Labour Relations Code, RSA 2000, c L-1.

Loewenberg, Madeleine, & Lorenzo Lisi, "Going into Overtime," *Canadian Employment Law Today* 520 (22 October 2008) at 4.

Macaraeg v E Care Contact Centers Ltd, 2008 BCCA 182.

Mathews Dinsdale, "An Overhaul of BC's Employment Standards Legislation: Bill 8—What Employers Need to Know," *In a Flash* (30 April 2019), online: <https://mathewsdinsdale.com/an-overhaul-of-bcs-employment-standards-legislation-bill8-what-employers-need-to-know>.

Mathews Dinsdale, "Ground Shifting Again for Alberta Employers—Premier Announces Employment & Labour Changes Under Bill 2—*An Act to Make Alberta Open for Business*," *In a Flash* (28 May 2019), online: <https://mathewsdinsdale.com/ground-shifting-again-for-alberta-employers-premier-announces-employment-labour-changes-under-bill2-an-act-to-make-alberta-open-for-business>

McCracken v Canadian National Railway Company, 2012 ONCA 445.

National Defence Act, RSC 1985, c N-5.

Offence Act, RSBC 1996, c 338.

Police Act, RSA 2000, c P-17.

Post-secondary Learning Act, SA 2003, c P-19.5.

PSS Professional Salon Services Inc v Saskatchewan (Human Rights Commission), 2007 SKCA 149, leave to appeal to SCC refused, 2008 CanLII 32715 (SCC).

Public Inquiry Act, SBC 2007, c 9.

Rosen v BMO Nesbitt Burns Inc, 2013 ONSC 2144.

Statistics Canada, "Benefiting from Extended Parental Leave," *The Daily* (21 March 2003), online: <https://www150.statcan.gc.ca/n1/daily-quotidien/030321/dq030321b-eng.htm>.

Statistics Canada, *Leave Practices of Parents After the Birth or Adoption of Young Children*, by Leanne Findlay & Dafna Kohen, Catalogue No 11-008-X (Ottawa: Statistics Canada, 30 July 2012), online: <https://www150.statcan.gc.ca/n1/pub/11-008-x/2012002/article/11697-eng.pdf>.

Tri Roc Electric Ltd v Butler, 2003 CanLII 11390 (Ont LRB).

Human Rights Issues 7

LEARNING OUTCOMES

After completing this chapter, you will be able to:

- Explain what constitutes discrimination under both the BC *Human Rights Code* and the *Alberta Human Rights Act*.
- Identify the key features of these statutes, including prohibited grounds and areas of discrimination.
- Understand the distinction between equal pay for work of equal value and employment equity.
- Outline the remedies available to complainants under these statutes.
- State the requirements of human rights legislation during the hiring process, including how they relate job advertisements, applications, and interviews.
- Understand the human rights issues raised by pre-employment testing, including medical and drug and alcohol testing.
- Understand the implications of human rights legislation during the course of employment, including the duty to accommodate disability, religion, sex, and family status.
- Explain the concept of undue hardship.
- Understand when on-the-job drug and alcohol testing is justifiable and when it is not.
- Outline the employer's obligations with respect to workplace harassment, sexual harassment, and sexual solicitation.

Understanding Discrimination and Human Rights Complaints

There was a time when even the most blatant forms of discrimination were legal in Canada. Under the common law, stores could refuse service, landlords could refuse housing, and employers could refuse to hire individuals for whatever reason they chose, including race, gender, or marital status. However, over the past 60 years, every jurisdiction in Canada has enacted human rights legislation that prohibits discrimination in key social areas, including employment, services (such as stores, restaurants, hospitals, and schools), and accommodation (housing).

Human rights requirements are a key consideration during the hiring process, and they continue to play a central role throughout the employment relationship. Human rights legislation in Alberta and British Columbia (BC) requires an employer to maintain a workplace that is free from discrimination and harassment. It must make all employment decisions, including those related to hiring, training, transfers, promotions, apprenticeships, compensation, benefits, performance evaluations, discipline, layoffs, and dismissals, on a non-discriminatory basis.

Unlike the *Canadian Charter of Rights and Freedoms* (Charter), which applies only to government actions (a topic that was discussed in Chapter 1), provincial human rights statutes apply to the actions of individuals and corporations as well. Moreover, the scope of human rights law has been steadily expanding.

Alberta's first comprehensive human rights legislation was passed in 1972 with the *Alberta Bill of Rights*. A companion piece of legislation, the *Individual's Rights Protection Act* (IRPA), was passed at the same time. The *Alberta Bill of Rights* was intended to protect citizens of the province from governmental abuse of power. The IRPA, however, was an indication of the province's new commitment to eradicating discrimination. The Act was passed as primacy legislation, meaning that it takes precedence over any other provincial legislation (unless specifically stated otherwise). The IRPA also required that a human rights commission be created to educate the public, promote human rights, and administer the law. It was the first legislation in Alberta that specifically outlined prohibited grounds of discrimination and initially protected primarily visible minorities. The IRPA has been amended several times. It became the *Human Rights, Citizenship and Multiculturalism Act* in 2000, and in 2010 it became the *Alberta Human Rights Act*. The Alberta Act prohibits discrimination in employment on 15 grounds.

BC introduced its first human rights legislation, the *Human Rights Code* (the BC Code), in 1973. The current version of the BC Code came into force in November 2018. Like the Alberta Act, it is primacy legislation, so if there is a conflict between the Code and any other provincial legislation, the Code prevails (s 4). It prohibits discrimination in employment on 15 grounds (if physical and mental disability are counted as separate grounds), but with a couple of differences from the Alberta Act. Amendments to the BC Code in 2016 added gender identity and expression to the list of protected grounds.

What Constitutes Discrimination?

The term "discrimination" is not defined in the *Alberta Human Rights Act* or given a single definition in the BC *Human Rights Code*. Its meaning has, however, been addressed by the courts. Initially, courts interpreted it to mean an intentional act of exclusion—for example, the placement of an advertisement specifying that individuals of a certain ethnic background need not apply. This overt type of discriminatory behaviour—also known as "direct" or "intentional" discrimination—is easy to identify.

However, many acts of discrimination are hidden or even unintentional: for example, policies or practices that on their face are not intended to discriminate but which have a discriminatory effect on individuals or groups. In older cases, courts did not apply human rights law to such cases of indirect or unintentional discrimination. In the 1970s and 1980s, however, courts began to recognize more indirect forms of discrimination and to provide remedies even when there was no intent to discriminate. The courts have developed a three-part test to establish a ***prima facie*** case of discrimination. The leading case for this general test is *Moore v British Columbia (Education)*, which sets out the test at paragraph 33. The test may be paraphrased as follows:

prima facie
evidence that, as it first appears, is sufficient to prove a proposition or fact, though it may still be rebutted

1. the complainant has a characteristic protected from discrimination by the human rights legislation;
2. the complainant experienced an adverse impact with respect to their employment; and
3. the protected characteristic was a factor in the adverse impact.

systemic discrimination
the web of employer policies or practices that are neutral on their face but have discriminatory effects; also called "institutional discrimination"

Once a complainant has provided enough evidence to prove each of these three elements, it is up to the employer to prove that its policy, practice, or conduct is justified. If it cannot do so, the court finds discrimination and provides a remedy.

FYI

Systemic Discrimination: What Is It?

Systemic discrimination (also called "institutional discrimination") is one of the more complex and subtle forms of indirect discrimination. It refers to the web of employer policies or practices that are neutral on their face but have discriminatory effects. For example, a company may have a culture that encourages informal mentoring through sports-related activities that take place after working hours. Employees with disabilities or whose family responsibilities make it more difficult for them to participate after hours may be less successful at building internal networks as a consequence. This in turn could affect performance evaluations and opportunities for promotion.

The existence of systemic discrimination is sometimes identified through numerical data. For example, data may show that there are few women in high-level positions in a particular advertising firm compared with the representation of female executives in the labour force in general.

FYI

Key Features of Human Rights Legislation

1. Human rights legislation applies to both the private and the public sector and to the conduct of individuals. Unlike the Charter, its application is not limited to the actions of government.
2. Discrimination in employment is prohibited on numerous grounds, which are similar but not identical in Alberta and BC:

Alberta	British Columbia
race	race
religious beliefs	religion
colour	colour
gender	sex
sexual orientation	sexual orientation
physical disability	physical disability
mental disability	mental disability
age	age
ancestry	ancestry
place of origin	place of origin
marital status	marital status
family status	family status
gender identity	
gender expression	
source of income	
	political belief
	conviction of a criminal or summary conviction offence that is unrelated to a person's employment

3. To infringe human rights legislation, it is not necessary to intend to discriminate.
4. The effect of an employer's action or rule matters as much as the intent. The employer has a duty to accommodate the special needs of protected individuals or groups unless doing so would create undue hardship for the employer.
5. No one can contract out of human rights legislation. For example, the negotiated terms of a collective agreement are void if they do not comply with the legislation.
6. Human rights legislation provides for civil remedies, such as ordering an employer to compensate employees for lost wages or mental suffering, or ordering it to change its employment policies. It does not provide for criminal penalties, such as imprisonment.
7. Human rights legislation is quasi-constitutional in that if there is a conflict between its provisions and those of another provincial statute, its requirements prevail.
8. Human rights legislation applies to every stage of the employment relationship, from recruitment through to termination.

Overview of Alberta's and British Columbia's Human Rights Legislation

The Preamble and Purpose of the Legislation

The *Alberta Human Rights Act* opens with a preamble that sets out the spirit and intent of the legislation. As with most provincial human rights statutes, the preamble was inspired by the United Nations 1948 *Universal Declaration of Human Rights*, which recognizes the "inherent dignity and … equal and inalienable rights of all members of the human family" and provides for equal rights and opportunities without discrimination to create a climate of understanding and mutual respect.

The Alberta preamble states:

> WHEREAS recognition of the inherent dignity and the equal and inalienable rights of all persons is the foundation of freedom, justice and peace in the world;
>
> WHEREAS it is recognized in Alberta as a fundamental principle and as a matter of public policy that all persons are equal in: dignity, rights and responsibilities without regard to race, religious beliefs, colour, gender, gender identity, gender expression, physical disability, mental disability, age, ancestry, place of origin, marital status, source of income, family status or sexual orientation;
>
> WHEREAS multiculturalism describes the diverse racial and cultural composition of Alberta society and its importance is recognized in Alberta as a fundamental principle and a matter of public policy;
>
> WHEREAS it is recognized in Alberta as a fundamental principle and as a matter of public policy that all Albertans should share in an awareness and appreciation of the diverse racial and cultural composition of society and that the richness of life in Alberta is enhanced by sharing that diversity; and
>
> WHEREAS it is fitting that these principles be affirmed by the Legislature of Alberta in an enactment whereby those equality rights and that diversity may be protected.

In BC, these basic principles are laid out in section 3 of the BC *Human Rights Code*, which defines the purpose of the legislation as follows:

> (a) to foster a society in British Columbia in which there are no impediments to full and free participation in the economic, social, political and cultural life of British Columbia;
> (b) to promote a climate of understanding and mutual respect where all are equal in dignity and rights;
> (c) to prevent discrimination prohibited by this Code;
> (d) to identify and eliminate persistent patterns of inequality associated with discrimination prohibited by this Code;
> (e) to provide a means of redress for those persons who are discriminated against contrary to this Code.

The preamble to the Alberta Act and section 3 of the BC Code do not contain specific legislative requirements. However, they can affect the interpretation of the legislation. Where an issue is ambiguous, and the legislation doesn't provide clear direction, courts and tribunals often use these introductory statements as an internal aid to guide interpretation of the statutes.

The scope of human rights protections is interpreted quite liberally in both provinces because of the preamble and purpose, and also because both statutes are considered **remedial legislation**. This means that they exist to right a societal wrong, not to allocate blame or punish an offender. In employment cases, courts and tribunals have consistently affirmed that such remedial legislation should be interpreted "in a broad and generous manner," with any uncertainty in the meaning of a provision resolved in favour of the employee. Accordingly, the emphasis is generally on conciliation and compensation for the victims. An employer who violates an employee's human rights may be required to alter its policies or practices, may be subject to a public declaratory order that they have violated human rights, or may be ordered to pay restitution to an individual who files a complaint against it, but there are no criminal penalties such as imprisonment.

remedial legislation
legislation that exists to right a societal wrong, not to allocate blame or punish an offender

Areas Covered

The statutes of both provinces provide that everyone has the right to be free from discrimination in five main areas of social activity:

1. publications and notices;
2. goods or property, services, accommodation (housing), and facilities;
3. tenancies;
4. employment practices, including equal pay, and advertisements; and
5. membership in trade unions and occupational associations.

The legislation also protects those who file a human rights complaint from retaliation through what are known as "anti-reprisal clauses." Such clauses are meant to give individuals the comfort to raise concerns and complaints without fear of discipline, termination, or other employment-related consequences.

Although employment is only one of the five areas covered by the legislation, the majority of complaints arise in the employment context. In 2017–18, 79 percent of the complaints in Alberta were related to employment (Alberta Human Rights Commission, 2019), and for the period 2018–19, 61 percent of the complaints in BC were related to employment (BC Human Rights Tribunal, July 2019, at 23). The term "employment" has been interpreted broadly to include full- and part-time employment; contract work; temporary work; probationary periods; and, in some cases, volunteer work.

Prohibited Grounds of Discrimination in Employment

Section 7 of the Alberta Act provides that every person is entitled to equal treatment with respect to employment, without discrimination on the basis of race, religious beliefs, colour, gender, gender identity, gender expression, physical disability, mental disability, age, ancestry, place of origin, marital status, source of income, family status, or sexual orientation. Prior to 2009, sexual orientation was not named as a specific ground in the Act. The addition of sexual orientation to the Alberta legislation was the result of a Supreme Court decision that determined Alberta's legislation was in and of itself discriminatory because it failed to protect an identifiable group that is frequently subjected to prejudice (see the discussion of *Vriend v Alberta* in Chapter 1).

Section 13 of the BC Code lists the grounds of discrimination related to employment. They overlap with the Alberta grounds, with some differences. The BC statute does not include source of income as a ground of employment discrimination, but it does include political belief and conviction for a criminal or summary conviction offence unrelated to a person's employment.

Each of the prohibited grounds is considered below. Because the BC Code does not define the grounds it lists, the information here is based on definitions from section 44 of the Alberta Act (these are designated with an asterisk) and supplemented with descriptions from the Alberta Human Rights Commission (2018). The following descriptions include some illustrative cases from BC and point out grounds that the BC Human Rights Tribunal and courts have interpreted differently from Alberta or other jurisdictions.

The Alberta and BC statutes both identify a few statutory exemptions that, in limited circumstances, expressly allow discrimination. For example, section 7(3) of the Alberta Act and section 13(4) of the BC Code make an exemption for bona fide occupational requirements (BFORs). Similarly, section 11 of the Alberta Act allows flexibility to interpret facts on a case-by-case basis. If a person or organization that contravened the Act can show that the contravention was "reasonable and justifiable in the circumstances," the Alberta Human Rights Commission will allow the discriminatory conduct to continue. The BC legislation does not have a comparable provision. However, it exempts non-profit social organizations that serve a protected group (s 41) and employment equity programs designed to help disadvantaged individuals or groups (s 42). (Exemptions are discussed more fully below under the heading "Exemptions: Where Discrimination Is Allowed.")

1. *Race.* Race is not specifically defined in the BC or Alberta legislation but can be considered as a group of people who are related by a common heritage. It can also be related to other grounds, such as colour, place of origin, or ethnic origin, and may include language as an element of the complaint.
2. *Religious beliefs.* This ground protects people from discrimination on the basis of their religion or faith. The Alberta Act and the BC Code prohibit one person from attempting to force another to accept or comply with a particular religious belief or practice. The legislation may also require an employer to take positive measures, such as allowing breaks for prayer at certain times. Religious beliefs and practices are protected, even if they are not essential elements of a particular religion, provided they are sincerely held. The Alberta Act also specifically recognizes that religious beliefs include "native spirituality."

3. *Colour.* Colour means the colour of a person's skin. Discrimination on the ground of colour may encompass racial slurs, jokes, stereotyping, and verbal or physical harassment.
4. *Gender.* Discrimination on this ground extends to male, female, and transgender individuals, as well as gender identity and gender expression. It also protects women who are pregnant. It is the ground cited in sexual harassment cases. The Alberta Human Rights Commission (2018) states that the term "transgender" refers to people who identify as transgender or transsexual and refers to the Ontario Human Rights Commission's definition of gender identity, which states:

> Gender identity is linked to a person's sense of self, and particularly the sense of being male or female. A person's gender identity is different from their sexual orientation. … People's gender identity may be different from their birth-assigned sex, and may include:
>
> > Transgender: People whose life experience includes existing in more than one gender. This may include people who identify as transsexual and people who describe themselves as being on a gender spectrum or as living outside the gender categories of "man" or "woman."
> >
> > Transsexual: People who were identified at birth as one sex, but who identify themselves differently. They may seek or undergo one or more medical treatments to align their bodies with their internally felt identity, such as hormone therapy, sex-reassignment surgery or other procedures.

In BC, the term "sex" is used instead of "gender." Although tribunals and courts in BC and Alberta have interpreted "sex" to prohibit discrimination against transgendered people, calls by transgender advocates for an explicit reference to transgender and gender-variant people in the legislation became louder in 2015, culminating in the BC government adding gender identity and gender expression to the BC Code in 2016. The BC Human Rights Tribunal (October 2019) defines gender identity and gender expression as follows:

> Gender expression is how a person presents their gender. This can include behaviour and appearance, including dress, hair, make-up, body language and voice. This can also include name and pronoun, such as he, she or they. How a person presents their gender may not necessarily reflect their gender identity.
>
> Gender identity is a person's sense of themselves as male, female or both, in between or neither. It includes people who identify as transgender. Gender identity may be different or the same as the sex a person is assigned at birth.

The first time the BC Human Rights Tribunal rendered decisions relating to the ground of gender expression and gender identity was in 2018.

CASE IN POINT

Discrimination Based on Sex

Morrison v AdvoCare, 2009 BCHRT 298

Facts

Morrison was a male registered care aide who applied to work in a residential care home on two occasions. AdvoCare refused to hire him. Despite several phone calls from Morrison, AdvoCare indicated that it had a confidentiality policy and could not divulge its reasons to him. The company continued to advertise for aides with the same qualifications as Morrison. The AdvoCare manager responsible for interviewing applicants indicated that the company did not hire new graduates without related experience. However, a review of hires that occurred during the same period showed that a number of new graduates were hired without related experience. Morrison was as qualified as (or more qualified than) the successful applicants. No males were hired during that period. There was also conflicting testimony about Morrison's interview and references. The manager who interviewed Morrison stated that she noted several "red flags" during the interview. She further testified that she felt harassed by Morrison's follow-up calls, although she did not pass along his requests for information to anyone more senior.

Relevant Issue

Whether the employer's refusal to hire the complainant constituted discrimination on the basis of sex.

Decision

The BC Human Rights Tribunal found that Morrison was not hired because of the employer's stereotypical sex-related assumptions that he was aggressive and therefore not suitable for the job. In its decision, the Tribunal raised questions about the employer's exaggeration of minor performance concerns and inconsistencies in its hiring documentation, including a "red flag" guide that tells interviewers: "trust your gut!" Although the employer did not intend to discriminate, intention need not exist for discrimination to occur. Morrison was awarded $3,150 in lost wages, $3,773 for gas and lodging, and $5,000 for injury to dignity, feelings, and self-respect.

The *Morrison* case is particularly helpful for two reasons. First, the Tribunal addressed the conflicting testimony issue common in discriminatory hiring cases. Citing *Faryna v Chorny*, the Tribunal stated:

> The credibility of interested witnesses, particularly in cases of conflict of evidence, cannot be gauged solely by the test of whether the personal demeanour of the particular witness carried conviction of the truth. … [T]he real test of the truth of a story of a witness in such a case must be its harmony with … [that] which a practical and informed person would readily recognize as reasonable in that place and in those conditions. (at para 8)

Second, the Tribunal applied the following test for establishing a *prima facie* (on the face of it) case of discrimination in the hiring stage:

> In an employment complaint, the complainant usually establishes a *prima facie* case by proving:

1. that the complainant was qualified for the particular employment;
2. that the complainant was not hired; and
3. that either
   a. someone no better qualified but lacking the distinguishing feature which is the gravamen of the human rights complaint (sex, religion, race, etc.) subsequently obtained the position, or
   b. the employer continued to seek applicants with the complainant's qualifications. (at para 117)

This test comes from the leading BC decision of *Oxley v British Columbia Institute of Technology*, which adapted the "*Shakes* test" from Ontario (*Shakes v Rex Pak Limited*) for *prima facie* discrimination in the employment context and the federal "*Israeli* test" for a discriminatory refusal to hire (*Israeli v Canadian Human Rights Commission*).

5. *Disability.* In the Alberta legislation, both physical and mental disability are extensively defined in section 44 of the Act. A physical disability is any degree of physical disability, infirmity, malformation, or disfigurement that is caused by injury, birth defect, or illness. This includes, but is not limited to, epilepsy, paralysis, amputation, lack of physical coordination, visual impairment, hearing impediment, speech impediment, or reliance on a service dog, wheelchair, or other assistive device. Tribunals have also found that weight can be a physical disability. Mental disability is defined as any mental, developmental, or learning disorder, regardless of the cause or duration of the disorder.

   It is also generally accepted that employers cannot discriminate on the basis of a "perceived disability." For example, in a case about the Canada Border Services Agency's refusal to hire an overweight BC man, the Canadian Human Rights Tribunal held that the employer had discriminated against a worker on the basis of "perceived obesity"—even though his weight was not a real physical disability, since it had no effect on his ability to do the job (*Turner v Canada Border Services Agency* [2014]).

   Both provinces recognize that there will be situations where the nature of a disability prevents an individual from performing a job. Section 7(3) of the Alberta Act and section 13(4) of the BC Code indicate that an employer may make an employment decision that is discriminatory, provided that the decision is based on a BFOR. For example, neither statute would require an employer to hire a blind school bus driver, because sight is a fundamental ability necessary to perform the job. Minor, temporary illnesses such as the common cold or flu are not considered disabilities (see e.g. *Goode v Interior Health Authority* [2010]).

6. *Marital status.* Marital status is defined as being married, single, widowed, divorced, separated, or living in a conjugal relationship outside marriage. It is particularly relevant in the area of spousal, pension, and survivor benefits. Prior to the revisions in 2009, the Alberta Act defined marital status as "being married, single, widowed, divorced, separated or living with a person of the

opposite sex in a conjugal relationship outside marriage" (emphasis added). This clause, like the exclusion of sexual orientation discussed above, was corrected to align the Alberta legislation with federally protected rights to same-sex marriage, as set out in the federal *Civil Marriage Act* and supported as constitutional in the Supreme Court of Canada's 2004 decision in *Reference re Same-Sex Marriage*.

7. *Ancestry.* Ancestry means belonging to a group of people with a common heritage.
8. *Place of origin.* Place of origin refers to a country or region of birth, including a region in Canada.
9. *Age.* In Alberta, age is defined in the Act as 18 years or older. Therefore, anyone over 18 can make a complaint based on this ground. For example, the Alberta Act protects a 19 year old who is denied a position because of negative stereotypes about teenagers as well as a 57 year old who is rejected because he does not "fit the company's youthful image." Anyone under the age of 18 can file a human rights complaint on any ground *except* age. Before January 2018, age was not a protected ground in the areas of goods, services, accommodation or facilities, and tenancy. Exemptions still exist for age-restricted condominiums, cooperative housing, and mobile home sites that existed prior to January 1, 2018, as well as for seniors-only housing and programs that provide benefits to minors or senior, such as reduced bus fares.

   In the BC Code, age-based discrimination is prohibited for anyone 19 years of age or older. An employee under the age of 19 may still make a discrimination complaint based on another prohibited ground, such as race or disability.
10. *Family status.* In Alberta, family status is defined as "being related to another person by blood, marriage or adoption" (at para 44(1)(f)). The BC Code does not define family status.

    Family status is a quickly evolving area of human rights law with multiple cases coming before the courts from varying jurisdictions. The struggle has been to develop a common test to determine when family status discrimination has occurred. The *Johnstone* case, described in the Case in Point box "Discrimination Based on Family Status" later in this chapter, illustrates the ongoing evolution of the jurisprudence.
11. *Source of income.* Source of income is defined in the Alberta statute as "lawful source of income" (at para 44(1)(n)). This ground is intended to protect individuals whose source of income might attract social stigma—for example, recipients of social assistance, disability benefits, or seniors' supplements. Income that is not a source of stigma is not covered by this section of the Act. The BC Code does not include source of income as a ground of discrimination in the area of employment.
12. *Sexual orientation.* This ground protects people based on a person's actual or presumed sexual orientation, which can include homosexual, heterosexual, or bisexual. It is particularly relevant in the area of spousal, pension, and survivor benefits. It includes protection from differential treatment on the basis

of a person's actual or presumed sexual orientation. BC added sexual orientation to the list of prohibited grounds of discrimination in 1992, the same year it added family status. As noted above, the Alberta government added sexual orientation in 2009.

13. *Criminal record.* The BC Code does not allow employers to discriminate against someone because they have "been convicted of a criminal or summary conviction offence that is unrelated to the employment or to the intended employment of that person." As with other grounds, there is an exemption for BFORs under section 13(4). One issue that arises is whether an employer may refuse to preserve the employment status of an employee who is unable to work because they are serving a prison sentence. There have been a number of cases where employees have alleged discrimination in the latter situation if the employer has been unwilling to hold their jobs for them until they are released. This argument was rejected by the BC Court of Appeal in the 2000 decision *BC Human Rights Commission v BC Human Rights Tribunal.* In its decision the Court cited the *obiter dicta* (commentary apart from the main decision) of the trial court judge, who said:

> 53. The intent of the legislation is to protect persons convicted of criminal offences unrelated to employment from the stigma attaching to the fact of conviction or record of conviction preventing the person from either continuing in their present employment or obtaining new employment.
>
> 54. The legislation on its face does not support the view it was intended to preserve the employment status of a person who is absent from work to serve a sentence of incarceration imposed because of their intentional criminal conduct. (at para 24)

Criminal record is not listed as a ground of discrimination in the Alberta Act.

Additional Grounds of Discrimination

Equal Pay for Equal Work

In addition to the grounds of prohibited discrimination listed in section 7, the Alberta Act protects individuals in the area of equal pay under section 6. When employees of any sex (male, female, or transgendered) perform the same or substantially similar work, they must be paid at the same rate. Furthermore, the employer is not allowed to reduce another employee's salary to meet the requirements of the legislation. The BC Code has a similar provision in section 12, although section 12(3) states that a wage difference between employees of different sexes that is based on a factor other than sex is permissible, provided that the factor reasonably justifies the difference.

The requirement to provide equal pay for equal work has existed for over 55 years, but before this requirement it was common for men and women to receive different rates of pay even when they were performing the same job.

To fall within the equal pay for equal work protection, the work of one employee must be substantially similar (but need not be identical) to the work of another. For example, male and female cooks working in the same restaurant must receive the same rate of pay, subject to the exceptions set out above, even though one makes salads and the other makes desserts. Similarly, a retail clothing store cannot reasonably argue that its female and male sales assistants receive different rates of pay because they work in separate sections of the store and therefore do different jobs. Section 12(2) of the BC Code specifies that "the concept of skill, effort and responsibility must … be used to determine what is similar or substantially similar work."

To prove a violation of the equal pay for equal work provisions, there is no need to show that an employer intended to discriminate. The law applies wherever women and men perform similar work but receive different rates of pay for reasons other than the exceptions noted above.

As with other standards under the BC Code or the Alberta Act, equal pay for equal work is enforced by the individual's filing of a complaint with the BC Human Rights Tribunal or the Alberta Human Rights Commission (though BC employees have the option of filing a claim in court). Although historically female employees have benefited most from equal pay laws, both men and women may file complaints.

What Is Equal Pay for Work of Equal Value?

Pay equity, or "equal pay for work of equal value," is a relatively recent concept that requires employers to compare totally different jobs and ascertain whether they are equal in value. The only jurisdictions in Canada that impose comprehensive compliance obligations on employers to achieve pay equity are those that are federally regulated and employers in Ontario and Quebec under their respective *Pay Equity Acts*. The federal *Pay Equity Act* was introduced in October 2018. It requires employers in the federal sector with ten or more employees to undertake a pay equity review and analysis to ensure they are providing equal pay for work of equal value. The Act requires that employers establish a pay equity plan that includes (1) an analysis of gender predominance of job classes, (2) estimates of the value of work performed by each job class, and (3) a comparison of pay between predominantly male and predominantly female job classes of similar value.

Neither the BC Code nor the Alberta Act actually uses the term "equal pay for work of equal value." Instead, BC uses the term "for similar or substantially similar work" (s 12(1)) and Alberta uses the wording "the same or substantially similar work" (s 6(1)). In both provinces, a comparison is made between the value of the jobs, not their content. Neither have assessment and planning requirements like those in the federal *Pay Equity Act*.

Pay equity arose from the concern that equal pay for equal work laws would never be able to achieve gender equality because, typically, men and women did not perform substantially similar work. Historically, women have tended to occupy a small number of relatively low-paying jobs collectively known as the "pink collar ghetto." Pay equity is premised on the idea that these jobs are poorly paid *because* they are primarily performed by women. In other words, the labour market has consistently undervalued jobs dominated by women. For example, parking lot attendants, who are usually men, are paid more than childcare workers, who are usually women.

The purpose of pay equity, therefore, is to reduce the wage gap between men and women by requiring employers to compare the underlying value of jobs performed predominantly by men with those performed predominantly by women. Pay for female-dominated jobs is then based on their value in relation to the value of male-dominated jobs, rather than on the value assigned to them by the labour market. This can be a challenging task, and the process required by the legislation is necessarily technical and complex.

IN THE NEWS

The Battle Starts at the Top: How Canadian Companies Can Close the Gender Pay Gap

Recently, female faculty members at the University of British Columbia, the University of Guelph and McMaster University received $3,000/year raises after salary audits at the universities found they were being paid less than their male colleagues.

Efforts such as these are praised as Canada's gender wage gap remains relatively unchanged from year to year. "The notion of [patriarchy] is so pervasive throughout our values and culture, and it also shows up in policies, programs and laws … it's not an easy thing to overcome and it will take a long time," said Anil Verma, a professor of industrial relations and human resource management at the Rotman School of Business. "The good news is that we're making progress."

But progress is slow. Canadian women earn 84 cents for every $1 earned by men. For women who are Indigenous, living with a disability, racialized, or newcomers to Canada, the gap is even larger.

Leadership commitment is the key to closing the gender pay gap according to Verma.

"The battle starts at the top," he notes. "The leader of the organization has to send a clear message through communication and through action to demonstrate that this is an 'equal opportunity' company."

Once leadership is on board, employers should speak with their employees on an individual level. Human resources departments responsible for recruitment, hiring, training, performance appraisal, and compensation can be key partners.

Charlotte Yates, provost and vice-president at the University of Guelph, says that a major barrier to closing the pay gap is that bias most often creeps in incrementally, not explicitly. This may include bias related to career arcs for women who may have different family and social obligations. It also includes assumptions about what leadership looks like.

"For example, the characteristics we think are successful, tend to also … be male characteristics. More aggressive, more assertive, more likely to say 'I'm the right person for this,'" says Yates. Women are less likely to behave in these ways, and the impact on pay equity is surprising.

SOURCE: Adapted from Collie, 2019.

employment equity addresses the broad social problem of the underrepresentation of certain groups of people, such as visible minorities and people with disabilities, in most workplaces, especially in better-paid and higher-level jobs

Employment Equity

Although the two terms are often used interchangeably, **employment equity** is not the same as pay equity. Employment equity addresses the broad social problem of the underrepresentation of certain groups of people, such as visible minorities and people with disabilities, in most workplaces, especially in better-paid and higher-level jobs. Neither Alberta nor BC has legislation that addresses employment equity. However, BC has legislation that addresses it indirectly: section 42 of the BC Code protects voluntary employment equity programs from claims of discrimination (see below under the heading "Exemptions: Where Discrimination Is Allowed").

In 1986, the federal government enacted the *Employment Equity Act*, which requires large federally regulated employers to implement employment equity programs in their workplaces. Although this federal Act is not covered in the current textbook, under the Federal Contractors Program provincially regulated companies with 100 or more employees that contract with the federal government for business worth $1 million or more must commit to implementing employment equity and are encouraged to seek additional information on the employment equity requirements contained in the program.

FYI

Strategies for Making Workplaces More Inclusive

Organizations that are most successful with employment equity link the full participation of designated group members to their business strategy. The following is a sampling of strategies that diversity award-winning employers in Canada have adopted:

1. partnering with outside organizations to find job candidates who are hard to reach through traditional recruitment strategies;
2. holding equity-awareness sessions for recruiters;
3. publishing and displaying recruitment materials in a variety of languages;
4. providing tools to help employees with disabilities;
5. surveying employees on whether they are treated respectfully and fairly at work;
6. recognizing candidates who have obtained their qualifications and experience in non-traditional ways;
7. building diversity training into management/supervisory preparation, including a training program on bias-free interviewing;
8. focusing on retaining employees from designated groups by incorporating a diversity component into their succession planning program;
9. hosting leadership seminars and networking breakfasts for senior-level female and minority employees; and
10. providing paid internships to people with disabilities.

Discrimination Through Reprisal

The *Alberta Human Rights Act* provides that people have the right to enforce their rights under the Act without reprisal. An employer may not retaliate against someone for making or attempting to make a complaint under the Act; giving evidence or participating in a proceeding under the Act; or assisting in any way with an investigation, settlement, or prosecution. The Act also prohibits anyone from making frivolous or vexatious complaints that are motivated by malice. British Columbia's legislation similarly provides parties with protection from "retaliation" after attempting to assert their rights under the BC *Human Rights Code* (s 43). Providing protection from reprisals for exercising rights under the legislation is important. Without this protection, it is likely that many legitimate complaints would go unreported out of fear of the consequences an employee might face.

Discrimination Not Covered by the Alberta Act or BC Code

To engage the protection of the Alberta Act or the BC Code, the discriminatory treatment *must be based on one of the prohibited grounds*. Although the grounds of prohibited discrimination are numerous and broadly defined, they are not exhaustive. Someone who is discriminated against on the basis of a ground not covered, such as social status, cannot file a complaint under the Act or the Code. Similarly, discrimination on the basis of physical appearance, for example, does not infringe the Act or the Code unless it touches on a prohibited ground, as would be the case if an employer discriminated against a person who wears a nose ring for religious reasons or who has a perceived disability that has more to do with appearance (e.g., weight in the *Turner v Canada Border Services Agency* decision mentioned above).

The prohibited grounds of discrimination in other provinces are similar but not identical to the grounds in Alberta and BC. For example, some provinces, such as Quebec, prohibit discrimination on the basis of assignment, attachment, or seizure of pay. Others do not include all the grounds found in Alberta; for example, neither BC nor Ontario includes source of income as a prohibited ground of discrimination in the area of employment.

Exemptions: Where Discrimination Is Allowed

The right to be free from discrimination in employment on the basis of the grounds discussed above is not absolute. The BC Code and the Alberta Act set out exemptions where even intentional discrimination is permissible.

Unlike the legislation of some other jurisdictions, the Alberta Act identifies very few specific exemptions. Instead it relies on the general defences to discrimination found in sections 7(3), 8(2), and 11 of the Act. Sections 7(3) and 8(2) allow an employer to discriminate in advertising, interviewing, or hiring if the reason is a BFOR. Section 11 allows discrimination as long as it is "reasonable and justifiable" in the circumstances. For example, a fitness club may hire only male attendants to work in the men's locker room. However, in such instances, the employer must consider whether accommodation could be made to enable a woman to work in the position. If working in the men's locker room is a minor part of the job, it should be determined whether the job could be redefined to eliminate that element and thus accommodate a female candidate.

Section 7(2) of the Alberta Act also contains special exemptions on the grounds of age and marital status for bona fide retirement plans, pension plans, or employee insurance plans. This allows insurance organizations to opt out of providing employees over a specified age with a pension or insurance plan and allows them to offer different plans to employees who are single rather than married. However, the age-based discrimination currently allowed in Alberta may soon come under fire. An Ontario Human Rights Tribunal decision in *Talos v Grand Erie District School Board* ruled that age-based distinctions in pension, benefit, and insurance plans for employees aged 65 and older are a violation of the Charter. The ruling stated that denying protection to workers aged 65 and older without regard to individual circumstances devalues the contributions of older workers and entrenches the stereotype that their labour is worth less. The Tribunal further held that this type of age discrimination could not be justified because there was actuarial evidence that it was not cost prohibitive to provide coverage to older workers and the decision to exclude them was arbitrary and not within a reasonable range of choices.

Similar to the Alberta Act, the BC Code allows employers to discriminate on any of the grounds listed so long as the employer's "refusal, limitation, specification or preference" is based on a "bona fide occupational requirement" (s 13(4)). The BC Code also allows certain organizations to grant "preference" to members belonging to "an identifiable group or class of persons." These identifiable groups or classes match the categories of persons discussed above with three exceptions—family status, sexual orientation, and conviction for an offence are not included. The exemption is granted where the organization has "as a primary purpose the promotion of the interests and welfare" of that identifiable group or class of persons and is "not operated for profit" (s 41). An obvious example of this is an agency that provides relief counselling to sexually abused women and hires only female staff.

Special (Affirmative Action) Programs in British Columbia

Section 42 of the BC Code permits discrimination in the case of persons disadvantaged because of race, colour, ancestry, place of origin, physical or mental disability, or sex. Under this exemption, an employer may implement a special program to relieve or promote people who typically suffer from employment discrimination on the basis of those prohibited grounds. The Code identifies this special program as an **employment equity program**. For example, where the employer has a bona fide affirmative action program to hire someone from a First Nations background, the employer may discriminate in favour of people who fall within that category. This provision is consistent with sections 6(4) and 15(2) of the Charter.

employment equity program
a special program to relieve or promote people who typically suffer from employment discrimination on the basis of prohibited grounds

Making a Human Rights Complaint

Provincial human rights tribunals have responsibility for accepting, screening, mediating, and deciding complaints made under the applicable human rights legislation. An employee who wants to file a claim of discrimination or harassment may obtain an application form from the website of the Alberta Human Rights Commission and BC Human Rights Tribunal. In both Alberta and BC, complaints should be filed within one year of the alleged discriminatory incident. Complaints in Alberta are assessed for completeness and to ensure the Alberta Human Rights Commission has jurisdiction before they are sent to the respondent, who is required to respond within a specified period. If the Commission does not have jurisdiction, the complaint has no prospect of success, or if it was filed for improper motives it may be dismissed at this stage. The BC Human Rights Tribunal similarly will review whether the complaint is filed within the statutory timeline and sets out alleged discrimination pursuant to the BC Code before notifying the respondent.

If a complaint is not dismissed at this earlier stage by the Alberta Commission or the BC Tribunal, there is normally an attempt to settle the dispute before going to a hearing. If conciliation is not successful through informal settlement discussions or mediation (a service provided by the BC Tribunal), a case management meeting is held and the parties prepare for a hearing.

A human rights hearing is quite similar to a hearing in the court system. The parties present documentary evidence and call, examine, and cross-examine witnesses. They may be represented by lawyers if they wish. The case is heard by a panel (also called a tribunal). The panel generally follows similar rules about the types of evidence it accepts, although it has more latitude than a court because the parties involved are often unfamiliar with courtroom processes and standards. Hearings are generally open to the public, although they may be heard privately if requested and if the panel feels there is good reason.

At the end of a hearing, the panel may give an oral decision, but will also provide a written decision at a later date. Decisions from human rights panels have the same force and effect as a court decision. If either party is unhappy with the outcome of their case, they can file for a reconsideration of the decision by the panel. This option is only available in limited circumstances. For example, a party may apply where there are new material facts or evidence that could not reasonably have been obtained earlier or where the decision is in conflict with established jurisprudence and it involves a matter of public importance.

Human rights complaints that arise from a matter covered by a collective agreement are usually heard by an arbitrator under the grievance procedure of the collective agreement, rather than by a human rights panel, although there is nothing that prevents an individual from filing a complaint against an employer under both jurisdictions. The human rights process may be put on hold while the grievance proceeds to prevent the same matter from being decided in two separate forums, but it may be revived afterward if the complainant is unhappy with the result. An employee covered by a collective agreement may also file a human rights complaint against their union.

Although human rights panels are not courts of law, some basic principles regarding civil proceedings still apply. Here are some things to keep in mind:

- Both sides must be given notice of the proceedings and must be given an opportunity to be heard before the decision is made. Hearings can proceed without the attendance of an affected party if notice was given and the party failed to show up.
- The complainant bears the initial burden of proof—that is, they must be able to show that discrimination occurred, after which point the respondent has the burden of showing that the discrimination was a BFOR or that its duty to accommodate would have caused undue hardship.
- The burden of proof is the lower civil standard of "proof on a balance of probabilities," not the criminal one of "proof beyond a reasonable doubt."
- In BC, there is no automatic right to appeal the panel's decision. A party must have valid grounds to have the decision reviewed by the BC Supreme Court. In Alberta, the Act includes the right to appeal to the Court of Queen's Bench. Higher courts generally have three options on appeal. They may confirm the panel's decision, reverse or alter the decision and order specific remedies, or remit the matter back to the panel for reconsideration.

Remedies

Section 32(1) of the Alberta Act allows a human rights tribunal to dismiss a complaint that is without merit. However, if a complaint does have merit (in whole or in part), the tribunal may order the respondent to:

- cease the discriminatory policy or behaviour;
- refrain from engaging in the same or similar discriminatory acts in the future;
- award the complainant any opportunities or privileges that were lost as a result of the discrimination (e.g., a tribunal may order that a complainant be reinstated to their position or be given a promotion that was denied);
- compensate the complainant for any or all wages, income lost, or expenses incurred because of the discrimination; or
- take any other action the tribunal considers proper to place the complainant in the position they would have been in but for the discrimination.

The tribunal may also order either party to pay the other for a portion of the costs associated with the proceeding.

In BC, the remedies are very similar. Additionally, the BC Code specifically allows the panel to order an employer to adopt and implement an employment equity program and to make a declaratory order, which can consist of a public statement confirming an employer's wrongdoing. Section 37(2)(d)(iii) enables the panel to order compensation to the complainant for "injury to dignity, feelings and self-respect." Nothing in the Alberta legislation prohibits a tribunal from making similar orders. It is not uncommon for Alberta tribunals to award between $10,000 and $15,000 in damages for hurt feelings or injury to dignity and self-respect. In BC, awards for injury to dignity have usually been in the same range and, generally, it has been understood that the de facto ceiling for injury to dignity awards was in the range of $25,000 to $35,000 until recently. In 2016, the BC Court of Appeal upheld an unprecedented award of $75,000 for injury to dignity in a case of discrimination on the basis of disability (*University of British Columbia v Kelly*). Subsequently, in *Araniva v RSY Contracting (No 3)*, the BC Tribunal awarded $40,000 for injury to dignity in a sexual harassment case (amounting to discrimination on the basis of sex). The Tribunal acknowledged that damages awards in previous comparable cases had been in the range of $22,500 to $25,000 but expressly endorsed an upward trend in damages awards:

> Ultimately, however, I do not find that the comparison with these cases undermines Araniva's claim. Those cases are now several years old. Since they were decided, the BC Court of Appeal has upheld an award of $75,000: Kelly. The trend for these damages is upward. (at para 145)

Unless there is a human rights element to a civil action, a human rights claim may only be made through the administrative system of human rights commissions and tribunals, or through grievance arbitration for unionized employees. There is no independent tort of discrimination under the common law (as held by the Supreme Court of Canada in the 1981 case *Seneca College v Bhadauria*); discrimination is a matter for human rights legislation. The BC Court of Appeal more recently applied the *Bhadauria* ruling when it held that there is no violation of the Charter in the requirement that "[a]ll human rights complainants [must] bring their complaints under the *Code* and before the Tribunal" rather than being allowed to go directly to the courts with a discrimination claim (*Gichuru v The Law Society of British Columbia* [2014]).

However, if an employee's claim of discrimination or harassment is part of a civil lawsuit, such as a claim for wrongful dismissal, the employee is usually not allowed to pursue a parallel human rights claim with a tribunal. In such cases, an employee has the option of either going to court and including the discrimination claim as part of the wrongful dismissal lawsuit or filing an application under the human rights legislation of the appropriate jurisdiction. The employee can file in both legal avenues, to ensure deadlines are met, but a decision by one adjudicative body will prevent the case from being heard by the other.

Human Rights Issues in Recruitment, Selection, and Hiring

It has been said that the selection process is probably responsible for more discrimination than any other area of employment practice. At the hiring stage, assumptions, often subconscious, about certain groups of people and their abilities can come into play. Recruiters are required to make decisions quickly based on information in a job application form and one or two interviews. Unspoken assumptions and first impressions lend themselves to subtle forms of discrimination. Indeed, tribunals sometimes find a "subtle scent of discrimination" that permeates certain workplaces and amounts to a violation of human rights (see e.g. the BC case of *Morrison v AdvoCare* [2009] and the federal case of *Turner v Canada Border Services Agency* [2014], mentioned above).

To protect themselves, employers should document all decisions made at each step of the hiring process and include the reasons for each decision. Clear and careful documentation, prepared at the time a decision is made, provides an employer with a credible basis to defend against allegations that the decision was made on discriminatory grounds. The Act is infringed even if a discriminatory ground is only one of several reasons for an employment decision.

The following is a discussion of the human rights issues raised at each step of the recruitment, selection, and hiring process.

Essential Requirements of the Job

An employer should ensure that a job description is current and accurately reflects the employer's needs and expectations. Particular duties or structures that made sense when the job was last filled may have changed in the interim.

The employer should review the job carefully to determine which requirements are essential for the job. Interpretation of BFORs would rely on an analysis of job duties. Only essential duties should be considered in deciding whether or not someone is capable of performing a job.

Job duties or requirements that are both essential and relate to a prohibited ground of discrimination should be scrutinized carefully. For example, requiring a driver's licence for a job that does not entail a lot of driving would unnecessarily bar a candidate who is unable to obtain a driver's licence because of physical disability, and therefore could infringe the Act. On the other hand, if the job involves a lot of communication with the public, it is reasonable to require fluency in English, but it is unacceptable to discriminate against someone who speaks English with a non-Canadian accent. (Although language is not a prohibited ground of discrimination, it is directly linked to other grounds, such as place of origin.)

Where an essential job requirement negatively affects a person or group on the basis of a prohibited ground of discrimination, an employer has a duty to accommodate the individual or group unless this causes **undue hardship**. The undue hardship standard was established in 1999, when the Supreme Court of Canada issued the watershed decision of *British Columbia (Public Service Employee Relations Commission) v BCGSEU* (known as the *Meiorin* case). Meiorin was a firefighter and long-serving employee who lost her job when her employer implemented a new physical fitness test as a bona fide occupational qualification. Although the *Meiorin* case occurred in the context of an ongoing employment relationship, the approach established by the court is important to employers during recruitment, testing, selection, and hiring.

undue hardship
occurs if accommodation creates "onerous conditions," "intolerable financial costs," or "serious disruption" to the business

CASE IN POINT

Three-Part Test Established for Justifying Discriminatory Rule

British Columbia (Public Service Employee Relations Commission) v BCGSEU, [1999] 3 SCR 3

Facts

Meiorin was a forest firefighter who had performed her job in a satisfactory manner for three years when her employer, the BC government, implemented a new policy under which all firefighters were required to pass a series of fitness tests. A team of researchers at the University of Victoria had designed the tests using a sample group of participants that consisted of many more men than women. To measure aerobic capacity, the test required employees to run 2.5 kilometres in 11 minutes or less. Meiorin tried to pass this part of the test on four separate occasions, but her best time was 49 seconds over the 11-minute limit. As a result, the government terminated her employment as a forest firefighter.

Relevant Issue

Whether Meiorin's termination amounted to discrimination and thus violated British Columbia's human rights legislation.

Decision

The Supreme Court of Canada found that the rule was discriminatory because Meiorin was able to show that the aerobic requirement screened out more women than men on the basis of their differing physical capacities. The issue was whether the discriminatory rule or standard could be justified. Reversing previous case law, the Court ruled that there should not be separate categories of discrimination: direct and constructive (adverse impact). Whatever form discrimination takes, job rules or qualifications that detrimentally affect people or groups on the basis of a prohibited ground of discrimination should be subject to the same analysis. The Court established a three-part test to determine when a discriminatory rule or qualification is justifiable. To successfully defend a discriminatory standard or rule, the employer must:

1. demonstrate that a *rational connection exists* between the purpose for which the standard was introduced and the objective requirements of the job;
2. demonstrate that the standard was *adopted in an honest and good-faith belief* that it was necessary for the performance of the job; and
3. establish that the standard was *reasonably necessary* to accomplish that legitimate work-related purpose. To establish this, the employer must show that it was *impossible to accommodate* employees who share the characteristics of the claimant without imposing undue hardship on itself.

The employer met the first two tests but failed the third one. It was unable to prove that the aerobic standard was reasonably necessary for a forest firefighter to perform the job safely and efficiently or that accommodation was impossible without undue hardship.

Under the third part of the *Meiorin* test, a discriminatory standard will be found reasonably necessary, and therefore justified, only if the employer can show that it was impossible to accommodate the individual or group negatively affected by the rule without suffering undue hardship. This is a very high standard for an employer to meet and one that requires it to consider differing needs when setting or creating a standard or rule. However, this does not mean that an employer must show that it is *impossible* to accommodate the individual or group at all. In its 2008 *Hydro-Québec* decision, the Supreme Court of Canada clarified the third part of the *Meiorin* test. It confirmed that the test is not whether it is impossible to accommodate, but whether it is impossible to do so *without undue hardship*. This simple caveat provided a much-needed clarification that the high standard of "impossibility" was limited by the concept of undue hardship. *Hydro-Québec* has already been applied in dozens of human rights cases in BC and Alberta.

Furthermore, the question of reasonable accommodation should be taken into consideration *from the beginning as part of setting the rule or standard.* In *Meiorin*, the BC government should have developed standards of aerobic fitness that recognized the different capacities of women and men and established requirements accordingly. The Court suggested some factors that might be determinative when assessing whether the duty to accommodate has been met:

1. Did the employer investigate alternative approaches that do not have a discriminatory effect, such as individual testing?
2. Were there valid reasons why alternative approaches were not implemented? What were they?
3. Can the workplace accommodate different standards that reflect group or individual differences and capabilities?
4. Can legitimate workplace objectives be met in a less discriminatory manner?
5. Does the standard ensure that the desired qualification is met without placing an undue burden on those to whom it applies?

6. Have other parties who are obliged to assist in the search for accommodation (e.g., the union representing an affected worker) fulfilled their roles?

Use of Employment Agencies

Sometimes employers use employment agencies to hire people temporarily. These workers are often referred to as "temps." In some situations, the agency remains the employer.

In BC, employment agencies are specifically identified in section 13(2) as having an obligation not to refuse to refer a person for employment on any of the 15 grounds of discrimination listed in section 13(1). An "employment agency" is defined in section 1 of the Code as including "a person who undertakes, with or without compensation, to procure employees for employers or to procure employment for persons."

In Alberta, employment agencies are not addressed specifically. However, human resources managers need to be aware that employment agencies are subject to the conditions of human rights legislation in the same way that employers are. Employers cannot ask, and employment agencies cannot accept or act on requests, to hire people on the basis of preferences related to prohibited grounds of discrimination. For example, an employer cannot legally ask an employment agency to send only "young blondes" to fill a position. An employment agency that accepted this directive would also be in contravention of the Act.

To ensure that it is not implicated in any discriminatory practices, an employer should include a term in its contract with the employment agency that requires the agency to comply with all human rights requirements. Similarly, the agency should make it clear that it will not accept or act on discriminatory directions.

Advertising a Job

Many jobs are filled through advertisements. It is the intention of both BC and Alberta human rights statutes that an employer consider many qualified candidates in the early part of the recruitment process so that suitable candidates are not eliminated inadvertently. This intention affects both where and how a position is advertised, as well as the contents of the advertisement.

Where and How Is a Job Advertised?

Jobs are often advertised informally, using internal postings or "word of mouth." The human rights problem with such informality is that it tends to perpetuate the current composition of the workforce. For example, if most of the current employees come from a certain ethnic background, filling the position by internal posting or word of mouth may perpetuate the ethnic status quo.

It is not illegal to advertise by word of mouth or in an ethnically based community paper, but this approach creates some risk. If there is a subsequent complaint about discrimination, an employer's hiring practices may affect a tribunal's view of the case. Broadly based advertising is best because it provides access to the largest pool of applicants. Senior or highly skilled positions may need to be advertised over a larger geographic area than other jobs.

Contents of Advertisements

Section 8(1) of the Alberta Act is very clear about what may be included in a job ad as well as the interview process. It provides as follows:

> 8(1) No person shall use or circulate any form of application for employment or publish any advertisement in connection with employment or prospective employment or make any written or oral inquiry of an applicant
>
> (a) that expresses either directly or indirectly any limitation, specification or preference indicating discrimination on the basis of the race, religious beliefs, colour, gender, gender identity, gender expression, physical disability, mental disability, age, ancestry, place of origin, marital status, source of income, family status or sexual orientation of that person or of any other person.

Section 11 of the BC Code is less detailed. It just prohibits advertisements from "express[ing] a limitation, specification or preference as to" any of the grounds listed in section 13 (except for prior offences), unless there is a BFOR.

Advertisements should not contain qualifications that directly or indirectly discourage people from applying for a job on the basis of a prohibited ground of discrimination. An advertisement should be geared to the qualifications and skills required for the position.

Advertisements should always use non-discriminatory language when describing a job. For example, gender-neutral words, such as "sales clerk" (rather than "salesman") or "server" (rather than "waitress"), should be used. Reference to preferred applicants as "mature" and descriptions of an employer as having a "youthful" culture tend to exclude candidates on the prohibited ground of age.

Employers should also avoid qualifications that, while not obviously biased, tend to touch on a prohibited ground. For example, if the advertisement states that Canadian experience is preferred, a qualified candidate whose work experience is largely outside Canada might be deterred from applying. This is related to the prohibited ground of place of origin. Previous work experience may be canvassed at the application and interview stage to the extent that it is relevant.

The BFOR exemption applies to the BC and Alberta rules for advertisements. Sometimes an essential job duty unavoidably touches on a prohibited ground. For example, a school bus driver needs a special driver's licence. This requirement may be stated in the advertisement even though it bars applicants who are unable to obtain such a licence because of a disability. But employers must make sure they state the essential job requirements rather than refer to personal characteristics. For example, where strenuous physical work is necessary, the advertisement should state that "heavy lifting is required," rather than that "the applicant must be physically fit." An advertisement can indicate that an employer is an equal opportunity employer or that candidates from diverse backgrounds are encouraged to apply.

Job Applications

Section 8(1)(b) of the Alberta Act prohibits employers from requiring job applicants to furnish any information regarding protected grounds. The Act thus expressly prohibits questions on an application form that directly or indirectly classify candidates by prohibited grounds. The intent is to avoid discouraging potential applicants from applying by creating the impression that they would not be acceptable.

Appropriate questions are limited to establishing the applicant's name, address, education, and previous employment history. The purpose of the job application form is to gather information on job qualifications and skills and to avoid eliciting information that directly or indirectly excludes individuals on non-job-related grounds. Table 7.1 provides examples of requests and questions that are recommended or should be avoided because they directly or indirectly touch on prohibited grounds. This list is not exhaustive.

TABLE 7.1 Recommended Guide for Pre-employment Inquiries

Unless there is a valid, job-related reason that constitutes a bona fide occupational requirement, employers should follow the guidelines below.

Common Question Areas	Recommended	Not Recommended
Gender, marital status, family status	Availability for shift work, travel, etc.	Plans for marriage, family, child care; any inquiries specific to gender or marital status (including common law relationships) or family status
Race, colour, ancestry, or place of origin	Legally permitted to work in Canada?	Place of birth, citizenship, racial origin, next of kin
Name	Previous names, only if the information is needed to verify the applicant's past employment or education and to do a reference check	Maiden name; "Christian" name; reference to origin of name; being related to another person by blood, marriage, or adoption
Languages	Ability to communicate in any language specifically required for a job	Other languages when not required in a specific job
Photographs	In rare situations such as modelling and entertainment	Requesting photographs (these can reveal race, gender, etc.)
Clubs or organizations	Membership in professional associations, clubs, or organizations; hobbies or interests, as long as they are job related	Specific inquiries about club and organization memberships that would indicate race, colour, religious beliefs, ancestry, or place of origin
Age	Old enough to work legally in Alberta or BC?	Specific age of applicants who are 18 years or older, including retirement information
Height and weight	Describing job duties that require heavy lifting or other physical requirements	Minimum/maximum height and weight requirements/stipulations

(Continued on next page.)

TABLE 7.1 Recommended Guide for Pre-employment Inquiries (Continued)

Common Question Areas	Recommended	Not Recommended
Disability	Indicating the job offer is contingent upon a satisfactory job-related medical examination to determine capability to perform the duties as outlined	General disabilities, limitations, present or previous health problems, workers' compensation claims or sick leave or absence due to stress or mental or physical illness
Smoking	Indicating the successful applicant will be required to work in a non-smoking environment	Asthmatic or permanent respiratory conditions that may be affected by smoke
Source of income	Job-related information such as former employment	Inquiries unrelated to the specific job to be performed
Education	Educational institutions attended; nature and level of education achieved	Inquiries about religious or racial affiliation of educational institution
Religious beliefs	Availability for shift work, travel, etc.	Inquiries about specific religious holidays observed by the applicant, customs observed, religious dress, etc.; requiring applicants to provide recommendations from a church or religious leader

Note: Once an offer of employment has been made and accepted, an employer may request photographs or other personal information for the purpose of employee identification, for tax purposes, or for the administration of benefits. The employer must handle and store the information in a secure manner to avoid possible or perceived misuse of the information.

SOURCE: Adapted from Alberta Human Rights Commission, July 2017.

The BC Code does not expressly deal with application forms or job interviews, and the BC Human Rights Tribunal does not have a guide to questions that should or should not be asked by employers. However, on a claim under section 13 of the Code, the Tribunal treats interview questions and application forms as evidence of discrimination in the hiring process—where the questions relate to prohibited grounds.

Job Interviews

As noted above, the BC Code is silent on what can or cannot be done or asked at a job interview. But any perception on the part of a job applicant that they were discriminated against would be sufficient grounds to file a complaint under the Code. The Alberta Act imposes the same restrictions at the job interview stage as it does for job application forms and advertisements.

However, the job interview process poses unique human rights challenges, and everyone who participates in the process should be knowledgeable about human rights requirements. For example, when meeting a candidate, an interviewer may be tempted to chat informally to create a relaxed atmosphere. During such a conversation, information may be elicited that touches on a prohibited ground. For example, a job candidate may comment about family pictures displayed in an interviewer's office. The interviewer should refrain from eliciting information regarding the candidate's family, even though it would be normal to do so in polite conversation. Even if the information is elicited without intent to discriminate, it may raise questions about whether the candidate's family status played a part in the eventual hiring decision. A candidate who is not hired could file a claim of discrimination and an employer would need to expend time and effort in responding to it.

The interviewer should resist any urges to form subjective impressions or observations that relate to prohibited grounds. The interviewer should also be conscious of human rights issues when placing notes on the interview file that are intended to help them remember a particular candidate. From a legal point of view, notes referring to "an older guy with a slight lisp" or a female candidate wearing a "tight rainbow sweater" will not be helpful.

There are several ways to limit the potential for human rights problems arising from the interview. These include the following:

1. *Accommodate disabilities.* If a job applicant is unable to attend an interview because of a disability, an employer must accommodate the candidate so that they have an equal opportunity to be interviewed.
2. *Have a standard set of questions and evaluation criteria.* Standardizing an interview keeps it on track and avoids the perception that candidates were treated differently on the basis of a prohibited ground. Using a standard evaluation rubric with descriptions of good, adequate, or poor responses also decreases the likelihood that raters will base their evaluations on factors not relevant to performance of the job.
3. *Use interview teams.* Teams allow interviewers to compare impressions and can reduce the impact of individual biases. If a candidate subsequently alleges discrimination, there are several people to recall what took place during the interview. There should be at least one interviewer knowledgeable about the position being offered.
4. *Beware of prohibited grounds.* An interviewer should not ask questions that relate to a prohibited ground unless the elicited information can legally form the basis of a hiring decision. If a response cannot be used in making a hiring decision, the employer takes a risk in asking it. The candidate may perceive that the information played a part in the decision not to hire and it may be difficult to prove otherwise.

   There is some debate about whether an interviewer should raise the issue of physical ability to perform the job at the interview stage. If the disability is obvious and relevant to the essential requirements of the job or if the candidate raises the issue, the employer should discuss the disability and possible accommodations. Otherwise, the candidate may get the impression that the employer has no serious interest in understanding how they can perform the job. However, if the disability is not obvious or is not raised by the candidate, it is probably safer for the employer not to introduce it. Once the employer is aware of the disability, an unsuccessful candidate could allege that the information played a part in denying them the job. It has been suggested that issues of accommodation should be discussed only after a conditional offer of employment is made unless the candidate requests accommodation at the interview stage or the disability is obvious (Ontario Human Rights Commission, 2008).

Generally speaking, a job applicant is under no obligation to voluntarily disclose during an interview a medical condition that qualifies as a mental or physical disability.

Similar considerations apply to discussions about the accommodation of religious practices. For example, if the position requires that the successful candidate work Friday nights and Saturdays, the employer would be wise not to discuss the candidate's availability for those shifts because this could elicit information concerning a prohibited ground. Even if shift work is an important part of the job, an employer is obliged to accommodate an employee unless accommodation would create undue hardship. Therefore, there is little to be gained by raising the issue during the interview stage and risking a discrimination claim unless accommodation is virtually impossible because of the employer's size or hours of operation. If accommodation is virtually impossible, it could be raised at the interview because the employer can justify its discriminatory rule under the three-part *Meiorin* test.

A final point to note is that, whether it is at the time of receiving a job application or resumé, during the interview, or after the interview, an employer should be cautious about automatically screening out applicants on the basis that they are overqualified for the position (Miedema & Hall, 2006, at 39). As shown in the following case of *Sangha v Mackenzie Valley Land and Water Board*, rejecting an applicant who is an immigrant because he is "overqualified" may be found to be discrimination on the basis of national or ethnic origin.

CASE IN POINT

Is Overqualification a Valid Reason Not to Hire?

Sangha v Mackenzie Valley Land and Water Board, 2006 CHRT 9, judicial review allowed, 2007 FC 856

Facts

Sangha had a PhD in environmental science and extensive work experience in this field. After he immigrated to Canada from India, however, he was unable to get a job in keeping with his employment background. Desperate to find a job in his field, he applied for one of four entry-level environmental positions advertised by the employer, Mackenzie Valley. Although Sangha was one of the best-qualified candidates, the employer's interview team decided he was unsuitable because he was overqualified for the position. The team felt he would be easily bored with the job and leave as soon as he found something better, and they already had a problem with high turnover. When Sangha found out that he did not get the job, given his credentials and how well he believed the interview had gone, he filed a complaint of discrimination based on race, national or ethnic origin, colour, and religion.

Relevant Issue

Whether rejecting a job candidate who is an immigrant on the basis that he is overqualified is contrary to the *Canadian Human Rights Act*.

Decision

The Canadian Human Rights Tribunal found that Sangha had been discriminated against on the basis of national and ethnic origin. The Tribunal noted that on the face of it, the employer's hiring process was non-discriminatory and neutral. There were no questions that touched on personal characteristics, such as race, colour, national or ethnic origin, religion, or age, and the interview was conducted professionally. However, relying on expert testimony at the hearing, the Tribunal found that the experience of applying for a job for which one is overqualified is disproportionately an immigrant experience. Visible minority immigrants are disproportionately excluded from the higher levels of the job market because of barriers to employment at this level. They therefore seek employment at lower echelons where their qualifications exceed the job requirements. The Tribunal held that "thus a policy or practice against the hiring of overqualified candidates affects them differently from others to whom it may also apply" (at para 202). As such, it is *prima facie* discriminatory.

Sangha was awarded $9,500 for pain and suffering. However, his request for compensation for three years' worth of lost earnings ($55,000 per year) and for an order that Mackenzie Valley hire him when a position became available was denied. In the Tribunal's view, Sangha had not established that his being hired was more than just a "mere possibility" had there not been discrimination. However, on appeal, the Federal Court found that Sangha had in fact shown that there was a "serious possibility" that he would have been hired but for the discriminatory overqualification standard. It therefore sent the decision back to the Tribunal for reconsideration as to the appropriate remedy.

Other cases alleging age-based discrimination related to an "overqualification" standard have also been filed (see e.g. *Yue v District of Maple Ridge* [2008] and *Reiss v CCH Canadian Limited* [2013]).

An employer is justified asking questions that appear discriminatory only when there is a BFOR. In BC, there are two other circumstances where an employer may ask questions about protected grounds: (1) where the employment pertains to a special service organization under section 41, or (2) where the employment is part of an employment equity program under section 42.

Conditional Offers of Employment

Once an employer has made an offer to a candidate, it is appropriate to gather information that would be forbidden in earlier stages of the recruitment process. The following are examples of information that should be requested only after an employer makes a conditional offer:

- a copy of a driver's licence, which contains information such as date of birth;
- a work authorization from immigration authorities, which contains information regarding date of arrival in Canada;
- a social insurance card, which may contain information regarding immigration status;
- a transcript or copy of professional credentials, which often indicate place of origin; and
- requests for medical examinations or health information necessary for pension, disability, superannuation, life insurance, and benefit plans, all of which may indicate physical disabilities (Ontario Human Rights Commission, 2008).

Pre-employment Medical or Fitness Examinations

Medical tests to determine a candidate's ability to perform the essential duties of a job should take place only after a conditional offer of employment is made and only if there is no other reasonable way for the employer to determine the applicant's ability to do the job. The examination must be directly relevant to the job as well as objectively necessary and appropriate. For example, a back X-ray may be appropriate for a job that involves heavy lifting but not for a managerial job. The results cannot be used to disqualify a candidate unless they directly undermine the candidate's ability to perform the essential duties of the job. Even then, the employer is obliged to accommodate the employee unless this would create undue hardship.

If medical testing is required, all candidates must be tested; employers who test only certain candidates may be vulnerable to allegations of discrimination. The results of medical tests must be maintained in confidential medical files, separate from human resources files, and accessible only to qualified medical personnel.

Where medical testing is appropriate, candidates should be so notified at the time that an offer of employment is made. Arrangements must be made for the competent handling of test materials and for keeping them properly labelled and secure at all times. Test results should be reviewed with the employee by the physician.

Pre-employment Drug and Alcohol Testing

Human rights legislation throughout Canada considers alcoholism and drug dependency to be forms of disability and therefore prohibited grounds of discrimination (see "On-the-Job Drug and Alcohol Testing," below). As a result, workplace alcohol and drug testing is quite restricted in this country. Pre-employment testing is where someone is not yet employed and is seeking employment. Post-employment drug and alcohol testing is discussed later in this chapter. However, such testing continues to be an important issue, especially in workplaces that are safety sensitive or that are affiliated with companies operating in the United States, where such testing is far more common. In the view of Canada's human rights commissions, drug and alcohol testing is risky during recruitment and before hiring. The best advice for most employers, including those in BC, is to not attempt such tests, since there is a strong chance they will be seen as discriminatory attempts to screen out applicants with dependency disabilities. Further, pre-employment drug testing does not measure current impairment, and pre-employment alcohol testing, while measuring impairment at the time of testing, does not predict a candidate's ability to perform the essential job requirements. It is, therefore, difficult to justify its potential discriminatory effect.

However, from the perspective of the Alberta Human Rights Commission, testing, in and of itself, is not prohibited. What does concern the Commission is what happens afterward. If there is discrimination based on a real or perceived disability, if there is a failure to accommodate a dependence disability, or if the employer has a policy that discriminates against employees with drug or alcohol dependence, the Commission may act to remedy the violation. For example, if an employer tests an applicant *before* or *after* offering employment, the test comes back positive, and the employer withdraws the offer or refuses to hire that applicant, it will look a lot like discrimination to the Commission. Alternatively, if an employer tests an applicant, the test comes back positive and the employer (1) checks to see whether the positive test is the result of a dependence disability and if it is, then (2) identifies ways to accommodate to the point of undue hardship, it will look a lot less like discrimination.

At this point, the Alberta Human Rights Commission continues to follow its reasoning in the *Kellogg Brown & Root* (*KBR*) case described below.

CASE IN POINT

Perceived Disability in Pre-employment Drug Screening

Alberta (Human Rights and Citizenship Commission) v Kellogg Brown & Root (Canada) Company, 2006 ABQB 302, rev'd 2007 ABCA 426, leave to appeal to SCC refused, 2008 CanLII 32723

Facts

Chiasson was hired as an inspector (a safety-sensitive position) at the Syncrude plant in Fort McMurray. He was told that his employment was conditional on passing a pre-employment drug test. He took the test, began work, and was on the job for nine days when the test results came back indicating that there were THC metabolites (residual effects of marijuana use) in his urine. He was summarily dismissed. Chiasson filed a complaint with the Alberta Human Rights and Citizenship Commission claiming that he was discriminated against on the basis of a perceived disability. Chiasson stated he was a recreational marijuana user, his use offsite did not affect his work, he had never had a safety incident, and he did not have a disability. Furthermore, his performance on previous jobs had been evaluated as superior to excellent.

Relevant Issue

Is mandatory pre-employment drug testing *prima facie* discrimination on the basis of a real or perceived disability? If it is discrimination, can it be justified?

Decision

The Alberta Human Rights and Citizenship Commission dismissed the case in June 2005 on the basis that Chiasson did not suffer from any real or perceived disability, and therefore no discrimination had occurred. In an interesting reversal, the Court of Queen's Bench reviewed the case and held that the company's screening policy had the effect of creating a class of people (those who tested positively for drug use) and systematically discriminating against them. Because dismissal was the automatic and absolute sanction for failing the test, the policy also had the effect of discriminating against both individuals with an actual disability (addiction) and those perceived to have a disability (recreational users).

The Alberta Court of Appeal subsequently reversed the Queen's Bench decision and restored the Alberta Human Rights and Citizenship Commission decision. The Court of Appeal held that the drug testing policy did not perceive that those who test positive have a drug dependence (disability). Instead, the policy treats those who test positive as being a safety risk in a dangerous workplace. The Court went on to discuss the link between casual drug use and lingering impairment that could create a safety hazard. It compared the drug testing policy to a policy prohibiting consumption of alcohol before a truck driver gets behind the wheel. The Appeal Court's decision does not remove perceived disability from the prohibited grounds of discrimination, nor does it give the all-clear to KBR's drug testing policy. But because there was no actual or perceived disability in this case, it chose not to determine whether the pre-employment policy would be discriminatory if a disability did exist. Unlike the Commission, the Court did not consider arguments about whether the policy would satisfy the duty to accommodate branch of the test for a BFOR. Leave to appeal to the Supreme Court of Canada was denied.

As shown in *KBR* and subsequent cases with similar fact situations (see e.g. *McNamara v Lockerbie & Hole Inc* [2010]), an employer may be entitled to engage in pre-employment testing. However, it must be able to show that it is reasonably necessary in the context of the job. Furthermore, the employer must accommodate an employee who tests positive, up to the point where it causes the employer undue hardship.

Employers must keep human rights requirements in mind throughout the hiring process. Human rights issues that arise after the employee begins to work are discussed in the remainder of this chapter.

Human Rights Issues During the Course of Employment

The Duty to Accommodate

The duty to accommodate has been part of an employer's obligation for many years. The principle that underlies the duty to accommodate is the belief that it is unfair to exclude people because, on the basis of a prohibited ground of discrimination, their needs are different from those of the majority.

The essence of accommodation lies in tailoring the workplace to meet the needs of the individual employee. According to the Ontario Human Rights Commission's "Policy on Ableism and Discrimination Based on Disability" (2016), the principle of accommodation involves three factors:

1. *Individualization.* There is no formula to determine when the duty to accommodate has been satisfied. Each person's needs are unique; a solution that meets one person's requirements may not meet another's.
2. *Dignity.* People must be accommodated in a manner that most respects their dignity, including their privacy, confidentiality, comfort, and autonomy. For example, a wheelchair entrance over the loading dock or garbage room is unacceptable.
3. *Inclusion.* Job requirements and workplaces must be designed with everyone in mind. An employer cannot base systems or requirements on "normal employees" and then make exceptions as people or groups request them.

The employer has primary responsibility for initiating accommodation. However, other parties have responsibilities as well: it is a shared obligation. The party requiring accommodation should make their needs known to the employer and supply information regarding the assistance required. Although an employer is not obliged to offer the perfect accommodation or an accommodation that is preferred by the employee, the accommodation offered must still be reasonable. Employers should make every effort to avoid imposing additional disadvantages to the employee (see e.g. *Finning Ltd v International Association of Machinists and Aerospace Workers* [1995] and *Edmonton (City) v Amalgamated Transit Union, Local 569* [2003]).

Unions also have a responsibility to help find solutions when accommodation conflicts with the collective agreement.

The Alberta Human Rights Commission (2010) provides the following accommodation guidelines for employers, employees, and unions, which are also useful guidelines for BC employers:

> *Rights and Responsibilities of the Employer or Service Provider*
>
> 1. Determine if the request falls under any of the areas and grounds protected under the [Act].
> 2. Be aware that once a request is received, the onus to accommodate is on the employer or service provider.
> 3. Respect the dignity of the person or group requesting accommodation.
> 4. Respect the privacy of the person requesting accommodation. Medical information is considered personal information, and employers must abide by applicable privacy legislation when they collect, use, or disclose an employee's medical information.
> 5. Listen to and consider the needs of the person seeking accommodation and their suggestions for accommodation.
> 6. Review medical or other information that the person seeking accommodation provides to support the request for accommodation.
> 7. Be willing to take substantial and meaningful measures to accommodate the needs of the person seeking accommodation.
> 8. Consult an expert such as a human resources officer or lawyer if more information is needed to assess the request.
> 9. Be flexible and creative when considering and developing options.
> 10. Discuss options with the person who needs accommodation.
> 11. Take reasonable steps to accommodate the person seeking accommodation to the point of undue hardship. If full accommodation is not possible without undue hardship, try to suggest options that may partially meet the needs of the person seeking accommodation.
> 12. Reply to the request for accommodation within a reasonable period of time.
> 13. Make a formal written agreement with the person being accommodated and ensure that the accommodation is given a fair opportunity to work.
> 14. Follow up to ensure that the accommodation meets the needs of the person seeking accommodation.
> 15. Provide details that justify a refusal to accommodate, if accommodation is not possible because it poses undue hardship or because of a bona fide occupational requirement. …
> 16. Be willing to review and modify the accommodation agreement if circumstances or needs change and the agreement is no longer working. (at 7-8)

Rights and Responsibilities of the Person Seeking Accommodation

1. Ensure that a concern falls under any of the areas and grounds protected under the [Act].
2. Inform the employer or service provider about the need for accommodation.
3. Bring the situation to the attention of the employer or service provider, preferably in writing. Include the following information:
   - Explain why accommodation is required … .
   - Support the request for accommodation with evidence or documents … .
   - Provide medical information that explains the employee's functional limitations and necessary accommodations … .
   - Suggest appropriate accommodation measures.
   - Indicate how long accommodation will be required.
4. Allow a reasonable amount of time for the employer or service provider to reply to the request for accommodation.
5. Listen to and consider any reasonable accommodation options that the employer or service provider proposes. A person seeking accommodation has a duty to accept a reasonable accommodation, even if it is not the one that the person suggested or prefers.
6. Consult an expert such as a human resources consultant, union representative, or lawyer if it is difficult to determine if the proposed options are reasonable.
7. Request details of the cost or other factors creating undue hardship, if the employer or service provider indicates that accommodation would pose an undue hardship. Provide more details about your needs if such information is helpful.
8. When an accommodation is provided, make a formal written agreement with the employer or service provider.
9. Cooperate to make the agreement work.
10. Advise the employer or service provider when accommodation needs have changed. Provide medical documentation to support these changes and assist the employer in the process of modifying the accommodation.
11. Be willing to review and modify the accommodation agreement if circumstances or needs change and the agreement is no longer working.
12. Tell the employer or service provider if the need for accommodation ends. (at 6-7)

The requirement for an employee to cooperate with the accommodation process was affirmed in *Anderson v Alberta* (2004), along with the principle that an employee cannot hold out for the perfect accommodation.

CASE IN POINT

Employee Obligation in Accommodation

Anderson v Alberta, 2004 ABQB 766

Facts

Anderson was employed by the Alberta Solicitor General's Department as a provincial protection officer. She had been off work for about a year recovering from back surgery. Her physician determined she was capable of returning, as long as she followed certain work restrictions. The employer looked for suitable accommodation, found a position that met her needs, and offered to accommodate her. Anderson felt that the position was undesirable and had been offered as a punishment for a previous complaint she had filed. She refused the position and was suspended without pay.

Relevant Issue

Whether an employee has an obligation to accept a reasonable accommodation or the right to hold out for the "perfect" accommodation.

Decision

The Court found that the position offered to Anderson fit within her medical restrictions and that the employer made an adequate attempt to accommodate, so the onus was on the complainant to accept. An employee is not entitled to be accommodated in a job of their choice, and the employee must be reasonable.

Employers should exercise caution when interpreting the *Anderson* decision. Although an employer is not obliged to offer the perfect accommodation, or even one that is preferred by the employee, the offered accommodation and the approach taken by the employer must still be reasonable.

All parties to an accommodation have obligations they must meet. This includes unions, if an employee is unionized. The obligations of unions were established by the Supreme Court in *Central Okanagan*, discussed below, and can be summarized as follows:

- Take an active role as a partner in the accommodation process.
- Share responsibility with the employer to facilitate accommodation, including suggesting and testing alternative approaches and cooperating when solutions are proposed.
- Respect the confidentiality of the person requesting accommodation.
- Support accommodation measures irrespective of collective agreements, unless doing so would create undue hardship.

CASE IN POINT

Union Violates Its Duty to Accommodate

Central Okanagan School District No 23 v Renaud, [1992] 2 SCR 970

Facts

Renaud was a Seventh Day Adventist working in a unionized position as a custodian for the school board. The work schedule, which was part of the collective agreement, included a Friday evening shift. Renaud's religion prohibits work on the Sabbath, which begins at sundown on Friday and continues through until sundown on Saturday. A number of options were proposed by Renaud, but the only practical solution was to create a unique schedule for him. The employer was willing; however, this was an exception to the collective agreement, which required union consent. The union refused and after a number of other failed attempts to accommodate Renaud, his employment was terminated.

Relevant Issue

Whether the union's decision to refuse the unique schedule amounted to a violation of BC human rights legislation.

Decision

The Supreme Court of Canada held that the union had violated its duty to accommodate. The Court stated that a union can become a party to discrimination in two ways. It may cause or contribute to discrimination by contributing to the development of a work rule that has a discriminatory effect (e.g., when the work rule is part of the collective agreement). It can also contribute to discrimination if it impedes the employer's efforts to accommodate. At the same time, the Court recognized that an accommodation that significantly disrupts a collective agreement or affects the rights of other employees may constitute undue hardship. However, in this case it was found that the impact of a unique schedule for Renaud was minimal for both the collective agreement and co-workers. The employer also failed in its duty to accommodate because it failed to pursue the accommodation through grievance and arbitration.

What Constitutes Undue Hardship?

Once an employee makes a *prima facie* case of discrimination, the onus shifts to the employer to present evidence showing that accommodating the employee would create undue hardship. Undue hardship is not defined in the Alberta or BC legislation. Instead, we draw inferences from case law regarding the factors that are normally considered when evaluating undue hardship. In the *Renaud* decision, the Supreme Court emphasized the importance of interpreting undue hardship reasonably and in consideration of each unique situation: "What constitutes [undue hardship] is a question of fact and will vary with the circumstances of the case" (at 984).

The Alberta Human Rights Commission's interpretive bulletin on the duty to accommodate (2010) provides some additional guidance. Undue hardship occurs if accommodation creates "onerous conditions," "intolerable financial costs," or "serious disruption" to the business. Some hardship may be unavoidable, but where the line is drawn in each case depends on the following factors:

1. *Financial costs.* These must be quantifiable, not merely speculation. For example, if an employee has multiple sclerosis and deterioration is expected over time, the fact that additional accommodation may be needed in the future cannot be used to assess the employer's current ability to accommodate. Costs must be so significant that they would substantially affect the productivity or efficiency of the employer. A tribunal would normally consider the costs to the entire organization, not just one branch or unit. Furthermore, a tribunal will take into consideration the ability to amortize costs (spread them out over time), as well as any tax exemptions, grants, or subsidies that will offset anticipated losses.
2. *Size and resources of the employer.* The costs of modifying premises or equipment and the ability to amortize those costs will be considered. The larger the

organization, the more likely it will be that it can afford a wider range of accommodations without reaching undue hardship.

3. *Disruption of operations.* This refers to the extent to which an employer is prevented from carrying out essential business functions. For example, if no productive work is available to offer an employee, then accommodation may create an undue hardship.
4. *Morale problems of other employees.* Morale problems refer to the effects of an increased workload for other employees. This might include excessive overtime, stress, sleep difficulties, or other health problems. It will not be undue hardship if co-workers are simply disgruntled and would prefer the employee was accommodated elsewhere.
5. *Substantial interference with the rights of other individuals or groups.* This ensures that an accommodation itself does not result in discrimination. The concerns of other employees must be well grounded. An example might include an accommodation that is a substantial departure from the terms and conditions of a collective agreement. For example, seniority rights of unionized employees are considered a cornerstone provision of a collective agreement and should not be interfered with lightly (see *Kelowna City and CUPE Local 338* [2003]).
6. *Interchangeability of workforce and facilities.* The ability to relocate employees to other positions on a permanent or temporary basis is a factor in evaluating undue hardship and makes it easier for larger organizations to accommodate.
7. *Health and safety concerns.* If an accommodation is potentially a safety risk, the employer must consider the level of risk and who bears the risk. If the potential harm is minor and unlikely to occur, or if the risk is primarily to the employee seeking accommodation, it is unlikely to be considered an undue hardship. The employer will be expected to consider ways of reducing the safety concern.

Fulfilling the Duty to Accommodate

The duty to accommodate applies to all grounds of discrimination, but it is most likely to arise in the context of disability, religion, sex (including pregnancy and breastfeeding), age, and family status, because these are the areas where special needs are most common. The following discussion considers the scope of the duty to accommodate in each of these areas and the types of accommodation that employers typically must consider. Although the exact scope of the duty is still unclear in some areas, the general trend is toward the expansion of an employer's obligation to accommodate.

Accommodating Employees with Disabilities

METHODS OF ACCOMMODATION

As a result of *Meiorin*, employers now know they must consider employees' special needs when designing their policies and workplace structures. Accordingly, when constructing or renovating buildings, buying equipment, or establishing new policies and procedures, employers should choose products or designs that do *not* create barriers for people with disabilities. For example, when upgrading a computer and phone system, an employer could incorporate large fonts, bright lighting, and volume into its design.

Accommodations may include making changes to the layout of the workplace to make it barrier free, such as building ramps and wheelchair-accessible washrooms or modifying equipment and vehicles. It may also require changing the way that work is done. This may involve providing stools, special software, or technical aids; modifying work hours; or reassigning disabled employees to vacant jobs that they are able to perform. Episodic disabilities (e.g., arthritis, multiple sclerosis, or migraines) may require accommodations such as flex time, providing a private area in the workplace in which to rest or take medications, project-based work (where the longer time frame allows for periods of disability), and ergonomically designed equipment.

For non-physical disabilities, such as learning disabilities, accommodation may include allowing the employee to work in a quieter area, providing clearer or written instructions, and specialized training.

Manager and supervisor training are also crucial: front-line supervisors need to be aware of how to respond to employees who disclose a disability; they need to be sensitized to the supports required and understand the types of accommodation available; and they need to be prepared for any co-worker issues that may arise. This latter point relates to addressing possible co-worker perceptions of favouritism toward the employee who is being accommodated. Where appropriate, employee education sessions may be helpful (Silliker, 2012).

Workplace accommodations need not be expensive. Often the largest investment is in taking the time to understand what the employee needs and being flexible in the range of accommodation possibilities considered. However, there may be situations where extensive changes are required. In some circumstances, performance standards or productivity targets may have to be modified.

An employer must also be sensitive to the duty to accommodate in preparing and applying its attendance policy. Requiring a specific level of attendance is discriminatory if it has a negative effect on employees on the basis of the prohibited ground of disability. The employer's attendance policy should establish whether an absence is the result of a medical condition and, if so, assist the employee in meeting its requirements. However, if serious attempts to accommodate have been made and employee absences are causing significant disruption, the employer is not required to maintain the employment relationship indefinitely. Where the level of absenteeism is excessive and there is no possibility of regular attendance in the future, the employer may dismiss a disabled employee for "innocent absenteeism." A word of caution is appropriate here. It is important that employers distinguish between culpable absenteeism (absence over which the employee has control, such as regularly arriving late for work) and innocent absenteeism (absence for reasons beyond the employee's control—that is, disability).

Where an employer uses disciplinary tactics to address innocent absenteeism, there is a risk that the employer will be found guilty of failing to accommodate.

Employers are required to test workers with disabilities individually to determine whether the disability affects their ability to perform the duties of the job. For example, an employer may have a general rule that truck drivers must not be epileptic. However, where the job involves only occasional driving, the applicant's epilepsy is controlled by medication, and the applicant's personal physician permits them to drive, a more individualized assessment is required (Gilbert, Burkett, & McCaskill, 2000, at 229).

MEETING THE REQUIRED STANDARD

Although employer size is a relevant factor in determining when the point of undue hardship has been reached, case law makes it clear that even smaller employers have a positive obligation (an obligation that must be pursued actively) to seriously consider how a disabled employee can be accommodated. As a point of interest, it is possible that a unionized employer that has met its duty to accommodate under the legislation will still be found by an arbitrator not to have met its duty under the collective agreement if the wording of the agreement sets a higher standard.

In other words, where negotiated provisions exceed human rights requirements, employees will be entitled to those higher standards. On the other hand, where negotiated provisions fall below human rights requirements, employees are entitled to the standards set by the legislation. A key tenet of human rights statutes is that one cannot "contract out" (i.e., cannot avoid) the statutory requirements of the legislation.

PROVIDING ALTERNATIVE WORK

How far must an employer go to meet its duty to accommodate a disabled employee? In *Human Rights at Work* (2008), the Ontario Human Rights Commission suggests that the following questions be considered in determining whether providing alternative work is appropriate when accommodation in the pre-disability job is not possible:

- Is alternative work available now or in the near future?
- If not, can a new position be created without causing undue hardship?
- Does the new position require additional training, and does the training impose undue hardship?
- Does the alternative work policy contravene the collective agreement?
- What are the terms of the collective agreement or individual contract of employment?
- What are the past practices of the workplace?
- How interchangeable are workers? Do they frequently change positions, either permanently or temporarily, for reasons other than disability accommodation?

Note that where an employee is placed permanently in a lower-paid, lower-ranked position as a result of accommodation, and all other alternatives have been exhausted, an employer can pay that individual the same as other employees who are performing the same work. As a result, a reasonable accommodation could result in a demotion of role and pay.

HOW DILIGENTLY MUST AN EMPLOYER PURSUE ITS DUTY TO ACCOMMODATE?

An employer's obligation depends on the circumstances, the nature of the disability, and the predictability and frequency of an employee's absences. The employee's prognosis is especially important: is the employee likely to return to work in the foreseeable future? The better an employee's prognosis, the greater the employer's duty to accommodate.

As the decision in *Jodoin* (discussed below) indicates, the employer's duty to accommodate is ongoing and must be pursued actively. An employer must not simply decide that an employee with a particular disability is incapable of performing a job. It must seek information, in an objective manner, to help it make that determination and to identify reasonable alternatives. Failure to make proper inquiries undermines an employer's contention that it attempted accommodation or that accommodation constitutes undue hardship. It can also result in significant liability for wages lost during the period that the employee should have been accommodated and for the employee's mental suffering.

CASE IN POINT

Employer Insufficiently Diligent in Pursuing Duty to Accommodate

Jodoin v City of Calgary, 2008 AHRC 13

Facts

Jodoin had worked in the waste and recycling department at the City of Calgary for about two and a half years when he injured his back while lifting a garbage can. His claim for compensation was accepted by the Workers' Compensation Board (WCB). Over the next five months, Jodoin underwent a series of medical tests followed by surgery. After a period of recovery, he was returned to his original job, on a modified program of half-days. A subsequent assessment by his physician resulted in a change to Jodoin's restrictions. It was recommended he not lift more than 20 pounds. A second return to work was attempted, but when Jodoin refused to move a refrigerator on a dolly, he was told to go home.

From that point forward, Jodoin remained off work. He participated in a number of vocational assessments in addition to functional capacity assessments. The return-to-work coordinator at the City sent several emails to various work units attempting to locate suitable work for Jodoin. There was little response. The WCB accused Jodoin of failing to cooperate and declared his functional capacity assessments "invalid" because of a lack of effort. A WCB case manager unilaterally revised his restrictions, indicating he was capable of a medium level of work. This was diametrically opposed to medical opinions that indicated Jodoin should be in a sedentary position. His WCB benefits were cancelled. The City accepted the opinion of the WCB without seeking further information. Eventually Jodoin was told that in order for the City to continue looking for accommodations, he had to apply for a leave of absence without pay or he would be terminated from his job. Jodoin did not understand and did not sign the application for leave.

Relevant Issue

Whether the employer fulfilled its duty to accommodate the employee.

Decision

The Tribunal found in favour of Jodoin, stating that the employer's search for permanent modified work was both limited and ineffective. Although emails were sent, there was no record of what positions were considered or why they were inappropriate. The return-to-work coordinator for the City did not follow City procedures. She failed to contact the union as required, there was little communication with Jodoin, she did not fill out necessary checklists, and the search was never extended to other departments.

The Tribunal concluded the following:

> At no time did the City inform Jodoin that they could not find appropriate sedentary work for him. Instead, they threatened him with termination if his WCB benefits were not reinstated or if he did not sign the [application for leave]. This was done with Jodoin being given no opportunity to seek or be provided with competent advice as to how he should proceed. (at para 150)

The City was also chastised for accepting the WCB change from sedentary to medium duties without consulting Jodoin's physicians. As a result, Jodoin was awarded damages of $5,000 and lost wages of $17,308 (plus 7.75 percent interest from July 2004 to the date of the decision in November 2008).

Another decision that illustrates the extent of an employer's duty to accommodate disability is *ADGA Group Consultants Inc v Lane* (2008). There, a consulting firm's cursory investigation of bipolar disorder was found to be insufficient to meet its duty to accommodate a new employee with that disorder. The Ontario Human Rights Tribunal found that the employer had not fulfilled its duty to accommodate under the Code. The Tribunal held that the duty to accommodate has two dimensions: *procedural* and *substantive*. From a procedural point of view, it found that ADGA's investigation of bipolar disorder was brief and superficial. On appeal to Ontario's Divisional Court, the Tribunal's decision in *ADGA* was upheld. The Court found that generalized fears, based on false stereotypes, and anticipated hardships about the impact of accommodation on the workplace are not sufficient to discharge an employer's procedural duty to accommodate. The employer should have more fully investigated the nature of bipolar disorder and the employee's own situation as an individual with that disorder and developed a better-informed prognosis of the likely impact of his condition on the workplace. As part of the final order, ADGA was ordered to establish a comprehensive, written anti-discrimination policy and to retain a qualified consultant to provide training on its obligations under the Code. These orders were also upheld on appeal.

EMPLOYEE'S OBLIGATION TO COOPERATE

Once hired, an employee has an obligation to let the employer know about the need for accommodation. There is also a duty to cooperate with the accommodation process, including responding to reasonable requests for medical documentation in the case of ongoing absence and keeping the employer informed of progress and recovery prospects. The *Renaud* case, discussed above, affirms this general duty. In *Star Choice Television Network Inc v Tatulea* (2012), an arbitrator dismissed the employee's claim for wrongful dismissal after finding that the employee had repeatedly refused to meet with the employer to discuss a return-to-work process and rejected its offer of reasonable accommodation. The BC Court of Appeal has affirmed that employees have a duty to facilitate accommodation, including voluntarily seeking assistance from programs the employer provides (see *Health Employers Assn of BC (Kootenay Boundary Regional Hospital) v BC Nurses' Union* [2006] and *Kemess Mines*

Ltd v International Union of Operating Engineers, Local 115 [2006], which are discussed briefly below under the heading "Accommodating Employees with Drug or Alcohol Dependence").

HOW SHOULD AN EMPLOYER TREAT ACCOMMODATION REQUESTS?

The following are guidelines for employers in handling requests for disability accommodation (adapted from LeClair, 2003, at 7). Note that regardless of the type of disability, the accommodation process usually starts with a conversation with the employee and, optimally, remains interactive throughout.

1. *Gather information to determine whether a disability exists and what the prognosis is for recovery.* The information should indicate when the employee will be returning (if off work), the scope of any medical restrictions, an estimate of how long the restrictions will be necessary, and the type of accommodation required. Employers must obtain the employee's written consent for the release of this information.

   Many legal issues can arise when the employer is seeking medical information because this must be balanced against the employee's right to privacy. For example, employer's may sometimes receive insufficient information or doubt whether the medical information provided by the employee is objective. In these cases, the employer cannot normally require that the employee be examined by another employer-selected physician (*Canada (AG) v Grover* [2007]). This is called an independent medical exam (IME). Nor can the employer discipline the employee for refusing to comply with the request for additional information. The employer's best option is to keep the employee off work until satisfactory medical information has been provided. That said, an employee's persistent refusal to cooperate in the accommodation process, including refusal to cooperate with reasonable requests for medical information, may ultimately exhaust the accommodation process and bring the employment relationship to an end.

   It should be noted that employers do not have a right to know an employee's diagnosis, but they are entitled to enough information to make decisions about how to accommodate the employee and to ensure a safe workplace. Such information should focus on the employee's prognosis and their capabilities and limitations as they relate to the job. Employers should be wary of asking employees to sign blanket releases that would give them access to more information than necessary to accommodate the employee. The longer the medical leave, the more information the employer is generally entitled to receive (see e.g. *Red Deer College and Faculty Association (Legault)* 2015). However, they should avoid contacting the employee's physician directly; this should be done through the employee or by an occupational health professional.
2. *Evaluate the employee's job to determine its physical and psychological demands to see if they can be altered without causing the employer undue hardship.* Possible job modifications include changing the way the work is

performed, altering office premises, changing work schedules, or using specialized equipment. Any accommodation must preserve the employee's dignity.

3. *If the employee cannot be accommodated in their pre-disability job, thoroughly review any other available jobs.* Consult with the union if a potential accommodation could impact other employees that are covered by a collective agreement. Consider placing the employee on a temporary assignment or assembling various tasks that the employee is capable of performing. The employee is obliged to cooperate in this process by, for example, giving the employer information concerning physical capabilities and restrictions.
4. *Determine whether the proposed accommodation would cause the employer undue hardship.* Relevant factors include the size of the employer's operations, the cost of the accommodation, outside sources of funding, and health and safety risks. Review the accommodation options with the employee and other stakeholders to ensure all options have been explored and the best option is selected. However, the employer does not have to offer the "perfect" or the employee's "preferred" accommodation.
5. *Monitor the situation regularly to ensure that it continues to fit the employee's needs.* The employee's health condition and work capacity may change, for better or worse, over time.
6. *Document all facets of the accommodation process.* Create a case file. Include a record of the accommodation options that were considered, reasons why they were or were not implemented, and notes and records of all discussions with the employee and union.
7. *Maintain confidentiality throughout the process.* Only co-workers who will need to do something differently because of the employee's accommodation should be told about the situation. Similarly, focus only on how the accommodation will affect their duties; don't discuss the details about the disability or a medical diagnosis. Co-workers should be advised that accommodation is a legal right, not a special favour (Merck, 2011).

FYI

Attitudes and Legal Expectations Are Changing: Accommodating Mental Illness in the Workplace

Gone are the days when an employer could equate the duty to accommodate for disability with "physical" disability. Given that about 20 percent of Canadians will have a diagnosable mental illness at some point during their lifetime, it's not surprising that the duty to accommodate employees with mental or psychological disabilities is a growing issue in the workplace (Canadian Mental Health Association, "Fast Facts"). Add to this the financial impact and heightened legal expectations related to accommodating mental illness and it is apparent that employers need to be proactive in this area. Proactive measures include increasing the flexibility in how duties are performed, addressing the stigmatization and social exclusion of people who have mental health issues through awareness education and training, and making sure front-line supervisors and managers are equipped to handle requests for accommodation of mental disabilities and are supported in the ongoing conversations surrounding it.

Unlike a workplace injury or visible physical ailment, mental illness is not always obvious. An employer needs to be able to recognize the possible need for accommodations for mental illness even when they are not directly requested (Jurgens, 2013, at 13). This is because an employee with mental illness may not be able to recognize or articulate the need for accommodation. Also, while awareness and attitudes are changing, there is a lingering stigma that makes some employees hesitant to come forward (Williams & Nave, 2013, at 4-2). Case law makes it clear that an employer must take the initiative where a problem is apparent: an employer "cannot turn a blind eye to suspicious behaviour and/or other manifestations of an actual disability and then be able to rely upon the absence of direct knowledge to argue that it is under no obligation to accommodate" (*Direct Energy v CEP, Local 975* at para 25; see also *Krieger v Toronto Police Services Board* and *Ontario Provincial Police Association v Ontario Provincial Police*).

Where an employer has reasonable and probable grounds to suspect an employee has a mental health condition that may be a safety concern or is seriously impacting the employee's performance, the employer may request medical confirmation that the employee is fit for work. That said, there are practical limits to what an employer is expected to deduce from an employee's behaviour. In *Stewart v Ontario (Government Services)*, a case decided by the Ontario Human Rights Tribunal, the applicant was a project manager who was dismissed for poor performance. She filed a human rights application alleging, among other things, that her performance issues were related to her disabilities—a learning disorder and adult attention-deficit hyperactivity disorder—and that her employer's failure to accommodate these disabilities constituted discrimination. While Stewart admitted that she did not expressly make her employer aware of these disorders, she maintained it knew or ought reasonably to have known about her disability on the basis of certain workplace behaviours it could readily observe: her preference for visual learning aids, her statements that her children had learning disabilities, her lack of organization, her forgetfulness, her poor time management, and her inability to stay on task. The employer therefore had a duty to make reasonable inquiries concerning possible accommodations. However, the Tribunal dismissed this portion of the application as having no prospect of success: it found that in the absence of a request for accommodation from the applicant, it was reasonable for the employer to assume that her performance-related difficulties were based on lack of skills rather than a disability. The fact that accommodation requests and plans were common in this particular workplace also supported the employer's position that it would have been receptive to such a request. This decision suggests that it takes more than evidence of poor performance to activate a duty to inquire about possible accommodations based on disability: there also needs to be a clear connection between the performance issue and the nature of the disability.

As with physical disability, the primary focus in accommodating a mental illness is job performance. For example, letting the employee know that certain behaviours have been noticed (e.g., the employee seems more stressed or less focused than normal) and that it's affecting performance can be the starting point. The employer can then ask what the employee requires to improve performance and offer ways to find that help (Crisp, 2013, at 13). This could include, for example, providing modified duties, offering flex time, and providing access to services, treatments, and supports, including peer support programs (Silliker 2012).

ACCOMMODATING EMPLOYEES WITH DRUG OR ALCOHOL DEPENDENCE

Canadian law defines alcohol and drug dependence as a disability and therefore a prohibited ground of discrimination. Employees who are dependent on these substances are entitled to be reasonably accommodated unless it causes the employer undue hardship. This typically obliges an employer to provide an employee assistance program (EAP) or to allow an employee time off work to attend such a program. However, accommodating substance abuse does *not* require an employer to accept lengthy, ongoing absences unrelated to rehabilitation. Moreover, as the *Chopra* case illustrates, if an employee does not benefit from rehabilitation efforts, an employer that is fair and consistent in applying its own policies is not required to hold a job open indefinitely.

CASE IN POINT

Employer Terminates Employee for Infringing Drug and Alcohol Policy

Chopra v Syncrude Canada Ltd, 2003 ABQB 504

Facts

Chopra worked for the employer for 14 years. Although his performance was adequate for most of that period, his alcoholism and depression became a problem eight months before his retirement. In March 1993, Chopra was found to have consumed so much alcohol while on the job that his supervisor had to escort him home. Chopra agreed that he would accept mandatory referral to the EAP, would never again violate the employer's drug and alcohol policy, and would attend supervisory and follow-up meetings as required. Both parties understood that failure to adhere to this plan would result in a termination hearing.

Chopra attended a treatment program but was soon asked to leave for violating its policies. He was, however, admitted into a relapse prevention program to help him deal with his disability. A third incident occurred a short time later, resulting in his absence from work because of intoxication. The employer's response was to require Chopra to submit to a medical tracking process and random drug and alcohol testing. In June 1993, he was again found to be under the influence of alcohol while at work. Consequently, a termination hearing was convened, and he was dismissed. He then filed a wrongful dismissal suit against the employer.

Relevant Issue

Whether the employer had adequately accommodated Chopra's disability.

Decision

The Alberta Court of Queen's Bench found that the employer had fulfilled its duty to accommodate. It had provided Chopra with counselling, allowed several breaches of its policy without resorting to termination, given him a paid leave of absence, and sent him to a treatment facility to receive help. The employer had handled his return to work appropriately. Chopra was not entitled to any further accommodation.

In *Chopra*, the employer fulfilled its duty to accommodate the employee's substance abuse because it was both consistent and persistent. It provided the employee with clear, written warnings that he would be dismissed if he did not cooperate in addressing the problem. It got the employee to commit, in writing, to attend therapy or counselling and submit to testing. While accommodating some relapses, it consistently let the employee know that his job was increasingly at risk if he failed to cooperate.

BC courts have taken a similar approach. In two cases decided together, the BC Court of Appeal dealt with two slightly different scenarios. In *Health Employers Assn of BC (Kootenay Boundary Regional Hospital) v BC Nurses' Union*, the hospital hired a nurse with a history of addiction that included two previous dismissals due to addiction to opiate drugs. He had been reinstated in those jobs after labour arbitrations, which required him to sign "last-chance" rehabilitation agreements. On hiring him, the hospital required him to attend monthly meetings to monitor his rehabilitation program. However, the employee failed to stick to his program, lied to the hospital about this, and stole discarded "wastage" drugs from the hospital. The hospital fired him, but an arbitrator ordered the hospital to reinstate him and attempt to place him in a position that would not give him access to opiates. The arbitrator acknowledged the employee's failure to assist in the accommodation process, but felt the employer had a greater responsibility in light of his addiction. The employer applied to the BC Court of Appeal for judicial review (in BC, reviews of labour arbitrations go directly to the province's top court). The Court overturned the arbitrator's decision and found that the employer had fulfilled its duty to accommodate. It took into account the employee's long history of drug use and his failure to stick to his recovery plans. In this case, the very act of hiring him was tantamount to accommodation, and the monthly meetings were also an accommodation. Citing *Renaud*, the Court stated that "[t]he employer's duty to accommodate [the nurse] was matched by his duty to facilitate the accommodation process" (at para 52).

In the *Kootenay Boundary Regional Hospital* decision, the employer and employee both knew of the addiction and the employer actively assisted the employee's rehabilitation. By contrast, in the companion case of *Kemess Mines Ltd v International Union of Operating Engineers, Local 115*, the employer had a zero-tolerance policy about substance abuse, and the employee was in denial about his addiction. Although the mining company did have an employee assistance program, the employee did not take advantage of the program because he was not fully aware of his addiction. The zero-tolerance policy required dismissal of an employee with an addiction who did not voluntarily enroll in the assistance program. The employer became aware of the addiction and dismissed the employee. The matter went to a labour arbitrator, who said that the employer had not done enough to accommodate the employee and ordered that he be reinstated but suspended without pay for ten months. The employer sought judicial review at the BC Court of Appeal. The Court held that the employee's lack of full awareness of his addiction did not absolve him of the need to facilitate accommodation. But it went on to say that his failure did not justify the employer's firing him. The employer argued that a duty to accommodate was "totally incompatible" with its zero-tolerance policy, which created an incentive for employees to voluntarily seek help before their addiction affected workplace safety. The Court ruled that the duty to accommodate overrides an employer policy. Safety is a factor in the duty to accommodate to the point of undue hardship, the Court said. But an absolute, fire-addicts policy is not justified. Intermediate steps were available—such as the ten-month suspension that the labour arbitrator had made in this case. The Court therefore upheld the arbitrator's award.

In both of these BC cases, the employer was able to satisfy the first two parts of the *Meiorin* test: the anti-drug policy was rationally connected to workplace safety, and the employer had adopted the policy in good faith. The Court accepted this even in the case of the zero-tolerance policy, which was meant to create an incentive to seek treatment. As in most cases, the more complex test is determining when the undue hardship line is crossed.

An employer that appears to condone substance abuse by ignoring it, then reacts suddenly in dismissing an employee, is in a different legal situation from an employer that offers programs or consistently enforces no-drugs policies. To meet its duty to accommodate an alcohol- or drug-dependent employee, an employer should require the employee to undergo counselling or rehabilitation and never create the impression that it is tolerating the abuse (Miller, 2003, at 3087).

The recreational use of drugs or alcohol does not qualify as a disability. This has become a particular concern for employers since the legalization of cannabis on October 17, 2018. However, legalization does not mean that employees can be impaired at work. Employers should have policies similar to those they have in place for alcohol consumption. They can prohibit the use of cannabis at work or during working hours and they can prohibit employees from being at work while impaired.

If an employee contravenes an employer's policy by having drugs or alcohol on the employer's property and the employer establishes that the employee does not have a substance abuse "problem," there is no statutory duty to accommodate. In this case, the employer may discipline the employee in the same manner as it would any other employee for misconduct. Moreover, an employee has to do more than simply say they have a substance abuse problem; there must be convincing, objective evidence from, for example, a credible medical expert who has treated the worker at the relevant time. Excessive drug or alcohol use does not necessarily mean that the individual is an addict. However, if an employer dismisses an employee who is subsequently determined to have a drug- or alcohol-related disability, the employee may be entitled to reinstatement and accommodation. In cases where possible drug or alcohol abuse seems a likely contributor to the situation, the employer should inquire about it before termination.

On the other hand, an employer does have a duty to accommodate an employee who has a valid prescription to use medical cannabis. These employees should be accommodated in the same way as any other employee with a medical prescription that could affect their ability to work in a safety-sensitive job. In a recent ruling, the Supreme Court of Newfoundland and Labrador held that an employer did not breach its duty to accommodate a medical cannabis user when it refused to place him in a safety-sensitive position on a construction project. The evidence established that the employee's regular use of the drug could cause residual impairment up to 24 hours after ingestion, which would be impossible to measure with the current technology. Placing the employee in a safety-sensitive position was an unmanageable risk that constituted undue hardship for the employer (*International Brotherhood of Electrical Workers, Local 1620 v Lower Churchill Transmission Construction Employers' Association Inc* [2019]).

IN THE NEWS

Cannabis Zero-Tolerance Common in Canadian Workplaces: Study

Canadian workplaces are globally trail-blazing cannabis policies, with nearly half of private-sector employers imposing a blanket ban on cannabis use, says a Conference Board of Canada survey.

While legalization has pushed Canadian employers to address that reality—76 per cent had updated their pot policies before the end of prohibition last October—many are still grappling with sensitive areas, said study senior researcher Monica Haberl.

And the survey of 163 employers found 48 per cent have adopted no-use-at-anytime rules for their workers despite the drug's legality, said the report titled Acting on the Cannabis Act.

"There's a zero-tolerance for use there, not just on the job but at all times, and that's because testing for cannabis isn't perfect, they choose to be on the safer side," said Haberl.

"In some cases, the employer would say, 'in order to get a job, you can't use cannabis.' "

That's weighted heavily in so-called safety-sensitive industries such as transportation or warehousing where heavy equipment is used, she said.

Among public sector employers, 29 per cent have adopted that strict approach, states the study.

"A zero-tolerance policy would not hold up legally in non-safety-sensitive workplaces—this is based mainly on legal precedence and not on legislation," said Haberl.

Only about one-third of respondents said they'd provide cannabis education or materials along those lines, she noted.

"With legalization, there are people trying it for the first time so there's certainly opportunities for education, especially with edibles coming onto the market soon," said Haberl.

"But I can see safety-sensitive workplace employers don't want to bring it up, thinking people will then try it."

The survey of employers across the country was conducted last November to January, soon after legalization took effect Oct. 17. It paints a picture of a national workplace that's been thrust into a leadership role, though largely without the guidance of legislation, said Haberl.

"Because Canada's the first G8 country to legalize it, other advanced countries looking at taking the same path are watching us," she said.

It shows organizations are less concerned with cannabis use as time goes by—52 per cent expressed fears about the drug's effect before last October, with that number dropping to 36 per cent after.

But those concerns are much higher among safety-sensitive industries such as transportation and warehousing, which reached 78 per cent.

Jamie McMillan said a zero-tolerance policy for his 20 truck drivers is non-negotiable.

"For anybody who handles heavy equipment, you can't have that, you could have another Humboldt Broncos situation," said the man who owns Medicine Hat-based McMillan Transport Ltd. "It can happen to anyone ... we just can't take the chances."

Drug testing, he said, is done "as much as it's needed," though he's confident his employees fully comply.

All members of pipeline inspection company In-line Pigging Solutions Ltd. are tested for cannabis and also face a zero-tolerance policy, even office workers, said its Health, Safety and Wellness manager David Geoffrion.

"It's to make it fair," he said, adding there has been pushback by those who want to use the CBD component of cannabis for medical purposes.

But he said that strict stance is really the product of the company's clients who insist on it, coupled with the fact the firm does business in the U.S., where regulations are even more stringent.

When impairment testing technology is better, that could change, said Geoffrion.

"Science has to catch up. I think it will," he said.

It's those same uncertainties that have left most employers grappling with the definition of cannabis impairment, when its active ingredient, THC, can remain detectable in the body long after consumption, she added.

SOURCE: Kaufman, 2019. Used with permission.

Accommodating Employees' Religious Beliefs and Practices

The requirement to accommodate an employee's religion or creed may arise in a number of areas, including dress codes, break policies, work schedules, and religious leave. According to *Meiorin*, flexibility should be built into an employer's policies. For example, break policies should be flexible enough to accommodate daily periods of prayer for employees whose religion requires them. The employer's policy should allow people to deviate from dress codes for religious reasons. If a dress code is designed to address a health and safety issue, the employer should try to modify the requirement. For example, a man who works in food preparation and who is required to have a beard for religious reasons could wear a hairnet over his beard.

In *Syndicat Northcrest v Amselem*, the Supreme Court of Canada defines religion as follows:

> a particular and comprehensive system of faith and worship. Religion also tends to involve the belief in a divine, superhuman or controlling power. In essence religion is about freely and deeply held personal convictions or beliefs connected to an individual's spiritual faith and integrally linked to one's self-definition and spiritual fulfilment, the practices of which allow individuals to foster a connection with the divine or with the subject or object of that spiritual faith. (at para 39)

Thus, human rights legislation protects more than well-known or mainstream religions. So long as a person's belief is sincerely held, regardless of how widespread that belief might be, the employee's religious beliefs are entitled to accommodation. Employers should be careful about making judgments regarding the legitimacy of any faith and take steps to accommodate. This is true even if people of the same faith don't all ask for the same accommodation. People's beliefs and practices exist on a spectrum. Some will feel it is important to observe all rites and rituals, while others may be more relaxed. This does not necessarily mean their beliefs are any less sincere (Boyle, 2016).

RELIGIOUS DAYS OFF

Human rights law requires an employer to accommodate the religious observances of employees who are unable to work on particular days by relieving them from working on those days unless this causes undue hardship. The following case, *Central Alberta Dairy Pool*, is a precedent-setting decision that elaborates on some of the issues that courts and tribunals consider in determining the dimensions of undue hardship. In this case, an employee who refused, for religious reasons, to work on Easter Monday was terminated. Although the employer argued that working on Mondays was an essential job requirement, the Supreme Court of Canada held that the employer had failed to show that it could not accommodate the individual without suffering undue hardship.

CASE IN POINT

Employer Must Accommodate Easter Monday Leave

Central Alberta Dairy Pool v Alberta (Human Rights Commission), [1990] 2 SCR 489

Facts

Christie worked for the employer, Central Alberta Dairy Pool, for three years before becoming a member of the Worldwide Church of God in 1983. This church observes five holy days throughout the year, some of which fall on Mondays. Followers are expected, although not required, to abstain from working on these five days. Christie requested permission from his employer to take an unpaid leave of absence on a Monday to observe a holy day. The employer denied this request on the basis that the dairy was especially busy on Mondays and made it clear that Christie would be fired if he failed to appear for work on the Monday in question. Christie was absent from work that Monday because of his religious observance. On his return the next day, he learned that the employer had hired another person to take his place. He filed a human rights complaint.

Relevant Issue

Whether accommodating Christie's religious observance would create undue hardship for the employer.

Decision

The Supreme Court of Canada ruled that the employer's failure to accommodate violated human rights legislation. The employer was justified in organizing its operations to require its employees to work on Mondays because mandatory Monday attendance was rationally connected to the job. Christie, however, was legally entitled to practise the religion of his choosing and to refuse to work on those Mondays that conflicted with the observance of his religious holidays. Therefore, the employer was required to demonstrate that accommodating the employee would create undue hardship. The Court listed the following factors as relevant to determining undue hardship: financial cost, disruption of a collective agreement, employee morale, interchangeability of the workforce, and facility requirements. None of these factors warranted a substantial concern in this case, nor did the facts suggest that Christie's Monday absences would become routine.

Although the employer in *Central Alberta Dairy Pool* was relatively small, the Court required it to accommodate the employee's religious convictions by allowing him to take Easter Monday off. However, *Re CANPAR* (2000) shows that the employer's accommodation need not be ideal from the employee's point of view, as long as the employer makes reasonable efforts. In *Re CANPAR*, the employee wanted to leave work early on Friday afternoons to accommodate his religious observance of the Sabbath. The employer discussed several accommodation options with him and eventually transferred him to a more central route where it was convenient for another driver to relieve him of his duties before sunset. As a result of this accommodation, the employee did not lose any meaningful work opportunities, nor were his wages affected. However, after a few months in his new position, the employee became unhappy and grieved his accommodation. The arbitrator found in favour of the employer because its choice of accommodation was reasonable, alleviating discrimination without impairing the employee's earnings or disrupting operations. The arbitrator stated that an employee cannot expect to receive a perfect accommodation.

In a third religious-observance accommodation case, *Ontario (Human Rights Commission) v Roosma*, a large employer (Ford Motor Company of Canada) succeeded in showing undue hardship. *Roosma* involved two employees who refused to work their Friday evening shifts after converting to a faith that observed its Sabbath at that time. Although the employer was very large, it successfully argued before the Ontario Human Rights Tribunal that accommodating the employees by allowing them to not work their Friday night shifts imposed undue hardship on the employer. On appeal, the Ontario Divisional Court upheld the Tribunal's decision, finding that it was reasonable and based on relevant factors. These factors included the high levels of absenteeism on Friday evenings; the disruption of the collective agreement; and the negative effect on other workers, safety, and the employer's competitive position. The effect of accommodation on existing seniority rights was a key consideration because of the large number of senior employees. The Court also found that the union's unwillingness to advocate for accommodation that significantly prejudiced other workers was not unreasonable.

In some ways it seems difficult to reconcile *Central Alberta Dairy Pool* and *Roosma*. However, in *Central Alberta Dairy Pool*, the employer was disputing its ability to accommodate the employee's absence for five days per year at most, whereas the employer in *Roosma* was disputing its ability to accommodate many more days. Moreover, in *Roosma* the employer had made several attempts, over a period of many months, to accommodate the employees before concluding that accommodation was not viable in the circumstances. An interesting situation that runs up the middle between these two cases is a BC case in which the Human Rights Tribunal seems to endorse a hair salon's every-other-Sunday accommodation of a Christian employee. The arrangement allowed the employee, a lifelong Pentecostal Christian, to attend church services every other Sunday and work at the salon on the other Sundays (*Balak v First Choice Haircutters* [2009]).

Another question that can arise is how employers accommodate conflicting belief systems in the workplace. In the following case, *Friesen v Fisher Bay Seafood* (2009), the BC Human Rights Tribunal determined that the employer had not discriminated against the complainant when it required him to stop preaching to other employees during his working hours.

CASE IN POINT

Is Requiring That an Employee Refrain from Preaching During Working Hours a Bona Fide Occupational Requirement?

Friesen v Fisher Bay Seafood, 2009 BCHRT 1

Facts

Fisher Bay operated a plant that processed seafood on Vancouver Island. The company had ongoing problems retaining workers because of the unpleasant nature of the work. Friesen was hired as a nightshift cleaner in January 2006. He was considered a good and reliable employee and was promoted to the position of night supervisor. Friesen sincerely believed that to obey the commandments of Jesus Christ he must "preach, teach, baptise and make disciples." Complaints about Friesen's preaching began about one month after he started work but were minor in nature. Over time, they became more frequent, and the complainers more upset. The employer attempted to discuss the problem with Friesen, but when this failed it began moving other employees to the day shift. The conflict escalated, and the employer warned Friesen that he could not continue telling the employees he supervised that they must accept his beliefs. Friesen refused to stop preaching and was discharged.

Relevant Issue

Whether accommodating Friesen's religious observance would create undue hardship for the employer.

Decision

The Tribunal found that Friesen was discriminated against. However, it also found that the employer standard of not preaching to others during work hours was a BFOR. The standard was adopted for a purpose rationally connected to maintaining a mutually respectful, functioning workforce at the plant. It was adopted in an honest and good-faith belief that it was necessary. The Tribunal further indicated that the employer had accommodated to the point of undue hardship. It had (1) attempted to coach Friesen about the rights of other employees, (2) dealt with employees who threatened to quit because of Friesen's preaching, (3) allowed Friesen to preach on his lunch hour, (4) adjusted scheduling to try to reduce conflict, and (5) offered to rehire Friesen if he would stop proselytizing. The Tribunal felt that the employer had done all it could and was not required, as Friesen had suggested, to create a solitary job for him because his conduct upset his co-workers. The complaint was dismissed.

When considering the duty to accommodate for a religious observance, there is one threshold question: does the employee genuinely believe that the religious practice is necessary? In the *Friesen* case, there was no question that Friesen's beliefs were sincerely held. Whether a particular practice or observance is required by official religious dogma or is in conformity with the position of religious officials of that faith is irrelevant except in extreme cases (i.e., where the existing practice is fabricated). Accordingly, while an employer may offer evidence regarding an employee's sincerity about the necessity of a particular religious practice, evidence concerning whether a particular practice is mandatory or even common is not relevant. That said, as with the other grounds, employees seeking accommodation for religious needs are required to work with their employers and other affected parties to find solutions to these issues (Krupat, 2013, at 2-6). As the *Friesen* decision illustrates, the need to balance the rights of all employees and the employer's efforts to promote a mutually respectful workplace is given considerable weight in human rights cases.

Accommodating Employees' Pregnancy and Breastfeeding Needs

Pregnant employees or employees who are breastfeeding may require temporary accommodation in the workplace. This could include temporary relocation from a work area that might endanger the pregnancy, a flexible work schedule, increased break time, and appropriate support for breastfeeding. *Sidhu v Broadway Gallery* addresses an employer's obligation to modify an employee's duties during pregnancy.

CASE IN POINT

Employer Fails to Meet Duty to Accommodate Pregnant Employee

Sidhu v Broadway Gallery, 2002 BCHRT 9

Facts

Sidhu became pregnant after working in a garden nursery for one year. She found it difficult to pull cans filled with sand and lift heavy objects. She obtained a note from her doctor stipulating that she could not lift objects greater than 40 pounds or spray the trees with pesticide but indicated that she wished to continue working full time. However, after she gave the note to her employer, her employer instead offered her a part-time position with drastically reduced hours. Sidhu then left her job and filed a complaint under the BC *Human Rights Code*.

Relevant Issue

Whether the employer's failure to accommodate Sidhu's request for work suited to her pregnancy constituted discrimination on the basis of sex.

Decision

The Tribunal held that the employer failed in its duty to accommodate Sidhu during her pregnancy. She established a *prima facie* case of discrimination because, but for the doctor's note, the terms and conditions of her employment would not have been altered. She was able to perform her job except for the heavy lifting. Given the nature of the work performed and the size of the workforce, the employer could have accommodated her by providing her with alternative full-time work. Because alternative full-time work existed, the proposed part-time position was not a sufficient accommodation.

Pregnancy-related accommodation extends to the area of benefits. An employee who requires time off before or after her pregnancy or parental leave arising from pregnancy-related health concerns is entitled to benefits under an employer's workplace sickness or disability plan.

In addition to accommodating pregnancy-related concerns, employers must also accommodate breastfeeding requirements. This may mean allowing the baby's caregiver to bring the baby into the workplace to be fed, making scheduling changes to allow time to express milk, or providing a comfortable, private area for breastfeeding.

Accommodating Employees' Family Status

Until recently, there were few cases in this area. The duty to accommodate for family status was generally taken to mean that employers have some obligation to assist employees who are balancing work and family responsibilities and to avoid policies that adversely affect them. For example, an employer may need to provide flexible work hours for an employee who is caring for aging parents or having difficulties arranging child care. Similarly, an employer who consistently holds business meetings after office hours may be contravening human rights laws because attending these meetings could adversely affect employees with small children (Ontario Human Rights Commission, 2008).

In the past few years, courts and tribunals have been asked to consider the extent to which employers have the duty to accommodate employees for their general family caregiving obligations. One of the first of these cases was *Health Sciences Assoc of BC v Campbell River and North Island Transition Society*. In that 2004 decision, the BC Court of Appeal found that the employer had discriminated against the complainant on the basis of family status when it changed her work hours, inadvertently causing her to be unable to take care of her son, who was a special needs child, after school. Relying on medical evidence affirming that the son required his mother's personal care after school, the Court distinguished this situation from the commonplace obligation of parents to arrange care for their children. It set down the principle that an employee has proven *prima facie* discrimination on the basis of family status where the employer's rule or requirement is a "serious interference with a substantial parental or other family duty" (at para 39).

This serious interference test remains the rule in BC for cases of discrimination based on family status and was recently given implicit approval by the Supreme Court of Canada when the Court refused to hear an appeal challenging the *Campbell River* approach to family status cases (*Brian Suen v Envirocon Environmental Services, ULC* [2019]). The debate, however, continues in the rest of Canada. A line of cases on this issue in the Canadian Human Rights Tribunal and Federal Court suggests that an employer's duty to accommodate extends to "ordinary," not just "substantial," family obligations. This line of cases, which led to the *Johnstone* decision discussed below, criticizes the *Campbell River* approach for applying a different standard to family status than to other prohibited grounds. It posits that concerns about serious workplace disruption should be addressed when determining whether the duty to accommodate has been met up to the point of undue hardship; they should not be used to restrict the definition of "family status" itself. The Alberta Human Rights Commission adopted this broader approach in 2014.

CASE IN POINT

Discrimination Based on Family Status

Canada (AG) v Johnstone, 2014 FCA 110

Facts

Johnstone and her husband were both employees of the Canada Border Services Agency (CBSA). As full-time staff, they worked rotating, variable shifts that had no predictable pattern. After the Johnstones had two children, one in January 2003 and a second in January 2004, Johnstone asked the CBSA to accommodate her childcare obligations by providing a fixed work schedule. Since Johnstone's husband was facing the same unpredictable schedule, neither could provide nor arrange alternative child care on a reliable basis. The CBSA declined and instead offered her part-time work, which affected her benefits, pension, and opportunities for promotion. The CBSA did not refuse to provide the fixed schedule because it would cause undue hardship. Rather, it refused on the ground that it had no legal duty to accommodate childcare responsibilities. Johnstone filed a complaint with the Canadian Human Rights Commission alleging discrimination on the basis of family status, contrary to sections 7 and 10 of the *Canadian Human Rights Act*.

Relevant Issue

Was Johnstone discriminated against on the ground of family status, and what is the correct legal test for discrimination on the ground of family status?

Decision

The initial decision of the Canadian Human Rights Tribunal in 2010 was that Johnstone had indeed suffered discrimination. The CBSA applied for judicial review by the Federal Court, arguing, among other things, that the Tribunal was wrong to find that family status includes childcare responsibilities and that it had applied too easy a test for *prima facie* discrimination. The Federal Court rejected these arguments in 2013. The CBSA appealed this decision to the Federal Court of Appeal. That Court first confirmed that parental obligations that engage a parent's legal responsibility, as opposed to personal choice, fall under the protection of the *Canadian Human Rights Act*. This includes childcare obligations.

The Court then reviewed prior jurisprudence regarding family status and previously developed tests to determine when discrimination with regard to child care has occurred. The Court of Appeal rejected the restrictive test in *Health Sciences Assoc of BC v Campbell River and North Island Transition Society* (*Campbell River*), which required that there be a change in a term or condition of employment imposed by an employer that results in a "*serious interference* with a *substantial* parental or other family duty or obligation *of the employee*" (at para 78; emphasis added). The Court of Appeal agreed with the Tribunal's analysis in *Hoyt v Canadian National Railway* (2006), which criticized the *Campbell River* decision for creating a hierarchy of human rights, and stated that the test for family status discrimination must be flexible and contextual and must be substantially the same as that which applies to other enumerated grounds. In consideration of these and other cases, the Court of Appeal developed the following test:

1. First, the claimant must demonstrate that the child is actually under their care and supervision.
2. Second, the claimant must demonstrate an obligation that engages the individual's legal responsibility for the child, rather than a personal choice. For example, the child must not have reached an age where they can reasonably be expected to care for themselves during the parent's working hours.
3. Third, the claimant must demonstrate that reasonable efforts have been made to meet the childcare obligations through reasonable alternative solutions, and that no alternative solution is reasonably accessible.
4. Fourth, the claimant must show that the workplace rule interferes with the childcare obligation in a manner that is more than trivial or insubstantial.

When the Court of Appeal applied its newly developed test to Johnstone's circumstances, it found that she had established a case of discrimination on the ground of family status resulting from childcare obligations. The Court awarded Johnstone lost wages, $15,000 for pain and suffering, and $20,000 for wilful and reckless discrimination. It also ordered the employer to develop and implement human rights policies and to provide related training to all partners and supervisory staff.

The *Johnstone* test suggests that the duty to accommodate for child care extends only to obligations, not to merely personal choices, and that the employee must have made reasonable efforts to self-accommodate before the duty is triggered (Zabrovsky, 2014). This aspect of the decision is consistent with decisions in BC and Alberta. The lower threshold set in *Johnstone* for what amounts to discrimination is, however, contrary to the test in BC.

Given the Supreme Court of Canada's recent refusal to hear the appeal in *Envirocon*, it's clear that Canada's top Court has given implicit approval of the *Campbell River* approach, or at the very least are not yet prepared to comment on it. The Supreme Court made no direct commentary on the test itself, which creates some uncertainty as to how *Johnstone* will be interpreted moving forward. What is certain is that the debate over whether the *Campbell River* or *Johnstone* approach applies will continue. It remains to be seen which provinces will adopt *Johnstone*'s approach to family status discrimination. Federal Court of Appeal decisions are only binding on the Federal Court and the Canadian Human Rights Tribunal, and *Johnstone* only applies to federal employees protected by the *Canadian Human Rights Act*. Until the Supreme Court of Canada interprets "family status" discrimination, the scope of this discrimination will likely be different from province to province.

To further complicate matters, it appears that Alberta's Human Rights Commission endorsed the Federal Court's approach by relying on *Johnstone* in *Clark v Bow Valley College* (2014). However, a 2019 Court of Queen's Bench decision, *United Nurses of Alberta v Alberta Health Services* (2019), has firmly rejected the self-accommodation requirement. Justice Hollins stated that the original decision made by a grievance arbitration board had improperly included self-accommodation in the test for *prima facie* discrimination. The board should have followed the reasoning of Alberta Queen's Bench Justice Ross in *SMS Equipment* (2015):

> A flexible and contextual application of the *Moore* test does not justify the application of an entirely different test of *prima facie* discrimination, and in particular does not justify including within that test a self-accommodation element that is not required with respect to other prohibited grounds of discrimination. This is unnecessary and contrary to the objects of human rights law. It is unnecessary because a finding of discrimination does not automatically follow once a *prima facie* case is established. It is only when the complainant establishes a *prima facie* case and the respondent fails to justify the rule or conduct that discrimination will be found. It is contrary to the objects of human rights law because it imposes one-sided and intrusive inquiries on complainants in family status discrimination cases. Complainants are not only required to prove that a workplace rule has a discriminatory impact on them, but that they were unable to avoid that impact. Thus the Grievor was subjected to an examination regarding her relationship or lack thereof with the biological fathers of her children, her choice of caregivers for her children and even her personal financial circumstances. She had to undergo this examination before the Employer would even consider a request for an accommodation in the form of a shift exchange that she had arranged with another willing employee. The search for accommodation is intended to be a "multi-party inquiry." … Converting this multi-party inquiry into a one-sided investigation could certainly deter complainants from pursuing claims for discrimination based on family status. (at para 77)

In BC, the requirement of a "serious interference with a substantial parental or other family duty or obligation of the employee" from *Campbell River* (at para 78) is still the law. The BC Human Rights Tribunal continues to follow it. Although the BC Tribunal and courts have not yet considered the 2014 *Johnstone* decision, the BC Supreme Court has rejected the Canadian Human Rights Tribunal's earlier criticisms of the *Campbell River* decision. Moreover, the recent decision by the Supreme Court of Canada in *Envirocon* to not hear an appeal involving the applicable test for family status accommodations further supports the view that *Campbell River* will remain the applicable interpretation of the law in BC for the foreseeable future.

The duty to accommodate for family responsibilities promises to be a dynamic area of human rights law and it will take some time before appeal courts settle this issue. However, the case law seems to be moving in the direction of expanding employers' obligations in this area, and an employer needs to take requests for accommodation seriously. Employers need to be prepared to be flexible, and even creative, with respect to requests for accommodation of an employee's family obligations, including elder care. Each case must be considered on its own merits. An employer should make sure that it understands what the employee is asking for, and why, and it should explore what options are available to meet this need, up to the point of undue hardship.

Accommodating Employees' Age

Age discrimination in employment has historically been viewed as a justifiable infringement on human rights because everyone ages and we have accepted that with aging there is a deterioration in physical and mental performance. However, in recent years there has been a significant shift in both social consciousness and the law of age discrimination.

Two of the early cases justifying age discrimination, *Douglas/Kwantlen Faculty Assn v Douglas College* (1990) and *Dickason v University of Alberta* (1992), involved university professors who challenged mandatory retirement policies. Both cases were heard by the Supreme Court of Canada, and although the Court confirmed that the mandatory retirement provisions were discriminatory, it held that the discrimination was reasonable and justifiable in the circumstances. The benefits of mandatory retirement, which included preservation of the tenure system, academic renewal, and the protection of "retirement with dignity," outweighed the harmful effects of these policies.

This change in attitude is also reflected in amendments to the Alberta *Human Rights Act* made in 2018 to prohibit age restrictions in the provision of tenancy and services (including insurance). The BC Code was also amended to prohibit mandatory retirement. Until 2008, the Code only prohibited age discrimination for those aged over 18 or below 65. As of January 1, 2008, age discrimination is prohibited for anyone aged 19 and up. Employers must therefore attempt to accommodate older workers and are not allowed to have a policy of mandatory retirement for any age.

The following Alberta case, *Cowling v Her Majesty the Queen in Right of Alberta*, illustrates other types of age-based discriminatory behaviour that the law seeks to eliminate, as well as the extent of remedies available.

CASE IN POINT

The Dangers of Making Assumptions About Age

Cowling v Her Majesty the Queen in Right of Alberta as represented by Alberta Employment and Immigration, 2012 AHRC 12

Facts

Cowling was first hired on contract as a provincial labour relations officer in 1999 when she was 59 years old. Her contract was renewed every two to three years and she received positive performance reviews and bonuses every year for eight years. Just before her final contract ended in 2007, Cowling was told that her department was restructuring and her position was being downgraded; it would become a permanent "growth" or "developmental" position. When Cowling applied for the new position, she found that the responsibilities were virtually identical to her former position; however, she wasn't hired. The new position was never filled, and the job description was then upgraded. Cowling filed a complaint with the Alberta Human Rights Commission.

Relevant Issue

Whether the employer's actions constituted age-based discrimination.

Decision

The Commission held that the employer's actions constituted age-based discrimination. Given the non-renewal of the contract after eight years of strong performance reviews, Cowling's exemplary qualifications, her ongoing pursuit of training opportunities, and her consistent achievement of bonuses, it was reasonable to infer that age was a factor in denying her continued employment (at para 169). Furthermore, the language used ("growth" and "developmental") to describe the "new" position supported the inference that the employer was looking for someone younger to fill Cowling's duties and that she was being targeted because of her age (at para 172). As the Commission stated, "discrimination is rarely practiced openly. Accordingly, it is appropriate to draw reasonable inferences based on circumstantial evidence" (at para 166). Cowling was awarded $15,000 in general damages, plus five years' pay (minus 30 percent to reflect the more tenuous nature of contract employment), plus interest and costs. The Commission also ordered that Cowling be reinstated.

IN THE NEWS

Ageism Is Alive and Thriving in Our Workforce, Limiting Older Employees, Say Experts

Embracing older employees and all they have to offer is the way forward for employers.

Although the average age of retirement in Canada is about 63, there is a steady increase in older workers postponing their retirements. According to a 2018 labour force report, Canadians over the age of 55 account for about 38 percent of the working population and have the fastest rate of employment growth.

Some believe that a youth-obsessed culture overshadows the value of older employees. It's a lost opportunity that has everything to do with ageism, suggests Cathie Brow, senior vice-president of human resources and communications with Revera, a leading owner, operator, and investor in the senior living sector.

Ageism comes in many forms. It can be subtle and unintentional, from jokes about "seniors' moments," to "overeducated or experienced" insinuations during job interviews, to job ads that ask for a "digital native—someone who grew up with computers." Sentiments like these are myths, according to Wanda Morris, vice-president of advocacy for the Canadian Association for Retired Persons. These and other common misperceptions (such as older workers aren't tech savvy, have more absences, or have limited longevity) need to be addressed and can be costly to businesses.

According to Morris, the "truth is, there is much more turnover among young people than older workers, who tend to be more loyal."

Employers may be pursuing the wrong demographic. Seniors don't stay for financial reasons, and they often take roles for less pay. They are healthy with experience to share. They are not ill-equipped to deal with today's workplace; they are simply not ready to throw in the towel on their professional lives.

Employment lawyer Doug MacLeod agrees with Morris: "It's going to be an issue that just keeps coming up more and more in the workplace. … They want to keep active, keep the brain operating. … in a capacity where they can mentor people and use their institutional knowledge to help move an organization forward."

SOURCE: Based on Nicholls Jones, 2018.

On-the-Job Drug and Alcohol Testing

As noted previously, an employer's ability to administer workplace drug and alcohol testing in Canada is restricted. The basic approach is that on-the-job testing is unjustified except in limited circumstances, such as in safety-sensitive positions where certain conditions apply or where an employee is involved in a workplace accident that reasonably suggests impairment (i.e., post-incident testing). Testing is also acceptable for Canadian trucking companies operating in the United States, where they must comply with American testing requirements or where positive role modelling is a BFOR (*Milazzo v Autocar Connaisseur Inc* [2003]; *Alberta Human Rights and Citizenship Commission v Elizabeth Metis Settlement* [2003]).

The seminal decision in the area of drug and alcohol testing is *Entrop v Imperial Oil Ltd.* In that 2000 case, the Ontario Court of Appeal drew a distinction between random alcohol testing and random drug testing. It found that Breathalyzers are minimally intrusive yet provide a highly accurate measure of both consumption and impairment; they may therefore be acceptable in safety-sensitive positions, especially where supervision is impractical. In contrast, drug tests are more intrusive (they require a urine sample) and fail to measure current impairment because there is a delay in obtaining test results; therefore, random drug testing is less likely to be acceptable, even in those restricted circumstances when random alcohol testing may be acceptable.

More recently, however, the Supreme Court of Canada has ruled on the legality of a unilaterally imposed policy requiring universal random testing in a unionized, safety-sensitive workplace. This decision throws into question the previous distinction between drug and alcohol testing and appears to raise the bar for justifying random testing.

CASE IN POINT

Raising the Standard for Random Substance Testing

Communications, Energy and Paperworkers Union of Canada, Local 30 v Irving Pulp & Paper, Ltd, 2013 SCC 34

Facts

In 2006, Irving's unionized paper mill in New Brunswick unilaterally implemented a workplace policy that required, among other things, that all employees in safety-sensitive positions be subject to testing for alcohol (but not drugs) on a random basis. The policy worked as follows: in any 12-month period, 10 percent of the employees in safety-sensitive positions were randomly selected for a Breathalyzer test. A positive result could result in discipline, up to dismissal. One of those randomly selected employees, Perley Day, was a man who had not consumed alcohol since 1979. Although his test results, unsurprisingly, showed a blood alcohol level of zero, the union filed a policy grievance challenging the reasonableness of the universal random testing policy under the management rights clause of the collective agreement. It argued that a Breathalyzer test (as an involuntary submission of bodily fluids) is highly intrusive and an unjustifiable breach of an employee's privacy rights.

The arbitration board agreed with the union, finding that although the mill was a dangerous workplace, there was insufficient evidence of alcohol abuse to justify such a privacy-invasive policy. (It noted that in the 15 years prior to implementing the policy, there had been only eight documented cases of alcohol-related impairment, and none of these had involved an accident, injury, or "near miss." Moreover, during the 22 months that the policy was in effect, none of the employees had tested positive for alcohol.) Therefore, it held that a policy requiring privacy-invasive, universal random testing was a disproportionate response.

The employer applied for judicial review, arguing that requiring that there be an accident, incident, or near miss before allowing random testing of all employees in safety-sensitive positions was unreasonable. The New Brunswick Court of Appeal agreed. It held that random mandatory alcohol testing is a reasonable exercise of management rights in workplaces that are inherently dangerous; no further proof of a particular workplace substance abuse problem is necessary. The union appealed this decision to the Supreme Court of Canada.

Relevant Issue

Whether proving that the workplace is inherently dangerous is sufficient to justify unilaterally implementing a universal random alcohol testing policy.

Decision

In a 6–3 split decision, the Supreme Court of Canada held that, except perhaps in the most extreme safety-sensitive workplaces, showing that the workplace is inherently dangerous is not enough. To warrant such a policy, the employer must demonstrate enhanced safety risks, such as providing evidence of a serious problem with substance abuse in the workplace. The majority decision found that in this case, the expected safety gains to the employer ranged "from uncertain ... to minimal at best" (at para 14), while the impact on employee privacy was much more severe. It concluded that the onus is on the employer to show that random testing is a proportionate response, based on the particular workplace involved, and the employer had not done this.

The majority decision in *Irving* clarified certain points, as well as raising others, concerning drug and alcohol testing in safety-sensitive workplaces. These include the following:

1. Selective drug or alcohol testing may be carried out when there is a reasonable suspicion of impairment—for example, when an employee exhibits slurred speech and appears to be under the influence of drugs or alcohol.
2. Selective drug or alcohol testing may be carried out when an employee has been involved in a workplace accident, incident, or near miss where it may be important to determine the root cause of what happened. This is often called "post-incident testing."
3. Random (unannounced) alcohol or drug testing may be carried out as part of an agreed rehabilitation and return-to-work program of an employee clearly identified as having a problem of alcohol or drug use.
4. The majority decision did not differentiate between the different standards applied to drug testing and alcohol testing that underlay *Entrop*. Instead, it suggests that a policy requiring universal random testing for either drugs or alcohol must be supported by evidence of reasonable cause (Essiminy & Weschler, 2013).
5. There may be a category of workplaces that are so extremely dangerous (e.g., a nuclear power facility) that universal random testing is acceptable without further inquiry. This, however, would be the rare exception.

The level of evidence that an employer provides to demonstrate a general problem with substance abuse in the workplace to justify random testing was tested in *Suncor Energy Inc v Unifor Local 707A*. In this case the Alberta Court of Appeal agreed with a lower court that it is not necessary for the employer to demonstrate a problem within a specific group of employees (in this case a bargaining unit). Demonstrating that it exists within the workplace as a whole may be sufficient.

In cases of post-incident or reasonable cause testing, the approach generally taken by adjudicators is to consider (1) the threshold level of the incident, (2) the degree of inquiry conducted before a decision was made, and (3) the link between the incident and the employee's situation (see *Communications, Energy and Paperworkers, Local 447 v Weyerhaeuser Co* [2006]). It is the employer's responsibility to demonstrate that reasonable cause for testing exists. If there are clear signs of impairment, and the cause is unknown, testing for both drugs and alcohol may be reasonable. This approach also indicates that an accident in and of itself may not be sufficient to justify post-incident testing. Rather, the employer must consider all of the circumstances and show a link between substance use and the cause of the incident. For example, in *Canadian Energy Workers' Association v ATCO Electric Ltd.* Justice Khullar of the Alberta Court of Queen's Bench confirmed that an employer was justified in requiring that two employees submit to post-incident testing after a low-speed collision at the worksite. Poor judgment was identified as the cause of the incident, and the employees failed to follow vehicle safety procedures despite training. Poor judgment or human error alone would not have been sufficient, but the combination of factors in this case indicated that the employer was justified.

Since most drug and alcohol testing decisions, including *Irving* and *Suncor*, are based in unionized workplaces and address reasonableness in exercising management rights under a collective agreement, their findings may not be directly applicable to non-union employers. However, it is quite likely that human rights tribunals will look to these decisions for guidance in trying to balance safety with human rights considerations (Standryk, 2013).

Therefore, union and non-union employers implementing random workplace drug or alcohol testing should carefully consider both rationale and scope. First, the need for such testing in relation to safety-sensitive positions and any indications that on-the-job alcohol or drug use is an actual problem should be analyzed. *If* random testing is implemented, it should be part of a broader, comprehensive substance abuse policy incorporating education, counselling, and rehabilitation. A positive test should not automatically disqualify an applicant or automatically result in termination of a current employee. The test should interfere as little as possible with employee privacy rights and be administered in a respectful way. The policy should also be reviewed regularly to ensure ongoing compliance with developing law (Mitchell, 2008, at 2).

Harassment

Human rights legislation in some provinces specifically prohibits "harassment," which may include both **sexual harassment** and abusive or annoying behaviour based on any of the prohibited grounds of discrimination. Alberta and BC do not define or specifically prohibit "harassment." However, harassment is prohibited if it is associated with any of the protected grounds. Examples of prohibited behaviours include:

sexual harassment a course of vexatious comment or conduct (based on sex or gender) that is known or ought reasonably to be known to be unwelcome; it may be practised by a male on a female, by a female on a male, or between members of the same sex

- verbal or physical abuse;
- threats, derogatory remarks, jokes, innuendo, or taunts about appearance or beliefs, or any other prohibited ground, including gender;
- the display of pornographic, racist, or offensive images;
- practical jokes that result in awkwardness or embarrassment;
- unwelcome invitations or requests (explicit or implied);
- intimidation, leering, or other objectionable gestures;

- condescension or paternalism that undermines self-confidence; and
- unwanted physical contact including touching, patting, pinching, or punching (Alberta Human Rights Commission, 2017).

In 2013, the BC government incorporated bullying and harassment into its occupational health and safety laws—including forms of harassment unrelated to the grounds in the BC *Human Rights Code*. Alberta followed suit with similar changes to their *Occupational Health and Safety Act* in 2018. Those laws require employers to train employees about bullying and harassment and how to avoid these behaviours, and WorkSafeBC has created a prevention toolkit (WorkSafeBC, "Bullying and Harassment").

Harassing comments or conduct need not explicitly refer to a prohibited ground of discrimination to be covered by human rights legislation. For example, if someone who is from a different ethnic background than the rest of their department is singled out for practical jokes, the jokes themselves need not have anything to do with their ethnic background to be in violation of the law. Harassment on the basis of ethnic origin may be inferred from other circumstances, such as a lack of employees from visible minorities in the workplace or a high turnover among these employees.

According to the Alberta Human Rights Commission (2017), when a supervisor harasses an employee on the basis of one of the prohibited grounds it is an abuse of authority and the employer can be held responsible. Similarly, if a co-worker harasses another employee, the employer can be held responsible. Employers are legally required to actively discourage and prohibit humiliating conduct or language that results in one employee's working conditions being less favourable than another's.

Behaviour that is acceptable to both parties involved, such as flirtation or good-natured jesting, is not considered sexual harassment. In cases of subtle forms of harassment, or where the harasser does not realize that the conduct is annoying, the harassed employee must let them know how the conduct is being perceived. In other words, there is an onus on the person experiencing harassment to inform the harasser that the behaviour is unwelcome. For example, someone may repeatedly tell jokes about a certain ethnic group to an employee from that ethnic group in the honest belief that they are being funny. However, once the recipient of the jokes lets the joke teller know that the jokes are offensive, the joke teller has been put on notice that the jokes are unacceptable and must stop.

The standard for determining whether harassment has occurred is objective: would a reasonable person think the comment or conduct is inappropriate? It does not require that most people view the behaviour as harassing, as long as the recipient does and that perspective is reasonable.

Although discrimination in Alberta and BC must be based on a prohibited ground to be heard by a human rights tribunal, there are other alternatives for resolving complaints of general workplace harassment. These complaints can be addressed through the employer's policies, a collective agreement grievance process, or the courts. (Complaints in BC may also be addressed through WorkSafeBC, including complaints with no connection to the grounds in the BC Code.) It is important to know that an employer who allows harassment to become intolerable (even if the harassment is not related to a protected ground) may be found guilty of constructively dismissing an employee who feels that there is no option but to resign (see e.g. *Shah v Xerox Canada Ltd*).

Another type of harassment involves a **poisoned work environment**. This refers to a workplace that feels hostile because of insulting or degrading comments or actions related to a prohibited ground of discrimination. It is not necessary that a person who perceives a hostile work environment be the target of the comments or actions. To constitute harassment, the comments or actions need only be ones that would influence and offend a reasonable person.

poisoned work environment
a workplace that feels hostile because of insulting or degrading comments or actions related to a prohibited ground of discrimination

Different workplaces tolerate different comments and conduct. However, when profanity or coarse conduct is directed toward a particular group—even if it is not directed at a particular individual—it is a human rights issue. In *Pillai v Lafarge Canada Inc* (2003), the BC Human Rights Tribunal found that racial slurs that were not made directly to the complainant contributed to a poisoned work environment because they were frequent and, like all racial slurs, beyond the bounds of normal social interaction.

An employer has an obligation to monitor, prevent, and respond promptly to harassment that could poison the workplace. For example, an employer that fails to erase offensive graffiti as quickly as possible may be liable for harassment for allowing a poisoned work environment. Similarly, an employer who knew or should have known about harassment, and could have taken steps to prevent or stop it, may be liable.

An employer can also be held responsible for harassment that occurs away from the workplace, such as at a company barbecue, conference, or Christmas party. Such events are often considered an extension of the workplace, putting a greater onus on the employer to ensure a healthy and safe environment is created for all employees in attendance. Conversely, an employer that fosters an inclusive workplace and trains its managers to recognize and respond promptly to harassment may avoid liability for harassment by non-managerial employees under human rights legislation. This situation differs from workplace *discrimination* where the employer is automatically liable for the conduct of all its employees, including non-managerial employees.

Sexual Harassment

Sexual harassment is not specifically identified in either the Alberta or BC legislation, but the Supreme Court of Canada has ruled that sexual harassment falls under discrimination on the basis of "sex" or "gender." In the seminal 1989 decision *Janzen v Platy Enterprises Ltd* (*Janzen*), the Court defined "sexual harassment" as:

> unwelcome conduct of a sexual nature that detrimentally affects the work environment or leads to adverse job-related consequences for the victims of harassment. …
>
> It is … an abuse of power. When sexual harassment occurs in the workplace, it is an abuse of both economic and sexual power. Sexual harassment is a demeaning practice, one that constitutes a profound affront to the dignity of the employees forced to endure it. (at 1284)

Sexual harassment is similar to other forms of workplace harassment in that it refers to a course of vexatious comment or conduct (based on sex or gender) that is known or ought reasonably to be known to be unwelcome. It may be practised by a male on a female, by a female on a male, or between members of the same sex. More than one incident is usually required to sustain a human rights complaint; a single incident is sufficient, however, if the conduct is serious enough that the harasser must have known it was offensive.

Under Canadian case law, the term "sexual harassment" covers a broad range of conduct. The common thread is that it is unwelcome conduct of a sexual nature that attacks the dignity and self-respect of the complainant and leads to negative job-related effects for the victim (*Janzen*). It can be physical or verbal. The more obvious cases of harassment involve unwelcome physical contact such as touching, patting, pinching, kissing, and hugging. However, it also includes offensive remarks, ostensibly flattering remarks about physical appearance, inappropriate staring, offensive jokes, displays of offensive pictures or other materials, questions or discussions about sexual activities, and paternalistic comments that undermine the recipient's authority.

As in the case of general workplace harassment, there may be instances where the harasser does not realize their comments are offensive. For example, if someone repeatedly questions a colleague about sexual matters, they may think they are simply being open and friendly. However, if the recipient lets the person know that their conduct is annoying and inappropriate, the harasser has been put on notice that the questions are unacceptable and should stop. The standard for establishing sexual harassment is objective: would a reasonable person in the recipient's position find the comments or conduct inappropriate? Again, it is not necessary that most people view the behaviour as harassing, as long as the recipient does and that perception is reasonable.

Sexual harassment can also include making comments that are not obviously sexual in nature. For example, in *Shaw v Levac Supply Ltd*, an employee repeatedly referred to a co-worker as a "fat cow" and said "waddle waddle" when she walked by. The Board held that the comments constituted sexual harassment by implying sexual unattractiveness.

In considering claims of sexual harassment, courts and tribunals recognize that there are different types of workplace culture: what's tolerated as "shop talk" in some workplaces might be considered inappropriate in others with a more formal atmosphere. However, a defence that it was only shop talk will not be helpful to employers who tolerate offensive sexist or racist behaviour. Moreover, an employer that allows questionable shop talk will find it more difficult to prove just cause for dismissing an employee who engages in such conduct. Just cause is necessary if an employer wishes to discharge an employee without notice or a separation package.

At the same time, tribunals have found that where a complainant initiates and willingly participates in sexual banter, co-workers cannot reasonably be expected to know that this type of conduct is no longer welcome unless the complainant communicates that fact. In *Kafer v Sleep Country Canada*, the complainant was unsuccessful because, on the basis of her earlier sexualized banter, the Tribunal found that "no reasonable person would conclude that she found the conduct in question unwelcome" (at para 9). However, it also held that once an employee lets co-workers know that conduct that was previously acceptable is no longer welcome, any continuation would constitute harassment contrary to the Code (Edstrom, 2013).

Human rights adjudicators have recognized that sending provocative and unwanted text messages (sexting), even outside of the workplace and office hours, can constitute sexual harassment as well. In *McIntosh v Metro Aluminum Products* (2011), the applicant filed a human rights complaint after the owner, with whom she had once had a consensual relationship, persisted in sending her sexually explicit and increasingly nasty texts after she broke the relationship off. The Tribunal rejected the employer's argument that McIntosh had participated in, and thereby consented to, the ongoing texting, noting that McIntosh's texts were entirely focused on trying to get him to stop sending her his vulgar messages. As a consequence of failing to ensure that McIntosh's workplace was free of harassment, the employer was ordered to pay the applicant approximately $15,000 in lost wages and a further $12,500 for injury to her dignity, feelings, and self-respect.

Remedies for sexual harassment are on an upward trend, with tribunals awarding significant damages for mental distress and injury to dignity and self-respect. For example, in *Corporation of the City of Calgary v Canadian Union of Public Employees, Local 37* (2018), a female truck driver was awarded three years of lost wages as well as $75,000 in general damages. The City was found responsible for the harassment and discrimination the driver experienced at the hands of her supervisor, foreman, and co-workers, as well as for an inadequate investigation. The figure for general damages considered the seriousness of the misconduct, the fact it was perpetrated and condoned by the foreman and supervisor, and there were many incidents that occurred over a prolonged period (18 months). The Tribunal also considered the impact on the grievor, who suffered significant long-term injuries, including the breakdown of her marriage, the loss of her home, and the loss of her work. Other cases (*Jane Doe v Canada*) have also held that even if the harassment and discrimination is not the sole cause of any injury to the employee, damages can be awarded if the degrading conduct exacerbates an existing condition.

Sexual Solicitation

Some provincial human rights codes identify "sexual solicitation" as a form of harassment (e.g., s 7(3) of the Ontario *Human Rights Code*). **Sexual solicitation** describes a situation where someone in a position of authority makes unwelcome advances or requests for sexual favours and where the threat of reprisals or promise of reward is explicit. Human rights laws in Alberta and BC do not specifically define sexual solicitation. Nonetheless, the cases dealing with discrimination on the basis of sex or gender have extended to include such conduct.

sexual solicitation
a situation where someone in a position of authority makes unwelcome advances or requests for sexual favours and where the threat of reprisals or promise of reward is explicit

Promoting a Harassment-Free Workplace

An employer may greatly reduce the chances of having sexual and other types of harassment occur by devising and enforcing a policy against harassment. This policy must include measures that educate employees about their rights and encourage employees to come forward with any complaints. It is also wise to regularly remind and refresh the memory of the workforce about their rights and their obligations as they relate to supporting a harassment-free workplace. Clearly communicating such a policy may also limit the employer's liability for harassment committed by non-managerial employees.

To be effective, Alberta or BC workplace and sexual harassment policies should do the following:

1. Encourage employees to come forward with complaints. How a policy sounds and is structured is important. Management has to demonstrate its commitment to eliminating all forms of harassment.
2. Ensure acceptance by all staff, unions, and employee associations. This can only be developed through consultation, input, and feedback. Time taken here will be more than repaid down the road.
3. Provide a clear definition of harassment as it relates to the protected areas and grounds in the Alberta *Human Rights Act* [or the BC Code].
4. Include guidelines for individuals seeking advice about making a sexual or other type of harassment complaint.
5. Maintain confidentiality of complaints and protect employees from retaliation.
6. Designate a person or persons to hear complaints. These individuals should be viewed by other employees as neutral but as having the authority to act. If possible, have more than one person assigned to this important, sometimes emotionally taxing, job.
7. Lay out the steps: Effective harassment policies provide a step-by-step description of what happens in the company when a complaint of harassment is made. To encourage prevention, also spell out the disciplinary consequences for harassing any employee.
8. Guarantee a fair and prompt reaction to anyone with a complaint of harassment.
9. [Include education so that everyone knows] about the policy and … understand[s] the true nature of harassment. (Alberta Human Rights Commission, 2012)

Investigating Harassment Complaints

Investigating sexual harassment complaints can be particularly challenging because the complainant may wish to remain anonymous or there may not be any witnesses, so the employer is must try to assess the credibility of the parties involved. However, this does not mean that an employer can ignore a complaint. The onus is on the employer to conduct a fair investigation. The following two cases show the importance of taking harassment allegations seriously and of investigating such complaints promptly, thoroughly, and in a way that is fair to *both* parties involved. In *Harrison v Nixon Safety Consulting (No 3)* (2008), a female safety officer alleged that she was sexually harassed and that her employer largely ignored her concerns. The *Harrison* case also illustrates the extent to which harassment cases often turn on the credibility of the parties and how issues of credibility are sometimes determined.

CASE IN POINT

Employers Need to Take Harassment Complaints Seriously

Harrison v Nixon Safety Consulting (No 3), 2008 BCHRT 462

Facts

Harrison, 28, was hired by Nixon Safety Consulting (NSC) to be a safety officer at a condominium construction site. NSC was contracted by Navigator to provide safety services at the site and Navigator, in turn, was contracted to do concrete work by Con-Forte, a construction company in charge of the project. Harrison worked in the site office with Ford, Navigator's project manager, and Goodman, head of onsite operations for Con-Forte.

On her second day of work, Harrison claimed that Ford told her he would "put in a good word for her" at work if she had sex with him. She also claimed that Ford had touched her shoulders and back and slapped her buttocks, as well as shown her pornography on his computer. Harrison spoke to Goodman about Ford's conduct, but he simply said she shouldn't worry; she would have her own trailer soon and would be away from Ford.

Harrison then spoke to her supervisor at NSC, and he suggested she stay home the next day. However, almost immediately she received a letter from Ford's lawyer warning her against making "slanderous and defamatory comments" or Ford would take legal action. At this point her NSC supervisor told her that Ford had complained about her, and NSC was worried about its contract with Navigator. Two months into her three-month probationary period, NSC terminated Harrison.

Harrison filed a complaint with the BC Human Rights Tribunal. In Ford's response, he denied making sexual remarks and claimed that Harrison sometimes wore inappropriate clothing to work, such as short skirts and tight jeans, and made inappropriate comments. He admitted there was "sexual banter" but said Harrison usually initiated it. Goodman agreed with Ford's account, adding that Harrison got more demanding and disruptive at the worksite as time went on.

Relevant Issue

Whether the employer's conduct contravened human rights legislation.

Decision

The Tribunal found Ford's and Goodman's version of events not credible. For example, there was no evidence that Harrison wore skirts to work, and their accounts of her other behaviour were unsupported. Ford's quick response with a letter from his lawyer following her complaint to her NSC supervisor seemed extreme for someone who felt he didn't have anything to worry about. Harrison, on the other hand, had made notes in her daily work journal that included records of Ford's behaviour and her complaints to Goodman and her NSC supervisor. Moreover, the Tribunal found the employer's investigation "cursory and superficial."

As a result, the Tribunal ruled that Harrison was subjected to unwelcome sexual misconduct that negatively affected her work environment and employment. Ford should have known his conduct was inappropriate, and as a result his conduct constituted sexual harassment. Her termination was directly linked to the harassment and constituted discrimination on the basis of sex. NSC, Ford, Navigator, and Con-Forte were held jointly liable for damages, which were four months' lost wages ($14,144); plus $15,000 for injury to Harrison's dignity, feelings, and self-respect; plus $3,000 from Ford, Navigator, and Con-Forte for improper conduct in trying to discredit Harrison.

Note that the fact that Harrison was terminated during her probationary period was irrelevant, because discrimination and harassment are prohibited regardless of when it occurs during an employee's employment. Another interesting point is that although Harrison was officially working for NSC, the Tribunal found that she had an employment relationship with Navigator and Con-Forte as well, because Ford and Goodman held positions of authority over her. All of the companies were therefore held jointly liable for the damages awarded.

The Tribunal in *Harrison* specifically criticized NSC for the superficiality of its investigation of its employee's complaint. The following case of *Elgert v Home Hardware Stores* also looks at the importance of a proper investigation, this time from the point of view of the alleged harasser.

CASE IN POINT

Employer's Investigation Must Be Fair to Both Sides

Elgert v Home Hardware Stores Limited, 2011 ABCA 112, leave to appeal to SCC refused, 2011 CanLII 75139

Facts

Elgert worked at the Wetaskiwin Home Hardware Distribution Centre for nearly 17 years when his employment was terminated for alleged sexual harassment. Christa Bernier, the daughter of the distribution centre's manager, worked directly for Elgert. Elgert had received numerous complaints about her performance with respect to her work with a male colleague with whom she had a romantic relationship. The performance issues were noted in Bernier's performance review, and Elgert transferred Bernier to another area to manage the problem.

Shortly afterward, two co-workers heard Bernier state she was unhappy with Elgert and that she would get even with him. She subsequently told her father about an incident that she alleged occurred four months earlier. Bernier said that Elgert followed her into a storage room and "belly bumped" her against a table, ending up with his legs between hers. Another employee, Diane Stengle, alleged that a similar incident had occurred between her and Elgert. Stengle had not initially reported it because she took it as a joke. Other workers testified that the "belly bumping" was something several employees did when everyone was in a good mood.

It is unclear how the complaint progressed through the company, but at some point Bernier's father notified his superior and friend, Don Kirck. In a teleconference with Bernier and the vice-president of human resources (Stew Gingrich), it was determined that Kirck would fly to Alberta to investigate. Kirck had no training or experience in investigations. He met briefly with Christa Bernier, then suspended Elgert, who begged him to do a thorough investigation. Kirck stated at the time that he was 100 percent certain that Elgert was guilty. Elgert was supplied no particulars, and when he asked what he had done, he was told "You know what you did." Gingrich invited Elgert to a meeting but refused to allow him to bring his lawyer. Elgert did not attend. Gingrich admitted he wanted to meet with Elgert alone to try to get him to confess. Elgert was terminated for cause without further investigation. Elgert was emotionally devastated by the allegations and struggled to cope with the damage to his reputation in the small community. He brought an action for wrongful dismissal and defamation.

Relevant Issue

Whether Elgert had engaged in sexual harassment that was just cause for dismissal.

Decision

A jury found that Elgert did not commit the acts of sexual harassment alleged by Bernier or Stengle and that each had defamed Elgert. He was awarded 24 months' salary in lieu of notice and $60,000 for defamation. The jury also found that Home Hardware's conduct during the course of the dismissal was in bad faith and ordered aggravated damages of $200,000. They further found that Home Hardware's conduct was harsh, vindictive, reprehensible, malicious, extreme in nature, and deserving of punishment in the form of punitive damages of $300,000. The Court of Appeal eliminated the aggravated damages and reduced the punitive damages award to $75,000.

The investigation in *Elgert* was improper in several respects. The investigator had a close relationship with the complainant's father. The investigator did not interview all the relevant witnesses and did not provide any information to the accused about the nature of the allegations. The accused was not allowed legal counsel, and the investigator had made up his mind before the investigation began. As the result in *Elgert* demonstrates, the compensation available to employees wrongfully dismissed for improperly investigated harassment claims can be considerable.

Investigating Harassment Complaints—Doing It Right

INVESTIGATE IN A TIMELY MANNER

Excessive delay reduces the effectiveness of the investigation (recollection of events gets more difficult; the working environment becomes strained). On the other hand, never rush to the point of undermining the accused's ability to respond to the allegations.

ENSURE THAT THE INVESTIGATOR IS UNBIASED

The investigator should not have a stake in the outcome (as in the case of a supervisor investigating a subordinate). It may be necessary to look externally for someone who is sufficiently objective.

GIVE THE ACCUSED A CHANCE TO RESPOND

Fairness demands that you give the accused an opportunity to defend themselves. In particular, provide the accused person with specific information about the allegations (e.g., dates and details) because it is difficult to respond adequately to vague or general accusations of harassment.

FOLLOW THE EMPLOYER'S OWN POLICIES AND PROCEDURES

This may seem obvious, but failure to follow set procedures (assuming they were well thought through in the first place) undermines the investigation unless there is a good reason to deviate from them. Investigators should be trained in human rights and in how to conduct a proper investigation.

MAKE SURE THAT WITNESSES ARE INTERVIEWED SEPARATELY

Interviewing witnesses together can influence their statements and lead to collaboration or intimidation. Where there is more than one accuser, they should be warned not to confer when putting their complaints in writing and that their complaint should only reflect their own individual experiences.

ASK NON-LEADING QUESTIONS

Leading questions are those that are phrased in a way that prompts the witness on how to respond (e.g., "Did the accused ever look at you in a way that made you feel uncomfortable?").

INTERVIEW THIRD-PARTY WITNESSES

Many harassment issues come down to credibility—he said/she said—so it is important, where possible, to get written statements from third-party witnesses.

DOCUMENT THE INVESTIGATION

As always, the investigator should thoroughly document each step of the investigation. For example, having a complete record of what witnesses said lends credibility to the investigation.

KEEP AN OPEN MIND

Some employers respond to a complaint by trying to sweep the matter under the rug, while other employers presume the accused must be guilty and overreact by dismissing the accused without a proper investigation. While this may be tempting, especially in the era of the #MeToo movement, where the public discourse encourages us to believe all accusers, this is not the appropriate stance to take to ensure a fair and neutral investigation.

CONSIDER THE ENTIRE CONTEXT

Where discipline is warranted, keep in mind the entire context in determining the appropriate response. For example, a higher degree of discipline, up to and including dismissal, may be called for where the accused is in a supervisory position but may be inappropriate for an accused who is not.

SOURCE: Adapted from information from Bongarde Media Co, 2009.

During the investigation, the employee should typically not be suspended without pay, since this may suggest guilt. Therefore, where warranted, the employee should be placed on a leave of absence, with pay, until the investigation is complete (Bernardi, 2011, at 4).

Employer Liability for Human Rights Violations

vicarious liability legal responsibility for the actions of another

Under section 44(2) of the BC Code, an employer is **vicariously liable** (legally responsible for the actions of another) for the discriminatory acts of its agents and employees in the workplace. The employer is directly liable for the actions of management. The Alberta legislation does not specifically recognize employer liability for employee actions in the statute. Instead, the Alberta Human Rights Commission relies on the 1987 Supreme Court decision in *Robichaud v Canada (Treasury Board)*. *Robichaud* states that an employer can be held responsible for "the unauthorized discriminatory acts of its employees in the course of their employment" (at para 1). Employers, therefore, are liable for all human rights violations of their employees while on the job, even if the employee is not carrying out their job duties when they commit the violation (at para 12). Therefore, under the BC statute and in the interpretation of the Alberta statute, there is no question that an employer can be held responsible for a manager who commits sexual harassment. However, an employer may be able to avoid liability for harassment by non-managerial employees if it can show that it was unaware that harassment was occurring, was diligent in attempting to prevent it (i.e., by having a robust policy, proactive policy training, and a well-known complaint process), and responded appropriately to it once aware. It is critical that the employer be diligent; a passive policy of merely waiting to receive complaints is unlikely to prevent liability.

An employer is generally not responsible for clients or customers who act in a discriminatory or harassing way. However, an employer may be liable for their behaviour if it knew of or had control over the situation, or if it could have done something to prevent or stop the behaviour but failed to act. Moreover, if there is a subsequent wrongful dismissal action, an investigation process that included all of the witnesses that the accused had asked to be interviewed about the situation is more likely to be seen as thorough and fair.

Competing Accommodation Claims

Employers can sometimes face difficult decisions when they encounter a situation where the rights of one employee appear to conflict with the rights of another. The Supreme Court of Canada in *R v NS* (2012) made it clear that "competing rights claims should be reconciled, through accommodation if possible, and if conflict cannot be avoided, through case-by-case balancing" (at para 9).

Unfortunately, this does not tell employers how to achieve that balance. The Ontario Human Rights Commission has tried to provide some guidance in its 2012 "Policy on Competing Human Rights," which is based on the following principles:

1. No rights are absolute.
2. There is no hierarchy of rights.
3. Rights may not extend as far as claimed.

4. The full context, facts, and constitutional values at stake must be considered.
5. Must look at the extent of interference (only actual burdens on rights trigger conflicts).
6. The core of a right is more protected than its periphery.
7. Aim to respect the importance of both sets of rights.
8. Statutory defences may restrict rights of one group and give rights to another.

The policy recommends a three-stage approach for employers to evaluate competing claims:

Stage One: Recognizing competing rights claims

1. What are the claims about?
2. Do claims connect to legitimate rights?
3. Do claims involve individuals or groups rather than operational interests?
   a. Do claims connect to human rights, other legal entitlements, or bona fide reasonable interests?
   b. Do claims fall within the scope of the right when defined in context?
4. Do claims amount to more than minimal interference with rights?

Stage Two: Reconciling competing rights claims

1. Is there a solution that allows enjoyment of each right?
2. If not, is there a "next best" solution?

Stage Three: Making decisions

1. Decisions must be consistent with human rights and other law, court decisions, and human rights principles.

This approach is exemplified in *Lidkea v Edmonton Public School Board*. The Alberta Human Rights Commission awarded the complainant $15,000 in damages for injury to dignity, feelings, and self-respect for failing to balance competing interests. Lidkea was teaching in a school for the deaf, and she was assigned to a small, isolated classroom after she advised her employer that she needed to bring a service dog to work every day. The school was concerned about potential health and safety concerns for students and staff. Assigning Lidkea to the separate classroom resulted in a sense of isolation, restricted her movements within the school, and made it difficult for her to function. The Commission held that the employer was justified in requiring Lidkea to stay off work for a short period of time so they could assess the situation. However, when the assessment did not substantiate valid health concerns from students or staff, the employer violated Lidkea's rights when she was not returned to a regular classroom, because it set a standard for workplace safety that was not reasonably required. Rights of other stakeholders are a valid consideration for undue hardship, but employers would be wise to go through a careful analysis to ensure the decisions they make achieve a reasonable balance and infringe as little as possible on the rights of the affected parties.

KEY TERMS

employment equity, **228**
employment equity program, **231**
poisoned work environment, **277**
prima facie, **217**
remedial legislation, **220**
sexual harassment, **275**
sexual solicitation, **279**
systemic discrimination, **217**
undue hardship, **235**
vicarious liability, **284**

REVIEW AND DISCUSSION QUESTIONS

1. Azar worked as a nurse for five years in various temporary positions for the same employer. She applied for a temporary position that was available from September 2020 to June 2021. Before the hiring decision was made, Azar advised the employer that she was pregnant and expected to commence her maternity leave in February 2021. Although she was the most qualified applicant for the job, the employer awarded the job to someone else. Azar filed a complaint with the Alberta Human Rights Commission.
   a. What is the alleged ground of discrimination?
   b. In your opinion, did the employer contravene the BC *Human Rights Code*? Explain your answer.
2. Monique applied for a position as a cashier at a cafeteria. The employer's dress code requires employees to be "neatly groomed in appearance" and to avoid displaying body piercings or tattoos. The employer refused to hire Monique because she wears a nose ring. Monique filed a complaint with the Alberta Human Rights Commission.
   a. What is the alleged ground of discrimination?
   b. In your opinion, did the employer contravene the *Alberta Human Rights Act*? Explain your answer.
3. Kimberley was assigned male at birth but started living as a woman at age 29. Following her sex-reassignment surgery, Kimberley experienced physical and emotional abuse in a relationship, and she was referred to an organization that assists battered women. Several years later, she responded to an advertisement for volunteers at a rape crisis centre. Being a woman was stipulated as a job qualification. During the training session, someone identified her as transgender, based solely on her appearance, and Kimberley was asked to leave. Kimberley filed a complaint with the BC Human Rights Tribunal.
   a. What is the alleged ground of discrimination?
   b. In your opinion, did the employer contravene the BC Code? Explain your answer.
4. Joe applied for a position in a daycare centre. The centre refused to interview him because it thinks that parents would be uncomfortable with having a man take care of their young children. Joe filed a complaint with the Alberta Human Rights Commission.
   a. What is the alleged ground of discrimination?
   b. In your opinion, did the employer contravene the Alberta Act? Explain your answer.
5. During his job interview, Zhou mentioned that he was recovering from an addiction to cocaine. The employer refused to proceed with the interview because the position being applied for was in a safety-sensitive area. Zhou filed a complaint with the BC Human Rights Tribunal.
   a. What is the alleged ground of discrimination?
   b. In your opinion, did the employer contravene the BC Code? Explain your answer.
6. The employer interviewed a number of candidates for a position in a nursing home that involves lifting patients and other physically demanding work. One of the candidates, Joan, had limited mobility in her arm, which was obvious at the interview. The employer did not address the issue, and the interview was brief. Joan was not hired and filed a complaint with the Alberta Human Rights Commission.
   a. What is the alleged ground of discrimination?
   b. In your opinion, did the employer contravene the Alberta Act? Explain your answer.
7. Joe has a medical degree from a university outside Canada. He applied for a position as an orderly because his degree is not recognized in Canada. The employer refused to give him the job because she felt that he was "overqualified" and would leave as soon as he found a position more in keeping with his education. Joe filed a complaint with the BC Human Rights Tribunal.
   a. What is the alleged ground of discrimination?
   b. In your opinion, did the employer contravene the BC Code? Explain your answer.

8. Human rights legislation in Canada was intended to end discriminatory practices in five social areas. It has been argued, however, that it has not been very effective. Critics have asserted that racist and sexist employers have found ways to circumvent the law. Discuss whether Canada's human rights laws have achieved their objective of eliminating discrimination. If they have not, how could they be made more effective?
9. Increasingly, employers are using social networking sites to find out more information about job candidates in the hiring process and basing their hiring decisions in part on this information. Is this a smart move or a human rights trap? What are some of the upsides and downsides of this approach?
10. Sarah, a salon owner, operates a trendy salon in Calgary. She advertises for a stylist. Nia calls in response to the ad and seeks an interview. At no time does Nia mention that she covers her head for religious reasons. Nia attends the interview, which lasts only ten minutes. During the interview, Nia makes it clear that she will not remove her headscarf while at work, and Sarah tells her that in that case, she cannot hire her. Sarah has a policy requiring all stylists to show their hair. She doesn't allow baseball caps or other hats to be worn by staff because, in her view, a stylist's hair is her "calling card" and that of the salon. As a result of Sarah's reaction to her headscarf during the interview, and the ultimate decision not to offer her the job, Nia files a human rights complaint alleging discrimination. She's been turned down by numerous salons, and she's tired of it. Sarah says she's a small salon, and the costs of responding to this complaint will put her into financial ruin. Assume that you are a member of the human rights tribunal deciding this case. On the basis of the *Alberta Human Rights Act*, what would your decision be? Support your conclusions.
11. Is it a violation of the BC Code for an employer to require proficiency in English?
12. McCormick was an equity partner at a prestigious law firm in BC. As per the terms of the partnership agreement, he was due to retire during the year in which he turned 65. When he and the firm were unable to reach an agreement that would allow him to work beyond this age, he filed a complaint with the BC Human Rights Tribunal alleging age-based discrimination. The law firm challenged the Tribunal's jurisdiction on the basis that McCormick was a partner, not an employee, of the firm. The BC Court of Appeal agreed: unlike a corporation, a partnership is not a separate legal entity. Therefore, McCormick, as a partner, could not be an employee of the partnership because he cannot employ himself.

    If this fact situation occurred in Alberta instead of BC, would the result likely have been different?
13. Can an employer have a "non-smokers only" hiring policy? Discuss.
14. You've just started your new job as human resources manager at a retail chain that sells teen clothing. A supervisor calls you with a question. She's been getting complaints from a couple of employees that other employees are speaking with each other during work hours in a language other than English (even though they speak English well). They say it's rude and makes them feel left out of the conversation. The supervisor is wondering if she can insist that all employees speak English during working hours. What advice should you give the supervisor?
15. Although weight discrimination is one of the most common forms of discrimination in the workplace, weight is not one of the prohibited grounds under Alberta or BC human rights legislation. Should it be added?
16. Mary was hired by Good Value Shop in 2012. She has suffered from and been treated for depression most of her life. Mary is seen as a difficult employee: her supervisor describes her as short-tempered, manipulative, and disruptive. One behaviour that is particularly resented by her manager is her habit, after receiving directions from a manager, of checking with other managers and co-workers in the store to see if those directions are being consistently applied. In 2020, Mary goes off work on stress leave for depression. The supporting documentation sent to the disability insurance provider makes it clear that her depression relates to her work situation. It indicates that several friends and co-workers have quit due to stress, she has had four different managers in less than two years, and there is frequent bullying and verbal abuse by managers. When she returns to work two months later, she continues with the behaviour that had most upset her supervisor: questioning instructions and checking with other managers to see if they are being consistently applied. Her supervisor repeatedly tells her not to do this, but she continues. As a result, her employment is terminated for insubordination, four months after she returned from stress leave. In your opinion, has the employer infringed the BC Code? Explain your answer.

17. Your employer intends to deny a 64-year-old female employee a training opportunity that is available to everyone else in her department because "she won't be around long enough to use the new information." How would you advise the employer?

18. Your employer is a religious person who seeks your opinion about displaying religious symbols in the workplace. What advice can you offer?

19. Your employer tells you that he's heard that a supervisor in the purchasing department made a pass at two employees at the company picnic. What should the employer do? Why?

20. You are an employer who wants to reinstate an employee who left work with a back injury. However, it's a small workplace and the only job that the employee can perform is one created out of all the "light duties" of the other six jobs. This would require the other employees to perform all of the heavier duties, which might lead to injury. What should you do to meet the requirements of the legislation in your province?

21. Your employer tells you of a major productivity project that will begin shortly and take six to nine months to complete. Under normal circumstances, he would assign the project to the operations manager, but she is seven months pregnant and will be on maternity leave for most of the project's duration. How would you advise your employer about the human rights issues involved?

22. An employee who has been on maternity leave calls you to say that she will need more flexibility in her schedule when she returns to work because of childcare needs. How should you respond?

23. Two employees, Joseph and Sean, have come to you complaining about verbal harassment on the job. Both employees are fundraisers for AIDS research, and several of their co-workers routinely tease them about being gay. How would you advise them? What steps would you advise their employer to take?

24. Your co-worker comes into your office Monday morning very angry. She tells you that she is tired of her Uncle Miguel always favouring his nephews over his nieces. At a family gathering on the weekend, he gave each of his nephews $1,000 but gave nothing to his nieces. She wants to know if she can lodge a complaint against her uncle by filing an application under human rights legislation. How do you advise her?

25. Julio, a supervisor, continually harasses and ridicules George, who works in his department. No one else in the department believes that Julio's criticisms of George are justified. It appears to them that Julio simply does not like George for a personal reason. Can George file a human rights application? Give reasons for your answer.

26. Datt had worked for McAdams Restaurant for 23 years (taking orders, cleaning) when she came down with a skin condition on her hands that was made worse by frequent hand washing. She took several short-term disability leaves but her condition always worsened after she returned to work. McAdams said that frequent hand washing was necessary to maintain acceptable sanitary conditions, to meet both government regulations and its own hygiene policies. For example, the restaurant has a timed system where a timer sounds each hour, and all crew members and the manager must wash their hands. Datt's doctor reported that she could not perform any job requiring frequent hand washing but there were duties she could perform, including cash, some food preparation, and some cleaning. However, the disability benefits provider told Datt she would not be able to return to work because "restaurant work was not good for her" and offered her a three-month job search program. McAdams terminated her. Datt filed a human rights application.

a. Did Datt have a disability?

b. Was this a case of *prima facie* discrimination?

c. Did the employer have a duty to accommodate Datt, and if so, did it fulfill that duty up to the point of undue hardship? Explain your answer.

27. Linda was a sales rep whose job involved a lot of driving. After she was diagnosed with cataracts and told that within two years she would be legally blind, her employer advised her to apply for disability leave. Although her vision did deteriorate over the next few years, it was not as severe as the original prognosis, so she wrote to her employer asking to return to perform light duties or take on part-time work. The employer indicated nothing was available. Several months later, Linda's disability benefits were terminated, as she was deemed capable of returning to work in some occupation. Although her employer was notified of the change and of Linda's wish to return to work, it took no action. Four years later, Linda filed a human rights complaint. The employer argued that it had relied on information from the disability benefits provider indicating that she was unable to perform the available jobs.

Do you think Linda's complaint will be successful? Explain your answer.

28. Clara was hired on a four-month fixed-term contract to perform crisis response work, including responding to calls from area hospitals to assess and provide support for persons who presented as being in crisis. She was terminated after eight weeks in the position because, the employer alleged, she was unable to perform essential parts of the job. For example, she was unable to respond quickly to verbal and non-verbal clues commonly found in individuals who are in crisis. Before her termination, the employer had raised its performance concerns, and Clara told them she was taking medication for epilepsy and among its side effects was an occasional difficulty with words and delays in completing tasks. However, when asked by the employer if she needed accommodation, Clara had said there was no need. When her performance did not improve, despite several poor performance reviews and a final written warning, the employer terminated her contract. Clara grieved her dismissal.

    Do you think Clara's complaint will be successful? Explain your answer.

29. Tiana has been acting strangely at work and it appears to be alcohol related. However, she denies that she has a drinking problem. Does the employer have any responsibility to accommodate a disability that the employee denies?

30. David was a machine operator in a cheese factory. After confiding in a colleague that he had had a brief affair with his supervisor's ex-wife, several co-workers began picking on him by making negative comments. This lasted over two years. Despite numerous complaints to his supervisor who witnessed some of these insults, nothing was done. Despite the employer's zero-tolerance harassment policy, when the employer's human resources department became aware of David's allegations, it launched only a superficial investigation: it did not ask who the perpetrators were or gather facts about the specific allegations. It accepted the supervisor's view that it was not a serious problem. After his lawyer's offer to the employer to meet to discuss the matter further was rejected, David filed a lawsuit alleging constructive dismissal based on the employer's failure to provide a harassment-free environment. The Court agreed, finding that in light of both the nature of the comments made and the length of time they continued, it was reasonable for David to leave his job. It awarded him 12 months' notice (a year's worth of compensation).

    What lessons does this case hold for employers?

31. Angry that her supervisor had disciplined her for calling him a "dirty Mexican" at work, Danielle posted about the incident on her Facebook page. The supervisor heard about the postings and filed a human rights complaint against Danielle (but not the employer).
    a. What is the likely legal basis for the supervisor's application?
    b. Can statements made on Facebook, or in any other social media forum, be considered "harassment in the workplace"?
    c. Given that the employer was not a party to the proceedings, what would be an appropriate remedial order (i.e., remedy)?

32. A mailroom clerk's employment was terminated after the employer conducted a brief investigation of a sexual harassment complaint made by an employee of its cleaning subcontractor. The alleged misconduct included blowing the cleaner a kiss and sometimes grabbing her buttocks when he caught her alone; this had gone on for five years. The mail clerk grieved his termination, alleging that while the incidents had occurred, they had been consensual. He also pointed to his six years of service, his clean disciplinary record, and testimony from another cleaner that he had stopped his objectionable behaviour with her as soon as she had demanded it (by showing him her fists). The complainant had also indicated that she did not necessarily want the mail clerk to lose his job; she simply wanted an end to the harassment. In this situation, what do you think would be an appropriate remedy?

REFERENCES

ADGA Group Consultants Inc v Lane, 2008 CanLII 39605 (Ont Sup Ct J (Div Ct)).

Alberta (Human Rights and Citizenship Commission) v Kellogg Brown & Root (Canada) Company, 2006 ABQB 302, rev'd 2007 ABCA 426, leave to appeal to SCC refused, 2008 CanLII 32723.

Alberta Bill of Rights, RSA 2000, c A-14.

Alberta Human Rights Act, RSA 2000, c A-25.5.

Alberta Human Rights and Citizenship Commission v Elizabeth Metis Settlement, 2003 ABQB 342.

Alberta Human Rights Commission, "Duty to Accommodate: Interpretive Bulletin" (2010), online: <https://www.albertahumanrights.ab.ca/Documents/Bull_DutytoAccom_web.pdf>.

Alberta Human Rights Commission, "Developing an Effective Harassment and Sexual Harassment Policy" (2012), online: <https://www.albertahumanrights.ab.ca/Documents/DevImplHarassPolicy.pdf>.

Alberta Human Rights Commission, "Harassment as a Form of Discrimination" (2017), online: <https://www.albertahumanrights.ab.ca/Documents/HarassFormOfDiscrim.pdf>.

Alberta Human Rights Commission, "A Recommended Guide for Pre-Employment Inquiries" (July 2017), online: <https://www.albertahumanrights.ab.ca/publications/bulletins_sheets_booklets/sheets/hr_and_employment/Pages/pre_employment_inquiries_guide.aspx>.

Alberta Human Rights Commission, "Protected Areas and Grounds " (16 November 2018), online: <https://www.albertahumanrights.ab.ca/publications/bulletins_sheets_booklets/sheets/Pages/protected_grounds.aspx>.

Alberta Human Rights Commission, "Quick Facts about Human Rights Complaints in the Area of Publications and Notices" (23 January 2019), online: <https://www.albertahumanrights.ab.ca/other/statements/Pages/quick_facts_complaints.aspx>.

Anderson v Alberta, 2004 ABQB 766.

Araniva v RSY Contracting (No 3), 2019 BCHRT 97.

Balak v First Choice Haircutters, 2009 BCHRT 84.

BC Human Rights Commission v BC Human Rights Tribunal, 2000 BCCA 584.

BC Human Rights Tribunal, *Annual Report 2018–2019* (July 2019), online: <http://www.bchrt.bc.ca/shareddocs/annual_reports/2018-2019.pdf>.

BC Human Rights Tribunal, "Personal Characteristics Protected in the BC Human Rights Code" (October 2019), online: <http://www.bchrt.bc.ca/human-rights-duties/characteristics.htm>.

Bongarde Media Co, "Sexual Harassment: 8 Traps to Avoid When Investigating Harassment Complaints," *HR Compliance Insider* (March 2009) 5:3 at 1.

Boyle, M, "Happy Himmelfahrt: 5 Employer FAQs About Religious Accommodation @Work," CanLII Connects (15 December 2016) online: <https://canliiconnects.org/en/commentaries/44275>.

Brian Suen v Envirocon Environmental Services, ULC, 2019 CanLII 73206 (SCC).

British Columbia (Public Service Employee Relations Commission) v BCGSEU, [1999] 3 SCR 3 [*Meiorin*].

Canada (AG) v Grover, 2007 FC 28.

Canada (AG) v Johnstone, 2014 FCA 110.

Canadian Charter of Rights and Freedoms, Part I of the *Constitution Act, 1982*, being Schedule B to the *Canada Act 1982* (UK), 1982, c 11.

Canadian Energy Workers' Association v ATCO Electric Ltd, 2018 ABQB 258.

Canadian Human Rights Act, RSC 1985, c H-6.

Canadian Mental Health Association, "Fast Facts About Mental Illness," online: <https://cmha.ca/fast-facts-about-mental-illness>.

CANPAR and United Steelworkers of America, Local 1976, Re 2000, 93 LAC (4th) 208.

Central Alberta Dairy Pool v Alberta (Human Rights Commission), [1990] 2 SCR 489.

Central Okanagan School District No 23 v Renaud, [1992] 2 SCR 970.

Chopra v Syncrude Canada Ltd, 2003 ABQB 504.

Civil Marriage Act, SC 2005, c 33.

Clark v Bow Valley College, 2014 AHRC 4.

Collie, M, "'The Battle Starts at the Top': How Canadian Companies Can Close the Gender Pay Gap," *Global News* (9 April 2019), online: <https://globalnews.ca/news/5121054/canada-equal-pay-day-gender-wage-gap-remedy>.

Communications, Energy and Paperworkers Union of Canada, Local 30 v Irving Pulp & Paper, Ltd, 2013 SCC 34.

Communications, Energy and Paperworkers Union of Canada, Local 447 v Weyerhaeuser Co, 2006 AGAA No 48 (QL).

Corporation of the City of Calgary v Canadian Union of Public Employees, Local 37, 2018 CanLII 53482 (Alta GAA).

Cowling v Her Majesty the Queen in Right of Alberta as represented by Alberta Employment and Immigration, 2012 AHRC 12.

Crisp, D, "We All Have Everyday Mental Health Issues," *Canadian HR Reporter* (7 October 2013) at 13.

Dickason v University of Alberta, [1992] 2 SCR 1103.

Direct Energy v CEP, Local 975, 2009 CarswellOnt 4343 (Arb Bd).

Douglas/Kwantlen Faculty Assn v Douglas College, [1990] 3 SCR 570.

Edmonton (City) v Amalgamated Transit Union, Local 569, 2003 AGAA No 71 (QL).

Edstrom, CJ, "Lewd, Sexual Workplace Banter Found Not Discriminatory" (18 December 2013), online: *Harris & Company LLP* <https://www.lexology.com/library/detail.aspx?g=981893d4-6554-4cc2-831e-6dc53b0168ec>.

Elgert v Home Hardware Stores Limited, 2011 ABCA 112, leave to appeal to SCC refused, 2011 CanLII 75139.

Employment Equity Act, SC 1995, c 44.

Entrop v Imperial Oil Ltd, 2000 CanLII 16800 (Ont CA).

Essiminy, Patrick, & Stephanie Weschler, "The Supreme Court of Canada Rules on Random Drug and Alcohol Testing in the Workplace" (21 June 2013), online: <https://www.mondaq.com/canada/employee-rights-labour-relations/246488/the-supreme-court-of-canada-rules-on-random-drug-and-alcohol-testing-in-the-workplace>.

Faryna v Chorny, 1951 CanLII 252, 1952 2 DLR 354 (BCCA).

Finning Ltd v International Association of Machinists and Aerospace Workers, 1995 AGAA No 103 (QL).

Friesen v Fisher Bay Seafood and others, 2009 BCHRT 1.

Gichuru v The Law Society of British Columbia, 2014 BCCA 396.

Gilbert, Douglas, Brian Burkett & Moira McCaskill, *Canadian Labour and Employment Law for the US Practitioner* (Washington, DC: Bureau of National Affairs, 2000).

Goode v Interior Health Authority, 2010 BCHRT 95.

Harrison v Nixon Safety Consulting (No 3), 2008 BCHRT 462.

Health Employers Assn of BC (Kootenay Boundary Regional Hospital) v BC Nurses' Union, 2006 BCCA 57.

Health Sciences Assoc of BC v Campbell River and North Island Transition Society, 2004 BCCA 260.

Hoyt v Canadian National Railway, 2006 CHRT 33.

Human Rights Code, RSBC 1996, c 210.

Human Rights Code, RSO 1990, c H.19.

Hydro-Québec v Syndicat des employé-e-s de techniques professionnelles et de bureau d'Hydro-Québec, section locale 2000 (SCFP-FTQ), 2008 SCC 43.

Individual's Rights Protection Act, RSA 1980, c I-2.

International Brotherhood of Electrical Workers, Local 1620 v Lower Churchill Transmission Construction Employers' Association Inc, 2019 NLSC 48.

Israeli v Canadian Human Rights Commission, 1983 CanLII 6 (CHRT).

Jane Doe v Canada (AG), 2018 FCA 183.

Janzen v Platy Enterprises Ltd, [1989] 1 SCR 1252.

Jodoin v City of Calgary, 2008 AHRC 13.

Jurgens, K, "Accommodating Mental Illness Strategically," *Canadian HR Reporter* (14 January 2013) at 13.

Kafer v Sleep Country Canada (No 2), 2013 BCHRT 289.

Kauffman, B, "Cannabis Zero-Tolerance Common in Canadian Workplaces: Study," *Calgary Herald* (13 August 2019), online: < https://calgaryherald.com/cannabis/cannabis-business/cannabis-zero-tolerance-common-in-canadian-workplaces-study>.

Kelowna City and CUPE Local 338, 2003 BCCAAA No 272 (QL).

Kemess Mines Ltd v International Union of Operating Engineers, Local 115, 2006 BCCA 58.

Krieger v Toronto Police Services Board, 2010 HRTO 1361.

Krupat, K, "Should Religious Employees Have Faith in Workplace Accommodation Law in Canada?" in *The Six-Minute Employment Lawyer 2013* (Toronto: Law Society of Upper Canada, 2013).

LeClair, Ron, "The Evolution of Accommodation," *Canadian HR Reporter* (24 February 2003) at 7.

Lidkea v Edmonton Public School Board, 2016 AHRC 20.

McIntosh v Metro Aluminum Products and another, 2011 BCHRT 34.

McNamara v Lockerbie & Hole Inc, 2010 AHRC 7.

Meiorin: see *British Columbia (Public Service Employee Relations Commission) v BCGSEU*.

Merck, "Just-in-Time Toolkit for Managers" (2011), online: <http://merckdisabilitytoolkit.com/toolkit.cfm?Tool=6>.

Miedema, Adrian, & Christina Hall, *HR Manager's Guide to Background Checks and Pre-Employment Testing* (Toronto: Thomson Canada, 2006).

Milazzo v Autocar Connaisseur Inc, 2003 CHRT 37.

Miller, J, "Addiction in the Workplace," *Canadian Employment Law Today* 395 (6 August 2003) at 3086.

Mitchell, Tim, "Impairment Testing: Implementing and Administering Testing Policies," *Canadian Employment Law Today* 504 (27 February 2008) at 2.

Moore v British Columbia (Education), 2012 SCC 61.

Morrison v AdvoCare and others, 2009 BCHRT 298.

Nicholls Jones, Sophie, "Ageism Is Alive and Thriving in Our Workforce, Limiting Older Employees, Say Experts," *CPA Canada* (9 August 2018), online: <https://www.cpacanada.ca/en/news/canada/2018-08-09-ageism-is-alive-and-thriving-in-our-workforce-limiting-older-employees-say-experts>.

NS, R v, [2012] 3 SCR 726.

Occupational Health and Safety Act, SA 2017, c O-2.1.

Ontario (Human Rights Commission) v Roosma, 2002 CanLII 15946 (Ont Sup Ct J (Div Ct)).

Ontario Human Rights Commission, *Human Rights at Work*, 3rd ed (Toronto: Thomson Reuters, 2008).

Ontario Human Rights Commission, "Policy on Competing Human Rights" (2012) online: <http://www.ohrc.on.ca/en/policy-competing-human-rights>.

Ontario Human Rights Commission, "Policy on Ableism and Discrimination Based on Disability" (2016), online: <http://www.ohrc.on.ca/en/policy-ableism-and-discrimination-based-disability>.

Ontario Provincial Police Association v Ontario Provincial Police, 2018 CanLII 82193 (Ont LA).

Oxley v British Columbia Institute of Technology, 2002 BCHRT 33.

Pay Equity Act, CQLR c E-12.001.

Pay Equity Act, RSO 1990, c P.7.

Pay Equity Act, SC 2018, c 27, s 416.

Pillai v Lafarge Canada Inc, 2003 BCHRT 26.

Red Deer College and Faculty Association (Legault) 2015, 250 LAC 4th 264 (Alta GAA).

Reiss v CCH Canadian Limited 2013 HRTO 764.

Robichaud v Canada (Treasury Board), [1987] 2 SCR 84.

Rudner, S, "Workplace Investigations and Suspensions" (22 November 2018), online: <https://www.rudnerlaw.ca/workplace-investigations-suspensions/>.

Same-Sex Marriage, Reference re, 2004 SCC 79.

Sangha v Mackenzie Valley Land and Water Board, 2006 CHRT 9, judicial review allowed, 2007 FC 856.

Seneca College v Bhadauria, [1981] 2 SCR 181.

Shah v Xerox Canada Ltd, 2000 CanLII 2317 (Ont CA).

Shakes v Rex Pak Limited, 1982 3 CHRR D/1001.

Shaw v Levac Supply Ltd, 1990 14 CHRR D/36 (Ont BI).

Sidhu v Broadway Gallery, 2002 BCHRT 9.

Silliker, A, "Workplaces Have 'Role to Play' in Mental Health," *Canadian HR Reporter* (4 June 2012), online: < https://www.hrreporter.com/news/hr-news/workplaces-have-role-to-play-in-mental-health/314506>.

SMS Equipment Inc v Communications, Energy and Paperworkers Union, Local 707, 2015 ABQB 162.

Standryk, Leanne, "Update on Random Drug Testing in Safety Sensitive Workplace: Supreme Court of Canada Quashes Random Testing" (5 July 2013), online: <http://lbwlawyers.com/update-on-random-drug-testing-in-safety-sensitive-workplace-supreme-court-of-canada-quashes-random-testing>.

Star Choice Television Network Inc v Tatulea, 2012 CLAD No 32 (QL).

Stewart v Ontario (Government Services), 2013 HRTO 1635.

Suncor Energy Inc v Unifor Local 707A, 2017 ABCA 313.

Syndicat Northcrest v Amselem, 2004 SCC 47.

Talos v Grand Erie District School Board, 2018 HRTO 680.

Turner v Canada Border Services Agency, 2014 CHRT 10.

United Nurses of Alberta v Alberta Health Services, 2019 ABQB 255.

University of British Columbia v Kelly, 2016 BCCA 271.

Vriend v Alberta, [1998] 1 SCR 493.

Williams, L & D Nave, "Meeting the Challenge: Considerations for Accommodating Mental Illness" in *The Six-Minute Employment Lawyer 2013* (Toronto: Law Society of Ontario, 2013).

WorkSafeBC, "Bullying and Harassment Resource Tool Kit," online: <https://www.worksafebc.com/en/health-safety/hazards-exposures/bullying-harassment/resource-tool-kit>.

Yue v District of Maple Ridge, 2008 BCHRT 379.

Zabrovsky, Andrew, "Federal Court of Appeal Upholds *Johnstone*, Clarifies Nature and Scope of Family Status Protections," *FTR Now* (5 May 2014), online: <http://hicksmorley.com/2014/05/05/federal-court-of-appeal-upholds-johnstone-clarifies-nature-and-scope-of-family-status-protections>.

Occupational Health and Safety Legislation

8

LEARNING OUTCOMES

After completing this chapter, you will be able to:

- Understand the internal responsibility system that underlies the health and safety legislation of British Columbia and Alberta.
- Outline the health and safety duties of the parties in the workplace.
- Identify workers' rights under workers' compensation legislation in British Columbia and occupational health and safety legislation in Alberta, including refusal of unsafe work, participation through the joint health and safety committee, and knowledge of workplace hazards.
- Understand the legal requirements surrounding workplace violence and harassment.
- State the accident-reporting requirements under the health and safety legislation of British Columbia and Alberta.
- Explain how the legislation and regulations are administered and enforced, and describe the test of due diligence.
- Identify the provisions in the *Criminal Code* related to the employer's health and safety obligations.

Introduction

Workplace health and safety must be embedded into the culture of every employer and workplace. It needs to be seen as a value of the organization, not simply a priority, because the cost of on-the-job accidents—in terms of human suffering, lost time and production, workplace safety and insurance claims, fines, and other penalties—is extremely high.

IN THE NEWS

Workplace Accidents on YouTube

To get the message across to cyber-savvy youth in British Columbia, WorkSafeBC is posting real life videos of tragic workplace accidents on YouTube at <https://www.youtube.com/user/worksafebc>. It appears that people are taking notice. A video showing how a 16-year-old forklift driver broke his back, together with an interview with the driver, was posted on YouTube on January 17, 2008. The video soon garnered over a million hits, and now had 3.8 million at the time of writing. Scott McCloy of WorkSafeBC hopes that the message will sink in and help change young people's perception of invincibility, and ultimately change their behaviour.

The Alberta Ministry of Labour has its own YouTube channels: "Bloody Lucky" (<https://www.youtube.com/user/bloodyluckyvids>), which posts videos to promote on-the-job safety to workers, and "Work Safe" (<https://www.youtube.com/user/AlbertaWorkSafe>), which posts videos and advertisements to promote occupational health and safety.

Several statutes and regulations address health and safety in the British Columbia (BC) and Alberta workplace. In BC there is the *Workers Compensation Act* (WCA), part 3 of which is devoted to occupational health and safety, as well as the *Occupational Health and Safety Regulation* (OHSR), an extensive set of rules created under that part of the WCA. In Alberta, the *Occupational Health and Safety Act* (OHSA), *Occupational Health and Safety Regulation* (OHSR), *Occupational Health and Safety Code* (OHS Code), and *Workers' Compensation Act* (WCA) and its regulations codify the legislation in this area. The OHS legislation focuses on promoting a safe and healthy workplace and preventing work-related accidents and diseases. In both provinces, the WCA also covers the compensation and rehabilitation of workers who are injured or who contract a disease related to the workplace (see Chapter 9).

IN THE NEWS

Recent Updates to Alberta Legislation

In Alberta, the exemption of farm and ranch workers from workplace safety standards has been an issue for a number of years. The ever-present risks associated with farm and ranch work, combined with the fact that Alberta was the only province where OHS standards did not apply to farm and ranch workers, caused the newly elected NDP government to review this exclusion in 2015 and table new regulations to protect these workers. The proposed legislation, titled *Bill 6: Enhanced Protection for Farm and Ranch Workers Act*, was tabled in the fall of 2015. The draft legislation received a mixed reception from Alberta farmers and ranchers, with serious concerns being raised.

Despite its good intentions, many farmers and ranchers protested that the draft legislation constituted an unwarranted imposition on their family farming/ranching operations and an assault on their cherished way of life. Responding to the strong backlash, the Alberta government clarified that the new rules were intended to target farm and ranch operations that employ paid workers; they would not apply to owners, family members of owners, or other related volunteer or educational activities.

The Bill was amended to reflect this focus, passed in Alberta's Legislature on December 10, 2015, and came into force on January 1, 2016. It provided that wage-earning farm and ranch employees in Alberta, like other provinces, are protected by basic OHS safety standards. Under those basic standards, the employer is responsible to ensure, as far as is reasonably practicable, the health and safety of their paid workers on their worksite and workers are responsible to work safely and to cooperate with the employer in maintaining a safe workplace.

Farms and ranches employing at least one paid, non-family worker are covered. However, the OHS standards apply to an operation only when a paid worker is present and only to the paid workers at the workplace. OHS standards do not apply to family members of the owner of a farm or ranch operation, to the private residence (which includes areas around the home like the lawn area, backyard, or garden), or when people are doing non-work-related activities on their land, such as recreational activities like horseback riding or hunting.

While the basic OHS standards came into effect in Alberta on January 1, 2016, the government also committed that it would undertake consultations with farmers and ranchers over the following 18 to 24 months to develop detailed technical rules and regulations for farms and ranches. These amended rules and regulations consider the unique aspects of this industry. For example, some of the changes include allowing the use of older equipment with procedures to ensure worker safety, the provision not to have to wear a seatbelt at low speeds, and the ability to use a front-end loader to raise a worker if there's no other option. The United Conservative government, elected in 2018, reviewed the changes to the legislation and introduced the *Farm Freedom and Safety Act*, which received Royal Assent in December of 2019. Farms and ranches are still required to follow the *Occupational Health and Safety Act* but are now exempt from the specific standards required by the *OHS Regulations* or the *Code*.

The Internal Responsibility System

Most provinces' health and safety legislation is based on a system of joint responsibility, which is referred to as the **internal responsibility system**. This is the "people framework" of an effective occupational health and safety management system. This system is based on the premise that government alone cannot effectively regulate all workplace risks. Instead, the law emphasizes the participation and accountability of all parties in the workplace to ensure a healthy and safe environment.

In the internal responsibility system, **joint health and safety committees (JHSCs)** play an important role. In most provinces (nine of ten), including BC and Alberta, these are mandatory in all workplaces with 20 or more workers or where required by order.

A JHSC is composed of management and worker representatives who collectively exercise specific powers. In BC workplaces with 10 to 19 workers, a single **health and safety representative** exercises most of the same powers. In Alberta, section 17 of the OHSA has the same rule for workplaces with between 5 and 19 workers.

The BC OHSR (s 3.12) and the Alberta OHSA (s 31) give workers the right and responsibility to refuse unsafe work. In BC, Workers Compensation Board officers

internal responsibility system
the "people framework" of an effective occupational health and safety management system, based on the premise that government alone cannot effectively regulate all workplace risks; instead, the law emphasizes the participation by and accountability of all parties in the workplace to ensure a healthy and safe environment

joint health and safety committee (JHSC)
an advisory health and safety body that is composed of equal numbers of management and worker representatives; generally required in workplaces with 20 or more workers

health and safety representative a person who exercises rights and powers similar to those of the joint health and safety committee; required in workplaces with 6 to 19 employees

and, in Alberta, occupational health and safety officers may be called in where the workplace parties are unable to resolve an issue. Parties who fail to fulfill their obligations are subject to significant fines.

Who Is Covered?

BC's OHSR and Alberta's OHSA cover most workers and workplaces in the provinces. Part I, division 2(a) of the BC WCA stipulates that the OHSR will apply to "every employer and worker whose occupational health and safety are ordinarily within the jurisdiction of the government of British Columbia." "Worker" is given a very broad, though detailed, definition in section 1 of the BC WCA; and section 1(aaa) of the Alberta OHSA defines a worker as "a person engaged in an occupation." An individual need not be an "employee" in the legal sense of the term to be covered by the legislation. Anyone paid to perform work or supply services, including an independent contractor, is protected.

"Workplace" is defined broadly in section 106 of the BC WCA as "any place where a worker is or is likely to be engaged in any work and includes any vessel, vehicle or mobile equipment used by a worker in work." The Alberta legislation uses the term "work site." Section 1(bbb) of the Alberta OHSA defines "work site" as "a location where a worker is, or is likely to be, engaged in any occupation and includes any vehicle or mobile equipment used by a worker in an occupation." The only workplaces that are not covered are workplaces under federal jurisdiction, which are subject to the *Canada Labour Code*, or workplaces where work is done by an owner, occupant, or servant in a private residence or its connected land. In other words, the only provincially regulated workers not covered by the OHS legislation are individuals who come into a residence and are directly employed by the occupant, as in the case of a nanny.

Duties of the Workplace Parties

The BC WCA and the Alberta OHSA place duties and impose accountability on everyone involved with the workplace: employers, contractors, supervisors, owners, suppliers, licensees, officers of a corporation, and workers. In BC, an "owner" includes a tenant, trustee, receiver, or occupier of the land on which the workplace is situated as well as a person who acts on behalf of an owner as an agent or delegate (s 106 of the WCA). The Alberta definition of "owner" is "the person who is registered under the *Land Titles Act* as the owner of the land on which work is being carried out or may be carried out, or the person who enters into an agreement with the owner to be responsible for meeting the owner's obligations under this Act, the regulations and the OHS Code, but does not include a person who occupies land or premises used as a private residence unless a business, trade or profession is carried on in that premises" (s 1(ll) of the OHSA). Where the OHS legislation is breached, several workplace parties, including supervisors and workers, may be found personally liable along with the employer and may be fined for breaching their duties under the

OHS legislation. These duties are set out in sections 115–117 of the BC WCA and section 3 of the Alberta OHSA.

The Alberta OHSA (amended in 2018) defines four new worksite parties and their responsibilities. The amended Act also expands the obligations of existing worksite parties. These new parties include supervisors, service providers, self-employed persons, and temporary staffing agencies. These groups now have the legal responsibility to protect workers under their supervision and in proximity to their worksite, to ensure workers are suitable for assigned tasks, and to report unsafe or harmful worksite acts or conditions to Alberta Labour. The updated OHSA also updates and expands the responsibilities of existing groups, including owners, employers, suppliers, prime contractors, and contractors.

FYI

Key Features of Occupational Health and Safety Provisions

1. The occupational health and safety legislation focuses on *prevention* of workplace accidents and diseases. It is for this reason that BC rebranded its Workers Compensation Board as WorkSafeBC.
2. The premise behind the legislation is that the workplace parties share the responsibility and accountability for occupational health and safety because they are best placed to identify health and safety problems and to develop solutions. This approach is called the *internal responsibility system*.
3. The framework of *general rights and responsibilities* of the workplace parties is complemented by the *specific requirements* related to particular industries and hazards, contained in numerous regulations enacted in support of the legislation.
4. *All "workers," not just employees*, are covered by occupational health and safety provisions. This includes independent contractors, workers engaged in subtrades, and employees or workers of other employers who happen to be in the workplace.
5. Under the BC *Workers Compensation Act*, the Alberta *Occupational Health and Safety Act*, and their respective regulations, workers have the following core rights:
   a. the right to participate in identifying and resolving health and safety concerns, primarily through the joint health and safety committee or, in smaller workplaces, the health and safety representative;
   b. the right and responsibility to refuse work they believe is dangerous to themselves or another worker; and
   c. the right to know about potential hazards to which they may be exposed, through training and the Workplace Hazardous Materials Information System (WHMIS).
6. Penalties for violating occupational health and safety provisions include fines and penalties or even terms of imprisonment.
7. In BC, occupational health and safety is administered by the workers' compensation board, which does business as WorkSafeBC and reports to the Minister of Labour. In Alberta, it is administered by the Ministry of Labour and Immigration.

Employer's Duties

Under both the BC WCA and the Alberta OHSA, employers have an overriding general duty to take every reasonable precaution to protect the health and safety of their own workers and any other workers present at a workplace where work for those employers is being carried out, and they are accountable for doing so. This accountability carries through all levels of management to the worksite, where the immediate manager or supervisor is responsible for carrying out the employer's duties as agents of the employer. In addition, employers have numerous specific obligations, including the duty to:

1. comply with all parts of the BC WCA or the Alberta OHSA, the Regulations, and specific orders (e.g., an order issued by an occupational health and safety officer);
2. ensure that workers are made aware of all known or reasonably foreseeable health or safety hazards associated with their work to which they might be exposed;
3. ensure that workers are made aware of their rights and duties under the Act and Regulations;
4. establish occupational health and safety policies and programs in compliance with the BC Regulations and, in Alberta, with the Regulations and OHS Code;
5. provide and maintain in good condition protective equipment, devices, and clothing and ensure that they are used;
6. provide workers with the information, training, and supervision necessary to ensure the health and safety of workers;
7. keep posted a copy of the WCA and Regulations in BC, and the OHSA, Regulations, and OHS Code in Alberta, readily available for workers at the worksite;
8. help JHSCs and health and safety representatives carry out their duties;
9. cooperate with WorkSafeBC, its officers, and other persons carrying out any duty under the WCA or the Regulations, or the Alberta workplace health and safety officers performing those duties;
10. refuse to employ underage workers (minimum age requirements depend on the workplace: a person must be at least 16 to work on a construction or logging project, 15 to work in a factory, and 14 to work elsewhere);
11. keep accurate records of biological, chemical, or physical agents as required by the regulations; and
12. report accidents, injury, or illness.

Workers' Duties

The BC WCA and the Alberta OHSA impose obligations on workers (including all levels of managers and supervisors, who are both agents of the employer and workers at the same time), including the duty to:

1. comply with the statutes and their regulations;
2. use or wear any equipment, protective device, or clothing required by the regulations;

3. report any missing or defective equipment or protective device that may create a danger and, in BC, to report proposed changes to equipment or machinery that may affect worker health and safety;
4. report any known workplace hazard;
5. refuse to engage in any horseplay or similar conduct that may endanger the worker or any other person (such as racing forklifts in a warehouse);
6. ensure that their ability to work without risk to themselves or others is not impaired by alcohol, drugs, or other causes;
7. cooperate with the joint health and safety committee or worker health and safety representative; and
8. cooperate with occupational health and safety officers, the workers' compensation board and its officers, and any other persons carrying out duties under the OHSA, WCA, or its Regulations.

WorkSafeBC and the Alberta Ministry of Labour and Immigration rarely charge a worker for violating the WCA or OHSA (Keith & Chandler, 2014, at 51). Employers, however, must effectively address situations where employees fail to comply with health and safety requirements. An employer who fails to do so is arguably condoning an employee's breach and therefore is in violation of its obligations.

Unless a breach is serious, employers typically respond with progressive performance management interventions. This involves the use of gradually escalating levels of discipline, starting with a verbal warning and counselling and moving to a written warning, possibly a suspension, and even dismissal. Appropriate corrective action for a minor breach might entail a mandatory safety talk and counselling regarding the violation (Keith & Chandler, 2014, at 17). However, if a worker intentionally disables a safety device in an effort to make their job go faster, for example, the breach is serious enough to warrant a written warning or suspension, assuming the worker previously received safety training and the employer consistently enforces safety rules. *USWA Local 862 v Canadian General Tower Ltd* involved an employee who grieved his dismissal for tampering with the safety button on a machine.

CASE IN POINT

Employee Dismissed for Tampering with Machinery

Canadian General Tower Ltd and USWA, Loc 862 (Schramm) (Re), [2003] OLAA No 801 (QL)

Facts

The employer's poor safety record had resulted in several accidents and charges from the Ontario Ministry of Labour. After an accident involving a paper rewinder, a ministry inspector issued an order that directed the employer to ensure that a safety button on this machine was not taped down. Taping the button did not improve productivity, but it allowed the machine to run without an operator's finger on the button. The employer posted the order in the workplace and presented a letter to each operator at individual meetings called to discuss the matter.

Despite these discussions, an employee, Schramm, taped down the button. The machine operator on the next shift, unaware that the button was taped down, was slightly injured as a result. Schramm apologized for the incident but was fired the next day. The employer claimed that it had taken every reasonable precaution but could not protect itself from an employee who knowingly put himself and others at risk. Schramm grieved the dismissal.

Relevant Issue

Whether the employer had just cause to dismiss the employee for tampering with the safety button.

Decision

The arbitrator refused to reinstate Schramm. He found that a company must be armed with the right to discharge employees for safety violations of the kind committed by Schramm or it will not be able to meet its due diligence obligations. He rejected Schramm's view that it was not a safety infraction because the button was not a safety mechanism, stating:

> The accelerator pedal on an automobile would not normally be a "safety" device but tying it down in some way could have significant consequences for the safe operation of a vehicle. (at para 31)

Supervisors' Duties

The BC *Occupational Health and Safety Regulation* applies to all employers, workers, and "all other persons working in or contributing to the production of any industry within the scope of Part 3 of the *Workers Compensation Act*" (s 2.1 of the OHSR). These "other persons" include supervisors, prime contractors, owners, suppliers, and directors and officers of a corporation. The duties of supervisors are spelled out in section 117 of the WCA and they include:

1. ensuring the health and safety of all workers under their supervision;
2. being knowledgeable about the WCA and its Regulations as they apply to the work being supervised;
3. complying with the WCA, its Regulations, and any applicable orders;
4. ensuring that workers under their supervision are made aware of all known or reasonably foreseeable health or safety hazards in the area where they work;
5. consulting and cooperating with the JHSCs and safety representatives; and
6. cooperating with the WCB, its officers, and anyone else carrying out duties under the WCA or its Regulations.

In Alberta, there is no specific reference to supervisors in the OHSA, but they wear two hats: they are agents of the employer and they are workers, as captured under the broad definition of "worker" in section 1(ccc). Their obligations include both those of employers and those of workers. As agents of the employer, supervisors must:

> (a) as far as it is reasonably practicable for the supervisor to do so,
>
> (i) ensure that the supervisor is competent to supervise every worker under the supervisor's supervision,
>
> (ii) take all precautions necessary to protect the health and safety of every worker under the supervisor's supervision,
>
> (iii) ensure that a worker under the supervisor's supervision works in the manner and in accordance with the procedures and measures required by this Act, the regulations and the OHS code,

(iv) ensure that every worker under the supervisor's supervision uses all hazard controls, and properly uses or wears personal protective equipment designated or provided by the employer or required to be used or worn by this Act, the regulations or the OHS code, and

(v) ensure that none of the workers under the supervisor's supervision are subjected to or participate in harassment or violence at the work site,

(b) advise every worker under the supervisor's supervision of all known or reasonably foreseeable hazards to health and safety in the area where the worker is performing work,

(c) report to the employer a concern about an unsafe or harmful work site act that occurs or has occurred or an unsafe or harmful work site condition that exists or has existed,

(d) cooperate with any person exercising a duty imposed by this Act, the regulations and the OHS code, and

(e) comply with this Act, the regulations and the OHS code.

An individual need not have the title "supervisor" or "manager" to be a supervisor. A lead hand who is covered by a collective agreement may qualify if they have supervisory functions.

Prime Contractors' Duties

Section 118 of the BC WCA and section 10 of the Alberta OHSA make reference to a "prime contractor." In Alberta, every worksite with two or more employers involved in work at the site must have a prime contractor (s 10(1)). The prime contractor is usually the directing contractor at **multiple-employer workplaces**—workplaces where workers of two or more employers are working at the same time. These prime contractors have duties that include:

multiple-employer workplaces workplaces where workers of two or more employers are working at the same time

1. ensuring that the activities of all parties at the workplace that relate to occupational health and safety are coordinated, and
2. doing everything reasonably practicable to establish and maintain a system or process in compliance with the BC WCA or Alberta OHSA and their Regulations.

Owners' Duties

Owners' duties include:

1. providing and maintaining premises being used as a worksite in a way that ensures the health and safety of anyone at or near the worksite;
2. providing employers or prime contractors at the worksite with any information necessary to identify and prevent hazards to the health or safety of persons at the worksite; and
3. complying with the BC WCA, the Alberta OHSA, their Regulations, and any applicable orders.

Suppliers' Duties

In BC, every person who supplies workplace equipment, tools, machines, or devices must ensure that they are in good condition and comply with the WCA and its Regulations. A supplier is defined in section 106 of the Act to be anyone who "manufactures, supplies, sells, leases, distributes, erects or installs" such equipment. Biological, chemical, or physical agents are also identified as being materials that can be supplied.

Similarly, in Alberta, every supplier "shall ensure, as far as it is reasonably practicable for the supplier to do so, that any tool, appliance or equipment that the supplier supplies is in safe operating condition" (s 6(1) of the OHSA). Furthermore, a supplier has to ensure that equipment, harmful substances, and explosives comply with the OHSA, the Regulations, and the OHS Code (s 6(1) of the OHSA).

Duties of Corporate Officers and Directors

Corporate officers and directors must take all reasonable care to ensure that their company complies with the BC WCA, the Alberta OHSA, the Regulations of both provinces, and any orders and requirements of WorkSafeBC or the Alberta Ministry of Labour and Immigration. By placing duties directly on officers and directors, the legislation encourages senior management to take a serious interest in compliance with health and safety requirements.

Workers' Rights

Under the BC WCA, the Alberta OHSA, and their Regulations, workers have three key rights:

1. to participate in the health and safety process,
2. to refuse unsafe work, and
3. to know about workplace hazards.

The Right to Participate in the Health and Safety Process

The JHSC and Health and Safety Representatives

Division 4 (ss 125–140) of the BC WCA and section 16 of the Alberta OHSA set out the rules regarding JHSCs and health and safety representatives.

The JHSC is an important element of an effective internal responsibility system. It is an advisory group of worker and management representatives that has statutory powers. Members meet regularly to discuss health and safety concerns, review progress, and make recommendations on health and safety issues.

In BC, a JHSC is required in every workplace where 20 or more workers are regularly employed, or in any other workplace where a WorkSafeBC order requires them. Section 126 of the WCA allows the WCB to make special variations from the usual and otherwise mandatory arrangements. In BC workplaces with between 10 and 19 workers, section 139 of the WCA allows a worker health and safety representative to take the place of a JHSC, exercising most of the powers and responsibilities of a JHSC. In Alberta, section 17 of the OHSA has the same rule for workplaces with between 5 and 19 workers. An employer cannot interfere in the choice of the worker health and safety representative; they must be selected by workers who do not exercise managerial functions. Where the workers are unionized, the union selects the representative.

Structure of the JHSC

The employer is responsible for ensuring that a JHSC is established in accordance with the requirements of the BC WCA or Alberta OHSA and OHS Code. These requirements are set out below:

1. In Alberta and BC, a JHSC in a workplace with 20 or more workers must have at least four members. Regulations can dictate a higher number for certain workplaces (s 127(a) of the WCA).
2. Worker members must be employed in the workplace covered by the JHSC. In BC, management members may be chosen from another of the employer's workplaces if there are no managerial employees at the workplace covered by the JHSC.
3. At least half of the JHSC members must be worker representatives selected by workers. An employer is prohibited from having any involvement in the selection of the worker members. If a trade union represents the workers, the worker members must be selected by the union.
4. A JHSC must be co-chaired by one member selected by the worker representatives and one member selected by the management representatives.
5. There is no maximum number of JHSC members.
6. The names and work locations of the JHSC members must be posted in a conspicuous location in the workplace.
7. The JHSC must meet at the workplace at least once each month, unless a regulation or order specifies otherwise.
8. The employer must pay JHSC members for time off to prepare for and to attend each JHSC meeting, and for time spent performing certain other committee duties, such as conducting monthly inspections.
9. In BC, the JHSC must complete a report for each meeting (s 137 of the WCA). A copy of that report must be sent to the employer, who must retain it for at least two years, and it must be accessible to committee members, workers, officers, and WorkSafeBC.
10. The BC WCA entitles each JHSC member to an annual educational leave of eight hours, or longer if necessary, to attend approved occupational health and safety training courses (s 135). There is no specific comparable entitlement in the Alberta legislation.

Powers and Duties of the JHSC

An effective JHSC plays a central role in spotting dangers in the workplace and looking for solutions to health and safety problems. The main functions of the JHSC in Alberta include the following:

1. *Identifying potentially dangerous situations in the workplace.* Machinery that lacks protective devices, harmful substances, and dangerous working conditions are some of the matters that should alert JHSC members. The workplace should be inspected at least once a month. Where the size of the workplace makes this impractical, the JHSC should set up an inspection schedule that ensures that part of the workplace is inspected each month and the entire workplace is inspected at least once a year.
2. *Obtaining information from the employer regarding workplace hazards.* The JHSC should obtain information from the employer regarding actual or potential hazards in the workplace, as well as the health and safety experience and standards in similar workplaces of which the employer is aware. It can also ask the employer for information concerning health and safety–related testing and have a worker committee member present at the beginning of the testing to validate the procedures and results.
3. *Making recommendations to the employer for improving workplace health and safety.* Recommendations could cover anything from new or modified safety training programs to additional protective devices. Although an employer need not comply with JHSC recommendations, it must respond in writing to any written recommendations.
4. *Investigating work refusals.*
5. *Investigating serious injuries in the workplace.*

In BC, the main functions of the JHSC include the following (s 130 of the WCA):

1. *Identifying unhealthy or unsafe situations in the workplace.* This includes giving advice on implementing effective systems for responding to such situations. It also involves considering and dealing as quickly as possible with all complaints relating to the health and safety of workers.
2. *Consulting with workers and employers on safety matters.* The JHSC is required to make recommendations to the employer and the workers for improvements in the health and safety and occupational environment of the workers. This includes recommending educational programs that serve to promote the health and safety of workers in compliance with the legislation and monitoring their effectiveness.
3. *Advising the employer on programs, policies, and changes under the regulations.* This advice can extend to proposed changes to the workplace or work processes that could affect the health or safety of workers. This ensures that accident investigations and regular inspections are conducted as required under the legislation.
4. *Participating in inspections, investigations, and inquiries relating to the legislation.*

The Right and Responsibility to Refuse Unsafe Work

Under section 3.12 of the BC OHSR and section 31 of the Alberta OHSA, every worker has the right (in fact, the duty) to refuse unsafe work. This right is restricted for some occupations, either because danger is an inherent part of the job or because exercising the right would expose others to danger. Restrictions apply to police officers, firefighters, and persons employed in operating a correctional facility, hospital, nursing home, or ambulance service. For example, a police officer cannot refuse to follow a suspect carrying a gun on the ground that the situation is dangerous. An officer can, however, refuse to operate a police car that they believe has faulty brakes because driving a defective vehicle is not a danger inherent to the job.

When Can the Right and Responsibility to Refuse Unsafe Work Be Exercised?

In BC, any worker may refuse work when they have reasonable cause to believe that:

- the equipment they are to use,
- the physical condition of the workplace, or
- a contravention of the legislation relating to the equipment or workplace would "create an undue hazard to the health and safety of any person" (s 3.12 of the OHSR).

In Alberta, no worker shall carry out any work if, on reasonable and probable grounds, the worker believes there exists an imminent danger or an imminent danger will be created either by the work or by the operation of any tool, appliance, or equipment (s 31(1) of the OHSA).

Generally speaking, the OHS legislation work refusal provisions have received a broad interpretation, provided that the refusal is based on genuine health and safety concerns.

In *Inco Metals*, the Ontario Labour Relations Board held that valid employee refusals can arise in a group setting if each employee shares a common safety-related concern. Moreover, if the employees genuinely and reasonably believe that the work is unsafe, it is irrelevant that subsequent investigation reveals that no real danger existed.

CASE IN POINT

Employees Entitled to Act in Concert

Inco Metals Co, [1980] OLRB Rep July 981

Facts

The employees, who worked in a copper refinery, saw a hole in the ceiling of an anode furnace. Shortly after they finished their shift, the hole was patched, but fire was later seen coming through the ceiling of the furnace, and two other employees refused to "tap" the furnace because they believed it would be unsafe. Management called Ontario Ministry of Labour inspectors, but copper sheeting and fireproof cloth prevented them from determining whether the problem was serious. Members of management who were familiar with anode furnaces assured them that the roof was unlikely to collapse, and the inspectors accepted their opinion that the furnace was safe. The inspectors directed that work proceed with an additional employee to detect any surges of molten copper.

When the employees returned for their shift, they found a patch over the hole and flames coming out the edges. They were informed that the tapper on the preceding shift had exercised his right to refuse work and that safety inspectors had been called in. The crew refused to tap the furnace. The foreman brought in a member of the JHSC, who called the inspector. The inspector, who had less experience than members of management, adopted their view and made an order allowing work to continue. However, the employees continued to refuse to work. The employer sent them home for the rest of their shift and placed a disciplinary note on their files. Employees on the subsequent shift agreed to tap the furnace, and after that job was safely done, the furnace was shut down and the hole was fixed.

The employees filed a complaint with the Ontario Labour Relations Board, alleging that they had been disciplined for exercising their right to refuse work under the Ontario OHSA. The employer argued that by acting as a group, they were engaging in an action akin to an unlawful strike and that they lacked reasonable grounds for believing that the work was unsafe.

Relevant Issue

Whether the employer's disciplinary actions were unlawful under the OHSA.

Decision

The Ontario Labour Relations Board ruled in favour of the employees. It held that legitimate work refusals can occur where several employees share a common safety concern. The issue is whether the employees had reasonable cause to believe that the work was unsafe when they exercised their right to refuse to work. It is irrelevant that subsequent events proved that there was no danger when the employees exercised their right. Moreover, the Board found that the employees were still acting within their rights when they refused to return to work after the inspector ordered that work proceed. Because they knew that the inspector was basing his decision on the assurances of management, they had no confidence that this order reflected a neutral assessment of the situation.

As a result of these findings, the employer was ordered to reimburse the employees for the hours of work they lost when they were sent home and to eliminate the disciplinary notes from their records (Gilbert, Burkett, & McCaskill, 2000, at 293).

In *Lennox Industries*, the employer was found to be in violation of the Ontario OHSA anti-reprisal sections when it disciplined a worker whose concern about safety originated because of his reaction to the supervisor's proximity during an argument. The arbitrator found that the work refusal provisions of the OHSA applied because the worker's belief that he was in danger of being hurt was genuine.

CASE IN POINT

Reaction to Supervisor's Proximity Justifies Work Refusal

Lennox Industries (Canada) Limited v United Steelworkers of America, Local 7235, 1999 CanLII 20394 (Ont LA)

Facts

On investigating a work slowdown, a production supervisor found that the problem stemmed from the fact that a worker was away from his workstation, talking to a co-worker. The supervisor told the worker to return to work, but the worker indicated that there were "no parts" to work on in his area. The discussion developed into an unpleasant confrontation, with the worker asking the supervisor, "Are you intimidating me?" and stating to the co-worker, "I can't work like this. Can you work like this?" The worker said that he felt unsafe and wanted a health and safety representative to be called. The supervisor did not call the health and safety representative.

Instead, he removed the worker from the line because production was backed up and gave him a two-day suspension for insubordination. In the log book, the supervisor wrote that the worker "refused to get back to work stating that it was unsafe to resume working *my [sic] being so close to him*."

The worker grieved the imposition of discipline, arguing that it constituted a reprisal for asserting his right under the Ontario OHSA to refuse unsafe work. The basis for his refusal was that the supervisor was standing 1 foot away "hollering, coercing, and intimidating him," his hands were shaking, and he was afraid that he would slip and cut himself on the steel edge of the materials he was handling. The employer argued that the worker did not fit within any of the protections allowed in the OHSA because he was making no claim that any "equipment, machine, device or thing" that he was "using or operating" was likely to endanger him.

Relevant Issue

Whether the employer violated the OHSA by disciplining the worker in these circumstances.

Decision

The arbitrator found in favour of the worker. During the first stage of a work refusal, a worker may refuse to work "where he has reason to believe" danger exists. On the evidence, the worker had a subjective belief that he was in an unsafe situation. Once the worker communicated his concern about the supervisor's proximity, the supervisor was obliged to investigate the complaint in the presence of the health and safety representative. The arbitrator ordered that the worker's suspension be rescinded, that he be compensated for all wages lost, and that his personnel record be amended by removing all references to this incident.

Procedure for Exercising the Right and Responsibility to Refuse Unsafe Work

The procedure for exercising the right to refuse unsafe work is set out in section 3.12 of the BC OHSR and section 31 of the Alberta OHSA.

FIRST STAGE OF REFUSAL

Initially, the right to refuse work is based on the worker's personal belief. In BC, as long as a worker has reasonable cause to believe that carrying out any work process or operating any tool, appliance, or equipment would create an undue hazard to the health and safety of themselves or another worker, they may refuse to work (s 3.12 of the OHSR). The perceived danger need not be imminent or likely to result in serious bodily injury. In contrast, in Alberta, a worker has a responsibility to refuse work if they believe, on reasonable and probable grounds, that an imminent danger exists or that carrying out the work would create an imminent danger (s 31(1) of the OHSA).

A worker who is exercising this right must immediately tell their supervisor or employer that they are refusing to work and state the circumstances. The supervisor or employer must immediately investigate the matter and either ensure that the unsafe condition is remedied without delay or inform the worker that in their opinion the report lacks validity.

The employer may require a worker to remain at the worksite and may reassign the worker temporarily to another work assignment. The employer must pay the worker during the first stage of refusal.

SECOND STAGE OF REFUSAL

If, in BC, the worker who refused unsafe work is not satisfied with the results of the supervisor's or employer's investigation, the supervisor or employer must conduct further investigation into the matter in the presence of the worker who made the report as well as a JHSC member or a trade union representative or, in the absence of either of those, "any other reasonably available worker selected by the worker" (s 3.12(4) of the OHSR). At this stage, the matter could be resolved and either the problem would be rectified or, if the employer believes the situation was not or no longer is unsafe, the employer may be able to persuade the worker to resume work.

In Alberta, however, there is no equivalent to this second stage of refusal. If the worker believes that an imminent danger still exists, or that carrying out the work would create an imminent danger, they proceed directly to filing a complaint with an occupational health and safety officer.

THIRD STAGE OF REFUSAL

In BC, if the matter has not been resolved and the worker still refuses to work after the second stage, the supervisor or employer and the worker must immediately notify an officer of WorkSafeBC of the matter (s 3.12(5) of the OHSR). This person "must investigate the matter without undue delay" and then issue whatever order is necessary. The perceived workplace hazard will be removed or rectified or the worker will be asked to resume their duties.

In Alberta, the investigating officer must investigate the refusal and provide a record to the employer as well as to the worker with respect to the cause of the work refusal, the investigation performed, and what action was taken to address the investigation results (s 32(3) of the OHSA).

In both BC and Alberta, the worker, while waiting for the results of the investigation, remains at a safe place near their workstation unless the employer assigns them temporary alternative work. There will be no loss of pay for this alternative work until the matter has been resolved. Alternatively, subject to an applicable collective agreement or employment contract, the employer may send the worker home if no other work is available and the inspection takes considerable time to complete. The employer must not send the employee home as a form of reprisal.

Pending the officer's decision, if the employer believes the situation was not or no longer is unsafe, they may ask another employee to do the disputed work only if that employee is advised of the work refusal and the reasons for it. The replacement worker has the same rights of refusal as the first worker.

The officer must make a decision in writing. If the officer finds that the situation is unsafe, they may issue an order requiring the employer to take the necessary corrective measures. Conversely, if the officer agrees with the employer's position, no order will be made. The officer's decision may be appealed by the party who disagrees with it.

No Reprisal

Section 151 of the BC WCA and section 35 of the Alberta OHSA prohibit an employer from penalizing a worker in any way for exercising their rights or carrying out any duty under the BC OHSR or Alberta OHSA, including the right and responsibility to refuse unsafe work. Such penalties constitute discrimination under section 150 of the WCA. An employee who believes they have suffered a reprisal may institute a grievance procedure if the workplace is unionized. Otherwise, the employee may file a written complaint with WorkSafeBC or with an Alberta occupational health and safety officer. In circumstances where the employer alleges that the refusal was improper, the onus is on the employer to prove that the refusal was improper.

Limits to the Right and Responsibility to Refuse Unsafe Work

The right to refuse unsafe work is broad but not unlimited. Employees cannot refuse to work for reasons unrelated to their own safety, such as pressuring the employer on a collective bargaining issue or retaliating for their belief that another employee is being required to perform unsafe work. Employees who refuse work must have a sufficiently close relationship to the perceived danger to justify an honest belief that they are in danger or that they would put another employee in danger by performing the work. An employee who refuses unsafe work cannot subsequently refuse other work that is not unsafe (Gilbert, Burkett, & McCaskill, 2000, at 295). Decision No 2001-2562 is a case involving an alleged employer reprisal for a work refusal.

CASE IN POINT

Refusal to Perform Unsafe Work

Decision No 2001-2562, Workers' Compensation Reporter (2001), vol 18, no 1 at 103 (BC Workers' Compensation Board, Appeal Division)

Facts

The employer operated a meat and other foods processing plant. Its employee guidelines stipulated that all workers were expected to have good personal hygiene, neat clothing, and proper footwear while on the job. The footwear was required to be left at the plant when the worker left; otherwise, it would have to be sterilized. The firm's policy was to buy boots for its workers or to reimburse them up to $25 to buy their own. The employer also kept on hand a supply of "common boots" for visitors on plant tours or who were there for other reasons.

The worker arrived at the plant on February 8 with boots that had holes in them. He asked for a replacement pair from the employer. Because ordering a replacement pair would usually take about three days, the employer suggested he buy a new pair and get reimbursed for $25. When the worker refused to accept this option, the employer offered him a pair of common boots. But he refused to wear these, saying that he thought this was unhygienic. He asked the employer to sanitize the boots by buying disinfectant spray and spraying the common boots. The employer told the worker to buy the spray himself. He refused. He asked to be given alternative employment elsewhere in the plant until his replacement pair came in. The employer told him to go home and refused to pay him for the days he was off work.

He finally returned to work on February 14 after he purchased some disinfectant spray and used it on the common boots. However, he filed a complaint through his union arguing that he was exercising his right to refuse to perform unsafe work under section 3.12 of the OHSR, and that he had been discriminated against contrary to section 151 of the WCA. The case went to a reviewing officer and was appealed further to the Appeal Division of the Board.

Relevant Issue

Whether the worker had refused to perform unsafe work and had been discriminated against by his employer for having done so.

Decision

The Appeal Division found that this worker was not exercising his right to refuse to perform unsafe work because his employer was not asking him to perform unsafe work. The employer was not compelling the worker to use the common boots, so the issue of their sanitation was a red herring.

The Regulations in fact made safe footwear primarily the responsibility of the worker, not the employer, and there was no legal obligation on the employer to provide him with common boots or any other kind once the worker's own pair was deficient.

The worker had no reasonable cause to believe that his employer was requiring him to carry out a work process that would create an undue hazard for him. The employer had a policy regarding footwear and the worker simply refused to comply with it. Because the worker was not properly exercising his right to refuse to do unsafe work, his employer could not have discriminated against him for doing so. Accordingly, the Appeal Division ruled that the worker was not entitled to any remedy.

Battle Mountain considers the actions of an employee who allegedly invoked the work refusal provisions of the Ontario OHSA without a bona fide belief that the work he refused was dangerous. The employee's termination for misusing the OHSA in this manner, and causing serious consequences for the employer and other employees, was upheld.

CASE IN POINT

Employee Lacks Honest Belief in Mineshaft Danger

Battle Mountain Canada Ltd v United Steelworkers of America, Local 9364, [2001] OLAA No 722 (QL)

Facts

The worker was employed by a mining company between 1989 and 1998 and had been a member of the JHSC since 1995. On December 14, 1998, he refused to take the cage, which transported workers underground, to his assigned work area, alleging that it was unsafe. His action closed down the mineshaft. The worker's refusal was based on an allegation that pits designed to catch loose rocks were full and therefore presented a danger.

Later in the afternoon, the worker revoked his work refusal after the employer provided him with documentation that he requested. It was therefore unnecessary for an Ontario Ministry of Labour inspector to investigate. However, shortly after the work refusal, the employer discharged the worker on the basis that his work refusal was unlawful and constituted serious culpable misconduct. The worker grieved his dismissal, arguing that it was a reprisal for exercising his rights under the Ontario OHSA and the collective agreement.

Relevant Issue

Whether the employer's termination of the worker violated the OHSA.

Decision

The arbitrator found that the employer's dismissal of the worker was justified. The "catch pits" were not situated on the side of the shaft that workers used and presented no danger. The employee's evidence was inconsistent and lacked credibility. The employee did not have an honest belief that his health and safety—or that of other workers—would be endangered by using the shaft cage. Instead, the evidence supported the view that the employee used the work refusal to "put forward his own personal agenda."

The arbitrator ruled that, as remedial legislation, the OHSA must be given a fair and liberal interpretation. However, to receive the protection of the OHSA, workers must comply with its legislative requirements, including having an honest, genuine, and bona fide belief that the refused work posed a danger. Misusing the right to refuse unsafe work was culpable misconduct that had significant negative effects for both the employer and his co-workers, who lost four hours' pay and their bonus. The arbitrator refused to reinstate the worker despite his 11 years' service, citing his lack of candour and noting that his prospects for rehabilitation were poor.

Notwithstanding the above, generally speaking, the OHSA work refusal provisions have received broad interpretation, provided that the refusal is based on genuine health and safety concerns.

The Right to Know About Workplace Hazards

Under sections 3.1–3.4 of the BC OHSR, employers are compelled to provide workers with instruction and supervision in the safe performance of their work. This must be done by the implementing of an occupational health and safety program that is designed to prevent injuries and occupational diseases. In Alberta, occupational health and safety programs are not compulsory, but employers may voluntarily establish programs for the purpose of injury prevention. However, an employer must ensure, pursuant to section 3(1)(b), that workers are aware of their responsibilities and duties under the OHSA, its Regulations, and the OHS Code. Workers have the right to know about potential hazards to which they may be exposed. This includes the right to receive training about the safe use of machinery, equipment, and processes. A significant part of this right relates to the right to know about hazardous substances at the workplace.

Designated Substances

In BC, part 5 of the OHSR (Chemical Agents and Biological Agents) and part 6 of the OHSR (Substance Specific Requirements) together form the designated substances provisions.

In Alberta, parts 1–3 of the OHS Code provide core technical requirements for all industries. Part 2 requires employers to proactively identify hazards, prepare a written report made available to workers, and explain how the hazards will be eliminated or controlled. Chemical and biological hazards are discussed in part 4.

In workplaces where designated substances are present, processed, used, or stored and where workers are likely to come into contact with, inhale, or absorb them, employers are required to take specific measures. These include limiting the amount of the designated substance that workers can be exposed to in a given time period and recording this exposure.

In BC, part 6 of the OHSR addresses specific hazardous substances. It sets maximum exposure limits for a number of specified listed biological and chemical substances or agents. Similarly, under part 4 of the Alberta OHS Code, employers must make certain that a worker's exposure to any of the approximately 800 substances listed in Table 2 of Schedule 1 of the OHS Code does not exceed the occupational exposure limit for that particular substance. Exposure means inhalation, ingestion, or skin contact. Measures to control or mitigate exposure include engineering controls, special work practices (administrative controls), and hygiene facilities (technical controls). Personal protective equipment is the last line of defence.

These hazardous substances provisions incorporate maximum exposure limits. Their requirements are separate from those of the Workplace Hazardous Materials Information System, discussed below, which focuses on the rights of the worker to know and be educated about hazardous substances in the workplace.

Workplace Hazardous Materials Information System

WHAT IS WHMIS?

Workplace Hazardous Materials Information System (WHMIS) a national information system designed to provide workers and employers with essential information about hazardous materials in the workplace

The **Workplace Hazardous Materials Information System (WHMIS)** is a national information system that applies to all industries and workplaces in Canada pursuant to the federal *Hazardous Products Act* and the *Hazardous Products Regulations*. It is Canada's first "right to know" legislation and is designed to provide workers and employers with essential information about using, handling, and storing hazardous materials in the workplace. As a national system, it provides a uniform level of protection throughout the country.

Effective February 2015, the federal legislation for WHMIS was amended to align with the Globally Harmonized System of Classification and Labelling of Chemicals (GHS), keeping Canada in line with its major trading partners and other nations around the world. As a result, significant changes to the federal WHMIS legislation have occurred:

- "Controlled products" will now be called "hazardous products."
- New hazard classes have been introduced.
- Different classification criteria have been implemented.
- New supplier labels and pictograms are in effect.
- New product safety data sheets (SDSs) replace the old material safety data sheets (MSDSs).
- Going forward, there is no requirement to update SDSs every three years.

The new labels will be the most visible change in workplaces. The harmonized system will continue to be called WHMIS in Canada (Government of Alberta, "Changes to WHMIS," 2015).

In BC, WorkSafeBC administers the requirements of the *Hazardous Products Act* through a cooperating agreement with other levels of government in Canada under section 114 of the WCA. The essential features of WHMIS are contained in sections 5.3–5.19 of the OHSR. The term "controlled products" used by the federal WHMIS legislation is essentially equivalent to the term "chemical agent or biological agent" in BC's OHSR. The parallel legislation in Alberta is part 29 of the OHS Code regarding controlled products used, stored, handled, or manufactured at worksites across the province. Alberta, like all other provinces and territories, has harmonized its legislative framework with the federal plan.

EMPLOYERS' RESPONSIBILITIES

Under WHMIS, an employer has the following responsibilities:

1. *Prepare and maintain an inventory of hazardous materials.* Employers must take and maintain an inventory of all hazardous materials and physical agents present in the workplace.
2. *Label hazardous materials.* Employers must ensure that every hazardous material in or out of a container in the workplace is labelled with a supplier

or a workplace label. Labels must contain certain information and hazard symbols. Labels that are illegible or removed must be replaced.

3. *Prepare or obtain product safety data sheets.* Employers must prepare or obtain from the supplier SDSs for every hazardous material in the workplace. SDSs must contain precautionary and first aid measures and identify the product and supplier. SDSs must be readily available to workers who may be exposed to the hazardous material and to JHSC members or to the health and safety representative. They must be in English as well as in the majority language of the workplace.
4. *Provide worker training.* Employers must ensure that workers who are exposed or likely to be exposed to a hazardous material or physical agent are trained concerning its safe use, handling, and storage. Employers must consult the JHSC or health and safety representative concerning the content and delivery of training programs and must review the program at least annually to see whether retraining is necessary. Safety training must begin with the orientation of new employees.

Employers who are concerned that the requirement to provide information on the label or SDS may result in the disclosure of confidential business information and trade secrets may request an exemption from disclosure by filing a claim with the federal Hazardous Materials Information Review Commission. If this exemption is granted, the employer must still disclose the confidential information in a medical emergency.

Workplace Violence

As a general principle, employers have a legal duty to address violence in the workplace stemming from their general duty to take every precaution reasonable in the circumstances to protect the health and safety of their workers. Part 27 of the Alberta OHS Code and sections 4.27–4.31 of the BC OHSR also impose a *specific* duty on employers to take steps to address workplace violence. Violence means the threatened, attempted, or actual conduct of a person that causes or is likely to cause physical injury. The philosophy of the OHS Code regarding violence is that prevention is preferable to intervention and that "workplace violence is considered a hazard." Under section 389, an employer must conduct a hazard assessment to identify:

- aspects of the workplace that may enhance opportunities for violence (such as poorly lit areas or unregulated building access),
- those individuals at highest risk, and
- the need for controls.

Section 4.28 of BC's OHSR is similar, requiring a "risk assessment" about workplace violence, but is not as specific about what the employer must identify. Instead, it requires employers to consider previous experience in that workplace and in similar workplaces and to look at all of the circumstances in which work takes place. The OHSR requires not only an assessment; it imposes on employers a duty to "instruct workers" on how to identify the potential for violence, how to respond to violence, and the employer's policies for violence in the workplace, including reporting procedures (s 4.30). In 2013 WorkSafeBC adopted new policies that expand the scope of violence to include bullying and harassment, and in 2018 new legislation in Alberta added "harassment" as a workplace hazard (see below).

An employer has a further obligation to develop a policy and procedures addressing potential workplace violence (s 390 of the OHS Code; ss 4.28–4.29 of the BC OHSR). These are required to be in writing and available to workers. In order to implement its workplace violence program, an employer must:

- instruct workers in how to recognize workplace violence (s 4.30 of the BC OHSR; s 391 of the Alberta OHS Code);
- communicate the organization's policy and procedures related to workplace violence;
- develop appropriate responses to workplace violence; and
- develop procedures for reporting, investigating, and documenting incidents of workplace violence (s 4.29 of the BC OHSR; s 391 of the Alberta OHS Code and ss 18(3) to (6) and 19 of the Alberta OHSA).

In 2013, the BC government expanded the scope of employer obligations related to workplace violence to address concerns about bullying and harassment. Through policies adopted that year, WorkSafeBC now requires employers to train all employees about bullying and harassment and to teach them how to avoid these behaviours. The policies are based on WorkSafeBC's interpretation of the general duties of employers, workers, and supervisors, set out in sections 115–117 of the WCA and sections 4.24–4.31 of the OHSR (WorkSafeBC, "Policies Workers Compensation Act"). To accompany this new training obligation, WorkSafeBC has created a prevention toolkit that includes templates for workshops (WorkSafeBC, "Bullying and Harassment Prevention Tool Kit").

In 2018, the Alberta government expanded the latitude of employer duties related to workplace violence by adding **harassment** as a workplace hazard, which requires employers to protect their employees from harassment under OHS legislation. In general terms, this means that employers and supervisors must ensure workers are not subject to, and do not participate in, violence or harassment at the worksite. Specifically, part 27 of the OHS Code has now been overhauled to require employers to take, among other things, the following steps to put a stop to workplace violence and harassment:

harassment any unwanted physical or verbal behaviour that offends or humiliates and persists over time; serious one-time incidents can also be considered harassment; specific definitions of harassment may be included in legislation that addresses this issue

- address both and harassment and violence as possible "hazards" when conducting hazard assessments and implementing measures to eliminate or control those hazards, as required by Part 2 of the OHS Code;
- develop and implement violence and harassment prevention in consultation with their joint worksite health and safety committee, health and safety representative, or affected workers, as applicable; and
- provide training to workers regarding recognizing, preventing, and responding to violence and harassment.

In Alberta, employers must now investigate any incident of violence or harassment and prepare an investigation report outlining the circumstances of the incident and the corrective action taken. Employers must retain the investigation report for at least two years after the incident and must ensure a copy of the report is readily available and provided to an Alberta OHS officer on request. An Alberta OHS officer may also conduct an investigation of a violence or harassment incident, and every person present when an incident occurs or who has information relating to the incident is required to cooperate with the officer.

The Canadian Centre for Occupational Health and Safety (<http://www.ccohs.ca/topics/hazards/psychosocial/violence>) provides further information on how to address workplace violence.

IN THE NEWS

Lori Dupont—A Workplace Murder

Lori Dupont was a recovery room nurse at Hôtel-Dieu Grace Hospital who began a relationship in 2002 with Dr Marc Daniel, an anesthesiologist at the hospital. After she broke off the relationship, he began making threats against her and her family. Following a suicide attempt, Daniel was required to take a medical leave and enroll in a health program. When he returned to work in May 2005, there were several conditions placed on his hospital privileges, including being monitored and restricted from working at the hospital during the weekends. However, by the fall some of these restrictions had been removed and on Saturday, November 12, 2005, Daniel and Dupont were scheduled to work together. With only a skeletal staff in the operating room, Daniel took the opportunity to stab Dupont to death. He committed suicide shortly thereafter. During the subsequent inquest, the coroner's jury heard that the hospital allowed Daniel to keep his hospital privileges, despite complaints about his threatening behaviour that included breaking a nurse's finger and destroying hospital equipment, as well as the ongoing harassment of Dupont.

SOURCE: Based on Schmidt, 2006.

Other Protections Under the British Columbia OHSR and the Alberta OHS Code

The BC OHSR is a very detailed code of safety regulations for the workplace and are regularly amended. There are 34 parts to the OHSR, and so far we have looked at matters dealt with in only the first six. Employers and workers in specific industries have an incumbent duty to heed the standards of safety that are stipulated in the remaining 28 parts of the regulation as they apply to their specific workplace. A list of the titles to those remaining parts of the OHSR is provided below to illustrate the comprehensive and detailed nature of these regulations:

Part 7 Noise, Vibration, Radiation, and Temperature
Part 8 Personal Protective Clothing and Equipment
Part 9 Confined Spaces
Part 10 De-energization and Lockout

Part 11	Fall Protection
Part 12	Tools, Machinery, and Equipment
Part 13	Ladders, Scaffolds, and Temporary Work Platforms
Part 14	Cranes and Hoists
Part 15	Rigging
Part 16	Mobile Equipment
Part 17	Transportation of Workers
Part 18	Traffic Control
Part 19	Electrical Safety
Part 20	Construction, Excavation, and Demolition
Part 21	Blasting Operations
Part 22	Underground Workings
Part 23	Oil and Gas
Part 24	Diving, Fishing, and Other Marine Operations
Part 25	Camps
Part 26	Forestry Operations and Similar Activities
Part 27	Wood Products Manufacturing
Part 28	Agriculture
Part 29	Aircraft Operations
Part 30	Laboratories
Part 31	Firefighting
Part 32	Evacuation and Rescue
Part 33	Repealed
Part 34	Rope Access

For example, suppose you are operating a janitorial business and you have several employees working for you. Parts 5 and 6 will regulate the use and storage of the chemicals that your workers might have to use, part 8 will have something to say about the clothing they may have to wear to protect them from those chemicals, part 13 will regulate what kind of precautions should be taken if they are going to be using ladders or scaffolding, and so on.

The depth and breadth of BC's OHSR coverage continues to evolve and expand, including amendments that reach beyond traditional industries. Consider, for instance, the 2017 amendment by the BC government to ban an employer from requiring employees to wear high-heeled shoes—a move targeted to protect servers in the restaurant industry.

IN THE NEWS

BC Regulation Means Employers Can't Require Women to Wear High Heels to Work

A move by the British Columbia government to ban mandatory high heels in the workplace is being lauded as a step towards ending discriminatory dress codes.

Requiring women to wear high heels on the job is a health and safety issue, said Labour Minister Shirley Bond. "This change will let employers know that the most critical part of an employee's footwear is that it is safe," she said in a statement on Friday. "I expect employers to recognize this very clear signal that forcing someone to wear high heels at work is unacceptable."

The high heels issue is broader than just footwear, said Robyn Durling, communications director with the legal-assistance group BC Human Rights Clinic. "It's part of the overall issue of sexualizing women in the workplace," he said. The new regulations will help prevent women from being forced to wear clothing they're not comfortable with and could prevent some sexual harassment in the workplace, Durling said. "I think there are gains being made. They're slow and they're prudent, but they're steps in the right direction."

Green party Leader Andrew Weaver introduced a private member's bill last month on International Women's Day that would have made it illegal for employers to require women to wear high heels at work. Instead of implementing the bill, the government amended the footwear regulation under the *Workers Compensation Act*.

The amended regulation says employers cannot force workers to wear footwear with a design, construction or material that inhibits the worker's ability to safely perform their job. It says employers have to consider slipping, ankle protection, foot support, muscle or bone injuries, and electrical shock when considering mandatory footwear.

Weaver said he welcomed the change, adding that he has recently heard from people in "countless sectors" who were forced to wear high heels at work.

"They talked about sexism, objectification, bleeding feet, sore knees, hips, and backs, long-term damage, and called for this practice be officially changed," he said in a statement.

"We are very far from an inclusive, gender-equal province. But this is an important step in the right direction." The changes will be enforced by WorkSafeBC, the body that oversees worker safety in the province.

SOURCE: Canadian Press, 2017.

The Alberta OHS Code is equally comprehensive, being composed of 41 parts in total. Again, employers and workers need to be aware of the safety standards contained in these parts.[1]

Given the degree of detail in the BC OHSR and the Alberta OHS Code sections, employers who fail to meet the requirements set out in them cannot argue that they were unaware of the requirements. They will face the principle that ignorance of the law is no excuse.

Accidents

Accident Reporting

Part 1, division 5 of the BC WCA provides for the reporting of injuries, disabling occupational diseases, or death to a worker. Section 53 stipulates that the worker (or their dependant in the case of death) must notify the employer of these occurrences as soon as practicable. Written particulars can be provided on a prescribed form. The employer in turn is obliged to report to WorkSafeBC within three days of its occurrence the particulars of the aforesaid injury. In the case of occupational disease, the worker (or their surviving dependant) must provide this information as soon as possible after learning of its occurrence.

1 The full text of the OHS Code is available online at <https://www.qp.alberta.ca/documents/OHS/OHSCode.pdf>.

Part 3, division 10 (ss 172–177) deals with situations where an accident resulted in serious injury or death, *or* involved:

- a major structural failure or collapse of a building, bridge, tower, crane, hoist, temporary construction support system, or excavation;
- the major release of a hazardous substance;
- a fire or explosion that had a potential for causing serious injury to a worker; or
- an incident that was by regulation required to be reported.

In these cases, the employer must inform WorkSafeBC "immediately." WorkSafeBC will order the employer to conduct an investigation, and it will be carried out by "persons knowledgeable about the type of work involved." Following the investigation, a report must be prepared and submitted to WorkSafeBC and any JHSC or health worker representative.

In Alberta, accidents may be investigated by an officer attending at the scene (s 19 of the OHSA). However, the procedure for accidents of a more serious nature is detailed in section 40 of the OHSA. Section 40(1) states:

> 40(1) When an injury or incident described in subsection (2) occurs at a work site, the prime contractor or, if there is no prime contractor, the employer shall report the time, place and nature of the injury or incident to a Director of Inspection as soon as possible.

Section 40(2) lists the types of accidents and injuries to be reported under section 40(1):

> (a) an injury or incident that results in the death of a worker;
> (b) an injury or incident that results in a worker being admitted to a hospital, and for the purposes of this clause, "admitted to a hospital" means when a physician writes admitting orders to cause a worker to be an inpatient of a hospital, but excludes a worker being assessed in an emergency room or urgent care centre without being admitted;
> (c) an unplanned or uncontrolled explosion, fire or flood that causes a serious injury or that has the potential of causing a serious injury;
> (d) the collapse or upset of a crane, derrick or hoist;
> (e) the collapse or failure of any component of a building or structure necessary for the structural integrity of the building or structure; or
> (f) any injury or incident or a class of injuries or incidents specified in the regulations.

New rules in the Alberta OHSA (as of 2018) expand the scope of injuries and incidents that must be reported and investigated, including any incident that results in a worker being admitted to a hospital (instead of a two-day stay) and any incident that occurred at a worksite having the potential of causing serious injury to a person, or "near misses."

The duty to report workplace injuries is taken seriously. In one case, an employer's failure to report a server's slip-and-fall accident in a restaurant and its cleanup of the accident site before the inspector arrived to investigate led to a $20,000 fine

(Keith & Chandler, 2014, at 115). In the event of any serious accident or injury, an employer should immediately:

1. arrange for medical assistance for the injured worker;
2. lock out the machinery or equipment;
3. secure the accident site; and
4. notify the following parties: the injured worker's family; the BC WCB Labour, Citizens' Services and Open Government, or the director of inspection pursuant to Alberta's OHSA; the JHSC or a health and safety representative; and its lawyer.

Accident Investigation Procedures

At least two managers should be trained in accident investigation techniques. One senior person should take charge of the investigation and the collection of all information and documents related to an accident. An employer should take the following actions:

1. Ensure that the investigation begins as soon as possible after an injured worker receives medical treatment. There should be a separate management investigation, apart from the investigation conducted by the Ministry inspector.
2. Prepare and file the requisite information for the WCB.
3. Obtain a statement from the injured worker, if possible.
4. Take photographs and, if relevant, samples of any hazardous materials. Examine the equipment or tools involved.
5. Interview all potential witnesses. Include questions about the steps that were taken to prevent the accident.
6. Ensure that all interviews are witnessed by a third party.
7. Prepare witness statements and have them signed by the witnesses.
8. Do not tamper with the site of the accident.
9. Develop and implement a remedial action plan that identifies and addresses the root cause(s) of the accident (Keith & Chandler, 2014, at 195).
10. During the ministry inspector's investigation, any person being questioned has the right to have counsel present and the right to remain silent. A management representative should accompany the inspector during the investigation and record their observations, comments, tests, and measurements.

Administration and Enforcement

Administration

Under the internal responsibility systems of BC and Alberta, workplace parties share responsibility for ensuring a healthy and safe workplace. WorkSafeBC officers and occupational health and safety officers (Alberta) provide specialized safety advice and expertise, but they become involved in enforcement only when the self-regulatory system based on joint responsibility breaks down.

Inspections

In addition to investigating work refusals, work stoppages, and serious injuries or fatalities, inspectors also conduct random, unannounced inspections of workplaces. During a workplace inspection, the inspector may be accompanied by a worker representative from the JHSC, the health and safety representative, or a worker knowledgeable in the field and by the employer or its representative.

Sections 179–182 of the BC WCA and section 51 of the Alberta OHSA give inspectors broad powers, including the power to:

1. enter any workplace without a search warrant, except where the workplace is also a personal dwelling;
2. conduct tests or have tests conducted at the employer's expense;
3. request the identity information of workers and employers at worksites;
4. question anyone in the workplace;
5. speak privately to any worker;
6. compel the production of drawings, specifications, licences, or other documents for examination and copy them, if necessary, before returning them to the employer; and
7. remove any equipment, machine, or device to test as necessary.

In certain circumstances, objects or other evidence may be seized, with the subsequent approval of a justice of the peace, if the inspector reasonably believes that a violation of the Act has occurred for which the object will provide evidence.

The employer should designate a member of senior management who is knowledgeable in health and safety matters to meet an inspector as soon as they arrive at the workplace. It is usually a good idea for the senior manager to accompany the inspector during the inspection to explain health and safety efforts and obtain feedback. The inspector should be debriefed at the end of the inspection so that management may benefit from their expertise and observations.

It is illegal to alter the scene of a serious workplace injury or fatality in any way without the permission of a ministry inspector. Exceptions exist where alterations are necessary to relieve suffering, maintain an essential service, or prevent unnecessary damage to property.

Enforcement

Under sections 187–198 of the BC WCA and section 32 of the Alberta OHSA, an officer who finds a contravention of the Act or Regulations may issue an order requiring the employer to comply with the law. If a contravention endangers the health or safety of a worker, the officer has the authority to issue a stop-work order.

In BC, section 191 of the WCA authorizes WorkSafeBC to order that work at all or any part of a workplace come to a stop until the stop-work order is cancelled by the Board. Such orders will be made whenever the Board has "reasonable grounds for believing there is a risk of serious injury, serious illness or death to a worker at the workplace."

In Alberta, section 60(1) of the OHSA authorizes an occupational health and safety officer to order that work be stopped, that any worker leave the area, and that an employer remove the source of danger or protect any person from it. In making its decision, the officer considers such factors as the employer's record of accidents, work refusals, and non-compliance with officers' orders.

A copy of an inspector's order must be posted in a conspicuous location in the workplace. An officer's order is binding as soon as it is issued. The *Border Paving* case demonstrates that a stop-work order may provide employee protection while the undetermined causes of an accident or series of accidents are investigated.

CASE IN POINT

Stop-Work Order for Contravention of Occupational Health and Safety Legislation

Border Paving Ltd v Alberta (Occupational Health and Safety Council), 2009 ABCA 37, aff'g 2006 ABQB 893

Facts

While moving down a 7 percent grade on Mountain Road Highway near Whitecourt, Alberta, a RayGo 304 road roller owned by Border Paving Ltd flipped over. The operator, Kelly, was thrown clear but was seriously injured. Although this particular machine had rollover protection, Kelly was not wearing a seat belt. Furthermore, it was discovered that at the time of the accident, the road roller was in neutral rather than in gear, as it should have been. Within several hours, an occupational health and safety investigator arrived on the scene. The next day, Border Paving brought in a replacement road roller; however, it was not equipped with rollover protection.

The investigator issued a number of orders associated with the accident, but in particular he issued an order that the work be stopped until the cause of the accident had been determined and until any replacement equipment had rollover protection installed on it. Border Paving appealed a decision to uphold the investigator's order regarding the necessity for installing rollover protection on equipment, first to the Occupational Health and Safety Council and then to the Alberta Court of Queen's Bench.

Relevant Issue

Whether the investigator's order was necessary to protect Border Paving employees from work being carried on in a manner that was unsafe for them.

Decision

The Alberta Court of Queen's Bench noted the following: evidence presented at the OHS Council hearing revealed that this accident was actually the third rollover of a Border Paving road roller, that the two earlier rollover accidents had also happened on hills, and that both previous operators had been injured as well. It was learned that Kelly had limited experience with Border, and that Border had provided no training to him in the operation of the RayGo roller. Although the Council varied or revoked several other orders written by the investigator associated with the same accident, the Council specifically confirmed the investigator's order under section 9 of the OHSA regarding a requirement for installed rollover protection on the road roller equipment.

In deciding what standard of review should be applied to the Council's decision, the Alberta Court of Queen's Bench took into consideration the standard of review established by the Alberta Court of Appeal in *Navrot v Alberta Occupational Health and Safety Council*, in particular the required functional and pragmatic analysis of both the OHS legislation and OHS Council conducted by the Court of Appeal. The Court of Queen's Bench then decided that the issue regarding the investigator's order was slightly less fact-intensive than the issues in the *Navrot* case, but that a standard of reasonableness nevertheless required a degree of deference to the Council's expertise.

After reviewing the evidence of three separate Border Paving equipment rollovers, the evidence of three operators having been injured, the unexplained causes of all of the accidents, and the lack of training provided to employees operating the road rollers, the Court of Queen's Bench found that the decision of the OHS Council to confirm the investigator's order was entirely reasonable and supportable:

> In my view, Border's record of roller rollovers and lack of demonstrated training of the operator Kelly made it entirely reasonable that it be required to have rollover protection for its RayGo 304 rollers. How could there be any better proof of the need for protection than this sorry record? How can Border suggest that it has been deprived of the legislative right to institute safe operating procedures? Its procedures have been shown to be unsafe. (at para 19)

The Alberta Court of Queen's Bench therefore dismissed Border's appeal. Although the employer appealed yet again, the Alberta Court of Appeal dismissed the appeal, confirming that the reasonableness standard that had been applied by the Court of Queen's Bench was correct and confirming that Border Paving had not been deprived of its statutory right to institute safe working procedures.

Any party may appeal an officer's order to be heard by a review officer pursuant to section 96.2(1)(c) of the BC WCA or section 71 of the Alberta OHSA. In BC, this request for review must be made within 90 days of the issuance of the order; in Alberta, it must be made within 30 days. Launching an appeal does not suspend the order, although the chief review officer has the discretion to suspend the order pending the appeal. In Alberta, the reviews and appeal aspect of the OHSA was recently (2018) completely revamped. For example, for some matters, a party can request a review that is conducted by a director of inspection. However, one of the director's discretionary steps is to refer the matter to the appeal body, which is no longer the Alberta OHS Council but is rather the Labour Relations Board. Certain other matters may be appealed directly to the Labour Relations Board.

An employer may appeal an order if it requires more time to comply, perhaps because of the costs of compliance. A successful appeal may reduce the likelihood of charges being laid under the legislation (Keith & Chandler, 2014, at 132).

On an appeal, the review officer may uphold or rescind the order or substitute its own findings. The review officer's decision is effectively final (s 96.4(9) of the BC WCA or s 72(11) of the Alberta OHSA), because the decision will be overturned on judicial review only if it was "patently unreasonable" or without jurisdiction, not merely incorrect.

Section 194 of the BC WCA allows an officer to compel an employer to prepare a compliance report indicating what has been done to comply with the order and, if compliance has not been achieved, what will be done to accomplish that. In Alberta, section 59(1) of the OHSA allows an officer to order that an employer comply with the OHSA, its Regulations, or the OHS Code within a certain time period specified in the order. Ultimately, the inspector determines whether compliance has been achieved.

strict liability offences offences where the doing of the prohibited act is sufficient proof of the offence and the accused has the burden of proving that it took all reasonable care to avoid the offence

Due Diligence Defence

Offences under the BC WCA and the Alberta OHSA and their Regulations are **strict liability offences** because the Ministry does not need to prove that the employer intended to violate the legislation or was negligent to obtain a conviction. Rather, if there is a workplace accident, the onus is on the accused employer to show that it complied with the WCA and its Regulations for "all known or reasonably foreseeable health or safety hazards" that workers might be exposed to in the workplace (s 115(2)(b) of the WCA). Similarly, in Alberta, employers must ensure the health and safety of their workers and others present at their worksite "as far as it is reasonably practicable for the employer to do so" (s 3(1) of the OHSA).

However, section 196(3) of the BC WCA stipulates that no employer will be liable to any administrative penalty under the Act if the employer exercised due diligence.

An attempt to show that every reasonable precaution was taken is a **due diligence defence**. For example, if a worker is injured in unguarded machinery, the employer may successfully defend itself if it can prove that it took all reasonable care to ensure that the machinery was guarded, including training employees about the importance of guards and disciplining employees who remove them.

due diligence defence
the onus on a party in certain circumstances to establish that it took all reasonable steps to avoid a particular event

Although the due diligence defence is set out in sections 196(3) and 215 of the WCA, it also exists at common law. Under this defence, an employer may also avoid liability if it reasonably believed in a mistaken set of facts that, if true, would have rendered its act innocent (Keith & Chandler, 2014, at 12).

Employers are not held to a standard of perfection. The defence of due diligence does not require an employer to anticipate and solve every possible problem in advance of its arising. It does require an employer to comply with the workplace health and safety legislation on an ongoing basis and anticipate reasonably foreseeable hazards. In *R v Lonkar Well Testing Limited*, for example, the Alberta Court of Queen's Bench overturned a Provincial Court conviction that the employer had failed to ensure the health and safety of a worker as far as it was reasonably practicable. The worker suffocated while working on a pressure vessel on a sweet gas well at its worksite.

CASE IN POINT

Employer Not Held to Standard of Perfection

R v Lonkar Well Testing Limited, 2009 ABQB 345, rev'g 2008 ABPC 385

Facts

Jonathan Audit had been a full-time employee of Lonkar Well Testing for two years when the meter run of Lonkar's horizontal pressure vessel, a machine that measured the service flow rate of a well, malfunctioned. Jerdan, the site supervisor, immediately contacted ProPipe, the manufacturer of the pressure vessel, to have the meter run replaced. ProPipe agreed to come to the worksite, close and cap the well head, shut certain valves in the pressure vessel, and turn off the burner in the separator. After taking these precautions, it would be safe for the ProPipe experts to dismantle the malfunctioning meter run and install a new one.

Jerdan decided to prepare for the arrival of the ProPipe experts in two ways. First, he asked Audit to remove 12 of the 24 flange bolts on the equipment, demonstrated or supervised the procedure for the removal of the first two bolts, and enlisted the help of one other worker to assist Audit. He warned Audit not to carry out any additional work beyond the removal of the first 12 bolts. Jerdan's second step in preparing for the arrival of the ProPipe experts was to drive about 60 kilometres to Grande Prairie to obtain parts.

Audit and the assistant commenced work on the removal of the remaining 10 bolts at approximately 11:00 a.m. When, at about 11:15 a.m., a driller visited the trailer that housed the malfunctioning equipment, the work had already been completed and the driller was told by Audit (the assistant had departed by that time) that no further work was to be performed on the meter run until Jerdan had returned from Grande Prairie.

When Jerdan got back, he discovered Audit lying dead on the floor of the trailer. He had a large bump or hematoma on his head. The meter run and back pressure valve (weighing approximately 375 pounds) had somehow been removed from the pressure vessel. Stratification of hydrocarbons, a product of sweet gas, may have occurred along the level of the trailer floor where Audit had fallen. An autopsy report confirmed that Audit had died as a result of suffocation due to an oxygen deficient environment.

The Alberta Provincial Court found Lonkar guilty, beyond a reasonable doubt, of the charge of failing to ensure the health and safety of its worker, Jonathan Audit. Lonkar appealed.

Relevant Issues

1. Whether the trial judge erred in characterizing the work in which Audit was engaged as the work of the employer.
2. Whether the trial judge erred by failing to construe the statutory wording in section 2(1) "as far as it is reasonably practicable" as part of the assessment of the Crown's burden of proof.
3. Whether the trial judge erred in concluding that Lonkar had not established its reasonable care defence on a balance of probabilities.

Decision

1. The Alberta Court of Queen's Bench found that the trial judge did not err in characterizing Lonkar as the employer responsible for having the malfunctioning meter run problem remedied, and that Jerdan, Audit, and the assistant had undertaken preliminary work in that regard. The fact that Audit had disobeyed a direct order from Jerdan did not detract from this characterization of Lonkar as Audit's employer.
2. The trial judge did not err in failing to construe the wording "as far as it is reasonably practicable" (at para 18) in the Crown's burden of proof. The "liability being imposed," the Court of Queen's Bench said, "is strict but not absolute" (at para 26). Citing *R v Sault Ste Marie*, the Court explained that there was a requirement to prove the *actus reus* element of the offence, but not the *mens rea* element, because of the "virtual impossibility in most regulatory cases of proving wrongful intention":

   > While the prosecution must prove beyond a reasonable doubt that the defendant committed the prohibited act, the defendant must only establish on the balance of probabilities that he has a defence of reasonable care. (at para 26)

3. The trial judge did err, however, in finding that the accused did not take reasonable care in the circumstances—suggesting that, because Jerdan did not provide a *specific* dire warning that death could result from not following his orders, it may not have been crystal clear to Audit that replacement of oxygen could—very quickly and without his knowledge—occur and therefore there was a specific risk of death from the vapours that might escape.

   The concept of foreseeability formulated by the trial judge was not accepted by the Court of Queen's Bench, which conceived the principle as follows:

   > For a potential danger to be foreseeable, there must be at least a reasonable prospect or expectation that it will arise. "Foreseeable" is not the equivalent of "imaginable." If s-s. 2(1)(a)(i) required not only addressing and foreseeing a potential danger so as to ensure the health and safety of workers, but imagining all the bizarre and unforeseeable situations which might create a further danger, then the employer's liability under this provision would be absolute. (at para 62)

The trial judge's approach to foreseeability had, in other words, essentially rendered meaningless the legislature's phrase "as far as it is reasonably practicable." It had substituted a standard of absolute liability for the appropriate standard, strict liability. To prove due diligence, it was therefore sufficient that Lonkar had foreseen the hazard of a gas leak, had taken steps to avoid danger, had assigned Audit to a specific task that involved no hazard of leakage, had warned Audit when he was provided with his instructions, and had trained Audit in the health hazards associated with his work—including training in working in confined spaces. It was reasonable, given Audit's age, experience, and previous work record, that the employer should expect he would not undertake unauthorized work.

There is no list of factors that guarantees that a court will find that an employer was duly diligent. However, typically an employer's safety record, the foreseeability of the risk, and the hazards inherent in the industry are considered. A court assesses whether the employer had safety procedures in place that it implemented, monitored, and enforced.

As part of exercising due diligence, an employer should document all of its efforts to prevent workplace accidents, including all discussions with employees regarding safety procedures. To increase the credibility of a due diligence defence, employers should take the following specific steps:

1. Designate a senior manager to be responsible for work safety compliance.
2. Prepare a *written* health and safety policy, as required by the OHS legislation.
3. Provide safety orientations for new employees and for existing employees with new job assignments.
4. Identify workplace hazards through internal and external safety audits. An outside safety expert may identify blind spots in the program.
5. Hold monthly safety meetings in every department or work group, and forward all recommendations or concerns to the JHSC or health and safety representative.
6. Support and respond to the JHSC or health and safety representative.
7. Ensure that senior executives actively support the JHSC or health and safety representative.
8. Train workers and supervisors to perform their duties safely, and document all training. Make sure employees actively participate—doing is better than watching—and double-check that employees actually *understand* the procedures. Training should also be specific to the workplace and the employee's job.
9. Hold regular safety meetings to update workers.
10. Take effective corrective measures for all workers and managers who fail to follow safety requirements.
11. Have a corporate director chair a committee to address OHS legislation and environmental compliance, and place its concerns on the board of directors' agenda at every general meeting.
12. Have specialized legal counsel conduct an annual compliance audit.
13. Implement a system of recognition and rewards for individuals and departments who reach safety goals.
14. Conduct regular safety inspections and safety audits.
15. Ensure that all managers and supervisors are instructed on the legislation, applicable regulations, work hazards, and control measures.
16. Ensure that all workers are instructed on their rights and responsibilities pursuant to the legislation and applicable regulations and are properly trained on work-related hazards. Retain confirming documentation (Keith & Chandler, 2014, at 16).
17. Keep equipment in good order.

The following BC decision illustrates a situation where an employer, despite having violated safety regulations, succeeded in showing that it had acted with due diligence.

CASE IN POINT

Employer Meets Obligation to Show Due Diligence Despite Safety Violation

Decision No 2001-0295, Workers' Compensation Reporter (2001), vol 17, no 2 at 257 (BC Workers' Compensation Board, Appeal Division)

Facts

The employer was engaged in some excavating at a worksite in January 2000. An occupational health and safety officer carried out an inspection and discovered that the excavation was in violation of the OHSR: the walls of the hole had not been shored up or adequately sloped to prevent the surrounding earth from collapsing into the hole, as is required by the OHSR where holes are more than 4 feet deep (the officer measured the hole to be 6 feet). He also noted that the surrounding soil (type-B) was of a kind likely to crack or crumble. Accordingly, sanction processes were set in motion, and ultimately a penalty of $7,500 was imposed on the employer for failing to comply with the regulation.

In its defence, the employer argued that the evidence as to whether the excavation was greater than 4 feet was based entirely on a very poor photograph from which it was not possible for even expert witnesses to determine just how deep it was. It also argued that because it was a very cold day, it was not possible for the surrounding soil to collapse. The employer had been using a safety manual that clearly outlined the proper requirements for excavation, its workers had been given proper training in digging trenches, and staircases for safe access and egress to excavated sites were often created. It argued that the evidence did not establish on a balance of probabilities that it had contravened the regulation; accordingly, it had exercised the requisite due diligence in the circumstances and so should not be penalized.

Relevant Issue

Whether the employer had shown due diligence despite its having contravened the safety legislation relating to the excavation.

Decision

The WCB Appeal Division noted that before a reviewing officer can levy an administrative penalty, they must be satisfied on a balance of probabilities that there is sufficient evidence the requirements for a penalty are met. The evidence does not have to show beyond a reasonable doubt (the criminal standard of proof) that a violation of the regulation has occurred, nor does there have to be conclusive proof of such a violation. Here the evidence did establish on a balance of probabilities that there was a violation of the regulation.

However, even after a violation has been established, the board must then make a finding of how much risk was associated with that violation. Here, the risk was relatively low because the surrounding soil was frozen. Hence, the low possibility of frozen soil collapsing rebuts, on a balance of probabilities, the presumption of high risk.

Section 196(1)(a) of the WCA compels an employer to prove, on a balance of probabilities, that it exercised due diligence to prevent the non-compliance to which the penalty relates. The Appeal Division found that the evidence of the employer's training of workers and its previous conduct with excavations indicated that it took its responsibilities and obligations under the regulation seriously, so it did not wilfully or deliberately violate it. Accordingly, the administrative penalty against the employer was cancelled.

Offences and Penalties

Any person who contravenes the legislation or who fails to comply with an order is potentially liable under sections 213 and 217 of the BC WCA or under sections 68,

73, and 74 of the Alberta OHSA. Neither the BC nor the Alberta legislation makes a distinction between individual offenders and corporations; however, it should be noted that corporations are included in the definition of a "person" (BC *Interpretation Act*, s 29, and Alberta *Interpretation Act*, s 28(1)(nn)).

In BC, administrative penalties may be imposed in amounts of up to $662,102.49 (s 196 of the WCA). If a person is charged and convicted of an offence under the WCA, the maximum penalty for a first offence is $724,644.41 and, in the case of a continuing offence, a further fine of not more than $36,232.25 may be imposed for each day during which the offence continues after the first day (s 217 of the WCA). Such penalties may be accompanied by imprisonment for a term not exceeding six months. In the case of a subsequent conviction, the maximum fine increases to $1,449,288.80 and another $72,464.44 for each day during which the offence continues after the first day, and imprisonment for up to 12 months. These fines, in effect as of January 2019, are reviewed for adjustment each fall. Imprisonment is very rare, as is the imposition of the maximum penalties. That said, many penalties are issued—in 2018, WorkSafeBC imposed 366 penalties totalling approximately $5.6 million (WorkSafeBC, 2019).

In Alberta, maximum penalties for offenders for a first conviction are fines up to $500,000 and further fines of $30,000 (s 74(1)(a) of the OHSA) for each day that the legislation continues to be contravened or imprisonment for up to six months, although, just as in BC, imprisonment is extremely rare. Maximum fines for subsequent convictions are $1,000,000, and if the offence continues a further fine of up to $60,000 (s 74(1)(b) of the OHSA) for each day that the legislation continues to be contravened or imprisonment for up to 12 months. In *R v Westcon Precast Inc*, the employer was fined for failing to meet the standard of care required under the OHSA when one of its employees was killed in a workplace accident. Fines for violations that do not result in a workplace injury are often imposed as a deterrent.

CASE IN POINT

Employer Fined for Failing to Provide for Workers' Safety

R v Westcon Precast Inc, 2007 ABPC 143

Facts

Evenson had been an employee of Westcon Precast Inc, based in Calgary, Alberta, for about six weeks. Westcon was in the business of producing pre-cast concrete septic tanks, among other items. Evenson was in the process of removing an interior mould from a concrete septic tank created the day before. To accomplish this, he manoeuvred a crane to insert a sling hook into a lug on the mould and lifted the 1,457 kilogram mould out of the septic tank. The next step of the process involved Evenson's going underneath the mould to cover four air holes on the bottom of the mould with a layer of masking tape. At some point in this sealing process, the mould slipped off the sling hook and dropped onto Evenson. He died at the scene. It was unclear whether the sling hook had a safety latch on it, although evidence established that Westcon usually purchased sling hooks that had safety latches. Further, an autopsy revealed that Evenson had used some form of cannabis several hours before he died, but it was unclear whether the drug had caused him to be functionally impaired.

Relevant Issue

Whether the employer met its duty to provide for the safety of workers under the Alberta OHSA.

Decision

Westcon pleaded guilty to a charge of failing to ensure the health and safety of its workers as far as it was reasonably practicable to do so, contrary to section 2(1)(a) of the OHSA. The Alberta Provincial Court noted that no safety cage was provided by Westcon to ensure that the mould could not drop on employees when they were working underneath it and found that the accident was completely foreseeable. It was also possible to predict the measures necessary to prevent the risk of material falling on a worker, as had occurred in this case.

Before a sentence was rendered, the Court took into consideration the fact that Westcon had installed safety cages for use under suspended loads, the fact that Westcon had joined the Manufacturers' Health and Safety Association and sent employees there for safety training, and the fact that Westcon had taken the initiative of forming its own safety committee at the company, which had begun meeting on a monthly basis. Pursuant to section 41(1) of the OHSA, the Court then sentenced Westcon as follows: it required that Westcon pay $195,000 to the Manufacturers' Health and Safety Association to be used to enhance its educational materials regarding the use of overhead cranes; it required a payment of $5,000 in default enforcement; and it required that a $750 victim surcharge be paid by Westcon.

Requiring an employee to work alone is a situation that may place extra responsibilities on the shoulders of the employer who creates that working arrangement. In July 2011 a Calgary security company was handed $92,750 in penalties for failing to ensure the safety of a female guard who had been issued her security guard licence just three weeks prior to experiencing a violent sexual assault at the worksite. She had had only one day of training before she was sent to work the night shift at a store in a strip mall that was under construction. The store occupied one main area and several smaller rooms—all of which were unlocked—and there were no windows, just an unsecured orange tarp covering the storefront. She was completely unarmed.

At about 3 a.m., the guard heard shouting and banging. Frightened, she hid in one of the smaller rooms, phoned her dispatcher, and asked her dispatcher to call 911. As she was speaking to 911, she was grabbed by a young man who had entered the business from the back of the store. Although the guard escaped and ran toward the tarp, she was caught and dragged back into the smaller room, where she was sexually assaulted, choked, and unlawfully confined. Her call to 911 had occurred at 3:02 a.m. It was 3:25 a.m. when the police arrived.

Part 28, section 393 of the Alberta OHS Code stated:

> (1) This Part applies if:
> (a) a worker is working alone at a work site, and
> (b) assistance is not readily available if there is an emergency or the worker is injured or ill.
> (2) Working alone is considered a hazard for the purposes of Part 2.

An assessment of whether assistance is "readily available" in the event of an injury, illness, or emergency depends on three factors:

1. *Awareness.* Will other persons capable of providing assistance be aware of the worker's needs?
2. *Willingness.* Is it reasonable to expect that those other persons will provide helpful assistance?
3. *Timeliness.* Will assistance be provided within a reasonable period of time?

In the Alberta Provincial Court, Garda Canada Security Corp entered a plea of guilty to section 2(1)(a)(i) of the OHSA for failing to ensure the health and safety of its worker. Its primary negligence, according to the judge, was "failing to conduct a specific site assessment" prior to assigning the guard to a dangerous location where it was foreseeable that a criminal act could occur. The company was fined $5,000 and ordered to pay a victim surcharge of $750. In addition, under section 41.1 of the OHSA, the company was ordered to pay $87,000 to the Southern Alberta Institute of Technology for the development of a hazard assessment education program for working alone. On an earlier date in a different courtroom, the intruder was sentenced to serve eight years in prison.

Criminal Liability of Organizations

Amendments to Canada's *Criminal Code* that came into effect on March 31, 2004 impose a significant duty on organizations to ensure workplace health and safety. Because this is criminal legislation, rather than employment law, it applies to both federally and provincially regulated organizations and supplements occupational health and safety legislation.

The amendments do not set out specific requirements. Instead, they state that everyone who undertakes or has the authority to direct how another person does work or performs a task is under a legal duty to take "reasonable steps" to prevent bodily harm arising from that work or task. It is likely that reasonable steps entail compliance with provincial occupational health and safety legislation (Keith & O'Reilly, 2004, at 3230).

The amendments were enacted in response to recommendations made by the inquiry into the Westray mine disaster in 1992, where serious safety violations resulted in the death of 26 Nova Scotia miners. These amendments are designed to make organizations more accountable for the safety of their workers.

Before these amendments, individuals could be held criminally liable for acts or lack of action that caused workplace accidents. However, the new law strengthened the earlier provisions in a number of ways. Courts can now hold an organization liable for the combined effects of actions by several employees. For example, if two workers each turn off a safety mechanism in the belief that the other's safety mechanism is still operative, the organization can be held legally accountable for the collective failure of the safety system (Vu, 2003, at 1).

Earlier law was also limited because an organization's criminal liability depended on whether a senior member of the organization with policy-making authority committed an offence. For example, in the Westray mine disaster in Nova Scotia, proving criminal liability depended on establishing what the people at the head office in Toronto were aware of. Although the new law is still focused on making senior members more accountable, the net is cast much wider. The group of people whose acts or omissions can legally implicate an organization now includes anyone acting within the scope of their authority in directing work. This includes senior officers, directors, partners, members of an organization, co-workers, agents, and contractors.

The new law also increased the maximum fine on **summary conviction** from $25,000 to $100,000. There is no limit on fines that can be imposed on conviction for

summary conviction
a less serious offence that is tried summarily

indictable offence a more serious offence than a summary offence

indictable offences. As a result of these amendments, individuals who are convicted of serious health and safety violations now face the possibility of life imprisonment in addition to serious penalties under provincial health and safety legislation (Keith & O'Reilly, 2004, at 3230). Factors in determining sentencing include the seriousness of the crime, the extent of the injury suffered, the degree of premeditation involved, and whether the individual has any previous convictions.

Although the amendments were designed to hold senior management more accountable for health and safety crimes, lower-level supervisors may face the greatest risk of being charged personally. In April 2004, less than a month after the amendments came into force, a 68-year-old construction supervisor became the first person charged under the new law. The supervisor was overseeing the repair of a drainage problem in the foundation of a house when a trench collapsed and a worker was trapped by heavy dirt. By the time an emergency crew reached the scene, the worker was dead. The supervisor was charged with criminal negligence causing death. Although the charges were later withdrawn as part of an apparent plea bargain, if the supervisor had been convicted, he would have faced the possibility of life in prison or a fine of an unlimited amount (Humber, 2004, at 3291).

The first corporation ever convicted of criminal negligence under these provisions was fined $100,000 in March 2008 for a workplace fatality after a young employee was crushed by heavy machinery. Although the machinery involved was equipped with a safety device, it had been disabled at the time of the fatality. Factors that were considered in determining the size of the fine included the small size of the employer and its subsequent large investments in safety improvements.

Emergency Response (Planning and Management): Planning for a Pandemic

Planning for emergencies such as widespread power outages and severe weather conditions has always been recommended practice. However, the SARS outbreak in 2003 and concerns about the avian and swine (H1N1 and H3N2) flu viruses and the Zika virus have added a sense of urgency to the discussion surrounding emergency planning and the need to prepare specifically for a possible pandemic. Pandemic plans require special policies and procedures because widespread contagious diseases affect the workplace in unparalleled ways. Some experts have estimated that at an influenza pandemic's peak, companies may experience absentee rates of between 15 and 30 percent as a result of sickness, quarantine, travel restrictions, family care obligations, and fear of contagion (Bongarde Media Co, 2008, at 15).

The COVID-19 pandemic of 2020 brought these fears to life. Canadian borders were closed, and travel within Canada was banned as quarantines were implemented around the world. Public and private sector organizations were forced to close their doors for months on end, and employers were completely unprepared for the rapidly evolving situation. Those allowed to stay open because they were classified as "essential services" scrambled to find personal protective equipment and to reconfigure their workplaces to abide by mandatory social distancing requirements. For some, the challenge proved too great, with disastrous consequences. Infection rates and deaths skyrocketed in some Alberta sectors, including long-term-care facilities and meat-packing plants.

IN THE NEWS

The Reopening of an Alberta Meat-Processing Plant Tied to Canada's Largest COVID-19 Outbreak

The Cargill meat-packing plant in High River, Alberta was linked to more than 1,200 COVID-19 cases. The plant supplies more than two-thirds of Canada's beef and was shut down for two weeks in April 2020 when hundreds of workers became ill and one woman died. An inspection by Alberta Occupational Health and Safety that was conducted after dozens of workers were already sick concluded that the plant was safe to remain open. But days later the outbreak had grown to hundreds, and after the death of 67-year-old Hiep Bui it was shut down.

Two weeks after the shutdown, Cargill announced it would reopen. Workers and their union, UFCW Local 401, were outraged and pursued legal action. According to union representatives, Cargill had not consulted with them or adopted recommended safety initiatives. Some employees accused the company of ignoring social distancing rules and trying to lure them back to work.

The company, however, stated that they worked with Alberta Occupational Health and Safety through virtual and in-person tours to develop new safety measures. These were being introduced prior to reopening and included new buses with protective barriers, reassigning lockers to allow for more spacing, production floor barriers, and the use of face shields.

The world's largest meat-packing companies, Cargill, Smithfield Foods Inc, JBS USA, and Tyson—all paused operations at around 20 slaughterhouses and processing plants in North America during the height of the pandemic. As of April 29, 2020, the virus was continuing to spread in Alberta's meat-packing plants; 276 employees tested positive at the JBS plant in Brooks, Alberta, about 180 kilometres southeast of Calgary.

Note: At the time of publication of this book, three deaths due to COVID-19 had been linked to the Cargill meat-packing plant in High River.

SOURCE: Adapted from Dryden, 2020.

From a legal perspective, occupational health and safety legislation does not currently require pandemic preparedness measures. However, such measures are an important part of an employer's general duty under the legislation to take every reasonable precaution to protect the health and safety of workers, as well as the employer's implied duty under the common law to ensure the health and safety of its employees. During a pandemic, an employer is responsible for taking all reasonable steps to ensure that the workplace is free from infection and to prevent the spread of infection. Moreover, by taking all reasonable measures to reduce exposure to an infected person, an employer can reduce the likelihood of an employee successfully invoking the right to refuse unsafe work during a pandemic. The legal impact arising from workplace exposure to COVID-19 remains to be seen, but there is little doubt that employers have been shocked into a new state of awareness regarding pandemic preparation.

There is no "boilerplate" approach to pandemic planning because requirements depend on factors such as the organization's industry, size, and location. Generally, employers need to review all of their policies and procedures to assess and develop a policy that addresses the special conditions of a pandemic. This policy should be made available to employees.

Components of a plan could include the following:

- Ensure that employees have credible, up-to-date details on what they should, and should not, do in the event of an emergency (e.g., a pandemic).
- Provide a channel, such as a website, that allows employees to post questions and comments.
- Minimize direct interactions between employees (social distancing) by, for example, limiting large gatherings or holding only essential meetings.
- Alter the physical workspace to create distance between employees.
- Allow employees to work from home whenever possible because isolation is the best defence against a contagious disease. This will require identifying job responsibilities that can be performed from home and ensuring those employees have the necessary training, as well as the hardware, software, bandwidth, and access to corporate information resources, to work from home. It is important that employees *test the new infrastructure before it is needed*; many companies during COVID-19 found out the hard way they were ill-equipped to deal with the forced closure of their business premises and the requirement for employees to work from home.
- Adopt higher standards of cleanliness, including frequently disinfecting desks and computer equipment, including mobile devices.
- Maintain an extra stock of critical supplies, such as hygiene products, hand sanitizers, and disinfectants.
- Ensure that absenteeism policies do not encourage "presenteeism" (when sick employees come to work). If employees fear job loss or disciplinary action, they will be more likely to come to work and infect co-workers. Employees should be required to complete a "fitness to work" questionnaire before they report to work.
- Screen customers, suppliers, and the public and encouraging those who have symptoms not to enter.
- Post notices at entry points advising staff and visitors not to enter if they have symptoms of influenza.
- Avoid unnecessary travel.
- Make personal protective equipment, such as masks or gloves, available to those at special risk.

Depending on the specific circumstances, employees who are made ill in the course of employment may be entitled to benefits under workers' compensation legislation. Otherwise, employees unable to work as a result of potential exposure to a virus may be entitled to employment insurance under the federal *Employment Insurance Act* (Torrance, 2009). The Canadian government not only made access to employment insurance easier during the COVID-19 pandemic, it also established several direct subsidies to individual Canadians (primarily through the Canada Emergency Response Benefit, which paid $2,000 for a four-week period that was extended several times throughout 2020) and businesses (through a 75 percent wage subsidy and interest-free loans) in an attempt to keep businesses from closing permanently.

Apart from the potential for a pandemic, occupational disease continues to be a leading cause of worker death in Alberta. In 2017, this accounted for 86 fatalities or 51.8 percent of all occupational fatality claims (Government of Alberta, 2018). This was down from 99 fatalities or 52.7 percent in 2013 (Government of Alberta, 2015). Although accidents and serious safety incidents continue to grab our attention and the headlines, occupational health considerations weigh equally heavily in the larger scheme.

KEY TERMS

due diligence defence, **323**
harassment, **314**
health and safety representative, **296**
indictable offence, **330**
internal responsibility system, **295**
joint health and safety committee (JHSC), **295**
multiple-employer workplaces, **301**
strict liability offences, **322**
summary conviction, **329**
Workplace Hazardous Materials Information System (WHMIS), **312**

REVIEW AND DISCUSSION QUESTIONS

1. British Columbia's and Alberta's health and safety legislation is based on an internal responsibility system. Explain this concept. In your opinion, is it an effective approach to ensuring safety in the workplace? Give reasons for your answer.
2. Name and explain the three core worker rights under the BC WCA and the Alberta OHSA.
3. What are the responsibilities of the members of a JHSC?
4. Explain the due diligence defence. What steps can employers take to establish this defence?
5. You are the human resources manager in a small manufacturing firm. An operations supervisor, Habrim, comes to you with a problem. The plant has just started working on a rush order from a major customer and now one of his production workers (Bruce) has refused to work because he says his machinery is unsafe. Habrim checked the machine, and it looked safe to him. He then contacted WorkSafeBC to further investigate the refusal, but he is wondering whether, in the meantime, he can get another employee to work on the machine that Bruce says is unsafe. Advise Habrim by explaining to him what the law requires in these circumstances.
6. Thompson, an experienced operator of the bar bundler packager at ABC Steel Co, noticed that bars had fallen into the basement of the packager. Contrary to his training and the employer's safety protocol, Thompson did not lock out the machine. Instead he placed the machine on automatic and entered the basement area. To get there he had to push open a self-closing swing gate, which displayed a sign warning that the packager had to be "locked out" before entry. Similar signage was on the guard rail fence. Nonetheless, Thompson continued into the basement area; within moments he was crushed to death by a movable portion of the bundler.

   The employer was charged with breaching a regulation under the OHSR, which requires machines with nip hazards to have a guard to prevent access to the pinch point—the point where moving machinery parts are strong enough to pull someone in and injure them. The employer argued that it had done everything reasonable in the circumstances—employee training, a gate that closed automatically, and ample signage. It claimed that it is impossible to foresee and therefore guard against "reckless" employees who do the totally unexpected—even a locked gate would not have deterred a "determined and intentioned" employee like Thompson.

   On the basis of these facts, answer the following questions:

   a. Is this a strict liability offence? If so, does the Ministry have to prove anything or does the entire burden of proof lie with the employer?
   b. The employer may avoid liability if it shows that it exercised due diligence in attempting to carry out its duties. What is the standard of proof in making out a due diligence defence: "beyond a reasonable doubt" or "on a balance of probabilities"? Research what these two different standards of proof mean.
   c. In light of all the circumstances, in your view, did the employer exercise due diligence in the steps it took to protect employees from this hazard? If not, what additional steps should it have taken?
7. Identify the key changes that have occurred in the federal WHMIS legislation as a result of Canada's efforts to align with the Globally Harmonized System of Classification and Labelling of Chemicals, and describe the implications for the provinces.
8. Describe the key changes to occupational health and safety legislation in relation to farms and ranches that came into force in Alberta effective January 2016.

RELATED WEBSITES

The website for WorkSafeBC, the Workers' Compensation Board of British Columbia <http://www.worksafebc.com>

The website for Alberta Occupational Health and Safety <https://www.alberta.ca/occupational-health-safety.aspx>

The website for the Workers' Compensation Board of Alberta <http://www.wcb.ab.ca>

REFERENCES

Battle Mountain Canada Ltd v United Steelworkers of America, Local 9364, [2001] OLAA No 722 (QL).

Bongarde Media Co, "Making the Business Case for Safety," *Safety Compliance Insider: Your Plain Language Guide to C-45, OHS & Due Diligence* 4:10 (October 2008) at 15.

Border Paving Ltd v Alberta (Occupational Health and Safety Council), 2009 ABCA 37, aff'g 2006 ABQB 893.

Canada Labour Code, RSC 1985, c L-2.

Canadian General Tower Ltd and USWA, Loc 862 (Schramm) (Re), [2003] OLAA No 801 (QL).

Canadian Press, "B.C. Regulation Means Employers Can't Require Women to Wear High Heels to Work," *Vancouver Sun* (7 April 2017), online: <https://vancouversun.com/news/local-news/b-c-regulation-means-employers-cant-require-women-to-where-high-heels-to-work>.

Criminal Code, RSC 1985, c C-46, as amended.

Decision No 2001-0295, *Workers' Compensation Reporter* (2001), vol 17, no 2 at 257 (BC Workers' Compensation Board, Appeal Division).

Decision No 2001-2562, *Workers' Compensation Reporter* (2001), vol 18, no 1 at 103 (BC Workers' Compensation Board, Appeal Division).

Dryden, Joel, "Alberta Meat-Processing Plant Tied to Canada's Largest COVID-A9 Outbreak to Reopen Within Days," *CBC News* (29 April 2020), online: <https://www.cbc.ca/news/canada/calgary/cargill-high-river-jon-nash-meat-packing-plant-covid-19-1.5549774>.

Employment Insurance Act, SC 1996, c 23.

Enhanced Protection for Farm and Ranch Workers Act, SA 2015, c 19.

Gilbert, Douglas, Brian Burkett & Moira McCaskill, *Canadian Labour and Employment Law for the US Practitioner* (Washington, DC: Bureau of National Affairs, 2000).

Government of Alberta, "2014 Occupational Health and Safety Statistics—Initial Analysis" (2015), online: <https://open.alberta.ca/dataset/c1c1b935-a5d5-456a-b86c-c9986fa5542d/resource/c1f148ae-c689-48ea-acfd-b26f2b604d08/download/2015-2014-occupational-health-safety-statistics-initial-analysis-2014-ohs-data.pdf>.

Government of Alberta, Occupational Health and Safety Bulletin, CH009—Chemical Hazards, "Changes to WHMIS Legislation" (February 2015), online: <https://open.alberta.ca/publications/ch009-chemical-hazards>.

Hazardous Products Act, RSC 1985, c H-3.

Hazardous Products Regulations, SOR/2015-17.

Humber, Todd, "Supervisor Facing Criminal Charges," *Canadian Employment Law Today* 421 (15 September 2004) at 3291.

Inco Metals Co, [1980] OLRB Rep July 981.

Interpretation Act, RSA 2000, c I-8.

Interpretation Act, RSBC 1996, c 238.

Keith, Norm, & Cathy Chandler, *A Practical Guide to Occupational Health and Safety Compliance in Ontario*, 4th ed (Toronto: Canada Law Book, 2014).

Keith, Norm, & Yvonne O'Reilly, "The New Health and Safety Crime," *Canadian Employment Law Today* 413 (12 May 2004) at 3230.

Lennox Industries (Canada) Limited v United Steelworkers of America, Local 7235, 1999 CanLII 20394 (Ont LA).

Lonkar Well Testing Limited, R v, 2009 ABQB 345, rev'g 2008 ABPC 385.

Navrot v Alberta Occupational Health and Safety Council, 2005 ABCA 398.

Occupational Health and Safety Act, SA 2017, c O-2.1.

Occupational Health and Safety Code, Alta Reg 87/2009.

Occupational Health and Safety Regulation, Alta Reg 62/2003.

Occupational Health and Safety Regulation, BC Reg 296/97.

Sault Ste Marie, R v, [1978] 2 SCR 1299.

Schmidt, Doug, "Why? Family, Friends Ask," *Windsor Star* (11 November 2006).

Torrance, Michael, "A/H1N1 Flu and Pandemic Preparedness: An Employment and Labour Perspective" (1 May 2009), online: *Norton Rose Fulbright Canada LLP* <https://www.lexology.com/library/detail.aspx?g=fc43e31b-40dc-47d5-975e-f2a809855190>.

Vu, Uyen, "Ottawa Proposes Corporate Killing Law," *Canadian HR Reporter* (14 July 2003) at 1.

Westcon Precast Inc, R v, 2007 ABPC 143.
Workers Compensation Act, RSBC 1996, c 492.
Workers' Compensation Act, RSA 2000, c W-15.
WorkSafeBC, "Bullying and Harassment Prevention Tool Kit," online: <https://www.worksafebc.com/en/health-safety/hazards-exposures/bullying-harassment/resource-tool-kit>.
WorkSafeBC, "Media Backgrounder: Preventing Workplace Injuries" (April 2019), online: <https://www.worksafebc.com/en/resources/about-us/news-and-events/backgrounders/preventing-workplace-injuries>.
WorkSafeBC, "Policies Workers Compensation Act," online: <https://www.worksafebc.com/en/law-policy/occupational-health-safety/searchable-ohs-regulation/ohs-policies/policies-for-the-workers-compensation-act>. See policies D3-115-2, D3-116-1, and D3-117-2 on workplace bullying and harassment.

Workers' Compensation Legislation

9

LEARNING OUTCOMES

After completing this chapter, you will be able to:

- Understand the historic trade-off that underlies the workers' compensation system.
- Identify the key features of workers' compensation legislation and the role of workers' compensation boards in British Columbia and Alberta.
- Understand eligibility requirements for statutory benefits and compensation.
- Explain the duty to cooperate and the purpose of vocational rehabilitation.
- Understand the system's funding and the assessment of employers.
- Understand effective claims management procedures.
- List the functions of the workers' compensation boards in British Columbia and Alberta and the appeals structure in each province.

Introduction

negligence
an act or omission that involves no intention to cause harm but that a reasonable person would anticipate might cause harm

contributory negligence
a common law defence in an action arising from negligence in which it is asserted that the plaintiff's own negligence directly caused or contributed to the injuries suffered

co-worker negligence
a common law defence in an action arising from negligence in which it is asserted that the plaintiff's injuries were caused by the negligence of the plaintiff's co-worker, not the employer

voluntary assumption of risk
a common law defence in which it is asserted that the plaintiff voluntarily assumed the risk of injury

The workers' compensation legislation in British Columbia (BC) is called the *Workers Compensation Act*; similarly, in Alberta, it is called the *Workers' Compensation Act*. For the sake of brevity, "WCA" is often used in this chapter to refer to both statutes. The WCA in Alberta is accompanied by a *Workers' Compensation Regulation*, which guides interpretation and application of the WCA.

The WCA, like occupational health and safety legislation in BC and Alberta, relates to workplace health and safety. However, while the focus of occupational health and safety legislation is primarily on prevention, the WCA deals with compensating and rehabilitating workers who suffer work-related injuries and illnesses.

The principles that underlie the BC and Alberta workers' compensation systems are the same as they were when the systems were devised more than 95 years ago. A workers' compensation system is an insurance system financed by employers that guarantees compensation to workers for work-related injuries or diseases, regardless of who was at fault. In exchange for a no-fault system, workers have given up their right to sue employers for work-related injuries or disease, provided their employer has purchased the workers' compensation insurance. Thus, employees receive immediate compensation for injuries without the delay, expense, and uncertainty of filing a court claim against their employer; and employers are relieved of the uncertainty of lawsuits and financially devastating claims.

The historic trade-off wherein workers relinquished the right to sue in exchange for guaranteed benefits has withstood occasional legal challenges from workers who have argued that preventing them from suing their employers infringed their rights under the *Canadian Charter of Rights and Freedoms* (Charter). In the often-cited case of *Medwid v Ontario*, the Ontario High Court of Justice held that any disadvantage to workers caused by this trade-off is offset by the advantage of immediate payment from an insurance fund on a no-fault basis. In fact, the principle underlying workers' compensation continues to be generally supported as benefiting both employers and workers.

FYI

Before There Was a Workers' Compensation System ...

A system of workers' compensation was implemented in BC in 1917 and in Alberta the following year. The primary goal was to address the social and economic injustice that resulted from the treatment of injured workers under the common law of tort and contract.

Common law compensation for disabled workers was based on the law of **negligence**. To receive compensation for an occupational injury, the worker was required to bring a negligence suit against the employer in court. This was a prohibitively expensive proposition for most workers, and employers had several powerful defences to allegations of negligence.

The first of these was the defence of **contributory negligence**. If a court found that a worker had contributed in some way to their own injury, the employer's liability would be reduced. The second defence was **co-worker negligence**. If an employer could show that an injury was caused by the negligence of a co-worker, the employer was not liable. Finally, there was the defence of **voluntary assumption of risk**. If the work was inherently dangerous, such as working in a mine, an employer could argue that the worker voluntarily assumed the risk of injury by taking the job. If the defence succeeded, the employer was not liable.

Because the law was biased in favour of employers and because lawsuits were expensive and time-consuming, most workers who were injured on the job received no compensation, and many were left destitute if their injuries rendered them unable to work. At the same time, employers occasionally faced ruinous damage awards. To address these problems, a no-fault workers' compensation system was established to provide compensation to workers and protect both workers and employers from the cost and risk of lawsuits.

However, the implementation of this general principle has generated a great deal of controversy over the years. Numerous government inquiries and legislative changes have grappled with the challenge of providing a compensation process and benefit structure that is both fair and financially sustainable. Questions related to benefit levels and eligibility criteria for claims based on such factors as stress, chronic pain, and environmental sensitivities continue to generate controversy.

IN THE NEWS

Farmers Protest Mandatory WCB Coverage at Alberta Legislature

When the Alberta government introduced Bill 6,* legislation that would make Workers' Compensation Board coverage mandatory for farms with non-family waged workers, protesters descended on the legislature to make their displeasure known. About 75 farmers and ranchers participated in the protest, and presented a petition with more than 14,000 signatures, calling for Bill 6 to be amended or scrapped altogether. Many protesters were concerned about the impact the legislation would have on small-scale family farms. Bill 6 was particularly controversial because it also requires that farms comply with labour relations, employment standards, and occupational health and safety legislation.

Labour Minister Lori Sigurdson explained that the intention of Bill 6 was to allow occupational health officers to investigate serious injuries or fatalities on farms with the aim of preventing them in the future. This type of legislation is already in place in every other province.

Clint Lewing, a rancher in Leduc County, said that although increased safety regulations are needed, the province was ignoring rural concerns. "They need to pump the breaks and consult with us," Lewing said in an interview with CBC Edmonton AM host Mark Connolly. "Just because you have it in the book and say you need to follow it this way, does not make the workplace a safer place. You need to have industry involvement."

* Bill 6 was amended to exclude farm family members from required coverage, and the *Enhanced Protection for Farm and Ranch Workers Act* came into effect January 1, 2016. The United Conservative (UCP) government elected in 2019 promised to repeal the legislation introduced by the New Democratic Party to allow farmers the option of third-party workplace injury coverage. The UCP followed through on that promise with the *Farm Freedom and Safety Act*, which received royal assent on December 5, 2019. The first thing to note is that this new Act does not touch the changes made by the NDP to the *Occupational Health and Safety Act*. Basic health and safety protections to paid, non-family farm and ranch workers is still required. However, farm and ranch owners are now provided with a choice between workers' compensation insurance and private insurance, and they are not required to insure workers employed on a farm or ranch with five or fewer employees. It remains to be seen how well these changes protect workers and their employers. Private insurance is not no-fault, so employees may still file legal action against their employers, and insurers may seek to limit their liability. It is also unclear whether the benefits provided by private insurers will be comparable to those under the *Workers' Compensation Act*.

SOURCE: Based on *CBC News*, 2015.

FYI

Key Features of Workers' Compensation in BC and Alberta

1. The workers' compensation systems in both Alberta and BC are no-fault insurance systems that compensate workers for work-related accidents or injuries regardless of whether the injury is the result of negligence by the employee or the employer. Workers may not sue employers for occupational injuries and illnesses.
2. Benefits for injured workers are funded entirely by employers in the province, who pay premiums based on their industry classification. The premium reflects the risks and rates of injury in a particular industry. However, employers with good safety records pay less than others in their industry group as a result of an experience-rating program, and employers with poor safety records pay more.
3. It is against the law for workers to contribute to workers' compensation premiums.
4. Workers may not waive their rights to benefits under the workers' compensation system—in other words, employers cannot require them to give up these benefits.
5. Coverage is mandatory for many employers; other employers, independent contractors, sole proprietors, and executive officers may opt into the system if they pay their own premiums. Exempted industries are listed in Schedule A of the Alberta *Workers' Compensation Regulation*. The BC Act applies to all employers and workers except those exempted by order of the Board.
6. Workers' compensation focuses on the early and safe return of disabled workers to work, and it requires workers and employers to cooperate in this effort. Workers must provide ongoing information concerning their functional abilities, and employers must look for suitable work to which workers can return.
7. If an injured worker cannot return to their employer, a labour market re-entry plan may be prepared by the workers' compensation board to assist them in re-entering the workforce.
8. The workers' compensation systems are administered by independent workers' compensation boards—called WorkSafeBC in BC and the Workers' Compensation Board in Alberta. The boards adjudicate and pay compensation claims, oversee rehabilitation and re-employment, collect employer premiums, set employer assessment rates, and manage investments. The boards also enforce workers' rights to reinstatement. Private insurance companies play no role in compensating workers for occupational injuries.

Role of Workers' Compensation Boards

Although Ministry names and portfolios change from time to time, at the date of publication of this book the Workers' Compensation Board (WCB) falls under the Ministry of Labour in BC and under the Ministry of Labour and Immigration in Alberta. The WCBs are independent statutory agencies that administer the WCAs. They run under the operating names of WorkSafeBC in BC and WCB Alberta in Alberta. They have a wide jurisdiction to perform a number of functions as set out in section 96 of the BC WCA and sections 17 and 97 of the Alberta WCA. They determine how much the assessments should be that are paid by employers in specific industries, including special additional assessments for specific employers who have not complied with safety standards or have been found to have unsafe working conditions.

The boards hear all claims that are allowed to be made under the WCA and make a determination as to whether an injury or industrial disease arose in the course of employment and whether compensation is payable. The WCBs also oversee workers' rehabilitation and re-employment, manage investments, enforce reinstatement rights, and prepare policies and guidelines for adjudicating claims to promote consistency.

All decisions of the WCBs can be appealed to the Workers' Compensation Appeal Tribunal (WCAT) in BC and to the Appeals Commission for Alberta Workers' Compensation. In 2018 WorkSafeBC received 155,753 new reports of work-related injuries, or an average of 427 injury reports per day. In that same year, WCB Alberta received 132,346 new claims, or an average of 363 new claims/day. It should be noted that there is no federal workers' compensation board: workers' compensation benefits for federal public sector employees are administered by the workers' compensation board in the province in which they work. They also receive the same level of benefits as other workers in that province.

Worker Coverage

Most industries, particularly those that entail higher risk—including manufacturing, construction, hospitals, hotels, restaurants, and theatres—are now covered under the WCAs. **Industry** is defined broadly in the BC WCA as including any "establishment, undertaking, work, trade and business" (s 1). This coverage includes all workers, from CEOs to independent contractors. Only when WorkSafeBC exempts an employer or industry from the Act is an industry excluded from the workers' compensation system, and the exemptions are narrow. They are limited to unincorporated owner-operator businesses (sole proprietorships, partnerships) with no other employees, incorporated financial investment firms where all the employees are shareholders, and those employing household or childcare help for a limited number of hours per week. In addition, while the employees of unincorporated businesses are covered, the owners of those businesses are not, unless they opt in by paying annual fees to WorksSafeBC. Aside from these exemptions, all employment relationships are covered, including independent contractors working for a client, even if those contractors are not registered with WorkSafeBC. There are, however, some special rules in the Act and Regulations for certain types of injuries in certain industries (e.g., mining, fishing, and firefighting), but no general exemptions.

industry
under the BC *Workers Compensation Act*, any establishment, undertaking, work, trade, or business; under the Alberta *Workers' Compensation Act*, an establishment, undertaking, trade, or business, whether it is carried on in conjunction with other occupations or separately

The definition of "industry" is similar in the Alberta WCA, including an "establishment, undertaking, trade or business, whether it is carried on in conjunction with other occupations or separately" (s 1). Some industries are not compulsorily covered. These are listed in Schedule A of the Alberta *Workers' Compensation Regulation* and include, for example, financial institutions, recreational and social clubs, broadcasting stations, and law firms. However, many of these low-risk industries apply for coverage because it protects them from lawsuits for work-related injuries at a relatively low cost. Similarly, certain workers who are not automatically covered—such as sole proprietors and executive officers—may opt into the system. Farming is one high-risk industry in Alberta that was previously exempt from workers' compensation legislation. Even though agricultural businesses currently require coverage, as highlighted in the In the News box, regulating agricultural operations continues to be controversial in Alberta.

WCB Benefits

When Are Benefits Available?

The WCA insures workers against only those injuries or diseases that relate to the workplace; non-occupational injuries or illnesses are not covered. The WCB determines whether a worker qualifies for benefits on the basis of requirements set out in the WCA. The following is a review of the general rules relating to eligibility for WCB benefits.

Arising out of and in the Course of Employment

Assume that Avivah, a flight attendant, is on layover in Amsterdam before returning to Toronto. Her purse is stolen while she is on her way to a café, and she suffers a concussion when she gives chase to the thief. Is Avivah entitled to workers' compensation benefits?

The BC wording "arising out of and in the course of the employment" (s 5) has been broadly interpreted—again, favouring compensation of the worker. Benefits are paid as long as a worker is performing work-related duties anywhere on the employer's premises during work hours. Similarly, section 24(4) of the Alberta WCA states that if the injury arises "out of the employment," it is presumed that it occurred "during the course of the employment" (and vice versa) unless proven otherwise. An accident arises out of the course of employment when an employment hazard has caused it, and an employment hazard is an employment circumstance that presents a risk of injury. "In the course of" or "during the course of" means that the accident occurs at a time and place consistent with the obligations and expectations of employment. Thus, an injury need not result from the performance of a worker's job as long as the activities that result in the injury are reasonably incidental to the job. In one case, Decision No 339/91, an employee who hurt her back when she reached around to do up a button while in the washroom before starting her shift was compensated because going to the washroom was reasonably incidental to her employment. What is reasonably incidental to the job can be difficult to determine sometimes, as can be seen from the following case.

CASE IN POINT

Injuries Sustained in the Course of a Worker's Employment

Decision No 2001-0417, Workers' Compensation Reporter (2001), vol 17, no 3 at 343 (BC Workers' Compensation Board, Appeal Division)

Facts

On November 28, 1998, while the worker was trying to pull open a frozen-shut trap door on a drilling deck where he was employed, he felt his "navel pop out." He sought medical attention that same day. His doctor's examination report diagnosed the worker's problem as an umbilical hernia; the report noted that he had never experienced previous problems in that area. After the worker made a claim for this injury with the WCB, an entitlement officer concluded from doctors' reports that the worker had a para-umbilical hernia.

According to the data in a claims manual used by the Board, this kind of hernia was considered to be a congenital hernia; hence, it could not have arisen from stress, strain, work effort, or trauma except in the most unusual circumstances. Accordingly, in December the entitlement officer denied the worker's claim for compensation. About a year later, the worker's doctor wrote the Board advising that his patient's hernia was clearly caused by his lifting a heavy object at work and so he should be entitled to compensation. The matter was appealed to the Review Board and it decided in the worker's favour. The employer appealed that decision to the Appeal Division.

Relevant Issue

Whether the worker's injury was compensable because it arose from what he did at work or whether his claim was barred because it arose from a congenital condition.

Decision

In BC, a claim for compensation for injuries under the WCA can only succeed if the worker can show, pursuant to section 5(1), that they arose in the course of the worker's employment. To assist it in considering the claim, the Board consulted the relevant WCB policy manual, which stated that umbilical hernias are clearly congenital in nature and not related to stress or strain at work, except in the most unusual circumstances.

Nonetheless, the weight of evidence in the case supported a conclusion that the worker's hernia, even if it was umbilical, arose out of the work incident when he was trying to open the frozen trap door. Despite the policy manual suggesting otherwise, the board is still required to determine each case in accordance with its merits and principles of justice. Regard must always be made to the particular circumstances of each claim to determine whether the policy standard should apply or not. This is a reflection of the general administrative law principle that an administrative agency must not fetter its discretion by mechanically applying a policy guideline without considering the specific circumstances of a specific case before it. The Appeal Division considered this case to be one that fell within the category of "unusual circumstances" and deemed his injury to be work related. Accordingly, the worker was entitled to recover compensation.

Workers who travel on business are usually covered for injuries suffered while participating in predictable activities, such as dining in a hotel, but are not covered for personal or social activities, such as going to a movie theatre. In Avivah's case, the Tribunal recognized that there was a personal aspect to Avivah's activities but decided that the injury was compensable because, but for the layover, the incident would not have occurred, and the layover was an inherent part of her job (Gilbert & Liversidge, 2001, at 24). Similarly, while a worker's regular drive to work does not likely occur in the course of employment, driving to a client's establishment for the purpose of work likely does. There is a **rebuttable presumption** that accidents sustained during employment arise out of and in the course of employment. If a worker suffers an injury while at work, an employer that wants to contest the worker's claim must prove that the injury did not arise out of employment. Where the evidence is inconclusive, the worker is given the benefit of the doubt, and the claim is resolved in the worker's favour. Section 4.1 of the Alberta WCA states "if the evidence in support of the opposite sides of an issue related to a claim for compensation is approximately equal, the issue shall be resolved in favour of the worker."

rebuttable presumption an inference that a court will draw unless the contrary is proven

A worker who experiences a secondary injury that is causally linked to a work-related injury may receive benefits for the secondary injury. For example, someone who has a work-related injury to their right leg and then develops a problem with their left leg because of their increased reliance on it may be compensated for their left leg problem. However, there must be a causal link. For example, in a recent case the Alberta WCB accepted responsibility for tears to the meniscus of a worker's right knee, but refused to accept additional responsibility for subsequent back, lower right leg, and lower left leg pain (*2017-0397 (Re)*). The worker believed that overcompensating for her right knee caused the problems in her back and legs and appealed the decision of the Board. The Appeal Commission had to determine if the weight of the evidence supported a causal relationship between the knee injury and the back and lower leg pain that arose 18 months after the injury. Substantial medical evidence was submitted at the hearing, and the Appeal Commission upheld the decision of the WCB. They found that the evidence suggested the worker's back and leg pain was related to her high body mass index, underlying osteoarthritis of the knee, and degenerative disc disease in her back rather than her workplace injury. This case shows how difficult it can be to distinguish the root cause of many health conditions. Pre-existing conditions can affect WCB outcomes even when the worker has had no symptoms of the condition prior to the workplace injury.

Secondary injuries are new and distinct impairments or injuries that occur because of complication of a compensable injury. They may qualify for compensation if they are a direct result of a WCB-approved medical or rehabilitation treatment or as a result of a weakened limb or failure of a prosthesis or appliance related to a compensable injury. A second accident that is not work related but that aggravates a compensable injury may also be compensable.

***but for* test**
this is a logic test commonly used to determine causation in law; the test asks "*but for* the existence of X, would Y have occurred?" and if the answer is yes, then factor X is an actual cause of result Y

The standard used by WCBs to determine causation is called the ***but for* test**. This is a finding that the work exposures were necessary for the accident or injury to occur: *but for* the work exposure, the injury or disease would not have happened. Work does not have to be the only factor or even the primary factor for an injury to be compensable. It must, however, be a necessary factor. If the injury or disability would have happened without the work exposure, it is not compensable. In making this determination, WCBs consider the weight of the medical and other evidence to see if it demonstrates that:

- the worker suffered an injury,
- as the result of an employment hazard, and
- at a time and place consistent with the obligations and expectations of employment (Decision No 2019-0504).

Wilful Misconduct

Assume that co-workers Vitaly and David get in a fight at work because Vitaly was teasing David for wasting too much time on the job. During the fight Vitaly punches David, and David suffers a broken jaw as a result. Is David entitled to workers' compensation benefits?

In BC, under section 6 of the WCA, a worker is entitled to WCB benefits if they suffer an injury or disability "arising out of and in the course of the employment." Similarly, in Alberta, under section 1 of the WCA, a worker is entitled to benefits for an injury or disability from an "accident" that "arises out of and occurs in the course of employment." However, the BC legislation does not cover an injury that is "attributable *solely* to the serious and wilful misconduct of the worker" (emphasis added), unless the injury results in death or serious or permanent disablement (s 5(3)).

A similar disqualification from eligibility usually occurs pursuant to section 24 of the Alberta legislation if the injury is "attributable primarily to the serious and wilful misconduct of the worker." Again, death or serious disablement may negate disqualification from eligibility. The rationale is that by reason of the misconduct, the worker has taken themselves "out of the course of employment."

What actions might remove a worker from the course of employment? The Appeals Commission for Alberta Workers' Compensation, in *Decision No 2010-542*, provides the following list (which is not intended to be all-inclusive) at para 8:

- a criminal act with gainful intent;
- intoxication, when drinking is not permitted or condoned by the employer and intoxication is the sole cause of the accident;
- an intentional self-inflicted injury;
- fighting, when the issue is purely personal with no employment relationship;
- horseplay, if the worker is the instigator and it is a serious deviation from or abandonment of employment duties;
- activities which are exclusively personal and have no relationship, directly or indirectly, to the worker's employment duties or the employer's operations.

In both provinces, the WCBs interpret "out of the course of employment" in a way that favours compensation rather than denial of benefits. Section 5(3) of the BC statute is interpreted so that it applies only to workers who are injured as a result of intentionally breaching a well-known rule, and not to workers who are injured because of carelessness or an impulsive action. The WCB may grant benefits even if an injury is caused by fighting where the fighting involves work and the claimant does not provoke the fight. However, if the altercation is not related to the workplace, or the employer has rules against horseplay that are strictly enforced, WCBs are less likely to provide benefits.

What constitutes serious and wilful misconduct under the Alberta legislation is interpreted similarly, as can be seen in Decision No 2014-0343 of the Appeals Commission for Alberta Workers' Compensation below.

CASE IN POINT

Impulsive Act Does Not Meet Threshold for "Wilful Misconduct"

2014-0343 (Re), Decision No 2014-0343, 2014 CanLII 29801 (Alta WCAC)

Facts

The employee was hired on September 27, 2012, and shortly afterward was provided with five days of specific training on the safe operation of the machinery involved in the job duties. The most basic rule included in the training was to ensure that the machine was unplugged or shut off before clearing any jams because the operating mechanism was dangerous and could cause fatal injury. On November 10, 2012, the worker suffered a broken arm when he reached into the moving mechanism of the machine to retrieve an object. The employer argued that the worker's actions were serious and wilful misconduct because he knew the dangers, purposely weighed the risks, disregarded them, and put his arm into the machine. In the employer's view, the employee had no regard for his safety or the employer's rules and should be held accountable for his actions. For his part, the worker stated that he was not sure as to his exact thought process at the time of the event, but his action was impulsive and showed a lapse of judgment. He recognized that it was a poor decision and that he violated the employer's safety rules.

The WCB agreed to accept the worker's injury claim and to authorize wage replacement benefits. The employer appealed to the Dispute Resolution and Decision Review Body (DRDRB), which upheld the WCB decision. In 2013, the employer appealed the DRDRB's decision to the Appeals Commission for Alberta Workers' Compensation.

Relevant Issue

Was the worker's action serious and wilful misconduct of a nature sufficient to deny him worker's compensation benefits?

Decision

The panel found that the worker's actions in this case were impulsive, not carefully thought out, and devoid of regard for the likely consequences. As such, they did not meet the requirements for "serious and wilful misconduct." In order to constitute "serious and wilful misconduct," the person's actions must be fully considered, carefully thought out, and not impulsive. In reaching this decision, the panel considered the principles of no-fault legislation, stating that workers should be covered even if the accident was their own fault. The panel cited the Court of Appeal in *Alberta (Workers' Compensation Board) v Buckley*, describing the purpose of mandatory universal workers' compensation schemes:

> They were "no-fault" regimes for two reasons. The first was to ensure that injured workers would be compensated, regardless of whether they were responsible for their own injuries. The injured worker is covered no matter how negligent, careless, inattentive, grossly negligent, unskilled, or stupid he (or his co-workers or employer) might be. The second principle of the worker's compensation regime is that compensation for the injured worker would come from within the system. Injured workers would no longer sue their co-workers or their employer, and they would not sue other workers or employers within the system. They would never have to worry about an under-insured co-worker or employer. The employers and the co-workers were immune from suit. This is the famous "historic trade-off." For that reason, the bar for concluding that a worker cannot receive WCB benefits because of "serious and wilful misconduct" is very high. (at para 52)

Disability Claims

Assume that Francesco, a cashier in a grocery store, suffers from carpal tunnel syndrome in his wrist. Is he entitled to workers' compensation benefits?

The presumption of work-relatedness does not apply to most disability cases. Where the onset of an injury is gradual—as in a repetitive strain injury—the onus is on the worker to show a relationship between the disability and the work. However, it is not necessary that the work be the primary or dominant cause of the injury. If the work contributed in a significant way to the injury, the worker is entitled to WCB benefits. Francesco will probably find it easy to show a connection between the repetitive wrist motion required in his job and the disabling carpal tunnel syndrome that he suffers.

Where the worker has a pre-existing condition, they may receive benefits for their entire disability, although the employer may be relieved of part of the costs of the claim. For example, where a worker has a hereditary form of arthritis and their job contributes to the symptoms, the worker may receive full benefits, and the employer may ask the WCB to charge part of the costs to the Board's accident fund (discussed below).

Occupational Diseases

Occupational diseases are compensable if there is a causal relationship between the disease and the employment. Industrial diseases that are known to arise from specific industrial processes are set out in Schedules B and D to the BC *Workers Compensation Act* and Schedule B to the Alberta *Workers' Compensation Regulation*. If a worker in one of these industries contracts one of these diseases, there is a rebuttable presumption that the disease results from employment. For example, a miner who contracts silicosis is presumed to have a work-related disease. An employer that wishes to dispute the miner's claim must challenge this presumption by demonstrating that the silicosis was not related to the mining job. There are no minimum exposure requirements.

A few specified diseases create a non-rebuttable presumption of work-relatedness. In these cases, the disease is deemed to have been the result of a worker's employment, and the employer cannot attempt to allege otherwise. For example, a worker in one of the processes set out in Schedule B to the WCA of both BC and Alberta who contracts asbestosis is deemed to have contracted the disease if the workplace was one where there was exposure to airborne asbestos dust. However, compensation for all injuries, or all aspects of an injury, linked to working with asbestos may not always be so easily achieved, as the following case illustrates.

CASE IN POINT

Psychiatric Condition Arising from Occupational Disease Found Compensable After Multiple Appeals

Alberta (Workers' Compensation Board) v Alberta (Workers' Compensation Board, Appeals Commission), 2005 ABQB 161

Facts

Jacques St Martin was an electrician who, many years earlier in the course of his employment, had been exposed to asbestos. When his wife died of malignant mesothelioma, a disease caused by exposure to asbestos, and it was learned that her asbestos exposure was linked to her having regularly handled and laundered his work clothes, he became clinically depressed. After his wife's death, St Martin requested a full medical examination for himself. It was discovered that there was a spot on one of his lungs. He was diagnosed with asbestos-related pleural disease and was said to be at a definite risk for mesothelioma, the same disease that had killed his wife. He attended counselling sessions at Cross Cancer Institute in Edmonton and was later referred to a psychiatrist for assistance. The Alberta Workers' Compensation Board accepted St Martin's claim for compensation for asbestosis and pleural disease but did not accept his claim for clinical depression. However, the Appeals Commission reversed the Board's decision, saying that St Martin's psychiatric condition had arisen from his asbestos exposure. The WCB appealed the decision to the Alberta Court of Queen's Bench.

Relevant Issue

Whether the Appeals Commission erred in finding that St Martin's psychiatric illness was related to his employment and was compensable.

Decision

Alberta WCB Policy 02-01 requires a two-step analysis to determine a worker's eligibility for compensation: the accident or illness must arise out of the employment, and the accident or illness must have occurred in the course of employment. With respect to his asbestosis and pleural disease, the WCB had already decided that St Martin had suffered an accident arising out of and occurring in the course of his employment as an electrician. But WCB policy also specifies that accidents can be both physical and psychological, and that the results can be either immediate or of a progressive nature, the latter having a less obvious but nevertheless relevant relationship to employment. In other words, but for his work and his bringing home asbestos on his clothes, St Martin would never have exposed his wife to asbestos. Furthermore, medical evidence confirmed that St Martin was justifiably fearful of being diagnosed with the identical asbestos-related cancer that his wife had suffered from. The Appeals Commission therefore ultimately decided that the death of his wife, because it had highlighted St Martin's own possible fate, was a work-related stressor underscoring his sense of his own vulnerability. The Court found the conclusion of the Appeals Commission to be reasonable when it determined that St Martin's psychiatric condition, when taken as a whole, satisfied the two-part legal test for eligibility in the WCB policy. As a result, the Court of Queen's Bench dismissed the WCB's appeal.

Because of the progressive nature of a disease like asbestosis, it is not only compensation for all injuries—or all aspects of an injury—that may prove a challenge to a worker seeking to prove that their injury is linked to working with asbestos. The amount of compensation due to them may also prove a challenge if the date of a formal medical diagnosis of a progressive occupational disease occurs decades after the worker's actual exposure to the hazard, as shown in *Schneider v Alberta (Appeals Commission for Alberta Workers' Compensation)*.

CASE IN POINT

Date of First Medical Treatment for a Progressive Disease Is Date of Accident

Schneider v Alberta (Appeals Commission for Alberta Workers' Compensation), 2009 ABCA 417

Facts

In the course of his employment between 1968 and 1972 as a plumber and pipefitter, the appellant, Maurice Schneider, was frequently exposed to asbestos. About three decades later, on March 10, 2003, he was clinically diagnosed as having asbestosis, and the WCB and its Appeals Commission both determined that he was therefore entitled to a lump-sum pension amount for his disablement from that date onward. Schneider appealed the Commission's decision to the Alberta Court of Queen's Bench and simultaneously sought judicial review. Both cases were dismissed, and a further appeal was denied. He appealed to the Alberta Court of Appeal.

Relevant Issue

Whether the date that Schneider was officially diagnosed with a progressive occupational disease was the "date of the accident" as contemplated by section 24(7) of the *Workers' Compensation Act*.

Decision

All of the parties agreed that Schneider's diagnosis of asbestosis was indisputable evidence that he had suffered a permanent clinical impairment. Disagreement centred on the question of the date of his "accident." The WCB had determined that the date was March 10, 2003—the date of Schneider's formal diagnosis of asbestosis. The Appeals Commission upheld this finding. The Court of Queen's Bench found the Commission's decision to be reasonable. With respect to judicial review, it found that no statutory right of appeal existed because there was no question of law except the meaning of the term "disablement."

The Court of Appeal found errors in the Appeals Commission's decision regarding what it had identified as the date of Schneider's disablement, or alternatively, the date that the potential disablement had come to the Board's attention. Section 24(7) of the WCA states that the date of the accident for the purposes of the Act is deemed to be:

> (a) in the case of disablement, the date the disablement occurs, and
> (b) in the case of potential disablement, the date the potential disablement comes to the Board's attention.

In order to properly interpret the "date of the accident," the Court of Appeal said that the Appeals Commission should have sought the guidance of Workers' Compensation Board Policy 03-01 and applied it to section 24(7)(a) of the statute. WCB Policy 03-01 stated:

> When there is a specific incident which results in injury, the date of accident is the date on which the incident occurred.
>
> When the compensable condition or disease is progressive (e.g., there is no specific incident), the date of accident is normally the first date on which medical treatment is provided. If, however, the worker experienced earlier layoffs or loss of earnings which medical evidence indicates were caused by the compensable condition, the date of accident will be the first day of that earnings loss.

In other words, to identify the date of the accident, the Appeals Commission had to decide whether Schneider's case fell under section 24(7)(a) or section 24(7)(b) of the WCA. If section 24(7)(a) applied, then WCB policy required the Commission to assess whether Schneider's condition arose from a specific incident or not, which would then lead to two other, mutually exclusive, questions. Even though the Appeals Commission acknowledged the medical evidence of Schneider's asbestosis, the Court of Appeal isolated an error in the Commission's reference to and consideration of "potential disablement," showing a vacillation in decision-making between choosing section 24(7)(a) or (b) of the Act.

The Commission should have immediately identified the asbestosis as a disablement and proceeded to the next question set forth by WCB policy: whether there was a specific incident that caused the disablement. Schneider's evidence demonstrated exposure to asbestos over several years, so it was therefore likely that his condition was progressive rather than one that had been triggered by a specific incident. Policy 03-01 then directs that the date of the accident be identified as "normally the first date on which medical treatment is provided" (at para 9). Although, as the Court of Appeal points out, "historical and radiograph evidence of asbestos-related pleural disease" had comprised part of Schneider's medical history, the Appeals Commission failed to consider it—even though it was the first of the two mutually exclusive questions that WCB policy required it to address. Instead, the Board focused on the second of the two mutually exclusive questions—Schneider's lack of evidence to demonstrate any earnings loss causally connected to the asbestosis. This failure to proceed "under the totality of [the relevant WCB] policy" (at para 34) meant, ultimately, that the date of Schneider's accident appears to have been completely overlooked. As a result, the Court of Appeal required a new hearing of Schneider's case. The Workers Compensation Appeals Commission reviewed the case in 2011 and reversed its decision. They established the effective date for permanent impairment as the midpoint between November 1987 when Schneider first experienced the impairment and March 10, 2003 when the impairment rating was determined to be 20 percent.

This case demonstrates that the gap in time between when a worker first receives medical attention following a period of exposure to a hazard from which they ultimately develop a progressive occupational disease to the eventual date when an official diagnosis of that disease is finally provided may be huge. To determine the date of the accident, and the amount of compensation due, the complete medical history of the worker should therefore be considered.

In 2005, the BC government amended the WCA by adding section 6.1, which creates a statutory presumption that if a firefighter has contracted a prescribed disease, "the disease must be presumed to be due to the nature of the worker's employment as a firefighter, unless the contrary is proved" by the employer. A statutory presumption is an assumption of fact that is automatically accepted until disproved. In other words, the employee does not have to try to prove that their illness has been caused by the job. Instead, this is an assumed fact unless it is proven otherwise. Similarly, in Alberta, the WCA presumes that certain types of cancer and heart attacks that occur within 24 hours of attending at an emergency have arisen out of employment for firefighters and paramedics (s 24.1). The Act further establishes a presumption that post-traumatic stress disorder arises out of the course of employment for firefighters, correctional officers, emergency dispatchers, as well as other first responders.

A presumption also exists for traumatic psychological injury claims for all workers who experience a traumatic event or series of events at work:

> 24.2(2) If a first responder, correctional officer, emergency dispatcher or any other class of worker prescribed by the regulations is or has been diagnosed with post-traumatic stress disorder by a physician or psychologist, the post-traumatic stress disorder shall be presumed, unless the contrary is proven, to be an injury that arose out of and occurred during the course of the worker's employment.
>
> (3) If a worker
>
> (a) is or has been exposed to a traumatic event or events during the course of the worker's employment, and
>
> (b) is or has been diagnosed with a psychological injury by a physician or psychologist,
>
> the psychological injury shall be presumed, unless the contrary is proven, to be an injury that arose out of and occurred during the course of the worker's employment.

In all other circumstances, the WCB must decide on the facts of a case whether a disease is work related and therefore compensable. In an Ontario case, Decision No 269/90, a worker who operated some vibratory tools on an intermittent basis suffered from white finger disease. Because he did not use the tools for two continuous years, he did not meet the Board's policy guidelines for automatic recognition of the disease. However, the Workers' Compensation Appeals Tribunal found that on a balance of probabilities, the disease was related to the work that the worker performed. Because there was no reasonable alternative explanation as to how the worker acquired the disease, he was entitled to benefits (Gilbert & Liversidge, 2001, at 30).

Hearing loss is compensable as an injury if it results from direct trauma to the ear, as in the case of an explosion. Hearing loss caused by hazardous noise levels over a long period of time may constitute an occupational disease, but WCB guidelines require a history of such exposure, generally over a period of five years or more.

Disability benefits may be available to a worker who is not physically disabled but who must remain off work to avoid exposure to a hazardous substance or to avoid infecting others. For example, a hospital worker exposed to a communicable disease during employment is entitled to compensation if they are required to stay off the job to avoid infecting others (Gilbert & Liversidge, 2001, at 31).

In 2020, when the world was grappling with the COVID-19 outbreak, many questions were raised about who would be able to claim workers' compensation benefits. How would people know if it was contracted through work or from somewhere else? The Alberta Workers' Compensation Board issued a fact sheet to address these questions. The underlying assumption was that most cases were not work related. However, if a worker contracted COVID-19 as a direct result of the duties of their employment, they would be entitled to compensation if the following conditions were met:

- the nature of employment involved sufficient exposure to the source of infection, and

- the nature of employment was shown to be the cause of the condition, or
- the nature of employment creates a greater risk of exposure for the worker.

As always, work-relatedness and benefit entitlement are based on the specific circumstances of each case. WCB Alberta indicated that a claim was more likely to be accepted if the worker contracted COVID-19 while performing what the province deemed to be "essential service" work that put the individual in regular contact with the general public. Workers were also likely be covered in the event of a widespread outbreak at their place of employment (WCB Alberta, 2020). WorkSafeBC took a similar approach, continuing to assess work-relatedness on an individual case basis. Workers' compensation benefits were not available to workers in either province who chose to withdraw from work for preventative reasons.

Mental Stress or Disorder and Chronic Pain

Claims for mental stress or disorder and chronic pain present special challenges in determining eligibility for benefits. According to the BC WCA, a claim for mental disorder alone can succeed only if it meets all three criteria set out in section 5.1 of the Act:

1. it is either a reaction to a traumatic event related to the employment, or predominantly caused by work-related stressors, including bullying or harassment but also including more general accumulated stressors;
2. it is diagnosed by a physician or psychologist as a mental or physical condition; and
3. it does not arise from the proceedings involved in making a claim for compensation.

This section was changed in 2012. It used to limit recovery to stress that was the result of a traumatic, unexpected event. The change has the effect of broadening the coverage considerably—not only to include stressors other than traumatic events, but also to remove the requirement that the stressor be something unexpected. In contrast to claims based on stress alone, mental stress that is the consequence of a compensable physical injury is covered, as long as it can be proved.

Importantly, the law and WorkSafeBC policy clarifies that a mental disorder claim cannot be related to an employer's decision relating to employment. This means that a mental disorder claim will be dismissed if it is caused by employment-related decisions, such as a decision to change the work to be performed or the working conditions, to discipline the worker, to terminate the worker's employment, or other decisions related to workload and deadlines, work evaluation, performance management, transfers, layoffs, demotions, reorganizations, and the like.

Alberta takes an approach similar to that in BC, with some subtle differences. Under section 6 of the Alberta WCA (powers of the board of directors to authorize policy) and WCB Policy 03-01 Part II (June 26, 2018), the WCB will consider a claim for psychiatric or psychological injury when there is a confirmed psychological or psychiatric diagnosis as defined in the most current version of the *Diagnostic and*

Statistical Manual of Mental Disorders (DSM), and the condition results from one of the following:

1. organic brain damage causally connected to a work-related head injury, exposure to toxic chemicals or gases, anoxia or other work-related injury, disease, or condition;
2. an emotional reaction to a work-related physical injury (e.g., depression related to amputation or prolonged disability);
3. an emotional reaction to a work-related treatment process (e.g., complicated recovery from surgery, added pain from treatment);
4. traumatic onset psychological injury or stress;
5. chronic onset psychological injury or stress.

Policy 03-01 describes "mental stress" as a commonly used term that describes an individual's non-specific physical and psychological response to events or changes that occur in that person's life. These events are known as "stressors." Some level of stress is a normal part of life; however, when a person's ability to cope with the stressor is overwhelmed, *distress*, a negative form a of mental stress, can develop and result in diagnosable psychological or psychiatric injuries. Stress is not an accepted medical diagnostic term but can result in psychiatric or psychological diagnoses such as adjustment disorders, anxiety disorders, or mood disorders, depending on the circumstances.

Claims for chronic onset injury or stress are compensable only if all of the following criteria are met:

- there is a confirmed psychological or psychiatric diagnosis as described in the DSM;
- the work-related events or stressors are the predominant cause of the injury; predominant cause means the prevailing, strongest, chief, or main cause of the chronic onset stress;
- the work-related events are excessive or unusual in comparison to the normal pressures and tensions experienced by the average worker in a similar occupation; and
- there is objective confirmation of the events.

Normal pressures and tensions include interpersonal relationships and conflicts, health and safety concerns, union issues, workload and deadlines, performance evaluation (including discipline), transfers, changes in job duties, layoffs, demotions, terminations, and reorganizations.

For example, a bank teller who suffers mental stress as a result of an armed robbery can probably expect to receive benefits. However, a worker who suffers stress as a result of workload pressure would probably not succeed under this policy.

A 2014 case from the Supreme Court of Canada, *Martin v Alberta (Workers' Compensation Board)*, affirms the approach taken by the Alberta WCB in determining whether a case of chronic stress has arisen out of and during the course of employment.

CASE IN POINT

Alberta Approach to Mental Stress Claim Evaluation Confirmed by Supreme Court

Martin v Alberta (Workers' Compensation Board), 2014 SCC 25

Facts

Martin, a 30-year employee of Parks Canada in Banff, made a disability claim based on mental stress to the Alberta WCB. Martin was an advocate of park wardens being permitted to carry firearms as a health and safety measure. As a result of his involvement in the issue, Martin was involved in several interactions with his employer of a labour relations nature. In December 2006, Martin received a letter from his employer requesting that he comply with an access to information request. The receipt of the letter, although a normal and ordinary event, triggered a stress reaction. Martin went on stress leave upon the recommendation of his physician. The letter from his physician in support of Martin's claim suggested a working diagnosis of post-traumatic stress secondary to the behaviours of administration.

Martin's claim was denied. The WCB indicated that the facts of his claim did not met the criteria for either traumatic stress or chronic stress. Martin appealed through the internal and external workers' compensation appeal mechanisms. The original decision was upheld. Martin then commenced a judicial review and appeal at the Court of Queen's Bench. The Court of Queen's Bench overturned the original decision, suggesting that the WCB's criteria were incompatible with the Charter because they create additional hurdles that are not required for claimants with physical disabilities (Factum of the Respondent, Workers' Compensation Board of Alberta):

> The third and fourth policy criteria for chronic onset stress in Alberta, requiring the work-related events to be *excessive* or *unusual* in comparison to normally experienced pressures and tensions and that there be objective confirmation of these events, are "add-ons" or additional "hurdles." (at para 22)

The case was then heard by the Alberta Court of Appeal, which reinstated the original WCB decision.

Relevant Issue

Are the criteria of "excessive" or "unusual" used by the WCB in accordance with the law?

Decision

The Supreme Court upheld the original WCB and Court of Appeal decisions. The Court found that the policy does not add extra requirements. Instead, the policy provides guidance in determining whether an accident has occurred and, if so, whether it is *caused by* (arises out of) employment. The Court accepted the interpretation of "excessive or unusual" described by the Workers' Compensation Board (Factum of the Respondent, Workers' Compensation Board of Alberta):

> The main idea behind workers' compensation is to compensate for injuries and conditions caused by work. Not every injury, condition, episode of discomfort or onset of anxiety is caused by work, even if it occurs at work. (at para 72) …
>
> The requirement of an *excessive* or *unusual* triggering event, when compared to the *normal pressures and tensions* of the job reflects a systemic desire to have an ascertainable standard for this type of injury. Mental injuries by their nature, as well their connection to the workplace, are indistinct. Unlike physical injuries, such as a broken arm or a repetitive strain injury, mental stress is less tangible, harder to see and less amenable to proof of causation. (at para 74)
>
> In light of the elusive nature of mental injuries and their connection to the workplace, the *excessive* or *unusual* standard was developed to provide an objective test of workplace causation. The application of this test is really an inquiry into whether it is probable that the reported mechanism of injury produced the injury that is claimed, an inquiry that is no different than in every case of a physical injury. In workers' compensation, different types of injuries are proven by different methods depending on the nature of the injury and its amenability to direct or physical proof of causation. (at para 75)

The *Martin* case is an important one for several reasons. In addition to affirming the Alberta approach to determining compensability in chronic stress cases, the Supreme Court also stated that the standard of review for workers' compensation cases is one of reasonableness (rather than correctness), because the workers' compensation tribunal is an expert in matters pertaining to workers' compensation and is therefore entitled to deference. This standard of review applies equally to cases in BC. The Court also affirmed that the workers' compensation legislation in Alberta and the policy with respect to chronic stress are consistent with the federal *Government Employees Compensation Act*, which assigns responsibility for adjudicating workers' compensation claims of federal employees to the provincial workers' compensation bodies.

Policy 03-01 also applies to chronic pain or chronic pain syndrome. Pain that is persistent or lingering and due to discernible organic diagnoses or psychiatric conditions is compensable. However, when pain and pain behaviour is inconsistent with organic findings, the WCB may compensate if all of the following conditions are met:

- all physical medical investigation and rehabilitation treatment is concluded,
- the pain results in marked life disruption,
- the pain and related symptoms develop as a consequence of a compensable injury or condition,
- the pain persists for six months or more beyond the usual healing time for the injury,
- complaints of pain and pain behaviour are inconsistent with organic findings, and
- pain impairs earning capacity.

In BC, Practice Directive #C3-1 indicates that, where the policy definition for chronic pain has been met, the condition will give rise to a compensable claim when the following conditions are met:

- the causal connection between the work injury and the worker's pain has to be more than insignificant,
- the work injury contributed to a material degree in the development of chronic pain,
- the worker's pain complaints are consistent with the work injury and/or effects of treatment,
- it is reasonably likely/biologically plausible that the reported pain symptoms are a consequence of the compensable injury, and
- there are no other medical factors unrelated to the compensable injury that are a more likely explanation for the worker's pain.

What Do Benefits Cover?

There are several kinds of compensation and benefits available under the WCA for accidents that arise from employment. These include compensation payments from the WCB's accident fund for injuries and disabilities, death, and vocational rehabilitation. Benefits can be permanent or temporary, as the case requires.

Assume that Robert is a 38-year-old head mechanic at Otto's Auto Body Shop, a family-owned business that has 21 employees. Robert has worked at Otto's Auto for the last four years. At the beginning of his eight-hour shift on February 12, 2015, Robert tore a ligament in the thumb of his right hand. This is the same ligament he damaged several years before, when he worked for a previous employer. Robert is in a lot of pain, and he tells his employer he cannot work the remainder of his shift. The employer asks a co-worker to drive Robert to the hospital. This is a work-related injury, and the employer files the necessary paperwork with the WCB, as required by the legislation, to start a WCA claim for Robert. At the hospital, the attending physician advises Robert that he has badly injured his hand and he will not be able to use it for at least four weeks. He will also need extensive physiotherapy if he hopes to recover its full use.

What benefits will Robert be entitled to under the WCA? (Robert's after-tax earnings, including his benefits package, are approximately $200 per day, or $1,000 per week.)

Lost Earnings on the Day of the Injury

In our example, Otto's Auto must pay Robert for the remainder of his February 12 shift. Section 25(1)(a) of the Alberta WCA provides that "[i]f an accident disables a worker for all or part of the day of the accident," the employer shall

> pay compensation to the worker for that day in an amount equal to the minimum normal net wage the worker would have received for that day if the worker had not been disabled and had been available for work in the normal course.

There is no similar provision in BC—compensation for lost wages usually starts with the first regular work shift missed.

Health Care Costs

Health care costs associated with a work-related injury or disease—such as chiropractic care, dental care, prescription drugs, and artificial limbs—are covered by the Act in both provinces. Therefore, the WCA system will cover all health care costs that result from Robert's injury. Also covered are modifications to a worker's home or vehicle. In most cases health care benefits start immediately (that is, on the day of injury).

Temporary Partial Disability

In our example, as long as the disability arising from the accident lasts, the WCB will compensate Robert for lost earnings from the first working day following his injury. Loss-of-earnings benefits are calculated in BC as 90 percent of the difference between the worker's average net earnings before the injury and what the WCB considers best reflects the injured worker's loss of earnings: the average net earnings he is earning after the injury, or the average net earnings the WCB estimates he would be capable of earning in a suitable occupation after the injury (s 30). The earnings take into account contributions to the Canada Pension Plan, employment insurance, and retirement funds (s 33). Robert will therefore receive $900 (90 percent of $1,000) per week while he is off work completely with his work-related injury. These benefits are non-taxable.

Similarly, in Alberta, pursuant to sections 56 of the WCA and WCB Policy 04-02 Part II, loss-of-earnings benefits for a temporary partial disability are calculated on the basis of the worker's estimated loss of net earnings (the difference between the worker's net earnings at the time of the accident and the greater of the worker's actual earnings after the accident and the worker's estimated earning capacity after the accident). The disability benefit is a proportionate part of 90 percent of the resulting earnings loss, taking into account the Alberta WCB's estimate of the degree to which the earnings loss is caused by the residual disability. While Robert is temporarily off work completely, he would receive 90 percent of $1,000, or $900 per week.

When, later, he partially resumes employment, he would receive 90 percent of the difference between his net pre-accident and net post-accident earnings if a suitable job, or a modified version of his pre-accident job, is made available to him.

Assume that after several weeks of physiotherapy, Robert's physician advises him that he can return to the workplace and perform modified work if he does not use his right hand. Otto's Auto agrees that Robert can work in the office for a few weeks while one of the office employees is on holidays. However, the net earnings of this position are only $500 per week. In this situation, in both BC and Alberta, Robert will be paid 90 percent of the difference between his pre-injury net earnings ($1,000) and his net earnings in the office job ($500). Therefore, while Robert is performing modified work, his WCB benefits will be $450 (90 percent of the $500 difference in pay between the two jobs). These partial benefits are also not subject to income tax.

While Robert is receiving WCB benefits, he is required to notify the WCB of any material change in his situation—that is, any change that would affect his entitlement to benefits and services. This could include a change in medical or employment status, earnings, or ability to cooperate with the Board. Failure to report a material change can result in disentitlement to benefits or being charged with an offence. Otto's Auto similarly has a duty to report material changes that may affect its obligations under the WCA, including changes in business activity, assessable payroll, operations, or ownership. Otto's Auto is also required to continue Robert's pre-injury employment benefits for the first year after his injury, provided that Robert continues to make any contributions he is responsible for during this year.

Permanent Total Disability

Suppose that Robert suffered a much more serious injury than previously described, an injury so serious that he was left permanently and totally disabled. In BC, WorkSafeBC would pay him a periodic payment equal to 90 percent of his average net earnings, which would be paid to him for the rest of his life (s 22). In 1996, that amount of compensation was stipulated to be no less than $1,623.32 per month, but this amount is indexed to inflation and was set at $1,802.04 in 2019. Sections 23.1

through 23.5 set out a scheme for continuing compensation after retirement in the case of permanent total or permanent partial disability.

In Alberta, pursuant to section 56(10) of the WCA, the WCB would pay Robert a non-economic loss payment, which is a lump-sum payment based on the measurable clinical impairment and an economic loss payment, which is a periodic payment based on the loss of earning capacity caused by the disability. The economic loss payment is 90 percent of his pre-accident net earnings. Pursuant to section 56(11) of the Act, compensation for a permanent total disability of not less than $1,640.90 per month would be paid to Robert throughout his lifetime.

Temporary Total Disability

If Robert were left 100 percent disabled as a result of his injury at work but only for a certain period of time, he would be paid periodic payments in the same amount as if he had been left permanently disabled. This rule applies in both BC and Alberta. However, that compensation would no longer be payable once he recovered.

Permanent Partial Disability or Disfigurement

Now suppose that Robert has been left with a permanent partial disability from his accident. The nature and degree of that injury can vary considerably. In BC, compensation is a periodic payment equalling 90 percent of the estimated loss of average earnings resulting from the impairment—that is, the difference between what Robert was able to earn before the disability and what he is now able to earn. Robert is entitled to this compensation throughout the remainder of his working life (s 23). Again, there is a set minimum amount that must be payable, which is based on the amount for permanent total disability (with adjustment for the extent of the partial disability and adjustment for inflation).

In Alberta, compensation will be a periodic payment equalling a proportionate part of 90 percent of Robert's net earnings (s 56(1)(b)) based on the WCB's estimate of impairment of earning capacity from the nature and degree of the disability. If Robert is under the age of 25 or was enrolled in a vocational or academic program at the time of the accident and if he was at least 50 percent disabled, the calculation would be based on his net earnings or the Alberta average weekly earnings (whichever is greater). This legislative change (s 68), which took effect in 2018, is intended to ensure severely injured young workers are compensated in a way that reflects their actual earning potential.

When a disability is permanent and partial, the WCB has to determine whether Robert will be able to continue in his former employment or whether it would be better for him to resume work in some other capacity with another employer. In the case of serious and permanent disfigurement as a result of the injury, the WCB may allow the worker to retain the same earnings as before but instruct that he be provided with a lump-sum payment of compensation.

Death and Survivor Benefits

Under section 17 of the BC WCA, there is a complex formula for determining who is entitled to receive death and survivor benefits and what they should be paid. A spouse and children are entitled to monthly payments based in part on the disability compensation the deceased worker would have received had the injury not been fatal. There are a number of factors that affect the amount, including the deceased worker's net average earnings, the number of dependent children, the dependants' entitlements to Canada Pension Plan benefits, and whether the surviving spouse is an invalid. A surviving spouse is also entitled to a lump-sum amount, which is indexed to inflation and which in 2019 was $2,500.

Under the Alberta legislation, the surviving spouse or adult interdependent partner of a worker killed in an accident, or subsequently succumbing to an injury sustained in an accident, is entitled to a pension (s 70). The amount and duration of the pension vary depending on factors such as the number of dependent children and the spouses' or adult interdependent partner's employability. Pursuant to section 89(2), the spouse or partner may access the same benefits and services (such as vocational rehabilitation) as the worker would have been entitled to use had they lived.

Vocational Rehabilitation

In many injuries or illnesses arising from the workplace, it is possible to have the worker resume employment in some other capacity. This almost invariably involves retraining the worker to obtain new knowledge and skills. The WCB can draw from the accident fund to finance this retraining of the worker. The retraining can also extend to the spouse and dependants of deceased workers.

Continuing with our example, assume that after six months of physiotherapy it becomes apparent that Robert will never recover sufficient use of his right thumb to perform his pre-injury mechanic's job. It is therefore unlikely that Otto's Auto will ever be able to re-employ him because all jobs comparable to Robert's require manual dexterity. As a result, the WCB gets involved. It works with Robert to assess his skills and interests. It then prepares a vocational rehabilitation plan to assist Robert in re-entering the labour market.

After assessing Robert's personal, physical, and vocational abilities and interests, the Board and Robert agree that he should return to school to become a qualified auto mechanics instructor (a "suitable occupation" based on his transferable skills). In this way, he can build upon his extensive experience and stay in a field he enjoys. With this additional qualification, Robert will probably eventually be able to earn a salary comparable to his pre-injury earnings. A vocational rehabilitation plan may require many different approaches, such as work placements, workplace modifications, and formal retraining.

The Duty to Cooperate

After an injury, the WCB monitors the claim. The goal is to return a worker to the pre-accident employer, where possible, as soon as it is safe to do so. Therefore, Robert and Otto's Auto are expected to keep in touch throughout Robert's recovery period, sharing information necessary to facilitate Robert's return to work. Robert must cooperate by consenting to the disclosure of medical information indicating his functional abilities so that Otto's Auto can assess his ability to return to work. By identifying gaps between Robert's functional abilities and the physical demands of his job, Otto's Auto can make any necessary modifications to facilitate an early return.

Pursuant to section 54 of the Alberta WCA, if a worker

> behaves in a manner that tends to imperil or retard the worker's recovery or refuses to undergo any medical aid that the board, based on independent medical advice, considers reasonably essential to promote the worker's recovery,

the Board may reduce or suspend the compensation payable to that worker. Virtually identical provisions appear in section 57 of the BC WCA.

Both Robert and Otto's Auto are required to keep the Board notified of material changes to their circumstances. The Act in each province prohibits anyone from providing false or misleading information, failing to report a return to work, or failing to inform the Board of a material change in a worker's circumstances that could affect that person's entitlement to compensation or other benefits under the Act.

The workers' compensation legislation in Alberta has provisions in section 88 that require an employer to offer to reinstate a worker who was previously employed with that employer for at least 12 continuous months on a full- or part-time basis. The employer is required to accommodate to the point of undue hardship. When the worker is able to perform the essential duties of the pre-injury job, the employer must offer to reinstate the worker to the same position or alternative employment of a comparable nature and with at least the same pay and benefits. If the worker cannot perform the work, the employer is required to offer the first suitable employment opportunity that becomes available. Furthermore, the employer is prohibited from terminating the employee within six months of reinstatement or while the employee is still receiving compensation under the WCA. Section 88 also requires that the employer and injured worker cooperate with the early and safe return to work of the worker. Employers are required to:

- contact the worker as soon as possible after the accident and maintain communication throughout the recovery period;
- attempt to provide suitable employment that is consistent with the worker's functional abilities and, where possible, restores the worker's earnings to pre-accident levels; and
- provide information to the Board as requested regarding the worker's return-to-work status.

Injured workers are similarly required to:

- contact the employer as soon as possible after the accident and maintain communication throughout the recovery period;
- assist the employer to identify suitable employment; and
- provide information to the Board as requested.

The BC WCA does not include any equivalent reinstatement provisions.

Funding the WCA System

Employer Assessments

Employers pay the full cost of the WCA system by means of premiums. It is illegal for employers to recover any part of their premium from workers.

An employer must register with the WCB after becoming an employer. Failing to register can result in an employer's being assessed for periods during which it did not pay premiums, plus interest and penalties. If an accident occurs before an employer registers, all or part of the accident cost may be charged directly to the employer.

For assessment purposes, there are, in BC, at least 11 different categories of employers as set out in section 37 of the WCA. The Act sets out the factors that determine what the assessment will be for a particular employer within each of those categories. These will include the number of employees at a particular worksite (size of payroll) and the employer's compliance or non-compliance with safe working condition requirements in the past. If the WCB thinks that an injury, death, or disablement was primarily due to an employer's gross negligence, it can levy and collect a special contribution that the employer will have to pay to the accident fund. These special levies have a maximum value that is indexed to the consumer price index. As of the fall of 2019, the maximum levy is $57,971.53.

In Alberta, section 98 of the WCA requires an employer to provide information that will permit the WCB to classify it and assign it a base insurance rate according to the type of industry and the potential hazards associated with it. Other reporting obligations of the employer, besides providing a description of the business, include reporting insurable earnings and reporting accidents. The employer's assessment is calculated as a percentage of the employer's payroll, up to a maximum amount per worker. The assessment for each worker can be calculated by multiplying the employer's assessment rate by the worker's annual earnings up to the maximum amount.

To calculate Otto's Auto's total WCA premiums for the year, multiply its total payroll (excluding amounts per individual worker that are above the earnings ceiling) by its assessment rate of 1.88 percent. For example, if the 21 employees at Otto's Auto earn a total of $630,000 (excluding earnings above the ceiling), the WCA assessments for that year amount to $11,844 ($630,000 × 1.88%).

Employers in Alberta have the opportunity to reduce their premiums by up to 20 percent if they participate in the Partnerships in Injury Reduction program. In order to participate, employers must achieve and maintain a Certificate of Recognition (COR). To achieve the COR, the employer's health and safety management system is audited and must receive minimum scores on each element of the audit and an overall score of at least 80 percent.

Effective Claims Management

To minimize the occurrence and costs of workplace accidents and illnesses, employers should, among other things, establish an effective claims management program. The following procedures are useful in this regard:

1. *Establish procedures for investigating workplace injuries and train management in these procedures.* Procedures include interviewing an injured worker, if possible, to obtain their recollection of an accident and any information about pre-existing medical conditions. Management should also interview witnesses about these matters, record the information, and photograph or sketch the accident scene without altering it, if possible.
2. *Complete and file an accident report with the WCB in the required format.* This initiates the claims process. The WCB must receive the report within three calendar days of the time that the accident came to the employer's attention in Alberta and within three business days in BC. There is a penalty for late filing. Provide all relevant data. Ask the injured worker to sign a medical release, which authorizes the employer to receive functional abilities information from the worker's physician.
3. *Document all claims, even those that appear to be minor.*
4. *Where the worker's entitlement to benefits is clear, make every effort to ensure that the worker is able to claim benefits promptly.* For example, respond promptly to WCB inquiries.
5. *Challenge only truly doubtful claims, but protest them from the outset because once a claim is established, it is difficult to question later.* For example, an employer who fails to challenge a doubtful medical aid claim because the initial costs are minor will find it difficult to appeal the mounting costs later on. No injury should be underestimated. For example, an apparently minor back claim can result in long-term compensation and medical costs in the $100,000 range.
6. *Keep notes concerning contacts with health and safety officials and the WCB.* Important information to include are the date, time, and substance of any conversations and the name of the WCB contact person. Follow up on any conversations with the WCB by letter, indicating any action or information that is required. Keep the file current.
7. *Establish a return-to-work plan and make necessary accommodations short of undue hardship.*
8. *Do not contact the injured worker's physician.* An employer may request clarification of a physician's report through the WCB or the worker. An employer may also request an independent medical examination to verify the nature of the claim or to determine the worker's ability to participate in modified work.
9. *Keep medical files separate from personnel files, and treat them in a confidential manner.*

Administration and Enforcement

The workers' compensation system is administered by the WCB in each province. Board employees perform many functions, including adjudicating and paying compensation claims to eligible workers. In Alberta, Board employees operate by a code of rights and conduct that establishes the rights of workers and employers, including the right to participate in decisions that affect them. It imposes procedures for ensuring fair handling of complaints. According to the Alberta WCB's Annual Report, the Alberta WCB dealt with 28,600 lost time claims and 162 fatalities in 2018 (Alberta WCB, 2018). In addition, the Board oversees workers' reintegration and re-employment, collects employer premiums, sets employer assessment rates, manages investments, and provides health and safety education for employers and workers. The WCB also prepares policies and guidelines for adjudicating claims to promote consistency. Medical specialists are available on staff to assist in complex claims, and outside specialists are used as required. In Alberta, Millard Health (operated by the WCB) provides occupational rehabilitation and disability management services.

WorkSafeBC operates similarly and received 155,753 injury reports in 2018, including 50,000 short-term disability claims and 131 work-related fatality claims (WorkSafeBC, 2019).

Appeals

In BC, a worker or employer who disagrees with a decision of WorkSafeBC may in some circumstances, and within 90 days of the decision, request that the decision be reviewed by a review officer (s 96.2 of the WCA). The review officer's decision will be made in writing and delivered to the Board and the interested parties. A party not content with the review officer's decision may file a written notice of appeal with the Workers' Compensation Appeal Tribunal within 30 days (s 243(1)).

In Alberta, if a worker, dependant, or employer is dissatisfied with the result of a WCB claim, they have one year to make a request in writing that a review body review the record of a compensation claim (s 46 of the WCA). One further appeal is permitted to the Appeals Commission for Alberta Workers' Compensation (ss 10–13.5), which can be made up to two years after the decision of the review body. Issues raised on appeal are far-ranging and include matters such as eligibility for benefits, health care, employer re-employment obligations, and the amount of premiums. So, if Robert or Otto's Auto disagreed with the WCB's award, either party could appeal it. Robert could also seek an interim financial relief during the review or appeal processes. Alberta has also added a medical dispute resolution panel that will adjudicate if doctors disagree about a worker's claim.

The BC WCAT and the Appeals Commission for Alberta Workers' Compensation are independent of their respective boards, although, like all tribunals in BC and Alberta, they are required to conduct their proceedings in compliance with the BC *Administrative Tribunals Act* and the Alberta *Administrative Procedures and Jurisdiction Act*, respectively. It is rare for workers' compensation issues to go to court, and few applications for judicial review of tribunal decisions succeed (Gilbert et al, 2011, at 300).

The Right to Sue

Under section 10 of the BC WCA and section 17 of the Alberta WCA, employers enjoy special protection from lawsuits. For example, if companies X and Y are employers and their workers are involved in a motor vehicle accident while on the job, the workers cannot sue each other and cannot sue either company X or company Y. However, independent contractors who have not opted for coverage under the WCA may bring a lawsuit against the company with whom they contract in the event they suffer a work-related injury. For this reason, employers may want independent contractors to agree to opt for coverage.

A 2012 decision of the BC Court of Appeal affirmed the breadth of this rule about the right to sue. In *Downs Construction Ltd v Workers' Compensation Appeal Tribunal*, an employee sought to sue her employer and a co-worker for mental stress that the co-worker had caused. When they relied on section 10 to bar her claim, she filed for compensation under section 5.1 of the WCA (see the discussion above under "Mental Stress or Disorder and Chronic Pain"). WorkSafeBC rejected the claim, and the WCAT affirmed the decision, stating that the employee had not satisfied the requirements of section 5.1 for a mental stress claim. The employee again sought to file a civil lawsuit. She argued that section 10 did not bar the claim, since the WCAT had refused to compensate her, arguing that the rejection of her claim amounted to a decision that her stress did not arise in the course of employment. The Court of Appeal rejected her claim. It ruled that section 10 bars civil lawsuits against employers for work-related injuries—even if the claim under the WCA has failed. If the incidents that gave rise to the claim were in the context of employment, there can be no civil lawsuit.

KEY TERMS

but for test, **344**
contributory negligence, **338**
co-worker negligence, **338**
industry, **341**
negligence, **338**
rebuttable presumption, **343**
voluntary assumption of risk, **338**

REVIEW AND DISCUSSION QUESTIONS

1. What have workers given up for their rights under the present injury compensation system? Do you think that they have benefited from this trade-off? Why? What do you think would happen if the right to sue was reintroduced to the system?
2. Why would an employer in an industry that is not required to be covered by the WCA opt for coverage?
3. Why is it important for an employer to have an effective claims management program?
4. Locate the WCB policy manual for your province online (see <https://www.wcb.ab.ca/about-wcb/policy-manual> for the Alberta manual and <https://www.worksafebc.com/en/law-policy/claims-rehabilitation/compensation-policies/rehab-claims-volumeii> for the BC manual). How is chronic pain treated under the current WCA system?
5. Sameera, an employee who worked in one of the retail outlets in a mall, slipped and fell on a patch of ice in the mall parking lot on her way to work. She injured herself and sued the owners of the mall for damages. The mall owners appealed to the WCB, arguing that she was eligible for WCB benefits. The parking lot was a "common area" owned by the mall's management company. The employee had parked in the portion of the lot designated by the employer for employees.
   a. Why would the mall owners want Sameera's injury to be covered by the WCB?
   b. In your opinion, is Sameera eligible for WCB benefits in these circumstances? Explain your answer.
6. Bob, aged 34, got a job at a call centre for mobile communication systems for drivers. He assisted clients with non-emergency concerns, but his department handled overflow emergency calls; he was taught to connect those subscribers to police or 911. One day, Bob received an overflow emergency call from a woman who asked him to track the location of her sister's vehicle. When he informed her that he could not track the vehicle of a third party unless police were involved, she said she was afraid that her sister intended to commit suicide. She became angry and abusive and refused to let him connect her to 911 or the police. Ten minutes later a supervisor took over the call and the supervisor eventually convinced the caller to contact emergency services. By the end of the call Bob was shaking and having trouble breathing. He went home and took the following day off. Two months after the call, Bob had a panic attack at work; he attempted to return to work three more times but was unable to function. Bob indicated that the call brought back emotional problems and experiences from his youth.

   Bob was diagnosed with post-traumatic stress disorder. He filed for workers' compensation benefits for mental stress from an unexpected traumatic event at work. Looking at the relevant sections of your province's WCA, did Bob's mental stress qualify as an illness warranting workers' compensation benefits?
7. Aisha sprained her ankle while she was on the picket line during a strike at her workplace. Is she entitled to workers' compensation benefits?
8. Pierre's job was marking locations for workers to build concrete building structures based on blueprints. One day his car was damaged while parked in the lot beside the construction site, which was fenced off for use by construction workers. A few days later, during normal working hours, Pierre approached the individual—an employee of a different firm working at the site—who he thought was responsible for the damage to his vehicle. That person swore at him and then attacked him. The perpetrator was charged and later convicted of assault for causing Pierre serious injuries. Pierre reported his injuries to his employer, who filed a WCB claim on the basis that the parking lot was part of the workplace.

   In your opinion, is Pierre eligible for workers' compensation benefits?
9. Cassandra and Jamal were working at a construction site and leaving for lunch in Cassandra's personal truck.

As they were leaving, Cassandra saw Michael walking down the road about 75 feet in front of the truck. As a joke, Cassandra started playing "chicken" with Michael. As she drove ahead, Michael looked back and waved his arms as if to say "come and get me." Michael jumped back and forth, and Cassandra swerved back and forth pretending to aim at him. Both were smiling and clearly joking around with each other. When they were about 10 feet apart, Michael jumped to the left and Cassandra accidentally turned to the left as well. She panicked and hit the gas instead of the brake. Cassandra hit Michael before she was able to stop. Michael suffered a broken leg and filed a WCB claim. In your opinion is Michael eligible for coverage?

RELATED WEBSITES

The official website for WorkSafeBC <http://www.worksafebc.com>

The official website for the BC Workers' Compensation Appeal Tribunal <http://www.wcat.bc.ca>

The official website for the Alberta Workers' Compensation Board <http://www.wcb.ab.ca>

The website for the Alberta Partnerships in Injury Reduction program <https://www.alberta.ca/partnerships-injury-reduction.aspx>

REFERENCES

2014-0343 (Re), Decision No 2014-0343, 2014 CanLII 29801 (Alta WCAC).

2017-0397 (Re), Decision No 2017-0397, 2017 CanLII 51057 (Alta WCAC).

Administrative Procedures and Jurisdiction Act, RSA 2000, c A-3, as amended.

Administrative Tribunals Act, SBC 2004, c 45.

Alberta (Workers' Compensation Board) v Alberta (Workers' Compensation Board, Appeals Commission), 2005 ABQB 161.

Alberta (Workers' Compensation Board) v Buckley, 2007 ABCA 7.

Alberta, Workers' Compensation Board, *2018 Annual Report*, online: <https://www.wcb.ab.ca/annual-report-2018>.

Alberta, Workers' Compensation Board, Policy 02-01 Part I, 1996. *Alberta WCB Policies & Information Manual*, online: <https://www.wcb.ab.ca/assets/pdfs/public/policy/manual/printable_pdfs/0201_1.pdf>.

Alberta, Workers' Compensation Board, Policy 03-01 Part II, 2004. *Alberta WCB Policies & Information Manual*, online: <https://www.wcb.ab.ca/assets/pdfs/public/policy/manual/printable_pdfs/0301_2_app6.pdf>.

Alberta, Workers' Compensation Board, Policy 04-02 Part II, 2019. *Alberta WCB Policies & Information Manual*, online: <https://www.wcb.ab.ca/assets/pdfs/public/policy/manual/printable_pdfs/0402_2_app1.pdf>.

Canadian Charter of Rights and Freedoms, Part I of the *Constitution Act, 1982*, being Schedule B to the *Canada Act 1982* (UK), 1982, c 11.

CBC News, "Farmers Protest Plan for Mandatory WCB Coverage at Alberta Legislature: Petition Against Enhanced Protection for Farm and Ranch Workers Act Has More Than 14,000 Signatures" (27 November 2015), online: <https://www.cbc.ca/news/canada/edmonton/farmers-protest-plan-for-mandatory-wcb-coverage-at-alberta-legislature-1.3340327>.

Decision No 269/90 (27 September 1990) (Ont WCAT) [unreported].

Decision No 339/91 (15 June 1993) (Ont WCAT) [unreported].

Decision No 2001-0417, Workers' Compensation Reporter (2001), vol 17, no 3 at 343 (BC Workers' Compensation Board, Appeal Division).

Decision No 2010-542, 2010 CanLII 38710 (Alta WCAC).

Decision No 2019-0504, 2019 CanLII 104589 (Alta WCAC).

Downs Construction Ltd v Workers' Compensation Appeal Tribunal, 2012 BCCA 392.

Enhanced Protection for Farm and Ranch Workers Act, SA 2015 c 19.

Factum of the Respondent, Workers' Compensation Board of Alberta, SCC No 35052.

Farm Freedom and Safety Act, SA 2019 c 19.

Gilbert, Douglas, et al, *Canadian Labour and Employment Law for the US Practitioner*, 3rd ed (Washington, DC: Bureau of National Affairs, 2011).

Gilbert, Douglas, & Les Liversidge, *Workers' Compensation in Ontario: A Guide to the Workplace Safety and Insurance Act*, 3rd ed (Aurora, ON: Canada Law Book, 2001).

Government Employees Compensation Act, RSC 1985, c G-5.

Martin v Alberta (Workers' Compensation Board), 2014 SCC 25.

Medwid v Ontario, 1988 CanLII 193 (Ont H Ct J).

Occupational Health and Safety Act, SA 2017 c O-2.1.

Schneider v Alberta (Appeals Commission for Alberta Workers' Compensation), 2009 ABCA 417.

WCB Alberta, "Worker Fact Sheet, COVID-19" (26 March 2020), online: <https://www.wcb.ab.ca/assets/pdfs/workers/WFS_COVID-19.pdf>.

WorkSafeBC, "Statistics 2018" (19 August 2019), online: <https://www.worksafebc.com/en/resources/about-us/annual-report-statistics/2018-stats?lang=en>.

WorkSafeBC, "Compensation Practice Direction: #C3-1—Chronic Pain" (1 January 2003), online: <https://www.worksafebc.com/en/resources/law-policy/compensation-practice-directives/chronic-pain?lang=en>.

Workers' Compensation Act, RSA 2000, c W-15.

Workers Compensation Act, RSBC 1996, c 492.

Workers' Compensation Regulation, Alta Reg 325/2002.

Privacy Inside and Outside the Workplace

10

LEARNING OUTCOMES

After completing this chapter, you will be able to:

- Recognize the need for greater protection for personal information and other privacy rights.
- Understand the application and function of the BC *Freedom of Information and Protection of Privacy Act* and the Alberta statute of the same title.
- Explain how federal privacy legislation affects provincially regulated employers in British Columbia and in Alberta.
- Identify the ten principles behind the federal *Personal Information Protection and Electronic Documents Act*.
- Understand the function of the Office of the Information and Privacy Commissioner as it relates to the two privacy protection statutes of British Columbia and the two parallel statutes in Alberta.
- Conduct a brief overview of the BC *Personal Information Protection Act* and the Alberta statute of the same title.
- Understand employee privacy rights in workplaces not covered by general privacy legislation, including an employer's ability to legally monitor computers and other devices that are used for personal as well as work-related purposes.

Introduction

Historically, the right to privacy has not been recognized as a separate right under the common law in Canada. In the past, the privacy of the average person has been protected by the practical difficulties of locating and compiling numerous records. However, in our increasingly electronic age, where personal information can be compiled and transferred in seconds, privacy concerns are now paramount. These concerns are currently reflected in legislation to safeguard the privacy of personal information and in legal decisions that, for example, restrict the admissibility of evidence gained through electronic means.

Canada's original privacy legislation related to personal information held only by governments. For example, in the 1990s, both British Columbia (BC) and Alberta passed legislation that covered personal information held by the provincial government as well as other *public* bodies in the province, such as hospitals. BC's *Freedom of Information and Protection of Privacy Act* (FIPPA), enacted in 1992, allows individuals to file a request for information held by the BC government and other public bodies in the province. A parallel statute of the same title was passed by the Alberta legislature in 1994. It performs a similar function with respect to a request for information held by the Alberta government and other public bodies in the province. Every province and territory has privacy legislation governing the collection, use, and disclosure of personal information held by government agencies (Office of the Privacy Commissioner of Canada, 2014).

More recently, the federal government, followed by several provincial governments, including BC and Alberta, passed the first privacy legislation that covers personal information held by organizations in the *private* sector. The federal law is called the *Personal Information Protection and Electronic Documents Act* (PIPEDA). In BC and Alberta, the statute is called the *Personal Information Protection Act* (PIPA). These Acts are the provincial equivalents of the federal PIPEDA.

FYI

Alberta's Personal Information Protection Act Amended

In November 2013, the Supreme Court of Canada struck down Alberta's PIPA and gave the province one year to bring its law in line with the *Canadian Charter of Rights and Freedoms* (*Alberta (Information and Privacy Commissioner) v United Food and Commercial Workers, Local 401*). In a 9–0 decision, Alberta's privacy law was ruled unconstitutional in a dispute over the right of a union to photograph people crossing a picket line.

In its decision, the Court addressed the importance of freedom of expression in the context of a labour dispute, noting that Alberta's privacy law, which was considered to be overly broad, imposed an undue restriction on the union's right to communicate its case during a legal strike. Writing for the Court, Abella and Cromwell JJ noted that Alberta's PIPA "imposes restrictions on a union's ability to communicate and persuade the public of its cause, impairing its ability to use one of its most effective bargaining strategies in the course of a lawful strike" (at para 5).

As a result, Alberta's privacy legislation was changed. Amendments to PIPA came into force on December 17, 2014 to address the concerns raised by the Supreme

Court's decision. The amendments focused on the collection, use, and disclosure of personal information by unions in connection with a lawful labour dispute. No other changes were made to the legislation at the time.

Alberta's PIPA underwent a comprehensive review in 2016, which resulted in ten recommendations; however, the Act has not been amended further at the time of publication of this text.

In addition to the privacy rules in FIPPA, PIPA, and PIPEDA—laws that are the focus of this chapter—employers and employees should also be aware of potential liability for the tort of invasion of privacy. Ontario courts recently recognized a common law privacy tort that may affect employers in that province (the Act was used in *TeBaerts*, discussed below). Other provinces may follow suit. BC courts do not recognize a common law privacy tort, but that is because the province has had a statute, the *Privacy Act*, since 1968. Section 1 of the statute permits a person to sue for invasion of privacy, even if there is no specific harm caused by the invasion (referred to as "actionable without proof of damage"). Employers can also be vicariously liable for privacy invasions that their employees commit while carrying out their duties—whether an invasion of another employee's privacy or the privacy of a customer or another member of the public (see Chapter 11 for a discussion of vicarious liability).

The following is an overview of BC's and Alberta's privacy statutes, the federal PIPEDA, and the information and privacy offices in those three jurisdictions.

Freedom of Information and Protection of Privacy Act (British Columbia and Alberta)

The *Freedom of Information and Protection of Privacy Act* of BC applies to provincial government ministries, Crown corporations, local governments, universities and colleges, school boards, municipal police forces, health boards and hospitals, and the self-governing professions. (A detailed list of these public bodies and professions is provided in schedules 2 and 3 at the end of the Act.) The *Freedom of Information and Protection of Privacy Act* of Alberta applies to those public bodies listed in section 1(p) of the Act.

In BC, section 2 of the Act says that one of the purposes of the legislation is to "make public bodies more accountable to the public and to protect personal privacy by … giving the public a right of access to records." The underlying philosophy of the legislation in both provinces is that providing citizens with free access to government and public body records ensures that citizens get good government, as it inevitably compels those governments and public agencies to be more fair, transparent, and creditable.

FIPPA limits the type and amount of information that the provincial government and other public bodies can collect from individuals. Although the word "privacy" is not defined in either Act, the legislation puts very definite limits on what information about individual citizens can be obtained, stored, or passed on to third parties and how it can be used. It provides individual citizens with numerous opportunities to gain access to information held by these agencies and government bodies. The Atwell report, described below under the heading "Using Technology to Monitor and Collect Information from Employees," is an example of FIPPA's application to workplace privacy, in the case of a public body as employer.

Despite the importance of FIPPA, more often than not it is PIPA, the provincial private sector legislation, that is most relevant in employment disputes revolving around privacy. However, before switching our focus to a specific discussion of the provincial PIPAs, it is worthwhile to take a closer look at some features of the federal PIPEDA because its requirements are relevant to provincial employers and its principles have been adopted in the PIPAs of BC and Alberta.

The Personal Information Protection and Electronic Documents Act and the Personal Information Protection Act

PIPEDA's Application Versus PIPA's Application

PIPEDA applies to all *federally regulated* organizations and affects how they collect, use, disclose, and retain personal information concerning their employees, customers, patients, and suppliers. As federal legislation, PIPEDA does not directly affect personal employee information held by provincially regulated employers because the federal government does not have jurisdiction over the employment relationship in those workplaces. On the other hand, the federal government does have constitutional authority over provincially regulated organizations for *commercial* purposes, so it would be possible for PIPEDA to directly apply to all personal information collected, used, or disclosed in provincially regulated organizations in the course of *commercial* activity. (Common commercial transactions include the selling, bartering, or leasing of donor, membership, or other fundraising lists.) However, when PIPEDA was passed, the federal government agreed that its requirements would not apply to organizations in provinces that have implemented "substantially similar legislation." Because both BC and Alberta have implemented substantially similar legislation—their respective PIPAs—the federal PIPEDA has narrower application in those jurisdictions. However, because the PIPAs of BC and Alberta are "comparable" pieces of legislation, PIPEDA's principles in handling personal employee information apply, and employers in these provinces must be aware of and follow those principles.

FYI

Key Features of the Federal PIPEDA

1. The purpose of PIPEDA is to balance the individual's right to have personal information kept private with an organization's need to collect, use, and disclose personal information where necessary.
2. PIPEDA applies to all organizations—both federally and provincially regulated—in Canada that collect, use, or disclose personal information in the course of *commercial* activities (s 4) unless the province in

which the organization is situated has passed comparable legislation. In that case, the provincial law applies (the Alberta and BC PIPAs, described in this chapter). PIPEDA also applies to interprovincial and international transactions involving personal information in the course of commercial activities.

3. As federal legislation, PIPEDA does not apply directly to personal *employee* information in provincially regulated workplaces.
4. The term "personal information" is broadly defined to include any factual or subjective information about "an identifiable individual" (s 2).
5. Subject to some limitations, PIPEDA requires an individual's consent before their personal information is collected, used, or disclosed. Information may be used only for the purpose for which consent was obtained. Further consent is necessary before the information can be used for any other purpose.
6. Organizations must take precautions to safeguard personal information in their possession.
7. With some limited exceptions, individuals have a right to gain access to their personal information and to challenge an employer's treatment of it or its accuracy.
8. An individual may make a complaint regarding the way an organization has handled their personal information to the Office of the Privacy Commissioner of Canada. The individual or the privacy commissioner may apply to the Federal Court for an order requiring the organization to change its practices. It may also award damages to the individual.

What Is Personal Information?

The term **personal information** is broadly defined in section 2 of PIPEDA. It includes any factual or subjective information about "an identifiable individual," whether recorded or not. Personal information that is protected under PIPEDA includes an individual's:

personal information any factual or subjective information about "an identifiable individual," whether recorded or not

- age, home address, and identification numbers (including social insurance number);
- residential telephone numbers and personal email address;
- sex, religion, ethnicity, social status, and marital status;
- employee files (formal and informal), performance appraisals, disciplinary actions, and evaluations;
- photographs, opinions, and income;
- relevant dates, such as a birth date;
- credit records, loan records, and purchasing and spending habits; and
- blood type, genetic information, and medical records.

According to the Office of the Privacy Commissioner, personal information also includes pay and benefit records, video and audiotapes, and records of web browsing, emails, and keystrokes. Personal information is collected in many forms: on paper, electronically, in a recording, or on a fax machine.

In section 1 of BC's PIPA, "personal information" is defined as:

> information about an identifiable individual and includes employee personal information but does not include
> (a) contact information, or
> (b) work product information.

Similarly, in section 1(k) of Alberta's PIPA, "personal information" means information about "an identifiable individual." Although no exceptions are articulated for "work product information" or for "contact information," "business contact information" arises as a specific exception to the application of the Act to personal information held by all organizations (s 4(3)(d)).

Regardless of the definition or form of personal information, its collection, use, protection, and disclosure should adhere to the ten PIPEDA principles set out below.

FYI

Amendments to PIPEDA: Bill S-4, the Digital Privacy Act

On June 18, 2015, Bill S-4, the new *Digital Privacy Act*, was proclaimed, amending PIPEDA. The key changes to PIPEDA are as follows:

- Where there has been a security breach (i.e., loss of, or unauthorized access to, personal information resulting from a breach of an organization's security safeguards or failure to establish such safeguards), and there is risk of significant harm to an individual, the organization must report and keep records of the breach.
- The definition of "personal information" has been changed to eliminate the exception regarding name, title, business address, or telephone number of an employee.
- PIPEDA now covers job applicants as well as employees.
- Business contact information is exempt where it is collected, used, and disclosed solely for the purpose of communicating with the individual for purposes related to their employment, business, or profession.
- The circumstances where personal information may be disclosed without the knowledge or consent of the individual involving breaches of agreements, illegality, fraud, and financial abuse have been broadened. Such disclosure could be to a third-party organization that is not a government institution or part thereof (Jacobs, 2014).
- The privacy commissioner can enter into compliance agreements that include terms necessary for statutory compliance (Emond Harnden, 2014).

Ten Fair Information Principles

PIPEDA recognizes two fundamental facts. The first is that individuals have a right to privacy concerning their personal information. The second is that organizations have a need to collect, use, and disclose personal information for appropriate purposes. The aim of legislatures is to achieve a fair balance between these two valid requirements.

fair information principles
the ten principles set out in schedule 1 of PIPEDA that underlie the collection, use, protection, and disclosure of personal information

Schedule 1 of PIPEDA sets out ten **fair information principles** that underlie the collection, use, protection, and disclosure of personal information. The standard in applying these principles is one of reasonableness. Section 5(3) states that an organization may collect, use, or disclose personal information *only for purposes that a reasonable person would consider appropriate in the circumstances.*

The fair information principles have been retained in the BC PIPA and the Alberta PIPA. Although the principles are not explicitly stated in these provincial Acts, they are apparent from the content of the legislation.

These ten principles, including some implementation suggestions in *Privacy Toolkit: A Guide for Businesses and Organizations* (Office of the Privacy Commissioner of Canada, 2015), are discussed below:

1. *Be accountable.* An organization that collects personal information must appoint one person to oversee its legislative compliance. An appointee should have the authority to intervene when a privacy issue arises, and employees should be aware of their name and title. The appointee is responsible for analyzing the organization's personal information handling practices: what personal information is collected and why; how it is collected; what it is used for; where it is kept; how it is secured; who has access to it; who it is disclosed to; and when it is disposed of.

   The appointee must then develop and implement policies and procedures to protect personal information. Front-line staff should be trained about policies and procedures and should know how to respond to inquiries. If personal information is transferred to a third party for processing, an organization should ensure, by contract or other means, that the information receives a comparable level of protection during processing.
2. *Identify the purpose of collection.* An organization must let an individual know why it is collecting personal information. Any forms or documents used to collect personal information must include:
   a. an explanation of why it is needed and how it will be used—for example, to open an account, verify creditworthiness, provide benefits, or process a magazine subscription; and
   b. a list of those to whom it will be disclosed.

   Furthermore, organizations should only use this information for the designated purpose.
3. *Get consent.* With limited exceptions, the individual to whom the personal information relates must consent to its collection. Consent must be voluntarily given and the individual must be aware of what is being collected and for what reason. Consent clauses should be easy to find and understand. Consent should be obtained at the time or before the personal information is collected. The form of consent depends on the sensitivity of the personal information. Typically, the more sensitive the information, the more formal the consent. Although consent must usually be express, it may be implied in some circumstances, such as where a magazine uses its subscription list to solicit a renewal. However, collection or use of medical, financial, or other sensitive data requires express consent. Similarly, employers should obtain the written consent of job applicants before contacting their references by including a request for consent on job application forms. All consents should be recorded by means of a note to file where consent is given orally, such as consent given over the phone, or by keeping a copy of emails or application forms where consent is given in writing.

   To continue using or disclosing information that was collected before the legislation came into effect, an organization must go back to the individual and obtain consent.

There are a number of exceptions to the need to obtain consent. Under section 7, an organization may *collect* personal information without an individual's knowledge and consent in circumstances that include the following:

a. collection is in the interests of the individual and consent cannot be obtained in a timely manner, as in the case of a medical emergency;
b. obtaining the individual's consent would compromise the availability or accuracy of the information, which is relevant to an investigation of a breach of an agreement or a contravention of law;
c. the information is contained in a witness statement and the collection is necessary to assess, process, or settle an insurance claim;
d. the information was produced by the individual in the course of their employment, business, or profession and the collection is consistent with the purposes for which the information was produced;
e. collection is for journalistic, artistic, or literary purposes; or
f. the information is publicly available.

Providing consent should not be made a condition for supplying a product or service, unless the information is necessary to meet a legitimate purpose that is specifically identified.

4. *Limit collection.* The organization must collect only information that is necessary for its stated purposes. For example, in the course of conducting a credit check, an organization should not collect information related to an individual's religious affiliation. Moreover, as noted above, collection of personal information—as well as its use, retention, and disclosure—is subject to the test of "reasonableness." For example, in 2010 the privacy commissioner in Alberta ordered an employer (Mark's Work Wearhouse) to stop collecting the personal credit information of job applicants, despite their consent, on the basis that such information was not reasonably necessary to evaluate prospective employees for retail positions. Mark's had argued that it required the information to assess whether an applicant posed a greater risk of committing in-store theft, but the privacy commissioner found that the information was not reasonably required to make this assessment (*HR Reporter*, 2010).
5. *Limit use, disclosure, and retention.* Subject to the exceptions noted below, organizations cannot use the information collected for any purpose other than the one stated. They must not disclose the information to third parties unless they obtain a new consent that authorizes the new disclosure. For example, information regarding dependants gathered for life insurance purposes cannot be transferred to a medical insurer for the purpose of obtaining medical coverage without obtaining a specific new consent.

   Personal information must be used only by those who need it and disposed of when it is no longer needed. If, for example, an employer provides personal information about employees to a payroll service provider, the service provider should commit to complying with PIPEDA and to using the information only for the purpose specified in its contract. For example, the information may not be used to create or sell mailing lists.

Under section 7, there are a number of exceptions to the rule that an organization may not *use* personal information without an individual's knowledge and consent. An organization may use this information in circumstances that include the following:

a. obtaining the individual's consent would compromise the availability or accuracy of information where the information is relevant to an investigation or a breach of an agreement or a contravention of law;
b. the information reasonably could be useful in investigating a contravention of law and it is used for that investigation;
c. the information is used in an emergency that threatens the life, health, or security of the individual;
d. the information is contained in a witness statement and its use is necessary to assess, process, or settle an insurance claim;
e. the information was produced by the individual in the course of their employment, business, or profession and its use is consistent with the purposes for which the information was produced;
f. the information is used for statistical or scholarly purposes, in which case the organization must notify the Privacy Commissioner of Canada before using it; or
g. the information is publicly available.

Under section 7, organizations may also *disclose* personal information without an individual's knowledge or consent in certain circumstances. Personal information may be disclosed when the disclosure is made:

a. to a lawyer who is representing the organization;
b. for the purpose of collecting a debt owed to the organization by the individual;
c. for journalistic, artistic, or literary purposes;
d. in circumstances where use or disclosure is required by law;
e. to assist in an emergency that threatens the life, health, or security of an individual (the organization must inform the individual of the disclosure);
f. for statistical or scholarly purposes, in which case the organization must notify the privacy commissioner; or
g. 20 years after the individual's death or 100 years after the record was created.

6. *Be accurate.* If use or disclosure of out-of-date or incomplete information would harm the individual, the employer should ensure that the information is accurate and current. Employees should also be given the opportunity to correct errors in information.
7. *Provide safeguards.* An organization should protect personal information against loss, theft, or unauthorized access. For example, written information should be kept in locked drawers with keys accessible only to those who need access. The most sensitive information should receive a higher level of protection through such devices as security clearances, passwords, firewalls, and encrypted computerized data. Employers should also consider separating

medical information that may have been collected as part of managing employee absence or disability claims from the employee's general file to limit access to these records.

8. *Be open.* Privacy policies and procedures should be readily available to customers, clients, employees, and suppliers. Front-line supervisors should be familiar with them.
9. *Give individuals access.* Subject to specified exceptions, organizations must provide individuals with details about the personal information being held about them and the means to gain access to it, upon request. For example, if a supervisor puts an informal note on an employee's file, the employee is entitled to gain access to the note on request. Employers should respond to employees' requests as soon as possible and no later than 30 days after the request is made.

   Case law indicates there is little information that an employer can keep from an employee unless it falls within one of the exceptions in section 9 of PIPEDA (Brown, 2003, at 11). Section 9 of PIPEDA, as well as section 23 of the BC PIPA and section 24 of the Alberta PIPA, specifically explain when access either *must* or *may* be denied. Section 9 of PIPEDA, for example, provides that access *must* be denied:

   a. if the information would reveal personal information about another individual unless there is consent or a life-threatening situation (however, if the third-party information can be removed, the remaining information must be released); or
   b. if the organization has disclosed information to a government institution for law enforcement or national security reasons and the organization is instructed by that institution to refuse access or not to reveal that the information has been released.

   Access *may* be denied under section 9 of PIPEDA if:

   a. the information is protected by **solicitor–client privilege**;
   b. disclosure could harm another individual's life or security (however, if the third-party information can be removed, the remaining information must be released);
   c. disclosure would reveal confidential commercial information (however, if this information can be removed, the remaining information must be released);
   d. the information was collected as part of an investigation into a breach of an agreement or a law; or
   e. the information was generated in the course of a formal dispute resolution process.

   Where access is denied, the organization should advise the individual in writing, provide reasons, and explain what recourse is available.
10. *Provide recourse.* Organizations must establish a procedure to deal with complaints about their compliance with privacy legislation. Organizations should investigate all complaints, notify the individual of the outcome of the

solicitor–client privilege
rule of evidence that protects a client from having to divulge confidential communications with their lawyer

investigation, correct any inaccuracies and instances of non-compliance, and record all decisions. If an organization refuses to provide the information or denies its existence, an individual may file a complaint with the **privacy commissioner**. The privacy commissioner has broad powers to investigate complaints and inquire into information practices. Although the privacy commissioner cannot issue a binding order against an organization, the commissioner or the individual may apply to a court for an order for damages or an order requiring the organization to change its practices related to personal information.

privacy commissioner the commissioner appointed to investigate complaints of failure to comply with the requirements of privacy legislation

It is an offence to obstruct the privacy commissioner, to "knowingly dispose" of personal information with an intent to evade a request for access to the personal information, and to retaliate against employees for asserting their rights under the legislation.

Role of the Federal Privacy Commissioner and the BC and Alberta Information and Privacy Commissioner

The Office of the Privacy Commissioner of Canada (OPC) oversees the operation of PIPEDA. Although independent and impartial, it reports directly to the House of Commons and Senate. The OPC can conduct audits and investigations into an organization's personal information handling practices. It has wide powers under the Act to summon witnesses, compel evidence under oath, and demand the production of records.

After conducting an investigation, where warranted, the OPC will make a report to the parties involved with recommendations as to how to resolve the matter. The OPC does not have the power to make binding orders, but it does have powers of disclosure—that is, it can make public the information it obtains about an organization that it has investigated. It can also have matters referred further to the Federal Court, if necessary.

In both BC and Alberta, the Office of the Information and Privacy Commissioner (OIPC) was created as a separate entity, independent from government. Its role is to monitor and to enforce the legislation in each province that relates to the collection of information and privacy—namely, the *Freedom of Information and Protection of Privacy Act* and the *Personal Information Protection Act*. FIPPA applies to information held by public bodies such as ministries, universities, and hospitals, and it determines how such bodies may collect, use, and disclose personal information. PIPA applies to information held by private organizations such as businesses, charities, and associations, and it governs how they may collect, use, and disclose personal information.

The OIPC in BC was established in 1993. It monitors the right of citizens to gain access to records held by more than 2,900 public agencies and over 380,000 businesses and other non-government organizations. The powers and duties of the commissioner are set out in part 10 of PIPA and part 4 of FIPPA.

The Alberta OIPC was established in 1995. The powers and duties of the commissioner are set out in part 4 of PIPA and part 4 of FIPPA.

In both provinces, the OIPC ensures that both statutes are administered so as to achieve their objectives. It investigates and resolves complaints, mediates and resolves appeals, conducts research, and educates the public.

PIPEDA Case Summary #2003-226 and *Eastmond v Canadian Pacific Railway* illustrate the kinds of issues that privacy commissioners may be called upon to investigate. Both cases involve federally regulated employers, to which PIPEDA applies; however, as noted above, the principles for handling personal employee information are similar under the provincial legislation, so these decisions are also relevant to privacy situations in BC and Alberta. *PIPEDA Case Summary #2003-226* involved a telecommunications industry employer's allegedly casual treatment of an employee's sensitive personal information. *Eastmond* involved an employer's use of non-surreptitious video surveillance in its workyard to deter theft and vandalism.

CASE IN POINT

Employer's Practices Regarding Medical Reports Too Lax

Officer of the Privacy Commissioner of Canada, *PIPEDA Case Summary #2003-226*, online: <https://www.priv.gc.ca/en/opc-actions-and-decisions/investigations/investigations-into-businesses/2003/pipeda-2003-226>

Facts

While applying for long-term disability benefits, the employee received a letter from her employer asking her to provide all the medical information necessary for her application. The employer's intention was to expedite the application process; however, only the insurance company actually required the information in question. The employee objected to providing this sensitive information, including her diagnosis, to her employer. She also objected to the employer's use of a fax machine to transmit her medical reports to its human resources office because employees who had no need for this information might accidentally see it. The employee filed a complaint with the privacy commissioner.

The employer argued that the fax machine was a secure method of transferring personal information since the machine was designated for human resources personnel only. The human resources department was located at one end of a largely empty floor, and it required card access, although all human resources employees had cards. The fax machine room was only locked when no employees were present, so it would be difficult (although not impossible) for other staff to enter the fax machine room when it was unlocked without human resources staff noticing.

Relevant Issue

Whether the employer's conduct contravened PIPEDA's requirements to:

1. limit collection and use of personal information to that which is necessary for the purposes identified by the organization; and
2. ensure that the information is properly secured, with more sensitive information being safeguarded by a higher level of protection.

Decision

The assistant privacy commissioner found that the employer contravened both PIPEDA requirements. With respect to the first issue, while a reasonable person might find nothing objectionable about the employer's facilitating the application process, it was unreasonable for the company to represent its collection of information as a requirement, rather than an option. Letters of notification concerning long-term disability should state that employees have the option of sending information directly to the insurance company.

With respect to the second issue, because of the sensitive nature of medical diagnoses, the level of protection provided was inadequate. Keeping a fax machine that receives personal information in an unlocked, accessible room was inappropriate. The assistant privacy commissioner also questioned the use of fax machines in general for relaying this sort of information and questioned the employer's practice of having human resources staff receive medical reports containing diagnoses.

She recommended that the employer inform all employees that they have the right to ensure that diagnostic information be kept confidential and that they have the option of sending reports to medical staff in health services rather than to human resources staff.

CASE IN POINT

Video Surveillance Cameras Justified in Workyard

Eastmond v Canadian Pacific Railway, 2004 FC 852

Facts

The employer installed video cameras in one of its workyards to reduce vandalism and deter theft, to reduce its potential liability for property damage, and to improve security for employees. One of the employees, Eastmond, launched a complaint under PIPEDA on the basis that theft and security were not serious problems in the workyard and that the cameras could be used to monitor the performance and conduct of employees. The privacy commissioner applied the following four-part test to determine the reasonableness of the placement of cameras:

1. Is the measure demonstrably necessary to meet a specific need?
2. Is it likely to be effective in meeting that need?
3. Is the loss of privacy proportional to the benefit gained?
4. Is there a way of achieving this benefit that involves less invasion of privacy?

After applying these tests, the commissioner recommended that the employer remove the surveillance cameras. Since thefts were relatively rare and lack of security was not a serious issue among employees, the employer failed to show a need for surveillance. It should have looked for alternatives, such as better lighting, that were less likely to invade privacy.

Because the employer did not comply with these recommendations, Eastmond applied to the Federal Court for an order.

Relevant Issue

Whether the employer's use of video surveillance cameras in the workyard violated the privacy rights of employees.

Decision

The Federal Court applied the four-part test set out by the commissioner, but it came to the opposite conclusion. In its view, the videotaping served a reasonable purpose. The cameras were not hidden from view, and they were placed in areas where employees had a low expectation of privacy. The tapes were reviewed only if there was a reported incident; otherwise, they were destroyed. The employer had considered alternatives, including fencing and security guards, but it had reasonably decided that these were not cost effective.

The employer was entitled to collect personal employee information through videotaping employees' movements without their knowledge and consent under the section 7 exception in PIPEDA related to an investigation of a breach of the law. Because the employer looked at the tapes only after a reported incident, requiring consent to review them would compromise its investigation of such a breach.

Employees to whom PIPEDA applies have substantive privacy protections. However, the Federal Court in *Eastmond* showed a willingness to temper those rights where an employer demonstrates that it used the least intrusive means practicable to accomplish a reasonable purpose. (The use of video surveillance and other electronic means to monitor employees is dealt with in more detail under the heading "Using Technology to Monitor and Collect Information from Employees" below.)

In BC and Alberta, complaints of privacy violations under PIPA and FIPPA must go through the administrative process of the OIPC. However, in addition to filing complaints with the provincial OIPC, employees may also have the option to file a lawsuit against an employer for violations of PIPA. Section 57 of the BC PIPA states:

> 57(1) If the commissioner has made an order under this Act against an organization and the order has become final as a result of there being no further right of appeal, an individual affected by the order has a cause of action against the organization for damages for actual harm that the individual has suffered as a result of the breach by the organization of obligations under this Act.

employee personal information personal information about an individual that is collected, used, or disclosed solely for the purposes reasonably required to establish, manage, or terminate an employment relationship between the organization and that individual, but does not include personal information that is not about an individual's employment; this is the definition used in the BC *Personal Information Protection Act*

personal employee information in respect of an individual who is a potential, current, or former employee of an organization, personal information reasonably required by the organization for the purposes of (1) establishing, managing, or terminating an employment or volunteer-work relationship, or (2) managing a post-employment or post-volunteer-work relationship between the organization and the individual, but does not include personal information about the individual that is unrelated to that relationship; this is the definition used in the Alberta *Personal Information Protection Act*

Section 60 of the Alberta PIPA is almost identical.

PIPEDA offers broader options for a lawsuit by those whose privacy has been violated. Section 14 allows them to file a complaint in court after the federal commissioner has released a report, regardless of its content, and even after the commissioner discontinues an investigation. And section 16 allows the court to award a range of remedies, including damages for actual loss or mere humiliation. In the employment context, although the PIPA provisions govern provincially regulated employees, PIPEDA applies this rule to federally regulated employers.

Personal Information Protection Act (British Columbia and Alberta)

The *Personal Information Protection Act* of BC and that of Alberta both apply to businesses and commercial enterprises, associations, trade unions, trusts, and charities and societies. As stated earlier, these statutes are essentially the provincial equivalent of the federal PIPEDA legislation. The purpose of this legislation is summarized in section 3 of the Alberta PIPA and in section 2 of the BC PIPA, in virtually identical language. Section 2 of BC's statute reads:

> The purpose of this Act is to govern the collection, use and disclosure of personal information by organizations in a manner that recognizes both the right of individuals to protect their personal information and the need of organizations to collect, use or disclose personal information for purposes that a reasonable person would consider appropriate in the circumstances.

The PIPAs of both provinces also define personal information in the context of employment. The BC PIPA uses the term **employee personal information**, while the Alberta PIPA uses the term **personal employee information**. The definitions of these terms are similar. In BC, "employee personal information" is:

> personal information about an individual that is collected, used or disclosed solely for the purposes reasonably required to establish, manage or terminate

> an employment relationship between the organization and that individual, but does not include personal information that is not about an individual's employment.

In Alberta, "personal employee information" is:

> in respect of an individual who is a potential, current or former employee of an organization, personal information reasonably required by the organization for the purposes of
>
> (i) establishing, managing or terminating an employment or volunteer-work relationship, or
>
> (ii) managing a post-employment or post-volunteer-work relationship between the organization and the individual, but does not include personal information about the individual that is unrelated to that relationship.

Note that the Alberta definition differs only in that it expressly includes "a potential, current or former employee," a "volunteer-work relationship," and "a post-employment or post-volunteer-work relationship." (A definition for "volunteer-work relationship" is provided in s 1(n).)

Two issues—whether an employee's right to protection of privacy is infringed when they are under video surveillance at work and when their employer monitors email and other forms of communication while the employee is on the job—are addressed by the BC PIPA in sections 13, 16, and 19. Employers should be aware of all three sections:

> 13(2) An organization *may not collect* employee personal information without the consent of the individual unless …
>
> (b) the collection is reasonable for the purposes of establishing, managing or terminating an employment relationship between the organization and the individual.
>
> 16(2) An organization *may not use* employee personal information without the consent of the individual unless …
>
> (b) the use is reasonable for the purposes of establishing, managing or terminating an employment relationship between the organization and the individual.
>
> 19(2) An organization *may not disclose* employee personal information without the consent of the individual unless …
>
> (b) the disclosure is reasonable for the purposes of establishing, managing or terminating an employment relationship between the organization and the individual. [emphasis added]

The parallel sections of the Alberta PIPA are, respectively, section 15(1) collection of personal employee information, section 18(1) use of personal employee information, and section 21(1) disclosure of personal employee information. Also, the Alberta PIPA was recently broadened to facilitate the use (s 17.1) and disclosure (s 20.1) of personal information by trade unions.

Thus, even in the absence of obtaining an employee's express consent to collect, use, or disclose personal information about that employee, an employer in both provinces would be able to do any of those things if they were *reasonable for the purposes of establishing, managing, or terminating* the employment relationship.

In BC, any employer using personal information for any decision relating to an employee must retain a record of that personal information for at least one year after using it so that the worker has a right to access it during that time frame (s 35). In contrast, Alberta employers are not specifically instructed with respect to retention of employee information. Instead, organizations "may retain personal information only for as long as the organization reasonably requires the personal information for legal or business purposes" (s 35). Employers in both provinces are required to destroy documents containing personal information within a reasonable time.

Section 34 of the PIPA of both provinces requires organizations, including employers, to make reasonable security arrangements to ensure that the information collected will be protected from improper access, use, disclosure, copying, modification, or disposal.

Applying PIPA to Privacy Issues in the Workplace

Privacy issues are increasingly being raised in the workplace. Technology makes it possible for employers to monitor employees' activities in unprecedented ways—for example, by recording keystrokes, websites visited, and emails; by tracking mobile device usage; and by conducting video surveillance.

As well, there continue to be infringement-of-privacy issues with respect to such activities as employers providing information to third parties for reference checks and their requesting that employees submit to drug or alcohol testing at work. In the case of the former, the law has to balance privacy with a long-established defence to defamation called "qualified privilege." With respect to the latter, it has to determine whether privacy/human rights infringements or safety concerns are most applicable.

Despite the obvious relevance of privacy issues in today's workplace, there are relatively few decisions rendered by the OIPC in either BC or Alberta so far. One reason for this is that the PIPAs of both provinces have only been in force since 2004. Furthermore, the Acts make allowance for the privacy commissioner to order a matter to be resolved by mediation (s 49 in both the BC and Alberta legislation), so many disputes may have been resolved that way. Finally, when introducing the legislation, the government made it clear that for the first couple of years, it would be monitoring rather than penalizing infringements to provide an educative atmosphere for workplaces and businesses.

However, now that the legislation has been in place for more than a decade, this lack of challenges will begin to change (as decisions such as the Atwell report suggest). The OIPC in BC reported 332 complaints in 2018–19, an increase from 273 the year prior (OIPC for BC, 2019). A decision of the Supreme Court of Canada in 2012 may also provide some further impetus for complaints and enforcement of privacy in the workplace under PIPA, FIPPA, and PIPEDA, as well as *Privacy Act* claims. In *R v Cole*, the Supreme Court ruled that an employee has a "reasonable expectation of privacy" in the information stored on employer-issued computer equipment. This is so even though the employer not only owns the device but has policies stating that it owns all data and messages on the device and "acceptable use" policies that authorize the employer to monitor use of the device. The Court acknowledged that such policies diminish an employee's privacy interest in devices such as a laptop computer, but do not eliminate it entirely. This case did not involve PIPEDA or PIPA, but rather a high school's handing over of a laptop to police after the school discovered that a teacher had copied nude images of a student onto the laptop. Because *Cole* was about whether the police needed a warrant to gain access to the data, the Court "[left] for another day the finer points of an employer's right to monitor computers issued to employees" (at para 60). However, the Court's reasoning has already begun to inform cases on PIPA, including the 2015 Atwell report and *TeBaerts* cases described below, under the heading "Using Technology to Monitor and Collect Information from Employees."

To understand the general approach taken to workplace privacy under the provincial PIPAs, it is useful to look at a few of the decisions that have been rendered by the OIPC in both provinces. In one BC case, *Tally-Ho Motor Inn*, a worker in the bar of a hotel lodged a complaint with WorkSafeBC about unsanitary conditions in the bar. The complaint was subsequently found to be unsubstantiated. However, the employer later told some of the complainant's co-workers that he had made the complaint. The worker filed a new complaint with the OIPC alleging that the employer had disclosed personal information about him—specifically, his name—to others that was unrelated to his employment. The privacy commissioner agreed that the employer's disclosing this information to other workers was not reasonable for the purposes of managing the employment relationship, so it was in contravention of section 19 of PIPA. The commissioner has wide powers under section 52 of PIPA when there has been an infringement of privacy, but he declined to make any order because the violation occurred shortly after the Act came into effect and the breach was not considered that serious. Nonetheless, the case does show how broad an approach the law is taking in protecting privacy in the workplace.

Several other cases, *Tsatsu Shores Homeowners Corporation*, *Cardinal Coach Lines Ltd*, *Suncor Energy Inc v Unifor, Local 707A*, and *Twentieth Century Fox Film Corporation*, are worth looking at a little more closely.

CASE IN POINT

Employer's Failure to Give Proper Notice, Disclosure Without Consent, and Improper Security of Private Information

Tsatsu Shores Homeowners Corporation (Re), 2006 CanLII 42695 (BCIPC)

Facts

The employer organization managed an 87-unit condominium development in BC. The complainants were former employees of that company. The employer collected letters about them that had been sent by condo owners and non-residents to the organization's board of directors. These letters were the subject of a performance evaluation of the complainants that was not positive. Some of these complaints were posted on the company's website and in the condominium building, visible to residents and visitors. They also were disclosed in the minutes of several board meetings. Information about one of the complainant's health and about a workers' compensation matter involving another complainant was also disclosed. The organization did not obtain the complainants' consent to disclose this information. Also, the organization had stored the complainants' job applications in an unlocked filing cabinet in a room that was sometimes left unlocked; later, that information was removed and destroyed, but this was done less than a year after it had been used. The complainants filed a complaint with the OIPC relating to these matters.

Relevant Issue

Whether the employer had failed to comply with PIPA in a number of particulars, including:

- collecting, using, and disclosing employee personal information without consent;
- failing to correct personal information when requested to do so;
- failing to ensure that the information it had collected was accurate and complete;
- failing to make reasonable security arrangements to protect personal information; and
- failing to retain employee personal information for the minimum time required.

Decision

The privacy commissioner found that the employer organization had collected and used information about the complainants' job performance without the complainants' consent. However, the commissioner did not consider this to be unreasonable in the circumstances:

> Information about how well the complainants were performing their tasks, and information about specific concerns regarding performance, is personal information "reasonably required" within the meaning of PIPA's definition of "employee personal information." (at para 15)

However, without the prior consent of the employees, the disclosure of improper job performance information to third parties was clearly in violation of section 19(2)(b) of the Act, as was the disclosure of information of a personal nature not related to employment. In this case, the employer did not receive such consent, nor did it correct that personal information when requested to do so.

The commissioner also determined that the measures the employer took to protect the complainants' personal information were not adequate:

> It was not reasonable to place their personal information in an unlocked filing cabinet in a basement room with ready access to any number of individuals, regardless of whether that room was locked. There is no indication that the room, once locked ... was accessible by only a restricted number of organization directors or employees. (at para 39)

With respect to the final issue, although the Act requires organizations using personal information to make a decision that directly affects them to retain such information for at least one year after using it so that the individual has a reasonable opportunity to access it, the employer was not in breach of that requirement. Apparently, most of the information was rendered into emails, which were sent to the complainants directly or in copy form, so their being disposed of or deleted by the employer subsequently was not, in the circumstances, a breach of the Act.

As in the *Tally-Ho* case, no order penalizing the employer was made in the *Tsatsu* case, largely because PIPA was only in the first year of its existence when the infractions occurred.

CASE IN POINT

Employer's Disclosure of Personal Employee Information Regarding Suspended Employee Unreasonable

Cardinal Coach Lines Ltd (Re), 2010 CanLII 98657 (Alta OIPC)

Facts

A bus driver randomly selected to take a drug test under Calgary-based Cardinal Coach Lines' drug and alcohol policy failed the test and was subsequently suspended. Although he signed a letter stating he fully intended to return to work at Cardinal post-suspension and agreeing to future random tests, he got a job with a competitor company to earn income in the meantime—after passing their substance test. When the south rural operations manager at Cardinal heard that the driver was working for a rival, she decided to investigate by phoning the second company. After checking their records, they confirmed that the driver was indeed working for them. They then asked her why she was asking. She said that she still considered the driver to be a Cardinal employee, that he was currently suspended, and that she was trying to determine whether he intended to return to Cardinal. When they asked why he was suspended, she said that his "suspension was a result of his not meeting Company policy and requirements" (at para 5). Not long afterward, the driver was called in by the second company's safety supervisor, who told him that someone at Cardinal had "made remarks that reflected on his capacity to safely perform his duties" (at para 6) and he was asked to submit to another drug test. The results were not satisfactory, and he was terminated. The driver resigned from Cardinal and filed a complaint against the company with the Alberta privacy commissioner.

Relevant Issues

1. Whether Cardinal had used or disclosed the complainant's personal employee information.
2. Whether Cardinal had consent to disclose the employee's personal information.
3. Whether Cardinal had a reasonable purpose for disclosing the information, and whether the disclosure itself was reasonable for that purpose.
4. Whether Cardinal was required to give notice to the employee of the disclosure.

Decision

1. Section 1(j)(i) of PIPA defined personal employee information as "personal information reasonably required by an organization that is collected, used or disclosed solely for the purposes of establishing, managing or terminating an ... employment relationship." Employment status, in the opinion of the privacy office adjudicator, qualified as information reasonably required by Cardinal to manage its relationship with its driver employee. Similarly, the driver's suspension from work arose in the course of managing his conduct. The privacy adjudicator concluded that all of the information disclosed by Cardinal regarding the driver's employment status and the reason for that present status met the definition of personal employee information.
2. Although consent to disclose may be given directly by an employee orally or in writing, consent may also be deemed. Section 8(2)(a) of PIPA explains that "an individual is deemed to consent to ... disclosure of personal information about the individual by an organization for a particular purpose if ... the individual ... voluntarily provides the information." The adjudicator found that the driver had voluntarily disclosed to the competitor bus company his past experience as a driver for Cardinal. By doing so, he implicitly authorized the rival company to confirm his past employment with Cardinal. However, that sequence of events was clearly not what occurred. Instead, it was Cardinal that initiated a call to the competitor company, and it was Cardinal that sought a confirmation of his employment status elsewhere. The adjudicator said she therefore could not find that the driver voluntarily provided information about his employment with Cardinal "for the reverse purpose—that Cardinal would be enabled to check with [the rival company] whether he was (also) employed there." Further, there was certainly no deemed consent by the driver that Cardinal could disclose information about his suspension or the reason for it.
3. If an employer has a reasonable purpose for disclosing personal employee information and the disclosure is reasonable for that purpose, then section 21(1) of PIPA may permit disclosure without the employee's consent. Cardinal's regional manager maintained that it was important to determine whether the driver was working for the competitor company because a position was still being held open for him at Cardinal. The privacy adjudicator found that investigating the driver's employment status was a reasonable purpose. She pointed out, however, that the disclosure itself must also be reasonable for the stated purpose. Cardinal disclosed, as the adjudicator carefully delineated, three distinct pieces of the driver's personal employee information: his employment status at Cardinal, the fact of his suspension, and the reason he was suspended. But the timing of these disclosures is significant: none of these facts were disclosed by Cardinal's manager until after she had the information that had prompted her to make the phone call in the first place. The competitor had already confirmed to her that the driver was currently working for them. Why, then, would she proceed to reveal three distinct pieces of personal employee information to the competitor? The adjudicator found that, given the timing of these events, the disclosure of all of this personal employee information was therefore not reasonable for the stated purpose of Cardinal's investigation. There was actually "no need for Cardinal to disclose" it at all.

4. Because the driver was still a current employee of Cardinal, Cardinal was required by section 21(2)(c) (now s 21(1)(c)) of PIPA to provide notice to him—prior to the disclosure—of what information it intended to disclose, and the purpose of that intended disclosure. Its failure to do so meant that Cardinal had violated its driver's privacy rights.

Having contravened the *Personal Information Protection Act*, Cardinal Coach Lines was ordered by the Alberta OIPC to cease disclosing personal information about the complainant driver and to educate its employees about its obligations to them under PIPA.

CASE IN POINT

Random Drug Testing in the Workplace

Suncor Energy Inc v Unifor, Local 707A, 2016 ABQB 269

Facts

In 2012, Suncor Energy implemented a random drug and alcohol testing policy for employees holding "safety-sensitive positions." The testing program caused the union to file a grievance, alleging that testing infringed on workers' privacy rights and human rights. The matter went to arbitration, and the arbitration tribunal allowed the grievance in favour of the union, finding that such random testing was an unreasonable exercise of management rights. The arbitration decision was overturned by the Alberta Court of Queen's Bench, finding that the arbitration tribunal made three key errors:

1. The Tribunal applied the wrong legal test to determine whether the threshold concerning the degree of evidence necessary to establish a workplace drug and alcohol problem was met.
2. The Tribunal misapplied the legal test again when it said that "it could only consider evidence demonstrating an alcohol and drug problem within the bargaining unit" (at para 78). The legal test was to be applied to the "workplace" rather than the "bargaining unit" as long as this does not result in an overbroad analysis.
3. The Tribunal "ignored or misunderstood the evidence in a manner that affects its decisions" (at para 88).

The matter was ordered by the Court of Queen's Bench judge to be sent back for a fresh arbitration. However, Suncor appealed the Court of Queen's Bench decision. The Court of Appeal upheld the Court of Queen's Bench decision, agreeing that the decision-making process used by the arbitration tribunal was flawed. The matter was appealed by Suncor to the Supreme Court of Canada. While waiting for a decision from the Supreme Court, Suncor tried to implement its random drug and alcohol testing, but Unifor was successful in obtaining an injunction stopping Suncor from doing so until a fresh arbitration was conducted or until the Supreme Court of Canada provided a decision. In June 2018, the Supreme Court denied the union leave to appeal. This meant that the issue of Suncor's random drug and alcohol testing policy would have to be considered by a fresh arbitration panel, and, in the interim, the injunction would remain in force. On November 29, 2018, Suncor and the union reached an agreement that random drug testing would commence at the beginning of 2019. The fresh arbitration that had been ordered never occurred.

Various unions and employers have watched this case closely in relation to other potentially dangerous worksites. With Suncor managing some of the most dangerous worksites, the question of whether a union could successfully challenge a random drug and alcohol testing is relevant as employers continue to weigh safety and employee privacy in deciding whether to conduct random drug or alcohol testing. To further complicate this issue, with the legalization of cannabis in Canada, random drug testing runs the risk of affecting many more employees, potentially causing an increase of complaints against employers who try to conduct random tests. Conversely, the legalization of cannabis puts employers at a greater risk that employees may arrive to work impaired and not fit for duty, resulting in risk to the safety of other workers and the public.

CASE IN POINT

Proper Use of Employee Personal Information

Twentieth Century Fox Film Corporation, Re, 2006 CanLII 37938 (BCIPC)

Facts

The complainant was an employee of Twentieth Century Fox ("Fox"), which was producing a film in BC. Fox had to establish whether its workers were residents of BC in order to successfully apply for and obtain certain tax credits. It did this by requesting workers to provide at least three of the following: a copy of their BC Medical Services billing statement, a billing statement from a utility company, a property tax statement, or a BC driver's licence. The complainant balked at having to provide this information and also asked for something in writing to show that this was Fox's policy. Fox advised the complainant that employment was contingent upon the information being supplied; as for its policy, Fox advised what that policy was orally but not in written form.

The employee later filed a complaint alleging that Fox had infringed the provisions of PIPA in a number of ways: the information that Fox collected was not "employee personal information," the personal information did not relate specifically to employment, the employee should have been provided with a written copy of policies and procedures upon request, and Fox had not made reasonable security arrangements with the information it collected (it had left photocopies of identification documents lying around without being adequately secured). Fox argued that residency-related personal information is not "employee personal information," but that if it is considered "employee personal information" within the meaning of PIPA, then Fox is authorized to collect and use that information for the purpose of "maintenance of the employment relationship with the individual" (at para 30).

Relevant Issue

Whether the employer had infringed the provisions of PIPA by collecting employee personal information that was not related to employment by:

1. not providing a written statement of its privacy policy to its employees upon request, and
2. not making reasonable security arrangements with the personal information it obtained.

Decision

The privacy commissioner noted the following. To qualify as "employee personal information," that information (1) must be *personal information* (i.e., information about an identifiable individual); (2) must be collected, used, or disclosed for the reasonable purpose of establishing, managing, or terminating an employment relationship; (3) must be collected *solely* for those purposes; and (4) must not be personal information that is not about an individual's employment.

The commissioner found that the personal information was collected, used, and disclosed by Fox solely for the purposes of establishing and proving employees' residency in BC and so was "employee personal information." Moreover, the collection, use, and disclosure of this personal information complied with PIPA. Although PIPA requires an organization to "make information available on request" about its "policies and practices" (at para 66), there is no duty for it to provide a copy of any written policies and procedures. In the circumstances, Fox's security arrangements with the information was "reasonable."

Using Technology to Monitor and Collect Information from Employees

The monitoring of employee emails, Internet activity, and mobile devices for misuse is another area where the employee's right to privacy and the employer's need to manage the workplace may come into conflict. Computer misuse can adversely affect an employer in a number of ways. These include reduced productivity if employees engage in personal activity on company time; an increased potential for defamatory statements to be made and widely disseminated or for confidential information to be leaked; and breaches of company policy against certain activities, such as viewing pornography at work. Computer misuse can also compromise an employer's ability to maintain a workplace free from discrimination and harassment if offensive materials are circulated or co-workers are bombarded with objectionable emails (Gilbert, Burkett & McCaskill, 2000, at 266).

R v Cole, discussed above, underscores that, while employees have a reasonable expectation of privacy, this expectation is not absolute. The Supreme Court of Canada stated that the degree of privacy an employee can expect is diminished when the employer not only owns the equipment the employee is using but has policies that state the employer owns data, including messages, on the computer and can monitor all computer usage. The more aware employees are of these policies (and the more they are reinforced) and the more closely tied the policies are to the protection of the employer's reasonable interests, the more likely it is that an employer's monitoring will not be a violation. The cases below illustrate this balancing act.

In *Poliquin v Devon Canada Corporation* an employer's right to promote and maintain its integrity as a corporate citizen and obligation to provide a workplace free from harassment are evaluated against an employee's expectation that the oil and gas industry's "culture of permissiveness" might excuse his specifically prohibited misuse of his employer's computer technology.

CASE IN POINT

Monitoring Employees' Email and Internet Use: How Far Can Employers Go?

Poliquin v Devon Canada Corporation, 2009 ABCA 216

Facts

Poliquin had been employed by Devon Canada Corporation for over 20 years and ended up as a senior productivity foreman for the firm with over 20 employees under his supervision. Then Devon Canada discovered that he had accepted free landscaping services at his residence from the firm's suppliers, and that he used the firm's computer equipment and Internet access to view and transmit pornographic and racist material, including some to fellow workers. Both activities were in violation of the employer's code of conduct, and Devon Canada terminated Poliquin's employment on the ground of just cause. However, he had been considered a valuable employee and his performance appraisals had been "very positive over several years" (at para 29). When Poliquin sued Devon Canada for damages for wrongful dismissal, the firm applied for summary judgment to dismiss his action.

The trial court rejected Devon Canada's application for summary judgment. Devon Canada appealed that ruling to the Alberta Court of Appeal.

Relevant Issue

Whether in these circumstances Poliquin had been terminated for just cause, which would justify the employer's application for summary judgment dismissing his action.

Decision

The Court of Appeal found that Poliquin's soliciting and receiving landscaping services in the circumstances was misconduct that in and of itself justifies dismissal for cause, even if it were not a condition in the employer's code of conduct. His misuse of a workplace computer for pornographic and racist purposes negatively affected the professional, ethical, and operational integrity of the firm, and it was particularly inappropriate given his responsibilities as a senior supervisor in the firm. That conduct also was clearly in violation of the employer's code of conduct, and he had been warned on at least one occasion not to use his workplace computer for pornographic purposes. On the issue of whether the employer was justified in monitoring the activities of the employee, the judge stated:

> [A]n employer is entitled not only to prohibit use of its equipment and systems for pornographic or racist purposes but also to monitor an employee's use of the employer's equipment and resources to ensure compliance. (at para 49)

In reaching a decision, the judge noted that the cumulative misconduct of both improper activities has to be taken into account by courts when assessing whether an employer had just cause to terminate a worker. The judge found that not only was just cause established, but these were also grounds for the employer to apply for summary judgment of the matter rather than proceeding to trial.

As the *Poliquin* case shows, if a computer is company property, the employer is permitted to monitor activities on that property and courts have generally been willing to admit email evidence. However, if an employer wants to use information obtained through monitoring to discipline employees, it should communicate this policy and enforce it consistently. Employers will also have greater success enforcing employee electronic usage standards and monitoring to uphold such standards if there are regular reminders. This can occur, for example, through refresher training, regular policy review sign-offs, or even policy statement reminders on login screens. Employees should be forewarned that they have no right to privacy with respect to emails sent on company computers and should adhere to established company standards when using this workplace tool.

To be most effective, an email and Internet use policy should set out in detail the uses that are and are not permitted. For example, an employer might stipulate that email is to be used for business purposes only. If personal emails are allowed, the policy should state any content restrictions. For example, emails containing discriminatory, pornographic, or threatening content should be prohibited, and the policy should indicate that violations will result in discipline, including termination without notice. The 2015 Atwell report, discussed in the Case in Point box below, reinforces the importance of explicit policies as well as a reasonable degree of monitoring.

There may be situations where the nature of the emailed material is so offensive that an employer may dismiss an employee for cause even in the absence of a clearly formulated policy. In *TELUS Mobility*, an employee who was dismissed for sending pornographic material through email filed a grievance. Although the employer had an email policy, the arbitrator stated that because of the nature of the material, the employer could have dismissed the employee for cause even without such a policy.

Although it is a case under FIPPA rather than PIPA, the Atwell report from the BC OIPC is instructive, since in this case the monitoring was as intrusive as possible—it included complete records of all keystrokes plus screen captures every 30 seconds—and the employer had advised computer users about monitoring in vague terms.

CASE IN POINT

Keystroke Monitoring and Screenshot Capture: Justifiable Collection of Information?

Re Saanich (District), 2015 BCIPC 15 [Atwell report]

Facts

In May 2014, managers in the municipal government of Saanich, BC, hired an information technology (IT) security consultant who identified flaws and recommended improvements in IT security at the municipal offices. The municipal administrators began to address the recommendations. In late November 2014, after the election of a new mayor, Richard Atwell, the IT manager was told to accelerate security improvements, supposedly because the new mayor had IT expertise and would expect a better system. The manager purchased monitoring software called "Spector 360," even though the security consultant had not recommended such software. This software allowed, among other things, the taking of screenshots every 30 seconds on all employee computers and the recording of every keystroke an employee typed. The software also recorded all websites visited and copied every email and instant message. Although Saanich's chief administrative officer (CAO) had notified various directors and executive assistants "in a general way" of the plan to install security software and had mentioned that the software included monitoring functions, the employees were unaware of Spector 360 or the extent of data being collected. Saanich also had a Network Access Terms and Conditions Form, which users of IT services had to sign, but the form just advised employees that there could be monitoring of their use of IT resources and made no reference to the extent of monitoring.

The mayor took office on December 1, 2014. The CAO and a director told the IT manager to install and activate Spector 360 on December 2, 2014. The mayor learned of the data collection nine days later. He complained to the police, who found that no crime had been committed. Reports came out in December that the new mayor had told the CAO in November that he would be dismissing him once taking office. In January, the media reported that the mayor had been involved in an extramarital affair. In response the mayor told the media that municipal staff were using software to spy on him. The resulting controversy prompted the BC Privacy Commissioner, Elizabeth Denham, to start an investigation under FIPPA on January 20, 2015.

Relevant Issue

Whether Spector 360's collection of personal information was permissible under FIPPA.

Decision

The OIPC's report found that the monitoring software violated FIPPA and was an unjustifiable intrusion into the privacy of employees. The commissioner cited both FIPPA and the Supreme Court of Canada's statement in *R v Cole* that employees have a reasonable expectation of privacy on work computers and other devices. Her findings indicate that one must balance that expectation against valid reasons for an employer to collect personal information. Among the important findings were (1) when an employer allows employees to use computers for personal reasons, even limited use, that raises a reasonable expectation of privacy; (2) the software was as intrusive as possible in the extent of information it collected; (3) much of the information that Spector 360 collected was of limited or no value to IT security.

Although FIPPA allows public bodies to collect personal information without the express consent of employees for certain purposes, the commissioner found that none of these purposes were satisfied here. The strongest argument was based on section 26(c), which allows collection of "information [that] relates directly to and is necessary for a program or activity of the public body." This paragraph includes IT security, but the commissioner found that the collection of this much information was not necessary for that purpose. Her conclusion on this point was unequivocal and applied to the use of Spector 360 on all employees' workstations, not just the mayor's. She also found that Saanich's Network Access Terms and Conditions Form was not adequate, even for the collection of information with a valid security purpose. The interpersonal controversies that the media reported do not figure in the commissioner's report. While they may have coloured her conclusions that the information was not being collected for valid reasons, it is clear from her report that the collection in this case was illegal, even in the absence of malicious intent.

Commissioner Denham ordered Saanich to uninstall Spector 360, delete all the data it collected, conduct a privacy/FIPPA audit, and implement a proper privacy policy, including proper notice to employees of any collection of personal information.

The Atwell report is about FIPPA, but the OIPC's findings are relevant to PIPA too. The definitions of "personal information" in the two Acts are similarly broad. And although FIPPA is more restrictive about the information that public bodies can collect and use, both Acts do not allow collection without consent unless there is a valid reason to do so. Sections 13, 16, and 19 of the BC PIPA allow collection, use, and disclosure of personal information without the employee's consent if "reasonable for the purposes of establishing, managing or terminating an employment relationship between the organization and the individual." There must be a reasonable basis for the collection. Employers are not entitled to monitor personal information unless that information is somehow relevant to the employment relationship (e.g., discovery of the leaking of confidential information). *R v Cole* and the Atwell report suggest that employers should limit the information they collect to only what is necessary, and that the more fully they inform employees the better.

By contrast to a deliberate monitoring program, the accidental discovery by an employer or co-worker of private information that occurs while the discoverer is carrying out a reasonable work duty is much less likely to be a violation. The BC case of *TeBaerts v Penta Builders Group Inc* reveals this point. Like *Poliquin*, it was a wrongful dismissal case, which included a privacy claim connected to the incident that led to the firing. The plaintiff's employer had discovered private emails on her work computer while doing some payroll work that required the use of that computer. The emails contributed to the reasons for her dismissal, but the Court found that this was not an invasion of her privacy. In its reasoning, the Court cited *Cole* and employees' reasonable expectation of privacy in using workplace computers but found that the accidental collection and use of personal information (emails) in this case did not violate this expectation. Had this case been a complaint under PIPA instead of a wrongful dismissal action, the employer's use of the information would likely have qualified as being relevant to the management or termination of the employment relationship and grounds for dismissal.

TeBaerts not only reveals how the *Privacy Act* can figure in IT-monitoring cases but reinforces that privacy violations can become issues in lawsuits, as well as in OIPC investigations. Employers should also be aware that violations of PIPA may not only lead to an OIPC investigation but also a lawsuit by the employee. As noted above in this chapter, section 57 of the BC PIPA and section 60 of the Alberta PIPA allow employees to pursue compensation for damages if the OIPC finds a violation of the Act and the employee has suffered harm due to the violation.

FYI

Employer Monitoring of Outgoing Emails

According to a 2017 survey by the Public Relations Society of America (2017), email is the most frequently used method of organizational communication, both internally (95 percent) and externally (91 percent). A second study by SimplyHired (2020) suggests that about 52 percent of employers are likely to actively monitor that email. Moreover, the study shows they are often monitoring browser histories, work cellphone use, personal cellphone use, in-office instant messaging, time spent in conversations unrelated to work, and social media use. While these studies were conducted in the United States, email and other types of surveillance also occur in

Canadian workplaces. The frequency and purpose of monitoring is often contextual. However, as emerging technologies create opportunities to monitor employee activity and as work and home life become increasingly integrated through these technologies, employers and employees should both be conscious of the privacy implications that can arise.

Another case in which emerging technology was used for the collection of personal information is *Wansink v TELUS Communications Inc.* The employer sought to collect biometric data—in this case, voice prints—as part of its voice recognition remote access system.

CASE IN POINT

Did Compulsory Speech Recognition Program Violate PIPEDA?

Wansink v TELUS Communications Inc, 2007 FCA 21

Facts

To improve its security system, Telus asked employees who worked in the field to create a voice print that would be used to allow them to remotely access its internal computer network. Under this new e-Speak system, the employee's voice print would be converted into a matrix of numbers unique to that individual. The voice sample, upon which the voice print data was based, would be destroyed shortly after being taken and the voice print itself would be digitally stored in a secure database. Although most of the employees agreed to provide a voice sample for the new security system, four employees objected. Threatened with discipline, they filed a complaint with the privacy commissioner challenging the employer's right to force them to consent to the collection of this biometric information.

Relevant Issue

Whether requiring employees to provide voice samples in these circumstances infringed PIPEDA.

Decision

The privacy commissioner ruled in the employer's favour, finding that the system struck an appropriate balance between the employees' right to privacy and the employer's security needs. The process did not provide substantial information about an employee because the employer showed that it could only use the voice prints to verify the employee's identity. Appropriate security measures for the voice prints had been taken.

On appeal, both the Federal Court and the Federal Court of Appeal upheld the commissioner's decision. They confirmed that employee voice prints are "personal information" and thus governed by PIPEDA but stated that a "reasonable person" would conclude that the collection and use of the voice prints for security purposes was appropriate in the circumstances. Factors considered included:

- the level of sensitivity of the personal information involved (here, the employee's voice sample was collected but only a voice print—a matrix of numbers—was used);
- the security measures implemented by the employer (this is critical);
- the bona fide business objectives (protecting sensitive customer and other data);
- the effectiveness of the voice prints in meeting those objectives;
- the alternative methods of achieving the same levels of security at comparable cost and benefits (it replaced a less secure password system); and
- the proportionality of the loss of privacy as against the employer's costs and operational benefits in the level of security it provides.

The courts had more difficulty with the issue of consent. The Federal Court of Appeal confirmed that all of the exceptions to collection, use, and disclosure of personal information without consent are set out exhaustively in section 7 of PIPEDA, and that none of them applied in these circumstances.

However, the Court noted that, by its very design, the employer's e-Speak system ensured that individual consent must be provided prior to collecting their voice prints, because without employees' active participation, the company could not create their voice print and forcibly enroll them into the system. The Court of Appeal left open the question of whether alleged threats of disciplinary measures against employees who refused to consent might negate meaningful consent under the Act.

FYI

What Is Biometric Data?

Biometric technology uses an individual's unique physical attributes, such as a fingerprint, voice print, or even a vein scan, to identify that individual. Typically, the technology involves scanning the physical attribute, reducing it to digital form, and storing it on a system so that it can be used for comparison purposes. For example, each time the individual wishes to gain access to the place or system protected by the biometric technology, the physical attribute is again scanned and the new scan is compared against the stored sample. If the two match within a preset threshold, the individual is granted access. Among other things, biometrics can now be used in time clocks to verify employee work hours, for security purposes in door locks, and in computer and telephone systems (York & Carty, 2006, at 1). While biometric technology is now in widespread use (consider, e.g., that many individuals unlock their smartphones with a fingerprint or facial recognition), this does not relieve the burden on an employer to ensure that the collection, use, retention, disclosure, and disposal of this data is done in a reasonable fashion consistent with privacy legislation.

TELUS's success in the case suggests that employers covered by privacy legislation can collect biometric data if there is a significant business purpose for the collection and the employer implements strict security measures and protections against misuse. A central issue is proportionality: weighing the level of intrusion into an employee's privacy against its importance to the employer's operational needs in terms of what information it wants to collect, why it is collecting it, and how it will be used. Courts will also look at the alternatives to see whether less privacy-intrusive measures are viable.

Where an employer conducts video surveillance of an employee outside the workplace, and that employee is covered under PIPEDA, arbitrators have generally applied the test of "reasonableness" to determine whether that evidence is admissible. In *Ross v Rosedale Transport Inc*, a federally regulated employer had conducted video surveillance of an employee outside the workplace to establish whether the employee on sick leave was as disabled as he claimed to be. The surveillance was conducted while the employee was in full public view and thus had a "relatively low expectation of privacy." The video surveillance showed the employee performing physical activities (carrying furniture) well beyond the capacity he claimed to have, and as a result he was dismissed for cause.

However, the videotaped evidence was ruled inadmissible because the employer had initiated the surveillance on the basis of a vague suspicion that the employee was exaggerating his injuries. Because there were no "reasonable" grounds for conducting the surveillance in the first place, the resulting evidence could not be admitted. As a result, the employer lost the dismissal case.

From the opposite perspective, when it is a union conducting the filming, "reasonableness" is again the standard that must be applied. However, as reported at the outset of this chapter, "reasonableness" must effectively balance legitimate rights—one of those rights being the right for a union to set up a picket line and communicate its cause during a lawful strike—with privacy rights.

In a case that ultimately ended at the Supreme Court of Canada and resulted in Alberta's PIPA being struck down as unconstitutional in 2013 (*Alberta (Information and Privacy Commissioner) v United Food and Commercial Workers, Local 401*), the balance was impeded by provisions in Alberta's privacy legislation itself. Those offending provisions have since been amended, with enactment in December 2014 of provisions that allow for the collection, use, and disclosure of personal information by a trade union without the consent of the individual to whom the personal information pertains where all of the following conditions are met:

1. The collection, use, or disclosure of personal information is for the purpose of informing or persuading the public about a matter of significant public interest or importance relating to a labour relations dispute involving the trade union.
2. The collection, use, or disclosure is reasonably necessary for that purpose.
3. It is reasonable to collect, use, or disclose the personal information without consent for that purpose, taking into consideration all relevant circumstances, including the nature and sensitivity of the information.

No other changes were made to Alberta's privacy legislation at the time; however, the province undertook a comprehensive review of its privacy legislation. A final report to the Legislative Assembly was provided in 2016. Ten recommendations were made, including that PIPA be amended to make the Act apply fully to all not-for-profit organizations, subject to a one-year transition period.

In general, in a unionized workplace the collective agreement may restrict use of video surveillance or other forms of employee monitoring, but such language is rare. An appropriate restriction would be to require the employer to notify the union and perhaps participate in discussions before implementing any decision to conduct such surveillance.

However, even in the absence of restrictions within the collective agreement, arbitrators have generally recognized a right to workplace privacy in unionized workplaces, although the right is not absolute (York & Carty, 2006, at 2). Generally speaking, employee monitoring that is disclosed to the affected employees is allowed where it is a reasonable exercise of management rights, given all the circumstances. For example, arbitrators have generally allowed video cameras to stay, provided they are trained on security points such as entrances and exits and not work areas, or provided they are only turned on outside of working hours (Michaluk, 2007, at 5).

In view of the above, employers in both union and non-union workplaces should ensure they have a clear and carefully drafted IT policy that does the following:

- Put employees on notice that they should not have an expectation of privacy when using employer technology and systems (including computers, cellphones, or other electronic devices).

- Provide an explanation of the purpose of the policy (e.g., security, deterring theft, safety).
- Provide an explanation of how the policy will apply, including the types of technology and applications that are covered and what the information may be used for.
- Provide guidance on what uses are permitted or not permitted. For example, an employer might stipulate that email is to be used for business purposes only. If personal emails are allowed, the policy should state any content restrictions. For example, emails containing discriminatory, pornographic, or threatening content should be prohibited.
- Provide an explanation of the potential consequences for a breach of the policy (Jakibchuk, 2011, at 5).

As with all workplace policies, they also must be effectively communicated and consistently enforced to be effective.

In addition to having an effective policy on the use of email, the Internet, and technological devices, employers should institute measures such as having lockdown codes on computers, laptops, photocopiers, printers, and all similar devices to prevent sensitive information from being misappropriated (Silliker, 2012, at 7).

Balancing the privacy interests of employees with the interests of employers to run their businesses effectively is a subjective process, and in unionized settings arbitration decisions in this area have often been divided.

In conclusion, when electing whether or not to monitor the personal information of employees by video surveillance, email, keystroke monitoring, or biometric data, employers would be wise to keep foremost in their minds the underlying principles of PIPEDA and their reflections in the BC and Alberta statutes.

FYI

BYOD: The Newest Frontier

BYOD—Bring Your Own Device—refers to the trend of employees using their own personal devices for work-related as well as personal purposes (Dobson, 2012). While many employers are embracing this development, allowing employees to access corporate networks through their own smartphones, tablets, or laptops raises potential privacy and security issues. Many employers take the position that since the employee is connecting to the organization's network, the same rules that apply to an employer-owned device should apply to an employee-owned device. However, as discussed above, courts have found that employees have a reasonable expectation of privacy when they are allowed to use work-issued devices for personal data, and this expectation is arguably even stronger where the employee owns the device. Therefore, an employer's BYOD policy needs to clearly state that employer monitoring is allowed on such devices, explain the reason for it, and indicate how the information collected might be used. Employees may also be asked to sign an agreement that consents to the "remote wiping" of data where an employee-owned device is lost or stolen. Such an agreement should also release the employer from liability for the loss of any data, including personal data, from wiping activities (Dobson, 2012, at 20). Some employers may decide that BYOD is more trouble than it is worth and prohibit the use of personal devices for work-related communication and data storage.

KEY TERMS

employee personal information, **380**
fair information principles, **372**
personal employee information, **380**
personal information, **371**
privacy commissioner, **377**
solicitor–client privilege, **376**

REVIEW AND DISCUSSION QUESTIONS

1. Although PIPEDA does not apply to personal employee information in provincially regulated workplaces, BC and Alberta employers should be aware of its requirements. Why?
2. In federally regulated workplaces, how do PIPEDA's requirements affect the following?
   a. Checking references and retaining the information
   b. Taking witness statements for internal investigations
   c. Conducting performance evaluations
3. What are the ten fair information principles that underlie PIPEDA and inform provincial privacy legislation? Choose four that you consider significant and discuss them.
4. PIPEDA is intended to reflect a balance between an individual's need for privacy and an organization's need to use, collect, and disclose personal information in certain circumstances. Is this balance achieved by the legislation? Explain your answer.
5. Why should an organization have a policy on electronic monitoring? What should such a policy include?
6. George was a unionized car mechanic with 25 years' service in an auto body shop. On Thursday, May 14, 2020, he reported an injury while handling an air brake valve, but he worked the balance of that day as well as the next. However, on the following Monday, George returned to work with a doctor's note stating he could only use his left arm. But because George was already doing modified work that required both arms, the employer said it could not offer him any modified work. The employer decided to undertake video surveillance of George while off duty. It was suspicious because George had a somewhat greater than average record of work-related incidents calling for medical attention and it wanted to see whether he was engaged in activities that went beyond the medical restrictions imposed on him by his physician. The surveillance revealed him carrying objects of significant weight and digging up his garden. George was fired by his employer. He grieved his dismissal, and an arbitrator had to rule on whether the surveillance evidence was admissible. If you were the arbitrator, how would you rule? Explain your decision.
7. In the *Wansink v TELUS Communications Inc* decision, the Federal Court and Federal Court of Appeal had some difficulty with the issue of employee consent. Discuss whether PIPEDA should be amended to remove the consent requirement with respect to personal *employee* information. In other words, should an employer be allowed to collect personal employee information without consent as long as the information is reasonably necessary for managing the employment relationship?
8. The employees of a transportation company complained to management that the men's washroom was very messy, despite regular cleaning. The employer implemented a log system that monitored the use and the state of the men's washroom. After three days of monitoring, the employer concluded that the facility required attention only after it was used by a particular employee, John. The employer gave John a disciplinary letter advising him that his behaviour had to stop; otherwise, progressive disciplinary actions would be taken. John filed a complaint with the federal privacy commissioner alleging that management had monitored his washroom visits without his consent and used the collected personal information for disciplinary purposes. Did the employer infringe PIPEDA in this situation? Explain your answer.
9. The federal privacy commissioner is limited to making recommendations. Complainants must go to the Federal Court to get binding orders. Would Canada's privacy legislation be more effective if it "had more teeth"? Discuss.
10. In 2013 the Supreme Court of Canada struck down Alberta's PIPA. Describe the primary reason for that decision, the time frame that was given for corrective action to be taken, and the response of the Alberta government in terms of amendments to the legislation.
11. In 2015 the *Digital Privacy Act* came into force. Describe some of the key changes to PIPEDA resulting from this change.

RELATED WEBSITES

Website for the Office of the Privacy Commissioner of Canada <https://www.priv.gc.ca/en>

Website for the Office of the Information and Privacy Commissioner of Alberta <https://www.oipc.ab.ca>

Website for the Office of the Information and Privacy Commissioner for British Columbia <https://www.oipc.bc.ca>

REFERENCES

Alberta (Information and Privacy Commissioner) v United Food and Commercial Workers, Local 401, 2013 SCC 62.

Brown, David, "10 Months to Get Ready," *Canadian HR Reporter* (24 February 2003) at 1.

Canadian Charter of Rights and Freedoms, Part I of the *Constitution Act, 1982*, being Schedule B to the *Canada Act 1982* (UK), 1982, c 11.

Cardinal Coach Lines Ltd (Re), 2010 CanLII 98657 (Alta OIPC).

Cole, R v, 2012 SCC 53.

Digital Privacy Act, SC 2015, c 32.

Dobson, Sarah, "Some Expectation of Privacy with Workplace Computers: SCC," *Canadian HR Reporter* (19 November 2012) at 1.

Eastmond v Canadian Pacific Railway, 2004 FC 852.

Emond Harnden, "Canada Amends Privacy Law with Introduction of Bill S-4—Digital Privacy Act" (1 May 2014), online: <http://www.ehlaw.ca/1405-focus1405-4>.

Freedom of Information and Protection of Privacy Act, RSA 2000, c F-25.

Freedom of Information and Protection of Privacy Act, RSBC 1996, c 165.

Gilbert, Douglas, Brian Burkett & Moira McCaskill, *Canadian Labour and Employment Law for the US Practitioner* (Washington, DC: Bureau of National Affairs, 2000).

HR Reporter, "Retailer Ordered to Stop Credit Checks" (24 February 2010), online: <http://www.hrreporter.com/articleview/7596-retailer-ordered-to-stop-credit-checks>.

Jacobs, Adam, "Updates to Canadian Privacy Law Ramping Up with the Introduction of the Digital Privacy Act (Bill S-4)" (12 June 2014), online: *Mondaq* <http://www.mondaq.com/canada/x/320084/Data+Protection+Privacy/Updates+To+Canadian+Privacy+Law+Ramping+Up+With+The+Introduction+Of+The+Digital+Privacy+Act+Bill+S4>.

Jakibchuk, Adrian, "Whose Hard Drive Is It Anyway?" *Canadian Employment Law Today* (15 June 2011) at 4, online: <https://www.sherrardkuzz.com/wp-content/uploads/2018/10/Jakibchuk.Whose_Hard_Drive.pdf>.

Michaluk, Dan, "Walking the Tightrope—Recent Developments in Employee Surveillance," Hicks Morley LLP (20 April 2007).

Office of the Information and Privacy Commissioner for British Columbia, *Annual Report, 2018–2019* (October 2019), online: <https://www.oipc.bc.ca/annual-reports/2347>.

Office of the Privacy Commissioner of Canada, "Summary of Privacy Laws in Canada" (2014), online: <https://www.priv.gc.ca/en/privacy-topics/privacy-laws-in-canada/02_05_d_15>.

Office of the Privacy Commissioner of Canada, *PIPEDA Case Summary #2003-226*, online: <https://www.priv.gc.ca/en/opc-actions-and-decisions/investigations/investigations-into-businesses/2003/pipeda-2003-226>.

Office of the Privacy Commissioner of Canada, *Privacy Toolkit: A Guide for Businesses and Organizations* (Gatineau, QC: Office of the Privacy Commissioner of Canada, 2015), online: <https://www.priv.gc.ca/media/2038/guide_org_e.pdf>.

Personal Information Protection Act, SA 2003, c P-6.5.

Personal Information Protection Act, SBC 2003, c 63.

Personal Information Protection and Electronic Documents Act, SC 2000, c 5.

Poliquin v Devon Canada Corporation, 2009 ABCA 216.

Privacy Act, RSBC 1996, c 373.

Public Relations Society of America, "Trends in Communications Show Companies Slow to Adopt New Tech," EMPLOYEEapp (20 June 2017), online: <https://www.theemployeeapp.com/press-releases/trends-in-communications-industry-show-companies-slow-to-adopt-new-technologies>.

Ross v Rosedale Transport Inc, [2003] CLAD No 237 (QL) (Ont).

Saanich (Disctrict), Re, 2015 BCIPC 15 [Atwell report].

Silliker, Amanda, "BC Ministry of Health Fires 5 for Privacy Breach," *Canadian HR Reporter* (8 October 2012) at 7.

SimplyHired, "Being Watched at Work: Workplace Surveilance Perceptions" (2020), online: <https://www.simplyhired.com/guide/studies/being-watched-at-work>.

Suncor Energy Inc v Unifor, Local 707A, 2016 ABQB 269.

Tally-Ho Motor Inn, Re, 2006 CanLII 32981 (BCIPC).
TeBaerts v Penta Builders Group Inc, 2015 BCSC 2008.
Telus Mobility and TWU (Lee), Re (2001), 102 LAC (4th) 239 (Alta) (Arbitrator: Sims).
Tsatsu Shores Homeowners Corporation (Re), 2006 CanLII 42695 (BCIPC).
Twentieth Century Fox Film Corporation, Re, 2006 CanLII 37938 (BCIPC).
Wansink v TELUS Communications Inc, 2007 FCA 21.
York, Andrea & Lisa Carty, "Balancing Technology and Privacy at Work," *Blakes Bulletin on Privacy Law* (August 2006) at 1, online: <https://www.mondaq.com/canada/employee-rights-labour-relations/42582/balancing-technology-and-privacy-at-work>.

Navigating the Employment Relationship

11

LEARNING OUTCOMES

After completing this chapter, you will be able to:

- Understand the effective use of an employer's policy manual.
- Outline the legal requirements for amending an employment contract.
- Identify ongoing management issues, including performance management, progressive discipline, and attendance management programs.
- Explain an employer's vicarious liability for damages caused by employees.

Introduction

While all statutes discussed in Part II affect the ongoing employer–employee relationship, for non-unionized employees the framework underlying that relationship remains the individual contract of employment. Whether written or oral, this contract contains the main terms and conditions governing employment, and the parties must always keep it in mind when dealing with both ongoing matters and significant changes to their relationship. As discussed in Chapter 5, an employment contract's terms include both those expressly agreed to by the parties and those that are implied into the agreement by the common law.

Common law principles of contract, such as the need for consideration to create a binding obligation, remain relevant throughout the employment relationship. They must be taken into account if either party seeks to change the contract or add terms that are disadvantageous to the other party after the employee starts work. Similarly, the parties must consider common law rules relating to constructive dismissal if an employer should attempt to change an employee's duties in any significant way or to impose certain types of discipline during the course of employment.

This chapter considers several legal issues and human resources practices that employers should keep in mind in navigating the ongoing employment relationship.

Employer Policy Manuals

All but the smallest organizations should have a policy manual that contains employment policies and procedures. Many large employers also have a more user-friendly version called an employee handbook that provides a quick reference guide to information about working for the organization. In general, an employee handbook answers the "when," "where," and "how" questions, while a policy manual also provides insight into "why" things are done in a particular way in the workplace. Where a handbook is used, it should be sufficiently detailed to cover basic day-to-day rights and responsibilities and direct employees to where policies can be viewed in their entirety (Milne, 2005, at 3-1). In the following discussion, reference to policy manuals includes employee handbooks.

A well-drafted employer's policy manual serves several legal and communicative functions. It is an effective way for an employer to provide information to employees in a convenient, centralized location. It usually includes company rules concerning such matters as dress codes, probationary periods, benefit entitlements, disciplinary procedures, office procedures, sick leave policy, and the employer's harassment policy, and thus communicates an organization's expectations in these areas.

A policy manual also provides a convenient means for making relatively minor changes to company rules, such as a slight alteration in coffee break times. In this case, it is sufficient that the employer amend the manual and notify the employees concerning the revised rule or procedure. However, in the case of significant changes, such as those that arguably affect fundamental terms of the employment agreement, the employer must take additional steps (discussed below under the heading "Changing Employment Terms and Conditions").

An employer's policy manual also helps ensure consistency in an employer's treatment of employees. It provides managers with a set of pre-established rules to guide them, for example, in responding to various employee requests. Treating all employees consistently and predictably is a fundamental part of being a fair employer and being perceived as such by employees. By letting employees know what is expected of them and what they can expect from the employer in return, the manual helps reduce the potential for dissatisfaction and disputes.

As noted in Chapter 5, a policy manual does not automatically bind the employee; the employer must take certain steps to ensure that it forms part of the employment contract. An employer that wants to maximize the benefits of a policy manual should:

- ensure the employment contract or letter of hire specifically incorporates the manual (this must be done with sufficient clarity that the employee knows these terms are incorporated into their employment);
- provide employees with a copy of the manual before they begin work;
- ensure that the manual is clearly drafted;
- apply the manual's policies consistently among employees;
- ensure that all employees have up-to-date copies of the manual;
- give as much notice as possible of significant changes to the manual policy;
- have employees indicate in writing (typically through a signed acknowledgment form) that they have reviewed the manual and any changes to it, perhaps on an annual basis (this form should note that employees are responsible for asking human resources staff or a supervisor about anything they do not understand in the manual; Leiper & Hall, 2006, at 14);
- ensure that employees are aware of the consequences of failing to adhere to the manual and that these consequences are fair;
- include a statement advising employees that the organization retains the sole discretion to make changes to any of the policies, procedures, and guidelines contained in the manual; and
- update the manual periodically to ensure compliance with current legislation, while informing employees of these updates.

A decision that aptly demonstrates the importance of effectively implementing an employment policy manual is *Daley v Depco International Inc.* In that case, the employer's progressive discipline policy was at the heart of its defence that it had just cause to summarily dismiss the employee. In finding for the employer, the Court noted with approval that Depco not only distributed the employee handbook to its employees, but also obtained employee sign-offs that acknowledged receipt of the handbook and indicated agreement to abide by its rules, policies, terms, and conditions. Furthermore, the acknowledgment included an explicit statement that failure to abide by the handbook's policies "may result in disciplinary action and/or dismissal." The thorough way in which Depco implemented its progressive discipline policy played a crucial part in the Court ultimately finding in its favour.

It should be noted that for a breach of a company rule (or policy) to constitute just cause for dismissal, several factors must exist. In addition to being well communicated and consistently enforced, the rule must itself be "reasonable," the implications of breaking the rule must be sufficiently serious to justify termination, and employees must be advised that they can be terminated for breaking it. A final consideration is whether a reasonable excuse for breaking the rule existed (Saint-Cyr, 2012).

Changing Employment Terms and Conditions

Chapter 5 discussed the benefits of having a written employment contract that sets out the rights and responsibilities of both parties during the employment relationship. However, what happens when, either because of changed circumstances or because of an oversight in negotiating the agreement, the employer wants to make changes to the contract after employment begins?

Introducing changes to an employment contract, whether oral or written, during the course of employment raises a number of issues. If an employer wishes to make a minor change, such as slightly modifying a procedure for applying for reimbursements, the employer can simply announce the change and distribute amendments to the policy manual. However, an employer that wishes to introduce a change that is more significant faces two potential legal problems. First, if the change alters the employment agreement in a fundamental way, it may constitute constructive dismissal, thus allowing the employee to bring an action against the employer for damages for wrongful dismissal. Second, if the employer negotiates the change with the employee, the employer must provide consideration for the new term or the employee may subsequently argue they are not bound by it. These two issues are discussed below.

Constructive Dismissal

constructive dismissal dismissal that occurs when an employer unilaterally makes substantial changes to the essential elements of the employment contract to the detriment of the employee

Constructive dismissal occurs when an employer unilaterally makes substantial changes to the essential elements of the employment contract to the detriment of the employee. Where an employer makes a unilateral and substantial change, an employee can either accept the change (or possibly negotiate changes of their own) and continue working under the new arrangement or inform the employer that the change constitutes constructive dismissal. Alternatively, the employee may quit and sue the employer for pay in lieu of proper notice, or stay in the position and sue the employer for the difference between the old and the new salary.

The Supreme Court of Canada's decision in *Farber v Royal Trust Company* remains the seminal decision in Canada that defined constructive dismissal as occurring when a *substantial* change is made to an *essential* term of an employee's contract. Examples might include the following:

- a substantial reduction in a term of the employee's employment, such as the amount of vacation time per year;
- a demotion or substantial reduction in an employee's remuneration;
- refusing to allow the employee to fulfill the conditions of employment (e.g., preventing the employee from entering the workplace);

- harassing or abusing an employee such that the environment becomes untenable; or
- giving the employee the choice of accepting the fundamental change or being fired (Minkin Employment Lawyers, 2012).

Subsequently, in *Potter v New Brunswick Legal Aid Services Commission* the Supreme Court dealt with some ambiguities that can arise in constructive dismissal by establishing a two-branch test. The first branch tests whether there has been a substantial breach of the employment contract. The second branch tests for constructive dismissal where there has been no clear, objective breach of the employment contract.

In the first branch, the court determines whether a substantial breach of an essential term of the employment contract has occurred. The first step is to decide whether the employer's unilateral conduct breached an express or implied term of the contract. If the employee consented to the conduct, it was not unilateral and therefore was not a breach of the contract.

If a breach is established, the court will then determine whether a reasonable person in the same situation as the employee would have viewed the breach as *substantially* altering an *essential term* of the contract. For example, a 25 percent reduction in pay or a significant downgrade in job duties clearly goes to the heart of the employment agreement; it is a repudiation of the existing terms and conditions of employment and would be considered constructive dismissal. On the other hand, where an employer wants to introduce a more modest change, such as slightly modifying an employee's commission package or proposing a relatively small across-the-board salary decrease in response to difficult market conditions, the situation is less clear. Every case must be evaluated on its own facts to decide how essential the change is to the employee's job. Ultimately, if the issue ends up in court, it will be up to a court to decide whether the change is a fundamental one (versus a minor or administrative change) and therefore constitutes constructive dismissal.

The second branch is a test for constructive dismissal where there is no clear, objective breach of the employment contract. The court will determine whether the employer's conduct (while not an obvious breach of a specific contract term) would lead a reasonable person to believe that the employer no longer intended to be bound by the contract. If the cumulative actions of the employer would lead a reasonable person to think the employer was attempting to force the employee out, constructive dismissal is clearly established. For example, in *Lavinkas v Jacques Whitford and Associates*, the Court found that an employee who was marginalized, made to feel he was not valued, and told he was perceived as a joke because of his personality was constructively dismissed:

> The series of events … though innocuous when considered individually, had this cumulative effect.
>
> Looked at objectively, the only reasonable conclusion that an employee in Mr. Lavinskas' circumstances could have arrived at … was that Jacques Whitford did not want him, and regardless of what changes he tried to make to his performance, it would never be good enough for the Jacques Whitford

> management. It was not reasonable to expect an employee, faced with these circumstances, to persevere in his employment. (at paras 90–91)

Two British Columbia (BC) cases that applied the second branch of *Potter* provide contrasting illustrations of the former employee's obligation to prove that the employer's conduct amounted to a wish not to be bound by the contract—or, put another way, to not have the employee working there anymore. In *de Vink v Schaffer Residences Inc*, a woman quit her job and sued for constructive dismissal, claiming that her employer had "created an intolerable, hostile and acrimonious workplace" for her. The 65-year-old woman's claim was that her employer had begun to mistreat her two years before she quit, after she had a confrontation with a co-worker and later asked for a raise. She alleged that the employer bullied, harassed, and isolated her and did not help her to improve her relations with the other employees. The result was, she claimed, an increasingly "oppressive" atmosphere at work. However, her claim failed because of lack of corroborating evidence of bullying of the plaintiff. Indeed, the Court seemed to find that the plaintiff was the cause of conflict with her co-workers and supervisor. The judge found that the employer had done nothing to make the workplace intolerable; quite the opposite. When the plaintiff quit, the Court found she did so "of her own volition."

In contrast, in *Frederickson v Newtech Dental Laboratory Inc* there was evidence of treatment that would make the workplace intolerable to a reasonable person, thus supporting the conclusion that the employer did not want to continue employing the plaintiff despite its offer to do so. Newtech dismissed Frederickson upon her return from medical leave, citing a slowdown in business. However, when she had a lawyer send a demand letter for severance pay, the employer directed her to return to work. She refused the offer of re-employment, stating that the business owner's treatment of her at the time of the original dismissal would make the workplace intolerable. This treatment included the secret recording of two conversations with her and a conversation with another employee in which the owner agreed that she would be too embarrassed to return to work there. The trial judge ruled that Frederickson had a duty to mitigate her loss by accepting re-employment. The question for the Court of Appeal was whether she did have such a duty in these circumstances. The Court ruled that she was justified in refusing to return to the workplace. The employer breached the confidence expected of the "boss" by recording private conversations with her and later using them against her and by talking about her with another employee. On the basis of the second branch of *Potter*, a return to such a workplace was intolerable, and a reasonable person could not be expected to accept it. She was not required to mitigate damages by returning to that employer, and was therefore entitled to full damages for wrongful dismissal.

The first branch of *Potter* is the more traditional one of a change to the employment contract. Examples of contractual changes that have resulted in findings of constructive dismissal include demotion, fundamental changes to job responsibilities, reducing the employee's pay, changing the employee's hours of work, relocating the employee, the unfair imposition of probation, and creating a hostile work environment that makes the employee's continued attendance at work intolerable. The key question here is how substantial the change must be to constitute a dismissal.

Making Changes to the Employment Contract

Where a proposed change to an employment contract is arguably a fundamental one, an employer can generally meet its legal obligations by doing any of the following:

1. *Including variation clauses.* A variation clause is an express term in an employment contract that states the employer may make unilateral changes to the employment contract. While not fool proof, a variation clause helps to support an employer's claim that more minor or administrative amendments were contemplated in the original employment contract.
2. *Seeking employee consent.* Written and informed employee consent to proposed amendments will minimize the likelihood of successful constructive dismissal assertions.
3. *Providing "fresh consideration."* If proposed amendments impact substantive employee rights, employers should provide the affected employees with "fresh consideration." This could be a signing bonus, additional vacation, or some other form of consideration for accepting the revised contract. As discussed below, such consideration must have true value to the employee and cannot be an attempt to offer something that has already been provided (e.g., an offer of continued employment for acceptance of the change).
4. *Providing reasonable notice of the change.* As a general rule, employees should be given proper advance notice of all proposed amendments. If the employee rejects the change, reasonable notice of termination with an offer of re-employment on the new terms and conditions is possible (Totan, 2016).

Employers should include an express declaration that the employee may not continue under the existing employment terms after the end of the notice period, as the Ontario Court of Appeal's decision in *Wronko v Western Inventory Service Ltd* indicates.

CASE IN POINT

Changing Employment Terms Mid-Stream

Wronko v Western Inventory Service Ltd, 2008 ONCA 327, leave to appeal to SCC refused, 2008 CanLII 53793

Facts

Wronko began working for Western, a Toronto-based inventory service provider, in 1987, and by 2004 he was vice-president of sales. With each promotion he executed a new employment agreement. The last contract, signed in December 2000, provided for a generous severance package of a lump-sum payment of two years' salary upon termination without cause. In 2002, Western's new president decided that Wronko's contract should be amended, and he presented Wronko with a draft agreement that provided him with only seven months' severance if terminated without cause. After seeking legal advice, Wronko refused to sign this amended agreement. On September 9, 2002, Western responded with a letter stating that the new contract would take effect in two years' time. Wronko made it clear that he still did not accept the change, but he continued working. Two years later, Western wrote Wronko a letter that stated "Effective September 9, 2004, the terms noted in the employment agreement … apply and are in full force and effect. If you do not wish to accept the new terms and conditions of employment as outlined, then we do not have a job for you." Wronko again refused the new terms and, taking the position that the employer's letter effectively fired him, sued for wrongful dismissal.

At trial, the employer argued that it had met its legal obligations by giving Wronko two years' notice of the change and that by not attending work after that, Wronko had resigned. The trial judge agreed. Under the common law, Western had the legal right to vary even a fundamental term of the contract—in this case the termination clause—upon proper notice to the employee. The Court therefore dismissed the wrongful dismissal claim. Wronko appealed.

Relevant Issue

Whether an employer is able to unilaterally change a fundamental term of an employment agreement simply by providing advance notice of the change to the employee.

Decision

The Ontario Court of Appeal unanimously found for Wronko. It held that where an employer attempts to make a unilateral and fundamental change to the terms of an existing employment agreement, and the employee clearly rejects that new term, the employer must do more than provide advance notice of the change. It must also advise the employee of the consequences of rejecting it. In this instance, Western could have done this by explicitly telling Wronko that if he refused to accept the new terms, employment under the terms of the *existing* contract would terminate at the end of the working notice period (September 2004). At the same time, it could have offered to rehire him under the *new* terms, starting at the end of the working notice period. However, because Western had allowed him to continue working in these circumstances without notifying him of the consequences of this decision, Wronko could legally insist that the notice was ineffective. Therefore, by the letter of September 2004, Western effectively terminated Wronko and he was entitled to wrongful dismissal damages. The Court of Appeal awarded Wronko two years' termination pay in lieu of notice ($286,000) pursuant to the terms of his existing employment contract. Western's leave to appeal to the Supreme Court of Canada was dismissed with costs.

The *Wronko* decision stands for the proposition that providing advance notice of a fundamental change to the employment contract may not be enough. To make it effective, it is advisable that the employer also explain to the employee the consequences of rejecting the change. In this instance, Western could have done this by explicitly telling Wronko that if he refused to accept the new terms, employment under the terms of the existing contract would terminate at the end of the working notice period (September 2004). At the same time, Western could have offered to rehire him under the new terms, starting at the end of the working notice period.

It thus appears that the *Wronko* decision has expanded the legal requirements surrounding an employer's ability to make a unilateral, fundamental change to an employment contract by simply providing advance notice. However, as always, the interpretation of the legal requirement depends on the specific circumstances of the case. For example, in the 2012 case of *Kafka v Allstate Insurance Company of Canada*, Allstate had advised all of its insurance agents that significant changes to their compensation structure would take effect in 24 months' time. The agents who refused to accept the changes resigned and filed a motion to have their claim certified as a class action. Basing their argument on *Wronko*, these agents claimed that once they rejected the employer's proposed changes to their contract, the employer had to provide them with reasonable notice of termination and offer to rehire them on the new terms. However, the Ontario Divisional Court rejected this argument. It found that, unlike in *Wronko*, the employer's notice of the changes made it clear that the changes would take effect within 24 months, regardless of whether or not the employees accepted the change. The agents could therefore have no reasonable expectation that continuing under the previous compensation system at the end of the 24-month period remained an option. Importantly, in *Wronko* the employer had been ambiguous about whether the change would actually be implemented and the employee had been allowed to continue working despite the fact that he had notified the employer he was refusing the change.

The Ontario Divisional Court's decision in *Kafka* interprets *Wronko* quite narrowly. However, an employer that wants to make a fundamental change to an employee's terms of employment by providing advance notice should clearly indicate that the change will take place at the end of the notice period regardless of the employee's acceptance or rejection of it. Without this clarity, where an employee rejects the change the employer would be well advised to provide notice of termination of employment under the existing terms, which can be accompanied by an offer to rehire the employee on the new terms at the end of the notice period (Channe, 2012).

One important question that arises from this discussion is "How does an employer determine the amount of advance notice required?" The answer is that what constitutes proper notice depends on the particular circumstances. First, the employer looks at the terms of the employment contract to see whether it sets out a period for notice of termination. In the absence of an enforceable termination clause, the common law implies a duty to provide reasonable notice, which, as is discussed in Chapters 13 and 14, depends on a number of factors, including the employee's age, position, and length of service.

Where more than one employee is affected by a significant change, an employer probably should provide the same notice to all employees based on the longest notice period to which any of the employees is entitled. The main difficulty with this approach is that the notice required under the common law is often extensive, ranging from periods of several months to periods of up to two years for long-term employees. If the change being proposed by the employer is urgent, such as an immediate 15 percent across-the-board salary decrease to keep itself solvent, the employer may be unable to provide sufficient notice to meet its common law obligations.

Even where proposed changes to the terms of employment involve the promotion of an employee, the employer should keep the common law notion of constructive dismissal in mind. Constructive dismissal normally requires that the change be detrimental to the employee, but a reluctant employee who is unhappy or struggles in the new position may successfully argue that the promotion negatively affects the foundation of the contract. Employers should not coerce employees to accept promotions. The decision must be mutual. Employers must also be prepared to assist employees in performing new jobs. If an employee accepts a promotion but is unable to perform the new job satisfactorily, in the absence of just cause an employer should be prepared to re-employ them in their previous job or provide proper notice of dismissal or pay in lieu.

An employer may also be faced with resentment and declining morale if it chooses to institute significant unilateral changes in the terms and conditions of employment. This is especially true after the *Wronko* decision since, to make a change effective in the face of an employee's rejection of it, the advance notice now must be accompanied by rather direct statements regarding the consequences of the rejection. In short, significant changes to the employment contract can be made with sufficient advance notice, but they should not be made lightly.

Providing Consideration

Another way to amend an employment contract is through negotiation. This approach is especially useful where the employer wants a new term, such as a non-competition clause, to be added immediately.

However, as discussed in Chapter 5, to create a binding contract under the common law, both parties must receive consideration—something of value—in exchange for the promise given. Without proper consideration, the agreement is unenforceable. The same requirement applies to the amendment of a contract. If an employer places a contract containing a disadvantageous new contractual term in front of an employee and simply asks them to sign it, a court may refuse to enforce the new term because it lacked consideration. This is what happened in the *Singh v Empire Life* case.

CASE IN POINT

Continued Employment Deemed Not to Be Consideration in Employment Contract

Singh v Empire Life Ins Co, 2002 BCCA 452

Facts

The plaintiff, Singh, was interviewed for the position of regional manager with the defendant, Empire Life Insurance Company, in August 1998. On September 1, Singh got a handwritten letter confirming that Empire was offering him the position with a total compensation package of $170,000. His employment was to begin that day, and he was told that a formal contract would follow. Singh started work September 1, 1998. That day, he received a "confirmation of offer" letter with greater details relating to his employment, although the letter stated that it was "not a contract." It said the initial start-up period would be two years commencing from September 1, 1998. However, it was not until February 1999 that the parties signed a "regional manager's agreement." In that agreement a termination clause read, "The termination will be effective at the end of the appropriate period of notice according to applicable provincial legislation." This agreement also said that it replaced all prior agreements between the parties.

Things did not work out well, and in the fall of 1999 the company told Singh that his manager's position was redundant and terminated his employment. Because Singh had only been employed for just over a year, the company gave him two weeks' notice, as required under the BC *Employment Standards Act*. Singh took the position that he was entitled to reasonable notice, which would be longer than the statutory two weeks, because the parties' contract was made on September 1, 1998, and the employer at that time told him he would be working for at least two years. The trial Court ruled in favour of Singh and awarded him damages for the ten months remaining in the two-year contract. The employer appealed to the BC Court of Appeal, arguing that Singh's continued employment after he signed the second contract was adequate consideration for that agreement to make it effective.

Relevant Issue

Whether the employee's continued employment was consideration for the new agreement, even though its terms relating to notice for termination were less generous than those in the original agreement.

Decision

The trial Court judge's award of damages for ten months was upheld. The parties' contract of employment began on September 1, 1998. That contract clearly stated that Singh's employment was for a two-year fixed term. The contract that the parties signed five months later was less favourable to Singh than the first one and modified some of its terms—namely, the termination notice was reduced. This change had to be supported by consideration to be enforceable against Singh. His continued employment for five months after the original agreement did not amount to consideration that would support modification of the terms in that agreement. The courts in BC and elsewhere have affirmed the general principle that modification of a pre-existing contract will not be enforceable unless there is some further benefit to both parties. That did not happen in this case, so Singh was entitled to a much longer period of notice than that required under the statute.

On the other hand, courts have found that where an employer is in a position to terminate an agreement with little or no notice, and clearly intends to do so if the new terms of the agreement are not accepted, a promise not to terminate if the employee agrees to a new term may constitute consideration. In *Techform Products Ltd v Wolda*, the employer successfully advanced such an argument. The employer was able to establish that it intended to terminate the employee under the terms of his agreement if he did not accept the amendment and that forbearing from doing so was sufficient consideration.

To ensure that a negotiated amendment to an employment contract is enforceable, the employer should follow many of the steps discussed in Chapter 5 with respect to drafting the initial employment contract. The employee should be given time to review the proposed changes and to seek independent legal advice before signing the amended contract. If the amendment is crucial and the employee refuses to sign, the employer may be faced with the last resort of telling the employee that they will be dismissed *with reasonable notice or pay in lieu* if they do not sign. (An employee's refusal to sign a disadvantageous new agreement does not usually constitute just cause for dismissal; therefore, notice or pay in lieu is required.) This last option should be considered an option of last resort because its effect on employee morale may be significant.

Monitoring the Contract

Employment contracts sometimes contain important dates. For example, many employers have probationary periods, during which they observe an employee's performance to ensure they have chosen the appropriate candidate for the job. To benefit from a probationary term, an employer must be prepared to take action before the end of the term, if necessary. Once the contractual probationary period has expired, it will probably be more difficult and costly to dismiss the now non-probationary employee.

Similarly, if an employment contract is for a fixed term, it is important that the employer monitor the date that the contract expires. Under a fixed-term contract, an employer need not provide notice of termination if employment ends when the fixed task or term is completed. However, the employer risks losing the benefit of the fixed term if it inadvertently allows an employee to continue to work beyond the expiry date. Should this occur, the employee automatically becomes covered by an indefinite-term contract under both the statutory requirements of the BC *Employment Standards Act* (s 65(2)) and the common law. As noted in *Lui v ABC Benefits Corporation*, the "burden of professionalism" rests with the employer:

> I want to reiterate the concern I made known to the Defendant during the course of these proceedings as to why, being such a large corporate employer, the Defendant chose not to document its contractual dealings with the Project employees, other than by the original letter of employment. Had the Defendant attended to documenting the extensions of employment contracts with the Project employees, or non-extensions as the case may be, it is likely that this matter would never have become the subject of litigation. (at para 118)

To avoid missing important dates, an employer should use some form of a reminder system so that it does not inadvertently let a probationary term expire without reviewing the employee's performance or let a fixed-term employment contract lapse. Moreover, even fixed-term contracts should contain a termination provision that allows either party to terminate the contract on a certain amount of notice. The notice period is typically two to four weeks but can be longer for more senior positions.

Finally, it is a good practice to periodically revisit *all* employment contracts to ensure they reflect the current employment relationship. A court will refuse to enforce contracts that it finds obsolete because they no longer reflect the terms and conditions of employment. This typically means that the termination clause negotiated by the parties at the outset of the employment relationship no longer applies. To avoid this result, the contract could contain a clause that allows it to be reopened and updated periodically. Alternatively, amendment of the existing employment contract could be a condition of all promotions and significant changes in duties.

Managing Employee Performance and Conduct

Performance Appraisals

Performance appraisals are a key tool in an employer's ongoing management of the employment relationship. Performance evaluation is not a form of discipline. Like a report card, it gives the employer an opportunity to provide regular feedback to an employee.

Performance appraisals serve several purposes. Done well, they motivate employees and foster an atmosphere of openness within an organization. They provide encouragement and alert both the employer and the employee to problems at an early stage, thus providing an opportunity for improvement. The process of setting expectations and discussing how the employee is doing meeting these expectations is a foundational step to effectively manage performance, whether good or bad. Performance appraisals may also help the parties realize that an employee's skills and aptitudes do not fit well with the position, and thus it is time to look at other opportunities with the current employer or elsewhere.

In the event that the performance of a struggling employee does not improve with coaching or retraining, performance appraisals can lay the legal foundation for dismissing the employee with cause. As discussed in Chapter 13, it is can be difficult for an employer to dismiss an employee on performance-related grounds. However, an employer that has created a paper trail by consistently documenting performance problems and efforts at providing assistance is in a stronger legal position than an employer who has failed to do so.

That being said, performance appraisals are useful only if they reflect the actual performance of an employee. Many supervisors have a natural reluctance to raise performance problems with employees for fear of a hostile response. They may therefore note only the more positive aspects of the employee's performance and remain silent on problematic areas. A series of inappropriately positive reviews makes it difficult for an employer to allege just cause for dismissing an employee. In light of this, supervisors should be trained to conduct fair and effective performance appraisals.

In small organizations, performance appraisals tend to be less formal than in larger ones. However, in either case, appraisals should be conducted regularly and objectively based on the following principles:

1. Be honest and balanced. Identify both strengths and weaknesses.
2. Clearly communicate job standards to each employee.
3. Use a standard form to ensure that employees are evaluated consistently.
4. Allow the employee an opportunity to respond to an evaluation, both on the form and orally.
5. Document the evaluation.
6. Provide employees with a copy of the evaluation and have them acknowledge in writing that they have received it. The acknowledgment should indicate that an employee's signature does *not* mean that they agree with the content of the appraisal, simply that they have read it.
7. Set goals for the future and revisit these goals at the next performance review.
8. Conduct performance appraisals separately from salary reviews. An across-the-board salary increase, for example, may send a mixed message to someone who has received a poor performance review.

Progressive Discipline

The practice of **progressive discipline** first arose in unionized workplaces but is now common in non-unionized workplaces as well. It is based on the idea that discipline for less serious infractions should be imposed in a series of increasing steps. For example, where an employee is absent from work without leave, an employer may give a verbal warning for a first occurrence, a written warning for a second occurrence,

progressive discipline
discipline that is imposed in a series of increasing steps

and suspensions of increasing lengths for subsequent occurrences. Each of these steps must be documented. If the misconduct continues despite these disciplinary actions, an employer may eventually be entitled to dismiss the employee for cause.

Generally speaking, when applying its progressive discipline policy the employer considers the type of misconduct, as well as any previous misconduct, the discipline applied, and the length of time over which all of the incidents took place. The level of discipline must be proportionate to the employee's misconduct. An employer may skip steps in the disciplinary process as long as the policy allows it this discretion and the incident is sufficiently serious to warrant this action.

FYI

Progressive Discipline: A Step-by-Step Guide for Employers

The primary goal of progressive discipline should be to correct behaviour, not punish it. The secondary goal should be to appropriately document and establish a basis for termination should such corrections not occur and the employer's reasonable expectations not be met. An employer may choose to include some of the following steps in a progressive discipline program:

1. Outline acceptable standards of conduct and the consequences of misconduct in the policy manual or elsewhere.
2. Describe the steps that may be taken as part of a disciplinary action: a verbal warning, a written warning, suspension(s) with or without pay, and dismissal. (However, employers should be cautious when applying suspensions without pay to non-unionized employees. Unless an employer has a well-known policy regarding suspensions, suspensions without pay may constitute constructive dismissal, because under the common law an employer has no inherent right to suspend an employee for any reason.)
3. Discipline imposed should be proportionate to the offensive behaviour. Therefore, employers should retain the right to disregard these steps and proceed immediately to suspension or dismissal where serious misconduct is involved.
4. Clarify that progressive discipline is a disciplinary procedure designed to correct unacceptable behaviour or conduct, not merely performance feedback.
5. Document every step of the process, including verbal warnings, indicating the time, date, and reason the step was taken.
6. Explain to the employee the problem, the acceptable standard, and the action necessary to meet this standard at every step.
7. Ensure that plans devised to correct the problem are realistic, including timelines for making the necessary improvements. Importantly, employees should be given adequate time to correct their behaviour.
8. Ask employees whether they have any comments to add to the disciplinary form. Employees should initial the form to prove that they have received a copy of it.
9. Set a date for a follow-up meeting, but state that management will respond immediately if further problems arise before the meeting.
10. Train managers to deal with performance issues and monitor employee performance.
11. Discipline can be applied in a progressive way even when the misconduct or behaviour may be unrelated. For instance, an employer may impose a written warning as a result of chronic lateness. If, within a reasonable period of time, this same employee engages in an unrelated form of misconduct (e.g., insubordination), the next progressive step may be taken such as a suspension (with or without pay, pursuant to the employer's policy).
12. If problems persist after taking other disciplinary action, give the employee a final written warning before termination. In the final warning, put the employee on notice that unless there is an improvement, they will be subject to immediate termination for cause and note the measures that management has taken to help the employee meet the job

standards. A final written warning usually accompanies a suspension letter, which concludes with the following warning: "Should you repeat or continue any of the above-noted conduct in the future, you will be subject to further discipline, up to and including termination of your employment."

Although there are some incidents, such as acts of violence, for which immediate dismissal is appropriate, most incidents of misconduct warrant a less severe response. In *Motta v Davis Wire Industries Ltd*, the employer failed to appropriately warn a poor-performing senior manager, but the termination for cause is upheld following an act of serious insubordination aggravated by dishonesty.

CASE IN POINT

Manager's Insubordination Warrants Dismissal Despite Poor Performance Management and Failure to Warn

Motta v Davis Wire Industries Ltd, 2019 ABQB 899

Facts

Motta worked for Davis Wire Industries from May 17, 1997 to May 17, 2013, when he was terminated based on a series of grounds that included:

- mismanaging the Davis Edmonton facility by hiring unnecessary staff, failing to train staff despite repeated requests and promises to do so, failing to achieve any production in Edmonton, and permitting employees to do little or no work;
- insolence in an inflammatory letter to David Lloyd, the owner of the company; and
- insubordination for transferring an employee to the Calgary office and retaining him there in direct contravention of Lloyd's instructions.

Motta vigorously refuted the allegations. He testified that he had dedicated his life to the company, gave his own personal time and energy to its success, and always had the company's best interests at heart. In his view, the insubordination was based on a misunderstanding. He also argued that his handling of the Edmonton office was both professional and the result of malfunctioning equipment. He acknowledged that he became aware something had to change in May 2013 but argued he was not given a fair chance to implement his plan for improvement.

Relevant Issue

Whether the accumulation of performance issues constituted just cause for terminating Motta's employment.

Decision

On the issue of performance, Devlin J reviewed the law on dismissal for incompetence, citing *Lowery v The City of Calgary*:

> Summary dismissal for incompetence is justified by significant breach of contract on the part of an employee. Where the employer alleges cumulative cause for such dismissal, it must prove:
>
> 1. The employee was given express and clear warnings about his performance.
> 2. The employee was given a reasonable opportunity to improve his performance after the warning was issued.
> 3. Notwithstanding the foregoing, the employee failed to improve his performance.
> 4. The cumulative failings "would prejudice the proper conduct of the employer's business." (at para 3)

Justice Devlin found that Motta had grossly mismanaged the Edmonton plant and there was a clear basis for discipline, but the employer failed in its duty to warn Motta or provide him with an opportunity to improve. Lack of documentation and proper performance evaluations meant the employer was unable to show that Motta had been warned or that performance expectations had been provided to him.

On the issue of insolence alleged in the letter to Lloyd, the judge did not find that anything in the letter insulted the employer in an irredeemable fashion or made it unrealistic for his employment to continue.

On the issue of insubordination for hiring an employee after being expressly prohibited from doing so, the judge found that while the prohibited employment only continued for four days, Motta intended it to be for longer and intended to disobey on an ongoing basis. The employee had recently been fired for incompetence and had responded with an act of violence, which Motta knew about. This elevated the importance of the directive, and Motta understood this. Motta refused to alter a situation he knew his employer found unacceptable. The judge also noted that while insubordination for something minor may not constitute cause for termination, insubordination by senior managers is more serious in character because it has greater potential to impact operational integrity and can be more difficult to detect. Furthermore, the insubordination was aggravated by two incidents of dishonesty that went to the heart of the employment relationship. As a result, Devlin J ultimately decided that despite the employer's failure to adequately manage Motta's performance, his conduct as a senior manager was sufficiently serious to warrant justifying his dismissal.

In most cases, applying discipline in a series of steps allows an employer to respond to an employee's inappropriate conduct in a measured way and, as previously noted, gives an employee the opportunity to improve. Moreover, where rules are clear and consistently applied, employees are less likely to resent discipline or see it as unfair. An employee who is eventually dismissed for cause after being subjected to progressive disciplinary measures is less likely to challenge the dismissal in court or elsewhere (e.g., before a human rights or employment standards tribunal). Similarly, where a progressive discipline policy is in place and consistently applied, any such challenge is less likely to be successful.

condonation implied acceptance by one party of the conduct of another party; once an employer is aware of an employee's misconduct and takes no disciplinary action within a reasonable time, the employer cannot dismiss the employee for that misconduct without any new misconduct

Another benefit of consistently applying a progressive discipline policy is that the employer avoids condoning misconduct. **Condonation** occurs when an employer is aware of misconduct and takes no disciplinary action within a reasonable time. An employer that condones misconduct arguably cannot later use the misconduct as a basis for discipline or dismissal. For example, an employer that fails to react within a reasonable time after becoming aware of an employee's contravention of a company policy against borrowing money from suppliers arguably has condoned the employee's behaviour.

Suspensions

There are normally two reasons that an employer may want to suspend an employee: (1) for administrative reasons (like investigating a workplace incident), and (2) as a disciplinary measure (Monkhouse, 2017).

Employers must follow particular rules with respect to administrative suspensions, as the courts are reluctant to support such action. The Supreme Court in *Cabiakman v Industrial Alliance Life Insurance Co* stated that the following are required to place an employee on administrative suspension:

- The suspension must be necessary to protect the legitimate business interest.
- The employer must be acting in good faith.
- The suspension must be for a relatively short time period for a fixed term.
- Other than in exceptional circumstances, the administrative suspension must be paid.

Disciplinary suspensions are a form of punishment that are implemented as a result of employee misconduct. In other words, the employer must have just cause to do so. Further, there is some question about whether an employer has the right to suspend a non-unionized employee without pay as a form of discipline. Unless there is an express or implied term in the employment contract allowing this form of discipline (terms may be contained within a properly incorporated policy manual), a suspension without pay may constitute constructive dismissal under the common law. This is because the right to work in exchange for pay is seen as a fundamental part of the employment contract. For example, in *Carscallen v Fri Corporation*, the Court found that a week-long unpaid suspension of a marketing executive, along with several other disciplinary measures, amounted to constructive dismissal. Unpaid suspensions were not, either explicitly or implicitly, a part of that employee's employment terms.

In *Haldane v Shelbar Enterprises Ltd*, the Ontario Court of Appeal stated that the right to suspend an employee may be an implied term of an employment contract based on custom and usage or based on the presumed intention of the parties. However, the onus is on the employer to prove that this implied term applies in the circumstances. An employer may therefore choose to include a contractual term that allows it to suspend employees without pay for cause. A clear, well-communicated, and consistently enforced progressive discipline process that specifically includes an unpaid suspension as one of the disciplinary steps probably also meets this requirement.

Alternatively, to avoid the possibility of a finding of constructive dismissal, many employers with non-unionized employees have adopted a discipline policy with only three or four steps that excludes suspensions:

1. verbal warning,
2. written warning (optional),
3. final written warning, and
4. termination.

Even if an employer is able to suspend an employee without pay, the employer must act reasonably, because an unreasonable suspension constitutes constructive dismissal under the common law. And, as shown in *Alberta v AUPE*, whether it occurs in a unionized or non-unionized environment, any suspension of an employee without pay must be approached in a measured and contextual way and be of an appropriate length pursuant to the seriousness of the conduct.

CASE IN POINT

Suspension Without Pay Unreasonable in the Circumstances

Alberta v AUPE, 2005 CarswellAlta 2097 (Arb Bd)

Facts

Rennich was a corrections worker at the Edmonton Remand Centre. He was also a union representative of his fellow prison guards, having been elected chair of the Alberta Union of Provincial Employees (AUPE), Local 3. The Remand Centre had begun to experience problems with powerful gangs, such as the Redd Alert, among its prison population and was in the midst of a hunger strike precipitated by a fight and consequent reduction in the amount of time that inmates were permitted to remain outside their cells. Rennich decided to participate in two interviews about the situation with CBC Radio. The director of the Remand Centre responded by suspending Rennich for two days without pay for contravening the employer's code of conduct and ethics and for breaching the Correctional Services oath of confidentiality. Rennich filed a grievance.

Relevant Issue

Whether the employer had just cause for discipline and, if so, whether a suspension without pay was excessive in the circumstances.

Decision

The Alberta Arbitration Board had to decide whether Rennich's statements to the media met the test for discipline, first by being inaccurate, as alleged, and second by being knowingly or recklessly false. Rennich's position as elected chair of Local 3 gave him certain leeway to speak out on issues that affected membership safety—a right to speak that otherwise could have been characterized as a breach of his duty of fidelity to his employer. But his statements had to be based on facts that were accurate, or at least not inaccurate.

The Board found that most of Rennich's statements were indeed based on fact, such as comments that inmates were designing weapons like match bombs and comments that guards might have to resort to an "imminent danger" refusal to work under occupational health and safety legislation. The Board said Rennich would also have been entitled to state his opinion that the tactical approach used by the director of the Edmonton Remand Centre—going directly to the inmates for talks—was less than ideal from the perspective of corrections officers, who would have preferred that their customary position as intermediaries in the traditional line of communication between management and prison population be honoured.

When, instead, Rennich insinuated that the director had not been impartial, that he had increased by tenfold the potential danger in the prison, and that he had been "blatantly disrespectful" of corrections staff, the Board found that Rennich had "crossed the line." Rennich had moved from making comments that might be unwelcome from the perspective of management but were nevertheless not inaccurate to making statements that could not be substantiated by fact and that were recklessly false and maliciously aimed at management. The employer therefore had just cause for discipline. However, given Rennich's 20 years of employment with Correctional Services, with only one letter of reprimand on his record throughout those two decades, the two-day suspension without pay was determined to be excessive. A letter of warning placed in his file, the Board said, would have been the appropriate discipline in all the circumstances.

Probation

probation
a period of time when an employee is monitored to determine their suitability for a job

Another form of corrective action that an employer may take with regard to an underperforming employee is to place the individual on **probation**. This puts the employee on notice that their performance is being watched for signs of significant improvement. In the absence of a contractual provision authorizing this action, the imposition of probation may constitute a fundamental change to the employment contract and give the employee the right to sue for damages for constructive dismissal.

An employer may reduce the likelihood of this result if it imposes a probationary period as part of a progressive discipline program and provides the employee with a reasonable opportunity to meet its performance requirements. It cannot cut short the probationary period without leaving itself open to a claim for wrongful dismissal, which is exactly what occurred in *English v NBI Canada Inc*. The defendant's general manager had advised the Calgary branch manager of its office equipment business that his performance was "not acceptable and that improvement would have to be made in the next two months," a letter that effectively put English on probation. English felt that the demands placed on him and his sales representatives were unrealistic, given the economic downturn that Alberta was experiencing at the time and the junior status of some of his sales staff. When the two men met face to face only three weeks later, the meeting escalated into a heated argument and English was summarily fired. When English sued, NBI alleged "gross negligence and disregard for … formally assigned responsibilities" (at para 9). The Alberta Court of Queen's Bench found, however, that English was in the process of making appropriate efforts to meet the general manager's directives and that "mere dissatisfaction with an employee's performance is not sufficient reason for dismissal" (at para 21). Instead, the employer is obliged to show real misconduct or incompetence on a balance of probabilities. English had not even been granted the opportunity to complete his period of probation and demonstrate the Calgary branch's recent achievements. Not surprisingly, the Court rejected the defences of incompetence and disobedience and awarded the plaintiff four months' notice, taking into account his two years of service to the company.

Placing employees on probation is increasingly uncommon among employers because it is not effective either at remediating employee performance or at protecting the employer from wrongful dismissal claims.

Temporary Layoffs

Although a temporary layoff is not a form of discipline, an employer that places a non-unionized employee on temporary layoff for economic reasons must consider the possibility that the employee will bring an action for damages for constructive dismissal. Unless the employment contract expressly allows for layoffs, a layoff constitutes a fundamental change in the terms and conditions of employment that triggers wrongful dismissal damages. However, generally speaking, a short-term layoff will not amount to constructive dismissal and is expressly permitted in both Alberta and BC employment standards legislation.

Employment standards legislation defines the circumstances under which a layoff is "temporary" and makes it clear that a true temporary layoff does not require advance notice. A longer-term layoff is more problematic. Moreover, a temporary layoff can become a permanent one, triggering termination pay under employment standards legislation (see the discussion in Chapter 14 under the heading "Temporary Layoffs").

In Alberta, the *Employment Standards Code* allows an employer to temporarily lay off employees for up to 60 days. An employer may consider layoffs when demand for its products or services is dwindling, when the company's outlook is unpredictable, or during uncertain financial times. Once a layoff period goes beyond 60 days, termination pay is triggered if the employer does not call the employees back to work (Taylor, 2012). Similarly in BC, the *Employment Standards Act* recognizes a temporary layoff as lasting up to 13 weeks in a 20 week period. Once this timeframe is exceeded, termination pay obligations are triggered.

In the *Vrana v Procor* decision, the Alberta Court of Appeal found that an employer must provide some form of notice to employees prior to a temporary layoff. The Court held that notice should be provided to uphold the "spirit" of the Code.

CASE IN POINT

Notice Required for Temporary Layoffs

Vrana v Procor Limited, 2004 ABCA 126

Facts

After 16 years of employment with Procor, Vrana was given a letter indicating that, owing to a shortage of work, the company was forced to lay him off effective March 21, 2000. The letter went on to say that Procor hoped the layoff would be of a short duration, and that when the situation improved Procor would notify Vrana of his recall. Vrana was the last of a number of employees to be laid off, and none were ever called back to work. Procor eventually closed. Vrana filed a statement of claim for wrongful dismissal. The trial judge concluded that although Vrana had been temporarily laid off, he had not been constructively dismissed since the Code allows an employer to temporarily lay off employees without terminating the employment relationship until 60 days after the layoff. Vrana appealed.

Relevant Issue

Does an employer have to provide fair notice of its intention to temporarily lay off employees under the Alberta Code?

Decision

Using the preamble of the Code as justification to its proper interpretation, the Alberta Court of Appeal sided with Vrana, stating:

> The invocation of these temporary layoff provisions is clearly intended to be at the employer's option alone and does not require the employee's consent. The combined effect of these provisions therefore leaves an employee in this position. The employee is without work and without pay, having been laid off; the employer is under no obligation to pay the employee any wages or benefits during the 60-day time frame; the employee cannot treat the layoff as a termination or repudiation of the employment contract before the expiry of the 60-day period; the employee has no assurance that the layoff will ever end; the employee is limited in a search for alternative employment during that 60-day period; and the employee has no assurance that if he or she returns to work for a period of time, for example 10 days, that the layoff will not recommence thereafter. All this means that the employee's life in these circumstances is economically and legally on hold.
>
> This being so, we have concluded that, at a minimum, the potentially negative consequences of a temporary layoff demand that when an employer elects to exercise its rights under s. 62, it should provide a fair notice to the employee of its intention to do so. To comport with the spirit and intent of the *Code* and to ensure that the employee is properly advised of the employer's intentions, the notice should contain not only the fact of the temporary layoff and its effective date but also the relevant sections of the *Code* outlining the effect of that layoff, that is ss. 62, 63 and 64. This minimal obligation on the part of the employer will assist in ensuring that there is no misunderstanding between employer and employee as to the respective rights and obligations of each, a goal stressed in the preamble to the *Code*. (at paras 12-13)

Similarly, in *Collins v Jim Pattison Industries Ltd*, the BC Supreme Court interpreted the comparable provision of BC's employment standards legislation and found that the legislation did not create a statutory right allowing all employers to temporarily lay off employees. Instead, it found that the legislation merely served to qualify employee agreements that already included layoff provisions. The Alberta Court of Queen's Bench accepted the reasoning of the BC Supreme Court when it rendered a decision in *Turner v Uniglobe Custom Travel Ltd*. In this case, the Court found that just because the employer had met the minimum requirements in sections 62–64 of the Code, the employee was not prevented from bringing an action against the employer for wrongful dismissal.

Attendance Management

Culpable Absenteeism

Under the law there are two kinds of absenteeism: culpable and innocent. **Culpable absenteeism** involves blameworthy absences, such as being late without good reason (including returning late from a break), leaving work without permission, or failing to follow absence notification procedures. An employer may apply progressive discipline for culpable absenteeism. For example, if an employee leaves work without permission to watch a soccer game, the employer may issue a verbal or written warning for a first occurrence and apply increasing levels of discipline for any subsequent instances of culpable absenteeism. It may not always be obvious whether an absence is innocent or culpable. However, where there is a consistent pattern—as when absences usually occur on Mondays or Fridays—an employer may wish to pursue the matter.

culpable absenteeism blameworthy absences, such as being late without good reason (including returning late from a break), leaving work without permission, or failing to follow absence notification procedures

Innocent Absenteeism

Innocent absenteeism involves absences that arise as a result of a legitimate medical or other cause. Innocently absent employees can never be subject to disciplinary measures. However, even non-blameworthy absences may cause an employer difficulty if they occur frequently or over a long period of time. Therefore, for frequent or lengthy absences, an employer should attempt to find out whether they relate to a "disability" as that term is used in human rights legislation. If an employee is absent owing to a disability, they are entitled to accommodation from the employer, unless the accommodation constitutes undue hardship. This usually means that the employer must accept disability-related absences for a reasonable period of time, especially if an employee's prognosis is good and their attendance is likely to improve to an acceptable level. An employee has additional protections under workers' compensation legislation if the absence relates to a workplace injury.

innocent absenteeism absences that arise as a result of a legitimate medical or other cause; innocently absent employees can never be subject to disciplinary measures

If an employee's absenteeism is likely to continue and there is little chance that they will ever return to regular attendance, an employer may consider dismissing the employee on a non-disciplinary basis for frustration of contract. However, this step cannot be taken lightly; it may take years to establish that the employment contract has been frustrated because the employee has no realistic chance of returning to regular attendance. Furthermore, the existence of long-term disability benefits must be considered if terminating the employee will lead to disentitlement to benefits

(Gilbert, Burkett & McCaskill, 2011). Given the requirements of human rights legislation and the difficulty of establishing just cause under the common law, non-disciplinary termination is a last resort.

Sample letters relating to the management of an employee's non-culpable absences appear in Appendix C.

Attendance Management Programs

The goal of an attendance management program (AMP) is to promote good attendance by identifying and motivating employees with a poor attendance record. This can be done by making employees aware that their attendance level is being measured against a certain standard. Employees whose absenteeism record significantly exceeds this standard are brought into a program that includes interviews and counselling. Although this process may eventually lead to termination for frustration of contract, that final decision must always be made on a case-by-case basis and should not follow automatically based on attendance alone.

The standards for "excessive absenteeism" under an AMP may guide but will not determine whether an employment contract has been frustrated. For example, in *Edmonton (City) v Amalgamated Transit Union, Local No 569*, the Court suggested that the AMP should not have created an employee-wide average against which all employees would be measured. They suggested that, for example, it was reasonable to expect a higher level of attendance for a healthy, 18-year-old employee than for a 64-year-old employee. In the City of Edmonton's AMP, employee absences could be considered "excessive" if the employee had been absent in excess of the applicable standard for at least three consecutive years. The standard was based on the average number of non-culpable absences in the same period for employees in a similar occupational classification. The averages during the relevant period were three "incidents," or 13–15 days of absence.

Prior to terminating the employee, the employer had met with and counselled him about his attendance on 19 occasions. However, the Court found the standard itself was problematic, noting the following:

1. Absences described in an AMP as "excessive" are not necessarily excessive for the purposes of considering whether an employee's attendance justifies dismissal.
2. In considering whether an employee will likely be able to return to reasonable attendance in the future, "reasonable attendance" is not necessarily defined by the provisions of the AMP; other relevant factors may be considered for the particular employee performing the particular type of work for that employer.
3. Employees may establish *prima facie* discrimination if they can demonstrate that one of the prohibited grounds of discrimination under the Alberta *Human Rights Act* was a factor in differential treatment, regardless of when the discrimination occurred.

On an individualized assessment of the AMP and the employee's circumstances, it was determined that although the employee might never be able to achieve the

AMP standard, he could likely achieve reasonable levels of attendance that would not impose any significant hardship on the employer in the future.

When developing or reviewing AMPs, employers should ensure they give individualized consideration to an employee's attendance record and particular circumstances prior to terminating employment for non-culpable absenteeism. They should also ensure that assessments of attendance take into account the employee's age, disability, family status, or any other relevant factors that may impact attendance.

Employers' Vicarious Liability for Employees' Actions

Employers have a duty to take reasonable care for the safety of their employees and others who come into contact with them. The common law makes employers **vicariously liable** (legally responsible for the conduct of another) for damages caused by the actions of their employees if those actions fall within the course and scope of their employment. As noted in *John Doe v Avalon*, an action is deemed to be in the course of employment if it is either:

vicarious liability
legal responsibility for the actions of another

- authorized by the employer; or
- unauthorized, but so connected with authorized acts that it may be regarded as a mode (albeit an improper mode) of doing an authorized act.

Determining whether an employee's wrongful act is so closely connected to their employment that the employer should be held vicariously responsible for it is often difficult. For example, in *John Doe v Avalon East School Board* (2004), a teacher sexually assaulted a student and was charged and found guilty of the offence. The student sued the school board, arguing that it was vicariously liable for the actions of the teacher. The Court found that although the employer did nothing to cause the assault and acted promptly when it found out about it, the employer nonetheless had given the teacher the authority to set up the circumstances where the assault occurred.

In contrast, as the *Royal Bank of Canada v Intercon Security Ltd* case shows, an employer will not be held vicariously liable for an employee's acts when they arise independently of the employment relationship or where the workplace merely provided the opportunity for the wrongful act.

CASE IN POINT

Was the Employer Vicariously Liable for an Employee's Theft?

Royal Bank of Canada v Intercon Security Ltd, 2005 CanLII 40376 (Ont Sup Ct J)

Facts

Hornett began working for Intercon as a security guard in 1991. At the beginning of each shift, Hornett was given a box of keys in numbered envelopes and only told which envelope to open when a client's alarm went off. During one of his shifts, an automated teller machine (ATM) alarm was accidentally set off by staff at a Royal Bank branch. While responding to this alarm, Hornett noticed some weaknesses in the branch's security system (e.g., there were no door or motion alarms). He also correctly guessed how to get the combination for the ATM locks from a nearby mini-safe because of similar colour-coding. A week later, Hornett went with a friend to the same branch and entered using a key (the evidence was inconclusive concerning where the key came from). They retrieved the lock combination from the mini-safe and then found a manual for the locked ATMs (helpfully) sitting on a nearby shelf.

They successfully opened the lock and stole the money inside. Hornett resigned from his job shortly thereafter, and over the course of the next two and a half years he and his friend committed a series of similar thefts at 11 Royal Bank branches. They stole over $1 million in total. Some of these branches were not serviced by Intercon and no key was used. Hornett and his accomplice later confessed, pleaded guilty, and served their sentences. The Royal Bank sued Intercon on the basis of vicarious liability.

Relevant Issue

Whether the employer was vicariously liable for the thefts committed by Hornett.

Decision

The Court found that Intercon was not vicariously liable for Hornett's actions. Intercon did not authorize him to be on Royal Bank's premises when not responding to an alarm or when off duty. Although Hornett's employment may have given him the idea to steal from the ATMs, it did not provide him with the means. Therefore, his conduct was not sufficiently connected to his employment to make his employer vicariously liable. In making its determination, the Court also considered the following factors:

- the wrongful conduct did not further the employer's interests;
- there was not a great deal of power conferred on Hornett; and
- the bank was vulnerable because of its own negligence—there were gaps in its security systems, the combinations to the ATM locks were usually retrievable, and the ATM manual was located beside the ATMs.

Many of the cases where an employer has been found vicariously liable for the actions of its employees have related to intoxication. The employer's responsibility is greatest when it serves alcohol to an employee at a work-related event. However, it may also be liable if it is aware that an employee is driving a company vehicle while intoxicated. The Court in *Mugford v Kodiak Construction Ltd* found exactly that. Although concerns were expressed that this interpretation would impose an excessive burden on employers, the Court of Appeal found it necessary for the protection of the public.

CASE IN POINT

Employer Liable for Employee's Impaired Driving

Mugford v Kodiak Construction Ltd, 2004 ABCA 145

Facts

Weber, a seasonal employee of Kodiak Construction from 1996 to 1999, was given the use of one of the company trucks each time he started working for the season. At the end of the workday, Weber drove the truck to his home and kept it there for the night. Each season that Weber commenced employment, he was required to sign a form agreeing to abide by the employer's vehicle use policy, which read in part as follows:

> I agree to adhere at all times to the terms of the company policy governing the use thereof namely that the same is not to be used for personal use in any manner. Without restricting the generality of the foregoing I agree

> that the vehicle is only to be used to travel directly to and from work. In the event that I am found in breach of these terms, I covenant and agree to be personally responsible for all costs related thereto including any damages sustained to the said vehicle .... (at para 3)

Weber's supervisor testified that he would have reminded Weber of the policy, and also would have warned him against drinking and driving.

One night, Weber did not drive directly home from work. He went first to his girlfriend's house, where he consumed food and alcohol. Afterward, he drove to a friend's house, where he consumed more alcohol. On his way home, he was involved in an accident with Mugford. Weber was charged with and later found guilty of impaired driving. The employee and his employer were sued by Mugford for injuries sustained in the accident.

Relevant Issue

When an employee has the employer's express consent to have possession of a company vehicle, but does not have express or implied consent to drive the vehicle at the time of the accident and is in breach of the conditions attached to the use of the vehicle, is the employer vicariously liable for the employee's negligence?

Decision

The Court of Appeal held that once an employer has consented to an employee driving a company vehicle, it becomes vicariously liable for the actions of that employee when the employee is behind the wheel. It does not matter if the employer places restrictions on what the employee can do with the vehicle. Therefore, if an employee has been given possession of a vehicle and is in an accident, the employer will be responsible, even if the employee was off duty, inebriated, and in violation of the employer's vehicle use policy. The Court went on to say that its decision ensures that innocent third parties are protected, and that the best way for employers to manage the risk is to exercise extreme care when entrusting their vehicles to employees and to obtain insurance in excess of the statutory minimums.

John v Flynn presents a contrasting situation where the employee was driving his own vehicle. In *John*, the Ontario Court of Appeal reversed a lower court's decision by finding that the employer was not liable where it was aware that the employee had a drinking problem but was unaware that the employee was drinking on its premises.

CASE IN POINT

Employer Not Liable Despite Knowledge of Employee's Alcohol Abuse

John v Flynn, 2001 CanLII 2985 (Ont CA)

Facts

Flynn worked in the employer's forge department. One night, he drank for several hours before reporting for his overnight shift. During his breaks, he drank in his truck in the employer's parking lot, and he continued drinking after his shift before he drove home. Shortly after he got home, he went out again. While driving with an open beer bottle between his legs, he was involved in an accident in which the plaintiff was seriously injured. At trial, the jury found Flynn 70 percent responsible and the employer 30 percent responsible for the plaintiff's damages. The employer appealed.

Relevant Issue

Whether the employer was vicariously liable to the plaintiff for the actions of its employee.

Decision

The Ontario Court of Appeal found that the employer was not liable. The employer neither provided Flynn with liquor nor knew that he was drinking on its premises during his breaks. When the accident occurred, Flynn was not at work, was not going to or leaving work, and was not travelling during working hours. An employer's duty of care does not extend to all members of the driving public who might come into contact with its employees. The Court acknowledged that the employer was aware that drinking occurred in its parking lot because it found empty beer bottles there. It also knew that Flynn had a substance abuse problem; he had participated in its employee assistance program and signed a "last chance agreement" some years before, wherein he agreed to abstain from alcohol consumption. However, the employer had no duty to monitor his compliance with this agreement. To hold the employer liable to a third party in these circumstances would discourage employers from setting up employee assistance programs. It was Flynn's responsibility to comply with the agreement, not the employer's duty to monitor it.

In *John*, the employer did not provide the vehicle or alcohol, nor did it condone its consumption. However, the common practice in certain industries of giving gifts of alcohol, or providing alcohol at work-related events, places employers in a different legal situation. Consider the case of *Hunt v Sutton Group Incentive Realty Inc* in this regard.

CASE IN POINT

Employer Liable After Serving Alcohol to Employee

Hunt v Sutton Group Incentive Realty Inc, 2001 CanLII 28027 (Ont Sup Ct J)

Facts

Hunt worked as a receptionist and secretary for a real estate sales office. The employer held an afternoon Christmas party on its premises for employees, agents, brokers, and customers. Hunt attended this party both as an employee and as a guest. Guests served themselves from an open bar, and no one was designated to monitor alcohol consumption.

After helping with the cleanup, Hunt went to a nearby pub with some co-workers at 6:30 p.m. She left the pub at approximately 8:00 p.m. At 9:45 p.m., she was involved in a car accident while driving home. The roads were slippery, and she appears to have slid into the opposite lane where she was hit by an oncoming vehicle. She suffered severe injuries. Blood samples showed that she was driving with a blood-alcohol level in excess of the legal limit. Hunt sued both the employer and the pub for negligence in failing to fulfill their duty of care to her.

Relevant Issue

Whether the employer was in breach of its duty of care to the employee.

Decision

The trial judge found Hunt 75 percent responsible for the accident and the pub and the employer 25 percent responsible for damages, which were assessed at $1,124,916. The employer knew or ought to have known that Hunt was intoxicated and intended to drive; it should have taken steps to protect her. The employer did not adequately discharge its duty of care to her by offering a cab to its employees generally or by offering to drive her home. It should have ensured that Hunt did not drive herself home by taking her car keys or insisting that she take a cab. The employer should have foreseen or anticipated that some employees would stop for a drink on the way home.

The employer appealed this verdict, and the Ontario Court of Appeal ordered a new trial on the basis that the trial judge failed to consider evidence suggesting that the employee was not intoxicated when she left the party. However, the case underscores the need for an employer to exercise caution when alcohol is served at employer-sponsored events. It may be prudent to make company functions alcohol-free events. If alcohol is served, an employer should consider adopting some or all of the following measures:

- Limit alcohol intake by providing a small number of drink tickets to each guest.
- Hire professional servers and instruct them to refuse to serve alcohol to anyone who appears to be intoxicated.
- Serve meals or appetizers with alcohol.
- Provide free transportation from office parties by means of taxi vouchers, and insist that guests use them.
- Provide designated drivers.
- Keep contact numbers of employees' family members.
- Appoint people to monitor alcohol consumption.

One emerging area of potential liability for employers is the use of handheld electronic devices by employees while driving. Assume that an employee gets into an accident while performing work duties, and evidence shows that they were using a cellphone at the time. Just as an employer can be liable for allowing employees to drive home impaired from a work event, employers can now be liable for letting an employee be impaired by a cellphone used for business purposes (Zinn, 2008, at 4). Those injured could sue the employer, as well as the driver, where the employee is acting in the course of employment, including checking voicemail, texting, or contacting the office.

Although there have not yet been any decided cases in Canada in this area, in the United States employers have been held vicariously liable as a result of car accidents caused by employees using mobile devices. In *Yoon v Wagner*, a Virginia lawyer accidentally struck and killed a 15-year-old girl while allegedly speaking to a client on her cellphone. Following a jury trial, the Court awarded the plaintiffs $1.9 million. The defendant lawyer lost her job and served one year in jail. Her employer was held vicariously liable and settled for an undisclosed amount.

In light of the foregoing, employers should take every reasonable step to ensure that employees comply with provincial bans on the use of cellphones and similar electronic devices while driving. Employees in all jurisdictions should be educated about the dangers of driving with such distractions and about the requirements of the legislation. A workplace policy should also be developed. Such policies may expressly prohibit any use of wireless communications or electronic devices while driving and require the driver to pull over to take or make any calls (Fitzgibbon & Zavitz, 2009, at 5). It may be prudent for employers to use equipment that disables cellphones when a company vehicle is in operation. Where the use of hands-free devices are allowed, the employer should provide the required equipment and training for hands-free use. These policies must be strictly monitored and enforced.

FYI

Distracted Driving in Alberta: Everything You Really Need to Know

There's no denying it—the laws governing distracted driving in Alberta are here to stay—and for good reason. This bad habit causes millions of collisions every year in North America, and many of those are unfortunately fatal. In Alberta, distracted driving includes the following activities:

- talking on handheld cellphones;
- texting or emailing;
- playing video games;
- writing, drawing, or painting;
- personal grooming;
- entering information on to a GPS system;
- referencing, adjusting, or looking at any electronic devices like laptops, tablets, or mp3 players;
- reading printed materials;
- having your vision of the road compromised by a pet; or
- being distracted by a pet in the front seat, on the driver's lap, or in the vehicle.

Reading a quick text message while waiting for your chai tea latte? A fast catch-up on email, even when stopped at a red light? While some may feel there is some ambiguity around distracted driving while in a drive-thru or while stopped at a red light, the truth of the matter is that both situations are indeed included and could lead to a distracted driving charge.

In Alberta, individuals charged with distracted driving will be handed a pricy penalty—a whopping $287 fine and three demerit points. In the case that the police officer laying the charges finds the driver to have been exhibiting an even more serious threat or risk, they may also fine the driver an additional $402 for driving carelessly.

STARTLING FACTS ABOUT DISTRACTED DRIVING

- Reading a text message while driving distracts a driver for a minimum of five seconds each time. This means that the chances of an accident occurring while reading a text is extremely high.
- It takes an average of three seconds after a driver's mind is taken off the road for any road accident to occur. This is the bare minimum amount of time it takes, and it is surprisingly small. Three seconds is the time it takes to turn your ignition when starting your car.
- Each year, over 330,000 accidents caused by texting while driving lead to severe injuries. This means that over 78 percent of all distracted drivers are distracted because they have been texting while driving.
- Texting and driving is six times more likely to get you in an accident than drunk driving. That's right—it is actually safer for someone to get wasted and get behind the wheel than to text and do it.
- Every day, 11 teenagers die because they were texting while driving. Ninety-four percent of teenagers understand the consequences of texting and driving, but 35 percent of them admitted that they do it anyway.

SOURCE: Adapted from Sadler Insurance Inc, 2020.

KEY TERMS

condonation, 414
constructive dismissal, 402
culpable absenteeism, 419
innocent absenteeism, 419
probation, 416
progressive discipline, 411
vicarious liability, 421

REVIEW AND DISCUSSION QUESTIONS

1. Describe the legal position of both parties to an employment contract when an employer wishes to make an amendment after the employee has started work.
2. What are some of the benefits of conducting regular employee performance appraisals?
3. What steps can an employer take to ensure that its policy manual becomes and remains part of the employment contract?
4. What is condonation? How can it be avoided?
5. Workplace romances, even where they are consensual relationships between co-workers, can create some difficult issues in the workplace. From a strictly legal perspective, employers may want to discourage office romances, but from a practical point of view it is virtually impossible to prevent them. Discuss some of the risks that an office romance poses from various perspectives—to the couple involved, to co-workers, and to the employer. Is a policy on office romances a good idea and, if so, what should it include? Are there any disadvantages to having such a policy?
6. The employer is a college campus that has several establishments that serve alcohol, such as pubs and bars. If an employee consumes alcohol during lunch at one of the campus bars and then returns to work and injures someone or gets into an accident, would the employer bear the responsibility for any resulting loss or damages? Explain your answer.
7. The employer, Yummy Biscuits Inc, has decided that it needs to make significant changes to its benefits package to cut costs in an increasingly competitive marketplace. Yummy Biscuits wants to know the best way to introduce the changes so that employees will respond positively and to avoid any legal problems. It has approximately 50 employees and there is no union. How would you advise this employer?
8. Systems Cycle hired John, an experienced computer programmer, in its IT department. Shortly after being hired, John used Systems Cycle's computer to register a domain name similar to that of his former employer, and he redirected traffic from the new domain to a pornographic website. The former employer sued John and Systems Cycle, arguing that the latter should be vicariously liable for John's actions. How do you think a court would rule in this case? Support your answer.
9. Among the multitude of human resources policies that an employer can have, what, in your view, are the five most important ones that every employer needs? Explain your answer.
10. After several verbal warnings about her lack of time management skills, Bev was placed on a performance improvement plan (PIP) that outlined detailed performance objectives and provided timelines for fulfilling those objectives. The PIP was framed as a "last chance agreement," and Bev was aware that her job was in jeopardy when she signed it—without improvement, she would be terminated. The PIP called for several managers to work with her to help her improve her performance. It was a busy time of year, however, and the managers did not follow-up until several months later when, noting that there had been no improvement in Bev's performance, Bev was fired for cause on the ground of poor performance. Do you think the employer had just cause to dismiss Bev?
11. Your employer is concerned that some of the clothing its employees are wearing, especially in the summer, suggests a lack of professionalism. The employer has asked you to implement a dress code policy. What are some of the considerations you should keep in mind in addressing this issue?
12. What kinds of issues can or should be covered in an organization's social media policy?

REFERENCES

Alberta v AUPE, 2005 CarswellAlta 2097 (Arb Bd).

Cabiakman v Industrial Alliance Life Insurance Co, 2004 SCC 55.

Carscallen v Fri Corporation, 2006 CanLII 31723 (Ont CA).

Channe, Bonnea, "Update on Constructive Dismissal: Is It Sufficient for Employers to Provide Reasonable Notice of a Fundamental Change? What's New in HR Law" (May 2012).

Collins v Jim Pattison Industries Ltd, 1995 CanLII 919 (BCSC).

Daley v Depco International Inc, 2004 CanLII 11310 (Ont Sup Ct J).

de Vink v Schaffer Residences Inc, 2015 BCPC 355.

Edmonton (City) v Amalgamated Transit Union, Local 569, 2007 ABQB 59.

Employment Standards Act, RSBC 1996, c 113.

Employment Standards Code, RSA 2000, c E-9.

English v NBI Canada Inc, 1989 CanLII 3359 (Alta QB).

Farber v Royal Trust Company, [1997] 1 SCR 846.

Fitzgibbon, Michael P, & Kate A Zavitz, "Employers Impacted by Cellphone Ban for Drivers," *Canadian Employment Law Today* 536 (17 June 2009) at 4.

Frederickson v Newtech Dental Laboratory Inc, 2015 BCCA 357.

Gilbert, Douglas G, Brian Burkett & Moira McCaskill, *Canadian Labour and Employment Law for the US Practitioner*, 3rd ed (Washington, DC: Bureau of National Affairs, 2011).

Haldane v Shelbar Enterprises Ltd, 1999 CanLII 9248 (Ont CA).

Hunt v Sutton Group Incentive Realty Inc, 2001 CanLII 28027 (Ont Sup Ct J), rev'd 2002 CanLII 45019 (Ont CA).

John Doe v Avalon East School Board, 2004 NLTD 239.

John v Flynn, 2001 CanLII 2985 (Ont CA).

Kafka v Allstate Insurance Company of Canada, 2012 ONSC 1035.

Lavinkas v Jacques Whitford and Associates, 2005 CanLII 63777 (Ont Sup Ct J).

Leiper, Pamela, & Christina Hall, "User-Friendly Employee Handbooks," *Workplace News* (November–December 2006).

Lowery v Calgary (City of), 2002 ABCA 237.

Lui v ABC Benefits Corporation, 2019 ABPC 125.

Milne, Catherine, *Canadian Forms and Precedents: Employment*, vol 1 (Toronto: LexisNexis Canada, 2005).

Minkin Employment Lawyers, "Constructive Dismissal—When Resigning May Actually Be Wrongful Dismissal," online: <https://www.minkenemploymentlawyers.com/employment-law-issues/constructive-dismissal-when-resigning-may-actually-be-wrongful-dismissal>.

Monkhouse, Andrew, "Suspensions in the Workplace—Paid or Unpaid?" (15 September 2017), online: *CanLII Connects* <https://canliiconnects.org/en/commentaries/46624>.

Motta v Davis Wire Industries Ltd, 2019 ABQB 899.

Mugford v Kodiak Construction Ltd, 2004 ABCA 145.

Potter v New Brunswick Legal Aid Services Commission, 2015 SCC 10.

Royal Bank of Canada v Intercon Security Ltd, 2005 CanLII 40376 (Ont Sup Ct J).

Sadler Insurance Inc, "Distracted Driving in Alberta: Everything You Really Need to Know [2020]" online: <https://www.sadlerin.com/distracted-driving-alberta>.

Saint-Cyr, Yosie, "Relying on Breach of Policy to Discipline Employees," *First Reference Talks* (23 February 2012).

Singh v Empire Life Ins Co, 2002 BCCA 452.

Taylor, Jamie, "Temporary Lay Off in Alberta—What Employers Should Know" (30 January 2012), online: *Spectrum HR Law LLP* <https://www.mondaq.com/canada/employee-rights-labour-relations/160846/temporary-lay-off-in-alberta-what-employers-should-know>.

Techform Products Ltd v Wolda, 2001 CanLII 8604 (Ont CA).

Totan, Titus, "Revisiting Unilateral Amendments to Employment Contracts and Policies" (1 February 2016), online: *Rubin Tomlinson LLP* <https://rubinthomlinson.com/revisiting-unilateral-amendments-to-employment-contracts-and-policies>.

Turner v Uniglobe Custom Travel Ltd, 2005 ABQB 513.

Vrana v Procor Limited, 2004 ABCA 126.

Wronko v Western Inventory Service Ltd, 2008 ONCA 327, leave to appeal to SCC refused, 2008 CanLII 53793.

Yoon v Wagner, Action No 05-2122, 2005 US Dist LEXIS 56145 (Urbana Ill Dist Ct 2004).

Zinn, Russel, "Employees Driving Under the Influence—Of a Cellphone," *Canadian Employment Law Today* 503 (13 February 2008) at 4.

PART III

The End of the Employment Relationship and Beyond

Part III explores the legal implications of the many different ways in which an employment relationship can come to an end. Chapter 12 examines resignation and retirement, where the employment relationship voluntarily comes to an end. Subsequent chapters consider the implications of terminations initiated by employers. Chapter 13 reviews requirements for dismissal with cause under both the common law and provincial legislation. Chapter 14 reviews dismissal without cause under both the common law and provincial legislation related to temporary and indefinite layoffs and such terminations. Chapter 15 looks at employee obligations that survive the end of the employment relationship.

Generally speaking, the common law distinguishes between two kinds of dismissals: dismissals with just cause and dismissals without just cause—that is, wrongful dismissals. This distinction is an "all or nothing" proposition. If an employer cannot establish just cause for dismissing an employee—which is usually difficult to do—the employee has been wrongfully dismissed and is entitled to all the legal remedies that are available in the circumstances. On the other hand, if an employer can establish just cause for dismissing an employee, it can dismiss the employee summarily without notice or pay in lieu of notice.

Chapter 13 considers issues related to dismissals for just cause, including the types of misconduct that constitute just cause under the common law. Chapter 14 explores dismissals, including constructive dismissals, in the absence of just cause and considers the remedies available to employees in these circumstances. It also looks at ways in which an employer can minimize the possibility of wrongful dismissal lawsuits.

An employer that dismisses an employee without just cause must consider both statutory and common law reasonable notice requirements. In most circumstances, the notice period considered reasonable under the common law is more generous than a notice period required under provincial employment standards legislation. However, while an employer and employee may not agree to terms that are less advantageous to the employee than those set out in the legislation, the parties may contract out of common law notice requirements by specifying an alternative notice period in their employment contract through a termination clause. In this case, if the contractual notice period at least matches the notice requirements in the applicable legislation, the employer need provide only the amount of notice specified in the contract.

Chapter 15 looks at employee obligations that survive the end of the employment relationship, known as post-employment obligations. These obligations include the common law duty not to disclose (or misuse) confidential information or, in some circumstances, not to solicit former customers of the employer.

Resignation and Retirement

LEARNING OUTCOMES

After completing this chapter, you will be able to:

- Explain why an employer should formally accept an employee's resignation in writing.
- Understand why a resignation must be voluntary and unequivocal.
- State why an employer should not dismiss an employee who gives notice of resignation.
- Explain an employee's obligation to provide notice of resignation.
- Understand the implications of the elimination of mandatory retirement at age 65.

Introduction

Two of the ways that the employment relationship may come to an end are when the employee resigns or retires. Although they may seem, and usually are, straightforward events, there are some potential legal issues that an employer should be aware of.

Resignation

Resignations Should Be Formally Accepted

Absent coercion, a letter of resignation is typically binding on an employee. However, there are some cases that suggest that an employee may retract a written resignation up to the time the employer formally communicates its acceptance of the letter. It is therefore a good practice for an employer who wishes to accept a letter of resignation to send a letter to the employee confirming its acceptance of the employee's letter as soon as possible after receiving it, thereby creating a binding agreement to end the employment relationship.

Resignations Must Be Voluntary

wrongful dismissal dismissal without just cause wherein an employer breaches its common law duty to provide reasonable notice of termination or pay in lieu of notice to an employee

Generally speaking, an employee who gives an employer notice of resignation is not legally entitled to **wrongful dismissal** damages. In that case, the only amounts owing to the employee are outstanding wages and vacation pay. Once the employee has given the employer notice of resignation, the employer may not reduce the employee's wages, wage rates, or any other term or condition of employment until the date that employment terminates, whether or not work is required to be performed during that period.

To be valid, the resignation must be voluntarily and freely given. For example, if an employer gives an employee a "choice" between resigning or being dismissed, the courts usually find that the resignation is not voluntary, and the employer is obliged to provide pay in lieu of reasonable notice or show just cause for the dismissal. Once a resignation is tendered, the onus is on the employee to show that the resignation was *not* voluntary. The legal test is an objective one: would a reasonable person believe that the employee voluntarily resigned?

An employee also may allege that they resigned because the employer changed a fundamental term of their employment contract. If a court determines that a reasonable person would believe that the employee resigned in response to such a contractual breach, the employee is entitled to damages for constructive dismissal. (See the discussion in Chapter 14 under the heading "Constructive Dismissal.")

Inferring Resignation from an Employee's Conduct

Resignation may be inferred from an employee's conduct. The two key elements required to confirm a resignation are intent and an action from the employee that reaffirms the decision. For example, if an employee angrily leaves a manager's office saying "I'm leaving and don't expect me back" and does not appear for work the next day, the employer may infer that the employee has ceased their employment, even though they did not use the words "I quit." Similarly, if an employee expresses the intention to stop work and then returns a uniform and keys or tells co-workers that they will not be back, the employer may conclude that the employee has resigned. A letter from the employer formally accepting the resignation confirms the binding agreement to terminate the employment relationship and is advisable, especially in circumstances where the employee's true intent is unclear.

Courts will not infer resignation when an employee's words are vague or equivocal. For example, if an employee tells an employer that they plan to leave as soon as they can or that they are looking for another job and cannot wait to leave, the courts will not find that the employee voluntarily resigned. Similarly, an employee who leaves work early without authorization out of anger or frustration would not typically be considered to have resigned by virtue of their departure alone—though leaving early without permission could attract discipline.

To be effective, a resignation must be clear and unequivocal: both the employee's subjective intention to resign and the employee's words and actions, objectively viewed, must support a finding of resignation (Brown, 2013).

Pollock v First Heritage Financial Ltd and *Gilbert v Tandet Transport Inc* illustrate the requirement that an employee's intention be clear and unequivocal before an employer can treat an employee's conduct as a resignation.

CASE IN POINT

Notice of Resignation Must Be Clear

Pollock v First Heritage Financial, 2002 BCSC 782

Facts

Six employees of a financial planning firm were unhappy with proposed changes to their employment, including changes to their compensation program. They wrote a memo to their employer asking for a meeting to discuss the matter. When the employer's representative refused, they sent a second memo stating that they were willing to continue under their existing terms of employment, but interpreted his refusal to meet as an indication that he did not want them to report for work under their existing terms and that, unless they received written notice to the contrary, they would "proceed accordingly." The employer wrote to the employees individually, indicating that he accepted their resignation. He told them to return their keys and expense account cards, and they were escorted out of the building.

Relevant Issue

Whether the plaintiffs resigned or were wrongfully dismissed and therefore entitled to pay in lieu of reasonable notice.

Decision

The Court found that the employees were wrongfully dismissed and were entitled to pay in lieu of notice. The memo was not an unequivocal notice of resignation; rather, the employees stated that they intended to continue working under the existing terms of employment. A reasonable person in the employer's position would not conclude that the employees were resigning from their jobs. The Court awarded the employees, who had between two and six years of service each, between four and eight months' pay in lieu of notice for wrongful dismissal.

CASE IN POINT

Employee Must Form an Intention to Resign

Gilbert v Tandet Transport Inc, [2002] CLAD No 196 (QL) (Arb Bd)

Facts

After seven years' employment, Gilbert was temporarily laid off. During the layoff, he found a part-time job. On June 5, 2000, the employer issued a recall notice, which stated that if Gilbert failed to return by June 9, 2000, he would be treated as having resigned. Gilbert left several urgent telephone messages with the employer asking whether he would be returning to part-time or full-time employment. He needed to know this because he did not want to give up his new job for another part-time position. The employer returned his calls but was unable to reach him. Later that month, he received notice that the employer had processed his resignation. Gilbert then filed a complaint against his former employer for statutory termination pay.

Relevant Issue

Whether the employee resigned or was dismissed.

Decision

The arbitrator found that Gilbert was dismissed. He never formed an intention to resign because he never had enough information to make that decision. The employer's letter of recall stating that failure to attend the workplace on June 9 would be treated as a resignation was not sufficient to establish Gilbert's intention to resign. Gilbert was therefore entitled to statutory termination pay.

FYI

Strategic Quitting: The Dip

Seth Godin, in his book *The Dip*, says that pushing through difficult times can lead to extraordinary results if you are in the right job. If you are not in the right job, leaving can be part of a long-term strategy to find the right place.

When quitting is strategic:

- Consider changing jobs if you are experiencing serious mental health impacts that are affecting you, your relationships, or your family.
- If there is upheaval at your workplace, it may be appropriate to plan an exit strategy. Perhaps you are being asked to move, or your workplace is restructuring and you are concerned your job will be eliminated. Be proactive: work on your resumé and build your professional network.
- If you get up every morning and dread going to work, take some time to identify what might be triggering this feeling. Do you have a conflict with someone at work? Do you find your job boring or are there some tasks that are particularly unpleasant? This will help you identify the problem and point you toward the best solution.
- If you feel disengaged, your productivity has dropped, and you find yourself wondering if you are making any difference at all, it may be the right time to leave. Ask yourself if your job is providing you with the identity and purpose you want. If not, take some time to figure out where your real interests or long-term goals lie.
- Another trigger for introspection is if you feel there is no growth opportunity in your current job. Thinking it through can lead to good outcomes apart from quitting. Explore the reasons growth opportunities are unavailable. Most employers are happy to have a conversation with employees who want to learn about or work toward greater responsibilities.
- What should you do if you feel like an outsider at your workplace? Think about the seriousness of the situation. You should leave as soon as possible if there is physical or sexual harassment, or if there is illegal or unethical activity at your workplace. If the culture is

negative or discouraging, take some time to look for better options.

- Leaving may also be the right thing if it is part of a bigger plan. Maybe you want to start your own business. If you have that business plan ready and have your finances in order, it may be time to take the big leap.

When not to quit:

- Don't quit on the spot because you are angry. This can burn bridges with your current employer or the people you work with. They are your references for future jobs and will remember a professional exit.
- For future employers, a resignation in the face of failure might seem like you were forced out. Instead of quitting, stand up, take responsibility, and focus on bouncing back.
- If you think your company is sinking, try to hang on until you have a plan or a new job. Helping your team and employer will build relationships and provide valuable lessons and stories that show experience and maturity in job interviews.
- Unless something is terribly wrong, don't quit until you have another job. Your ability to negotiate is negatively affected if you are not employed, making your job search desperate and emotionally challenging.

Before quitting, you should ask yourself if you really can afford it. Check your financial health and figure out the number of days you can survive without a new source of income. Remind yourself why you need the salary from your current job.

SOURCE: Adapted from Chakravarty, 2018.

Employee Rescission of a Resignation

As discussed briefly above, an employee may seek to rescind their notice of resignation before such notice becomes effective. The question becomes whether an employee can rescind their resignation after an employer has formally accepted it. In *English v Manulife Financial Corp*, the Court contemplated whether a rescission was valid despite the employer having accepted the notice. In this case, the Court concluded that the employer was not obliged to rescind and provides some helpful commentary on why it came to this conclusion.

CASE IN POINT

Employee Must Form an Intention to Resign

English v Manulife Financial Corp, 2018 ONSC 5135

Facts

A long-term employee informed her supervisor that she would be retiring at the end of the year after Manulife announced that it would be converting its customer information to a new computer system at the start of the new year. She was told by her supervisor at that time that she could rescind or reconsider her resignation. Manulife decided to eliminate English's position once she retired. Manulife changed its mind about converting the customer information to a new computer system, and English told her supervisor that she wished to rescind her resignation. The supervisor did not accept this request but notified Manulife's human resources department of the request. Manulife rejected the request to rescind the resignation and indicated that it would continue to honour her notice of resignation. English worked until Manulife said she was finished, at which point she brought a suit for wrongful dismissal.

Relevant Issue

Whether the employee could rescind her notice of resignation.

Decision

The Court found that English's letter was a clear and unequivocal notice of retirement or resignation, that her notice of retirement was accepted by her supervisor after a discussion that allowed English to reflect on her decision, and that she could have revoked her resignation at that time. English's offer to retire as an employee was accepted by Manulife, resulting in a binding contract between the parties. Manulife was not obliged to allow her to rescind or resile from her resignation notice. English chose to retire willingly and freely and was in no way coerced, and the acceptance of her resignation by Manulife bound her to that resignation.

Even where an employee utters the words "I quit" or words to that effect, but does so while clearly distressed, the employer should not treat that as a resignation without giving the employee a cooling-off period. In *Robinson v Team Cooperheat-MQS Canada Inc*, the plaintiff was a long-service employee who became very upset during a meeting when he was unexpectedly accused by several of his staff of being "a bully." He repeatedly stated that if the accusations were not withdrawn, he would be "forced to resign." The next morning Robinson met with his boss and tried to retract his resignation. His boss refused. Robinson sued, arguing that he had been wrongfully dismissed, and the Court agreed. The Court found that Robinson had not expressed a clear and unequivocal intention to resign. Moreover, even if he had said "I quit," this would not necessarily constitute a valid resignation. A resignation given when emotions are running high can be withdrawn later, when emotions have cooled off. The Court found that a reasonable employer would not have concluded that Robinson had quit. Robinson was awarded one year's salary and costs in damages.

As the *Robinson* case shows, employers that receive a resignation from an employee who is emotionally upset should realize that it may not be binding. They need to consider all of the circumstances surrounding it. Was it expressed unambiguously? Was the resignation put into writing? Was it accepted verbally or in writing? Did the employee try to retract the resignation? Are there special circumstances that suggest the employee was under emotional duress at the time? Has the employer already acted in reliance on the resignation (Levitt, 2009)?

A 2008 British Columbia (BC) Supreme Court case, *Bru v AGM Enterprises*, is worth looking at in this context, because it considered the *Robinson* decision and applied the principles of the landmark case *Honda Canada Inc v Keays* regarding punitive or aggravated damages to a situation in which the employee had spoken of quitting. (For a full discussion of *Keays*, see Chapter 14, under the heading "Other Types of Wrongful Dismissal Damages.")

CASE IN POINT

Resignation Must Not Always Be Assumed

Bru v AGM Enterprises Inc, 2008 BCSC 1680

Facts

The plaintiff, Bru, worked at the defendant's deli market for two and a half years before her dismissal. She claimed that she had been harassed by her co-workers to the extent that she ended up staying home from work for several days. Then she called her employer and told them she was quitting her job. However, the following day she called her employer again and said she would be coming back to work, at which time the employer informed her that her employment was terminated. The plaintiff sued for wrongful dismissal, claiming she should have been given notice, and she also claimed damages for mental distress arising from the dismissal.

Relevant Issues

1. Whether the plaintiff had resigned or was wrongfully dismissed.
2. Whether the plaintiff was entitled to damages for mental distress arising from her dismissal.
3. Whether the principles of *Honda Canada Inc v Keays* regarding employers' obligations in a dismissal also apply to employers' receiving notices of resignation.

Decision

The BC Supreme Court ruled that from the facts it was not apparent that the plaintiff had clearly resigned from her position. Employers cannot always take at face value an employee's expressed intention of resigning; instead, they must take into account all the surrounding circumstances. Hence, the defendant in this case had in fact wrongfully dismissed this employee. In reaching this conclusion, the Court pointed out that the onus of proving the dismissal was on the employee. Bru had to convince the Court that she had not, in fact, resigned, which she was able to do in this case. At that point the onus shifted to the employer to prove that she had resigned (and that it had therefore not dismissed her) or that its dismissal was for just cause. This employer was able to do neither.

Turning to damages and the second and third issues, the Court found that the plaintiff was not entitled to punitive damages for mental distress arising from her dismissal because there was no evidence that there was intentional infliction of mental suffering upon her. Because of the *Keays* decision, such damages could only be awarded in the case of breach of contract or where the foreseeability principle of *Hadley v Baxendale* applies (i.e., where such mental suffering should have been foreseeable by the employer at the time the employee was dismissed). Nonetheless, the plaintiff was awarded **non-pecuniary damages** (monetary damages designed to compensate for a plaintiff's pain, suffering, or other injuries that are not readily quantifiable or valued in money) because her employer had failed to act fairly and with sensitivity and it had breached its good-faith obligations to her in the manner of how it dismissed her.

The Court held that the principles of *Honda Canada Inc v Keays* show that employers' obligations in a situation where an employee resigns are the same as those where an employee is dismissed.

Dismissing a Resigning Employee

non-pecuniary damages monetary damages designed to compensate for a plaintiff's pain, suffering, or other injuries that are not readily quantifiable or valued in money

Sometimes an employer who receives advance notice of an employee's resignation does not want the employee to work during the notice period because, for example, the employee may have access to sensitive business information or have extensive contact with customers. However, the employer should be careful in these circumstances not to pre-empt the employee's resignation. If the employer reacts by dismissing the employee, it has effectively fired that individual and may be liable for wrongful dismissal damages. The damages will likely be limited to the notice period provided by the employee on the principle that no wages are owing after the resignation date. However, where the employee has no other position to go to, the employer may be held liable for full wrongful dismissal damages. Statutory and common law compensation for wrongful dismissal is discussed in Chapter 14.

In Alberta, employees who have been employed by the employer for over three months are generally required to provide advance written notice of resignation, although some exceptions apply. If an employee has provided the employer with the minimum advance written notice of resignation required under the Alberta *Employment Standards Code*—one week if the employee has been employed by the employer more than three months but less than two years, or two weeks if the employee has been employed by the employer for two years or more—the employer may terminate the relationship prior to the end of the employee's notice period. In this case, the employer must pay the employee an amount at least equal to the wages the employee would have earned if they had worked their regular hours to the end of the notice period.

Consider, on the other hand, an employee who gives advance notice of resignation that is longer than the minimum required under the Alberta Code but less than (or equal to) the notice required of the employer if the employer had initiated the termination. In this case, an employer who wishes to advance the termination date must pay the regular wages that would have been payable if the employee had worked to the end of the notice period provided by the employee.

There is no statutory requirement for an employee to provide notice of resignation in BC. However, if an employee in BC with more than three months' service gives notice of termination to the employer and the employer terminates the employment during that notice period, the employer is liable to pay the employee an amount equal to the lesser of (1) an amount in money equal to the wages the employee would have earned for the remainder of the notice period, or (2) an amount in money equal to the amount the employer is liable to pay on termination.

In the rare case where the employee gives notice of resignation that is longer than that required of either the employee or the employer under legislation or the common law, the employer may terminate the relationship by paying the amount that would have been required had the employer initiated the termination (and no more).

Therefore, an employer that does not want a resigning employee to continue working during the notice period should accept the employee's resignation and advise the employee that they will be paid throughout the (applicable) notice period but should not attend work. This subtle but important distinction may avoid potentially costly litigation.

Wrongful Resignation

Under the common law, just as an employer has an implied obligation to provide reasonable notice of termination or pay in lieu, the employee has a reciprocal obligation to provide reasonable notice of resignation. This obligation has been codified under the applicable employment standards legislation in some provinces—for example, section 58 of the Alberta *Employment Standards Code* (there is no equivalent provision in the BC *Employment Standards Act*). In practice, in all jurisdictions, employers rarely sue employees for failure to provide notice because in most situations it is difficult for an employer to show that it suffered damage as a result of the employee's failure. It usually takes an employer less time to replace an employee than it takes a dismissed employee to find new employment.

However, there are situations in which an employee's specialized expertise or key role in an organization will lead a court to award damages to an employer for wrongful resignation. In the 1991 Alberta decision *Tree Savers International Ltd v Savoy*, for example, two employees who left their employer on only two weeks' notice to set up a competing business were held liable for failing to provide reasonable notice of resignation. Damages, which included the cost of retraining and replacing employees on short notice, totalled $73,100. More recently, in *GasTOPS Ltd v Forsyth*, four software executives who quit and started a competing business using the former employer's confidential software information were ordered to pay their former employer almost $20 million for, among other things, failure to provide reasonable notice of resignation. The Court found that, given all of the circumstances, including the fact that the executives were key employees with technical expertise and intimate knowledge of the business, the employer was entitled to ten months' notice of resignation, rather than the two weeks each employee provided. The Court noted that during that ten-month period they would have continued to owe the employer a duty of loyalty and good faith, thereby preventing them from starting their own company and competing with their former employer within that period. This decision was upheld on appeal.

As with a dismissed employee, an employer has a responsibility to lessen or mitigate its losses—in this case, by attempting to find a replacement for the employee—and it should document these efforts.

To reduce uncertainty, an employer may choose to include a policy in its employment manual or to negotiate a term in the individual contract of employment that sets out the notice of resignation that an employee is required to provide. In most cases, this is a period of approximately two weeks, and written notice is required. In Alberta, in cases where an employee is required to give advance notice of resignation but terminates employment without doing so, the employer is required to pay the employee's earnings no later than ten consecutive days after the date on which the notice would have expired if it had been given. The BC *Employment Standards Act* does not require employees to give notice (although, as in other provinces, the common law may in some cases require notice from employees, which would be considered on the individual circumstances). In both provinces, even if there is a required notice period in the employment contract, the employer cannot force an employee to continue working during the notice period. Its only recourse is to sue the employee for breach of contract.

Exit Interviews

Interviewing employees who resign may be useful in a number of ways. It can provide an employer with valuable information, including feedback about why an employee has chosen to leave. These insights can be used to identify causes of turnover and to develop improved retention programs. They may also identify issues that, left unaddressed, could lead to harassment or discrimination claims. As well, it provides an opportunity to gather "competitive intelligence" on what other companies are offering their employees (DiFlorio, 2012). To encourage an open discussion, someone other than the employee's direct supervisor should be involved. At an exit interview, an employer can ensure that all company property is returned and the employee understands the outstanding legal obligations of both parties. Such obligations might include the employee's duty not to disclose confidential business information and the employer's duty to provide the employee's record of employment for employment insurance purposes.

Retirement

Abolition of Mandatory Retirement at Age 65

Although public and most private pension plans are based on a retirement age of 65, there has never been legislation requiring employees to retire at age 65 in Canada. In fact, all provinces and territories have eliminated the general age ceiling relating to the protection provided under human rights legislation, although an exemption exists in some cases where the employer has a bona fide retirement or pension plan (discussed in the next section). Effective December 2012, the government of Canada repealed mandatory retirement for employees governed by federal human rights and employment legislation. This change created greater alignment of the legislative framework in this regard across Canadian jurisdictions.

Exemption to the Prohibition Against Age-Based Discrimination

No employer can maintain a retirement plan that contravenes the prohibition against age-based discrimination unless it can show that the plan is bona fide. In the absence of such a bona fide retirement or pension plan, the employer must show that age is a bona fide occupational requirement (BFOR) and satisfy the test established by the Supreme Court of Canada in the *Meiorin* case (*British Columbia v BCGSEU*). Under the test, which applies to the BFOR defence in all jurisdictions across the country, the employer must show not only that the policy is rationally connected to the job and implemented in good faith but also that it is reasonably necessary—that is, it is impossible to accommodate the employees affected without creating undue hardship for the employer. For example, it has been held by the Supreme Court of Canada that in the university context, mandatory retirement is "reasonable and justifiable" given the protections offered to faculty under tenure and pension systems. However, many universities have moved away from requiring retirement at age 65.

Implications of Employee Retirement for Employers and Human Resources Staff

Making retirement a matter of employee choice rather than employer policy raises a number of issues. In the absence of a bona fide retirement or pension plan, employers must accommodate an aging workforce on a case-by-case basis to the point of undue hardship. Although the effects of aging differ, in time they can be expected to influence the ability of many employees to meet the physical and mental demands of their jobs. Because employers have a legal obligation under human rights legislation to accommodate disabilities—including age-related disabilities—to the point of undue hardship, employers that do not have a bona fide retirement or pension plan in place may experience increased demands for accommodation.

Employers without a bona fide plan also need to consider their approach to performance management as it relates to older workers. Whereas employers with bona fide plans may be willing to accept marginal decreases in productivity as employees edge toward retirement, employers without bona fide plans may be more likely to use the same approach with older workers that they use with all workers: a consistent and formal performance management program with all relevant documentation.

Also, employers without a bona fide plan need to carefully document the reasons for terminating an employee who is age 65 or older since they face the possibility of both an age discrimination complaint and a claim for damages for wrongful dismissal. Should a human rights commission, tribunal, or panel conclude that age was a factor in an employer's decision to dismiss an employee, the employee may be entitled to a significant damages award, including possible reinstatement or compensation for lost wages and an award for mental anguish. While reinstatement is rarely ordered, due to the practical challenges associated with trying to repair the employment relationship, compensation for lost wages in a human rights forum will often include an accounting for future wages in lieu of reinstatement.

Typically, anyone who raises a wrongful dismissal complaint will include allegations of a breach of the common law notice requirement and not pursue a separate human rights complaint. If an individual receives pay in lieu of notice through a court action, it is likely that any damages awarded pursuant to a concurrent human rights complaint will be limited by the award of damages for breach of the common law notice requirement.

In the absence of a bona fide retirement plan, the common law rules that require an employer to give reasonable notice of termination, in the absence of just cause, apply to all employees. Because many older employees also have lengthy service with the employer, if they are to receive a separation package upon termination the amount of money involved may be significant.

Finally, some benefit plans limit benefits to employees over the age of 65. Unless these plans are deemed a "bona fide group or employee insurance plan" under the *Alberta Human Rights Act* or the BC *Human Rights Code*, any limits may be challenged as discriminatory under the law.

KEY TERMS

non-pecuniary damages, **437**

wrongful dismissal, **432**

REVIEW AND DISCUSSION QUESTIONS

1. Why should an employer inform an employee in writing of its acceptance of their resignation?
2. What should an employer do if it does not want an employee who has given notice of resignation to continue working?
3. How might an employer benefit from an exit interview with a resigning employee?
4. How are employers and employees affected by legislation relating to the retirement of employees?
5. You return to your office to find a letter of resignation on your desk from Stuart. This letter indicates that Stuart will be leaving in four weeks' time. You are actually pleased with the resignation because Stuart has been a poor performer for some time. However, you are concerned that his performance will deteriorate even further during the notice period, so you would like Stuart to leave immediately. What should you do?
6. You are a human resources consultant. One of your clients, an employer (Joseph), has contacted you about the following situation. He has just finished a performance evaluation meeting with one of his employees, Allan. Allan became very upset during the meeting, and at the end of it he got up and shouted, "Okay, if that's the way you feel about me, I quit!" Joseph is delighted with the resignation because Allan has been a difficult employee from the time he was hired three years ago, but he wonders if there's anything he needs to know about the law in this area before he starts hiring a replacement for Allan. Advise Joseph.
7. Janyce, aged 52, had worked at the employer's food market for ten years when a fire destroyed her house. The next day she called her employer, indicating that she did not know when she would be able to return to work. When a month went by without hearing from Janyce, the employer had its payroll department prepare a record of employment (ROE), which indicated that Janyce had "quit" her job. Several weeks later, Janyce was diagnosed with anxiety and depression, stemming from the fire and its surrounding circumstances, and she called the employer for her record of employment, because she needed it to claim sick leave employment insurance benefits. When she picked it up, she discovered that the ROE indicated that she had quit her job. Janyce sued the employer for wrongful dismissal. The employer countered that Janyce had resigned.

   Do you think that Janyce was wrongfully dismissed? Support your answer.

REFERENCES

Alberta Human Rights Act, RSA 2000, c A-25.5.

British Columbia (Public Service Employee Relations Commission) v BCGSEU, [1999] 3 SCR 3 [*Meiorin*].

Brown, David, "'Did He Just Quit?': The Rules on Resignations" (18 November 2013) *The Barristers' Lounge* (blog), online: <http://barristerslounge.wordpress.com/2013/11/18/did-he-just-quit-the-rules-on-resignations>.

Bru v AGM Enterprises, 2008 BCSC 1680.

Chakravarty, Devashish, "7 Right Reasons to Leave Your Job and When Not to Quit" (4 July 2018) *The Economic Times*, online: <https://economictimes.indiatimes.com/wealth/earn/7-right-reasons-to-leave-your-job-and-when-not-to-quit/articleshow/64803340.cms?from=mdr>.

DiFlorio, Laura, "9 Risks of Neglecting to Conduct Exit Interviews," *Canadian HR Reporter* (12 March 2012) at 19.

English v Manulife Financial Corp, 2018 ONSC 5135.

Employment Standards Act, RSBC 1996, c 113.

Employment Standards Code, RSA 2000, c E-9.

GasTOPS Ltd v Forsyth, 2012 ONCA 134.

Gilbert v Tandet Transport Inc, [2002] CLAD No 196 (QL) (Arb Bd).

Hadley v Baxendale (1854), 9 Ex 341, 156 ER 145.

Honda Canada Inc v Keays, 2008 SCC 39.

Human Rights Code, RSBC 1996, c 210.

Levitt, Howard A, "Resigning Worker Entitled to Cooling-Off Period" (10 March 2009), online: *Lexology* <http://www.lexology.com/library/detail.aspx?g=dfc7db55-a5c2-412a-ac03-f298e6d217db>.

Pollock v First Heritage Financial Planning Ltd, 2002 BCSC 782.

Robinson v Team Cooperheat-MQS Canada Inc, 2008 ABQB 409.

Tree Savers International Ltd v Savoy, 1991 CanLII 3952 (Alta QB), var'd but aff'd on this point, 1992 CanLII 2828 (Alta CA).

Dismissal with Cause 13

LEARNING OUTCOMES

After completing this chapter, you will be able to:

- Differentiate between a good reason for dismissal and just cause for dismissal under the common law.
- Understand the contextual approach to determining just cause for dismissal.
- Identify the elements of procedural fairness in dismissals for just cause.
- Discuss specific grounds for just cause, including dishonesty, insolence and insubordination, incompatibility, off-duty conduct, absenteeism, sexual harassment, intoxication, and incompetence.
- Understand related concepts, such as condonation.

Introduction

Generally speaking, under the common law in Canada an employee may be dismissed summarily—without advance notice or pay in lieu—only for just cause. All other terminations require reasonable notice or pay in lieu, unless there is a clearly expressed and enforceable term in an employment contract that establishes an alternative notice requirement. A dismissal without just cause and without notice or pay in lieu exposes the employer to a lawsuit for "wrongful dismissal" (see Chapter 14).

Under the common law, the term "just cause" has a particular meaning in the context of dismissal: it does not simply mean that an employer had a good reason, such as a need to downsize, for dismissing an employee. The essential legal question is whether an employee breached the employment contract in such a fundamental way that the employer is no longer bound by the common law obligation to provide reasonable notice of termination or pay in lieu of reasonable notice.

This is a very high standard for employers to meet, and the existence of just cause is decided on a case-by-case basis. Whether an employer has demonstrated just cause will ultimately be determined by a court, assisted by legal precedent (previous cases involving similar fact situations in which other courts have decided what constitutes just cause). Unfortunately for the parties, this determination is made only after the matter comes before a court in a wrongful dismissal action brought by a dismissed employee. At the time that the employer makes the decision to dismiss the employee, it can be uncertain that the employee's conduct constitutes just cause for dismissal under the common law.

However, by reviewing previous cases that have dealt with misconduct similar to that of the employee, the employer often will be able to get a sense of whether or not it can successfully defend a wrongful dismissal action in a particular situation. Furthermore, an employer can take certain measures, such as using progressive discipline and ensuring procedural fairness, to improve its chances of a successful defence.

Although courts primarily look to past wrongful dismissal lawsuits as precedents for determining just cause, if there are few such decisions involving a similar kind of misconduct, courts will also look at labour arbitration decisions. That is because arbitrators usually apply similar standards when they apply the just cause provision found in most collective agreements ("Common-Law Doctrine," 2004, at 3200). The cases discussed in this chapter therefore include some arbitration decisions.

onus of proof
the burden of proving a case or the facts involved in a dispute

balance of probabilities
the degree of proof required in civil law cases wherein a proposition is established as fact if it is shown that the proposition is more likely than not to be true

Overview of Just Cause Requirements

Onus of Proof

Because the consequence of a finding of just cause—dismissal without notice or pay in lieu of notice—is severe for the employee, the courts are reluctant to reach this result. The **onus of proof** is on an employer to show, on a **balance of probabilities**, that an employee breached an employment contract in a fundamental way. This standard of proof requires the ultimate decision-maker to be satisfied that, based on all of the available evidence, the thing that must be proven is more likely than not to have occurred. The analysis is contextual; it depends on the particular circumstances of the case. In *Health Sciences Association of Alberta v Alberta Health Services* (2010), for example, the Alberta Arbitration Board determined that in the health profession, both employers and employees are "reposed with a public trust" (at para 50) on behalf of "unwary or vulnerable patients [who] may be placed at risk of covert, surreptitious, furtive or seemingly accidental sexually tinged contact" (at para 44). Despite his awareness of the hospital's clear policy against it, a respiratory therapist (RT) at Chinook Regional Hospital in Lethbridge, Alberta, used a work computer to access pornography sites because if he did so at home, porn-monitoring software would instantly notify his wife by email that he had relapsed. The RT admitted to a psychiatrist a lifelong craving for pornography and a fixation with breasts, yet his job required daily medical examinations of female patients in a state of undress or partial undress.

The Arbitration Board found that his obsession was not amenable to progressive discipline. The overriding concern of the Board was "the heightened level of discomfort for any female patient, young or old, if they knew that their attending RT, with whom they have been left alone in an examining room" (at para 59) was suffering from such an addiction. The hospital terminated the therapist for seriously compromising its professional integrity. The Board agreed that because of the nature of the public trust reposed in health professionals, a fundamental breach of the bond of trust had occurred and the RT's grievance was dismissed.

Just cause is an "all or nothing" proposition. If an employee's misconduct or incompetence is not proven on the balance of probabilities, or fails to meet the threshold for just cause, an employer is obliged to provide reasonable notice or pay in lieu under the common law. There is no reduction in the notice period owed to an employee if the employee did something wrong but the misconduct was not serious enough to warrant immediate dismissal. In other words, the punishment must be proportionate to the level of misconduct.

Proportionality and the Contextual Approach

Over the past three decades, courts have increasingly recognized the unequal relationship that exists between most employers and employees, especially at the time of dismissal, and they have adopted several ways to protect employees. One relevant development is the concept of **proportionality**—that is, the idea that any sanction must be proportional to the conduct to which it relates. There are a few acts of misconduct (such as theft, assault, or a significant incident of sexual harassment) that may warrant **summary dismissal** even if they occur only once, because they go to the heart of the employment relationship. However, most other types of misconduct or performance-related incidents must usually occur more than once to constitute just cause.

proportionality
the idea that any sanction must be proportional to the conduct to which it relates

summary dismissal
dismissal without notice, usually based on just cause

For example, in *Henson v Champion Feed Services Ltd* (2005), the Alberta Court of Queen's Bench considered the dismissal of an employee, in the context of the "mad cow disease" outbreak, after the employee attempted to cover up his decision to use an unmarked bag of feed in the preparation of an order. The employer alleged that it had just cause to dismiss the employee, citing a buildup of problems over his seven-year work history. The employer had responded to prior performance issues with five verbal warnings and one written warning but had also lulled the employee into a sense of complacency with inconsistent messages, such as a promotion and successive wage increases. Because the employer's decision to dismiss in reaction to the incident was viewed by the Court as disproportionate, the plaintiff was entitled to six months' pay in lieu of notice.

contextual approach
the increasing tendency of courts to view employee misconduct within the overall context of the employment relationship, including length of service and work and disciplinary record, in determining whether the employer had just cause for dismissal

As noted above, the courts have adopted a **contextual approach** to just cause. In the past, courts often focused on the nature and seriousness of an employee's conduct to determine whether it warranted dismissal without notice. Using a contextual approach, courts now consider the nature and seriousness of an alleged offence in the context of the overall employment relationship. The Supreme Court of Canada in *McKinley v BC Tel* (2001), discussed in the next section, determined that relevant contextual matters include the employee's length of service, the employee's performance and disciplinary history, and any mitigating circumstances, such as personal factors or actions of the employer that could have influenced the employee's conduct or performance.

For example, in *Soost v Merrill Lynch Canada Inc* (2009), a high-performing financial adviser employed by a large investment firm violated some of the employer's policies and rules. However, the Alberta Court of Queen's Bench found that the company did not have just cause to dismiss Soost because some of the conduct for which he was dismissed had been tolerated by the employer until shortly before the termination. Soost's other transgressions were not so grave as to warrant dismissal and the destruction of his career. Initially, Soost was awarded $2.2 million in damages that included 12 months' pay in lieu of notice and an additional $1.6 million for damage to reputation and goodwill. However, this was partly overturned by the Alberta Court of Appeal in a ruling that determined there was no legal basis for awarding the $1.6 million on top of the pay in lieu of notice.

Another stark example of a contextual approach to the assessment of just cause is evident in *Dryco Drywall Supplies Ltd v Teamsters Local Union No 213* (2013), which concerned the dismissal of an employee for setting his co-worker on fire. The employee, as a prank, set fire to some fabric hanging from the back of a co-worker's safety vest. Though the employee initially extinguished the flame, the vest reignited and was ultimately put out by a customer who smothered the flames with his hands. As a result, the customer suffered burns and blisters to his hands, which took approximately two weeks to heal. The employee was fired, for cause. The union argued that termination was an excessive response and sought the employee's reinstatement. An arbitrator adopted a contextual approach, which included consideration of the employee's largely unblemished 32 years of service, the spur of the moment nature of the misconduct, and the less than "zero tolerance" approach to horseplay in the workplace, as well as the employee's genuine and immediate apology. Ultimately, the arbitrator concluded that while the misconduct in question was "careless and stupid" (at para 36), it did not provide just cause for dismissal in consideration of all the surrounding circumstances.

Procedural Fairness

Regardless of what type of misconduct or incompetence it alleges, an employer improves its chances of successfully demonstrating just cause under the common law if it follows certain rules of **procedural fairness**. As a general rule, an employee should be given ample opportunity to respond to the allegations against them before an employer makes the decision to terminate. The employee may have a reasonable explanation for their actions or may describe extenuating circumstances that an employer should consider in determining a fair disciplinary response. Allegations should be investigated in good faith, thoroughly, and promptly. The investigation should remain confidential. A decision must be made in good faith—that is, not arbitrarily or for an ulterior motive.

procedural fairness certain process rights that one party provides to another, such as an employer giving an employee an opportunity to respond to allegations against them

IN THE NEWS

Court Awards $50,000 in Aggravated Damages for Unfair, Bullying, Bad Faith Conduct

A recent decision by the Supreme Court of British Columbia is an important reminder that employers should not be too quick to terminate an employee even when they believe they have just cause. Before resorting to the extreme of terminating the employee, employers must ensure their conduct is justifiable, or they potentially face severe consequences.

In *Acumen Law Corporation v Ojanen*, Melissa Ojanen was hired as an articling student by Acumen Law. Partway through her articling term, Acumen found that Ojanen had been writing a personal blog that included similar legal information to that posted on the employer's website. Acumen believed this was hindering its marketing efforts, and the blog was the trigger for termination. Unfortunately, Acumen had not told Ojanen of its discovery and did not involve her in the investigation.

Instead, Ojanen was served with a termination letter and a notice of civil claim in front of her entire class. Acumen alleged that Ojanen had entered their premises after hours without permission, taken client materials home without permission, failed to attend a court appearance as scheduled, engaged in insubordination, avoided responsibility, and demonstrated that she was unfit to practise law. Acumen also reported her alleged dishonest and deceitful conduct to the Law Society of British Columbia.

Ojanen countersued her former employer for wrongful dismissal, seeking damages for Acumen's conduct in the manner of her dismissal.

The Court concluded that none of the alleged acts of misconduct, individually or collectively, amounted to "just cause" for termination. They ordered Acumen pay $18,934 for lost wages and vacation pay owing for the time remaining in her 12-month articling period.

Furthermore, the Court concluded Acumen's conduct was "unfair, bullying, [and done in] bad faith" (at para 137), causing serious and prolonged emotional distress well outside the norm for dismissed employees. Justice Gomery found that serving Ojanen with the notice in a public place was "unnecessary and psychologically brutal" (at para 128). The employer's failure to discuss its concerns about the blog with her before termination and accusing her of deceit and dishonesty were based solely on unfounded suspicions. As a result, Ojanen was awarded $50,000 in aggravated damages.

TAKEAWAY

This decision highlights the importance of the duty of good faith and fair dealing in termination of the employment relationship. The misconduct at issue must not only rise to the level of "just cause," but the employee must also be provided with a fair opportunity to present their side of the story prior to dismissal. Moreover, "employers must also ensure that the manner of termination is respectful, fair and sensitive to the vulnerability of the employee being terminated."

SOURCE: Adapted from Hoopes, 2019.

If an allegation of misconduct is substantiated, the employer should ensure that the sanction is proportionate to the misconduct within the overall context of the employment relationship. For example, the employer should:

1. consider whether the misconduct was planned and deliberate or a momentary error in judgment;
2. assess the misconduct in the context of the employee's position, length of service, performance record, and previous conduct;
3. consider extenuating circumstances, such as provocation, mistreatment, or external circumstances such as a serious illness in the family, that may have prompted the incident; and
4. consider the employee's response to the allegations, such as admission, remorse, denial, or further challenge. For example, if the employee denies that their actions constitute misconduct, there is less chance that their behaviour will change.

An employee's response to allegations of wrongdoing is important for another reason besides ensuring that the punishment is proportional to the misconduct. Under the contextual approach, courts look not only at the employment relationship up to the date of the alleged misconduct but also at how the employee responds to those allegations (Rudner, 2009, at 6). A court may uphold a dismissal for just cause based not on the seriousness of the alleged misconduct but on the fact that the employee lied or tried to conceal material information during the investigation. The case of *Obeng v Canada Safeway Limited* underscores the importance of how an employee responds to allegations of wrongdoing during an investigation.

CASE IN POINT

Employee's Failure to Be Truthful During Investigation Justifies Dismissal

Obeng v Canada Safeway Limited, 2009 BCSC 8

Facts

Obeng was an assistant manager at a Vancouver-area Safeway store. His actions, as observed by several other staff members, raised suspicions that he was stealing groceries. When asked for an explanation, Obeng became upset and denied all of the allegations made against him. For example, he vehemently denied placing groceries in a shopping basket (or even having a basket in his arms that afternoon), although several people reported him doing so. As a result of Obeng's failure during several investigatory meetings to provide any alternative explanation for his actions, Obeng was dismissed for theft. He sued the employer for wrongful dismissal damages.

Relevant Issue

Whether the employer had just cause for dismissal.

Decision

The Court held that Safeway had just cause for termination, not based on the alleged theft of groceries, for which there was insufficient proof, but because of Obeng's failure to be totally honest and forthright during the employer's investigation. Crucial to this finding was Obeng's admission at trial that he did have a grocery basket in his hands on the day in question, which, he explained, he had used to collect misplaced merchandise for later reshelving. Although this was a reasonable explanation for his actions, his failure to provide it during the employer's investigation was a breach of his obligation to provide full and truthful disclosure. Referring to the contextual approach laid out in *McKinley*, the Court stated:

> Mr. Obeng was well aware that theft was endemic in the grocery business and a serious problem, and he knew that Safeway considered it grounds for dismissal. He appreciated that, as a manager, his behaviour must be seen to be beyond reproach, and he knew that Safeway's Code of Business Conduct required that he make full and truthful disclosure in the course of an investigation. ... A denial is not an explanation, nor was it full and truthful disclosure. ...
>
> Mr. Obeng's dishonesty in relation to the investigation of his conduct on August 28 justifies his termination. (at paras 37-38)

In short, Obeng's failure to provide a complete and truthful explanation for his behaviour during the employer's investigation was a breach of his implied duty of honesty, which constituted just cause for dismissal.

Stating Grounds of Dismissal

On occasion, an employer may dismiss an employee without alleging just cause and later, when the employee sues for wrongful dismissal, assert that it actually had just cause. The employer is not necessarily prevented from changing its position. As shown in *Letendre v Deines Micro-Film Services Ltd*, justification for dismissal can be based on facts discovered after dismissal ("after-acquired cause") or on grounds that differ from those alleged at the time of dismissal.

CASE IN POINT

Best Reason for Discharge Not Discovered Until After Termination

Letendre v Deines Micro-Film Services Ltd, 2001 ABQB 26

Facts

Letendre had worked for Deines as vice-president of operations for 16.5 years when he was terminated for, among other things, insubordination. After the dismissal had occurred, Deines learned that two years before the termination Letendre had submitted a false claim to the company's insurers for an expensive laptop computer.

Relevant Issue

Whether the employer could rely on after-acquired knowledge about the employee's fraudulent insurance claim to support the dismissal, and if so, whether the fraud was sufficient to destroy the necessary trust between an employer and a key employee.

Decision

The judge found that an employer may justify termination without notice by relying on subsequently ascertained cause. Further, she applied the following general principles associated with revelation of character: (1) the more senior the employee, the more likely it is that the employer will be able to justify dismissal on the basis of the employee's untrustworthy character; (2) the character of the employment is relevant in determining whether the revealed character flaws relate to the employee's duties and make continued employment intolerable; and (3) dishonest conduct is, arguably, a character flaw that will almost always justify dismissal. The judge cited the BC Court of Appeal to underscore her point that honesty is still important—and perhaps the more serious and responsible the position held, the more that honesty must be not only inherent but patent. As vice-president, Letendre was second in command at Deines. His subsequently ascertained act of fraud demonstrated that he was unfit for a position of trust, and this revelation of character, although different from the ground initially alleged, could be used by the employer as cause for dismissal.

Sometimes an employer dismisses an employee for cause but still wants to provide them with some money as a gesture of goodwill. In this situation the employer should clarify in writing that the payment is made on a **without prejudice** basis—that is, the payment does not imply that the employer owes the employee reasonable notice of termination. Such a goodwill payment may also help to avoid litigation if it is comparable to the amount that an employee would be awarded in a successful suit for wrongful dismissal.

without prejudice without an admission of wrongdoing in a legal dispute

Condonation

An employer must be careful not to condone misconduct that it intends to rely on as just cause for termination. **Condonation** occurs when an employer who discovers an employee's misconduct or poor performance fails to respond within a reasonable time. If, for example, an employer discovers that an employee lied about his expense account and the employer fails to respond until two years later, the courts will not allow the employer to rely on the expense account incident in terminating the employee for cause.

condonation implied acceptance by one party of the conduct of another party; once an employer is aware of an employee's misconduct and takes no disciplinary action within a reasonable time, the employer cannot dismiss the employee for that misconduct without any new misconduct

In considering whether an employer has condoned an employee's behaviour, courts allow the employer a reasonable amount of time to consider its response to an incident. It is entitled to time to investigate the matter and decide how best to handle the situation. It must also know the full nature and extent of the misconduct in order to be held accountable for having condoned it.

Principles Pertaining to Dismissal for Just Cause

There are 11 commonly recognized principles pertaining to dismissal for just cause. A useful summary of these principles appears in the 1995 BC Supreme Court case of *Graham v Canadian Cancer Society* at para 39 (citations omitted):

> 1. The employee is entitled to be made aware of the responsibilities and restrictions imposed on him or her by the employer.
> 2. The employee is entitled to be advised of the employer's dissatisfaction and notified that his position is in jeopardy.
> 3. Cumulative causes may justify dismissal without notice where the events taken individually would not.
> 4. But mere inadequacies and errors of judgment ought not to be so put together.
> 5. Positions requiring a higher degree of public confidence may impose a higher standard of duty.
> 6. Abuse of authority and misuse of credit cards may justify dismissal.
> 7. Wilful disobedience may justify dismissal without notice but the onus is on the defendant to establish that the acts were in defiance of clear and unequivocal instructions or were known to be contrary to the

employer's objectives. The question is whether the act disregarded essential or fundamental terms of the contract of service.

8. The defendant may rely on grounds only known to it after dismissal, but not conduct after dismissal.
9. Conflict of interest that would cause an employer to lose trust may be a cause for dismissal.
10. The employer is entitled to set any guidelines it wishes provided the same are not contrary to law, dishonest or dangerous.
11. An employee may be terminated for cause while on sick leave.

In addition to the grounds mentioned in the above list, there are other grounds that may, on their own or in combination, provide just cause for dismissal, including (1) engaging in criminal conduct, (2) recklessness or negligence costing the employer money, (3) undermining the morale of co-workers, (4) harming the employer's reputation, (5) competing with the employer, and (6) committing a breach of trust.

Establishing Just Cause Under the Common Law

There are two general types of employee conduct that can justify dismissal without notice: misconduct, such as acts of theft or insubordination, and problems related to job performance. The more common grounds for dismissal for cause are:

- dishonesty (and related misconduct),
- insolence and insubordination,
- incompatibility,
- off-duty conduct harmful to the employer,
- conflict of interest,
- excessive absenteeism and lateness,
- sexual harassment,
- intoxication and substance abuse, and
- incompetence.

The following is a review of these grounds and their treatment in the courts.

Dishonesty

Dishonesty in the workplace is one of the most serious acts of misconduct because it undermines the crucial element of trust that should exist between an employee and an employer. Some examples of dishonesty include fraud, such as submitting inaccurate claims for overtime pay or sick leave benefits, accepting kickbacks from suppliers, or stealing company property.

However, an employer's ability to dismiss an employee for dishonesty is no longer a cut-and-dried issue. In the past, employers could assume that virtually any dishonest conduct constituted grounds for summary dismissal, because the employer could no longer be expected to trust the employee. However, as discussed above, recently courts have applied the contextual approach to assess whether an employee's dishonest conduct was serious enough to warrant dismissal without notice in light of all the relevant factors, including the employee's length of service and work record. If a single act of theft is seen as an error in judgment rather than a reflection of an untrustworthy character, the courts will probably find that dismissal without notice is unjustified and that progressive discipline should be applied instead. This contextual approach to dishonesty was highlighted in the landmark case of *McKinley v BC Tel*, where the Supreme Court of Canada found that dishonesty that does not go to the root of an employment relationship does not constitute just cause for dismissal.

CASE IN POINT

Employee's Dishonesty Must Be Assessed in Context

McKinley v BC Tel, 2001 SCC 38

Facts

McKinley occupied a senior financial position with the employer when he began suffering from high blood pressure. In mid-June 1994, he took a leave of absence. He told his supervisor that he wanted to return to work in a position that involved less responsibility than the position he left. In August 1994, he was dismissed. The employer offered him a separation package that he found unsatisfactory, and he sued for damages for wrongful dismissal. Shortly after the trial started, the employer applied to the Court to include the defence of just cause based on dishonesty. The alleged dishonesty related to the fact that McKinley's doctor had advised him that taking a certain medication would help control his blood pressure and thus assist him in returning to his former position. The employer alleged that McKinley was dishonest in failing to reveal this possibility.

Relevant Issue

Whether McKinley's failure to reveal the doctor's information constituted dishonesty that warranted dismissal for cause.

Decision

The Supreme Court found that although McKinley had been dishonest, the nature and extent of the dishonesty in the circumstances did not fundamentally undermine the employer–employee relationship. The employer's response should have been proportional to McKinley's conduct, taking into account its nature and seriousness and the context of his situation, including length of service, work history, and other relevant factors. In the circumstances, McKinley's dishonesty was not so fundamentally inconsistent with his obligations to the employer that it violated an essential condition of the employment contract. The employer was required to provide McKinley with pay in lieu of reasonable notice of termination.

Although the Supreme Court found for the employee in *McKinley*, it set out circumstances in which dishonest conduct would warrant dismissal without notice. It would do so if it violated an essential condition of the employment contract, breached the bond of trust between the parties, or was fundamentally or directly inconsistent with an employee's obligations to an employer. A serious breach of this bond of trust resulted in the dismissal of a City of Calgary truck driver in *Calgary (City) v Amalgamated Transit Union*. In this case, the arbitrator applies *McKinley* and provides a thorough review of contextual circumstances that might affect the penalty imposed.

CASE IN POINT

Employee's Misconduct Constitutes Just Cause for Dismissal

Calgary (City) v Amalgamated Transit Union, Local 583, 2016 CanLII 95890 (Alta GAA)

Facts

Charles Dodds, the grievor, drove his truck to work at a City of Calgary transit garage. During the day he picked up a door and some windows he had purchased for a personal construction project. A foreman came by to help him load the windows and strap down the load in his truck box. During this time the foreman loaded a jackhammer belonging to a contractor into the backseat of the truck. Dodds helped the foreman load the jackhammer because he was worried about the seats in his truck getting torn. The contractor reported to management that the jackhammer was missing, and an email was sent to staff asking employees to keep an eye out for it. Dodds went to a supervisor and told him his truck was parked where the jackhammer was stored, with the windows open, but that he had no knowledge of how the jackhammer disappeared. A few days later Dodds met the foreman and loaded the jackhammer into the foreman's truck. By this time Dodds' knew the jackhammer had been stolen. Unbeknownst to Dodds and the foreman, a co-worker had observed the initial theft and reported it to the city.

The city's corporate security adviser interviewed Dodds, who initially denied any knowledge of how the jackhammer disappeared. The investigator warned Dodds he knew a lot more about the theft than Dodds thought and reminded him of his obligation to be honest. Dodds was given an opportunity to discuss the matter with his union representative, after which he admitted to helping the foreman steal the jackhammer.

Relevant Issue

Whether the City of Calgary had just cause to terminate the grievor for theft and dishonesty.

Decision

The Arbitration Board relied on the contextual approach in *McKinley* when it upheld Dodds' discharge. The case provides a useful summary (at para 58) of both mitigating and aggravating factors that play a role in determining the appropriateness of discharge as a penalty in cases of dishonesty.

Mitigating factors may include:

1. a lengthy period of satisfactory employment;
2. a discipline-free history such that the employee's misconduct can be considered an isolated event;
3. the dishonest conduct was undertaken in the spur of the moment without premeditation;
4. any reasonable confusion as to whether the employee knew what they were doing was wrong;
5. the prompt and honest acknowledgement of the misconduct at the earliest reasonable opportunity;
6. the economic impact of the discharge given the employee's personal circumstances;
7. genuine remorse by the employee and apologies at the earliest reasonable opportunity;
8. the nominal value of the stolen property;
9. the employee is unlikely to engage in any future misconduct; and
10. uneven application of discipline by the employer for cases of theft and dishonesty.

Aggravating factors may include:

1. a disciplinary record, especially where there is previous discipline for matters relating to dishonesty;
2. the employee was in a position of trust and responsibility;
3. the dishonest conduct was planned and premeditated;
4. the failure to acknowledge the misconduct at the earliest reasonable opportunity;
5. continued dishonesty throughout the investigation with attempts to cover up the misconduct; and
6. a lack of genuine remorse.

The Arbitration Board found in this case that Dodds had to be highly suspicious of the foreman and had a duty to make inquiries of the foreman (who was not his supervisor and had no authority over him). He lied to cover up the theft and his role in the theft, and when he knew without a doubt that he was in possession of stolen property, he delivered it to the thief. Despite seven years of service, a clean disciplinary record, and a significant economic impact on the grievor, the discharge was upheld.

Litster v British Columbia Ferry Corp and Taylor highlights another issue that an employer must keep in mind when dismissing an employee for conduct that it alleges is dishonest: the employer must be able to prove its case. In *Litster*, the employee was successful in her wrongful dismissal action because her credible explanation for her conduct defeated the employer's allegations of theft.

CASE IN POINT

Employee's Credible Explanation Defeats Allegations of Theft

Litster v British Columbia Ferry Corp and Taylor, 2003 BCSC 557

Facts

Litster, age 44, had worked for the BC Ferry Corporation for more than 20 years when she was terminated for cause for removing paints from the employer's premises without permission. Litster admitted to removing the paints for the purpose of taking them to a recycling depot. However, for various personal and work-related reasons, she stored the paints in the shed at her home for several months. When the employer became aware that Litster had its paints in her possession, it investigated and decided that the six-month delay was not reasonable. It concluded that Litster had stolen the paints and dismissed her. Her termination letter—which was sent to several other employees, including the payroll manager—outlined the alleged theft. The employee sued the employer for wrongful dismissal. She also sued the author of the termination letter personally for defamation.

Relevant Issues

1. Whether the employer had just cause for dismissal based on dishonesty.
2. Whether the termination letter constituted defamation and, if so, whether the employer had a defence.

Decision

The BC Supreme Court found that the employer did not have just cause to terminate Litster, because her explanation for the delay in taking the paints to a recycling depot was credible. The Court noted that allegations of theft "must be proven on clear and cogent evidence and withstand the strict scrutiny appropriate for such a serious allegation" (at para 86). She was awarded 15 months' salary in lieu of reasonable notice. However, the Court did not find that the employer acted in bad faith, and therefore no additional damages were awarded (see the discussion of moral damages, formerly called *Wallace* damages, in Chapter 14).

With respect to the claim of defamation, the Court decided that the letter was defamatory because alleging theft had "the effect of lowering Ms. Litster in the estimation of others" (at para 123). The defence of "justification"—that is, that the statements were true—was not available to the author of the letter because the Court expressly found that Litster had not committed theft. The defence of "qualified privilege" was accepted, however. This defence applies where a person who makes a statement honestly and reasonably believes that the statement is true and has an interest in making it or a duty to make it; the recipients must have a corresponding interest in receiving it or a duty to receive it for the defence to succeed.

If an employee's dishonesty involves theft, the value of the stolen article need not be significant to warrant dismissal for just cause if the employee is aware that such conduct is prohibited. Though this is a factor some adjudicators may take into consideration, Arbitrator Swan argued in *Air Canada and International Association of Machinists and Aerospace Workers, District Lodge 148* (1978) that "[t]he value of the goods stolen, however, is not in my opinion a proper consideration. The same mental state is required to pilfer as to plunder, and an employee's dishonesty is equally cast in doubt whatever the value involved" (at 404).

In *Mutton v AOT Canada Ltd* (2002), the Court supported this line of reasoning when it found that an employee with less than a year's service was justifiably terminated for stealing stretch wrap from the employer for personal use without permission. Although the value of the item stolen was insignificant, the employee was aware that this behaviour could lead to termination, so the Court found that his misconduct violated the trust necessary in an employment relationship. Citing the contextual approach used in *McKinley*, the Court also took into account the employee's short length of service.

In dealing with instances of employee dishonesty, an employer can put itself in the strongest legal position possible by using the following three strategies:

1. *Provide clear written policies that outline required behaviour.* Key policies should state that violations will be cause for dismissal. To be effective, the policies must also be clearly communicated to employees and consistently enforced.
2. *Get the facts.* An employer must ensure that it has its facts right. Not only is there arguably a higher standard of proof required in cases where dishonesty is alleged, but the employer may also be required to pay additional compensation to an employee if it makes harmful accusations without sufficient evidence to support them. Employers should investigate incidents thoroughly—obtaining witness statements and listening to an employee's explanation—before deciding whether or not to dismiss the employee for dishonesty. If the employee has a reasonable explanation for their actions, such as taking computer equipment home to finish a report on the weekend, a court will probably not find that the employer had just cause for dismissing the employee. Proving that an employee committed fraud or was dishonest requires convincing evidence.
3. *When allegations cannot be proven, provide a reasonable separation package.* If the employer cannot prove that the employee committed the dishonest act but no longer wishes to retain the employee's services, it should dismiss the employee "without cause" and provide a reasonable separation package. This will protect the employer against additional damages that it could be required to pay to an employee if it makes unsubstantiated allegations of dishonesty in a wrongful dismissal suit.

Insolence and Insubordination

It is rare, but not impossible, that a single act of insubordination will provide just cause for termination. Such an act might be, for example, an assault on a supervisor or a deliberate contravention of an important employment policy that results in a significant loss for an employer. In *Donaldson v Philippine Airlines Inc* (1985), the employee disobeyed a directive from management by extending credit to a certain customer and deliberately withholding information from the employer. The employer lost money as a result. The Court found just cause for dismissal.

Usually, however, an employer must show a pattern of insubordinate or insolent behaviour that continues despite clear warnings before it can establish just cause. Courts will consider the context in which all conduct occurs. For example, if arguments are common in a workplace, a court will take into account "shop talk" in deciding whether an employee's behaviour is acceptable. Similarly, courts will consider whether the employee has been provoked by the supervisor.

Henry v Foxco Ltd demonstrates the courts' reluctance to disentitle an employee to reasonable notice for a single episode of insolence, even where the insolence was serious.

CASE IN POINT

Single Episode of Insolence Rarely Justifies Summary Dismissal

Henry v Foxco Ltd, 2002 NBQB 277, rev'd 2004 NBCA 22

Facts

Henry had worked for the employer as a body repair technician for nearly eight years when, one day, his supervisor asked him to remove decals from two vans. Several hours later, his supervisor said that he hoped Henry was working on the second van, not the first. Henry became angry and, according to the employer's evidence, said several times, "If you want to fire me, go ahead and fire me." The supervisor tried to calm Henry down but eventually said, "Okay, you're fired." Henry sued for wrongful dismissal. The trial judge held that the supervisor was justified in firing Henry because the supervisor's comments were part of his duties as manager, Henry became abusive to the supervisor, and the incident took place in front of other employees whom the supervisor supervised. In these circumstances, the employee's insolence went to the heart of the employment relationship. Henry appealed this decision.

Relevant Issue

Whether the single episode of insolence constituted just cause for dismissal.

Decision

The New Brunswick Court of Appeal found that the employer wrongfully dismissed Henry. While a single incident may completely undermine an employment relationship, the circumstances in this case were insufficiently extreme to do so. A court must apply the principle of proportionality. Termination would be warranted where:

1. the employee and supervisor could no longer maintain a working relationship;
2. the incident undermined the supervisor's credibility in the workplace; and
3. as a result of the incident, the employer suffered a material financial loss or loss of reputation, or its business interests were seriously prejudiced.

In Henry's case, these factors were not present. The incident did not occur in front of customers or the public. The employer should have imposed a "cooling-off period" before deciding on an appropriate penalty. Henry was awarded $14,200 plus interest as wrongful dismissal damages.

Even where there is gross insubordination, employers should be wary of acting hastily. An Ontario Divisional Court set aside a lower court's decision of just cause in *Caskanette v Bong-Keun Choi Dentistry Professional Corporation* because the employer had not provided any warning to the employee that her failure to return to work could result in termination. In January 2013, Choi acquired a dental practice and continued to employ the receptionist, Caskanette. However, Choi distrusted Caskanette because patients were not being booked on Fridays. He staged a "secret shopper" call to schedule an appointment for a Friday morning. Caskanette attended work on the Friday, but received a call cancelling the appointment and subsequently left. The office manager called and left her a message instructing her to return to work immediately. Caskanette did not return and was dismissed the following Monday. The trial judge decided Caskanette's insubordination warranted summary dismissal. The decision of the trial judge was overturned, though, affirming that the employer is required to provide an opportunity for an employee to atone. Even where the insubordination is significant, there is a duty to warn and a duty to apply progressive discipline.

An isolated instance of insubordination by a long-term employee usually requires an employer to impose a form of discipline that is less severe than immediate dismissal without notice. Only if an employee repeats the behaviour despite several warnings, including one that advises them that their job is in jeopardy if the insubordination continues, is termination for just cause likely sustainable.

Incompatibility

Generally speaking, it is difficult for an employer to dismiss an employee for cause simply because they do not fit in or has personal habits that are considered somewhat unpleasant in the workplace. General incompatibility is usually too vague to constitute just cause for termination without notice. Moreover, incompatibility or lack of fit with the "corporate culture" is sometimes a mask for discrimination in the workplace. However, in certain situations courts have upheld dismissals based on an employee's incompatibility with the dominant workplace culture. For example, in *Essery v John Lecky & Co* (1986), the dismissed employee was a hairdresser who had greasy hair, smoked heavily, and neglected his appearance. The employer successfully defended itself against a claim for wrongful dismissal by showing that the employee's personal habits harmed its business.

Off-Duty Conduct

Generally, conduct that takes place outside the workplace does not provide just cause for termination. However, an exception arises if an employer can demonstrate that an employee's off-duty conduct harmed its business or reputation. Much will depend on the employee's position, the nature of the off-duty conduct, and how the matter reflects on the employer's business. There are many cases of off-duty conduct related to the online activities of employees who disparage their employers on Facebook (e.g., *Bell Technical Solutions v Communications, Energy and Paperworkers Union of Canada* [2012]) or who make discriminatory or offensive comments on Twitter that can affect the reputation of their employers (e.g., *Toronto (City) v Toronto Professional Firefighters Association, Local 3888* [2014]).

Online activity was also the key issue in *Kelly v Linamar Corporation*. In that case a court had to decide whether a well-respected manager with 14 years' service could be dismissed for just cause for being charged with possessing child pornography on his home computer.

CASE IN POINT

Is Possession of Child Pornography on an Employee's Home Computer Just Cause?

Kelly v Linamar Corporation, 2005 CanLII 42487 (Ont Sup Ct J)

Facts

Kelly was the materials manager at Emtol, a subsidiary of Linamar, Guelph's largest employer. His duties included supervising 10 to 12 employees as well as being in regular contact with suppliers and customers. On January 21, 2002, Kelly was arrested and charged with possession of child pornography (on his home computer). Although he was a well-respected and trusted manager with an unblemished 14-year work record, the employer decided to terminate his employment based on that charge. On January 24, 2002, it sent him the following termination letter:

> Dear Mr. Kelly:
>
> Subject: Termination of Employment
>
> As you are aware you have been charged with a criminal offence, on or about Monday, January 21, 2002. Indeed, newspapers have published to the community that you have been criminally charged with possession of child pornography. As a result of our investigation, which includes statements made by yourself, you have been involved in inappropriate conduct in relation to the community at large and children in particular.
>
> As you are also aware, Emtol Manufacturing and its parent company, Linamar Corporation, actively promote and contribute to the community and children's programs, including a focus on elementary aged school children for the purpose of furthering a business and community reputation.
>
> As a result of your misconduct, which has been published to the community at large, the Company's legitimate interests have been negatively affected. In addition, your conduct has impacted upon the workplace and employee morale to such an extent that employees have indicated a refusal to work with you.
>
> Under these circumstances, and in light of your management position, you have left us no alternative but to terminate your employment effective immediately on a for cause basis.

Subsequently, Kelly pleaded guilty to the charge of possessing child pornography. He then brought an action against his employer for wrongful dismissal.

Relevant Issue

Whether the employer had just cause to terminate the employee on the basis of his off-duty misconduct.

Decision

The Court found that the employer did have just cause to terminate Kelly because he had breached his duty to ensure that his off-duty conduct did not adversely affect his employer. In the judge's words:

> Linamar has over a long period of time built up a good reputation which it jealously protects. That reputation includes the promotion of its activities with young people outlined earlier. A company is entitled to take reasonable steps to protect such a reputation and the termination of Philip Kelly was just such a step. (at para 31)

The Court noted that although at the time of dismissal Kelly had only been charged with the offence and had not yet pleaded guilty, he had admitted his guilt to the employer early on in the employer's investigation. The Court did caution that not every employee charged with possession of child pornography or a similar crime is subject to termination without compensation. Relevant factors include the employee's level of responsibilities and the degree to which the employer's reputation in the community will likely be affected. In this instance, dismissal was justified because Kelly was a senior manager with extensive contacts outside the organization. Moreover, his employer was a prominent and active member of the local community.

As always, employers should discipline for off-duty conduct only after a fair and thorough investigation. The employer in *George v Cowichan Tribes* learned this the hard way when the BC Supreme Court awarded 20 months' reasonable notice and $35,000 in aggravated damages to a long-service employee with an exemplary record who had been dismissed for an off-duty altercation with a woman at a pub. The employer failed to prove its allegations. The aggravated damages were awarded because the employer acted in a "cavalier, reckless and negligent manner" (at para 264) when it relied on an inadequate investigation and tarnished the employee's reputation in the community.

FYI

Can Blogging Get You Fired?

While social networking has been around since before the first water cooler was invented, employee use of personal blogs and online social networking websites is a more recent phenomenon. Should employers care about what an employee blogs or posts on their own time?

In some respects, the issues raised by employee blogging are familiar ones. Concerns about employees leaking confidential data, making harassing or defamatory comments about co-workers or managers, or damaging the employer's reputation are not new. What has changed recently is the size of the potential audience, the permanence of the record created, and the (often mistaken) perception of anonymity by the author.

Can an employee be disciplined or fired for cause based on online postings, tweets, or blogs made outside of working hours? The same principle applies here as to other off-duty conduct. Usually, what an employee does on their own time is not relevant to the employment relationship. However, if the off-duty conduct seriously damages the employer's reputation or business, the employer has a right to take action. Generally speaking, simply complaining about the boss or employer online will not be considered just cause for termination. The comments must be so disparaging that they undermine the employment relationship. Although there have not yet been any common law decisions in Canada on when blogging can be just cause for dismissal, there are a number of arbitral decisions that provide some early guidance in this area.

One of the first Canadian arbitration decisions to deal with the termination of an employee for the contents of her blog is *Grievance of "R": Discharge for Contents of a Personal Blog* (2008). Although the employee worked in a sensitive area of the provincial government (workers' compensation), her blog identified who she was, that she lived in Edmonton, and that she worked for the Alberta government. She made postings such as "I work in a lunatic asylum" and referred to being in an office populated by "imbeciles and idiot savants." She used aliases for her co-workers, but they were easily identifiable by details given in her posting. One sample posting, under the heading "Aliens Around the Coffee Table," read:

> Roberta likes to talk—unfortunately she's menopausal—she might have short term memory problems—always forgets the people's names she's talking about, or the point of her story, or the ending—most of the time we just listen for a few minutes until we figure out who made eye contact with her, then we ditch the person from the conversation for the rest of the break. … If I had to choose a planet that she came from, I'd say it was some dark planet, with very little oxygen. …

When confronted with printouts of blog entries, the employee stated that she was merely exercising her right to freedom of expression. The employer terminated her for cause, arguing that the employee's blogs had potentially damaged its reputation. The Arbitration Board dismissed the employee's grievance, stating that although the employee had a right to create a personal blog, her public statements went well beyond what was permissible. Especially disturbing were her disparaging remarks about at least seven co-workers with whom she regularly worked. The Board also considered several other factors. The frequency of her postings showed that it was not a momentary lack of judgment, she took no steps to prevent access to the general public, and perhaps most seriously, she failed to express serious regret over the effect that her behaviour had on her co-workers. This last point seems to have been especially important, since a co-worker who had also written blogs criticizing the workplace but who later apologized to the people she had offended received only a two-day suspension (Harris, 2008). Although this decision was later struck down on judicial review, the Court did so because of procedural concerns.

Another relevant arbitration decision is *Chatham-Kent (Municipality) v CAW Local 217* (Clark Grievance, 2007). The grievor was a personal caregiver at a retirement home with eight years of service. She set up a personal, publicly accessible blog in which she made disparaging remarks about her employer, expressed her dislike for the residents, and posted several pictures of herself with residents. The arbitrator upheld her termination on two grounds: breach of confidentiality for posting residents' pictures and insubordination for the contemptuous comments made about management.

On the other hand, in *EV Logistics v Retail Wholesale Union, Local 580* (Discharge Grievance, 2008), an arbitrator decided that a lengthy suspension was a more appropriate penalty than termination for a warehouse employee who was fired for the contents of his personal blog. The employee's publicly accessible blog contained a number of racist comments and violent fantasies. In reducing the penalty, the arbitrator noted several factors. These included the employee's personal problems, including a history of depression, and the fact that his violent fantasies were not directed at his employer. Nor were individual employees, customers, services, or products targeted. Finally, the employee had made a "sincere, complete, and without reservation" apology, as well as posting an apology on the blog's former site.

To minimize potential problems in this area, employers should develop a policy that sets out the ground rules on personal blogging as well as the consequences for breaching those rules. A well-drafted policy will alert employees that online posts, even those done on their own time and posted under a pseudonym, can have an impact on their jobs. It will also encourage employees to think about how their co-workers, customers, or supervisors could be affected by inappropriate postings. The following are some points to address in a blogging policy:

- The employer's general code of conduct applies to employee blogs, even if the employee posts under a pseudonym.
- Any confidentiality or non-disclosure obligations to the employer apply to the Internet in general and specifically to blogs, tweets, and social networking sites.
- The posting of defamatory or derogatory comments about fellow employees, customers, or management is expressly prohibited. Author anonymity, use of aliases, or omitting the names of people or organizations does not change this requirement.
- Bloggers who identify themselves as employees or who discuss substantive work issues in the blog should include a disclaimer stating that the opinions expressed are those of the author only (Pigott, 2005).
- Employees must use their own equipment and time for personal blogging purposes.
- Published materials that are damaging to the employer's business or reputation are expressly prohibited.
- Failure to follow the policy will, depending on the circumstances, result in disciplinary measures up to and including dismissal (Pushor Mitchell LLP, 2006).

As always, an employer should ensure that its policy is clearly drafted, regularly brought to the attention of its employees (at least annually), and applied consistently. Where relevant, employees should be made aware that the employer regularly reviews online journals and blogs for defamatory or other inappropriate material.

When investigating a suspected breach of its blogging policy, an employer should start by gathering as much information about the online conduct as possible. The employee should be shown the offending postings and instructed to remove them, within a reasonable time frame, and to apologize to the individuals affected. If the employee then refuses or fails to follow through with these measures, the employer is in a better position to justify the level of discipline imposed (Farahani, 2009, at 16-6).

Conflict of Interest

One of the implied duties that employees owe to their employers is the duty of faithfulness, or loyalty. Consequently, engaging in activities that create a conflict of interest with the employer's interests may justify dismissal for cause (Echlin & Thomlinson, 2011, at 206).

For example, an employee's "moonlighting" may adversely affect an employer. Moonlighting does not usually constitute just cause unless it harms an employer's interests as it can, for example, if an employee moonlights for a competitor or at a job that involves the employer's customers. By knowingly placing themselves in a situation that conflicts with the interests of the employer, the employee breaches their common law duty of loyalty. As shown in the *Patterson* decision below, in these circumstances it is important for the employer to have a clearly communicated conflict of interest policy that sets out the conduct that will justify dismissal. Moreover, the potential harm to the employer must be significant to justify dismissal for cause.

CASE IN POINT

Conflict of Interest Justifies Dismissal for Cause

Patterson v Bank of Nova Scotia, 2011 BCPC 120

Facts

Patterson was a customer service supervisor whose job occasionally involved her dealing with customers and recommending various types of services. When first hired, Patterson had signed Scotiabank's guidelines for business conduct, which required her to inform her manager if there was a risk of a conflict of interest. It also stated that she "should not commence or continue a business which competes with the Bank or engage in *any activity likely to compromise the position of the Bank*" (at para 29; emphasis added). About 12 years after Patterson started with the bank, she got her real estate licence and began working with a realtor on evenings and weekends. When the bank found out about this (Patterson had distributed her realtor business cards within the office), it insisted she either change positions with the bank or leave, because it was concerned about a perceived conflict of interest. Assuring the bank that she would not abuse her position, Patterson refused to make a change. The bank terminated her employment, alleging just cause.

Relevant Issue

Whether the employer had just cause to dismiss the employee.

Decision

The Court found that the employer had just cause. The employer's guidelines were reasonable and clear, requiring employees to discuss outside business interests with it where a potential conflict of interest was involved, and the employee was aware of those guidelines. Moreover, the employer gave Patterson an opportunity to remedy the conflict before dismissing her; when she refused, the employer was entitled to enforce the terms of its employment agreement (*Canadian HR Reporter*, 2011).

Absenteeism and Lateness

There are two types of absenteeism under the common law: culpable (blameworthy) and innocent (blameless). They are treated differently under the law.

Culpable Absenteeism

culpable absenteeism blameworthy absences, such as being late without good reason (including returning late from a break), leaving work without permission, or failing to follow absence notification procedures

Culpable absenteeism occurs when an employee is absent from work without a good reason. For example, if an employee sleeps in or decides not to go to work because they prefer to do something else, their absence is culpable. An employer is entitled to impose disciplinary action for culpable absenteeism or lateness. However, a single incident rarely justifies dismissal. Culpable absenteeism or repeated lateness is best addressed through a clearly communicated and consistently enforced policy and the application of progressive discipline to breaches of that policy.

In assessing whether ongoing lateness or absenteeism constitutes just cause for dismissal, an employer should consider the context of the employment relationship, including:

1. how long the employee has worked for the employer;
2. whether the lateness or absenteeism started suddenly or has been chronic since employment began;
3. how frequently the employee is late or absent;
4. what reasons the employee gives for their lateness or absences;
5. whether the lateness or absenteeism harms the employer; and
6. whether the employer consistently enforces its attendance policy—for example, if it tolerates the repeated lateness of other employees, the employer has little chance of justifying the dismissal of a particular employee on this basis.

Teck Coal v United Mine Workers of America, Local 1656 (2010) provides a clear illustration of culpable absenteeism amounting to just cause for dismissal. Kyle Norman, aged 26, commenced employment as a mine worker at the Cardinal River Operations of Teck Coal near Hinton, Alberta, in 2007. His work schedule consisted of two 12-hour day shifts and two 12-hour night shifts followed by four consecutive days off. By November 2008, Teck had issued to Norman a counselling interview report to warn him about his high rate of absenteeism (186 hours "year to date 2008," whereas the average annual absentee rate was between 9 and 11 hours). At the interview, Norman agreed to improve his attendance, to provide medical notes for future absences, and to contact his foreman prior to missing work. However, between January 1, 2009, and May 27, 2009, little had changed. Norman was absent because of illness another 196 hours, and therefore a further warning notice was provided, this time underscoring the fact that "his job was on the line."

As well, a new issue regarding Norman was becoming evident to Teck Coal. It gradually came to light that Norman was not always sick on the occasions when he was calling in sick:

- On July 15, 2009, he called in sick, but it was later discovered that he had taken time off because of the death of a friend. The employer, in this instance, granted him time off for compassionate reasons.
- On September 26, 2009, he was seen at a local bar called the Zoo, where he remained until well past midnight, "drinking and inebriated." When questioned about this absence, he denied being at the Zoo.

- On October 1, 2009, he called in sick, claiming to have a doctor's appointment. The employer learned that he did not see the doctor that day.
- On October 2, 2009, he reported he was too ill to attend work but was observed to be at another local bar. He asked the witness who saw him not to reveal his presence at the bar, but she said she would not lie for him. He then claimed to be there only as a designated driver, but the witness reported that he smelled of alcohol and appeared drunk.
- On October 3, 2009, when he was supposedly too sick to work, he hosted a party at his house. When questioned, he denied this to his employer, saying "a real party is when the police shut it down at midnight."

His high rate of absenteeism combined with these incidents of dishonesty, in the aggregate, led Teck Coal to dismiss Norman on October 28, 2009, telling him it could no longer rely on him or trust him as an employee. The union filed a grievance, claiming Norman suffered from a mental disability and that his termination had been discriminatory. A 5.75-hour psychiatric assessment was scheduled for Norman. The conclusion of the specialist, however, was that Norman did not suffer from an addiction to alcohol.

The Alberta Arbitration Board determined that the union had not, on a balance of probabilities, made out a case that Norman suffered from a mental disability that had affected his attendance at work, as he had claimed. Instead, the specialist described him as "impulsive and self-damaging" as well as "immature and irresponsible" (at para 20). His apparent dishonesty with his employer did not causally arise "from a medical or psychiatric disease or illness" (at para 21). In the Board's view, Norman's "clear preference was to drink, party and be with friends" (at para 24) rather than work, an attitude confirmed by the clinical notes of his family physician. The Board saw him as a "person who [had] yet to grow up," but in the opinion of the Board, such a character weakness "cannot be laid at the feet of employers" (at para 27). Given his brief 27 months of employment, his chronic unreliability, and his "appalling attendance record and two incidents of discipline during his short service" (at para 38), the Alberta Arbitration Board found that Teck Coal had dismissed Norman for just and reasonable cause. His grievance was therefore denied.

Innocent Absenteeism

Innocent absenteeism occurs when an employee cannot come to work for reasons that are beyond the employee's control. In these circumstances, an employer cannot impose discipline. Under human rights legislation, where absenteeism results from a disability, an employer has a duty to accommodate the employee unless this causes it undue hardship. (See the discussion of the duty to accommodate disability in Chapter 7.) Clearly, an employer who does not specifically articulate to the employee its shift from accommodating a disability to taking a disciplinary approach toward the absenteeism will not have just cause for dismissal.

innocent absenteeism absences that arise as a result of a legitimate medical or other cause; innocently absent employees can never be subject to disciplinary measures

In *Whitford v Agrium Inc* (2006), an employee with 22.5 years of service developed an alcohol addiction. His supervisor supported his attendance at a rehabilitation centre, but his treatment was not completely successful and he took further time off.

However, with the exception of one period of three to six days, Whitford was always honest with the employer, did not intentionally engage in misconduct or jeopardize others, informed the employer of the circumstances when he was absent, and sought the employer's permission and approval. When, therefore, the employer relied on Whitford's failure to prepare a return-to-work plan as a ground for dismissal, Whitford said it was never communicated to him that failure to create the plan would result in termination. The Alberta Court of Queen's Bench found that Agrium had not met the first part of the two-part test developed by the Supreme Court of Canada in *Cie minière Québec Cartier v Quebec (Grievances arbitrator)* (1995). Part one requires the employer to establish that, looking at the context of the employment relationship as a whole, the employee's ability to fulfill his workplace duties was impaired by his alcohol problem. Part two asks whether any improvement was likely in the foreseeable future. The Court said it was not necessary, however, to address part two of the test since Agrium had not met the requirement of part one.

Not all instances of innocent absenteeism resulting from sickness are protected under the disability provisions of human rights legislation. For example, in *Ouimette v Lily Cups Ltd* (1990), an Ontario case, an employee was dismissed after a series of absences during her probationary period. The absence that led to her termination was a three-day absence arising from an asthmatic reaction to aspirin (one day) and the flu (two days). The employee filed a complaint with the Ontario Human Rights Commission, alleging that because she had been absent because of illness, her termination violated the Ontario *Human Rights Code*. The board of inquiry found that minor illnesses do not qualify as disabilities under the Code. To treat temporary illnesses that are common to the general population as "disabilities" would trivialize the purpose behind this prohibited ground of discrimination. As a result of this decision, minor temporary illnesses are not protected as disabilities, and human rights legislation does not apply.

However, *Ontario (Human Rights Commission) v Gaines Pet Foods Corp* demonstrates that if any part of an employee's absences results from a disability, an employer cannot rely on these absences in determining whether it has just cause to dismiss an employee for excessive absenteeism.

CASE IN POINT

Employer Cannot Rely on Absences That Result from Disability in Dismissals

Ontario (Human Rights Commission) v Gaines Pet Foods Corp, 1993 CanLII 5605 (Ont Sup Ct J)

Facts

The employee had an extremely poor attendance record for several years before she was away from work for six months because of cancer. When she returned, the employer gave her a letter stating that she must maintain, over the next 12-month period, a level of attendance equal to or better than the average for the hourly-rated employees in the plant. When she failed to do so, the employer dismissed her for excessive absenteeism. She filed a human rights complaint. The board of inquiry held that because she had a serious absenteeism record, even without the six months off for cancer, the termination did not constitute discrimination on the basis of disability. The employee appealed.

Relevant Issue

Whether termination for excessive absenteeism in these circumstances constituted discrimination under the Ontario *Human Rights Code*.

Decision

The Ontario Divisional Court held that the employer contravened the *Human Rights Code* in dismissing the employee for excessive absenteeism. The 12-month attendance condition that it imposed was a direct result of her absence because of cancer, which is a disability. Her disability was therefore a proximate cause of her termination.

The Court noted that because of the employee's prior record of absenteeism unrelated to disability (only 25 percent of the total days off related to cancer), the employer could have dismissed her without reference to her cancer absences. However, the employer had admitted that it included those days in deciding that termination was appropriate. To constitute discrimination under the Code, the prohibited ground of discrimination need not be the only reason for termination, as long as it is one of the reasons.

In determining the appropriate remedy, the Court found that the employer had not acted in bad faith. It had been patient and given the employee several chances to improve her absenteeism record over the years. In the mid-1980s, when the employer decided to dismiss the employee, it may not have been clear that cancer was a disability under the Code. Therefore, the employee was awarded six months' pay for loss of earnings but no further damages.

For absences that relate to disabilities, employers are required to accommodate employees to the point of undue hardship. This may require them to accept irregular attendance or tolerate lengthy absences over a long period of time. However, where there is no realistic chance that an employee will ever be able to return to work on a regular basis, even with accommodation, an employer may eventually be able to prove undue hardship and thus dismiss the employee. This will depend on the employer's circumstances, the employee's prognosis, and the employee's attendance record over time.

Under the common law, a permanent illness that prevents an employee from returning to the workplace can result in a finding of frustration of contract. This principle of contract law applies when an employment contract becomes impossible to perform. However, findings of frustration are rare, particularly if the employee is not central to the employer's operation and has been employed for a long time. (See Chapter 14 under the heading "Frustration of Contract.")

In addition, where there is a long-term disability plan in the workplace and dismissing an employee would disqualify them from receiving benefits, such dismissal may be seen as a breach of the employment contract.

Sexual Harassment

Many types of sexual harassment, such as offensive humour or comments, warrant progressive discipline. However, in more serious cases of sexual harassment, especially those involving supervisors, courts have long upheld employers' decisions to dismiss employees for just cause even in the absence of progressive discipline. The courts' concerns in these types of cases are set out in *Bannister v General Motors of Canada*.

CASE IN POINT

Sexual Harassment Constitutes Just Cause for Dismissal

Bannister v General Motors of Canada, 1994 CanLII 7390 (Ont Sup Ct J), rev'd 1998 CanLII 7151 (Ont CA)

Facts

Bannister worked at General Motors as a security supervisor during the evening and night shifts. Most of the female staff in his department were summer students between 18 and 23 years of age. Bannister, who was in his late 40s, had worked for GM for 23 years when one of the summer students complained about his unwanted sexual approaches and comments. GM's investigation revealed that at least five women had similar complaints, alleging that he tried to kiss them, asked them to sit on his knee and give him a kiss, and described pornographic movies using sexual gestures.

During its investigation, the employer interviewed Bannister four times, and each time he denied any wrongdoing. He remembered some of the alleged incidents but did not believe they constituted sexual harassment. The employer terminated him for cause, and Bannister sued for wrongful dismissal.

The trial judge found that Bannister was not "beyond redemption," and in light of his 23 years' service granted him 21 months' pay in lieu of reasonable notice (roughly $120,000). The employer appealed.

Relevant Issue

Whether Bannister's conduct constituted just cause for dismissal.

Decision

The Ontario Court of Appeal found that the employer had just cause to dismiss Bannister. It acted with "care, responsibility and sensitivity" (at para 3) in investigating the initial complaint. The trial judge erred in focusing on Bannister's length of service and good record because it ignored two important duties of the employer: the duty to protect the members of its workforce from offensive conduct and the duty to protect the corporation against civil suits. The Court of Appeal emphasized Bannister's supervisory role. A supervisor who abuses his power by condoning or creating a poisoned work environment for women is not doing his job. As for the argument that a modern industrial plant is a rough work environment where offensive commentary is common, the Court stated:

> It is not a question of the strength or mettle of female employees, or their willingness to do battle. No female should be called upon to defend her dignity or to resist or turn away from unwanted approaches or comments that are gender or sexually oriented. It is an abuse of power for a supervisor to condone or participate in such conduct. (at para 35)

As a result of the Court's finding of just cause, Bannister was not entitled to any damages for wrongful dismissal.

In *Bannister*, the employer's proactive stance on the issue of sexual harassment and the procedural fairness it exhibited in its investigation helped it justify the dismissal. It had permanently posted a copy of its sexual harassment policy throughout the plant. The employee had attended a sexual harassment seminar designed for supervisors, where the employer informed supervisors that sexual harassment could result in dismissal for cause. The employer's investigation of the complaint was thorough and well documented. During the initial interviews with other employees, the name of the employee under investigation was not mentioned. The other employees were asked whether they had general information with respect to any human rights or sexual harassment issues. Bannister acknowledged that the employer had given him every opportunity to explain his side of the story and had interviewed everyone that he had asked to be interviewed about the situation. Furthermore, the fact that the employee repeatedly denied that his actions constituted misconduct raised a question as to whether his behaviour could change.

IN THE NEWS

How #MeToo Changed the Workplace

Since 2017, when allegations of sexual harassment and assault against film producer Harvey Weinstein became public, the way businesses approach workplace misconduct has shifted dramatically. In Canada, harassment allegations against Jian Ghomeshi (CBC), Albert Schultz (Soulpepper Theatre), and Paul Bliss (CTV) led to these men being publicly fired from their high-profile occupations in media and entertainment. But in the corporate sphere, most harassment complaints are settled quietly and shrouded in confidentiality. Except for the few cases that land in human rights tribunals or court, the public doesn't hear about them.

Surveys show workplace harassment continues to be widespread. A 2018 poll of 2,000 Canadians found that 34 percent of women and 12 percent of men reported being sexually harassed at work. Of those, two out of five indicated that the harassment came from someone with direct influence over their careers. Most believed their organizations had a culture where sexual harassment was not tolerated. However, fewer than half said they were adequately informed about what to do if they were harassed at their workplace.

This can be contrasted with a 2017 survey of 153 Canadian executives (95 percent of whom were men) conducted by KPMG. Ninety-four percent of those surveyed believed that sexual harassment was not an issue within their own workplaces, although they recognized it was rarely reported. Half also believed sexual harassment was less of a problem now than years ago, and most were sure their businesses had appropriate policies in place to address it.

This disconnect between the experiences of employees and the beliefs of organizational leaders indicates that there is much work to be done despite the awareness brought on by the #MeToo movement. According to Chris McKinnon, a former manager with the Ontario Human Rights Commission who now investigates harassment complaints, companies that don't rise to the challenge risk being outed online. He points out that victims who once felt isolated can now easily connect with others.

As employers reconsider how they respond to allegations of harassment, they must also be aware of fears that innocent people will fall prey to false allegations. Ninette Bishay was an 18-year-old student when a male colleague circulated a grossly inappropriate email about her to others in the office she was working at. She went directly to her boss and complained. Her harasser was fired the next morning. While grateful that her complaint was taken seriously, Bishay would advise that harassers be afforded more due process than what occurred in her situation. "I was harassed, don't get me wrong," Bishay says. "But I think a fair and rigorous process of investigation of complaints is expected in this day and age." Employers must find a balance between taking allegations seriously and maintaining fairness.

SOURCE: Adapted from Tanner, 2019.

Intoxication

The human rights issues that arise when an employee's substance abuse problem constitutes a disability are discussed in Chapter 7. Subject to these rights, violation of a policy that prohibits the use of alcohol or drugs or intoxication on the job or at lunch may constitute grounds for dismissing an employee. However, a single violation by an employee who is not in a safety-sensitive job will probably not be considered just cause for summary dismissal. *Ditchburn v Landis & Gyr Powers Ltd*, involving intoxication during working hours of an employee with 27 years of service, underscores the need to view misconduct in the context of the entire employment relationship.

CASE IN POINT

Single Incident of Intoxication Not Just Cause in Context of Entire Employment Relationship

Ditchburn v Landis & Gyr Powers Ltd, 1995 CanLII 7290 (Ont Sup Ct J), rev'd in part 1997 CanLII 1500 (Ont CA)

Facts

Ditchburn was a sales executive with 27 years of above-average performance. However, he began to have difficulty keeping up with a recent change in sales strategy that depended more on computers and less on strong interpersonal skills. The employer demoted him. As a result of the changes in his job, Ditchburn arranged a goodbye lunch with a long-time client, Deason. At lunch they drank several beers and then they drank some more at a local strip club. After Ditchburn drove Deason back to his workplace, they had an argument, which led to a physical altercation in the parking lot where both men suffered minor injuries. Ditchburn reported the incident to the employer, and the employer dismissed him for cause on the basis that he had violated the company policy against intoxication at work and by driving a company car while impaired during work hours while engaged in company business.

Relevant Issue

Whether intoxication during work hours and fighting at the client's workplace constituted just cause for dismissal.

Decision

The trial judge found that although Ditchburn had engaged in a flagrant breach of company policy, the incident was isolated and reflected uncharacteristically bad judgment. In light of Ditchburn's age (59), his many years of loyal service, and the fact that the incident was an isolated event, the employer should at least have given him the "benefit of the doubt" and been less rigid in the application of its policy. Instead, the employer used the incident as an excuse to rid itself of an employee who was not keeping up with technology.

Ditchburn was awarded pay in lieu of 22 months' reasonable notice plus $15,000 damages for mental distress, since it was foreseeable that he would suffer significant stress in these circumstances. He was also awarded an additional 2 months' pay because the employer failed to provide him with an adequate letter of reference.

On appeal by the employer, the Court of Appeal upheld the 22 months' pay in lieu of notice and the $15,000 awarded for mental distress. However, it held that the extension of the notice period by 2 months as a result of the inadequate letter of reference was inappropriate because the inadequate letter did not impair Ditchburn's job search.

Despite the result in *Ditchburn*, the contrasting decision in *Dziecielski v Lighting Dimensions Inc* shows that long service and a good employment record alone will not insulate an employee from a finding of just cause where the consequences of a single incident of misconduct involving intoxication are especially serious.

CASE IN POINT

Dismissal for Single Incident of Intoxication Upheld

Dziecielski v Lighting Dimensions Inc, 2012 ONSC 1877, aff'd 2013 ONCA 565

Facts

Dziecielski was vice-president of quality control of a small, privately owned automotive supplier. He had worked for the employer for 23 years when, after taking the company's pickup truck without permission to a client meeting and later consuming four beers over a one-hour lunch, he was in a single-vehicle accident. The company truck was destroyed and he was left with life-threatening injuries. On the basis of blood samples taken at the hospital, Dziecielski was charged with, and later pleaded guilty to, a criminal offence related to drunk driving. Several weeks after the accident, while recuperating, Dziecielski received a letter from his employer terminating his employment. He sued for wrongful dismissal, claiming reasonable notice damages of 24 months plus punitive, aggravated, and exemplary damages.

Relevant Issue

Whether the employer had just cause to dismiss the employee.

Decision

The trial Court's decision, upheld on appeal, was that the employer had just cause. In reaching this conclusion, the Court acknowledged that a single, isolated incident by a long-service employee with a clean record rarely justifies dismissal. Similarly, intoxication on the job does not automatically justify termination. However, in this case, summary dismissal was appropriate for a number of reasons. Drinking and driving is a serious criminal offence and widely condemned by society. The misconduct was prejudicial to the employer's interests because it put the employer at risk of both reputational damage and of vicarious liability to third parties if the employee had injured or killed others. Moreover, despite pleading guilty to the criminal charge, Dziecielski maintained that he was "not drunk" at the time of the accident. This ongoing denial spoke to a failure to accept responsibility for his actions. As a result, his lawsuit was dismissed and the Court awarded the employer legal costs of almost $29,000. Dziecielski's appeal to the Ontario Court of Appeal was unsuccessful, and that Court awarded further legal costs of about $11,000 to the employer (Filion Wakely Thorup Angeletti, 2013).

It is not clear whether this case foreshadows a more rigorous approach by the courts to workplace intoxication-related misconduct than that taken in the *Ditchburn* decision. The Alberta Court of Queen's Bench was similarly unwilling to tolerate a single incident of alcohol-induced misconduct when it upheld the dismissal of a long-term employee who sexually harassed a colleague after becoming intoxicated at a company function in *Clarke v Syncrude Canada Ltd* (2013). Certainly each of these cases can be distinguished based on the severity of the consequences of the misconduct, as well as other elements. What is clear is that when dismissal based on just cause is alleged, each case will be considered on its own facts by balancing the seriousness of the misconduct against other contextual factors.

In determining an appropriate response to an employee who is intoxicated during work hours, an employer should consider the following factors:

1. Did the intoxication harm its business interests?
2. How has it treated intoxicated employees in the past?
3. Does the employee work in a safety-sensitive area? If so, did the intoxication endanger the employee or others?

4. Was the employee's performance affected by the intoxication?
5. Is there a company policy or a term in an employment contract that addresses intoxication during work hours?

If alcohol is regularly consumed at business lunches as a means of engaging with customers, for example, an employer may have difficulty justifying the dismissal of an employee for being intoxicated during working hours.

Substance Abuse

As discussed in Chapter 7, substance abuse is considered to be a disability and thus a prohibited ground of discrimination. An employer therefore cannot discipline an employee for substance abuse; instead, it must accommodate the employee to the point of undue hardship. Even a perceived rather than an actual addiction may be protected in some cases.

In reality, accommodating an employee with a substance abuse problem means providing rehabilitation services or allowing time off work to attend these services. There is no rule of thumb concerning how long an employee must be given to overcome their disability: every case depends on its facts. At a certain point, however, if rehabilitation efforts are not successful and the employee's continued dependency adversely affects the workplace, an employer can dismiss an employee on the basis of just cause or frustration of contract.

Substance abuse should be distinguished from substance use and impairment at the workplace. Substance use has been a particular concern for employers with the legalization of marijuana. There has been fear that off-duty consumption may result in workplace impairment. There is also concern that more employees will use cannabis and that it cannot be as easily detected as alcohol. Finally, it is unclear how employers should deal with employees who are prescribed cannabis for the treatment of health issues.

On the whole, the impact on the workplace, from a legal perspective, has been less than dramatic. Most employers (particularly those in safety-sensitive industries) already have policies that deal with drugs, alcohol, intoxication, and prescription medications that may impact an employee's ability to safely perform their jobs. Even if an employee has a prescription, there is no absolute right to use cannabis at work. An employee who is impaired at work, from any type of drug (prescription or otherwise), has likely violated employer policy. If it is a safety-sensitive workplace, an employee who is impaired at work and does not have an addiction issue may be terminated. As always, whether a termination for impairment at work will stand up in court depends on a contextual analysis that considers the nature of the workplace, the circumstances, and the severity of the incident.

Incompetence

Although general incompetence is one of the most common reasons for dismissing an employee, it is also one of the most difficult grounds to prove. An employer must show that an employee has fallen below an objectively determined level of performance and that the problem lies with the employee, not with other factors, such as lack of adequate training.

However, it is possible for an employer to dismiss an employee for cause on the basis of incompetence if it has laid the necessary groundwork. The principles applied to performance or incompetence as just cause for dismissal have been articulated in numerous cases. A concise summary is provided in *Boulet v Federated Co-operatives Ltd* (2001) at para 3:

1. Each case must be decided on its facts.
2. An employer's displeasure at an employee's performance is not enough to warrant dismissal. There must be some serious misconduct or substantial incompetence.
3. The onus of proving just cause rests with the employer and the standard of proof is beyond a balance of probabilities.
4. The performance of an employee … must be gauged against an objective standard.
5. The employer must establish:
   (a) the level of the job performance required,
   (b) that the standard was communicated to the employee,
   (c) that suitable instruction and/or supervision was given to enable the employee to meet the standard,
   (d) the employee was incapable of meeting the standard, and
   (e) the employee was warned that failure to meet the standard would result in dismissal.
6. Where the employee's performance is grossly deficient and the likelihood of discharge should be obvious to the employee, warnings and reasonable notice are not required.
7. While the standard of incompetence to warrant discharge for cause is severe, the threshold of incompetence necessary to warrant dismissal for cause is significantly lower where dismissal is preceded by many warnings indicating unsatisfactory performance.
8. In considering whether an employer has provided adequate warning to an employee, where the dismissal is for repeated instances of inadequate work performance, the employer must show:
   (a) it has established a reasonable objective standard of performance,
   (b) the employee has failed to meet those standards,
   (c) the employee has had warnings that he or she has failed to meet those standards and the employee's position will be in jeopardy if he or she continues to fail to meet them; and
   (d) the employee has been given reasonable time to correct the situation.
9. An employer who has condoned an inadequate level of performance by his employee may not later rely on any condoned behaviour as a ground for dismissal.
10. Condoned behaviour is relevant if the employee fails to respond after appropriate warnings. Condonation is always subject to the implied condition that the employee will be of good behaviour and will attempt to improve.

On-the-job conduct falling within the scope of incompetence may also include a lack of requisite tact, discretion, and sensitivity for the particular demands of the position. In *Lowery v Calgary (City of)* (2000), a former paramedic was hired as the city's public relations officer. On at least four occasions he made media advisory statements that his superiors viewed as inappropriate. For example, he said that "previous patients who have suffered similar injuries have rarely lived" and referred to a patient as being "very combative and missing half his face." The Alberta Court of Appeal found that despite clear, express warnings and a reasonable opportunity to improve, Lowery failed to portray the requisite professionalism for the job. These cumulative failings, the Court said, would "prejudice the proper conduct of the employer's business" (at para 3).

However, even where preconditions are satisfied, it will be difficult for an employer to demonstrate just cause for dismissing a long-term employee whose performance it has accepted for years. In these circumstances, employers usually provide pay in lieu of notice instead of attempting to dismiss such an employee for cause. An employer may dismiss an employee for cause on the basis of a single instance of incompetence in only the most extreme of circumstances, such as recklessly incompetent behaviour that leads to serious financial losses for the employer.

Grounds That Cannot Constitute Just Cause

British Columbia's and Alberta's employment-related statutes prohibit employers from dismissing employees on certain grounds, including an employee's assertion of their statutory rights. A list of statutes and their prohibitions follows:

1. *BC Human Rights Code and Alberta Human Rights Act.* An employer cannot dismiss or otherwise penalize an employee for asserting their rights under these statutes.
2. *BC Employment Standards Act and Alberta Employment Standards Code.* An employer cannot dismiss or otherwise penalize an employee for asserting their rights under these statutes, including the right to pregnancy, maternity, or parental leave.
3. *BC Occupational Health and Safety Regulation and Alberta Occupational Health and Safety Act.* An employer cannot dismiss or otherwise penalize an employee for asserting their rights under this legislation, including the right to refuse unsafe work.
4. *BC Workers Compensation Act and Alberta Workers' Compensation Act.* An employer cannot dismiss or otherwise penalize an employee who is absent from work for a work-related cause and has a right to be reinstated under these statutes.
5. *BC Labour Relations Code and Alberta Labour Relations Code.* An employer cannot dismiss or otherwise penalize an employee for lawful union-related activity.

If an employer dismisses an employee for asserting their rights under these employment-related statutes and regulations, a court or tribunal may order the employer to reinstate the employee and pay the employee a monetary award.

KEY TERMS

balance of probabilities, 444
condonation, 450
contextual approach, 446
culpable absenteeism, 462
innocent absenteeism, 463
onus of proof, 444
procedural fairness, 447
proportionality, 445
summary dismissal, 445
without prejudice, 450

REVIEW AND DISCUSSION QUESTIONS

1. Define the following terms:
   a. Contextual approach
   b. Condonation
   c. Without prejudice
2. Explain the difference between culpable absenteeism and innocent absenteeism. Give an example of each.
3. According to case law, what type of off-duty conduct justifies summary dismissal?
4. Nicole, a 27-year-old mother of four, had worked at the counter of a Tim Hortons doughnut shop for three years. One day she was seen giving a Timbit to a crying child who came into the shop with a regular customer. When the manager of the store confronted her about it, Nicole readily admitted to giving the Timbit away without paying for it. She was aware that this was against the employer's policy, but she had been busy at the time and did not go to her purse to get the 16 cents at the time. Also, knowing that day-old Timbits were given away to small children in the store regularly, she expected to get a reprimand at most. However, the manager fired her on the spot. Nicole was so upset that she called her local newspaper when she got home and her firing became headline news (see Curtis Rush, "Tim Hortons Rehires Mother Fired over Timbit," *Toronto Star* [8 May 2008]). (A day later the owner of the franchise called and offered Nicole a job at another of his franchises.) Given the media attention the story garnered, it is clear that in the "court of public opinion" the employer did not have just cause to dismiss Nicole. However, did the employer have just cause under the common law? Explain your answer by referring to the principles upon which just cause dismissal of non-union employees is based.
5. Bert owns a small five-person consulting firm. He wants to terminate one of the consultants, George, for performance-related problems. George, who is 38 years of age, has been with the firm for 6.5 years and the quality of his work is excellent. Furthermore, he's a really nice guy. The problem is that he is a perfectionist and is extremely slow at getting anything done. He keeps missing crucial client deadlines, and clients are starting to take their business elsewhere. It has reached the point where none of the other consultants are willing to work with him. Bert has spoken to George about this many times over the years (and this problem has been noted in all of his performance reviews), but there has been no improvement. George is just incapable of picking up the pace. Bert wants to know whether he has just cause under the common law to dismiss George. Discuss.
6. Greg had worked for two years as games supervisor at a casino. His job was to monitor the dealers. He enjoyed his job and he joked around with his boss, Michael, all the time. One day Michael saw Greg spending a lot of time with one dealer who had nobody at her table and he told Greg to do his job and keep his eyes on his tables. Greg started to make loud kissing sounds and, suggesting that Michael was "sucking up" to management, started making very crude gestures. When Michael asked him to stop, Greg continued. All of this was witnessed by a security guard and customers at nearby card tables. A week later, Greg was brought into the office and terminated for just cause with no pay in lieu of notice. This was not the first time Greg had been disciplined for a lack of etiquette and professionalism, but it was the most serious incident. Greg sued for wrongful dismissal. In court he denied making the crude gestures, saying he only made kissing sounds and it was part of their ongoing banter. Did the employer have just cause under the common law to dismiss Greg? Explain your answer.
7. Maxine was a 35-year-old machine operator who had worked for the employer for six years when she was dismissed for cause for slapping a co-worker across the face during a verbal argument. Accordingly, she was not given notice or pay in lieu. Maxine sued the employer for wrongful dismissal, arguing that she was

entitled to reasonable notice. What factors do you think the court would consider in deciding whether the employer had just cause in this situation?

8. Art and Brian had eight and nine years' service, respectively, with the employer call centre and both had good work records. However, they were dismissed for cause after it was discovered that they had received about a dozen adult pornographic emails from a mutual friend. While they did not solicit or distribute the emails, the employer based the dismissals on breach of its computer use and harassment policy that, among other things, prohibited "accessing, transmitting, receiving, or storing discriminatory, profane, harassing, or defamatory information." The employer argued that it had done everything it could do to reinforce the importance of this policy: employees were required to read and sign off on it, they were reminded of it upon logging in, and they were made aware of the company's network monitoring system implemented to enforce compliance.

   Did the employer have just cause to dismiss Art and Brian?

9. Denise was hired in March 2019 as vice-president of operations for a software development company. At an annual salary of $125,000, she was the employer's highest-paid executive and had a wide range of functions. Although the employer was located in Vancouver, it agreed when Denise was hired that, for family reasons, she could work from her home in Alberta. However, the employment agreement indicated that the employer had the right to require her to move to Vancouver in the future. In December 2019, Denise requested vacation time to go to Mexico (where she had recently bought a house), and several times over the next six months Denise went to Mexico for short visits, sometimes claiming one or two sick days for those periods. In mid-August 2020, after arranging Internet and phone service and thereby confirming that she could work remotely from Mexico, Denise advised her employer that she and her family had decided to move to Mexico. The CEO said he felt betrayed by this sudden announcement and, uncertain about its tax and other implications, asked Denise for a written proposal, which he would present to the board of directors to show how this arrangement would work. Denise responded that she could work just as effectively from Mexico as from Alberta, and her employment agreement allowed her to work from home without any country restriction. Upset by Denise's position, the employer dismissed Denise in late November 2020 with two months' severance pay, shortly after Denise had finalized a major business deal for the employer. The termination letter stated that the dismissal was for cause for relocating to another country without permission and for dishonesty related to falsely claiming sick leave. Denise sued for wrongful dismissal damages equivalent to 12 months' salary. She denied that the employer had just cause and argued, in the alternative, that even if it did, by delaying her termination for several months the employer had condoned her decision to move to Mexico.

   Did the employer have just cause to dismiss Denise? If so, did its three-and-a-half-month delay amount to condonation?

10. ABC Company had recently become unionized after a highly contentious organizing drive. Two employees (Bob and Jeff), who had been very active in the organizing campaign, started posting derogatory statements on their Facebook accounts about their supervisor. Over the course of two months, the comments became increasingly negative and started implying violence. For example, one post said, "If somebody mentally attacks you, and you stab him in the face 14 or 16 times, … that constitutes self-defence doesn't it????" Another said: "Don't spend your money at ABC Company as they are crooks out to hose you."

   Together, the employees had hundreds of "friends" on Facebook, including several co-workers and a manager at ABC, who alerted the employer about these postings. After monitoring the postings for several weeks, ABC spoke to Bob and Jeff to hear what they had to say. Both initially denied their involvement, saying that their accounts had been hacked. Finding their explanation not credible, ABC decided it had just cause to dismiss them, despite their previously clean disciplinary records. They filed a grievance with their union, challenging their dismissal for cause.

   Describe the arguments that both the employer and the union, on behalf of Bob and Jeff, could make regarding the alleged just cause. Who do you think would be successful and why?

11. Three Toronto firefighters were fired in 2013 for making sexist tweets that were degrading to women. Examples of the tweets included the following:
   - One quote from the TV show *The Office* read: "Reject a woman and she will never let it go. One of the many defects of their kind. Also weak arms."

- Another was a line from the TV show *South Park*: "I'd never let a woman kick my a—. If she tried something, I'd be like HEY! You get your b— a— back in the kitchen and make me some pie!"
- One tweet, referencing a woman ordering coffee and overusing the word "like," queried: "[W]ould [swatting] her in the back of the head be considered abuse or a way to reset the brain?"

City officials indicated that these and similar tweets violated the city's social media guidelines, which state that employees should "not engage in harassment, personal attacks or abuse toward individuals or organizations," and "not use language that is discriminatory, hateful, or violent towards identifiable groups or that incites others to discriminate [or] practice hate or violence."

The three unionized firefighters grieved their dismissal. Referring to the principles discussed in the chapter, discuss whether the employer had just cause to dismiss these employees.

12. Sasha was a bank employee with 21 years' service whose IT role entitled her to virtually unlimited access to confidential documents. One day Sasha decided to access sensitive information concerning priority parking, without permission, to satisfy her curiosity about where she was on the list for the most prized parking spots. As soon as the employer found out about this action, it dismissed Sasha for just cause. Sasha sued the employer for wrongful dismissal, arguing that as a long-service employee with an unblemished work record, dismissing her for just cause for a single, isolated act was a disproportionate response. Did the employer have just cause in your view?

REFERENCES

Acumen Law Corporation v Ojanen, 2019 BCSC 1352.

Air Canada and International Association of Machinists and Aerospace Workers, District Lodge 148 (1978) 18 LAC (2d) 400.

Alberta Human Rights Act, RSA 2000, c A-25.5.

Bannister v General Motors of Canada, 1994 CanLII 7390 (Ont Sup Ct J), rev'd 1998 CanLII 7151 (Ont CA).

Bell Technical Solutions v Communications, Energy and Paperworkers Union of Canada, 2012 CanLII 51468 (Ont LA).

Boulet v Federated Co-operatives Ltd, 2001 MBQB 174.

Canadian HR Reporter, "Employer Can't Bank on Moonlighting Employee," *Canadian Employment Law Today* (5 October 2011) at 8.

Caskanette v Bong-Keun Choi Dentistry Professional Corporation, 2015 CanLII 31307 (Ont Sup Ct J (Sm Cl Ct)).

Chaba v Ensign Drilling Inc, 2002 ABPC 131, 116 ACWS (3d) 382.

Chatham-Kent (Municipality) v CAW Local 217 (Clark Grievance), [2007] OLLA No 135 (Williamson).

Cie minière Québec Cartier v Quebec (Grievances arbitrator), [1995] 2 SCR 1095.

Clarke v Syncrude Canada Ltd, 2013 ABQB 252.

"Common-Law Doctrine of Just Cause Provides a Blueprint for Employers," *Canadian Employment Law Today* 409 (17 March 2004) at 3197.

Ditchburn v Landis & Gyr Powers Ltd, 1995 CanLII 7290 (Ont Sup Ct J), rev'd in part 1997 CanLII 1500 (Ont CA).

Donaldson v Philippine Airlines Inc (1985), 10 OAC 217 (CA).

Dryco Drywall Supplies Ltd v Teamsters Local Union No 213 (Sobieski Grievance), 2013 CanLII 7695 (BCLA).

Dziecielski v Lighting Dimensions Inc, 2012 ONSC 1877, aff'd 2013 ONCA 565.

Echlin, Randall, & Christine Thomlinson, *For Better or For Worse: A Practical Guide to Canadian Employment Law*, 3rd ed (Toronto: Canada Law Book, 2011).

Employment Standards Act, RSBC 1996, c 113.

Employment Standards Code, RSA 2000, c E-9.

Essery v John Lecky & Co (1986), 60 Nfld & PEIR 219 (PEISC).

EV Logistics v Retail Wholesale Union, Local 580 (Discharge Grievance), [2008] BCCAAA No 22 (Laing).

Farahani, Sheri, "Employee Use of Blogging and Social Networking Sites: Understanding and Managing Threats to Employers," in *The Six-Minute Employment Lawyer 2009* (Toronto: Law Society of Ontario, 2009) 16-1.

Filion Wakely Thorup Angeletti, "Ontario Court of Appeal Upholds for Cause Dismissal of Employee Caught Driving Company Vehicle While Intoxicated" (14 December 2013), online: <http://filion.on.ca/ontario-court-of-appeal-upholds-for-cause-dismissal-of-employee-caught-driving-company-vehicle-while-intoxicated> (offline as of July 2020).

George v Cowichan Tribes, 2015 BCSC 513.

Graham v Canadian Cancer Society, 1995 CanLII 2866 (BCSC).

Grievance of "R": Discharge for Contents of a Personal Blog, 2008 (Alta Arb Bd), online: <http://onlinedb.lancasterhouse.com/images/up-Ponak_GovtofAlberta.pdf>.

Harris, Lorna, "Staff Fired After Bad-Mouthing Colleagues, Management in Blog," *Canadian HR Reporter* (8 September 2008) at 18.

Health Sciences Association of Alberta v Alberta Health Services, 2010 CanLII 96491 (Alta GAA).

Henry v Foxco Ltd, 2002 NBQB 277, rev'd 2004 NBCA 22.

Henson v Champion Feed Services Ltd, 2005 ABQB 215.

Hoopes, Jaime H, "Court Awards $50,000 in Aggravated Damages for Unfair, Bullying, Bad Faith Conduct" (3 September 2019), online: *Harris* <https://harrisco.com/court-awards-50000-in-aggravated-damages-for-unfair-bullying-bad-faith-conduct>.

Human Rights Code, RSBC 1996, c 210.

Human Rights Code, RSO 1990, c H.19.

Kelly v Linamar Corporation, 2005 CanLII 42487 (Ont Sup Ct J).

Labour Relations Code, RSA 2000, c L-1.

Labour Relations Code, RSBC 1996, c 244.

Letendre v Deines Micro-Film Services Ltd, 2001 ABQB 26.

Litster v British Columbia Ferry Corp and Taylor, 2003 BCSC 557.

Lowery v Calgary (City of), 2002 ABCA 237.

McKinley v BC Tel, 2001 SCC 38.

Mutton v AOT Canada Ltd, [2002] OJ No 696 (QL) (Sup Ct J).

Obeng v Canada Safeway Limited, 2009 BCSC 8.

Occupational Health and Safety Act, RSA 2000, c O-2.

Occupational Health and Safety Regulation, BC Reg 296/97.

Ontario (Human Rights Commission) v Gaines Pet Foods Corp, 1993 CanLII 5605 Ont Sup Ct J).

Ouimette v Lily Cups Ltd (1990), 12 CHRR D/19 (Ont Bd Inq).

Patterson v Bank of Nova Scotia, 2011 BCPC 120.

Pigott, Mary, "Employers Need to Address Workplace Blogging" (May 2005), online: *HRinfodesk* <http://www.hrinfodesk.com/articles/addressworkplacebloggingl.htm>. Provided by Great Library Digest from the Law Society of Upper Canada.

Pushor Mitchell LLP, "Employers Addressing Employee Blogging" (3 April 2006), online: <http://www.pushormitchell.com/2006/04/employers-addressing-employee-blogging>.

Rudner, Stuart, "Digging a Deeper Hole," *Canadian Employment Law Today* 530 (25 March 2009) at 1.

Soost v Merrill Lynch Canada Inc, 2009 ABQB 591; rev'd in part *Merrill Lynch Canada Inc v Soost*, 2010 ABCA 251.

Tanner, Adrienne, "How #MeToo Changed the Workplace" (12 November 2019) *Pivot Magazine*, online: *CPA Canada* <https://www.cpacanada.ca/en/news/pivot-magazine/2019-11-12-after-metoo>.

Teck Coal v United Mine Workers of America, Local 1656, 2010 CanLII 98274 (Alta GAA).

Toronto (City) v Toronto Professional Firefighters Association, Local 3888, 2014 CanLII 62879 (Ont LA).

Whitford v Agrium Inc, 2006 ABQB 726.

Workers' Compensation Act, RSA 2000, c W-15.

Workers Compensation Act, RSBC 1996, c 492.

Dismissal Without Cause and Wrongful Dismissal

14

LEARNING OUTCOMES

After completing this chapter, you will be able to:

- Understand the relationship between statutory and common law notice of termination requirements and how to determine notice periods under each.
- Identify the benefits and drawbacks of providing working notice rather than pay in lieu of reasonable notice to a dismissed employee.
- Understand the definition of "temporary layoff" under employment standards legislation and cases in which a layoff may trigger notice requirements.
- Explain the implications of mass notice of termination and notice requirements where there is a change in ownership of the employer organization.
- Identify when frustration of contract occurs.
- Understand how to structure a separation package.
- State the types of damages that can be awarded to a wrongfully dismissed employee.
- Discuss an employee's common law duty to mitigate their damages after dismissal.
- Explain constructive dismissal.
- Identify strategies for avoiding wrongful dismissal claims.
- Outline issues related to providing employee references and record of employment.

Introduction

As discussed in Chapter 6, employment standards legislation gives employees a basic level of protection in setting the terms and conditions of employment. Although the parties to an employment contract may negotiate standards that are more beneficial to an employee than those set out in the legislation, they may not agree to standards that are less generous.

Under employment standards legislation, employees are entitled to receive a minimum amount of either notice of termination or termination pay, except where the termination is for "just cause" or falls within one of the limited statutory exceptions. Unless an employer is able to prove that an employee fundamentally breached the terms of the employment contract, any dismissal must proceed on a without-cause basis. Dismissal with cause is covered in Chapter 13.

The statutory notice pay requirements are, however, just minimums. The common law imposes much higher notice or compensation obligations on employers where the employment contract is silent about notice. The employment contract is the first place to look for notice requirements agreed upon between an employer and an employee. However, if an employment contract lacks a provision that governs notice of termination, or if the provision is unenforceable, an employer has an implied duty to provide reasonable notice of termination or pay in lieu of reasonable notice under the common law. When the employment contract is oral, the employer also has an implied duty to provide the employee with reasonable notice. What is "reasonable" depends on the facts of each case, but courts have developed a number of factors to consider in determining the appropriate length of the notice period. The reasonable notice standard under the common law exists *in addition to*, and usually significantly exceeds, the minimum statutory standards for termination.

The purpose of providing termination notice, when the employer does not have just cause to terminate the employee, is to allow an employee time, while still being paid, to look for another job.

As noted above, statutory termination requirements are modest compared with the common law obligation to provide reasonable notice of termination. For example, a middle manager with 20 years' service with an employer is entitled to 8 weeks' notice of termination or termination pay under Alberta's *Employment Standards Code* (ESC) and British Columbia's *Employment Standards Act* (ESA). The courts, by contrast, would likely award this manager between 12 and 20 months' worth of "reasonable notice." Generally speaking, an employee in this situation who felt that the employer had failed to offer an acceptable separation package would sue for wrongful dismissal rather than file a claim under the ESC or the ESA.

For many employees, however, the statutory termination notice and termination pay requirements provide the only meaningful entitlements. For example, an entry-level employee who is laid off after two years of service is entitled to two weeks' termination notice or pay in lieu under employment standards legislation. If the employer fails to provide this notice or pay in lieu, the employee will probably seek to enforce their statutory rights by filing a claim. It is unlikely that the employee would hire a lawyer and launch a time-consuming and expensive lawsuit in the hope of obtaining a few more weeks' pay in lieu of reasonable notice under the common law. That said, an employee who is not intimidated by the court system could file a claim in small claims court at a much lower cost.

While most employees fall between these two extremes, in general only relatively senior employees or those with many years of service with an employer choose to go to court to assert their right to reasonable notice under the common law.

Overview of Statutory Notice/Compensation Requirements

In Alberta, an employer must provide between one and eight weeks' written notice of termination (or pay in lieu of that notice period) when dismissing an employee who has been employed by the employer for more than three months. The length of the notice period depends on the length of an employee's service. Exceptions to this requirement are limited and are discussed below, under the heading "Exceptions to Notice of Termination Requirements." In British Columbia (BC), under section 63 of the ESA, an employer is not required to give notice, but it must pay an employee who has been working for more than three months "compensation for length of service" unless the employer provides a comparable amount of notice or dismisses the employee for just cause (or the employee quits or retires).

An employer can choose to provide an employee with (1) advance notice of termination and have the employee work throughout the notice period ("working notice"), (2) wages in lieu of notice in Alberta or, in BC, compensation for length of service (CLOS), or (3) a combination of notice and pay in lieu or CLOS. Employers commonly give "working notice" when they dismiss many employees at the same time for economic reasons. When dismissing employees individually, however, employers usually provide departing employees with pay in lieu of notice.

In Alberta, but not in BC, employees are required to give notice when they quit. Under section 58 of the ESC, an employee who has been employed for more than three months must provide written notice of termination to the employer: one week if employed for more than three months but less than two years, and two weeks if employed for two years or more. There are a number of exceptions to this requirement, including the following:

- there exists a custom or practice in an industry respecting notice of termination that is contrary to the requirements noted above;
- the employee's health or safety would be in danger if they continued employment;
- the continuation of work has become impossible as a result of unforeseeable and unpreventable circumstances beyond the control of the employee;
- the employee has been temporarily laid off;
- the employee is not provided with work by the employer by reason of strike or lockout;

- the employee is employed on a casual basis and has the opportunity to accept or decline temporary work requested by the employer; or
- the employee's wage rate, overtime rate, or holiday or vacation pay has been reduced.

In Alberta, when an employee provides notice of termination that is at least equivalent to the minimum notice required under section 58 of the ESC, the employer may, under section 59, expedite the termination by paying the employee for the remaining notice period. If an employee has provided the employer with the minimum written notice of termination, the employer may advance the termination by paying an amount at least equal to the wages that the employee would have received if the employee had worked regular hours to the end of the notice period. However, if an employee gives advance notice of resignation that is *longer than the minimum* required under the ESC *but less than (or equal to) the notice required of the employer* when the employer is initiating the termination (and the employer wishes to advance the termination date), the employer must pay the regular wages to the end of the notice period provided by the employee. In the rare case where the employee gives notice of termination that is longer than that required of either the employee or the employer under the ESC, the employer may terminate the relationship as soon as the employee has worked the notice period that would have been required of the employer had the employer initiated the termination. In other words, the employer is not required to provide additional notice.

Once notice of termination has been given by either the employer or the employee, neither wages, nor wage rates, nor any other term or condition of employment may be reduced by the employer under section 61 of the ESC. In BC, a similar prohibition exists under section 67(2) of the ESA for notice by an employer. After the employer gives notice, it may not alter an employee's wage rate or any other condition of employment without the written consent of the employee.

Temporary Layoffs

A temporary layoff is a temporary ceasing of work with intent to recall. Under section 62 of Alberta's ESC, an employer that wishes to maintain an employment relationship without terminating the employment of an employee may temporarily lay off the employee. However, if the layoff lasts 60 consecutive days or longer, the layoff is no longer temporary and the employer is considered to have terminated the employee and must provide statutory termination pay. This 60-day period may be extended if a longer layoff and recall time frame is contemplated within the terms of an applicable collective agreement, or if the employer, through an agreement with the employee, continues making regular payments to or on behalf of the employee, such as pension contributions or employee benefit package contributions.

In short, there are several different circumstances in which a layoff is defined as "temporary." The common thread is that an employer is allowed longer layoff periods before triggering the termination provisions if it shows a continuing commitment to the employment relationship.

The law in BC is set out in sections 1, 62–63, and 65 of the ESA. It treats temporary layoffs more narrowly than Alberta's ESC. There is no general right of an employer to temporarily lay off an employee. An employer may temporarily lay off an employee only if the contract of employment specifically provides for it or if the employee agrees to it in a particular instance, or where temporary layoffs are a standard practice in the employer's industry. Section 1 of the ESA defines a "temporary layoff" to mean either (1) for employees under a collective agreement, a layoff that goes beyond the date on which the employee has a right of recall under the agreement; or (2) for other employees, a layoff that lasts up to 13 weeks in any period of 20 consecutive weeks. In BC, a layoff is not limited to full layoff. If an employee earns less than 50 percent of regular wages during a week, section 62 of the ESA deems that week to be a "week of layoff."

The CLOS requirement in section 63 of the ESA and the group-termination notice requirement in section 64 apply only to employees who are terminated, not to employees during a period of legitimate temporary layoff. However, if a temporary layoff exceeds the upper limit in section 1 (more than 13 weeks in a 20-week period), section 63(5) specifies that this layoff is in fact a termination, with the termination date being the start of the layoff. The compensation rules apply.

Section 65 of the BC ESA also deals with temporary workers, seasonal industries, and other employment arrangements in which work hours are not usually regular or continuous throughout the year. It specifies that the compensation and notice provisions in sections 63 and 64 do not apply in such situations. These are not technically temporary layoffs but are worth noting here.

Continuity of Employment

Both Alberta's ESC and BC's ESA address the consequences of a change in an employer's status on an employee's length of service. Section 5 of Alberta's ESC states that

> the employment of an employee is deemed to be continuous and uninterrupted when a business, undertaking or other activity or part of it is sold, leased, transferred or merged or if it continues to operate under a receiver or receiver-manager.

Section 97 of BC's ESA includes a similar provision:

> If all or part of a business or a substantial part of the entire assets of a business is disposed of, the employment of an employee of the business is deemed … to be continuous and uninterrupted by the disposition.

In both provinces, if an employee continues to work for a new owner of the former employer's business, the employee retains their rights and length of service as if there had been no sale or transfer of the business. For example, an employee who worked for Seller Company for five years and continued working for Buyer Company for another four years is entitled to termination notice/pay in lieu/CLOS on the basis of nine years' service. (Note that because the employee's employment continued under Buyer Company, Seller Company did not have a statutory obligation to provide termination notice [or pay in lieu/CLOS] at the time of the sale.)

An exception to this rule applies if there is a gap in employment. In Alberta, the gap must be more than three months. For example, if Buyer Company, operating in Alberta, hires an employee more than three months after either the employee's last day of work with Seller Company or the date of Seller Company's sale to Buyer Company (whichever is earlier), the employee does not retain their years of service with Seller Company. This three-month rule affects the employee's length of service for the purpose of calculating termination notice or pay entitlement and other employment standards rights that depend on length of service, such as vacation time. This exception can also apply in the absence of a sale: if a person works for an employer for three years, resigns, and is then rehired more than three months later, only the employment after rehiring is taken into account for the purpose of entitlements under Alberta's ESC. BC does not have a similar three-month rule. However, gaps due to temporary layoff or unpaid leave do not affect the calculation of the employee's length of service for the purposes of the ESA's rules for CLOS or group termination.

Communicating Termination Notice

Where notice of termination by the employer is required, it must be in writing; it must be addressed to the employee; and it must be given in person or by mail, fax, or email, as long as delivery can be proven. In Alberta, posting the notice on a bulletin board is not sufficient.

In BC, there are additional requirements under section 64 of the ESA for notice of group terminations. The notice must go to each employee, the Minister of Labour, and, if applicable, the employees' union. The notice must also specify how many employees are being terminated, the effective date of termination, and reasons for termination (s 64(2)).

Working Notice

An employer that provides working notice rather than pay in lieu (Alberta) or CLOS (BC) must abide by the following rules during the notice period:

1. the employer cannot reduce an employee's wage rate or alter any other term or condition of employment; and
2. the employer must pay the employee the wages they are entitled to, and this amount cannot be less than the employee's regular wages for a regular workweek; in Alberta, an employee who does not have a regular workweek is entitled to the average amount that they earned in the 13 weeks immediately before notice was given.

Calculating Statutory and Common Law Notice

Alberta's ESC sets out a minimum statutory notice requirement. Since 1995, BC's ESA has taken a different approach. Except for group terminations of 50 or more employees, the ESA does not require an employer to give notice; instead, it requires the employer to pay an employee "compensation for length of service" (CLOS). The duty to do so is removed if the employer meets certain notice requirements (or dismisses an employee for just cause). If the employer does give notice, the Alberta and BC regimes can look quite similar. But the CLOS is not equivalent to the common law "payment in lieu of notice"; it is a form of "deferred compensation" for past work. Therefore, in the following discussion, the Alberta and BC rules will be considered separately.

In both Alberta and BC, the statutory requirements are triggered when an employee's employment is terminated. Termination occurs when an employer:

1. dismisses or stops employing the employee (including bankruptcy or insolvency situations);
2. lays the employee off for a period exceeding that of a temporary layoff, as defined in the applicable statute (see above); or
3. constructively dismisses the employee and the employee resigns in response within a reasonable period.

Constructive dismissal occurs when an employer makes a fundamental change to an employee's job without providing reasonable notice and without explaining the consequences of rejecting the change or obtaining the employee's consent. Constructive dismissal is discussed in depth later in this chapter and in Chapter 11.

Alberta's Statutory Notice Requirements

In Alberta, the statutory requirements relating to termination notice or pay in lieu are covered under sections 54–64 of the ESC.

Individual notice periods range from one to eight weeks, depending on an employee's length of service. An employer may provide an employee with a combination of written notice and termination pay as long as together they equal the required number of weeks' notice. Alternatively, the employer may provide an employee with payment in lieu of notice for the entire period.

The Alberta statute requires employers to provide minimum notice periods to employees who are being terminated, unless they fall within one of the limited exceptions discussed below under the heading "Exceptions to Notice of Termination Requirements."

In Alberta, the minimum notice periods for employer-initiated terminations are as follows:

- less than 3 months' service: nil;
- 3 months' but less than 2 years' service: 1 week;
- 2 years' but less than 4 years' service: 2 weeks;
- 4 years' but less than 6 years' service: 4 weeks;
- 6 years' but less than 8 years' service: 5 weeks;
- 8 years' but less than 10 years' service: 6 weeks; and
- 10 or more years' service: 8 weeks.

The employer must continue paying the employee's benefits during the statutory notice period, including a situation in which the employee receives termination pay instead of working during all or part of the notice period.

Sample Calculation of Termination Pay for Alberta

Assume that Caitlin earns $700 per week by working 35 hours at $20 per hour. After six years' employment, she is about to have her employment terminated. The employer wants to know how much notice or pay in lieu of notice she is entitled to. Since Caitlin has worked between six and eight years, she is entitled to five weeks' notice of termination or pay in lieu of notice. The employer has a choice: it can give her five weeks' notice and require her to work during the notice period; it can give her five weeks' termination pay and ask her to leave immediately; or it can provide a combination of pay and notice, provided that it accounts to Caitlin for the entire five-week period.

If the employer chooses to provide pay in lieu of notice for the entire amount, it owes Caitlin $3,500 ($700 × 5 weeks = $3,500). It must also provide vacation pay on the termination pay. Given that Caitlin has been employed for over six years, she is entitled to a vacation payout equivalent to 6 percent ($3,500 × 6% = $210). Caitlin is therefore entitled to receive $3,710 ($3,500 + $210 = $3,710) pay in lieu of notice when her employment is terminated without notice.

In Alberta, when appropriate termination notice has been provided by either the employer or the employee, the employer must pay the employee's earnings not later than three consecutive days after the last day of employment. When the employer or the employee terminates the employee's employment and no notice is required, the employer must pay the employee's earnings not later than ten consecutive days after the last day of employment. When an employee is required to provide notice, but does not provide the required notice, the employer must pay the employee's earnings not later than ten consecutive days after the date on which the notice would have expired, had it been given.

Employment standards termination pay is not required where an employee has quit (and the resignation is not a constructive dismissal), retires, or is dismissed for just cause.

British Columbia: Compensation for Length of Service and Notice of Group Termination

In BC, sections 63–64 of the ESA set out the requirements for termination. Section 63 applies to all employees whose employment is terminated by an employer, even if the termination is part of a group termination. The employer must provide CLOS payments to all employees based on their years of work for the employer (as set out below). Section 64 is an additional requirement for group terminations. Unlike section 63, it requires notice of termination or pay in lieu of notice. We will consider each requirement in turn.

Section 63 of the ESA requires CLOS payments as follows:

- less than 3 months' service: nil (no CLOS is required in this period);
- 3 months' but less than 1 year's service: 1 week's pay;
- 1 year's but less than 3 years' service: 2 weeks' pay;

- 3 years' but less than 4 years' service: 3 weeks' pay;
- 4 years' but less than 5 years' service: 4 weeks' pay;
- 5 years' but less than 6 years' service: 5 weeks' pay;
- 6 years' but less than 7 years' service: 6 weeks' pay;
- 7 years' but less than 8 years' service: 7 weeks' pay; and
- 8 or more years' service: 8 weeks' pay.

The pay is based on the employee's regular wage. It includes vacation pay, but it excludes overtime and weeks in which the employee's hours were shortened by illness or other reasons. If an employee's hours varied from week to week (compared with, e.g., a regular 40-hour week), section 63(4) requires the employer to base the CLOS on the average weekly pay for the last eight weeks that the employee worked "normal or average hours of work." The BC Employment Standards Branch, which is the body that settles disputes about the interpretation of section 63, interprets this requirement to exclude weeks the employee was off work due to illness or had reduced hours in a given week due to a change in the schedule.

As an alternative to paying CLOS, an employer may provide written working notice of termination to the employee (s 63(3)(a)). If the written notice period matches the number of weeks required for a CLOS payment, the employer does not need to provide CLOS. An employer also has the option of giving notice for a portion of the required weeks and paying CLOS for the rest (s 63(3)(b)).

An employer does not need to pay CLOS (or to give notice instead) if an employee quits or retires or is dismissed for just cause (s 63(3)(c)).

If a BC employer gives notice rather than pays CLOS, it must continue paying the employee's regular wages and benefits during the notice period. An employer must pay CLOS, as well as any back wages owing, within 48 hours if the employer terminates employment or within six days if the employee terminates (s 18).

Sample Calculation of CLOS Pay for British Columbia

Assume that Roger earns $700 per week by working 35 hours at $20 per hour. After six years' employment, he is about to be laid off indefinitely. The employer wants to know how much it will have to pay him in CLOS—or how much notice he is entitled to. Since Roger has worked between six and seven years, he is entitled to six weeks' wages as CLOS. The employer has a choice: it can give him six weeks' notice and require him to work during the notice period; or it can pay him the six weeks' CLOS and ask him to leave immediately; or it can provide a combination of CLOS payment and notice, provided that it accounts to Roger for the entire six-week period.

If the employer chooses to provide the full amount of CLOS instead of giving notice, it owes Roger $4,200 ($700 × 6 weeks = $4,200). It must also provide vacation pay on the CLOS payment at the rate of 6 percent ($4,200 × 6% = $252). Roger is therefore entitled to receive $4,452 ($4,200 + $252 = $4,452) as CLOS when his employment is terminated without notice. If he also pursues a claim in court for wrongful dismissal, any award of damages that he wins will be on top of this CLOS payment: it is not deducted from the award.

Although the CLOS-or-notice rule can have a similar effect to Alberta's statutory minimum notice, there is a basic difference in approach between the two. The BC Employment Standards Branch and courts have affirmed that CLOS is separate from a contractual requirement to pay severance or from the common law concept of payment in lieu of notice as damages for wrongful dismissal, even though notice replaces the need for CLOS. Payment in lieu is wages for the period after the dismissal (equal to a reasonable notice period); in contrast, CLOS is a statutory benefit, a form of "deferred compensation" that is treated as wages for past work.

Employer's should pay particular attention to section 64 of the ESA, which applies to "group terminations" of 50 or more employees. If an employer dismisses 50–100 employees at a single location within a two-month period, the employer must provide 8 weeks' written notice (with pay during the notice period); 12 weeks' notice if it is 101–300 employees; and 16 weeks' notice if it is 301 or more employees. The employer can, under section 64(4), opt instead to give "termination pay" equal to the required number of weeks times the employee's usual weekly wages (s 1 defines "termination pay").

The obligation under section 64 for notice or termination pay is in addition to the CLOS requirement in section 63. So if an employer dismisses 60 employees and one of those employees had been working there for five and a half years, the employer must give that person 13 weeks' notice or 13 weeks' pay (eight weeks under s 64, plus five weeks of CLOS under s 63).

Reasonable Notice in Common Law

Even if an employer fulfills the statutory requirements for termination set out above, the employer must assess what constitutes reasonable notice under the common law. The answer to this question depends on the unique circumstances of each employment relationship, but it is almost always much higher than the statutory minimums in Alberta or the notice-instead-of-CLOS provisions in BC.

The classic case on the issue of reasonable notice is *Bardal v The Globe and Mail Ltd* (1960), which highlights the main (although not the only) factors that affect the length of the reasonable notice period:

1. the employee's age;
2. the employee's position;
3. the employee's length of service;
4. the employee's level of compensation; and
5. the availability of similar employment given the employee's experience, training, and qualifications.

Although *Bardal* lists a number of relevant considerations in determining the reasonable notice period, many employers think there is a "rule of thumb" that employees who are dismissed without just cause are generally entitled to—for example, one month's notice (or pay in lieu) for each year of service. However, in 1999 the Ontario Court of Appeal rejected this rule in *Minott v O'Shanter Development*

Company Ltd, stating that it undermined the flexibility of the *Bardal* test by overemphasizing the length of service factor. Although one month per year is often the amount a court finds, the case law demonstrates that employees who have been working for short periods often receive more than one month's notice for each year of service, while long-term employees frequently receive less than that "standard."

Historically, senior, managerial, and executive employees generally received longer notice periods than other employees. This reflected the traditional view that it is more difficult for them to find jobs comparable to those from which they were dismissed. In fact, in the past it took exceptional circumstances for a lower-level employee to be awarded more than 12 months' pay in lieu of notice. Similarly, there was an unofficial cap for senior or highly skilled employees of 24 months. More recently, however, courts have questioned these ceilings, as well as the emphasis given to the "character of employment" factor in determining reasonable notice damages (see e.g. *Dussault v Imperial Oil Limited* [2018]). Notice periods are starting to harmonize across a range of types of job.

Courts also generally assume that it will be more difficult for older workers to find comparable employment. Accordingly, an employee who is dismissed when they are in their 50s, for example, will often receive a longer notice period than a similarly placed employee who is much younger at the time of dismissal. Reasonable notice awards to older workers have also been affected by the end of mandatory retirement at age 65. For example, in *Kotecha v Affinia Canada ULC* (2014), a 70-year-old machine operator with 20 years of service was awarded 18 months' pay in lieu of notice. This decision illustrates that being over 65 is no longer a barrier to receiving significant reasonable notice damages. It also reflects the declining importance given to "character of employment" in determining the reasonable notice period, as Kotecha was a non-managerial employee (Meehan, 2014).

With respect to the availability of similar employment, cases have held that the reasonable notice period is not determined by the actual length of time it takes an employee to obtain a new position. *Bain v ICBC* demonstrates that an employer is not required to fully compensate an employee for having the misfortune of entering the job market when comparable jobs are particularly difficult to find.

CASE IN POINT

Appropriate Notice Period Not Equivalent to Time It Takes to Find a New Job

Bain v ICBC, 2002 BCSC 1445

Facts

The 57-year-old Bain had worked as a junior manager for seven years in the employer's information technology (IT) department when the employer dismissed him as a result of restructuring. The employer gave him seven months' pay in lieu of notice, but he felt this was inadequate and sued for additional damages. Because of the scarcity of IT positions in the current economic climate, he argued that he should receive 18 to 20 months' notice instead.

Relevant Issue

Whether wrongful dismissal damages should reflect the current economic climate.

Decision

The BC Supreme Court held that the appropriate notice period is not equivalent to the length of time it takes a dismissed employee to find a new job. Otherwise, employers would be held solely responsible for the lack of positions available during an economic downturn. A court should consider a lack of job opportunities in determining reasonable notice, but this factor should not receive undue weight. In this case, the Court held that Bain was entitled to 12 months' notice on the basis of his age, position, length of service, marketable skills, and—to some extent—the current economic climate.

Another factor that affects the availability of similar employment is the degree to which the employee's position is specialized. In *Jamieson v Finning International Inc* (2009), the Court awarded the employee a longer notice period because his job skills as a millyard systems manager in the heavy equipment supply industry were so specialized that there were limited opportunities for him to find similar employment.

In addition to the primary factors listed in *Bardal*, there are several secondary factors that courts consider relevant in determining reasonable notice. For example, if an employer lures an employee away from a secure position and later dismisses the employee without just cause, a court may require the employer to provide a longer notice period than would have been necessary without such an enticement. This is especially true for short-service employees.

The fact that an employee is pregnant at the time of dismissal is another "*Bardal*-type" factor that can be used to determine a reasonable notice period. Although an employee's pregnancy should not be an overriding consideration, the Court in *Ivens v Automodular Assemblies Inc* (2002) found that being pregnant probably will affect an employee's ability to find a new job and therefore should be considered. The Court awarded the 27-year-old pregnant employee, who had two months of service with the employer as an assembler, eight weeks' pay in lieu of notice. It felt that this was the appropriate reasonable notice period when the factor of her pregnancy was balanced with her type of work, probationary status, age, and length of service.

Other factors that may be taken into consideration include an employee's poor health, an employee's poor language skills, and the employer's refusal, without justification, to provide a letter of reference. In *Ostrow v Abacus Management Corporation Mergers and Acquisitions* (2014), the Court confirmed another relevant factor: the existence of a non-competition clause in the employment contract. In that case, the Court cited the non-competition clause as one of the factors it considered in awarding the plaintiff, who had been employed by the defendant for only nine months, reasonable notice damages of six months. Rejecting the employer's argument that the non-compete provision should not be considered because it had not sought to enforce it, the Court held that it was the fact that the plaintiff was led to believe that he was bound by the clause that made it relevant in establishing the reasonable notice period (at para 84).

In the past, some courts have recognized the notion of "ballpark damages" in deciding the length of reasonable notice. This meant that where an employer offered an employee a separation package that was within the range of what a court considered reasonable and fair, it would defer to the employer's assessment. However, more recently this notion has been rejected by several courts because it allows an employer to usurp the court's function of establishing notice periods. For example, in the 2003 case of *UPM-Kymmene Miramichi Inc v Walsh*, the New Brunswick Court of Appeal upheld an award of 28 months, even though it was not much higher than the employer's offer of 24 months' pay in lieu of notice.

Which Is Better: Working Notice or Pay in Lieu of Notice?

An employer is entitled to choose whether to pay an employee while they work during the reasonable notice period (working notice) or to pay the employee a sum that is equal to the amount they would have earned during the reasonable notice period, including both wages and benefits, and to ask the employee to leave immediately. An employer may also combine these options, provided that the combination of payment and notice equals the notice period to which the employee is entitled under law.

Providing working notice by giving employees notice and requiring them to work through the notice period may seem more cost effective for the employer than providing pay in lieu of notice. In some situations, working notice is a sensible decision for an employer. For example, where an employer indefinitely lays off many employees because of its economic circumstances, the affected employees may be able to remain productive and motivated throughout this period. It will help if the employer continues to treat these employees with respect and does not leave them "out of the loop" during the working notice period.

Employees who work during the notice period should be given generous opportunities to search for a new job during working hours by, for example, making telephone calls, sending faxes and emails, and going to interviews. There have been few cases in this area. However, in *Kelly v Monenco Consultants Ltd* (1987), the employer gave the employee working notice while he was on assignment in Nigeria. The Court found that the notice was illusory because he had no practical opportunity to look for a new job until he completed his Nigerian assignment. As a consequence, the employee was awarded pay in lieu of reasonable notice.

On the other hand, there are situations in which it is inappropriate for an employer to require an employee to work throughout the notice period. For example, where an employer dismisses an employee as a result of performance problems that fall short of just cause, it may be counterproductive to leave the employee in the workplace during the notice period. It is likely that the employee's efforts will, if anything, deteriorate further, and their attitude will affect the morale of the remaining staff. The case for providing pay in lieu of notice is even stronger where the employee works with sensitive business information, in sales, with customers, or with the public. *Elg v Stirling Doors* is a cautionary tale for employers who decide to leave an employee who is dismissed for having an antagonistic attitude in the workplace during the statutory notice period.

CASE IN POINT

Working Notice Is Not Always Appropriate

Elg v Stirling Doors, [2002] OJ No 2995 (QL) (Sup Ct J)

Facts

Elg, a 54-year-old manual labourer, had worked for a manufacturer of kitchen cupboards for approximately 14 years. She was one of eight employees. In late 1999, the employer sensed that morale in the workplace was deteriorating as a result of Elg's attitude. The problem worsened when the employer addressed it in a meeting with Elg. Several weeks later, the employer dismissed her, providing eight weeks' notice as required under the Ontario *Employment Standards Act*.

During the first two days of her working notice period, Elg did little work and attempted to slow production down. When the employer confronted her, she told him that her notice period would be "eight weeks of hell," and there was nothing he could do about it. She also said, "You are the kind of employer that employees shoot." The employer reported the statement to the police and immediately dismissed the employee on the ground of wilful misconduct. Elg sued for wrongful dismissal.

Relevant Issue

Whether Elg's conduct during the working notice period constituted just cause for immediate dismissal.

Decision

The Ontario Superior Court found that the employer lacked just cause for dismissal. In the Court's view, "working notice is an institution almost invariably predestined to fail." Elg's conduct was a predictable consequence of the employer's decision to provide termination notice rather than pay in lieu. Before the controversy, Elg had been a competent worker. There was no criticism of her work or attitude before the 1999 meeting, and the employer had never disciplined her. The Court found that eight weeks' notice was insufficient to satisfy the employer's common law obligation to provide reasonable notice. Elg was entitled to eight months' notice instead.

The decision in *Elg v Stirling Doors* appears to be somewhat anomalous because it effectively questions the concept of working notice, a strategy that can benefit both the employer and the employee, provided that both parties act in a reasonable manner. However, *Elg* underscores the need for an employer to exercise caution in deciding to provide working notice instead of pay in lieu to an employee who is dismissed for disruptive behaviour.

Structuring a Separation Package

An employer that decides to dismiss an employee immediately and provide a separation package instead of working notice must consider how best to structure the package. One option is to offer an employee a lump sum that reflects both minimum employment standards and common law notice requirements. This approach has both advantages and disadvantages.

On the positive side, many employees prefer to receive lump-sum payments and may be willing to settle for a smaller total amount than if the employer paid the parting settlement over time. One of the disadvantages for an employer is that it must pay the employee a potentially large sum of money at one time.

Alternatively, an employer may continue an employee's salary and benefits during the notice period. In this case, there should be a written statement specifically indicating that these payments include any statutory entitlements under Alberta's ESC or BC's ESA. The termination letter or agreement should also state that if the employee finds new employment, or self-employment, during the notice period, these salary continuation payments will end. The arrangement could also provide that the dismissed employee will receive a final lump-sum payment equal to, for example, 50 percent of the amount the employee would have received if their salary had been continued for the remainder of the reasonable notice period. This type of arrangement motivates an employee to find a new job because the employer is obliged to pay a lump sum even after the employee begins a new job. At the same time, it potentially lowers the total amount that the employer must pay the former employee.

Employers are required to continue to make benefit payments throughout the statutory and common law notice periods. It is important that employers check benefits policies to make sure that coverage can be maintained after the employee is no longer working. Although an employee is entitled to receive regular employment benefits during the notice period, the parties may negotiate other arrangements—for example, the employer may compensate the ex-employee for any lost benefits.

In addition to salary and benefits, an employer must consider what else an employee would have received if they had worked throughout the reasonable notice period. As discussed below, this can include bonus payments (where they are integral to the employee's compensation package), commissions (those the employee probably would have earned), stock options/equity compensation and pension plan contributions (based on the plans' provisions), and other benefits, such as a company car (if personal use was allowed) or club memberships (Stehr, 2012, at 20). *Carroll v ATCO Electric Ltd* (2018) addresses a number of issues associated with benefits. In this case Carroll was a long-serving senior executive who was terminated without cause. His compensation included an executive bonus plan, stock options, share appreciation rights, a defined benefits pension, and a supplementary employee retirement plan. In its decision, the Alberta Court of Appeal confirmed that entitlements to certain benefits during the notice period are strictly governed by the terms of those plans. For example, discretionary bonus payments are not a required component of a severance package provided plan language is clear and the employer is not acting in bad faith. The Court also endorsed the "rough upper limit" of 24 months' pay in lieu of notice for long-serving employees. Employers should regularly review their bonus and incentive plans to ensure the contractual language is unambiguous and reflects their intentions for what occurs post-termination.

Employees who are entitled to statutory termination notice or termination pay cannot be required to sign a release before receiving their minimum statutory entitlements. However, an employer may withhold payments that relate to the common law reasonable notice period until the employee has signed a full and final release. In such a release, an employee expressly forfeits their right to bring any legal action against the employer that is related to their employment or dismissal in exchange for the monetary settlement the employee receives.

Employees who are entitled to statutory termination pay have the right to receive a lump-sum payment within 48 hours of termination in BC; in Alberta, such payment must be provided within three days of the termination of employment or on what would have been the employee's next payday, whichever is later. A salary continuation termination package does not meet these requirements. Therefore, a salary continuation offer should state that it includes any statutory notice and termination entitlements. An employer should make no payment unless the parties agree in writing that the package constitutes a greater right or benefit than termination pay under employment standards legislation.

Finally, an employer should not give working notice to an employee who is unable to use the notice period to look for a new job, such as an employee who is on sickness, pregnancy, or parental leave. This is because the purpose of the notice period is to give the employee a reasonable opportunity to find comparable employment. Provided that an employer does not infringe human rights or employment standards legislation in terminating an employee, it may give the employee notice of termination or pay in lieu of notice after the leave ends and the employee comes back to work.

Mass-Termination Requirements

Employees often find it especially difficult to obtain new jobs when they are terminated as part of a mass layoff because so many other workers are seeking employment at the same time. During the mid-1980s, BC and other provinces experienced a large number of plant closures, and the government responded by instituting special mass-termination rules to govern these situations.

In Alberta, a mass ("group") termination is defined in section 137 of Alberta's ESC as one in which 50 or more employees are terminated at a single location in a four-week period. When that happens, the employees, the union (if there is one), and the Minister of Labour must be provided with notice, as follows:

- 8 weeks' notice where 50 or more but less than 100 employees are terminated,
- 12 weeks' notice where 100 or more but less than 300 employees are terminated, and
- 16 weeks' notice where more than 300 employees are terminated.

If an employee is affected by a mass termination, the notice they receive as part of that will suffice for the needs of individual termination notice. Group notice can be paid out in a lump sum or have a combination of pay/notice if the employer wishes to terminate employment before the end of the applicable notice period.

In BC, a mass ("group") termination is defined in section 64 of the ESA as one in which an employer terminates 50 or more employees within a two-month period. In this situation, as described earlier, mass-termination notice requirements apply as follows:

- 8 weeks' notice where 50 to 100 employees are terminated,
- 12 weeks' notice where 101 to 300 employees are terminated, and
- 16 weeks' notice where more than 300 employees are terminated.

Under section 63, an employer must also provide individual notice or CLOS to any employees terminated in these circumstances. The notice requirements in section 64 do not apply to an employee who has bumping rights based on seniority and who refuses to exercise them.

Because mass-termination notice requirements arise only when 50 or more employees are terminated within any two-month period in BC, an employer may reduce the notice owing by staggering layoffs. For example, an employer who lays off 150 workers over a two-month period would have to provide 12 weeks' notice to all the workers. If instead the employer laid off only 100 workers in the first two-month period and then the remaining 50 workers in the next two-month period, only 8 weeks' notice would be required in each two-month period. Recall, however, that the CLOS requirement under section 63 is still payable to each individual employee and that common law notice requirements would also apply.

Exceptions to Notice of Termination Requirements

In certain situations, an employer is not required to give either notice of termination or pay in lieu of notice to a dismissed employee. These exceptions are set out below.

Probationary Employees

In Alberta, an employer is not required to give termination notice to an employee who has been employed for three months or less, unless the employment contract states otherwise. Similarly, in BC CLOS is not required for employees who have worked less than three months.

Term or Task Employees

An employer is not required to provide notice of termination to an employee hired for a definite term of less than one year or for a specific task that will take less than a year to complete. This exception does not apply if employment ends before the end of the term or the completion of the task.

Temporary Layoffs

In Alberta, an employer is not required to provide notice of termination to an employee who is on temporary layoff, as defined in the ESC. An employee may be laid off without notice or pay in lieu for a period of up to 59 consecutive days. The layoff is deemed a termination on the 60th day (with some exceptions under s 63 of the ESC) and pay in lieu of notice is required.

In BC, section 67(1) of the ESA states that a notice of termination has no effect if the notice period coincides with a temporary layoff, which is defined in section 1 as being a layoff of up to 13 weeks in any period of 20 consecutive weeks. But recall that a temporary layoff is only permitted at all if it is a term of the employment agreement between the employer and employee (or a term of a collective agreement).

Just Cause

without prejudice without an admission of wrongdoing in a legal dispute

No notice of termination is required where there is "just cause" for termination. Just cause involves conduct that is serious and is discussed in Chapter 13. Where misconduct is less serious, the employer may decide to handle the matter on a **without prejudice** basis. This means that the employer's notice payment is made on a voluntary basis and is not an admission that there is no just cause under the law. The payment cannot later be used by the dismissed employee in court to argue that the employer effectively admitted lack of just cause and must now provide reasonable notice under the common law. A "without prejudice" payment may be made where an employer has a strong just cause case but wants to reduce the chance of litigation.

Refusal of (Reasonable) Alternative Work

An employer is not required to provide notice of termination if an employee refuses an offer of reasonable alternative work or employment or refuses work that is available through a seniority system, where one exists (normally in a unionized workplace). Therefore, an employee who has the right to bump a more junior employee in a layoff but chooses not to exercise that right forfeits the right to termination notice.

Where the alternative work does not involve bumping rights under a seniority system, an employer's offer of alternative work or employment must be reasonable. For an offer of alternative work to be reasonable, the employee should be able to perform the work or, if training is needed, it should be included as part of the offer. The alternative work should have similar pay and benefits (unless circumstances warrant a substantial change). Other factors, such as level of responsibility, duties, security, and reporting relationships, should also be considered. An employer that offers an employee a job that involves a significant demotion or wage reduction will probably be required to provide notice of termination because the job does not fall within the exemption. Further, the offer should be made in writing and convey details such as duties, hours of work, wage rate, and benefits (unless these are commonly known to employees). The offer must be presented in a way that makes it clear that alternative employment is available and that a choice or decision is to be made.

strike a refusal to work by a group of unionized employees following the expiry of a collective agreement or a failure to reach a first collective agreement, typically while the employer and union are attempting to negotiate a new collective agreement

Return After Recall

In Alberta and BC, an employee who does not return to work within a reasonable time (seven consecutive days in Alberta; a "reasonable time" in BC) after being recalled from a temporary layoff is not entitled to statutory notice of termination.

lockout an employer's refusal to let unionized employees into the workplace following the expiry of a collective agreement or a failure to reach a first collective agreement, typically while the employer and union are attempting to negotiate a new collective agreement

Strikes or Lockouts

An employee who is not provided work during or as a result of a **strike** or **lockout** at the employee's workplace is not entitled to notice of termination. This exception applies to both employees in the striking or locked-out bargaining unit and other employees in the workplace who are laid off as a result of the lockout or strike. The employee is not, however, dismissed as a result of a legal strike or lockout and is allowed to return to work at the end of the stoppage.

Casual Employees or Employees Who Elect to Work

Employees who may elect to work or not when asked to do so are not entitled to notice of termination. This exception applies to employees who are free to refuse work without penalty. For example, employees of a catering company who are called to work at special functions may fall within this exception if they are entitled to reject the offer without risk of any penalty, including being taken off the list of workers whom the employer contacts.

Frustration of Contract

In unusual circumstances, an employment contract comes to an end without notice because the contract has become impossible to perform for reasons such as floods, fires, or explosions that prevent the work from being performed. A contract cannot become frustrated as a result of foreseeable problems, such as the breakdown of machinery or an employer's economic difficulties.

Frustration of employment may also occur if an employee goes to jail or loses professional credentials, thereby rendering them incapable of performing the job. For example, if a member of an engineering department loses their engineering designation, and the designation is needed to do the job, the employer could argue that the employment contract has been frustrated.

A more problematic example is when an employer alleges frustration of contract because of an employee's prolonged illness. An employee who is absent from work because of disability is protected under the *Alberta Human Rights Act* and the BC *Human Rights Code*. In such cases, an employer must accommodate the employee unless doing so creates undue hardship. However, in exceptional circumstances, an employer might advance an argument that the employment contract has been frustrated. In *Demuynck v Agentis Information Services Inc*, the BC Supreme Court found frustration of contract on the basis of an employee's disability.

CASE IN POINT

Contract Frustrated Because of Employee's Physical Incapacity

Demuynck v Agentis Information Services Inc, 2003 BCSC 96

Facts

Demuynck worked for the employer as an accounts clerk for 18 years. In 1996, she injured her right elbow in a fall unrelated to work. She continued working until mid-1997, but then she left work and began to receive short-term disability benefits. Her doctor postponed her date of return four times. She returned to work for three weeks but left and collected long-term disability benefits for the maximum two-year period, which ended in January 2000. In April 1999, the employer dismissed Demuynck. The letter of termination did not refer to frustration of the employment contract; instead, it stated that the employer was undergoing considerable change. It offered Demuynck the equivalent of 12 months' salary if she remained unemployed or a "top-up" of her earnings if she became employed. She rejected this offer and sued for damages equivalent to 16 to 18 months of salary in lieu of notice.

At trial, the employer alleged that the employment contract had become frustrated by Demuynck's physical incapacity.

Relevant Issue

Whether the contract of employment had become frustrated by the employee's physical incapacity.

Decision

The BC Supreme Court found that the employment contract had become frustrated. It noted that frustration of contract occurs when an employee's incapacity is of such a nature, or is likely to continue for such a period of time, that the further performance of employment duties either is impossible or would be radically different from that originally contemplated in the employment contract. In making this determination, the Court considered the following factors:

- *The terms of the contract, including provisions relating to sick pay.* If an employee returns to work or is likely to return to work within the period during which sick pay is available, the contract is not frustrated.
- *How long the contract was likely to last in the absence of sickness.* An employment contract of indefinite duration is less likely to become frustrated than a contract related to temporary employment.
- *The nature of the employment.* If the employee is one of many employees who do the same job, the contract is more likely to survive than if the employee is a key individual who must be replaced quickly.
- *The nature of the illness or injury, the length of the employee's absence, and the prospects of recovery.* For example, where an employee is expected to make a full recovery, it is unlikely that the employment contract will be frustrated even if the absence is prolonged.
- *The employment history.* A contract covering a longstanding employment relationship is not as easily frustrated as one covering a short relationship.

In this case, the Court concluded that an absence of between 18 and 24 months was the limit of a temporary absence. Demuynck had been off work for 20 months, and there was no evidence that she would be able to return to work in the future. She had exhausted disability benefits. If her incapacity was not permanent, it was of such a duration that further performance was impossible or radically different from that contemplated in the original employment contract. The employment contract was therefore frustrated, and Demuynck was not entitled to wrongful dismissal damages.

Although the Court in *Demuynck* determined that the employment contract had been frustrated by the employee's physical incapacity, findings of frustration of contract are rare. Where the impossibility of performance stems from a disability, the employer must accommodate the employee to the point of undue hardship before considering any further steps. A court is less likely to find frustration of contract if an employee continues to be eligible for long-term disability benefits, because the existence of long-term benefits indicates that the parties to the employment contract contemplated and provided for the possibility of long-term disability. As a rule of thumb, an employer should wait for two years before considering severance of an employment relationship based on frustration caused by an employee's absence. Even after that time, an employer should obtain an up-to-date prognosis from the employee's physician to establish that a return to work is not imminent.

Seasonal Work

In Alberta, no notice of termination is required for employees hired for seasonal work (such as snow removal) at the end of the season. If an employee's employment is terminated prior to the end of the season, or if they are kept on after the season has ended, then the requirement for notice applies.

In BC, an employer is not obliged to provide CLOS or notice of termination to unionized workers where they are employed in "a seasonal industry in which the practice is to lay off employees every year and to call them back to work" (ESA, s 65(3)(b)(i)). Nor is it obliged to give CLOS or notice to employees who get "laid off or terminated as a result of the normal seasonal reduction, suspension or closure of an operation" (ESA, s 65(4)(b)) or to employees who are employed at one or more construction sites by an employer whose principal business is construction (ESA, s 65(1)(e)).

Employee Terminates Employment

Employees are not entitled to notice if they terminate employment on their own initiative. In Alberta, the ball is then in the other court, and it may very well be that they should have provided notice of termination to the employer, as set out in section 58 of Alberta's ESC.

BC's ESA does not require employees to give notice. However, common law principles apply, and employees may be expected to give the employer reasonable notice. Reasonable notice can be several weeks or even months in the case of key employees. For example, in *Consbec Inc v Walker*, the BC Court of Appeal found that when determining the amount of damages for an employee's failure to provide notice, a court must first determine the amount of notice the employee should have provided to the employer and then determine what damages, if any, the employer suffered due to the employee's failure to give notice. When measuring the damages, the Court stated that it is not the cost to the company that is measured, but the cost of the failure to give notice. In the *Consbec* case, the Court found that it was reasonable for the company to send another employee to carry on the business after the unexpected departure, but they were not entitled to relocation costs because they would have had to pay those even if they were given proper notice. They also took into consideration the fact that the company saved the departing employee's salary. In the end, the company did not suffer any damages.

Wrongful Dismissal

The following discussion relates to **wrongful dismissals**, which are dismissals without cause where employers have not provided reasonable notice or pay in lieu of reasonable notice. A dismissed employee has two years from the date of dismissal to bring an action for wrongful dismissal.

wrongful dismissal dismissal without just cause wherein an employer breaches its common law duty to provide reasonable notice of termination or pay in lieu of notice to an employee

Employees file wrongful dismissal claims in court, rather than file a complaint with Employment Standards (Alberta) or the Employment Standards Branch (BC). The branches hear complaints about unpaid wages or violations of the legislative requirements for notice/pay in lieu/CLOS, not for wrongful dismissal.

In Alberta, an employee with a claim of less than $50,000 usually files an action for wrongful dismissal in small claims court, where the adjudication process is relatively fast and informal. If the claim exceeds $50,000, the claim is filed with the Alberta Court of Queen's Bench. The civil claim form sets out the key elements of the claim and the damages sought. In BC, a wrongful dismissal claim for $35,000 or less can be heard in small claims court. A claim exceeding that amount will be heard in the BC Supreme Court, and the plaintiff will have to issue a notice of civil claim.

If the dispute involves allegations of just cause, a trial is necessary. If, however, the only issue in dispute is the amount of reasonable notice or damages in lieu, an application for summary judgment may be allowed (*Alberta Rules of Court*, r 7.3(1)(c) and BC *Supreme Court Civil Rules*, r 9-6). Summary judgment applications are most appropriate when the parties agree on the essential facts of the case but disagree on the amount of notice that is required given those facts.

However, this option has recently been challenged in the Alberta courts. In *Coffey v Nine Energy Canada Inc*, the Alberta Court of Queen's Bench determined that summary judgment was not appropriate for assessing damages for pay in lieu of notice in wrongful dismissal cases. In the view of the Court, assessing reasonable notice involves contentious issues of fact that require the weighing of evidence, which is beyond the scope of a summary judgment process. How this plays out on appeal and in other jurisdictions is yet to be seen.

costs
compensation for legal fees and expenses that the other party in a lawsuit is entitled to recover

Generally speaking, a successful party is entitled to partial **costs** from the other party. More generous costs are usually awarded only if one of the parties has acted poorly—for example, if an employer has made serious unjustified accusations in its pleadings.

In Alberta, the unsuccessful party in small claims court can appeal to the Alberta Court of Queen's Bench (*Provincial Court Act*, s 46(1)). Queen's Bench decisions can only be appealed to the Alberta Court of Appeal if the dispute exceeds the $50,000 monetary limit of the Provincial Court Civil Division (*Provincial Court Civil Division Regulation*, s 1.1).

In BC, similarly, a party can appeal without leave for most matters to the BC Court of Appeal from a decision of the BC Supreme Court (*Supreme Court Civil Rules*, r 18-3). Appeals to the Supreme Court of Canada on wrongful dismissal cases require leave of the Court. To receive leave, the case must raise a question of public importance, a significant issue of law, or a significant issue of mixed fact and law.

Reasonable Notice Damages: The Basic Entitlement

Under the common law, courts do not reinstate employees who are wrongfully dismissed. Instead, the remedy for wrongful dismissal is based on principles of contract law. An employer is required to compensate a wrongfully dismissed employee for lost wages and benefits during the reasonable notice period to put the employee in the same position they would have been in had the employer not breached the contract by failing to provide reasonable notice.

Damages for wrongful dismissal are calculated from the date on which an employer breaches the contract. If an employer dismisses an employee, damages are calculated from the date of dismissal. If an employer constructively dismisses an employee (constructive dismissal is discussed in detail below and in Chapter 11), damages are calculated from the date the employer makes the unilateral change to the fundamental terms of the contract of employment.

The calculation of these damages can be complicated because, in addition to lost salary or wages, the employee is entitled to all benefits and other compensation that they would have received during the reasonable notice period. For example, if a former employee is entitled to a reasonable notice period of 12 months, they are entitled to have the employer maintain the entire benefit package for that period or to be compensated for its loss. Except for the statutory notice periods during which benefits must be maintained, the parties may negotiate the manner in which the employer will compensate the employee for benefits during the common law notice period.

The following is an overview of a wrongfully dismissed employee's entitlements during the reasonable notice period:

1. *Salary.* The employee is entitled to receive the amount of salary they will lose during the reasonable notice period as a result of the wrongful dismissal. This includes any increases in salary that would have occurred during this period. If overtime pay or commissions are a fundamental part of the employee's pay package, lost earnings include overtime pay or commissions that the employee was likely to receive during the notice period.
2. *Benefits.* Benefits to which an employee is entitled include club memberships, rent-free residences, room and board, meal expenses, subsidized mortgages, professional fees, loans, and employee discounts. The value of staff loans and employee discounts is calculated by determining the difference between the market value of these benefits and what an employee would have paid for them during the notice period. An employee is also entitled to the personal-use aspect of benefits such as car allowances. They are not entitled to receive benefits that relate to job performance only, such as use of a company vehicle provided for business purposes only.
3. *Company vehicle.* An employer is not required to compensate an employee for the use of a company vehicle that was provided exclusively for company purposes. However, if an employee has use of a company vehicle for personal as well as for company purposes, or if use of the vehicle forms part of the employee's total compensation, an employer must compensate the employee for loss of use of the vehicle during the notice period.
4. *Insurance.* Benefits may be owing for the following types of insurance: life, accidental death and dismemberment, disability or medical, drug, and dental. If possible, an employer should continue coverage for insured benefits throughout the reasonable notice period. However, sometimes it is impossible to continue coverage. For example, in Alberta and BC, disability insurers are required to cover employees during a working notice period, but it is unusual for coverage to go beyond this period, since eligibility is usually based on an employee being actively employed with the employer that arranged the coverage. If an employee is no longer actively employed during a reasonable notice period, an employer can reimburse the employee for the cost of obtaining their own coverage during the remainder of the notice period. In *Prince v T Eaton Co Limited* (1992), a dismissed employee became totally disabled after receiving notice of termination but before the reasonable notice period

expired. The employee sued the employer and was awarded damages for the loss of long-term disability benefits. The employer was required to provide the employee with benefits because the insurer had removed the employee from coverage during the notice period. A similar result was reached in *Egan v Alcatel Canada Inc* (2004). In that case, the employer was found liable for the dismissed employee's disability benefits when the dismissed employee became disabled outside the notice period provided by the employer but within the reasonable notice period subsequently established by the court.

5. *Bonuses.* If an employer was required to pay an employee bonuses as part of the employee's compensation package, the employee must be compensated for their loss during the period of reasonable notice. The amount is based on what the employee would probably have received if they had worked throughout the notice period. If the bonus cannot be determined in this manner, the employer should calculate the average of past bonuses. Bonuses that were gratuitous payments made at the employer's discretion do not have to continue during the reasonable notice period.
6. *Stock options.* An employee who is dismissed without cause may continue to accrue and exercise stock options until the end of the reasonable notice period unless the employment contract or stock option plan unequivocally states otherwise.
7. *Pension entitlements.* An employer must compensate an employee for any loss of pension entitlement during the reasonable notice period, including the value of anticipated employer contributions. For pension purposes, the employee's length of service includes the reasonable notice period. The pension benefit calculation includes any salary increases that the employee would probably have received during the notice period.

aggravated damages damages awarded to compensate a party for non-monetary losses intentionally or maliciously caused by the other party's conduct

punitive damages damages awarded to punish the employer for its malicious or oppressive conduct, rather than to compensate the employee

***Wallace* damages** damages (given by extending the reasonable notice period) formerly awarded to a dismissed employee because of the employer's bad-faith conduct in the manner of dismissal

Note that damages do not include work-related expenses, such as a car allowance based on work kilometres travelled, because they are not incurred unless an employee is working.

Generally speaking, an employer should not dismiss an employee when the employee is on disability leave. An employee who becomes disabled during the notice period is entitled to both pay in lieu of notice and disability benefits because these are separate legal rights.

Other Types of Wrongful Dismissal Damages

In addition to the basic entitlement to pay in lieu of reasonable notice, the common law allows for other damages against an employer in certain circumstances.

In 2008, the Supreme Court of Canada issued a landmark decision in *Honda Canada Inc v Keays* that revisited the law of wrongful dismissal damages. Up to that time, in addition to reasonable notice damages, there were three main headings of damages in wrongful dismissal actions: **aggravated damages** (for mental distress); **punitive damages**; and, the most common, extended-notice ***Wallace* damages** for bad-faith conduct in the manner of dismissal.

The changes made by the Supreme Court in *Honda* are significant and provide the basis of what are now called "moral damages." They include reformulating when and how bad-faith conduct damages are awarded and clarifying the circumstances in which punitive damages are appropriate. The decision also provides guidance to employers concerning their ability to monitor and manage their workforce in the context of the duty to accommodate.

CASE IN POINT

Supreme Court of Canada Restates the Law of Damages for Wrongful Dismissal

Honda Canada Inc v Keays, 2008 SCC 39

Facts

Keays worked for Honda for 14 years, first on the assembly line and later in data entry. He received positive work assessments but had a poor attendance record because he suffered from chronic fatigue syndrome (CFS). Keays was enrolled in Honda's disability program, which allowed employees to miss work if they provided doctor's notes confirming that their absences were disability related.

When Keays began missing more days of work than his doctor had predicted and his medical notes changed in tone, becoming more "cryptic," Honda began to question whether Keays' absences were being independently evaluated by his doctor. Honda decided to cancel Keays' accommodation and stop accepting doctor's notes. Instead, it asked Keays to meet with Dr Brennan, an occupational medical specialist, so that they could decide how best to accommodate his disability. Keays had earlier met with another doctor at Honda's request and, fearing he was being "set up," retained a lawyer. The lawyer advised Honda that Keays would meet with the specialist only if the purpose, methodology, and parameters of the consultation were provided. Honda did not respond to the lawyer; it later advised Keays that it had a practice of only dealing with associates directly. Instead, it sent Keays a letter that included a medical opinion from Dr Brennan and the previous doctor that they could find no diagnosis indicating that he was disabled from working. It also stated that Honda supported his full return to work but that he would be dismissed if he continued to refuse to meet with Dr Brennan. He did not change his mind and shortly thereafter was terminated for cause, on the ground of insubordination. Keays sued for wrongful dismissal damages, as well as damages for discrimination and harassment.

The trial judge found Honda's actions not only unwarranted but outrageous. The judge held that Keays had been wrongfully dismissed and awarded him the following:

- 15 months' pay in lieu of reasonable notice;
- a 9-month extension to the notice period (for a total of 24 months) for the employer's bad-faith conduct in his dismissal (*Wallace* damages); among other things, the trial judge criticized Honda for requiring a doctor's note for every absence for CFS, something it did not do for other illnesses; and
- punitive damages of $500,000. This was by far the largest punitive award ever given in a wrongful dismissal action. The trial judge justified the award by stating that it takes a "large whack to wake up a wealthy and powerful defendant to its responsibilities" (at para 18).

On appeal, the Ontario Court of Appeal reduced the punitive damages award to $100,000 on the basis that it was disproportionately large. However, the Court of Appeal supported much of the lower Court's reasoning under the other headings of damages. Honda appealed.

Relevant Issue

Whether the damages awarded were appropriate.

Decision

The Supreme Court of Canada struck down all the damages awarded except the reasonable notice award of 15 months. It found that the trial judge made several "palpable and overriding" errors in his decision. The Court stated that the case presented an "opportunity to clarify and redefine some aspects of the law of damages in the context of employment" (at para 21). It made the following rulings:

1. It upheld the 15 months' general reasonable notice damages.
2. It struck down the 9-month extension of the notice period (*Wallace* damages) and made the following key findings:
   a. Honda did not deliberately misrepresent its doctor's views;
   b. an employer is entitled to rely on its doctors' medical opinions;
   c. there is nothing inappropriate about an employer using doctor's notes to manage attendance; and
   d. an employer is entitled to seek confirmation of disability or request clarification of accommodation needs; stopping the accommodation process was not a reprisal because its purpose was to allow Dr Brennan to confirm the disability.

   The Supreme Court went on to revisit when and how *Wallace* damages are awarded. If an employee can prove that the manner of dismissal caused actual damage (i.e., for mental distress), he should be compensated for it. Moreover, the award should be based on the employee's actual losses rather than given as an extension of the wrongful dismissal notice period.
3. It struck down the $100,000 punitive damages award. Punitive damages are reserved for exceptional cases where the employer's conduct is so malicious and outrageous that it is deserving of punishment on its own. In this case, Honda's conduct did not demonstrate "egregious bad faith" (at para 8). There was no discriminatory conduct here; the employer's disability program was designed to accommodate specific types of disabilities and was not itself discriminatory.

With the decision in *Honda Canada Inc v Keays*, the Supreme Court of Canada redefined many aspects of the law of wrongful dismissal damages.

Key Points Addressed in Honda

Determining Reasonable Notice

The Supreme Court confirmed that the main factors in determining "reasonable notice" are the nature of the job, the employee's age and length of service, and the availability of similar employment (the *Bardal* factors). No factor should be given undue weight, and each case turns on its own facts.

Moral (Formerly Wallace) Damages/Aggravated Damages

Damages attributable to bad-faith conduct in the manner of dismissal should be determined on the same basis as other compensatory damages. The test is: What damages were within the "reasonable expectation" of the parties as flowing from a breach of contract? Since *Wallace v United Grain Growers* (1997) established that an employer has a duty of good faith and fairness in the manner of dismissal, damages for breach of that obligation are foreseeable and the employee is entitled to compensation. The Court also held that *Wallace* damages should not be given through an arbitrary extension of the notice period. Instead, they should be given in the same manner as all compensatory damages—through a monetary award that reflects proven damages. Consequently, there must be proof of damages, such as treatment for mental distress, for a damage award to be made (Echlin & Thomlinson, 2011, at 254).

In *Honda*, the Supreme Court also eliminated the distinction between *Wallace* (now moral) damages resulting from conduct in the manner of termination and "aggravated damages" resulting from a separate cause of action. There is no longer a requirement for an independent actionable wrong to support an action for aggravated damages.

One effect of *Honda* that is specific to BC is that moral damages are now calculated separately from other damages. Before 2008, BC courts did not separately calculate *Wallace* damages (by, e.g., adding a percentage such as 33 percent to the basic damages award). Courts calculated what they called a "global amount" that did not specify how much the *Wallace* factor increased the award. An example of such a decision is *Clendenning v Lowndes Lambert (BC) Ltd*, a 2000 decision of the BC Court of Appeal. After *Honda*, BC courts now deal with *Wallace*-style moral damages as part of aggravated damages, which are separate from the basic award.

Punitive Damages

The Supreme Court also confirmed that the bar for awarding punitive damages is a high one. Damages should only be awarded for conduct that is harsh, vindictive, malicious, and reprehensible and when compensatory damages are not enough to punish, deter, and denounce the bad behaviour.

An award of punitive damages continues to require a finding that the employer committed an "independent actionable wrong." However, a breach of the contractual duty of good faith can serve as the independent actionable wrong (Echlin & Thomlinson, 2011, at 255).

Finally, courts should not award multiple forms of damages arising out of the same facts. The Supreme Court found that the lower courts' decisions indicated some confusion between damages for the employer's conduct in dismissal and punitive damages. It clarified the distinction and underscored the fact that punitive damages are only to be awarded in extreme cases.

Bad Faith in Dismissal

Since *Honda*, the courts are generally requiring proof of damages suffered from the bad-faith dismissal. For example, in *Elgert v Home Hardware Stores Limited* (2011) (described in Chapter 7), the Alberta Court of Appeal set aside the original award of $200,000 in aggravated damages. The Court indicated that while there was sufficient evidence to conclude that the manner of dismissal was unfair, in bad faith, misleading, and unduly insensitive, there was little or no evidence showing the amount of actual damages resulting from that treatment. The Court of Appeal also reduced the jury's original award of $300,000 in punitive damages to $75,000. The Court stated that the punitive damages award was not proportional, referring (at para 82) to six dimensions of proportionality that should apply:

1. *Proportionate to the blameworthiness of the conduct.* The more reprehensible the employer's conduct is, the higher the potential award will be. Factors to consider include outrageous conduct for a lengthy period of time without any rational justification, awareness of the hardship being inflicted, whether the misconduct was planned and deliberate, the intent and motive behind the conduct, whether there was an attempt to conceal or cover up the misconduct, whether the employer profited from its misconduct, and whether the interest violated by the misconduct was known to be deeply personal to the employee.
2. *Proportionate to the degree of vulnerability of the employee.* The financial or other vulnerability of the employee, and the consequent abuse of power by an employer, is highly relevant where there is a power imbalance.
3. *Proportionate to the harm or potential harm done to the employee.*
4. *Proportionate to the need for deterrence.* An employer's financial power may become relevant if the employer chooses to argue financial hardship, or if it is directly relevant to the employer's misconduct, or other circumstances where it may rationally be concluded that a lesser award against an employer with deep pockets would fail to achieve deterrence.
5. *Proportionate, even after taking into account the other penalties, both civil and criminal, that have been or are likely to be imposed on the employer for the same misconduct.* Compensatory damages also punish and may be all the "punishment" required.
6. *Proportionate to the advantage wrongfully gained by the employer from the misconduct.*

Bad-faith analysis is fact driven but generally will refer to conduct that could be considered untruthful, misleading, insensitive, or humiliating. Examples include:

- false allegations of cause or incompetence,
- harming the employee's reputation or causing embarrassment at the time of dismissal,
- harassment or sexual harassment prior to dismissal,
- dismissal connected to disability, and
- reprisals.

Bad-faith conduct can also occur after the dismissal for behaviours like pressuring the employee to sign a severance package, refusing to communicate with the employee, refusing to provide a reference letter when there is no performance concern, or failing to provide a record of employment (Nolan, 2019).

Furthermore, as *Boucher v Wal-Mart* illustrates, where courts find compelling evidence of both bad-faith conduct on the part of the employer and compensable losses by the employee, the amount of the awards given seems to be increasing. In *Boucher*, the Ontario Court of Appeal was asked to consider whether a much greater total award—$1.45 million in aggravated, punitive, and tort damages—was appropriate given the employer's actions and those of its manager, which led to an employee's constructive dismissal.

CASE IN POINT

Major Damages Awarded Against Wal-Mart and Its Manager

Boucher v Wal-Mart Canada Corp, 2014 ONCA 419

Facts

Boucher, aged 43, was an assistant manager at a Wal-Mart store in Windsor. A good worker, Boucher got along well with her manager, Pinnock, until May 2009, when he asked her to falsify a temperature log and she refused. After this, Pinnock started belittling and humiliating her in front of co-workers. In June, Boucher availed herself of Wal-Mart's Open Door Communication Policy by asking to meet with the district manager to discuss this issue. However, in breach of that policy, Pinnock was advised of the meeting and thereafter his behaviour toward Boucher became even worse. In October, Boucher asked to meet with senior management representatives, who said they would investigate her concerns. However, they warned her that she could suffer negative consequences if her concerns were found to be unjustified and, in mid-November, after finding that her complaints were "unsubstantiated," they told Boucher she would be "held accountable for making them" (at para 2). A few days later, Pinnock again humiliated her in front of other employees, this time by grabbing her by the elbow and telling her to prove to him that she could count to ten. He prompted her by initiating the count, then told her to count out loud along with him. Boucher was so humiliated that she left the store and soon after tendered her resignation. As one witness later testified, Pinnock seemed "overjoyed" when he heard she had quit.

Boucher sued Wal-Mart and Pinnock for constructive dismissal and related damages. In a jury trial, Boucher was awarded the following:

- 20 weeks' salary as required under her employment contract (2 weeks' salary per year of service);
- $1.2 million against Wal-Mart ($200,000 in aggravated damages for the manner in which she was dismissed and $1 million in punitive damages); and
- $250,000 damages against Pinnock ($100,000 for the tort of intentional infliction of mental suffering and $150,000 for punitive damages).

The defendants appealed both their liability and the amount of damages. Boucher cross-appealed for $726,691 for future income loss until retirement, arguing that, but for the defendants' wrongful conduct, she would have stayed at Wal-Mart until her retirement.

Relevant Issues

1. Whether the special damage awards against Pinnock and Wal-Mart should be set aside or reduced for being unnecessary or excessive.
2. Whether the employee is entitled to future income loss until retirement.

Decision

The Court found that Boucher had proven all three elements of the tort of intentional infliction of mental suffering:

- the defendant's conduct was flagrant and outrageous (Pinnock continuously and publicly demeaned Boucher over a period of nearly six months);
- the defendant's conduct was calculated to harm the plaintiff (evidence showed that Pinnock was "overjoyed" at having accomplished his goal of getting Boucher to quit); and
- the defendant's conduct caused the plaintiff to suffer a visible and provable illness (Boucher's family doctor confirmed that her symptoms—abdominal pain, weight loss, and inability to eat or sleep—arose from work-related stress).

The Court of Appeal also upheld the amount of the award ($100,000), even though it was unprecedentedly high against an individual employee in a breach of employment contract case. As the Court explained: "The jury represents the collective conscience of the community. The magnitude of their award shows that they were deeply offended by Pinnock's mistreatment of Boucher" (at para 56).

Regarding punitive damages, the Court found that Pinnock's mistreatment of Boucher met the high standard required for such damages. However, it reduced the amount of the award from $150,000 to $10,000 on the basis that the high $100,000 damages award for the tort of intentional infliction of mental suffering already carried a "strong punitive component" (at para 64).

Similarly, the Court upheld the $200,000 award for aggravated damages against Wal-Mart but reduced the punitive damages award from $1 million to $100,000.

The Court held that the $200,000 aggravated damages award was justified on several grounds: Wal-Mart failed to take Boucher's complaints seriously; it failed to discipline Pinnock or stop his ongoing mistreatment of her; it failed to follow and enforce its own workplace policies; and it threatened Boucher with retaliation for making her complaints. These actions warranted a substantial award for aggravated damages, separate from Pinnock's tort of intentional infliction of mental suffering (for which Wal-Mart was also vicariously liable).

On the other hand, as with Pinnock, the Court found that while the extent of Wal-Mart's misconduct warranted punitive damages, the amount of those damages should be reduced because the high aggravated damages award already contained an element of punishment and denunciation.

Boucher's Cross-Appeal

The Court of Appeal upheld the trial judge's ruling that Boucher was not entitled to an award for future loss of income. The evidence showed that Boucher had recovered from the effects of the wrongdoer's action. She was able to work (although she had not found a job), and therefore she had not suffered a loss of earning capacity. Accordingly, Boucher was only entitled to the loss of income provided for in her employment contract, which was 20 weeks. (The Court noted that Boucher did not have an employment contract that guaranteed her employment to age 65. She was entitled to be put in the position she would have been in if the contract had been performed—in other words, employment subject to dismissal in accordance with the terms of her contract.)

FYI

Employer Misconduct That Attracts Punitive Damages at the "High End of the Scale"

One of the reasons the Ontario Court of Appeal in *Boucher* cited for reducing the amount of punitive damages awarded against Wal-Mart was that its misconduct, while serious, fell far short of the "gravity and duration of the misconduct in other cases that have attracted high punitive damages awards" (at para 88). For example, the Court contrasted this case with the employer's actions in *Pate Estate v Galway-Cavendish and Harvey (Township)* (2013), where a wrongfully dismissed employee was ultimately awarded $450,000 in punitive damages. In *Pate*, the employer alleged that the employee had engaged in criminal activity and threatened to call the police if the employee refused to resign. When that failed, the employer instigated a police investigation that led to criminal charges and a four-day trial at which the dismissed employee was acquitted and it was revealed that the employer had withheld exculpatory information from the police. Moreover, this case was widely publicized over several years, causing the employee ongoing humiliation within the community. By contrast, the Court noted that Wal-Mart was already liable for compensatory damages, the misconduct lasted less than six months, and it (unlike its manager, Pinnock) did not set out to force Boucher's resignation.

Conclusions

Although the Ontario Court of Appeal scaled back the historically high punitive damage awards against both Wal-Mart and its manager, the total amount awarded

($410,000 in special damages alone) remains a significant sum. In fact, it's been reported that the awards both for aggravated damages and for intentional infliction of mental distress are the highest of their type in employment law in Canadian history (Schwartz & Portman, 2014). Thus, this decision signals the court's willingness to uphold large special damages awards where the circumstances are particularly egregious.

FYI

Galea v Wal-Mart: Executive Awarded Record Damages over Wal-Mart Canada's Conduct

In *Galea v Wal-Mart Canada Corp*, Ontario Superior Court Justice Michael Emery found that Wal-Mart's conduct was "misleading at best, and dishonest at worst." He awarded Gail Galea $250,000 in moral damages and $500,000 in punitive damages. Galea had been fired without any allegation of cause in 2010. Through various delays, which Galea could not have been pleased with, the case only reached trial in 2018.

Galea began her career with Wal-Mart in 2002 and was quickly promoted through the ranks to vice-president, general merchandising by 2008. Throughout her time, she was consistently praised, rewarded, and groomed for leadership.

That is why what happened next appeared entirely out of the blue.

In January 2010, then-president and CEO of Wal-Mart Canada, David Cheesewright, sat Galea down, took away her V-P title, and told her that he "did not know what to do with her." Confused, Galea was simultaneously told that her role no longer existed, but that she was still valued.

Thus began the long goodbye.

Galea was moved into an ad hoc position with no defined duties. From there, empty promises of international positions were made although no offers from any Wal-Mart Companies in India, Brazil, Chile, or the U.K. materialized. Hollow reassurances were made about Galea's value as an employee and future with the company.

Ten months later, Galea received a letter stating that it was in her best interest that her employment be terminated immediately.

Galea sought two sets of damages in her claim. The first stemmed from the wrongful dismissal. The second, for moral and punitive damages, flowed from Wal-Mart's conduct before, during, and after her termination. In addition, she sought moral damages for the mental distress and aggravating circumstances Wal-Mart caused over the course of the litigation, including trial.

In December 2017, Emery J awarded Galea $200,000 for the mental distress that Wal-Mart knew its actions would cause her. He found the 10 months Galea was left to fend for herself in vain was unduly insensitive. He awarded an additional $50,000 in moral damages for Wal-Mart's post-termination conduct, which included its discontinuation of her transition payments and health and dental benefits short of its contractual obligations, as well as its uncooperative behaviour throughout the litigation.

Justice Emery indicated that a higher award for punitive damages was required to deter Wal-Mart from conducting itself similarly in the future. He found that Cheesewright's "callous indifference" and "reprehensible conduct" was made on behalf of the company and awarded $500,000. This is the highest award for moral damages in employment law in the country and one of the largest amounts for punitive damages.

... In 2014, in *Boucher v Wal-Mart Canada Corp*, the Ontario Court of Appeal reduced an award of punitive damages against a Wal-Mart manager from $150,000 to $10,000, and against Wal-Mart itself from $1 million to $100,000. The Court of Appeal in that decision found that the significant compensatory damages alone were sufficient retribution to the plaintiff and were substantial enough to denounce and deter Wal-Mart's conduct. As well, the award was disproportionate to that awarded for more egregious conduct.

Perhaps it was Wal-Mart's past history and its economic power that caused Emery J to award such a cumulatively high amount. If that was the rationale, it provides a windfall for employees who are treated badly by larger corporations.

Two key differences [that exist] between these Wal-Mart decisions is that, in *Boucher* the misconduct lasted less than six months, whereas Galea was subject to mistreatment for almost a year within the workplace, and another several years through Wal-Mart's behaviour in the course of litigation. Secondly, the employer-employee power imbalance and the fact that Wal-Mart did not set out to force Boucher to resign were key factors in reducing the punitive damages. By contrast, Emery J explicitly found that Wal-Mart's actions were intended to "dismiss or denigrate" Galea to the point where she might resign.

That being said, employers in a non-union environment generally have the right to implement personnel changes within the workplace and to structure management authority as they see fit, without it leading to extraordinary damages beyond the costs of a wrongful or constructive dismissal. Surprisingly, this decision was not appealed. For now, this decision signals the significant financial risk corporate employers may face when they fumble through executive personnel changes and fail to place themselves into the minds and emotions of the impacted employee.

SOURCE: Levitt, 2018.

The Duty to Mitigate

Under the common law, but not under Alberta's ESC or BC's ESA, an employee who has been wrongfully dismissed has a duty to mitigate their damages. This means that the employee must take all reasonable steps to find comparable alternative employment during the reasonable notice period. Earnings from an employee's new job are usually deducted from the amount that the employer is required to pay to the employee as damages for wrongful dismissal. This duty flows from the principle that wrongful dismissal damages are meant to compensate the employee for the employer's failure to provide the required notice, not to penalize the employer for the dismissal itself.

The attributes of a reasonable job search are based on what a reasonable person would do in the circumstances; it is an objective standard. Employees who have been dismissed without notice are entitled to a period to accustom themselves to the new situation before beginning their job search. They are not expected to start making phone calls to prospective employers the morning after they have been dismissed. However, after a reasonable time has passed, they must start to look for a new position.

An employer that alleges that an employee failed to adequately mitigate damages bears the onus of proof. It must prove two things: that there were comparable jobs available during the notice period that were suitable for the former employee, and that the employee did not make reasonable efforts to obtain one of those jobs. Courts rarely scrutinize a dismissed employee's job search efforts. However, on occasion courts have found that an employee's job search was insufficient, and this finding has affected the reasonable notice period. In *Chambers v Axia Netmedia Corporation* (2004), the trial judge reduced the reasonable notice period from 11 months to 8 months because, among other things, the employee had limited his job search almost entirely to the Internet. In the Court's view, using only one job search approach was not "taking all reasonable steps" to mitigate damages.

Dismissed employees are expected to look for and accept only work that is comparable to their former job. Whether a job is comparable depends on the specific facts of the case, but generally the courts look at similarity in salary, location, status, skill, and training. Where a potential job would require a former employee to move to a different city, the courts consider the employee's family circumstances and the housing market. For example, if the former employee's spouse has a job in the community, it is less likely that the duty to mitigate would require relocation.

On occasion, discharged employees decide to make a career change. For example, a person who is dismissed from a position as a computer technician may decide to go into the tourist industry as a matter of personal preference. If jobs in the new industry are lower paying than available jobs in the previous industry, the former employer could argue that it should not be required to compensate the employee for the salary difference during the notice period. On the other hand, courts may accept an employee's decision to mitigate by starting a new business or retraining where this approach is realistic and there are few job opportunities in the former employee's previous industry or field.

Employers are legally liable for a former employee's out-of-pocket job search expenses. These could include expenses for long distance telephone calls, resumé preparation, postage, and travelling to job interviews.

In the Supreme Court of Canada's 2008 decision in *Evans v Teamsters Local Union No 31*, the Court was asked to consider whether a wrongfully dismissed employee's duty to mitigate could require him to return to work for the employer that dismissed him.

CASE IN POINT

Does Duty to Mitigate Require Returning to the Job the Employee Was Fired From?

Evans v Teamsters Local Union No 31, 2008 SCC 20

Facts

Evans was employed for over 23 years as a business agent in the Teamsters union. After the election of a new union executive, Evans was terminated. During settlement negotiations, Evans indicated that he was prepared to accept 24 months' notice of termination, possibly through 12 months of continued employment followed by a payment of 12 months of salary in lieu of notice. When the parties still had not reached an agreement after five months of negotiations, the employer offered Evans his job back so that he could work out the balance of his 24-month notice period. The employer also indicated that refusal would be treated as just cause for dismissal. Evans refused the offer and sued for wrongful dismissal. The trial Court agreed with Evans and awarded him 22 months' pay in lieu of notice totalling $100,000. The employer appealed. The Court of Appeal set aside the award, finding that Evans had not acted reasonably in refusing the former employer's job offer. Evans appealed to the Supreme Court of Canada.

Relevant Issue

Whether the employee failed to reasonably mitigate his damages when he refused to return to the job he was fired from.

Decision

In a majority decision, the Supreme Court held that Evans had failed to mitigate because his refusal was not reasonable in the circumstances. Whether a refusal is reasonable depends on the particular facts of each case. The Court found that where "the salary offered is the same, where the working conditions are not substantially different or the work demeaning, and where the personal relationships involved are not acrimonious" (at para 6), the employee has a duty to accept the temporary work offered. At the same time, the Court emphasized that an employee is not obliged to mitigate by returning to work in "an atmosphere of hostility, embarrassment or humiliation" (at para 6) and that an objective standard will be used to evaluate this factor. Would a reasonable person in the employee's position perceive it that way? The majority decision noted that at one point in negotiations, Evans indicated that he was prepared to return to work if certain of his conditions (including one that involved his wife's employment) were met. In light of these findings, his refusal to resume work temporarily was not reasonable and constituted a failure to mitigate.

There was a single dissenting opinion from Abella J in the *Evans* decision that is worth noting. She stated that requiring a dismissed employee to accept temporary employment with the same employer that wrongfully dismissed him disregards the uniqueness of an employment contract as one of "personal service." In her view, an employer can either offer working notice or provide pay in lieu of notice. What it cannot do is fire an employee and then, when negotiations fail, fire him again for failure to accept its subsequent offer to work out his notice period. In contrast, the majority decided that there is little practical difference between providing an employee with reasonable notice of termination and terminating employment immediately but offering new employment for the same time period.

The most apparent effect of this decision on employers is that it offers an additional option in negotiating a settlement in wrongful dismissal actions. However, this option is only available where the conditions set out in *Evans* are met—the salary remains the same, the working conditions are not substantially different or the work demeaning, and the personal relationships involved are not acrimonious. In practice, meeting all of these conditions may be difficult; otherwise, the employer probably would have given working notice in the first place. Nonetheless, this decision underscores the desirability of maintaining as positive a relationship as possible with an employee who is being dismissed without cause throughout the dismissal process and in any subsequent negotiations.

Constructive Dismissal

constructive dismissal dismissal that occurs when an employer unilaterally makes substantial changes to the essential elements of the employment contract to the detriment of the employee

Constructive dismissal is a type of wrongful dismissal. In this situation, an employer does not explicitly dismiss an employee. Rather, constructive dismissal occurs under the common law when an employer unilaterally makes a fundamental (and unfavourable) change to the employment agreement without providing reasonable notice and explaining the consequences of rejecting the change. Generally, this fundamental breach by the employer entitles the employee to resign in response and claim damages from the employer for pay in lieu of reasonable notice.

Constructive dismissal was introduced in Chapter 11, which describes the current leading case on this topic, *Potter v New Brunswick Legal Aid Services Commission* (2015). That case establishes clearly that there are two branches to constructive dismissal. The first branch is the employer's unilateral change of a term or terms of the contract. The second branch is conduct by the employer that indicates a desire to end the employment relationship, such as creating a hostile working environment. It is worth reviewing that discussion in Chapter 11 in the context of the following summary of basic principles for constructive dismissal.

Before turning to the test for whether a constructive dismissal occurs, we should consider why an employer may "constructively dismiss" an employee. Sometimes an employer modifies the terms of an employment agreement or changes other aspects of the employment relationship because it wants the employee to resign and believes that its actions will eliminate the need to formally terminate the employee and provide reasonable notice or pay in lieu. However, more often an employer makes the changes because of factors such as business necessity and hopes that the employee will accept the modified terms. In these situations, which are especially common during an economic downturn, the employer has no intention of repudiating the employment contract.

However, the employer's motives as well as the employee's perceptions are usually irrelevant. In either of the two scenarios above, the employer may have constructively dismissed the employee and will be liable for wrongful dismissal if the employee quits as a result of the changes. The test is an objective one: would a reasonable person in the employee's position find the changes imposed by the employer unreasonable and unfair?

What Constitutes Constructive Dismissal?

As noted above, constructive dismissal can occur as a result of changes to the terms of the contract (the first branch), or as a result of changes in the working relationship (the second branch). We will address the first branch before turning to the second—looking at different ways an employer can change employment terms to a degree that amounts to dismissal. Under this first branch of constructive dismissal, we will look at changes in compensation, duties (including reporting relationships), location of work, and hours and scheduling. We will then look at the classic example of the second branch: a hostile work environment.

Changes to Compensation Package

A minor change in an employee's compensation package probably does not result in constructive dismissal. For example, a 5 to 10 percent reduction in the salaries of all employees because of difficult market conditions is unlikely to be enough. On the other hand, a 30 percent reduction in pay undoubtedly would amount to constructive dismissal. Changes between these two extremes would need to be examined by a court to determine whether, given all the circumstances, they constitute a fundamental breach of the employment contract. It is also worth bearing in mind that it is not just big changes but also the cumulative effect of several small changes that can result in a finding of constructive dismissal ("Bongarde Media Co. Layoffs and Restructuring," 2009, at 2).

The Supreme Court of Canada's landmark decision in *Farber v Royal Trust Co* shows that constructive dismissal depends on an objective comparison between the employee's current job and the job that the employer offers, based on the facts known at the time the employer makes the fundamental change.

CASE IN POINT

Constructive Dismissal Requires Objective Analysis

Farber v Royal Trust Co, [1997] 1 SCR 846

Facts

Farber was a regional manager at Royal Trust Company who supervised 400 real estate agents and earned approximately $150,000 per year including commissions. The employer advised him that his job was being eliminated, along with that of most other regional managers. It offered him a lower managerial position that he had held eight years earlier. He rejected this offer because there was no guaranteed base salary, and the branch was experiencing serious difficulties. However, Farber was willing to accept a position as manager at a more profitable branch or a guaranteed base salary. Royal Trust rejected this counteroffer, and Farber sued for constructive dismissal. Both the trial Court and the Court of Appeal rejected Farber's action on the basis that the employer's offer was reasonable. Farber appealed to the Supreme Court of Canada.

Relevant Issue

Whether the change in the terms of employment, including potentially reduced compensation, constituted constructive dismissal.

Decision

The Supreme Court found that Farber had been constructively dismissed. An employer that unilaterally makes significant changes to an employee's duties signals that it is repudiating the employment contract. Constructive dismissal need not be based on bad faith by the employer. It depends on an objective comparison of the features of the new job with those of the current job. In this case, the new job offered was a demotion without a guarantee of base pay. The Supreme Court further held that evidence of a subsequent "turnaround" at the branch where Farber was offered a position (which meant that he might have been able to match his previous earnings) was irrelevant because it was not reasonably foreseeable at the time of the dismissal. The Supreme Court awarded Farber a year's pay in lieu of notice—$150,000—for the breach of his employment contract.

Changes in Duties

Proposed changes in an employee's duties constitute constructive dismissal if they are so significant that they represent a fundamental change to the employment contract. Increased job duties may fall into this category if, for example, the core responsibilities change and the job becomes much more stressful as a result. More typically, however, claims of constructive dismissal arise where the change in duties represents a demotion—a downgrade in responsibilities, authority, or status. In *Hainsworth v*

World Peace Forum Society (2006), an executive director who lost her title and had to report to one of her former co-directors was found to have been constructively dismissed. However, in *Carnegie v Liberty Health*, the Court found that a new reporting relationship that did not affect an employee's duties did not alone constitute constructive dismissal.

CASE IN POINT

New Reporting Relationship Does Not Create Demotion

Carnegie v Liberty Health, 2003 CanLII 25428 (Ont Sup Ct J)

Facts

Carnegie had 13 years' service and an excellent performance record. She earned approximately $100,000 a year, plus bonuses, as a director reporting to a vice-president. In 2000, the employer changed its sales structure to create the position of assistant vice-president. Carnegie and another worker applied for the new position; the other worker was the successful candidate. The employer presented Carnegie with three choices: (1) continue in her present job and report to the new assistant vice-president instead of the senior vice-president as before, (2) be named director of underwriting, or (3) take a new position as director of special projects. She quit, stating that she was not prepared to report to the assistant vice-president or accept what she perceived to be a demotion. She sued the employer for constructive dismissal. At trial, she was successful; the employer appealed.

Relevant Issue

Whether Carnegie was constructively dismissed.

Decision

The Ontario Divisional Court determined that Carnegie was not constructively dismissed. The trial judge had misconstrued a change in reporting obligations as being a transfer of responsibility. In fact, there was no evidence of this. Carnegie would have remained in the same job and exercised the same duties as before the restructuring. The change in reporting relationships that required Carnegie to report to someone who was previously her corporate "equal" did not amount to constructive dismissal.

Geographic Relocations and Changes in Travel Time

Geographic relocations must be significant to constitute constructive dismissal. A minor geographic change, such as moving an office or plant from one part of a city to another part, generally does not qualify. However, if an original workplace was accessible by public transit and a new workplace is not, an employer may be found to have constructively dismissed employees who are dependent on public transit, even though the workplaces are as little as 20 kilometres apart. In contrast, it may be an implied term in the contracts of senior executives of national or international companies that the employer is entitled to require the employee to relocate, unless there is an express contractual provision to the contrary.

Significantly increasing the time that an employee spends travelling in the course of a job may also be considered a fundamental change in the employment contract. In *Antworth v Fabricville*, the Court found that a newly imposed job requirement that increased the time that a district manager was on the road and away from home from 9 days to 20 days per month constituted constructive dismissal.

Changes to Hours and Scheduling

Depending on the circumstances, a significant reduction (or increase) in hours can be considered constructive dismissal. In *Pimenta v Boermans*, an optometrist cut an employee's hours from 40 to 35 per week. The Ontario Labour Relations Board found that this change, in conjunction with reductions in salary and duties, constituted constructive dismissal. In another case, a court found that increasing the hours of a part-time bookkeeper from 20 hours to 30 hours per week and requiring her to start her days one hour earlier was constructive dismissal under the circumstances.

It is not just the number of hours added or subtracted but also changes to when those hours are scheduled (e.g., from weekdays to weekends) that matter. Each case will be specific to the facts and will also depend on whether there was an express or implied term in the contract relating to when the hours will be worked.

Layoffs

Under Canadian common law, an employer does not have the right to lay off employees unless layoffs are authorized by an express or implied term in the employment contract or, arguably, the prevailing statutory scheme. If there is no such contractual agreement, in certain circumstances a temporary layoff may constitute constructive dismissal, in which case the employee can sue the employer for wrongful dismissal. To be safe, an employer should ensure that its employment agreements give it the right to lay off an employee temporarily. To be considered temporary, the period of layoff must not go beyond that set out in employment standards legislation.

Hostile Work Environment

Under the Supreme Court of Canada's 2015 decision in *Potter*, the second branch of constructive dismissal is not about changes to specific terms of employment. It is about the working relationship more generally—and more subtly. If the employer's treatment of the employee would make a reasonable person think the employer does not want to continue the employment relationship, the courts will find a constructive dismissal. The classic version of this branch is the creation of a hostile work environment or the employer's allowance of such an environment to continue.

Under this branch, an employer's failure to protect an employee from harassment can lead to a claim of constructive dismissal. Courts have found that employers have an implied duty to maintain a safe workplace and to treat employees with civility and respect. As set out by the Ontario Court of Appeal in *Shah v Xerox Canada Ltd* (2000), where this duty is breached and the employer's treatment of the employee (or its tolerance of offensive conduct) makes continued employment intolerable, the employee has been constructively dismissed. In other words, employers have an obligation to prevent workplace bullying.

If bullying in the workplace relates to one of the prohibited grounds of discrimination under the *Alberta Human Rights Act*, such as disability, race, or sex, an employee may file a complaint under the Act. However, a claim for constructive dismissal resulting from a hostile workplace can be made regardless of the underlying basis for the bullying. A constructive dismissal claim is based on an employer's failure to eliminate bullying, thereby repudiating the employment relationship. Examples of unacceptable conduct include rude, demeaning, abusive, and intimidating conduct directed against an employee that goes beyond a mere personality clash. If a reasonable person could not be expected to persevere with the job in the face of the conduct, the employee is entitled to resign and sue the employer for damages for constructive dismissal.

Chapter 11 provides more detail about this branch of the test for constructive dismissal, which *Potter* has expanded and redefined. This branch now clearly includes situations that are less starkly objectionable than harassment of the employee. If a series of events in the workplace, each innocuous on its own, accumulates enough to reasonably support the employee's conclusion that the employer does not want that employee to remain working there, the employee is constructively dismissed.

The Duty of a Constructively Dismissed Employee to Mitigate Damages

As discussed above, the duty to mitigate requires a wrongfully dismissed employee to make bona fide efforts to find a new job to limit the damages they suffer as a result of a dismissal. This duty also applies in constructive dismissal situations. Traditionally, courts have held the view that employees should not be required to mitigate their damages by continuing to work for an employer in a job that is inferior to the one from which they were constructively dismissed. However, the Ontario Court of Appeal in *Mifsud v MacMillan Bathurst Inc* (1989) (and, subsequently, the Supreme Court in the *Evans* case discussed above) has held that the duty to mitigate requires the employee to continue working if:

- the salary offered in the new position is the same as in the former position,
- the working conditions are not substantially different or demeaning, and
- the relevant personal relationships are not acrimonious.

Whether the duty to mitigate requires an employee to accept a new position offered by an employer depends on the circumstances of each case. Often the relationship between the parties has become hostile, or an employee would be humiliated by accepting the new position; in these cases, the employee is not required to mitigate damages by accepting the new job. However, where the situation meets the criteria in *Mifsud*, an employee may be required to work through the reasonable notice period while looking for alternative employment.

Thus, an employee who is presented with significant changes in their employment contract faces a difficult legal dilemma and should seek expert legal advice. On the one hand, if the employee decides to continue working, they may be condoning the change. An employee is allowed a reasonable amount of time in a new position to determine whether it represents a fundamental breach of contract or to negotiate further changes with the employer. However, if the employee remains on the job for more time than is reasonable, they will be accepting the new terms of employment. In these circumstances, the employee cannot subsequently leave and claim constructive dismissal.

On the other hand, if an employee resigns and alleges constructive dismissal, but a court subsequently finds that the change was not sufficiently fundamental to constitute constructive dismissal, as in *Carnegie*, or that the employee should have stayed to mitigate their losses, the employee is out of a job and unable to claim damages.

To avoid this result, an employee might advise the employer in writing that they do not accept the proposed changes and do not condone the constructive dismissal, but they are staying on the job under the new terms in an attempt to mitigate their damages. Probably because of the employee's difficult position, constructive dismissal suits are relatively rare (Gilbert et al, 2011).

As noted above, however, courts are unlikely to require an employee to mitigate damages by returning to work if the dismissal was due to the employer making the workplace intolerable to the employee, under the second branch of constructive dismissal. A recent example of such a ruling is *Frederickson v Newtech Dental Laboratory Inc* (2015), discussed in Chapter 11.

Avoiding Wrongful Dismissal Claims

Given the time, cost, and impact on staff morale involved in wrongful dismissal actions, it makes sense for an employer to avoid such actions, if possible. A number of suggestions to minimize the potential for lawsuits from dismissed employees follows. Even if an employee proceeds with litigation, an employer that has followed these suggestions is less likely to face a court that is unsympathetic to its point of view.

Hire Intelligently

An employer should do its homework when hiring. Thorough reference checks and comprehensive interviews reduce an employer's chances of hiring an employee who is unsuitable or unqualified for a job.

Include and Update a Termination Clause in Employment Contracts

An employer should negotiate a termination provision in an employment contract that sets out the amount of advance notice, or pay in lieu, that it must provide if it dismisses an employee. The notice period does not override the minimum requirements of employment standards legislation, but it need not be as generous as reasonable notice under the common law. Termination provisions must be written carefully. For example, a termination clause that is ambiguous or can be interpreted in any manner that could be deemed inconsistent with the minimum statutory requirements will be unenforceable.

In BC, the CLOS requirement under section 63 of the ESA is in addition to any contractual severance terms. However, if the contract specifies a period of working notice that exceeds the length of the CLOS entitlement, and the employer gives such notice, there is no need to pay CLOS. It is also permissible for a contract to specify that an employee will only be entitled to CLOS upon dismissal without cause, as required under the ESA, and no other notice or pay in lieu thereof will be required.

An employer must ensure that its contracts are kept up to date so that termination provisions remain enforceable over time. Otherwise, changes in an employee's duties or title may render the contract obsolete and therefore unenforceable. The employer can update the contract by, for example, negotiating the update with the employee and providing additional legal consideration, or planning the change to coincide with consideration such as a wage increase or promotion. Alternatively, the employer may make the change by giving the employee reasonable notice of it and offering employment under the new terms at the end of the notice period.

Make Use of Probationary Periods

A written contract or employment policy should state that the employee acknowledges that employment is subject to a set probationary period. This provision or policy should provide that the employer may terminate the employee at any time and for any reason within the first three months of employment without providing notice or pay in lieu of notice. If the probationary period is longer than three months, the obligations under Alberta's ESC and BC's ESA are triggered, but the probationary term may influence a court's assessment of notice in the event of a wrongful dismissal suit. An employer should monitor an employee's performance during the probationary period to identify any difficulties while its legal obligations are minimal.

Create a Paper Trail

An employer should document problems with employees as soon as they occur and in a precise and chronological way. If an employer makes an employee aware of a problem, the way in which it can be corrected, and the consequences of not correcting it, the employer has helped the employee meet the job requirements. If eventually there is no improvement, the employer has created a paper trail to support a decision to dismiss the employee. Such a trail is critical because an employer bears the burden of proof in establishing just cause for dismissal.

Provide Reasonable Notice of Changes

An employer may change even significant terms and conditions of employment unilaterally if it provides an employee with reasonable notice of the change and offers employment under the new terms at the end of the notice period. Reasonable notice may be several months or more, depending on an employee's age and other factors, such as length of service and position.

Determine Whether a Just Cause Claim Is Sustainable

An employer should apply progressive discipline to most types of misconduct—such as insolence or disobedience—before deciding to dismiss an employee. Where alleged misconduct is particularly serious, an employer has a duty to investigate any allegations fully and fairly before deciding to terminate. If, after such an investigation, an employer has compelling evidence of serious misconduct and no reasonable alternative explanation, it may dismiss for just cause. If, however, the evidence falls short of the required standard of proof, the employer should provide appropriate notice or a separation package.

Absent Just Cause, Determine the Appropriate Notice Period

Where there is no just cause under the common law for dismissing an employee and no enforceable termination clause in the employment contract, an employer should review reasonable notice periods determined by the courts in similar fact situations. There is no formula for establishing reasonable notice under the common law. Relevant factors include an employee's age, length of service, character of employment, and the availability of similar employment. Other factors that may come into play are whether an employer lured an employee away from a secure job.

Handle Terminations Professionally

Callous conduct during the termination process can increase an employer's liability. It can cause a court to award compensatory damages for any damages the employee suffered because of the manner of dismissal. In extreme cases, unprofessional conduct can also lead to punitive damages.

FYI

Tips for Being Professional When Dismissing an Employee

Below are general guidelines for an employer to follow when dismissing an employee:

1. Hold the termination meeting in a private location, such as the employee's office or meeting room, preferably near an exit. This way, the employer controls the length of the meeting and can leave, while the employee can remain in a private place until they are ready to encounter other employees.
2. Hold the termination meeting early in the week so that the employee has time before the weekend to obtain legal advice and make any other necessary arrangements. Consider holding the meeting late in the afternoon or at another time when the employee can leave immediately afterward.
3. Consider an employee's personal circumstances before terminating them. For example, do not terminate an employee on their birthday or around a holiday.
4. Keep the meeting focused on the termination, and keep the meeting brief: a maximum of 15 minutes. If the employee is being dismissed for cause, the employer should briefly state the reasons for dismissal but should not recite a litany of the employee's

shortcomings. An employer cannot benefit from attacking an employee when or after they are terminated, and an attack will make negotiations more confrontational. However, be clear that the decision to dismiss is final.

5. Make no unsubstantiated allegations. In the past, bad-faith damages have most commonly been awarded when an employer makes allegations without strong factual support. Do not misrepresent the reasons for the dismissal.
6. Ensure that the employee's supervisor and another manager are at the meeting to show that management supports the decision to dismiss the employee. The additional manager can also act as a witness to what is discussed.
7. Ensure that all representatives of management at the meeting make notes, date them, and sign them.
8. Confirm the termination of employment in writing (written notice is required under the employment standards legislation). The letter should include the effective date of the termination. It should briefly set out the reasons for the termination and confirm the reasonable notice provided or the just cause alleged. An employer can also use the letter to remind an employee of any post-termination obligations, such as those contained in a non-competition clause in the employment contract.
9. Pay outstanding wages, commissions, expenses, and vacation pay. Failure to pay these amounts violates employment standards legislation and makes an employee more likely to sue. It also places the employer in an unsympathetic light if the matter ever comes before a judge.
10. Provide employment standards termination and severance payments immediately if the dismissal is without cause, whether or not an employee signs a release. Unless cause is alleged, the employee is entitled to these payments. Withholding them as a tactic to pressure an employee into signing a release could result in additional damages for bad-faith behaviour if the matter goes to court.
11. Where a separation package is provided, give the employee the name of a contact person who can answer any questions related to the separation package. The contact person must be knowledgeable about the package and the related legal requirements.
12. Ask the employee to return all company property in their possession. Specify the items and a date by which they must be returned. Determine whether expense accounts are outstanding and advise the employee to submit an expense claim as soon as possible.
13. Offer outplacement counselling services where appropriate. Do not make the offer conditional on whether the employee signs a release. These services usually help an employee find other work quickly, thereby reducing the amount an employer owes for wrongful dismissal damages. An offer of counselling also sets a positive tone.
14. Let the employee know their entitlements under the law, such as those relating to benefits.
15. Be honest and forthright.
16. Do not offer a separation package if the termination is for just cause. An employer might offer the employee some money as a gesture of goodwill, but it must make the offer on a "without prejudice" basis so that it is clear the offer is not an admission of liability.
17. Explain all terms of any separation package. List the support being offered: financial compensation, relocation counselling, letter of reference, and cooperation concerning references, for example. Leave the employee with two copies of the severance letter and a release to review. Provide the employee with a contact person for their response.
18. Do not accept the employee's agreement to a separation package, and do not accept a signed release, during the termination meeting. The employee needs time to consider their position and to seek independent legal advice. Otherwise, a court may find the agreement unenforceable.
19. Avoid humiliating the employee. For example, do not escort them out the door when others are present. Any conduct that unnecessarily undermines an ex-employee's dignity may encourage a court to increase the damage award.
20. Prepare the employee's record of employment within five days of the last day of work for employment insurance purposes. Unjustifiably delaying an employee's receipt of employment insurance benefits could lead to additional damages.

21. Allow the employee some input into the way news of their dismissal is announced to other employees, clients, and suppliers while retaining control of the situation. An employee, for example, may prefer to keep the reason for their dismissal confidential. Do not make critical remarks about the employee to co-workers.
22. Designate someone to meet the dismissed employee's immediate co-workers as soon as possible to let them know about the dismissal. Indicate the assistance that the employer is offering them in finding another job. Let them know how the employee's responsibilities will be handled and how clients or customers will be notified of their departure. Send an internal memo to other employees. Quick action can minimize rumours and misunderstandings.
23. If a letter of reference is being provided, provide it unconditionally. Do not tie it in with reaching a settlement.

Get a Signed Release, Where Possible

To receive amounts in excess of statutory entitlements, an employee should be asked to sign documents in which they agree to release the employer from all legal claims related to their employment or its termination. Since the release is a "contract," this additional amount also acts as "consideration" for the employee's signing of the release. Furthermore, a release is enforceable only if a court is convinced that (1) an employee signed it willingly and without undue pressure from the employer, and (2) the employee understood its impact.

The employer should provide a dismissed employee with a reasonable opportunity to obtain independent legal advice before signing a release so that they cannot later argue they were unaware of its implications or felt unduly pressured to sign it. In *Stephenson v Hilti (Canada) Ltd* (1989), the trial Court found the release unenforceable on the basis of unconscionability. In that case, a 61-year-old employee with nine years' service signed a release providing him with 3.5 months' notice damages when his common law entitlement was later found to be 11 months. The employer did not suggest he seek independent legal advice. Stephenson signed because he was distraught at the thought that his pay would be cut off, as he needed money to pay his rent. The Court found that these facts fit the three-part test for unconscionability:

- there was inequality of bargaining position arising out of ignorance, need, or distress of the weaker party (Stephenson was unsophisticated in business matters and was evidently feeling desperate);
- the stronger party had unconscientiously used a position of power to achieve an advantage (the employer did not intentionally mislead him, but neither did it give any real thought to his well-being); and
- the agreement reached was substantially unfair to the weaker party or was "sufficiently divergent from community standards of commercial morality that it should be set aside" (at para 9; the settlement offer was one-third of the employee's common law entitlement).

The judge in *Stephenson* acknowledged that even on these facts the decision was "a close call" (at para 10). Generally, releases are not readily set aside. However, it is important that an employer be aware of the need to be clear, balanced, and honest when asking an employee to sign a release and to encourage the employee to seek independent legal advice.

It is important that releases specifically reference all possible claims relating to the employment relationship, including human rights and employment standards claims, although the ability of a release to effectively foreclose a subsequent human rights claim is questionable at law and at best partially dependent on the facts of the case.

Carefully Consider All Issues When Providing a Letter of Reference

An employer is not required by law to provide a letter of reference to a dismissed employee. However, an employee without such a reference will probably find it more difficult to find a new job, and this may increase the wrongful dismissal damages that the employer owes to the employee. Similarly, an employer that withholds a letter of reference to coerce an employee into signing a release may find itself paying additional damages if the employee suffers actual damages as a result of its tactics. This is especially true where withholding a letter of reference is part of a pattern of unfair conduct.

An employer that chooses to provide a reference has an obligation to avoid recklessness in doing so. As a general rule, a former employer is not liable for providing a negative reference if it sincerely believes that its statements are true and there is a reasonable basis for them. In other words, a claim will only succeed if the comments are not only inaccurate but also malicious (Levitt, 2017). Although such claims are rare, negative statements made carelessly or maliciously may result in a successful claim against a former employer for defamation or negligence. *Miller v Bank of Nova Scotia* demonstrates the matters that a court considers in determining an employer's liability for providing negative references.

CASE IN POINT

Employer Not Liable for Providing Negative Reference

Miller v Bank of Nova Scotia, 2002 CanLII 22030 (Ont Sup Ct J)

Facts

Miller worked part time for the employer bank but did not like working evenings. When she complained, the employer reminded her that she had been hired to work evening hours but stated that it would try to make alternative arrangements after its busy RRSP season ended. She agreed to wait, but shortly thereafter received a conditional offer of employment from another bank for daytime work. She accepted this position and resigned from the employer without giving notice. The new job offer was conditional on checking references.

When the new bank contacted the employer, Miller's supervisor was surprised; she did not know that Miller had given her name as a reference. She indicated that she was upset with the manner in which Miller had left her job and that she did not want to give a reference. When pressed, she stated that Miller had performed adequately as a trainee, but that she had left her job irresponsibly without providing advance notice. Notes taken by the reference checker suggested that the supervisor said that she thought Miller was underhanded, uncooperative, and always complaining. The new employer did not hire Miller, and Miller sued her former employer for slander.

Relevant Issue

Whether the former employer was liable for the tort of slander for comments made during the reference check.

Decision

The Ontario Superior Court of Justice dismissed Miller's action. It found the reference checker's notes to be unreliable, and it accepted the supervisor's evidence as to what she said about Miller. However, even if the statements recorded in the notes were made, they were protected by the defence of qualified privilege because they were genuine views based on reasonable grounds. There was no malice on the supervisor's part to undermine this defence. The defence of qualified privilege also requires that the person giving the reference have an interest in giving the information (i.e., it is given within the context of the person's job), as was the case here.

In deciding if it should provide a job reference, an employer must consider several issues. If it dismisses an employee without cause, and there have been no serious performance issues, it is preferable to provide the letter. It may assist the employee to find a new job more quickly, limiting any pay in lieu of reasonable notice. In these situations, it may be helpful to use a standard form reference letter that allows specific information concerning salary, position, dates of employment, and duties to be added for each employee. This will ensure consistency and help avoid claims based on discrimination under human rights legislation. Comments concerning the contributions of individual employees to the employer's organization may then be added, if they are accurate.

On the other hand, if an employee is dismissed for cause, the former employer must proceed with caution. A former employer that provides too positive a reference could face a lawsuit for negligent misrepresentation from a new employer who relies on the reference to its own detriment. For example, if an employee was dismissed for theft and a new position involved handling cash, the new employer could potentially sue the former employer for losses it suffered when its new employee stole from it, if the information provided in the reference was untrue. That said, there does not appear to be a single instance in Canada in which a successful claim has been made by a new employer against a former employer on the basis of misrepresentation in a letter of reference that it relied on to its detriment (Kent Employment Law, 2019).

An employer that dismisses an employee for just cause must also take care not to undermine its own position by providing an overly positive letter of reference that contradicts its allegations of cause. One approach is to give the employee a letter that confirms their period of employment, position, and salary but that does not comment on performance. This is the safest approach, although it may not be of much assistance in the employee's job search and therefore may potentially result in a longer notice period if the employer's just cause defence is not successful.

Letters of reference should be drafted with care. Where the employee has been dismissed without cause, the referee (the person who writes the reference letter) should try to portray the individual as positively as possible while at the same time being truthful. The information given should be supported by company records, such as performance reviews (Goulart, 2013, at 9-3). Potential employers in search of a reference should be directed to an experienced staff member who is familiar with the employee's situation. This will assist an employer in ensuring a consistent approach in the treatment of former employees. When an employer is contacted for a reference, usually it is a good idea for the employer to get back to the person seeking the reference after the referee has had a chance to review the file. It also provides an opportunity to confirm the identity of the person or organization seeking the reference, if that issue is in question.

Provide the Record of Employment in a Timely Manner

A record of employment form must be issued for employment insurance (EI) purposes within five calendar days of an interruption of an employee's earnings or the date on which the employer becomes aware of the interruption. An interruption of earnings occurs when an employee resigns, is laid off, is dismissed, or generally has had or is expected to have seven consecutive calendar days without both work and insurable earnings from the employer. An interruption of earnings may also occur when an employee's salary falls below 60 percent of their usual weekly earnings as a result of illness, injury, quarantine, pregnancy, or a parent's need to care for newly born or adopted children.

Under the federal *Employment Insurance Act*, an employer must deduct and account to Service Canada for any amount of pay in lieu of notice that an employee receives during a period when the employee also receives EI benefits. The employer and the former employee are jointly responsible for the repayment of benefits to the receiver general. However, the employer's obligation arises only where it has reason to believe that the employee received EI benefits.

If an employer has reason to believe there may have been an overpayment of benefits to a dismissed employee, the employer has two choices. Before providing an employee with a separation package, an employer can either obtain an acknowledgment from the employee stating that they have not received EI benefits or obtain a statement from Service Canada confirming that the employee has not received benefits during the relevant period. If Service Canada indicates that there has been an overpayment, the amount of the overpayment should be deducted from the severance amount and remitted directly to the receiver general.

KEY TERMS

aggravated damages, 500
constructive dismissal, 510
costs, 498
lockout, 494
punitive damages, 500
strike, 494
Wallace damages, 500
without prejudice, 494
wrongful dismissal, 497

REVIEW AND DISCUSSION QUESTIONS

1. Explain the difference between statutory and common law termination requirements. Discuss when an employee might pursue a common law rather than an employment standards complaint. Do you think the two systems complement or contradict each other?
2. Is an employer required to provide a recall date for a layoff to be considered temporary? Explain your answer.
3. Statutory notice of termination and compensation for length of service requirements under employment standards legislation serve different purposes for employers and employees. Describe those different purposes.
4. Identify and describe five exceptions where an employer is NOT required to provide notice of termination or pay in lieu of notice.
5. Discuss the employer's statutory requirements in the case of an employer that has purchased another company and then plans to terminate the employment of an employee from the purchased company.
6. You are an HR consultant. You are approached by a BC employer that currently has 500 employees but must, for economic reasons, permanently lay off 102 of these employees over the next several weeks. Explain to the employer how much statutory termination notice or termination pay it must give to these employees. Describe the other requirements that apply in a mass-termination situation.
7. Discuss the legal issues that arise when an employee who was not dismissed for cause but whose performance was less than satisfactory requests a letter of reference from an employer.
8. What are the factors that a court considers in determining reasonable notice when an employer dismisses an employee without just cause?
9. Discuss the legal dilemma of an employee whose employer makes a significant change in the terms of employment without providing reasonable advance notice.
10. Identify and discuss ways in which an employer may reduce the potential for wrongful dismissal actions.
11. From an employer's point of view, what are some of the benefits and drawbacks of providing an employee with working notice rather than pay in lieu of notice?
12. What are the factors that a court considers in determining whether a contract of employment has been frustrated due to an employee's physical incapacity?
13. Suzanne owns a small restaurant. Robert, the restaurant's chef, is an excellent cook, but he is very temperamental; he becomes angry and abusive with the other kitchen staff and waiters over the slightest mistake. It has reached the point that many members of staff dread working with him. Suzanne has spoken to Robert about this issue many times over the years, but if anything, it is getting worse. Robert simply tells her that he cannot tolerate "incompetence" among the staff and that shouting and yelling at them is just his way of coping with stress. Suzanne has decided that enough is enough—she is going to terminate Robert's employment. (Robert is 39 years old and has worked for the restaurant for seven and a half years. He earns $1,000 per week, including vacation pay. The restaurant's annual payroll is $850,000.)

    Answer the following questions related to this fact situation.

    a. Under your province's employment standards legislation, how many weeks' notice, or pay in lieu of notice, is owing to someone with Robert's length of service who is terminated?
    b. In your opinion, is it likely that a court would find that Suzanne had just cause under the common law to terminate Robert's employment? Explain your answer.
    c. Suzanne wants to avoid a lawsuit, so she decides that she will offer Robert a package. In your opinion, what would be a reasonable offer in these circumstances? Explain your answer by identifying

at least three factors that a court takes into consideration in determining the appropriate amount of reasonable notice of termination (or pay in lieu) required under the common law.

d. Suzanne feels nervous about dismissing Robert (given his temper) and she would like to avoid having to tell him about it face to face. She's thinking of just leaving a message on Robert's answering machine telling him that his services are no longer required and making the severance offer. Is this a good idea? If not, does she have an alternative to telling him in person? Explain your answer.

14. In the Supreme Court decision of *Evans v Teamsters Local Union No 31*, the majority held that the duty to mitigate wrongful dismissal damages may, under certain circumstances, require an employee to return to their former job to work out the remainder of the notice period. However, there was a strong dissenting opinion in that decision by Abella J. Discuss which opinion you find most compelling and explain the reasons for your view.

15. Hussain, a 66-year-old lab technician with 36 years' service, was dismissed without cause. Assuming that Hussain does not have an employment contract with an enforceable termination provision, what would be the amount of reasonable notice damages he would be entitled to receive? Support your answer.

16. Ramond, aged 46, was a chartering manager with a shipping company. His contract stipulated that he was to be paid $7,000 per month, paid semi-monthly. His employer was frequently late in paying him: his first paycheque was three days late; the next two were paid on time, but the next five were all three to four weeks late. This put Ramond in a difficult position with his landlord and, since it happened around Christmas, he was unable to buy gifts for his family. When he questioned his employer about the situation, the employer provided unhelpful responses, saying the delays related to problems with an offshore account. In January, Ramond resigned and sued the employer for constructive dismissal. Do you think his claim would be successful?

17. Tamara was an administrative assistant at a security services company. She worked for both the IT and the human resources departments at head office. Pursuant to a restructuring of the business, Tamara's IT support duties were largely removed, and she lost the right to a bonus, although her salary was increased to reflect the amount lost (around $1,300). Her reporting relationship also changed: she was now reporting to a lower-level HR professional rather than to the IT and HR managers. Several months later, Tamara resigned and sued the employer for constructive dismissal. Do you think she would be successful? Support your answer.

18. Greg, aged 52, was one of nine heating technicians who was permanently laid off due to a work shortage. He had worked for the employer for 12 years and was paid on an hourly basis, averaging earnings of about $55,000 per year. The employer offered Greg 16 weeks' pay in lieu of notice in exchange for a signed release, which he rejected. He sued the employer, claiming that his reasonable notice period should be 12 months. The employer countered that, had Greg worked through his claimed notice period, there would have been little work to do because of the slowdown in business, and his entitlement should be correspondingly reduced.

Do you think this argument would be successful? Support your answer.

19. Ethan was 48 years old and had worked for Happy Hardware for 18 years as a supervisor when a sexual harassment complaint was lodged against him. One of the complainants was the daughter of his manager, Stephan. When he heard about the complaint, Stephan arranged for a friend and colleague, Kyle, to conduct the investigation. Kyle met with Ethan to advise him that he was doing an investigation, but he refused to tell Ethan what he was alleged to have done. Kyle simply said, "You know what you did." At one point, Ethan told Kyle he thought someone might be out to get him; however, this allegation was never pursued and the complainants were never questioned about their motives. Within a week, Ethan was suspended, escorted from the workplace, and dismissed for cause. Ethan sued for wrongful dismissal and other damages. At the trial (by a jury), the jury heard evidence that one of the complainants had been overheard saying that she would "get even" with Ethan for having her transferred. On the basis of this and other evidence, the jury found that the complainants lacked credibility and that the employer had acted in bad faith in its investigation. The jury awarded Ethan 24 months' reasonable notice damages, aggravated damages of $200,000 (although no evidence of mental distress losses were put forward), and punitive damages of $300,000.

a. Do you agree that the employer acted in bad faith? Support your answer.

b. Do you think a court of appeal would support the award of damages?

20. Were the changes made to *Wallace* (bad-faith) damages by the Supreme Court in *Honda Canada v Keays* generally a good or a bad idea?

RELATED WEBSITE

This website covers wrongful dismissal and other employment matters and includes articles from a wide range of legal firms. <www.mondaq.com>

REFERENCES

Alberta Human Rights Act, RSA 2000, c A-25.5.
Alberta Rules of Court, Alta Reg 124/2010.
Antworth v Fabricville, 2009 NBQB 54.
Bain v ICBC, 2002 BCSC 1445.
Bardal v The Globe and Mail Ltd, 1960 CanLII 294 (Ont H Ct J).
"Bongarde Media Co. Layoffs and Restructuring: Beware of 'Constructive Dismissal' Risks" (April 2009) 5:4 *HR Compliance Insider.*
Boucher v Wal-Mart Canada Corp, 2014 ONCA 419.
Carnegie v Liberty Health, 2003 CanLII 25428 (Ont Sup Ct J).
Carroll v ATCO Electric Ltd, 2018 ABCA 146.
Chambers v Axia Netmedia Corporation, 2004 NSSC 24.
Clendenning v Lowndes Lambert (BC) Ltd, 2000 BCCA 644.
Coffey v Nine Energy Canada Inc, 2018 ABQB 898.
Consbec Inc v Walker, 2016 BCCA 114.
Demuynck v Agentis Information Services Inc, 2003 BCSC 96.
Dussault v Imperial Oil Limited, 2018 ONSC 1168.
Echlin, Randall, & Christine Thomlinson, *For Better or For Worse: A Practical Guide to Canadian Employment Law*, 3rd ed (Toronto: Canada Law Book, 2011).
Egan v Alcatel Canada Inc, 2004 CanLII 2553 (Ont Sup Ct J).
Elg v Stirling Doors, [2002] OJ No 2995 (QL) (Sup Ct J).
Elgert v Home Hardware Stores Limited, 2011 ABCA 112.
Employment Insurance Act, SC 1996, c 23.
Employment Standards Act, RSBC 1996, c 113.
Employment Standards Act, RSO 1990, c E.14 [repealed].
Employment Standards Code, RSA 2000, c E-9.
Evans v Teamsters Local Union No 31, 2008 SCC 20.
Farber v Royal Trust Co, [1997] 1 SCR 846.
Frederickson v Newtech Dental Laboratory Inc, 2015 BCCA 357.
Galea v Wal-Mart Canada Corp, 2017 ONSC 245.
Gilbert, Douglas, et al, *Canadian Labour and Employment Law for the US Practitioner*, 3rd ed (Washington, DC: Bureau of National Affairs, 2011).
Goulart, Ruben, "Mitigation: An Employer's Toolkit" (Paper delivered at the Law Society of Upper Canada Six-Minute Employment Lawyer program, 13 June 2013, Toronto).
Hainsworth v World Peace Forum Society, 2006 BCSC 809.
Honda Canada Inc v Keays, 2008 SCC 39.
Human Rights Code, RSBC 1996, c 210.
Ivens v Automodular Assemblies Inc, [2002] OJ No 3129 (QL) (Div Ct), rev'g [2000] OJ No 2579 (QL) (Sup Ct J).
Jamieson v Finning International Inc, 2009 BCSC 861.
Kelly v Monenco Consultants Ltd, [1987] OJ No 563 (QL), 5 ACWS (3d) 26 (H Ct J).
Kent Employment Law, "Employer Reference Letters: What Are You Afraid Of?" (13 March 2019), online: <https://kentemploymentlaw.com/2019/employer-reference-letters-afraid>.
Kotecha v Affinia Canada ULC, 2014 ONCA 411.
Levitt, Howard, "Executive Awarded Record Damages over Walmart Canada's Conduct," *Financial Post* (15 February 2018), online: <https://business.financialpost.com/executive/careers/executive-awarded-record-damages-over-walmart-canadas-conduct>.
Levitt, Howard, "Go Ahead, Give A Negative Employment Reference," *Financial Post* (26 June 2018), online: <https://business.financialpost.com/executive/careers/howard-levitt-go-ahead-give-a-negative-employment-reference>.
Meehan, Kathryn, "Court of Appeal Reduces 24.5 Months' Notice Granted to 70 Year Old Employee," *Case in Point: Legal Developments in Human Resources Law* (12 June 2014), online: *Hicks Morley* <https://hicksmorley.com/2014/06/12/oca-reduces-24-5-months-notice-granted-to-70-year-old-employee>.
Mifsud v MacMillan Bathurst Inc, 1989 CanLII 260 (Ont CA), leave to appeal to SCC refused (1990), 68 DLR (4th) vii.
Miller v Bank of Nova Scotia, 2002 CanLII 22030 (Ont Sup Ct J).
Minott v O'Shanter Development Company Ltd, 1999 CanLII 3686 (Ont CA).

Nolan, Ned, "Bad Faith in the Manner of Dismissal" (14 November 2019), online: *Nolan Ciarlo LLP* <http://www.nolanlaw.ca/2019/11/14/bad-faith-in-the-manner-of-dismissal>.

Ostrow v Abacus Management Corporation Mergers and Acquisitions, 2014 BCSC 938.

Pate Estate v Galway-Cavendish and Harvey (Township), 2013 ONCA 669.

Pimenta v Boermans, 2003 CanLII 26300 (Ont LRB).

Potter v New Brunswick Legal Aid Services Commission, 2015 SCC 10.

Prince v T Eaton Co Limited, 1992 CanLII 5968 (BCCA).

Provincial Court Act, RSA 2000, c P-31.

Provincial Court Civil Division Regulation, Alta Reg 329/1989.

Roy v Metasoft Systems Inc, 2013 BCSC 1190.

Schwartz, Jeremy, & Frank Portman, "Court of Appeal in Wal-Mart Case Scales Back Historic Punitive Damages Award" (26 May 2014), online: *Stringer LLP* <http://www.stringerllp.com/court-of-appeal-in-wal-mart-case-scales-back-historic-punitive-damages-award>.

Shah v Xerox Canada Ltd, 2000 CanLII 2317 (Ont CA).

Smith, Jeffrey R, "Constructive Dismissal: Employee Jumps Ship After Late Paycheques," *Canadian Employment Law Today* (22 September 2010) at 7.

Stehr, Craig, "Severance Pay Key Issue in Terminations," *Canadian HR Reporter* (13 August 2012) at 15.

Stephenson v Hilti (Canada) Ltd, 1989 CanLII 191 (NSSC).

Supreme Court Civil Rules, BC Reg 168/2009.

UPM-Kymmene Miramichi Inc v Walsh, 2003 NBCA 32.

Wallace v United Grain Growers Ltd, [1997] 3 SCR 701.

Post-Employment Obligations 15

LEARNING OUTCOMES

After completing this chapter, you will be able to:

- Explain a former employee's duty not to disclose (or misuse) confidential information.
- Understand the additional post-employment duties of fiduciaries.
- Describe the implications of an employee's implied duty to provide reasonable notice of resignation.
- Understand the implications of an employee's implied duty to act in good faith, including a management employee's duty to try to retain employees.

Introduction

Under the common law, it is an implied term of every employment contract that an employee serve an employer honestly and loyally. Aspects of this obligation continue after the employment relationship ends.

The two main aspects of this implied term are the duty not to use or disclose confidential information and the duty of good faith. The extent of these duties depends in part on the role of the employee: "fiduciary" employees have more substantial duties, including some restrictions on their ability to compete with the ex-employer. Moreover, as discussed in Chapter 2, contract terms can expand the scope of the restrictions on former employees. Contract terms may also require a departing employee to repay the employer for specialized training the employer provided to the employee.

Duty Not to Use or Disclose Confidential Information or the Prior Employer's Intellectual Property

Regardless of whether an employee leaves their job voluntarily or through dismissal, there is a common law rule that they cannot use or disclose trade secrets or confidential information obtained as a result of their employment. For example, generally speaking, an employee cannot copy a list of an employer's customers to use after their employment ends.

Tree Savers International Ltd v Savoy, a decision of the Alberta courts from 1991, provides a good summary of the general rule:

> an employee may leave his employment and lawfully compete against his former employer, taking with him knowledge gained in his former employment, *but he may not take or use against his employer any of his employer's trade secrets, confidential information or customer lists, whether during or after his employment.* (at para 12; emphasis added)

This duty not to disclose or use against a former employer confidential or proprietary (owned by the employer) information applies equally to managerial and non-managerial employees. However, the amount of sensitive, confidential, and proprietary information to which a senior manager has access typically exceeds that to which other employees have access.

Duty Not to Solicit or Compete with a Former Employer

General Employees

The general prohibition against using or disclosing confidential information obtained during employment is the only restriction that courts impose on most former employees, unless there is an enforceable restrictive covenant in their employment contract that provides otherwise. (On restrictive covenants, see below, and see also Chapter 2.) As affirmed in the 1977 Ontario case *Alberts v Mountjoy*, employees may start a business that competes with their ex-employer, work for a competitor, or solicit clients of the former employer after they leave employment unless doing so violates a restrictive covenant:

> He [the employee] may do so by establishing a business in direct or partial competition and he may bring to that business the knowledge and skill which he acquired while in the former service. (at para 15)

In fact, as decided in *RBC Dominion Securities Inc v Merrill Lynch Canada Inc*, non-fiduciary employees are free to compete against their former employer immediately following their departure, even if they fail to provide their employer with reasonable notice of resignation (though damages may arise from the failure to give reasonable notice of their resignation). This case is reviewed in more detail in a Case in Point later in this chapter.

As noted above, however, an individual employment contract may extend the post-employment restrictions on employees to include a duty not to compete. Contract terms called restrictive covenants can expand or clarify the common law restriction on an employee's use or disclosure of trade secrets or confidential information by defining specific information that the employee must keep secret and may not use after employment ends—for example, recipes or other trade secrets or, most commonly, customer lists. Such terms can also limit the employee's ability to compete with the former employer, regardless of whether the employee quit or was dismissed.

If, however, a restrictive covenant limits an ex-employee's ability to work, a court will be reluctant to enforce it. When employers seek **injunctions** to enforce covenants—for example, to prevent an employee from working for a competitor or setting up a new business—courts will assume that the restrictive covenant is unenforceable (see the discussion of injunctions below, after the summary of *KJA Consultants Inc v Soberman*). It is up to the employer to prove that the restriction is reasonable. The narrower and more specific the scope of the covenant, the more reasonable it is. If a covenant makes it too difficult for a former employee to continue to work in that employee's field, the courts are likely to reject the covenant as a "restraint of trade."

injunction
a legal remedy that prohibits another party from doing something

One element that can help to make a restrictive covenant enforceable is to tie it closely to the employee's access to the employer's confidential information. Mere competition with the former employer is usually acceptable to the courts, even if there is a restrictive covenant prohibiting such competition. Courts take a stricter view when the employee has taken customer information and other confidential information from the former employer. In such a case, they may even grant an injunction—though usually the injunction is against using the information rather than working for a competitor. The BC Supreme Court granted an injunction in the 2014 case *Phoenix Restorations Ltd v Drisdelle* but limited it to a prohibition on the ex-employee using the ex-employer's confidential information. Drisdelle was a construction coordinator for a property restoration firm. He quit his job after three years to work for a competitor. On the eve of quitting, he emailed a number of documents to himself that would be useful in his new job, and which Phoenix Restorations viewed as confidential. Phoenix sued him for breaching his non-compete covenant and for taking information. It then immediately applied to the court for an **interlocutory injunction** to prevent Drisdelle from using the information prior to a trial about his alleged breach of the contract. In its application, the employer did not rely on the non-competition/non-solicitation covenant, but on the contract's terms about confidentiality. The Court granted the injunction. In doing so, it stated that it was applying a less strict test than it would have applied to an argument that Drisdelle should not be allowed to work for the competitor at all. Phoenix obtained an injunction that it would probably not have obtained if it had relied on the clauses against competing or soliciting customers.

interlocutory injunction a temporary injunction granted by a court before the final determination of a lawsuit for the purpose of preventing irreparable injury

Although courts may grant interlocutory injunctions pending a trial in cases such as *Phoenix Restorations*, the ultimate remedy at a trial is usually damages. *Jones v Klassen*, discussed in Chapter 2, is a case in which the former employer sought damages rather than an injunction. Klassen quit working for the plaintiff brokerage and joined a competitor. Edward Jones sued, arguing that Klassen had his ex-employer's clients and had taken client lists and other customer information, all in violation of covenants. The Alberta Court awarded not only compensation to the employer, but punitive damages as well, mostly because of the clear breach of confidentiality. The Court noted that the latter also violated the general common law duty of confidentiality and Klassen's duties as a fiduciary.

Fiduciary Employees

In contrast to the common law rule for general employees, a **fiduciary employee**—that is, a senior or key employee who holds a position of trust and who could significantly affect an employer's interests—has additional post-employment obligations to a former employer. Even without a written agreement, a fiduciary may not solicit a former employer's customers or prospective clients if the fiduciary took part in developing a relationship with these clients while employed. Restrictions on fiduciaries last for a reasonable time after their employment ends. What is reasonable depends on the type of industry and the length of time it usually takes an employer to form a relationship with customers after the fiduciary leaves employment. This period of time typically ranges from 6 to 12 months, but may extend to as long as 18 months in extreme cases.

fiduciary employee a senior or key employee who holds a position of trust and who could significantly affect an employer's interests

The term "fiduciary" is narrowly interpreted because the obligations it places on an individual employee are considerable. Whether or not an employee is a fiduciary depends on the employee's role within an organization, rather than their job title. Senior managers are usually considered fiduciaries, but other employees can also be fiduciaries if they hold discretionary power that can materially affect an employer's business or legal interests. Sales representatives are not generally treated as fiduciaries.

The leading Canadian case on fiduciary duties is *Canadian Aero Service Ltd v O'Malley*. In this decision, the Supreme Court of Canada held that fiduciaries owe a duty not to take a corporate opportunity for their own benefit, and that this duty continues after the employment relationship ends.

CASE IN POINT

Fiduciary Employees Cannot Usurp Corporate Opportunity for Their Own Benefit

Canadian Aero Service Ltd v O'Malley, [1974] SCR 592

Facts

The president and executive vice-president of the employer corporation were in charge of obtaining a contract for topographical mapping and aerial photography in Guyana. The employer had already spent a large sum of money pursuing this contract when these two employees resigned and bid on the contract themselves. Their bid was successful.

Relevant Issue

Whether the employees owed a duty to the employer not to take advantage of the employer's business opportunity.

Decision

The Supreme Court found that the employees were fiduciaries and therefore owed the employer a duty of loyalty and a duty to avoid a conflict of interest. These obligations continued after the employment relationship ended. The employer was entitled to damages of $125,000, the amount that the employees gained under the contract.

The following factors are relevant in determining whether a fiduciary duty has been breached:

- the position held by the employees;
- the nature of the corporate opportunity, its "ripeness," its specificity, and the fiduciaries' relation to it;
- the amount of knowledge possessed by the employees;
- the circumstances in which the knowledge was obtained and whether it was special or private; and
- the circumstances under which the relationship was terminated: retirement, resignation, or discharge.

As this case shows, even without a restrictive covenant in an employment contract, a fiduciary cannot take advantage of corporate opportunities presented because of their employment. In a subsequent case, *KJA Consultants Inc v Soberman*, the trial judge extended the duties of fiduciaries by finding that the fiduciary employee breached his duty by accepting a contract offered to him by a former client.

CASE IN POINT

Fiduciary Duty Extended to Unsolicited Contract with Former Client

KJA Consultants Inc v Soberman, 2003 CanLII 13546 (Ont Sup Ct J), aff'd 2004 CanLII 36050 (Ont CA)

Facts

Soberman worked for 13 years for an employer that specialized in providing personal consulting services to the elevator industry. With 11 employees, it was the largest firm of its type in Canada. Soberman had been its general manager for four years when he resigned and set up a competing engineering consulting business. There was no non-competition or non-solicitation clause in his employment contract. Soberman gave notice of resignation on August 20, 2001, effective September 17, 2001. By the end of September, he had sent 70 to 80 letters to potential clients. He followed this mailing approximately one month later with 400 more letters to potential clients, this time intentionally including the former employer's clients.

Shortly before leaving his job, Soberman met with a client of his employer with whom he had worked closely as a consultant in putting together an elevator modernization project. At that meeting Soberman announced that he was leaving the employer to start his own consulting business and stated that the employer was capable of continuing the project without him. Later the client called Soberman to ask whether his new firm would submit a proposal for the project. When the client told the employer that his firm was taking its business to Soberman's new firm, the employer applied for an interim interlocutory injunction to prevent Soberman from soliciting its customers. The injunction was granted, and later the issue of breach of fiduciary duties went to trial.

Relevant Issue

Whether Soberman breached his fiduciary duties to the employer when he

1. took over the client's elevator modernization project, and
2. wrote to the employer's clients in the fall of 2001.

Decision

The Ontario Superior Court of Justice found that Soberman breached his fiduciary duties on both accounts and that because Soberman was the person with whom the employer's clients dealt, a one-year prohibition against soliciting the employer's clients was reasonable. Furthermore, the Court found that Soberman breached his fiduciary duties when he accepted the client's request that his new company present a proposal for the elevator project. There was no evidence that Soberman resigned in order to take over this project, and he did not approach the client; the client approached him. However, in the Court's opinion, Soberman took the project away from the employer, not because of his innate abilities or reputation, but because of his detailed familiarity with the project, which he had obtained solely by virtue of his position with the employer.

The employer was entitled to damages for Soberman's breach of fiduciary duties in the amount of $68,400 for the loss of its contract with the client's firm and $57,954 for the loss of contracts with other clients that Soberman had solicited. The Ontario Court of Appeal dismissed his appeal.

This case suggests that former fiduciary employees of businesses that rely on personal services, such as consulting firms, may not compete against former employers for a reasonable period of time after leaving employment, even where a client of the former employer seeks them out.

It should be noted that where a court decides that an award of damages is not an adequate remedy, it may grant an injunction. As noted above in the discussion of restrictive covenants, an injunction is a legal remedy that prohibits another party from doing something. In this context, an injunction would bar employees from continuing their unlawful competition. In rare cases, courts may grant an injunction prohibiting a person from competing with an ex-employer—where there is a restrictive covenant that the court is willing to enforce this way (see the discussion on restrictive covenants in Chapter 2). Courts also sometimes grant temporary injunctions to prevent unfair competition while the main dispute awaits a trial, called an interlocutory injunction. To succeed in getting such an injunction the employer must prove three things:

- there exists a substantial issue that should go to trial (*i.e., the plaintiff/former employer has a strong case*);
- irreparable harm is likely to occur to the former employer if the injunction is not granted (*i.e., harm would result that could not be adequately compensated for by a damage award, such as loss of protection of trade secrets*); and

- granting the injunction will result in a balance of convenience in favour of the former employer (*i.e., harm to the employer without an injunction is likely to be greater than harm to the employee if the injunction is granted*) (Echlin & Thomlinson, 2011, at 281).

Phoenix Restorations Ltd v Drisdelle, discussed earlier in this chapter, applied this test and granted an interlocutory injunction, which would remain in place until the full trial on the issue of breach of the employment contract. However, the injunction in that case was only against the use of the ex-employer's confidential information. It did not prevent the employee from working for a competitor. Even when an employment contract contains a potentially enforceable non-compete restrictive covenant, it is increasingly difficult for employers to obtain an order, whether interlocutory or permanent, that may prevent a former employee from earning a living.

Implications of an Employee's Implied Duty of Good Faith

In 2008, the Supreme Court issued an important decision that deals with the duties that departed employees owe to their employer upon termination. The case arose when the local branch manager of a brokerage firm coordinated the departure of virtually his entire office to its main competitor. Among other things, the Supreme Court found that although none of the employees involved were fiduciaries or subject to a restrictive covenant, the branch manager's actions were a breach of the implied duty of good faith he owed to his employer. He was required to pay his former employer approximately $1.5 million in damages for lost profits that resulted from breach of this duty.

CASE IN POINT

Manager Breaches Implied Duty of Good Faith

RBC Dominion Securities Inc v Merrill Lynch Canada Inc, 2008 SCC 54

Facts

In 2000, Delamont, the RBC branch manager in Cranbrook, BC, helped orchestrate the exodus of almost all of RBC's investment advisers and assistants to Merrill Lynch, its local competitor. The investment advisers left without notice and took with them client records, documents, and files that they had surreptitiously copied over the course of several weeks. The mass departures resulted in the near-collapse of RBC's Cranbrook office. None of the employees, including Delamont, was bound by a restrictive covenant or was a fiduciary. RBC sued Merrill Lynch and its former employees.

The trial Court made the following findings:

- The employees had breached the implied terms of their employment contracts. The contracts (1) required reasonable notice of departure (which the Court set at two and a half weeks each, or $40,000 in total) and (2) prohibited unfair competition with their employer.

- The brokers were jointly and severally liable for $225,000 in damages for lost profits for breaching their implied duty not to compete during the reasonable notice period. Merrill Lynch was also jointly and severally liable for this amount for inducing the brokers to breach this implied duty.
- As a manager, Delamont had breached his implied duty of good faith, which required him to attempt to retain employees under his supervision, and certainly not to coordinate their departure. The Court awarded almost $1.5 million against Delamont for loss of profits during the notice period plus future loss of profits for a five-year period flowing from breach of his duty of good faith.
- Merrill Lynch should pay $250,000 and the investment advisers $5,000 each in punitive damages for removing the client records from the employer's office.

On appeal, the BC Court of Appeal reversed the nearly $1.5 million award against Delamont and the $225,000 award against the other brokers and Merrill Lynch. RBC appealed to the Supreme Court of Canada.

Relevant Issue

Whether the Court of Appeal properly overturned those awards.

Decision

The Supreme Court restored the $1.5 million damages award against Delamont. By organizing the mass exodus, Delamont breached his implied duty to perform his employment duties in good faith. The Supreme Court reiterated the lower Court's decision that it was indeed part of his job as a manager to retain employees, not to facilitate their departure. Citing the *Hadley* principle, the Court ruled that damages for loss of profits for breach of this duty were within the reasonable contemplation of the parties when they entered into their new employment contracts. Therefore, RBC was entitled to claim all of the losses flowing from that breach, not just losses that were associated with the period of notice of resignation he should have given. The Court further found that, given the evidence at trial, the loss of profits was reasonably measured on the basis of five years.

The Supreme Court upheld the (total) $40,000 in damages awarded against the other employees for failing to provide reasonable notice of their departure. This amount was based on the profit that RBC lost by not having these brokers employed in the two and a half weeks after their departure. However, it rejected the trial judge's award of an additional (total) $225,000 against the brokers for unfairly competing with RBC during those two and a half weeks based on loss of profits flowing from that breach. It found that, in the absence of any non-competition agreement or fiduciary duty, once the brokers left, they were free to compete against their former employer, even during what should have been their notice period. The Supreme Court confirmed that there is no general duty not to compete.

The Supreme Court upheld the punitive awards related to removing the client records.

Several points concerning the duties of departing employees flow from or are highlighted by this decision:

- All employees, regardless of whether they are fiduciaries, have an implied duty of good faith in the performance of their job duties—that is, they have a duty to advance the interests of their employer. It is the paramount duty of an employee.
- A management employee's implied duty of good faith includes the duty to try to retain employees and certainly not to organize their departure. Significantly, damages for breach of this duty will be awarded to compensate for lost business beyond the reasonable notice period itself.
- All employees must provide their employers with advance notice of resignation. However, in most situations the required notice period will be short.

- A non-fiduciary employee who fails to give notice of resignation is not liable for competing against their former employer during the reasonable notice period. There is no general duty "not to compete" in such circumstances. Although it is difficult to enforce non-competition covenants, the result in this case highlights their desirability.
- Employees owe a duty of confidentiality to their employers. This duty exists regardless of whether or not it is articulated in a written contract. However, this duty does not necessarily extend to client contact lists (as opposed to client documents) in every industry. In this case, because of the nature of the relationship between investment advisers and clients, the Court did not award damages for the removal of the actual client lists, although punitive damages were awarded for removal of client documents. This finding is a unique outcome that turned on the particular circumstances before the Court—in most cases, and in most industries, an employee's duty of confidentiality *will* extend to client contact lists.
- A new employer may be held liable for damages where it induces an employee to breach contractual duties (implied or explicit) owed to the former employer.

The duty of good faith is also important in dismissal cases. For employees, it means that dishonesty can be a ground for dismissal (see *McKinley v BC Tel* in Chapter 13). And although employers do not have a general implied duty of good faith, there is such a duty for the manner of dismissal (see *Wallace v United Grain Growers Ltd* and *Honda Canada Inc v Keays* in Chapter 14). An employer's mistreatment of an employee can also amount to a constructive dismissal (see *Potter v New Brunswick Legal Aid Services Commission* in Chapter 11). A 2014 decision of the Supreme Court of Canada, *Bhasin v Hrynew*, has the potential to expand the scope of the duty of good faith, for both employees and employers. In that case, the Supreme Court speaks of a duty of good faith in the performance of contracts generally. This case is not about an employment contract, so it is too early to say whether it may eventually have application to employment law. However, it is a precedent that some lawyers may use to try to increase the expectations of honesty and good faith from both employees and employers.

Recouping Investment in Training Costs

Occasionally an employer will agree to pay for training of a new employee on the basis that if the employee leaves before a certain date, they will have to repay a prorated portion of those training costs. This is sometimes known as a training bond. For example, in *North Cariboo Flying Services Ltd v Goddard*, the employer agreed to pay between $25,000 and $40,000 for specialized training for an employee who was being hired as a chief pilot. When the employee resigned with one month's notice after only six months, the employer successfully sued that employee in small claims court for a prorated portion of the training costs.

The following factors are key to ensuring the enforceability of this type of training agreement:

- the training must at least in part enhance the employee's own marketability in the industry—it cannot simply be for the employer's benefit;
- the terms must be made clear before the employee accepts the training;
- the obligations placed on the employee must be clearly set out in writing;
- the employee must have time to consider the commitment involved and the opportunity to negotiate the terms of the agreement;
- there must not be coercion or any suggestion that the commitment is "unlikely to be enforced"; and
- the terms should be fair (e.g., any amount owed will be reduced on a prorated basis, depending on how long the employee works for the employer; Mitchell, 2011, at 13).

Conclusion

Employers and employees are bound together by many legal obligations that begin before an employer makes a decision to hire and which may continue beyond the end of the employment relationship. At every stage, legal issues present ongoing challenges and opportunities for business and human resources professionals. The focus of this text has been to equip you with the legal knowledge you will need to perform your job and to keep you mindful of the requirements of the law as it tries to balance the rights and obligations of employers and employees.

It has been said that the study of law is not the learning of rules but the continuing process of attempting to solve the problems of a changing society. Understanding the law as it tries to establish, maintain, enforce fair and practical rules in the workplace, and respond to evolving needs will undoubtedly be one of the most challenging and interesting aspects of your career.

KEY TERMS

fiduciary employee, **532**

injunction, **531**

interlocutory injunction, **532**

REVIEW AND DISCUSSION QUESTIONS

1. Describe the difference between the post-employment obligations of fiduciaries and those of other employees.
2. In your opinion, does the *KJA Consultants Inc v Soberman* decision go too far in protecting the interests of employers by prohibiting a former employee from accepting work that he did not solicit from a former employer's client? Why or why not?
3. There was a dissenting opinion in the *RBC Dominion Securities Inc v Merrill Lynch Canada Inc* case by Abella J. Locate the Supreme Court's decision on the CanLII website and review Abella J's dissent. It begins at paragraph 26 with the statement:

   > In the best of all possible worlds, employers and employees would treat each other with mutual respect, consideration and empathy. In the real world, however, as the dispute before us demonstrates, this aspiration is not always realized. The question, then, is at what point does the breakdown of an employment relationship cross the legal line from conduct that is disappointing to conduct that is compensable.

   Review the arguments that Abella J makes in her dissent. Do you agree or disagree with them? Support your position.
4. The employee, Abigail, signed a training agreement whereby she agreed to repay the employer (a Dairy Queen franchisee) the costs of her training as a store manager if she left before working there for two years. The subjects covered and assessed by Dairy Queen in this course included leadership, attitude, customer focus, financial, personnel management, product, equipment, and operations. Abigail resigned after only four months, and the employer sued her to cover the $5,000 worth of training she had received. Do you think the employer would be successful?

REFERENCES

Alberts v Mountjoy, 1977 CanLII 1026 (Ont H Ct J).
Bhasin v Hrynew, 2014 SCC 71.
Canadian Aero Service Ltd v O'Malley, [1974] SCR 592.
Echlin, Randall, & Christine Thomlinson, *For Better or For Worse: A Practical Guide to Canadian Employment Law*, 3rd ed (Toronto: Canada Law Book, 2011).
Hadley v Baxendale (1854), 9 Ex 341, 156 ER 145.
Honda Canada Inc v Keays, 2008 SCC 39.
Jones v Klassen, 2006 ABQB 41.
KJA Consultants Inc v Soberman, 2003 CanLII 13546 (Ont Sup Ct J), aff'd 2004 CanLII 36050 (Ont CA).
McKinley v BC Tel, 2001 SCC 38.
Mitchell, Tim, "When the Employer Is the Victim," *Canadian HR Reporter* (17 January 2011) at 13.
North Cariboo Flying Services Ltd v Goddard, 2009 ABPC 219.
Phoenix Restorations Ltd v Drisdelle, 2014 BCSC 1497.
Potter v New Brunswick Legal Aid Services Commission, 2015 SCC 10.
RBC Dominion Securities Inc v Merrill Lynch Canada Inc, 2008 SCC 54.
Tree Savers International Ltd v Savoy, 1991 CanLII 3952 (Alta QB), var'd 1992 CanLII 2828 (Alta CA).
Wallace v United Grain Growers Ltd, [1997] 3 SCR 701.

Sample Indefinite-Term Contract

EMPLOYMENT AGREEMENT

B E T W E E N:

Employer

– and –

Employee

WHEREAS the Employer and Employee have agreed to enter into an employment relationship for their mutual benefit;

THE PARTIES agree that the terms and conditions of their employment relationship shall be as set forth below.

1. **Scope of Duties**
   1.1 The Employer agrees to employ Employee in the position of Plant Manager, to perform the duties inherent in the position, including the duties set out in the job description attached as Appendix "A" to this Agreement. Employee will report to ____________.
   1.2 Employee agrees to devote their full-time efforts to the position and perform their duties to the best of their abilities. Employee further agrees not to engage in any other employment or self-employment.

2. **Term**
   2.1 The Employer agrees to employ Employee for an indefinite period of time, subject to the termination clause in paragraph 9 of this Agreement.
   2.2 During the first three months of Employee's employment, Employee will be working in a probationary period. The Employer reserves the right to terminate the employment of Employee for any reason without notice or pay in lieu thereof during this probationary period, notwithstanding the provisions of paragraph 9 of this Agreement.

3. **Compensation**

3.1 The Employer shall provide Employee with a gross salary of $____ per week from which standard deductions will be made.

3.2 Employee will also be entitled to earn an annual bonus not to exceed $__________. The payment of the annual bonus will be at the sole discretion of ________________ and should not be considered to be an expected part of Employee's remuneration.

3.3 Should Employee resign or have their employment terminated, Employee will not be entitled to any bonus for that year or any subsequent year.

4. **Benefits**

4.1 Employee will be entitled to participate in all of the Employer's medical/dental benefit plans generally available to its management employees in accordance with the terms thereof.

4.2 The Employer will provide Employee with a car allowance of $__________ per month. This allowance will include any and all vehicle operating costs.

5. **Vacation**

5.1 During this Agreement, Employee shall be entitled to three weeks' vacation per year. Such vacation shall be taken at a time or times acceptable to the Employer having regard to its operations. Vacation may only be carried over from year to year with the written authorization of ____________.

6. **Expenses**

6.1 Employee shall be reimbursed for reasonable and authorized business expenses, including travel, parking, and other necessary business expenses incurred as a result of Employee's work on behalf of the Employer. The Employer shall reimburse Employee for such expenses upon presentation of supporting documentation satisfactory to the Employer in accordance with the tax principles applicable in Canada for such reimbursement and the Employer's established reimbursement policies, as those policies may be modified from time to time in the Employer's discretion. Reimbursement for any such expenses will be at the sole discretion of the Employer.

7. **Confidentiality, Non-Competition, and Non-Solicitation**

7.1 Employee acknowledges that Employee is in a fiduciary position and, in the course of their employment, they will have access to and be entrusted with confidential information and trade secrets of the Employer and its subsidiaries.

7.2 Employee agrees to sign Confidentiality, Non-Competition, and Non-Solicitation Agreement attached as Appendix "B" to this Agreement and understands that it forms an integral part of Employee's employment contract.

8. Return of Property

8.1 Upon the termination of Employee's employment under this Agreement, Employee shall at once deliver or cause to be delivered to the Employer all books, documents, effects, money, securities, or other property belonging to the Employer or for which the Employer is liable to others, which are in the possession, charge, control, or custody of Employee.

9. Termination

9.1 Employee may terminate this Agreement upon two weeks' notice at any time by providing a written notice of resignation. Upon such termination of this Agreement, Employee will not be entitled to any further compensation under this Agreement.

9.2 The Employer may terminate the employment of Employee without notice or any payment at any time during the course of this Agreement with just cause. Just cause is defined as serious and wilful misconduct, and specifically includes but is not limited to theft, fraud, unauthorized absence without good reason, assault, gross insubordination, harassment, and breach of the attached confidentiality agreement.

9.3 The Employer may terminate the employment of Employee without notice and without cause at any time by providing written notice of termination to Employee. If the Employer elects to terminate the employment of Employee without cause after the completion of Employee's probationary period, Employee shall be entitled to a lump-sum payment of two weeks' base salary plus an additional two weeks' base salary for each completed year of employment. This lump-sum payment will be in lieu of and include all of Employee's entitlements under statute and common law and under this Agreement, including all compensation, benefits, and perquisites of any kind whatsoever, and specifically including any entitlements under the British Columbia *Employment Standards Act.*

10. Severability

10.1 If any provision of this Agreement is determined to be invalid or unenforceable in whole or in part, such invalidity or unenforceability shall attach only to such provision or part thereof and the remaining part of such provision and all other provisions thereof shall continue in full force and effect.

11. Modification of Agreement

11.1 Any modification to this Agreement must be in writing and signed by the parties or it shall have no effect and shall be void.

12. Governing Law

12.1 This Agreement shall be governed by and construed in accordance with the laws of the Province of British Columbia.

13. Independent Legal Advice

13.1 Employee acknowledges that they have obtained or have had the opportunity to obtain independent legal advice with respect to the terms and conditions contained herein.

Signed this _____ day of __________, 20___, in the City of Vancouver in the Province of British Columbia.

_______________________________ _______________________________

Employee Witness

____

Employer

Sample Fixed-Term Contract

B

EMPLOYMENT AGREEMENT

BETWEEN:

Employer

– and –

Employee

WHEREAS the Employer and Employee have agreed to enter into an employment relationship for their mutual benefit;

THE PARTIES agree that the terms and conditions of their employment relationship shall be as set forth below.

1. Scope of Duties

1.1 The Employer agrees to employ Employee in the position of President, to perform the duties inherent in the position, including the full authority to deal with all operational issues of the Employer and its subsidiaries including staffing, bidding, customer and supplier approval, performance reviews, organization, hiring, firing, corporate acquisitions, and protection of the Employer's intellectual property rights. Employee will report to the Employer's Chair.

1.2 Employee agrees to devote their full-time efforts to the position and perform their duties to the best of their abilities. Employee further agrees not to engage in any other employment or self-employment for the life of this Agreement.

1.3 Notwithstanding paragraph 1.1 of this Agreement, Employee must obtain written authorization from the Employer's Chair in respect of any acquisition, expenditure, or contemplated acquisition or expenditure the cost of which exceeds or could potentially exceed $1 million.

2. **Term**

2.1 The Employer agrees to employ Employee from ________ to ________, unless Employee's employment is terminated earlier pursuant to section 11 of this Agreement. Upon the expiry of this Agreement, Employee will not be entitled to any notice of termination or pay in lieu thereof.

3. **Compensation**

3.1 The Employer shall provide Employee with a gross salary of $4,000.00 per week from which standard deductions will be made.

3.2 Employee will also be entitled to earn an annual bonus for the fiscal years ending on the last Saturday in September in each of 2020, 2021, and 2022. The annual bonus will be equivalent to 5% of the increase in the net profit of the Employer from one fiscal year to the next fiscal year. "Net profit" is the earnings before income taxes and the deduction for management fees reflecting the shareholder profit distribution as disclosed in the Employer's audited consolidated financial statements.

3.3 Employee's bonus entitlement each year, if any, will be paid within 150 days of the end of the fiscal year.

3.4 Should Employee resign or have their employment terminated during any fiscal year, they will not be entitled to any bonus for that fiscal year or any subsequent fiscal year.

4. **Benefits**

4.1 Employee will be entitled to participate in all of the Employer's medical/dental benefit plans generally available to its executive employees in accordance with the terms thereof.

4.2 The Employer will provide Employee with a car allowance of $1,000.00 per month. This allowance will include any and all vehicle operating costs.

4.3 Employee will be entitled to the benefit of a golf club membership at the golf club of their choice for the period of this Agreement, the cost of which shall not exceed $30,000.00. The equity share or membership in the golf club will be owned by the Employer. The Employer will pay the annual golf club membership dues associated with the golf club membership on Employee's behalf. Before entering into any agreement with a golf club, Employee must satisfy the Employer that the golf club membership can and will revert back to the Employer upon the termination of Employee's employment or the expiry of this Agreement, whichever occurs first.

5. **Vacation**

5.1 During this Agreement, Employee shall be entitled to three weeks' vacation per year. Such vacation shall be taken at a time or times acceptable to the Employer having regard to its operations. Vacation may be carried over from year to year only with the written authorization of the Employer's Chair.

6. **Professional Development and Expenses**

6.1 Upon presentation of receipts, Employee shall be reimbursed for professional development expenses to a maximum of $5,000.00 per fiscal year commencing in Fiscal Year 2020.

6.2 During the term of this Agreement, Employee shall be reimbursed by the Employer for approved expenses, including travel, parking, and other necessary business expenses incurred as a result of their work on behalf of the Employer. The Employer shall reimburse the executive for such expenses upon presentation of supporting documentation satisfactory to the Employer in accordance with the tax principles applicable in Canada for such reimbursement and the Employer's established reimbursement policies, as those policies may be modified from time to time in the Employer's discretion. Reimbursement for any such expenses will be at the sole discretion of the Employer.

7. **Confidentiality**

7.1 Employee acknowledges that they are in a fiduciary position and, in the course of their employment, they will have access to and be entrusted with confidential information and trade secrets of the Employer and its subsidiaries.

7.2 The term "confidential information" when used herein shall include all information of a confidential or proprietary nature that relates to the business of the Employer including, without limitation, trade or business secrets, formulae, designs and design methods, other methodologies, computer software programs and modifications and enhancements thereto, business plans and policies, sales and marketing information, training materials, business records, intellectual property, intellectual technology, and any other information not normally disclosed to the public.

7.3 Employee acknowledges that all of the Employer's confidential information is its exclusive property and that all such property is held by Employee in trust. Except as their duties during their employment with the Employer may require, Employee shall keep secret and confidential and shall not make any copies of, and shall never disclose or use, either during or after their employment with the Employer, any confidential information of the Employer, except as required to fulfill their obligations to the Employer or as explicitly directed by law.

8. **Non-Solicitation**

8.1 Employee agrees that they shall not, during the term of this Agreement or within one year after the date of the expiry of this Agreement or the termination or cessation of Employee's employment pursuant to this Agreement, either directly or indirectly, in partnership or jointly or in conjunction with any other person or persons, firm, association, syndicate, company, or corporation, whether as principal, agent, shareholder, director, officer, employee, consultant, or in any other manner whatsoever, at any time solicit or accept any business from or the patronage of, or render any services to, sell to, or contract or attempt to contract with any person, firm, or corporation who is a customer or prospective customer of the Employer or an employee or former employee of the Employer.

8.2 Employee confirms that the restrictions in paragraph 8.1 above are reasonable and valid and all defences, if any, to the strict enforcement thereof by the Employer are waived by Employee. Employee further agrees that any breach of paragraph 8.1 will entitle the Employer to injunctive relief, as monetary damages would not be an adequate remedy.

9. Non-Competition

9.1 Employee shall not, at any time within one year of the expiry of this Agreement or the termination or cessation of Employee's employment pursuant to this Agreement, either individually or in partnership or jointly or in conjunction with any person as principal, consultant, agent, employee, shareholder, director, officer, or in any other manner whatsoever carry on, or be engaged in, or be concerned with, or interested in, or advise, lend money to, guarantee the debts or obligations of, or permit their name or any part thereof to be used or employed by, any person engaged in or concerned with or interested in a business similar to or in competition with the Employer in the Province of Alberta.

9.2 Employee confirms that the restrictions in paragraph 9.1 above are reasonable and valid and all defences, if any, to the strict enforcement thereof by the Employer are waived by Employee. Employee further agrees that any breach of paragraph 9.1 will entitle the Employer to injunctive relief, as monetary damages would not be an adequate remedy.

10. Return of Property

10.1 Upon the termination of Employee's employment under this Agreement or the expiry of this Agreement, Employee shall at once deliver or cause to be delivered to the Employer all books, documents, effects, money, securities, or other property belonging to the Employer or for which the Employer is liable to others, which are in the possession, charge, control, or custody of Employee.

11. Termination

11.1 Employee may terminate this Agreement upon one month's notice at any time by providing a written notice of resignation. Upon such termination of this Agreement, Employee will not be entitled to any further compensation under this Agreement.

11.2 The Employer may terminate the employment of Employee without notice or any payment at any time during the course of this Agreement with just cause. "Just cause" is defined as serious and wilful misconduct.

11.3 The Employer may terminate the employment of Employee without notice and without cause at any time during the course of this Agreement by providing written notice of termination to Employee. If the Employer elects to terminate the employment of Employee without cause prior to September 30, 2020, Employee shall be entitled to a lump-sum payment of $100,000.00, less deductions. This lump-sum payment will be in lieu of and include all of Employee's entitlements under statute and common law and under this Agreement, including all compensation, benefits, and perquisites of any kind whatsoever, and specifically including any entitlements under the Alberta *Employment Standards Code*.

11.4 If the Employer elects to terminate the employment of Employee without cause after ___________, but before the expiry of this Agreement, Employee will be entitled to a lump-sum payment of $200,000.00, less deductions. This lump-sum payment will be in lieu of and include all of Employee's entitlements under statute and common law and under this Agreement, including all compensation, benefits, and perquisites of any kind whatsoever, and specifically including any entitlements under the Alberta *Employment Standards Code*.

12. Severability

12.1 If any provision of this Agreement is determined to be invalid or unenforceable in whole or in part, such invalidity or unenforceability shall attach only to such provision or part thereof and the remaining part of such provision and all other provisions thereof shall continue in full force and effect.

13. Modification of Agreement

13.1 Any modification to this Agreement must be in writing and signed by the parties or it shall have no effect and shall be void.

14. Governing Law

14.1 This Agreement shall be governed by and construed in accordance with the laws of the Province of Alberta.

15. Independent Legal Advice

15.1 Employee acknowledges that they have obtained independent legal advice with respect to the terms and conditions contained herein.

Signed this _____ day of __________, 20___, in the City of Calgary in the Province of Alberta.

______________________________	______________________________
Employee	Witness

____

Employer

Sample Absenteeism Letters

C

Sample First Letter to Employee

Dear Mr/Ms X:

Re: Poor Attendance Record

This letter is sent to express our concern over your poor attendance record.

We are aware of your health-related problems and we do realize that these problems are not your fault. Unfortunately, however, your attendance record with ABC Company has now become very poor. In this year alone, you have been absent from the workplace [since/on the following dates …]. Moreover, when someone is absent from work, ABC Company is less able to meet its obligations and an extra burden is placed on your fellow employees.

Unless your attendance record improves, your continued employment with ABC Company may not be possible. Furthermore, I wish to advise you that the Company will require you to produce a doctor's note to support any future absence in the next twelve months. This warning is not a disciplinary notation.

We look forward to your full recovery and sincerely hope that you can be a valued member of our workforce.

Yours very truly,

ABC COMPANY

Per: ______________________

Sample Second Letter to Employee

Dear Mr/Ms X:

Re: Continuing Attendance Problem

This letter is sent to express our continued concern over your poor attendance record.

As you are aware, your attendance record is extremely poor. Our concerns were first brought to your attention in our letter dated [insert date] and when we met with you on [insert date]. Unfortunately, however, your attendance record with ABC Company has still not improved. Our records indicate that you have been absent from the workplace for the following periods:

[set out updated history of employee absenteeism]

We realize that these health/illness problems are not your fault. However, the cost of your time off to ABC Company and your fellow employees is substantial. This letter is a further non-disciplinary warning that your attendance record is not acceptable and that your continued employment with ABC Company will not be possible unless your attendance record improves.

In view of your continuing attendance problem, we will meet with you again in [three/four/etc.] months' time to determine if the necessary improvement has taken place.

We sincerely hope that your health/illness problems improve so that you can attend to work on a regular basis.

Yours very truly,

ABC COMPANY

Per: ______________________

Sample Second Letter to Employee with Request for Detailed Medical Assessment

Dear Mr/Ms X:

Re: Request for Detailed Medical Assessment

We are extremely concerned to see that your health/illness problems have again required you to take time off work. As you know, your attendance record is extremely poor. Our records indicate that you have now been absent from the workplace for the following periods:

[insert dates]

We realize that these health/illness problems are not your fault. However, the cost of your time off to ABC Company and your fellow employees is substantial. You previously received notice that ABC Company had a concern regarding your absenteeism on [insert dates]. We now wish to advise you that unless your attendance record improves, your continued employment with ABC Company will not be possible. This warning is a non-disciplinary notation.

In view of your ongoing attendance problems, we now require a more detailed medical certificate that addresses the following questions:

1. Are you fit to perform the essential duties of your regular position? In order for your physician to answer this question, please provide your doctor with the enclosed job description and physical demands analysis.
2. If you are not fit to perform the essential duties of your regular position, what limitations/restrictions exist on your ability to perform these essential duties? This information is required to determine whether suitable modified work can be made available to you.
3. What is the future prognosis on whether you will be able to maintain regular attendance in the foreseeable future, either with or without limitations/restrictions?
4. What is the expected duration of any limitations/restrictions that may exist on your ability to perform the essential duties of your regular position?

Please provide the above-requested information no later than [insert date]. We are enclosing an extra copy of this letter for you to provide to your doctor. Kindly sign the consent to the release of this information found at the bottom of this letter. Thank you in advance for your immediate attention to this matter.

We sincerely hope that your health/illness problems improve so that you can attend at work on a regular basis.

Yours very truly,

ABC COMPANY

Per: ______________________

(cont.)

I, ______________, hereby authorize and consent to Doctor ______________ [name of doctor] releasing all of the above-requested information to my Employer at the following address: [insert name and address of information recipient].

DATED this _____ day of ______________, 20____.

Sample Final Warning Letter to Employee

Dear Mr/Ms X:

Re: Unacceptable Absenteeism

This letter is sent to express our continuing concern over your extremely poor attendance record. As you are aware, our ongoing concern over your continuing attendance problems has been brought to your attention on numerous occasions, including [reference dates of previous letters and meetings].

Our most recent letter to you, dated [insert date], indicated that we would review your attendance record in [X] months' time to determine whether the necessary improvement in your attendance had taken place. Regrettably, however, your attendance problems have still not improved to an acceptable standard. Our records indicate that in the most recent [X] months alone, you have been absent from the workplace on the following occasions:

[insert dates]

We recognize that these ongoing health/illness problems are not your fault. However, the cost and disruption of your time off to ABC Company can no longer continue. Accordingly, this letter constitutes a final warning that your employment with ABC Company will be terminated in [X] months' time unless there has been an improvement in your attendance record to minimum acceptable standards. This warning is a non-disciplinary notation.

We will review this matter with you again in [X] months' time. We sincerely hope that your attendance problems will improve in order that your employment at ABC Company may continue.

Yours very truly,

ABC COMPANY

Per: ______________________

Sample Termination Letter to Employee

Dear Mr/Ms X:

Re: Employment Termination

This letter will confirm our meeting of today's date wherein you were advised that your employment is being terminated effective [immediately/specify date] due to the frustration of your employment contract caused by ongoing attendance problems.

Our records indicate that you have been absent from the workplace for the following periods:

[outline history of employee absenteeism]

Our concern regarding your ongoing attendance problems has been brought to your attention on numerous occasions since [insert date]. Most recently, you were issued a final warning on [insert date] advising that unless your attendance record improved by [specify time frame], your continued employment would not be possible. Regrettably, the necessary improvement did not occur.

Your record of absenteeism is excessive and, in the circumstances, it does not appear that you will be capable of regular attendance in the foreseeable future.

We regret having to take this action. However, your ongoing attendance problems have reached the point where your continued employment is no longer possible.

[add appropriate paragraphs relating to any employee entitlements under applicable provisions of the BC *Employment Standards Act*]

Yours very truly,

ABC COMPANY

Glossary

administrative agencies lower tribunals in the administrative hierarchy empowered to investigate complaints, make rulings, and sometimes issue orders

administrative tribunals a quasi-judicial authority whose rules are typically governed by a subject-specific statute

agency shop a type of union security where non-members within the bargaining unit pay the union for the costs of collective bargaining, rather than pay regular dues that cover a broader range of union activities

agent a person who can bind an organization to a contract with customers or other parties, even without the organization's knowledge

aggravated damages damages awarded to compensate a party for non-monetary losses intentionally or maliciously caused by the other party's conduct

anticipatory breach of contract when one party indicates it has no intention of living up to its obligations under the employment contract; this rejection—through either its statements or its conduct—is anticipatory because it occurs after the contract has been made but before employment begins

appellant the party requesting the appeal

attestation clause a clause on a job application form that states that the information provided is true and complete to the applicant's knowledge and that a false statement may disqualify the applicant from employment or be grounds for dismissal

balance of probabilities the degree of proof required in civil law cases wherein a proposition is established as fact if it is shown that the proposition is more likely than not to be true

bargaining unit the group of employees for which the union negotiates a collective agreement

binding requiring a lower court to follow a precedent from a higher court in the same jurisdiction (see also *stare decisis*)

bridging refers to a collective agreement that applies to the parties at the time notice to bargain is served continuing to apply to the parties until (1) a new collective agreement is in place, (2) the right of the union to represent the employees is terminated, or (3) there is a strike or lockout

burden of proof the obligation to prove a fact, a proposition, guilt, or innocence

***but for* test** this is a logic test commonly used to determine causation in law; the test asks "*but for* the existence of X, would Y have occurred?"; if the answer is yes, then factor X is an actual cause of result Y

case citation a reference for locating a case that sets out the case name, year in which the decision was made or in which it was published in a case reporter, volume number of the case reporter, series number, page number, and court

case law law made by judges, rather than legislatures, that is usually based on previous decisions of other judges

civil law law that relates to private, non-criminal matters, such as property law, family law, and tort law; alternatively, law of jurisdictions, such as Quebec, that is not based on English common law

closed shop a type of union security whereby a person must be a member of the union before getting the job; the employer is only allowed to hire current members of the union to work in a particular bargaining unit

common law law that has developed over the years through court decisions

condonation implied acceptance by one party of the conduct of another party; once an employer is aware of an employee's misconduct and takes no disciplinary action within a reasonable time, the employer cannot dismiss the employee for that misconduct without any new misconduct

consideration a mutual exchange of promises required, along with an offer and an acceptance, to create an enforceable contract; for example, in an employment contract, consideration is a promise of payment in exchange for a promise to perform the work

constitutional law the *Canadian Charter of Rights and Freedoms*; the "supreme law of the land"

constructive dismissal dismissal that occurs when an employer unilaterally makes substantial changes to the essential elements of the employment contract to the detriment of the employee

contextual approach the increasing tendency of courts to view employee misconduct within the overall context of the employment relationship, including length of service and work and disciplinary record, in determining whether the employer had just cause for dismissal

contra proferentem the doctrine of interpreting ambiguous contract language against the interests of the party that drafted the language

contract law an area of civil law that governs agreements between people or companies to purchase or provide goods or services

contributory negligence a common law defence in an action arising from negligence in which it is asserted that the plaintiff's own negligence directly caused or contributed to the injuries suffered

costs compensation for legal fees and expenses that the other party in a lawsuit is entitled to recover

co-worker negligence a common law defence in an action arising from negligence in which it is asserted that the plaintiff's injuries were caused by the negligence of the plaintiff's co-worker, not the employer

culpable absenteeism blameworthy absences, such as being late without good reason (including returning late from a break), leaving work without permission, or failing to follow absence notification procedures

defamation a tort claim based on a false statement or statements made to the detriment of an identified individual or organization and which are published or broadcast to an audience; defamation can be spoken (slander) or written (libel)

distinguishable when the facts or other elements in the previous case are so different from those of the current case that the legal principle in the previous decision should not apply

due diligence defence the onus on a party in certain circumstances to establish that it took all reasonable steps to avoid a particular event

employee personal information personal information about an individual that is collected, used, or disclosed solely for the purposes reasonably required to establish, manage, or terminate an employment relationship between the organization and that individual, but does not include personal information that is not about an individual's employment; this is the definition used in the BC *Personal Information Protection Act*

employment equity addresses the broad social problem of the underrepresentation of certain groups of people, such as visible minorities and people with disabilities, in most workplaces, especially in better-paid and higher-level jobs

employment equity program a special program to relieve or promote people who typically suffer from employment discrimination on the basis of prohibited grounds

essential services public services that, if interrupted, would endanger the life, safety, or health of the public; this includes services necessary to maintain the rule of law and public security; essential services are defined in statute and may vary by province

fair information principles the ten principles set out in schedule 1 of PIPEDA that underlie the collection, use, protection, and disclosure of personal information

fiduciary employee a senior or key employee who holds a position of trust and who could significantly affect an employer's interests

first contract arbitration a legislated requirement for interest arbitration in the place of a strike or lockout that applies only when a workplace is newly unionized and the parties are unable to reach their first agreement

good-faith bargaining the parties meet and make genuine efforts to reach agreement; this does not require that they agree to proposals from the other side, but they cannot deliberately sabotage bargaining efforts to avoid reaching agreement

grievance arbitration also known as "rights arbitration," occurs when a collective agreement is in force; a form of dispute resolution where an arbitrator decides on the correct application or interpretation of an existing collective agreement clause

harassment any unwanted physical or verbal behaviour that offends or humiliates and persists over time; serious one-time incidents can also be considered harassment; specific definitions of harassment may be included in legislation that addresses this issue

health and safety representative a person who exercises rights and powers similar to those of the joint health and safety committee; required in workplaces with 6 to 19 employees

implied terms default or mandatory rules that the courts assume are part of an employment agreement, even if they have not been expressly included in the employment contract

incorporated by reference when a second document is included as part of a first document because it is listed or named within the first document

indemnity clause a provision in a contract under which one party commits to compensate the other for any harm, liability, or loss arising out of the contract

independent contractor a self-employed worker engaged by a principal to perform specific work; an independent contractor is not an employee

indictable offence a more serious offence than a summary offence

individual employment contracts negotiated between an employer and each employee individually, without the involvement of an association or regulatory agency

industry under the BC *Workers Compensation Act*, any establishment, undertaking, work, trade, or business; under the Alberta *Workers' Compensation Act*, an establishment, undertaking, trade, or business, whether it is carried on in conjunction with other occupations or separately

injunction a legal remedy that prohibits another party from doing something

innocent absenteeism absences that arise as a result of a legitimate medical or other cause; innocently absent employees can never be subject to disciplinary measures

interest arbitration a form of dispute resolution that occurs when a collective agreement is being negotiated; the parties propose the terms and conditions of the collective agreement, and the arbitrator decides the content of any clauses that are in dispute

interlocutory injunction a temporary injunction granted by a court before the final determination of a lawsuit for the purpose of preventing irreparable injury

internal responsibility system the "people framework" of an effective occupational health and safety management system, based on the premise that government alone cannot effectively regulate all workplace risks; instead, the law emphasizes the participation by and accountability of all parties in the workplace to ensure a healthy and safe environment

joint health and safety committee (JHSC) an advisory health and safety body that is composed of equal numbers of management and worker representatives; generally required in workplaces with 20 or more workers

judicial review a request to a court to review the decision of an administrative tribunal

jurisdiction the authority granted to a legal body to administer justice within a defined area of responsibility; legislation applies only to a specific jurisdiction (area of responsibility), and courts and tribunals are limited to making decisions about issues that fall within a specific jurisdiction

just cause serious employee misconduct that warrants dismissal without notice

Labour Relations Board (LRB) the government agency responsible for interpreting, applying, and enforcing provincial labour relations codes; LRBs oversee certification and decertification processes and act as tribunals hearing disputes over unfair labour practices, strikes, lockouts, and any other matters related to the *Labour Relations Code*

litigation legal action

lockout an employer's refusal to let unionized employees into the workplace following the expiry of a collective agreement or a failure to reach a first collective agreement, typically while the employer and union are attempting to negotiate a new collective agreement

members (of administrative tribunals) adjudicators appointed pursuant to a statute

mitigate to make reasonable efforts to reduce damage or harm; the law imposes a duty to mitigate on anyone who suffers a loss, even if someone else is at fault; in employment law, mitigation means seeking a new job upon dismissal

multiple-employer workplaces workplaces where workers of two or more employers are working at the same time

negligence an act or omission that involves no intention to cause harm but that a reasonable person would anticipate might cause harm

negligent hiring failing to take reasonable care in the hiring process that results in foreseeable injury to a third party

neutral citation a form of citation that includes the traditional case name; the core of the citation, containing the year of the decision, a court or tribunal identifier, and a number assigned to the decision; and possible optional elements, such as paragraph numbers or notes

non-pecuniary damages monetary damages designed to compensate for a plaintiff's pain, suffering, or other injuries that are not readily quantifiable or valued in money

onus of proof the burden of proving a case or the facts involved in a dispute

open shop a system whereby union membership is optional and payment of dues is also optional

parallel citations references to a case published in two or more different case reporters

peace obligation a prohibition on strikes or lockouts during the term of the collective agreement

perk short for "perquisite," a bonus or benefit, particularly one owed to a job incumbent

personal employee information in respect of an individual who is a potential, current, or former employee of an organization, personal information reasonably required by the organization for the purposes of (1) establishing, managing, or terminating an employment or volunteer-work relationship, or (2) managing a post-employment or post-volunteer-work relationship between the organization and the individual, but does not include personal information about the individual that is unrelated to that relationship; this is the definition used in the Alberta *Personal Information Protection Act*

personal information any factual or subjective information about "an identifiable individual," whether recorded or not

persuasive when a court is persuaded to follow a precedent from another jurisdiction or from a lower court, although it is not bound to do so

poisoned work environment a workplace that feels hostile because of insulting or degrading comments or actions related to a prohibited ground of discrimination

precedent what previous courts have decided in cases involving similar circumstances and principles

prima facie evidence that, as it first appears, is sufficient to prove a proposition or fact, though it may still be rebutted

principal the party who contracts for the services of an independent contractor; the party who can be bound by its agent

privacy commissioner the commissioner appointed to investigate complaints of failure to comply with the requirements of privacy legislation

privative clause a provision limiting appeals to the courts from decisions of administrative tribunals

probation a period of time when an employee is monitored to determine their suitability for a job

procedural fairness certain process rights that one party provides to another, such as an employer giving an employee an opportunity to respond to allegations against them

progressive discipline discipline that is imposed in a series of increasing steps

proportionality the idea that any sanction must be proportional to the conduct to which it relates

punitive damages damages awarded to punish the employer for its malicious or oppressive conduct, rather than to compensate the employee

qualified privilege in the context of libel or slander, an exemption from liability for a statement made without malice, usually in the performance of a duty, and not communicated more widely than is appropriate

Rand formula shop a variation of the open shop union and what most labour legislation requires employers to accept if the union requests it; in a Rand formula shop, the employees do not have to be union members, but they are still required to have union dues deducted from their pay

ratification a process where employees in the bargaining unit vote to accept or reject a contract negotiated by the union on their behalf

read into when it is determined there is extra meaning in the language of a piece of legislation, which may not have been originally intended

reasonable care the level of diligence that is reasonable under the circumstances

rebuttable presumption an inference that a court will draw unless the contrary is proven

regulations rules made under the authority of a statute

remedial legislation legislation that exists to right a societal wrong, not to allocate blame or punish an offender

respondent the party opposing the appeal

restrictive covenant a promise not to engage in certain types of activities during or after employment

reverse onus a provision within a statute that shifts the burden of proof onto the individual specified to disprove an element of the information; typically, this provision concerns a shift in burden onto a defendant rather than the claimant

sexual harassment a course of vexatious comment or conduct (based on sex or gender) that is known or ought reasonably to be known to be unwelcome; it may be practised by a male on a female, by a female on a male, or between members of the same sex

sexual solicitation a situation where someone in a position of authority makes unwelcome advances or requests for sexual favours and where the threat of reprisals or promise of reward is explicit

solicitor–client privilege rule of evidence that protects a client from having to divulge confidential communications with their lawyer

standard of care the level of diligence the employee is expected to exercise

standard of review the level of scrutiny that an appeal court will apply to the decision of a lower court or tribunal

stare decisis a common law principle that requires lower courts to follow precedents emanating from higher courts in the same jurisdiction; Latin for "to stand by things decided"

statute law a statute is a law passed (i.e., created) by the federal or provincial government

strict liability offences offences where the doing of the prohibited act is sufficient proof of the offence and the accused has the burden of proving that it took all reasonable care to avoid the offence

strike a refusal to work by a group of unionized employees following the expiry of a collective agreement or a failure to reach a first collective agreement, typically while the employer and union are attempting to negotiate a new collective agreement

summary conviction a less serious offence that is tried summarily

summary dismissal dismissal without notice, usually based on just cause

systemic discrimination the web of employer policies or practices that are neutral on their face but have discriminatory effects; also called "institutional discrimination"

third party someone other than the employer or employee

tort law a branch of civil law (non-criminal law) that covers wrongs and damages that one person or company causes to another, independent of any contractual relationship between them

unconscionable in the context of an employment contract, something that is unreasonably one-sided

undue hardship occurs if accommodation creates "onerous conditions," "intolerable financial costs," or "serious disruption" to the business

union density the percentage of workers who are unionized, as opposed to working under individual contracts of employment; also called union coverage

union member a person admitted to membership in the union organization

union security refers to any requirements in the collective agreement that employees in the bargaining unit either be members of the union or pay dues to the union

union shop a type of union security whereby *all* employees in the bargaining unit *must* become members of the union within a specified period of time (usually after a probationary period); employment is conditional on joining the union

vicarious liability legal responsibility for the actions of another

voluntary assumption of risk a common law defence in which it is asserted that the plaintiff voluntarily assumed the risk of injury

***Wallace* damages** damages (given by extending the reasonable notice period) formerly awarded to a dismissed employee because of the employer's bad-faith conduct in the manner of dismissal

wildcat strike a work stoppage initiated by bargaining unit workers without proper authorization or approval; it may be started while the collective agreement is still valid or during bargaining but without notice being given or a strike vote taken

without prejudice without an admission of wrongdoing in a legal dispute

Workplace Hazardous Materials Information System (WHMIS) a national information system designed to provide workers and employers with essential information about hazardous materials in the workplace

wrongful dismissal dismissal without just cause wherein an employer breaches its common law duty to provide reasonable notice of termination or pay in lieu of notice to an employee

Index

Credits

Chapter 2

Christina Rexrode, "Yahoo CEO Scott Thompson resigns after scrutiny of his resume," *The Associated Press* (13 May 2012). Used with permission.

Chapter 3

Photo 3.1 (c) Rawpixel/Shutterstock.

Chapter 7

"Cannabis Zero-Tolerance Common in Canadian Workplaces: Study." Material republished with the express permission of Calgary Herald, a division of Postmedia Network Inc.

Embracing older employees and all they have to offer is the way forward for employers. <https://www.cpacanada.ca/en/news/canada/2018-08-09-ageism-is-alive-and-thriving-in-our-workforce-limiting-older-employees-say-experts>

Chapter 8

"B.C. regulation means employers can't require women to wear high heels to work," *The Canadian Press* (7 April 2017). Used with permission.

Chapter 12

"The Right Reasons to Leave Your Job and When Not to Quit," *The Economic Times*. <https://economictimes.indiatimes.com/wealth/earn/7-right-reasons-to-leave-your-job-and-when-not-to-quit/articleshow/64803340.cms?from=mdr>

Chapter 13

"How #MeToo Changed the Workplace" (excerpts). Postmedia Network Inc.